ST. JAMES'S PLACE
WEALTH MANAGEMENT

TAX GUIDE

2012–2013

CONTENTS

PREFACE

The *St. James's Place Tax Guide* has evolved over the last 41 years as a handy and reliable source of reference for our clients, advisers and other professionals.

The author, Walter Sinclair, supported by Barry Lipkin, works hard to produce a guide that contains the technical information required in a format that can be understood by most. Being a taxpayer myself, I find it really is a helpful source of information.

The tax regime in the UK is complex, and understanding the basics of income tax, capital gains tax and personal allowances is important to all of us as we experience the increased burden of taxation.

Of course, in an ideal world, the *Guide* would be very much shorter because our tax system would be much simpler. However, dealing with the implications of our complicated tax system will continue to be an important challenge for those individuals looking for advice.

Being in the wealth management business, it is no surprise to us at St. James's Place that, for most of our clients, tax management is a vital part of their financial planning. The information contained within this *Guide*, and the knowledge offered by the award-winning St. James's Place Wealth Management Group, is therefore more important than ever in helping you take the necessary steps to preserve and increase your wealth.

SIR MARK WEINBERG
Life President
St. James's Place Wealth Management

ST. JAMES'S PLACE
WEALTH MANAGEMENT

TAX GUIDE

2012–2013

WALTER SINCLAIR, FCA

with

BARRY LIPKIN, LLB FCA ATII TEP

palgrave
macmillan

PPP	personal pension plan
PRAS	pension relief at source
PRO	protected rights only
PRP	profit related pay
REIT	real estate investment trust
RPI	retail prices index
RTI	real time information
S (Ss)	section (sections) of an Act
S2P	state second pension
SAA	special annual allowance
SAYE	save as you earn
Sch/s	schedule/s of an Act
SDLT	stamp duty land tax
SERPS	state earnings related pension scheme
SFO	Superannuation Funds Office
SI	Statutory Instrument
SIP	share incentive plan
SIPP	self-invested personal pension
SME	small or medium enterprise
SSAS	small self-administered scheme
SSP	statutory sick pay
TA	Income and Corporation Taxes Act 1988
TCEA	Tribunals Courts and Enforcement Act 2007
TCGA	Taxation of Chargeable Gains Act 1992
TESSA	tax exempt special savings account
TMA	Taxes Management Act 1970
UAP	upper accrual point
UEL	upper earnings limit
USM	Unlisted Securities Market
VAT	value added tax
VATA	Value Added Tax Act 1994
VCT	venture capital trusts
WFTC	working families tax credit
WTC	working tax credit

INTRODUCTION

Originally establishing itself as the *Hambro Tax Guide* 41 years ago, this book has appeared annually ever since, more recently being called the *J. Rothschild Assurance Tax Guide*. The book has been designed to be used both by the professional and non-professional. Solicitors, accountants and company secretaries will find it especially useful as a concise ready reference. Many others, company directors and executives, partners and sole-traders, employers and employees, will find in it much helpful information and advice when dealing with problems of personal and company taxation.

It illustrates the working of income tax, capital gains tax, corporation tax, inheritance tax and VAT in the UK. It is intended to continue revising the book annually in order to keep it up to date in accordance with the annual changes to the law.

This, the 41st edition, deals with the tax system at the time of writing for the 2012–13 fiscal year and in some cases for subsequent years. Every chapter has been amended to reflect the many tax changes which have been made since the previous edition, including those relating to income tax and personal reliefs, investments, pensions, National Insurance, capital gains tax, corporation tax, inheritance tax, VAT, stamp duty, anti-avoidance and many, many others. To help keep track of the changes, Chapter 1 summarises this year's tax changes and is referenced to the relevant paragraphs in the *Guide*. In addition, tax planning pointers relative to this year's tax changes are included in this chapter.

This book has been appearing since 1972–73 and it is interesting to consider some of the tax changes over its life, comparing that year with 2012–13.

		1972–73	**2012–13**
Income tax	Standard/Basic rate	38.75%	20%
	Top rate – from taxable income		
	£15,000 including surtax	88.75%	
	£150,000		50%
	Single personal relief	£460	£8,105
Capital gains tax rates (individuals)		30%	normally 18%/28%
Estate duty/inheritance tax threshold		£15,000	£325,000
	Top rate at £500,001	75%	
	Only rate in most cases		40%
VAT from 1 April 1973		10%	20%

Previous editions of the book recorded falling rates for most taxes, apart from National Insurance contributions. What is more, many reliefs and taxes have come and/or gone, such as:

- Capital transfer tax.
- Development gains tax and development land tax.
- Surtax.
- Earned income relief.
- Investment income surcharge.
- Stock relief.
- Life assurance relief on new policies.
- Mortgage interest relief.
- Married couples allowance (unless born before 6 April 1935).
- Stakeholder pensions.
- Advance corporation tax and the imputation system.
- Working tax credits and child tax credits.
- Income tax starting rate going from 6 April 2008.

However, the deep recession resulted in stiffer taxes being imposed from 2010–11 such as the new 50 per cent additional rate and allowances being restricted. Furthermore, the May 2010 General Election gave rise to more changes such as a 20 per cent VAT rate. Also, many future changes have been announced, including the replacement of the 50 per cent tax rate with one of 45 per cent from 2013–14. But of one thing we can be sure, there will be very many tax changes to include in the pages of subsequent editions.

Due to the volume of changes, it is not possible to retain in each new edition full information for previous years. Thus for the tax rules for previous years, reference to past editions is occasionally necessary.

Because the book concisely covers a very wide field, it has been necessary to omit some of the exemptions and qualifications with which tax law abounds: to adopt a familiar saying, 'When I say never, I mean hardly ever and when I say always, I mean almost always.' The book is intended to be only a general tax guide. If it cannot solve a problem, the time has come to look at one of the multi-volume tax textbooks or to consult a tax specialist.

Ideas on straightforward tax saving appear throughout the book. However, Chapter 26 deals with *tax-saving hints* and has many references to the other chapters for easy location of topics. Furthermore, this chapter contains particular reference to future tax planning in a section entitled 'The way ahead' (26.8).

A particular feature to note is that all indexing and cross-referencing uses chapter and topic numbers. Thus 7.6 means the sixth-numbered topic in Chapter 7. Similarly 7.6.3 would mean the third subsidiary topic within that main heading. Cross-references to related chapter and topic numbers appear throughout the *Guide* in brackets and you will also find references to tax legislation where relevant under the appropriate topic title. Also, a glossary to help with the meanings of certain terms appears at the end of this book.

Since its inception, the *Guide* has included references to the tax legislation. Over the years, this has been consolidated into a number of Acts such as the Inheritance Tax Act 1984 (IHTA), Value Added Tax Act 1994 (VATA), Capital Allowances Act 2001 (CAA), Income and Corporation Taxes Act 1988 (TA), Income Tax (Trading and Other Income) Act 2005 (ITTOIA) and Income Tax Act 2007 (ITA). The book is now referenced mainly to the consolidating Acts, using the abbreviations shown above and following the Preface.

The *St. James's Place Tax Guide 2012–2013* brings together in a single volume all of the main taxes which are operating at present, enabling their total effect to be borne in mind. In planning for the future, however, account should be taken of the various avenues for short-term reform, as well as the longer term possibilities for capital gains tax, inheritance tax, income tax etc. As new developments are crystallised, they will be covered in the future annual editions of this book.

We are most grateful to all those who have written to us with kind and helpful comments concerning the previous editions, some of which have been taken into account in the preparation of this volume.

We gratefully acknowledge the help given to us on this edition by Malcolm Cooper-Smith of St. James's Place and Rob Gaines LLB.

WALTER SINCLAIR
and
BARRY LIPKIN

Chapter 1

THIS YEAR'S TAX CHANGES

1.1 Introduction

This chapter summarises many of the changes to the tax rules and rates which take effect for 2012–13. Also included are some important changes announced for future years. Tax planning pointers have been included in italics and these are amplified in Chapter 26. At the end of this chapter you will find a table of key rates and allowances for 2012–13.

You should remember that not all the changes included in the 2012 Budget take effect for 2012–13, which gives a planning interval in some cases.

1.2 Income tax

The rate bands have changed.

1.2.1 Income tax rates (5.0)

- The basic rate ceiling for 2012–13 becomes £34,370.
- The basic rate is 20 per cent from 2008–09.
- The 10 per cent starting rate for savings income applies to any that you have within your top slice of income but below £2,710 for 2012–13.
- The 50 per cent additional rate applies to taxable income over £150,000 for 2011–12 and 2012–13. A lower rate of 45 per cent replaces this for 2013–14.

The additional rate (50 per cent) provides greater scope for wealthy couples to save tax by equalising their income (26.2.11).

- After 6 January 2013, child benefit starts to be taxable if your net income or that of your partner exceeds £50,000 (5.2.2).
- From 6 April 2013, a cap is planned on unlimited tax reliefs. This will apply at £50,000 or 25 per cent of the income if greater, if more than £50,000 is claimed. Relief for donations to charities will remain unlimited.

1.2.2 Allowances and reliefs

Allowances such as personal allowance and age allowance have been increased (3.3).

- From 2010–11, personal allowance for those with taxable 'adjusted' net income over £100,000 will be reduced by £1 for every £2 of the excess, down to nil.
- For 2011–12, the personal relief for those under 65 went up to £7,475 and then £8,105 for 2012–13.
- From 2011–12, the basic rate limit has been reduced so that higher rate payers do not benefit from the increase in personal relief.
- From 2013–14, age allowance (3.2.7) will be drastically reduced.

- The pensions relief annual allowance remains at £50,000 but the lifetime allowance is now £1.5m (14.3.1 & 14.6.2).

Elements of child tax credit (3.4.4) and Working Tax Credit (WTC) increase for 2012–13 (3.4.4), although 50+ return to work payments have ended.

1.2.3 Charities

The entitlement to gift aid of community amateur sports clubs has been concessionary and now becomes statutory.

1.3 Tax on employments

- The company car benefits tax scheme becomes progressively harsher for years up to and including 2016–17.
- From 2016–17, petrol and diesel fuelled cars will become similarly taxed.
- The car and van fuel benefit charges for 2012–13 and 2013–14 will be respectively increased.
- The EMI threshold (10.9.8) goes up to £250,000.

1.4 Business taxation

- From 6 April 2012 (1 April 2012 for companies) writing down allowance goes down to 18 per cent for your main pool of plant and machinery.
- The special rate on the pool of assets including long life ones is 8 per cent from April 2012.
- From 6 April 2012 (1 April for companies) writing down allowance for cars is reduced to 8 per cent but only where the carbon dioxide emissions exceed 160 grams per kilometre (11.9.12); otherwise 18 per cent applies. Similar rules apply for car lease payments.
- From April 2012, annual investment allowance at 100 per cent is only available on the first £25,000 plant etc., instead of £100,000.
- Holiday lettings relief (7.7) continues for UK and EEA properties.
- Business premises renovation allowance (11.11.2) will be extended until April 2017.
- From 1 April 2013, companies can elect to put a proportion of their patents etc. (starting at 60 per cent) into a *Patent Box* to be taxed at 10 per cent.
- A 100 per cent first year allowance is available for plant and machinery for use primarily in designated assisted areas in enterprise zones.

1.4.1 Corporation tax (13.2 & 13.6)

- The main companies rate becomes 24 per cent from 1 April 2012 and 23 per cent from 1 April 2013 (13.2).
- The small companies rate is 20 per cent from 1 April 2011.
- The controlled foreign companies scheme is being reformed from 1 January 2013 (13.22).

1.5 Capital gains tax

1.5.1 Rates and exemptions

- For 2011–12 and 2012–13, the capital gains tax rate is 18 per cent, 28 per cent for higher tax payers and 28 per cent for trustees and personal representatives.
- The tax rate for entrepreneur's relief remains at 10 per cent, and the lifetime amount is £10m from 6 April 2011.
- The main annual exemption for 2011–12 and 2012–13 is £10,600 and £5,300 for many trusts.

1.6 Tax-efficient investments

- From 2012–13, the ISA limits will be indexed by reference to the Consumer Prices Index (8.12).
- Junior ISAs will be available from autumn 2011 for UK resident children under 18 who do not have a child trust fund.
- Income tax relief for investment in EIS shares after 5 April 2011 increases to 30 per cent.
- Enterprise investment schemes (11.26) and venture capital trusts (8.13) have been simplified, with higher thresholds.

1.7 Trusts

For 2012–13, the tax rates for trusts remain at 50 per cent, with a dividend rate of 42.5 per cent. (As before, the first £1,000 of income attracts less – 21.2.)

- The main trust rate for 2013–14 becomes 45 per cent with a dividend rate of 37.5 per cent.

1.8 Pensions taxation

- The pensions annual allowance was drastically reduced to £50,000 from 2011–12 and the lifetime allowance went down to £1.5m from 6 April 2012.
- A three-year carry forward facility has been introduced for unused annual allowances.
- Various changes take effect, including the abolition of contracting out (14.2.1) for money purchase schemes from 6 April 2012.

The new rules are complicated regarding transitional relief and otherwise, and you should consider seeking expert advice if appropriate.

1.9 Inheritance tax

1.9.1 Rates

The nil rate band increase to £325,000 for 2009–10 was frozen and remains the same for 2012–13, 2013–14 and 2014–15, after which it is indexed in line with the CPI.

The nil rate band provides scope for tax-free gifts by will and during your lifetime.

1.9.2 Civil partners

The tax exemptions covering civil partners in accordance with the CPA (from 5 December 2005) are particularly valuable in the field of inheritance tax. In the same way that married couples normally are free from inheritance tax on assets passing between them, so are single-sex partners under the new rules.

Partners within the CPA should take full advantage of the scope for passing on assets free of inheritance tax to the surviving partner. However, as with married couples, the nil rate band should not be wasted.

1.9.3 Unused nil rate band

If a surviving spouse or civil partner dies after 8 October 2007, any nil rate band which was unused at the first death can be transferred to the estate of the survivor (22.5.2).

In order to preserve the second nil rate band, it is no longer necessary to leave it to others than the surviving spouse or civil partner.

1.9.4 Charitable bequests

From April 2012, the inheritance tax rate on death is reduced to 36 per cent where at least 10 per cent of the net estate is left to charity.

1.10 Anti-avoidance etc.

- Certain VAT anomalies and loopholes are closed.
- New and changed legislation is introduced including capital allowances, debt buybacks, property business loss relief, offshore trusts, stamp duty and life insurance.

Artificial tax avoidance schemes should always be approached with the utmost caution, but if you effect one, remember your responsibility to report it to HMRC. If you are considering such a scheme, require the promoters to provide you with full information about the results of previous reports by them to HMRC relevant to that scheme including the scheme reference number.

1.11 International matters

1.11.1 Residence, ordinary residence and domicile

The reforms and definitions announced for April 2012 have been postponed for a year. The new measures include the abolition of ordinary residence and new legislation to protect relief for certain overseas employment (at present under SP1/09).

1.11.2 The remittance basis

From April 2013, the annual charge on those UK resident for 12 or more years becomes £50,000, but remittances for commercial investment will be tax-free. These measures come in one year later than originally announced.

If you are non-UK domiciled, you should carefully consider no longer claiming the remittance basis or perhaps ceasing to be UK resident.

1.11.3 Future statutory residence test (17.0 & 17.5)

The new residence test is still at consultation, but so novel that its key features are described to show how they could affect you.

1.12 Landfill tax (7.14)

The standard rate of landfill tax increases to £64 per tonne from 1 April 2012 and to £72 from 1 April 2013.

1.13 Value added tax

Changes include the following:

- The registration threshold increases to £77,000 from 1 April 2012 (23.5).
- The VAT rate remains at 20 per cent (5 per cent reduced rate).
- The VAT fuel scale charges (23.11.1) are increased for accounting periods beginning after 30 April 2012.

1.14 Stamp duty

- A higher rate of SDLT of 7 per cent applies for completions from normally 21 March 2012 for residential property where the consideration exceeds £2m.
- Where a company etc. envelopes a residential property, and the consideration exceeds £2m, SDLT will be at 15 per cent with effect from 21 March 2012.

1.15 National Insurance contributions

The details for 2012–13 include the following:

- Class 1 – the weekly earnings level below which you pay no contributions as an employee is £146.
- Class 2 (self-employed flat rate) – the weekly rate is £2.65.
- Class 3 (voluntary) – the weekly rate becomes £13.25.
- Class 4 contributions start at an annual earnings level of £7,605 and the charge at 9 per cent applies up to £42,475.
- From 2012–13 the excess of income over the main rate limits attracts a charge of 2 per cent for employees' and employers' contributions under Class 1 and under Class 4.
- Consultation will take place over a number of years on merging income tax and national insurance contributions.

1.16 Key rates and allowances 2012–13

See table below.

				Reference
INCOME TAX				5.0
Taxable income £	**Slice £**	**Rate %**	**Tax on slice £**	
34,370	0–34,370	20	6,874.00	
115,630	34,370–150,000	40	46,252.00	
Remainder		50		

Note: Savings income in your £0–2,710 band is taxed at 10 per cent. Dividends within your £0–34,370 band carry a 10 per cent tax credit (non-refundable) and attract no further tax.

Income tax allowances	**£**	3.0
Personal allowance	8,105	
Reduced by £1 for every £2 of income above £100,000		
Age allowance	10,500	
Age 75 or over	10,660	
Income limit for age allowance	25,400	
Married couple's allowance*		
Either partner over 75 in year of assessment	7,705	
Minimum amount	2,960	
Life assurance premium relief – only on pre-14 March 1984 policies	12.5%	

* relief restricted to 10 per cent.

COMPANIES (Year to 31 March 2012)		**%**	
Corporation tax – small companies rate		20	13.6
full rate		24	13.7.1
CAPITAL GAINS TAX			
Rate (individuals) from 23 June 2010	18%/28%		20.1
Annual exemption (individuals etc.)	10,600		20.5
INHERITANCE TAX			
Band £	**Death rate %**		22.5
0–325,000	Nil		
325,000 upwards	40		
Annual exemption		£3,000	22.17
VAT			
Main rate from 4 January 2011		20%	23.1
Registration threshold from 1 April 2012		77,000	23.5

Chapter 2

THE BASIS OF YOUR TAX LIABILITY

2.1 Who is taxable?

Individuals, partnerships, estates, trusts, companies, and certain other organisations that are resident in the UK are taxable on their income arising here. They are also liable on income arising abroad subject to the rules outlined later in this book. The taxation of the income of individuals is covered first; partnerships, estates, trusts and companies being dealt with in later chapters.

The UK income of non-resident individuals, companies and other entities may also be subject to tax here (19.1).

Similarly, capital gains tax is payable on certain capital profits made by UK residents anywhere in the world (20.3). Non-residents, however, are not always liable to UK capital gains tax.

2.2 The taxes payable (ITA Ss6–9)

A unified system of personal taxation operates under which there is, for 2012–13, a basic rate of 20 per cent, a higher rate of 40 per cent and an additional rate of 50 per cent (5.0). Your savings income falling within your basic rate band generally attracts 20 per cent (8.7). Certain different rates apply for previous years (26.2).

The capital gains tax rate for individuals is generally 18 per cent and 28 per cent. However, the first £10,600 of your net capital gains is not taxed (20.1).

Special rules apply to companies which are taxed on both income and capital gains at corporation tax rates (13.2).

Inheritance tax applies to wealth passing on death and in some other circumstances (Chapter 22).

2.3 What income is taxable? (TA 1988 Ss1 & 15–20)

The table below summarises the classes of income that are subject to income tax, or corporation tax for companies. Prior to 6 April 2005, when ITTOIA (2.10) was introduced, a schedular system applied although the basic tax rules remain.

2.3.1 Classes of income (from 6 April 2005)

Trading income including:

Trades (11.1)
Professions (11.1)

Employments (including directorships).There are normally three classes:

- The employee is resident in the UK and the work is done here (10.1)
- Work done here by a non-resident (10.2)
- Work done wholly abroad by a UK resident whose salary is sent here during the overseas employment excluding income taxed as above (10.3).

Property income – from land and buildings including rents and certain premiums from leases (7.1).

Savings and investment income (8.4 etc.).

Miscellaneous income (15.1).

2.4 Deduction of tax at source and tax credits

Tax at now 20 per cent is frequently deducted at source from savings income by the payers and the recipients get the net amount. The former pay the tax over to HMRC. Company dividend payments, however, are made without any tax deductions although the recipients are 'imputed' with a credit of 1⁄9 of the dividend.

Thus suppose that for 2012–13 you receive a dividend of £90: you will get a tax credit of £10 (£90 × 1⁄9) which is not reclaimable even if your income is low (16.7). If your income is high enough, however, you may be taxed at higher rates (5.0.1 and 5.6.1) on £100 (90 + 10).

Tax is also deducted at source in the case of certain annual payments (4.1) and income from wages and salaries (see 2.3.1). In the former case the payer of the income is entitled in certain circumstances to retain the tax deducted and need not pay it over to HMRC.

2.5 The distinction between capital and revenue profits

Most of your income is subjected to income tax at the basic and perhaps higher rate, whereas, normally, capital profits are liable to capital gains tax or are tax-free. The tax rates borne by income and capital gains are now broadly similar. However, the rules and reliefs are very different. The question is then: What is a capital profit?

Generally speaking, a capital profit is a profit which you realise on the sale of an asset where it is clear that you are not making it your business to buy and sell assets of that type. On the other hand, if you conduct a business in such assets your profits will be income.

2.5.1 Examples of capital transactions

- The sale of the house in which you live (also normally free of capital gains tax unless used for business) (20.23).

- The sale of your private motor car (also free of capital gains tax).
- The sale of shares you held as investments.
- The sale of a plot of land you inherited.
- The sale of the goodwill of your business.
- The receipt of an inheritance (also free of capital gains tax).
- The sale of a property which you had bought for investment purposes.
- The sale of a picture unless you are the artist or a picture dealer.
- The receipt of the proceeds of a 'qualifying' life assurance policy (9.3). (This is also normally free of capital gains tax.)

2.5.2 Examples of revenue transactions

- The sale of houses and land if you are a property dealer.
- The sale of motor cars if you are a car dealer.
- The sale of shares if you are a share dealer.
- The sale of pictures if you created them or are a picture dealer.
- The receipt of salaries, commissions, interest, dividends, rent, royalties etc.

2.6 Revenue and capital expenses

In the same way that income and capital profits must be distinguished, you must separate revenue and capital expenses for tax purposes. The latter can only be charged against capital profits and the former against income. For example, the commission on the sale of shares acquired for investment is deducted in calculating your capital gains but if you are a share dealer then it is a revenue expense.

Also, in determining the assessable profits of a business, only revenue expenses may be deducted and capital expenses are prohibited as a deduction (11.3.2).

2.6.1 Tax-free income

Certain items in your income may be entirely free of tax. These are listed below.

(1) Casual gambling profits (for example pools, horse racing etc.).
(2) Premium Bond winnings.
(3) Lottery prizes.
(4) Interest on authorised holdings of National Savings Certificates (TA 1988 S46).
(5) Bonuses paid at the end of 'save as you earn' contracts.
(6) Maturity bonuses payable on Defence Bonds, British Savings Bonds and National Development Bonds.
(7) Interest on Post-war Credits.
(8) Wedding and certain other presents from your employer that are in truth not given in return for your services as an employee.
(9) Certain retirement gratuities and redundancy monies paid by your employer (10.12).
(10) Any scholarship or other educational grant that you receive if you are a full-time student at school, college etc.
(11) War widows' pensions; also comparable payments overseas (TA 1988 S318).

(12) Certain social security benefits (25.3.1) including:
  (a) earnings-related supplement of unemployment benefit (but not unemployment benefit itself)
  (b) sickness benefit (but not statutory sick pay)
  (c) maternity allowance and grant (but not maternity pay)
  (d) attendance allowance
  (e) child benefit (some tax after 6 January 2013 if your own or partner's net income exceeds £50,000)
  (f) family income supplement (but retirement pensions under the National Insurance Scheme are assessable)
  (g) mobility allowance
  (h) certain payments of income support, family credit or housing benefit; but taxable up to given limits if related to trade disputes or conditional upon availability for employment (TA 1988 S617)
  (i) short-term incapacity benefit paid during the first 28 weeks of incapacity (FA 1995 S141).

(13) Housing grants paid by local authorities etc.
(14) German compensation payments to victims of National-Socialist persecution. This now includes payments made by foreign and UK banks and building societies. Also Austrian and German state pensions paid to such victims.
(15) Wound and disability pensions.
(16) Allowances, bounties and gratuities paid for additional service in the armed forces.
(17) The capital part of a purchased life annuity (but not the interest portion).
(18) Your first £70 of interest each year from National Savings Bank Ordinary Deposits. This exemption from tax applies separately to husband and wife (TA 1988 S325).
(19) Certain allowances paid under job release schemes, as described in the Job Release Act 1977, within a year of pensionable age.
(20) Additional pensions and annuities paid to the holders of certain gallantry awards by virtue of those awards (TA 1988 S317).
(21) Compensation for mis-sold personal pensions (FA 1996 S148).
(22) Jobfinder's grant, generally before 2003–04 (FA 1996 S152).
(23) Income from PEPs (8.10) and ISAs (8.12).
(24) Financial support to adopters by local authorities and adoption agencies (TA S327A).
(25) In-work credit, in-work emergency discretion fund and in-work emergency fund from 6 April 2008.
(26) The provision for employees of one health-screening and one medical check-up each year including through non-cash vouchers.
(27) Subsistence allowances paid by a UK located EU body to seconded UK experts from 1 January 2011.
(28) Certain fees relating to monitoring schemes regarding vulnerable persons from 2011–12.
(29) The first £30,000 of certain resettlement payments from April 2012 made to MPs.

2.7 Bank and building society interest

Any bank or building society interest which you receive normally has 20 per cent income tax deducted from it at source (8.6). If your income is sufficiently high, however, you will be charged an additional tax on the grossed up equivalent of the interest as if you had suffered tax on it at 20 per cent. The additional tax payable consists of higher rate income tax on the grossed up equivalent of the income, less tax on it at 20 per cent. Thus if you receive building society interest of £80 in the year then £100 (the grossed up equivalent) will be included in your total taxable income. The grossed up equivalent is determined by the formula:

$$\text{Interest received} \times \frac{100}{80} \text{ (that is, 100 less 20 per cent).}$$

2.8 Year of assessment

Income tax is an annual tax; thus it is your total income over each 12-month period that is assessed to tax. The year of assessment runs from 6 April to the following 5 April and so the tax year 2012–13 means the year ending 5 April 2013.

The income chargeable to tax for each year of assessment is computed according to the rules relevant to the various classes (see 2.3.1) as described later in this book. In general, an 'actual' basis is now required in which the income received during a particular year is assessable for that year.

The year to 5 April also forms the year of assessment for capital gains tax.

2.9 Period of assessment less than full year

It is possible for a taxpayer to have a period of assessment of less than 12 months. For example, a baby born during any year has a period of assessment running from the date of its birth until the next 5 April. If a taxpayer dies, his period of assessment runs from 6 April to the date of his death.

Notwithstanding that the period of assessment may be less than a year, the taxpayer receives the personal reliefs applicable to a whole year of assessment.

2.10 Where to find the law

Tax law is to be found in certain Acts of Parliament, case decisions, regulations and statutory instruments. The former are the normally annual Finance Acts and so called Taxes Acts, such as the Inheritance Tax Act 1984, the Taxation of Chargeable Gains Act 1992 and the Income and Corporation Taxes Act 1988 (ICTA).

Originally, ICTA consolidated the existing legislation regarding income tax and tax on companies, including that from trading, investment, land and employments. However, starting with the Capital Allowances Act 2001, areas of the legislation have been removed from ICTA and transferred to new legislation, where it is rewritten in a clearer style, generally without changing the meaning.

A major step in this process took place with the Income Tax (Earnings and Pensions) Act 2003 (10.0) which is described in Chapter 10. An even more sweeping consolidation and rewriting of ICTA took place from 6 April 2005. Its scope includes trading, property, savings and miscellaneous income, hence its lengthy title – the Income Tax (Trading and Other Income) Act 2005 (ITTOIA).

A summary of ITTOIA follows, so as to provide a broad outline of its contents. Since the old references are likely to prove helpful for the present, some are retained in this edition, together with some references to ITTOIA. Note that the classification of income into Schedules no longer applies.

2.10.1 Income Tax (Trading and Other Income) Act 2005 (ITTOIA)

Part		Sections	Schedules
1	Overview	1–2	1
2	Trading overview	3–4	2 (Parts 1–2)
	Income taxed as trading profits	5–23	2 (Part 3)
	Trading profits – basic rules	24–31	
	rules restricting deductions	32–55	
	rules allowing deductions	56–94	
	receipts	95–106	
	gifts to charities	107–110	
	herd basis	111–129	
	films and recordings etc.	130–148	
	other specific trades	149–172	
	Valuation of stock and work in progress	173–186	
	Unremittable amounts	187–191	
	Disposals and acquisitions of know-how	192–195	
	Basis periods	196–220	
	Averaging and adjustment income	221–240	
	Post-cessation receipts	241–257	
	Supplementary (trustees and insolvency)	258–259	
3	Property income	260–364	2 (Part 4)
4	Savings and investment income	365–573	2 (Parts 5–7)
5	Miscellaneous income	574–689	2 (Part 8)
6	Exempt income	690–783	2 (Part 9)
7	Rent a room and foster care reliefs	784–828	2 (Part 10)
8	Foreign income – special rules	829–845	2 (Part 11)
9	Partnerships	846–863	
10	Supplementary and general	864–886	3 and 4

2.10.2 Income Tax Act 2007 (ITA)

Most of the remaining income tax provisions from ICTA have been consolidated into the new Act (ITA) with effect from 6 April 2007. Exceptions are double tax relief, capital allowances (CAA) and pension schemes.

Chapter 3

PERSONAL RELIEFS

According to your circumstances you can claim certain personal tax reliefs which are deducted from your total income in arriving at the amount on which you pay income tax.

3.0 Personal reliefs at a glance 2012–13

Type	Circumstances	Relief
Personal allowance		£8,105*
Life assurance relief (3.2.5)	Policy effected before 14 March 1984 on your own or wife's life – deduction from premium	12½% of premiums
Blind person's allowance (3.2.6)		£2,100*
Age allowance (3.2.7)	Age 65–74 – Single Age 75 or over – Single	£10,500* £10,660*
	Reduced by £1 for every £2 of excess income over £25,400 down to personal reliefs level	
† Married couple's allowance (3.2.1)	Age under 75 Age 75 and over Minimum amount	NIL £7,705* £2,960
Income limit for personal allowance £100,000		

* These allowances will be increased for future years in line with the consumer prices index (unless the Treasury otherwise orders).

† These allowances are restricted to 10%.

3.1 Earned and unearned income

For tax purposes income is classified as being either 'earned' or 'unearned'. Earned income includes the following:

(1) The salary or wages from your job including any taxable benefits.
(2) Certain pensions or retirement annuities paid to you, including those under a Revenue approved scheme (10.11).
(3) Any income from a trade or profession in which you engage.
(4) Any income from a partnership provided that you work in it and are not merely a sleeping partner.
(5) Old age pensions and widow's pensions received under the National Insurance Act.
(6) Income from a patent or copyright if you actually created the subject matter.
(7) After leaving your employment, trade or profession, any taxable amounts that you receive from that source.
(8) Income from holiday lettings as defined (7.7).

The rest of your income is 'unearned' and includes:

(1) Dividends.
(2) Bank deposit interest.
(3) Building society interest received.
(4) Rents from property investments.
(5) Income from trusts.
(6) Interest from government or local authority stock.

3.2 Personal allowances (ITA Ss33–58)

For 2009–10 and 2010–11 there was a personal allowance of £6,475 (previously £6,035). This was available to individuals generally. However, a higher allowance may apply to those who have attained their 65th birthday (3.2.7). For 2011–12 the personal allowance increased to £7,475, becoming £8,105 for 2012–13, but the basic rate limit has gone down.

3.2.1 Personal allowance – income related reduction from 2010–11

Your basic personal allowance from 2010–11 is reduced by £1 for every £2 by which your income exceeds £100,000.

3.2.2 Example: Restriction of personal relief

	£
Mr B's income for 2011–12 is	110,000
Excess over £100,000	10,000
50 per cent thereof	5,000
Full personal relief	7,475
Restricted personal relief	**2,475**

3.2.3 Married couple's allowance (ITA Ss42–55)

From 6 April 1990, according to the rules, each married couple obtained a married couple's allowance, depending on their ages attained during the tax year. The following applied from 2007–08 to 2012–13:

	2007–08 £	2008–09 £	2009–10 & 2010–11 £	2011–12 £	2012–13 £
Husband and wife both aged under 65	Nil	Nil	Nil	Nil	Nil
Husband or wife aged 65–74	6,285	6,535	Nil	Nil	Nil
Husband or wife aged 75 and over (or born before 6 April 1935)	6,365	6,625	6,965	7,295	7,705
Income limit	20,900	21,800	22,900	24,000	25,400

For 1994–95 relief for married couple's allowance was restricted to the lower rate (20 per cent) and to 15 per cent subsequently. From 1999–2000, the rate is 10 per cent.

The higher allowances for older people are reduced if the husband's annual income exceeds a set limit, currently £25,400. For every £2 of income received in excess of £25,400, the higher allowances are reduced by £1 until the minimum allowance (£2,960) is reached.

After 5 April 2000, married couple's allowance is only available where at least one of you was born on or before 5 April 1935. It was withdrawn for younger couples.

You can elect for the married couple's allowance to be split equally between you or go entirely to the wife. Otherwise, it goes automatically to the husband. This election is needed before the start of the first tax year to which it applies. The wife may elect for the equal split but both must elect for her to receive it all. Any unused balance may be transferred to the wife. To do this, an election must be made to your Inspector of Taxes within six years of the end of the tax year.

In the year of marriage, if available, the allowance is reduced by one-twelfth for each complete month from 6 April until your marriage date.

3.2.4 **Child benefit**

Tax-free child benefit has applied since 4 April 1977. It applies in respect of your children under age 16 and those under 19 receiving full-time education, satisfying the necessary rules. From 14 April 2010, the weekly rate is £20.30 for the first child and £13.40 for each other child (previously £20.00 and £13.20). The special rate for lone parents (previously £17.55) was abolished from 2007–08. These rates continue until 6 April 2014. In addition, some guardians are entitled to an allowance of £15.55 per child.

Child benefit paid from 7 January 2013 may result in a tax charge if you and/or your partner has adjusted net income over £50,000 for the tax year. An income tax charge is made at 1 per cent on each £100 of the income between £50,000 and £60,000, above which the tax covers the full child benefit and the latter can be waived.

3.2.5 **Life assurance relief** (TA 1988 Ss266–274)

Tax relief in respect of pre-14 March 1984 life assurance policies is given based on the premiums paid in the tax year. You now normally deduct the relief from your premium payments (see table below). The relief only applies to policies taken out *prior to 14 March 1984*. Premiums in respect of policies effected after that date attract no relief. Similarly, relief is not due on existing policies for which the benefits are enhanced after that date, for example, by exercising an option to increase the policy term.

3.2.6 **Rules for life assurance relief – pre-14 March 1984 policies**

(1) The policy benefits must include a sum payable on death or in certain circumstances provide for a deferred annuity.

(2) The policy must be effected with a UK, Dominion or Irish insurance company or one carrying on business here; or a Lloyd's Underwriter; or a registered friendly society.

(3) The policy must be on your own or your wife's life and either of you may pay the premiums.
(4) Special relief is given for sums paid under an Act of Parliament or under the rules of your employment to secure a deferred annuity for your widow or children after your death. The relief is given according to your income level by deducting the following percentages of the premiums from your tax bill:

Total income	**% relief**
Not over £1,000	half of basic rate of income tax
£1,001–£2,000	three-quarters of basic rate
Over £2,000	basic rate of income tax

(5) Policies taken out after 19 March 1968 or changed after that date have to be 'qualifying policies' (9.3).
(6) A fixed percentage of each premium is deducted by you on payment and you keep this relief. The premium limit is the larger of $\frac{1}{6}$ of your total income (after charges) and £1,500. Any over-deduction by you will be adjusted in your assessment at the end of the tax year or you may be directed by HMRC to pay premiums without the deduction of tax relief.
(7) From 6 April 1989 the relief percentage is $12\frac{1}{2}$ per cent.
(8) Relief will be withdrawn for any premium due and payable after 5 April 2015 and also if paid after 5 July 2015.

3.2.7 **Example: Life assurance relief restrictions for 2012–13**

	£	**Date effected**	**2012–13 premium £**
Policy A – Sum assured	10,000	1.1.80	1,000
Policy B – Sum assured	20,000	5.4.82	1,500
Policy C – Sum assured	25,000	1.5.84*	2,000

* Policy C was effected after 13 March 1984 and thus does not qualify for relief. If total income for year = £12,000

Premiums eligible for relief restricted to $\frac{1}{6}$ × £12,000 = £2,000

Life assurance relief for year = £250 ($12\frac{1}{2}$% × £2,000)

3.2.8 **Blind person's relief** (ITA Ss38–40)

(1) The relief is given to registered blind persons.
(2) For 2012–13, the relief is £2,100.
(3) For 2011–12, the relief was £1,980.
(4) If a spouse cannot use all his or her allowance, it can be transferred to the other spouse even if he or she is not blind.

3.2.9 **Age allowance** (ITA Ss36 & 37)

(1) This applies for 2012–13 if you are over 65 by 5 April 2013.
(2) The personal allowance is increased to £10,500 if your age on 5 April 2013 is between 65 and 74 and to £10,660 if you have reached your 75th

birthday. For the extra age allowance for married people, only one of you needs to be 75 by that time.

(3) The above allowance figures are restricted if your income exceeds £25,400. The restriction is one-half of the excess of your income over £25,400. Thus if your income is £26,400 your allowance is restricted to £10,500 – £500 = £10,000. Note that the £25,400 restriction is based on your 'total income' (5.2), which is before tax but after certain deductions. If you have any life policy gains, these must be included without top slicing relief (9.7).

(4) If your income is sufficiently high your personal relief is restricted to the normal rate (£8,105), but not below this.

(5) From 2013–14, the age allowances will be frozen at £10,500 if you were born before 6 April 1948 and £10,660 if you were born before 6 April 1938.

3.2.10 Vocational training

If you paid for your own vocational training, tax relief was available from 6 April 1992 to 5 April 2000, subject to the rules. Relief was given for training leading to National Vocational Qualifications and Scottish Vocational Qualifications. The relief is not available for 2000–01 and subsequently, when an Individual Learning Accounts scheme took over (10.6.23).

3.3 Indexation of personal reliefs (ITA S57)

For 1981–82 and subsequent years, certain personal reliefs were to be increased from their previous levels by not less than the proportionate increase in the Retail Prices Index for the last calendar year. Starting with 1993, the year for comparison runs to September. With Parliamentary approval, however, a lower increase (or none at all as for 1993–94, 1994–95 and 2003–04 personal allowance) may be ordered by the Treasury. Similarly, FA 2010 fixed the allowance rates for 2010–11 at their 2009–10 levels. From 2012–13, the Consumer Prices Index will be used instead of the Retail Prices Index.

The reliefs concerned are personal allowance, married couple's allowance (3.2.1) and age allowance (3.2.7). Also, blind person's allowance (3.2.6) is indexed for 1998–99 and subsequently. Of course, indexation ceased to be relevant from 2000–01 for the reliefs which have been removed such as married couple's allowance for those under 65.

3.3.1 Example: Personal reliefs – general illustration

Mr A lives with his family at 1 Bridge Street. Their income consists of:

	Income assessable for 2012–13	
Name	**Earned** £	**Savings** £
Mr A	15,670.00	5,435.00
Mrs A	5,705.00	2,600.00

Mrs A pays an annual premium of £200 on a qualifying life assurance policy on Mr A's life taken out before 14 March 1984. How much income tax is payable by Mr A and Mrs A for 2012–13?

	Mr A	Mrs A
	£	£
Earned income	15,670.00	5,705.00
Savings income	5,435.00	2,600.00
Total Income	21,105.00	8,305.00
Less:		
Personal allowance	8,105.00	8,105.00
	13,000.00	200.00
Income tax payable: at 20%	2,600.00	40.00

Notes:

(a) On the levels of income shown above Mr A is not liable to higher rate (5.0).

(b) Life assurance relief of 12½% × £200 = £25 will be obtained by deduction from the premium payments.

(c) The savings income normally will have been subject to 20% tax at source, which is set against the liabilities shown. It is assumed that no dividends are included since these are differently treated (8.1).

3.4 Working tax credit and child tax credit etc.

As you have seen, there are reliefs and allowances which reduce your taxable income. There are also tax credits which are offset against your income tax, so that you pay less and may even receive a net repayment. However, these tax credits are effectively social security benefits which are in general only available to those with lower incomes. An outline follows of the rules. In particular, note that a revised system operates from 2003–04 (3.4.4).

3.4.1 Working families tax credit (WFTC)

Operating from October 1999, WFTC replaced social security family credit. If you were employed, from 6 April 2000, the tax credit was put through the PAYE system and went into your pay packet.

3.4.2 Disabled person's tax credit (DPTC)

DPTC replaced social security disability working allowance for 2001–03. There was a weekly basic tax credit for 2001–02 of £56.05 for a single person and £86.25 for a lone parent or a couple. These went up to £61.05 and £91.25 respectively in June 2001 and then £62.10 and £95.30 for 2002–03. Also, there were child tax credits as for WFTC as shown above, with that for a disabled child (£30.00) applying throughout 2001–02 and £35.50 for 2002–03. As for WFTC, there were net income thresholds, above which tax credit was lost at 55p per £.

3.4.3 Children's tax credit (CTC)

This tax credit commenced on 6 April 2001. It replaced married couple's and other related allowances now phased out, including additional personal allowance and widow's bereavement allowance.

You qualified for the allowance if you had one or more children under 16 living with you. Relief was given at 10 per cent on £5,290 for 2002–03 (on

£5,200 for 2001–02). However, if you were a higher rate tax payer, your CTC could be reduced or removed altogether.

For 2002–03 CTC increased to £10,490 for the year of a child's birth. Thus you received this increased amount where a baby was born in that year.

3.4.4 **Revised system**

From 2003–04, WFTC, DPTC and CTC have been absorbed into a new system comprising two new tax credits. These are child tax credit (CTC) and working tax credit (WTC). There are also pension credits (PC) to help retired lower income persons by topping up their incomes.

The new tax credits carry various advantages compared with the old ones such as higher levels. The annual details for 2010–11, 2011–12 and 2012–13 are shown below.

The various WTC and CTC elements to which you are entitled are aggregated and your total credits are reduced if your income is too high. For 2012–13, if you are entitled to only WTC, your tax credits are reduced by 41 per cent of the excess over £6,420. If you are entitled to CTC, your tax credits are reduced by 41 per cent of the excess of your income over £15,860, but the family element remains as above.

		2010–11 £	2011–12 £	2012–13 £
CTC:	Family element	545	545	545
	Baby addition	545	withdrawn	n/a
	Child element	2,300	2,555	2,690
	Disabled child element	2,715	2,800	2,950
	Severely disabled child element	1,095	1,130	1,190
WTC:	Basic element	1,920	1,920	1,920
	Couples and lone parent element	1,890	1,950	1,950
	30 hour element (for couples – both must work 30 hours jointly with one working at least 16 hours each week)	790	790	790
	Disabled worker element	2,570	2,650	2,790
	Severe disability worker element	1,095	1,130	1,190
	Childcare element:			
	For 1 child	9,100	9,100	9,100
	For 2 or more children	15,600	15,600	15,600
	Percentage of eligible costs covered	80%	70%	70%
PC:	Standard minimum income guarantee per week:			
	Single	132.60	137.35	142.70
	Couple	202.40	209.70	217.90

Chapter 4

ANNUAL INTEREST AND OTHER PAYMENTS

4.0 General scope

It is important as an individual taxpayer to ascertain whether or not you have an obligation to deduct income tax from any interest or other recurring payments which you propose to make. Subject to the detailed rules, a useful guideline is to check the position before making payments to overseas residents or any payments (other than UK interest) which are for commercial purposes.

This chapter surveys the history of income tax relief for business and personal interest payments. Although the tax law rewrite, which ran from 2003 to 2010, removed the long-standing terms 'charges on income' and 'income brought into charge', the principle of deducting tax from certain payments and accounting for it was preserved, where necessary substituting statutory provisions for old case law. For income tax purposes these changes applied from 6 April 2007 and this chapter now reflects the pattern of the current legislation.

On 27 March 2012 HMRC launched a broadly based consultation into many aspects of the taxation of interest and transactions of a similar nature with a view to bringing forward revising legislation in FB 2013. Many of the points raised aim to clarify anomalies and uncertainties of the established regime, including the tax deduction responsibilities of interest payers, the taxation status of interest elements of legal compensation of various kinds and the blocking of one offshore tax avoidance opportunity for large corporate groups. There may yet be some further proposals pursuant to a previous consultation, which closed on 28 May 2010 and addressed deduction of tax at source. The initial consultation period closed on 22 June 2012 and draft legislation is due be published during Autumn 2012.

4.1 Duty to deduct income tax at source

The majority of circumstances in which a duty to deduct income tax from interest and 'qualifying annual payments' at source is imposed by law relate to payments made by companies and financial institutions (13.9.1), so you will generally encounter them as a recipient.

In the few cases where this duty does apply to an individual, the rules can be complicated and HMRC publish their views on the location (in or outside the UK) of debts and obligations. If you are uncertain whether you have a duty to deduct tax or how to proceed, you should take advice, because failing to deduct tax when you should or deducting tax when you should not can have equally unwelcome consequences.

4.1.1 Deduction of tax from interest payments (ITA 2007 Ss874, 884 & 888)

As an individual, you are required to deduct a sum representing income tax from payments of yearly interest which are payable to a recipient whose usual place of abode is outside the UK, if they relate to a debt or other obligation that is located in the UK. Generally a mortgage on foreign property or a debt enforceable in a foreign court will be located outside the UK. If, however, you pay 'annual interest' in this country on an advance from an overseas bank which carries on business in the UK, you should not deduct income tax and, if you are uncertain as to the location of the obligation, you should take advice.

The tax deduction should equal tax at the basic rate (20 per cent) which is treated as tax paid on account by the recipient.

Your relief will be by way of an adjustment to your self-assessment, which gives relief at whatever rate is appropriate. However, if you have insufficient income taxed at the basic rate to cover the interest paid, a claw-back will be made.

4.1.2 **Deduction of tax from patent royalties and annual payments other than interest** (TA 1988 Ss898–905)

As an individual, you are required to deduct a sum representing income tax, from 'qualifying annual payments' arising in the UK and paid for genuine commercial reasons in connection with your trade, profession or vocation.

In addition you are required to make a similar deduction from any payment of patent royalties that is not a 'qualifying annual payment' but arises in the UK and is chargeable to UK income tax or corporation tax.

Interest, qualifying donations, gift aid, certain payments made by trustees, and annual payments for dividends or other non-taxable consideration, are not 'qualifying annual payments'. Although that leaves royalties and similar payments from intellectual property and certain telecommunication rights and certain employment-related annuities within the definition, these will seldom arise outside the context of your business activities.

The required tax deduction is of tax at the basic rate (20 per cent), which is treated as tax paid on account by the recipient. You will generally be required to account for this tax in calculating your self-assessment liability. Exceptionally, if you are involved with manufactured dividend payments by UK residents, your obligation to account to HMRC for any tax deducted is immediate.

A gap in the tax rewrite legislation, whereby HMRC had no statutory authority to make regulations to manage the 'immediate' collection of such tax deductions, having presumably dealt with it under their 'general care and management' powers, was remedied by F3A 2010.

4.2 Special schemes for deduction of income tax at source

You may encounter obligations to deduct income tax from payments under schemes that deal with particular types of transaction. The commonest is Pay As You Earn (PAYE) which applies to employment income paid by employers based in the UK and is described at length in Chapter 10 (10.14). Two further schemes – those for 'Non-resident Landlords' and 'Foreign Entertainers and Sportsmen' are described below.

4.2.1 **Deduction of tax from non-UK resident landlords**

If you pay to a UK non-resident rent or certain other payments relating to the occupation of UK property, you may be required to deduct income tax at the basic rate (currently 20 per cent) from each payment and account for this to HMRC under the 'non-resident landlords' deduction scheme'. This applies both to tenants and to property managers based in the UK. However, owners approved by HMRC may be exempted (if they pay on self-assessment) or granted a lower rate of tax (if available under a tax treaty) on application.

4.2.2 **Deduction of tax from visiting performers**

If you are involved in the engagement of UK non-resident entertainers or sportsmen, you may have an obligation to deduct income tax under the tax deduction schemes for 'foreign entertainers and sportsmen' (19.6) from fees and certain other expense paid to or for them. The deduction is normally at the basic rate (currently 20 per cent), but exemption or a lower rate of tax may be approved by HMRC on application. There is a specific exemption for certain visiting sportsmen concerned with the the 2012 Olympiad (15.2.2).

4.3 Interest payments and receipts – miscellaneous

Subject to the above, you must not deduct income tax from any payments of interest that you make. This means that most types of interest payments made by you for personal purposes will be gross without any tax deduction.

Companies and local authorities must normally deduct income tax in making 'annual interest' payments and this applies to a partnership of which a company is a member. However, rules have applied since 1 April 2001 permitting gross payments between companies (13.9.1). Interest paid by a bank in the normal course of its business is normally paid subject to the deduction of income tax, but interest on certain 'qualifying certificates of deposit' and 'qualifying time deposits' of £50,000 upwards is excluded (8.6 and 8.7) and paid gross.

However, from 6 April 2012 all new time deposits fall within the general tax deduction regime. This follows informal consultations announced in the previous year.

As indicated above (4.0), further changes to the tax deduction scheme for interest and like payments could appear in the 2013 Finance Bill.

Subject to the rules outlined in the following paragraphs, certain interest payments are allowed as deductions in computing your total income for income tax at the various rates.

4.4 Interest paid for business purposes

Note that interest paid for business purposes is allowable against your taxable business profits provided the loan is used wholly and exclusively for the purposes of your business, profession or vocation. This basic rule includes interest on bank overdrafts as well as that on other loans. These rules apply equally to interest paid for the purposes of your property business, whether relating to UK or foreign properties.

4.5 Tax relief for other interest payments (ITA Ss383–412)

In order to obtain relief for interest paid other than for business purposes, you must show that it is 'eligible for relief'. This term specifically excludes bank overdraft or credit card interest.

4.5.1 Tax relief for specified interest payments

Your interest is 'eligible for relief' if it is paid on loans raised for the following purposes:

(1) Subject to various restrictions, the purchase and improvement of buildings and land in the UK or Eire (4.6).
(2) Buying plant and machinery for use in a partnership which gets capital allowances on it where you are one of the partners.
(3) Buying plant and machinery which is used in connection with an office or employment that you hold and for which you personally get capital allowances (not available for cars, vans etc. from 6 April 2003 (10.6.6)).
(4) Acquiring ordinary shares in a close company (13.18) or lending it money for use in its business. (This does not apply to a close investment company, or for shares bought after 13 March 1989 on which BES or EIS relief is claimed – 11.25 and 11.26.) To qualify for relief you must either own more than 5 per cent of its shares, or own some shares and work for the greater part of your time for the company. Shares owned by 'associates' (13.18) are included in the 5 per cent but not, after July 1989, if owned by an employee trust of which you are a beneficiary.
(5) Purchases by employees of shares in their company as part of an employee buy-out. (Employees and their spouses must together own more than 50 per cent of the company, ignoring excesses over 10 per cent holdings.)
(6) Purchasing a share in a partnership, or lending it money for use in its business if you are a partner. This applies whether or not you work in the partnership and also extends to investing in a co-operative.
(7) Paying inheritance tax arising on death. The personal representatives of the deceased obtain relief for interest paid within a year of raising the loan. If the interest cannot be relieved wholly in the year of payment it can be spread forward or backwards.
(8) Purchasing certain life annuity 'home income plans' before 9 March 1999 (4.6).

Note: Relief for interest on loans to purchase plant and machinery (see (2) and (3) above) is given for three years after the year of assessment in which the loan is taken out. Special rules apply to investments in film partnerships ((6) above) and commercial woodlands (excluded from (4) above).

4.6 Loans for purchase and improvement of buildings and land (ITTOIA Ss29 & 272)

This section is largely historical, but may assist readers to understand the source of the limited relief that remains available to some individuals.

Within the limits mentioned below, any interest which you pay on a loan raised to buy land or buildings, or to improve them, was 'eligible for relief'. This did not include overdraft interest but covered fixed bank loans and building society mortgages etc. (Improvement loans only qualified for relief if applied for this purpose before 6 April 1988.) *Interest on a loan to buy your home was generally withdrawn from 6 April 2000.*

The interest on any loan that you raised to pay off another loan previously obtained to buy property was also 'eligible for relief'. However, no relief was available on a loan obtained after 5 April 1988 to replace money borrowed to improve property.

The Revenue gave sympathetic consideration to cases where, for example, the husband bought the property and the wife paid the interest – the couple would usually get tax relief.

Concerning a property loan raised after 26 March 1974, you only obtained tax relief if either (a) it was to purchase or improve your only or main residence and in general the interest pre-dates 6 April 2000 or (b) you let the property at a commercial rent for at least 26 weeks in the year and it was available for letting at other times. However, from 6 April 1995, interest is treated as a deduction from property income in the same way as other expenses are allowed. At the same time, the old rules (including the 26 weeks letting requirement) ceased to have effect. (The old rules continued to apply for corporation tax purposes.)

Under (a) your interest was restricted to that on a loan of £30,000 and if your borrowing exceeded this figure your interest relief was proportionately restricted. (In considering the £30,000 limit, no account was taken of interest which had been added to capital up to £1,000.) Before 6 April 1991, relief was available at the basic and higher rates of income tax. However, from that date, relief was only granted at the basic rate.

From 6 April 1994, relief was restricted to 20 per cent on existing and new loans. An exception was made for people over 65 who took loans against their homes to buy life annuities and will continue to obtain relief at the basic rate for the duration of existing loans. However, no relief is available for interest on loans taken out after 9 March 1999.

Regarding general home mortgages, from 6 April 1995 relief was further restricted to 15 per cent with 10 per cent applying from 6 April 1998 until 5 April 2000, after which the relief was withdrawn.

Under (b) you are only allowed interest relief against your income from letting property. You continue to obtain higher rate relief under this category.

You also obtained relief up to 5 April 2000 for interest on a loan which you obtained before 6 April 1988 (but not subsequently) to buy a house for a former or separated spouse, or a dependent relative of your wife or yourself. This interest counted, however, towards the £30,000 limit. Loans obtained for these purposes after 5 April 1988 did not qualify for relief.

Your interest relief was not restricted because you did not reside in your property, if you lived in job-related accommodation (10.6.13) and intended to make your property your main residence in due course (TA 1988 S356). A similar rule applied to interest paid on a loan to buy job-related accommodation where you were self-employed.

4.6.1 **Temporary relief** (TA 1988 Ss353 & 365)

You obtained relief for interest on a bridging loan of up to £30,000 for normally up to one year (or longer at the discretion of the Revenue) when you changed houses. Higher rate relief continued after 5 April 1991 on your existing but not your new bridging loan, if both were in place by that date. This included where there had been a formal offer and binding contract. This higher rate relief would normally only continue for up to one year, but could be extended at the discretion of the Revenue.

Similar rules continue to apply if you are over 65 and have a life annuity 'home income plan'. You may now leave your home without losing relief on the loan to buy your annuity. Again, you need to have the property up for sale and relief continues for 12 months from when you move out. In both cases, the Revenue have a discretion to extend this period. For such loans existing on 9 March 1999 (and certain remortgages) that still qualify for relief, the relief rate was fixed at 23 per cent and the limit at £30,000 from 6 April 2000.

4.7 Deduction of tax from mortgage interest payments
(TA 1988 Ss369–370)

Up to 5 April 2000, you were able to deduct tax from mortgage interest payments, provided the loan qualified for relief. Income tax was deducted at the basic rate from interest paid up to 5 April 1994. Subsequently, lower deduction rates applied. From 6 April 1994, the MIRAS (mortgage interest relief at source) rules applied using the 20 per cent lower rate instead of the basic rate of tax. Similarly, from 6 April 1995, the deduction rate was 15 per cent and from 6 April 1998 it was 10 per cent with no deduction being made after 5 April 2000.

Chapter 5

COMPUTING YOUR INCOME TAX BILL

Your 'total income' (see below) less your allowances for the tax year (3.0) will be subjected to income tax at the basic higher and additional rates according to the following table:

5.0 Income tax rates for 2012–13

Slice of income £	Rate %	Total income (after allowances) £	Total tax £
34,370 (0–34,370)	20	34,370	6,874
115,650 (34,370–150,000)	40	150,000	53,126
Remainder	50		

Note: A 10 per cent starting rate applies for any savings income in the £0–£2,710 band taking other income first.

5.0.1 Income tax rates before 2012–13

From 2008–09 to 2011–12, the basic rate was 20 per cent and the higher rate was 40 per cent (27.3). From 2010–11, there is also an additional rate (5.0.2). Before 2008–09, the basic rate was 22 per cent. However, there was a 10 per cent starting rate for earned income, pensions and savings income (on £2,230 for 2007–08).

5.0.2 Additional rate from 2010–11

For 2010–11 and subsequently you are liable to an additional rate of income tax of 50 per cent on any of your taxable income which exceeds £150,000. Special rates apply to investment income (5.6.2).

5.1 Indexation of income tax bands (ITA S21)

Prior to 6 April 1988 there was a basic rate band followed by five higher rate bands. Each of those bands was to be increased in line with the Retail Prices Index. The index comparison was made for the previous December each year and the figures rounded up to the next £100. However, from 1993 onwards, September is used.

As with the indexation of personal reliefs (3.3), Parliament has the power to modify the effects of indexing the income tax bands. In fact no indexation increases were made at all for some years, whilst increases above the index were made for others. Starting with 1988–89, one higher rate of 40 per cent replaced the previous five. From 6 April 1992 a lower rate band applies. The starting levels for the income bands continue to be indexed, although no indexation increases were made for 1993–94, 1994–95, 2010–11 and 2011–12. From 2012–13, the Consumer Prices Index will replace the Retail Prices Index for the above purposes.

5.2 What is total income? (TA 1988 S835)

Your total income comprises your income for the tax year less specified deductions (5.3). The following classes of income will be included for each tax year:

(1) *Income as assessed for the tax year under the following headings:*

Details	**Para.**
Property income	7.1
Trades and professions	11.1
Savings and investment income	8.4
Foreign income	18.2
Miscellaneous income	15.1
Earnings from employment (see also below)	10.0

(2) *The gross income actually paid to you in the tax year under the deduction of income tax at the source.* You will receive the net amount after suffering income tax but you will pay the higher rate of tax if appropriate on the gross amount. You will obtain a tax credit for the income tax suffered at source which will be deducted from your tax bill. The following would come within this category:

- The income portion of annuities.
- Interest on certain investments.
- Any annual payments which you receive (4.2).

Prior to 1996–97, tax was deducted at the basic rate, but up to 5 April 2008 a special 20 per cent rate applied regarding deductions from savings income which has now been merged with the 20 per cent basic rate. Annual payments are likely to have tax deducted at the basic rate (20 per cent).

(3) *Income distributions from discretionary and accumulation settlements* (21.4). Net payments made to you must be grossed up at 40 per cent and carry with them a tax credit of this amount which represents income tax effectively suffered by the settlement. Thus if you receive £60 this is included in your total income together with a tax credit of £40. If you have an interest in possession (22.30), then your income only carries 20 per cent tax from 2008–09 in the settlement (previously 22 per cent). To the extent that the income from 6 April 1993 consists of dividends, your tax credit was 20 per cent and from 6 April 1999 it is 10 per cent.

(4) *Dividends received together with the relevant tax credits.* From 6 April 1999, the tax credit on dividends is 10 per cent of the gross, but you pay no more tax unless you are a higher rate (40 per cent) payer (5.6).

(5) *Your gross income taxed at source under PAYE* (10.14). This consists of your salary etc. derived from your employment; it is subjected to lower,

basic and higher rate income tax at source. The tax suffered at source is naturally deducted from the tax bill on your total income.

(6) *The grossed up equivalent of any building society interest received.* This income is subject to 20 per cent income tax deducted at source but must be included in your total income gross. You gross it up by multiplying the income received by

$\frac{100}{100-20}$ (that is, $\frac{100}{80}$). You obtain a credit for the tax. For example, if you receive £80 building society interest, your total income will

include £80 $\times \frac{100}{80}$ = £100 and you obtain a tax credit of £20.

(7) *The grossed up equivalent of any bank interest etc. paid to you* (8.7).

5.3 Total income – deductions

As well as normal business expenses etc., which are deducted in arriving at the various income tax assessments, the following are deductible:

(1) Loan interest subject to the relevant rules (4.3).
(2) Business losses and capital allowances.
(3) Certain annual payments under partnership agreements to retiring partners or their widows.
(4) Annual payments to individuals under deeds of covenant entered into after 6 April 1965 and before 15 March 1988. In general these are not deductible from your income for higher rate income tax purposes, however, they reduce your total income for the purposes of the life assurance relief one-sixth rule (3.2.4).
(5) Certain annual payments which you make in connection with the purchase of a business where the payments are made to the former owner of the business or his widow or dependants.
(6) Covenanted donations and gifts of cash or other assets to charities under the 'gift aid' scheme (15.2.1).
(7) Allowable personal pension contributions, retirement annuity premiums and additional voluntary contributions (AVCs) (14.3.3).
(8) A proportion of certain transfers to reserves made by underwriters at Lloyd's or other approved underwriters.
(9) Personal reliefs and allowances (see Chapter 3). (These are, strictly speaking, deductions which are made from your total income rather than in its computation.)

5.3.1 Cap on unlimited tax reliefs

From 2013–14, subject to consultation, there will be a cap on those tax reliefs which are otherwise unlimited. The cap will be the greater of £50,000 and 25 per cent of income. Relief for donations to charities will remain unlimited.

5.4 Annual payments (ITA S448)

The annual payments mentioned above (3), (4) & (5) as well as various other annual payments (4.1) are paid under the deduction of basic rate income tax (20 per cent) (as was your allowable mortgage interest for 1993–94 (4.7)). From 1995–96 to 1999–2000, mortgage interest was generally payable under the deduction of lower tax rates, being 10 per cent for 1999–2000. To the extent that your income less allowances is not sufficient to cover your annual charges payments, your personal allowances etc. must be restricted. (This restriction did not apply regarding mortgage interest.)

Thus, if your income for 2012–13 is £7,500 and your personal allowances and reliefs total £6,500, you can pay up to £1,000 annual payments without restriction. The £1,000 is paid by you under deduction of basic rate income tax. Thus you actually pay only £1,000 – 20 per cent × £1,000 = £800. You also pay to HMRC tax at 20 per cent on £1,000 = £200. If your annual payments were £1,500, your total reliefs would be reduced to £5,000 so that your taxable income after allowances (£1,500) would be sufficient to cover your payments.

The income tax which you deduct from your annual payments must effectively be paid over to HMRC. This is done by paying tax on that part of your income which is equal to such annual payments. Where, however, the payments in question are allowed as deductions in computing your total income (for example, (5), (7) & (8) in 5.3) you get relief for the excess of your higher rate (and additional rate) tax over basic rate tax or tax credit on income covered by those payments.

5.5 Deductions from tax payable

When your total tax liability is computed certain deductions from the tax payable must be made, either because you have already paid part of it or because of special reliefs. These deductions include the following:

(1) Life assurance relief on policies effected before 14 March 1984 only (3.2.5). Normally 12½ per cent of your qualifying premiums (9.3) (subject to the various rules) is deductible from your tax payable. You normally obtain this relief by deducting it from each premium payment.

(2) 20⁄80 of your building society interest received; similarly 20⁄80 of bank deposit interest etc. (8.7). From 6 April 1991, this tax is capable of being repaid.

(3) Tax credits on dividends received (8.1). The tax credit is 1⁄9 of each dividend received, which is 10 per cent of the gross. This applies from 6 April 1999 (8.1.7) and covers tax on dividends within your £34,370 (previously £35,000) band. Above that, your gross dividends are taxed at 32.5 per cent and the 10 per cent tax credit offset and from 2010–11 over £150,000 the rate is 42.5 per cent.

(4) Tax paid under PAYE (10.14).

(5) Income tax deducted at the source at 20 per cent on certain investment interest paid to you (such as on company debentures).

(6) Basic rate tax deducted from annual payments made to you during the year which are included in your total income.

(7) Trust rate tax on income distributions made to you during the tax year by discretionary settlements and accumulation and maintenance trusts (21.5). The tax is computed on the gross equivalent of the distributions.

5.6 Investment income (ITA Ss7–9 & 12–19)

Certain discretionary and accumulation settlements (21.5) are subjected to additional tax. In this case, the charge is made on all the income including that from both investments and otherwise. (See Chapter 21, 21.5, for fuller details.)

If you are a basic rate payer, your tax on dividend income is limited to 20 per cent. A similar position applies regarding the 10 per cent tax credit from 6 April 1999.

For individuals, the tax rates on investment income follow exact rules. In general, property rents etc., are taxed at the same rates as earned income (5.0.1). Your savings income (including building society, bank interest and dividends) is taken as the top slice of your income and the appropriate tax rates applied (5.6.1). Tax deducted at source and tax credits are offset, but for 1999–2000 and subsequently the 10 per cent tax credit on dividends cannot be reclaimed. (Tax deducted from interest is still reclaimable.)

5.6.1 New rates for investment income from 2010–11

From 2010–11 if you have dividends otherwise taxable at 50 per cent, they are taxed at 42.5 per cent. Also from that year, the dividend trust rate becomes 42.5 per cent and the trust tax rate (21.5) goes up to 50 per cent.

5.6.2 Income tax rates on investment income (before tax credits)

Within income band –	Dividend tax credit on gross %	Dividends %	Other savings income %
2007–08 up to £34,600	10	10	20
over £34,600	10	32.5	40
2008–09 up to £34,800	10	10	20
over £34,800	10	32.5	40
2009–10 up to £37,400	10	10	20
over £37.400	10	32.5	40
2010–11 up to £37,400	10	10	20
£37,401–£150,000	10	32.5	40
above £150,000	10	42.5	50
2011–12 up to £35,000	10	10	20
£35,000–£150,000	10	32.5	40
above £150,000	10	42.5	50
2012–13 up to £34,370	10	10	20*
£34,370–£150,000	10	32.5	40
above £150,000	10	42.5	50

* 10 per cent applies for savings income in the £0–£2,710 band taking other income first

5.7 The assessment and payment of your income tax (TA 1988 Ss2–5 & TMA S59B)

This matter is considered in detail in Chapter 16. A uniform set of dates for the payment of income tax and capital gains tax was introduced as a part of the new self-assessment system. These dates apply for 1996–97 and subsequent years of assessment. The earliest payments under the new rules were due on 31 January 1997. Further payments on account of your 1996–97 liability were due on 31 July 1997, the final balance being payable on 31 January 1998, based on your income tax return. A similar scheme applies for subsequent years.

5.7.1 Example: Income tax computation

Mr B has his own business from which his assessable profit for 2012–13 is £46,000. His other income for 2012–13 consists of £1,200 net building society interest and £9,000 dividends received (notional tax credits £1,000). (Mr B is married, and for 2012–13 his wife's income will be taxed separately.) From the above, compute Mr B's income tax liability.

Mr B – Income tax computation for 2012–13		**£**	**£**
Earned income – business assessment			46,000.00
Investment income – building society interest:		1,200.00	
Add: 20% income tax			
	£1,200 × 20/80	300.00	
		1,500.00	
Dividends		9,000.00	
Add: Tax credit		1,000.00	
			11,500.00
Total income before personal reliefs and allowances			57,500.00
Less: Personal allowance			8,105.00
Taxable balance			49,395.00
Tax payable:			
Earned income	£34,370 at 20%		6,874.00
	£3,525 at 40%		1,410.00
Building Society	£1,500 at 40%		600.00
Dividends	£10,000 at 32.5%		3,250.00
	£49,395		
Total tax			12,134.00
Less: Tax credit on dividends		1,000.00	
Tax credit on building society interest		300.00	
			1,300.00
Net further tax payable			10,834.00

Note: If Mr B's taxable income exceeded £150,000, some 50 per cent additional rate tax (5.0.2) would be due.

5.8 Interest on overdue tax (TMA S86 etc.)

If you are late in paying your income tax you may be charged interest at 3.0 per cent from 29 September 2009. Previous recent rates have been:

From	Rate %	From	Rate %
6 May 2001	7.5	6 August 2007	8.5
6 November 2001	6.5	6 January 2008	7.5
6 August 2003	5.5	6 November 2008	6.5
6 December 2003	6.5	6 December 2008	5.5
6 September 2004	7.5	6 January 2009	4.5
6 September 2005	6.5	27 January 2009	3.5
6 September 2006	7.5	24 March 2009	2.5

This interest is not deductible for income tax purposes. The detailed rules are described later (16.8.2).

5.9 Fluctuating income

Because of the graduated nature of income tax rates, if your income fluctuates greatly from year to year you may find that your tax liability is high in some years and low in others. The result is that your total income tax over the years is more than it would have been had your income been spread evenly over those years. Certain special rules exist which have the effect of spreading lump sums of income over the period during which they have been earned.

So-called 'top slicing' relief is obtained when you receive certain large taxable sums in one year. You may effectively spread these sums over a stated period and recompute your tax liability on the basis that the income had been paid in this way. (The tax is payable for the year when you receive the income but the rate is normally lower.) What you do is to divide the lump sum (L) by the stated period (P) and calculate the tax payable (T) for the year on your other income plus (L/P). You then calculate the tax payable on your other income by itself and deduct it from (T). This gives the total tax payable on (L/P) and this tax is multiplied by P to give the total tax payable on (L).

A particular example where 'top slicing' applies is regarding the profit element in the proceeds of non-qualifying life assurance policies (9.7). Such policy proceeds are taxed at the excess of higher rate income tax over income tax at the basic rate, subject to the relief outlined above.

Chapter 6

HUSBAND, WIFE, CIVIL PARTNERS AND CHILDREN

This chapter deals, in particular, with the taxation of husband and wife as from 6 April 2000. From 5 December 2005, the rules generally also apply to civil partners (6.9). The concept of the present independent taxation system goes back to 6 April 1990 and reference should be made to previous editions of this book for intervening changes or for the rules which applied for 1989–90 and earlier years. The latter included an optional form of separate taxation of spouses, which merely allocated their joint liability, and an elective form of truly separate taxation limited to a wife's earnings. (Some of the rules for independent taxation have been mentioned in Chapter 3.)

6.1 Independent taxation of husband, wife and civil partners

(ITA Ss42–55)

You and your spouse or civil partner are each taxed separately on all of your income and capital gains. You each have a single person's relief and income tax rates (5.0.1) and a full capital gains tax annual exemption of £10,600 for 2012–13 (20.5).

Up to 5 April 2000, married couple's allowance (3.2.1) amounting to £1,970 for 1999–2000 was available for those under 65, but an income-tested higher married couple's allowance was available to those entitled to age allowance (3.2.7). The rate of relief became 10 per cent for 1999–2000. From 6 April 2000, the relief was generally withdrawn, but has remained available at the higher rate (3.2.1) where at least one party to the marriage was born before 6 April 1935.

If you married before 5 December 2005, married couple's allowance goes initially to the husband, but if his income is insufficient to use it, part or all can be transferred to the wife. If you marry or enter a civil partnership on or after 5 December 2005, the allowance goes initially to the spouse or civil partner with the higher income. Couples who married before 5 December 2005 can elect for this rule to apply.

However, under both sets of rules, either of you can elect for the married couple's allowance to be split equally between you and both of you can elect jointly for it to go entirely to the other spouse or civil partner (3.2.1). Such elections must be made before the start of the tax year for which they are first to apply and generally run on from year to year. Otherwise the allowance will be allocated as above.

Income from jointly owned property is taken as split equally between husband and wife or civil partner, subject to the right to make a joint declaration to the contrary. The effect of this action is to split the income in the ratio of your respective shares in the asset. Interest payable on loans in your joint names, if allowable for income tax, will generally create a deduction from income of a specific source, so that the relief for the interest will follow the split of the income between you. From 6 April 2004, distributions from jointly owned shares in close companies (13.18) are no longer automatically split equally between spouses or (from 5 December 2005) civil partners, but according to the actual ownership.

6.2 When you marry or form a civil partnership

When you marry or form a civil partnership, various rules apply to both of you (6.1). Essentially you will continue to be taxed separately on your income and capital gains, remaining responsible for your own tax returns. Thus at the end of the year in which you marry or become civil partners both of you may have to complete income tax returns.

6.3 Separate assessment (TA 1988 Ss283–285)

Prior to 6 April 1990, although the husband was normally taxed on both his own and his wife's income, it was nevertheless possible for a married couple to be assessed separately and to pay their respective shares of tax separately. However, from 6 April 1990, husband and wife are each taxed and assessed on their own income (6.2). Separate assessment was not the same as the separate taxation of your wife's earned income (6.4). Full details are given in earlier editions of this book.

6.4 Separate taxation of wife's earnings (TA 1988 Ss287 & 288)

Before the introduction of independent taxation from 6 April 1990, it was still possible to elect for the wife to be separately taxed on her earnings up to 5 April 1990 as if she were a single person. The husband was then taxed on the balance of their joint incomes (including the wife's unearned income) as if he also were single. Fuller details appear in previous editions of this book.

6.5 Deeds of covenant (FA 1988 Ss36–38)

Historically, payments under deeds of covenant provided a most tax-efficient and convenient means of passing money regularly to charities (15.2.1), but usually involved a minimum commitment for four years. Such payments were a class of annual payment (4.1), from which income tax could be deducted at the basic rate and in respect of which higher rate relief was generally available. Charitable covenants became far less important following the introduction of gift aid (15.2.1) and a relaxation of rules effected from 6 April 2000. Consequently, although there may still be some charitable covenants in place, your tax relief derives primarily from the gift aid regime.

Beneficial treatment also applied to payments under deeds of covenant to individuals, which usually involved a minimum commitment for seven years. They provided a popular way of assisting student children (if adults) and also grandchildren, but their tax benefits were withdrawn for new covenants from 15 March 1988. Deeds entered into before that date and displayed to an

Inspector of Taxes by 30 June 1988 were treated as annual payments (4.1) and income tax could be deducted at the basic rate for a transitional period.

In rare cases an old arrangement may still be in place in connection with alimony or child support, thus attracting a modest tax allowance for 'qualifying maintenance payments' (6.8.3), if you were born before 6 April 1935. In all other respects, payments under such deeds are disregarded for tax purposes and no tax deductions should normally be made at source, without specific instructions from HMRC.

Currently, except as described in the previous paragraph, the existence of a deed of covenant does not of itself create a stream of 'annual payments' for income tax purposes or a right to tax relief, nor a right or obligation to deduct income tax when making payment. Only the nature, purpose and circumstances of the payment can do that (4.1–4.3).

6.6 The income of your children

No matter how young they are, there is nothing to prevent your children earning income in their own right and being taxed on that earned income. This also applies to investment income unless the investments were given by your spouse or yourself and the child is neither married nor over the age of 18 at the time that the income is paid.

Settlements and arrangements made by you through which your child receives investment income normally result in your being taxed on that income if the child is neither married nor over 18. However, if the child's investment income which could potentially be treated as your own is less than £100, you will normally not pay tax on that income (ITTOIA S629). (This test is applied separately for income attributable to each parent.)

You should obtain a tax return each year for each of your minor children who has any income (including trust income). Completing a return will often prove beneficial since, if the child has suffered tax at source on any income (apart from dividends), this may be reclaimable in whole or part depending on its nature and on how much other income there is to set against the child's tax allowances. In such circumstances a repayment claim form can be submitted instead of a normal tax return (16.7).

If the child's income is small enough then the tax can be reclaimed on his or her behalf, because he or she has the benefit of the full personal allowance (£8,105 for 2012–13).

Historically, if the child had little or no other income, then it was of benefit for him or her to be paid an annual amount under deed of covenant (6.5) by a friend or relative (not the parents, unless the child was over 18 or married). From 15 March 1988 the rules were changed, but certain pre-existing deeds of covenant attracted relief as before for a transitional period.

Although covenanted payments used to be made under deduction of income tax at the basic rate, this is no longer the case and currently such payments are disregarded for most income tax purposes.

6.6.1 Example: Income of child

Mr A has one child, B, aged fourteen years, whose income for 2012–13 is as follows:

	Gross £
(1) Dividends, including tax credits, on shares given to B by Mr A	420
(2) Dividends, including tax credits (10% of gross), on shares given to B by his grandfather	3,800
(3) Interest on bank deposit (capital gifted by grandmother)	5,600

How much income tax is reclaimable on behalf of B for 2012–13?

Item (1) is not treated as B's income for tax purposes because it is regarded as the income of Mr A who gifted the shares to his child B.

The income tax payable by B for 2012–13 is calculated as follows:

	Gross £	Income tax deducted or tax credits £
(2) Dividends including tax credits on shares from grandfather	3,800	380.00
(3) Deposit interest	5,600	1,120.00
Total income	9,400	1,500.00
Less: Personal allowance of	8,105	
Taxable amount	1,295	
Income tax due £1,295 at 10% (dividend income)		129.50
Add: restriction on repayment £2,505 at 10%		250.50
		380.00
Less: Income tax suffered by deduction at source and tax credits		1,500.00
Net income tax reclaimable		1,120.00

6.6.2 Child trust fund (CTF)

The CTF scheme started as from 6 April 2005 and is not a single fund, but a Government sponsored series of investment accounts offered by banks, building societies and others.

Subject to meeting the detailed rules, children living in the UK, for whom child benefit is being received and who were born from 1 September 2002 to 2 January 2011, became eligible for the new tax-efficient CTF. Initially, each had £250 allocated to the fund at birth or 6 April 2005, if later and this was increased to £500 for children from low-income families qualifying for full child tax credit. Parents and others are permitted to add up to a total of £1,200 to the child's CTF each year and at age 18 the full fund will be available, without restriction on the assets. The Government was due to make further CTF payments when each child in the scheme reached age 7, amounting to £500 for children from lower income families and otherwise £250. CTFs operate on a tax exempt basis and will not prejudice entitlement to child tax credit.

Although there are special rules to cover children who are in care, disabled or terminally ill, the general rules are that, during the currency of the CTF, the parents can change the investment, but they cannot remove any money from the fund, and, once the child is 16, he will gain control of the management and at 18 can do whatever he wants with the money.

If in doubt as to the possible implications of these rules, you should take advice before adding your own money to such an account.

From 2009–10 the Government undertook to add £100 annually to the CTF for all eligible disabled children (£200 for the severely disabled), which will not count towards the £1,200 annual contribution limit.

On 24 May 2010, the new coalition Government announced plans to reduce and curtail its contributions to this scheme. Consequently, following the Savings Accounts and Health in Pregnancy Grant Act 2010, the following changes were made:

(1) From 1 August 2010 contributions at birth were reduced by 80 per cent to £100 for children from lower income families and otherwise £50, but no further payment will be made to children reaching age 7 from 1 August 2010 or for children born from 1 January 2011. However, the planned dates were changed to 1 September 2010 and 3 January 2011 respectively.
(2) From 6 April 2011 no further payments will be made to or for disabled children.
(3) A child entering local authority care between 1 August and 31 December 2010 who did not have a CTF should have had a single contribution of £100 placed in an account for them by HMRC.
(4) Although new CTF vouchers will no longer be issued, existing vouchers remained valid until their designated expiry date and HMRC opened accounts for any child whose expiring vouchers remained unused.
(5) All existing CTF accounts will continue and be subject to the existing rules as to non-Government contributions, management and maturity.

6.6.3 Junior ISAs

It was intended that Junior ISAs (8.12.1), which became available in autumn 2011, would serve as a replacement for Child Trust Funds (CTFs) (6.6.2).

6.7 Death of husband or wife

The death of your spouse or civil partner does not in general interrupt the tax treatment of the survivor. Each of you has been separately assessed to income tax and capital gains tax and, as the survivor, you will not alter the periods for which you make your own returns nor, with two possible exceptions (see below), the amount of the tax allowances that you claim.

It will be necessary for you or the executor or administrator of the estate to prepare a tax return for your former spouse or civil partner covering the part year to the date of death (21.10.1). This will attract a full year's personal allowance (£8,105) or higher age-related allowance, if appropriate. It is possible that the length of the period from 6 April to the date of death will result in a significant drop in the income assessable, so that a greater amount of age-related allowance might be available than would have been expected for a full year. Moreover, if the death occurred in the tax year, in which he or she was due to reach 65 or 75, then the higher allowance was potentially available, even if death intervened before the relevant birthday.

Conversely, if you too are entitled to an age-related personal allowance and your income increases, because of the death, your allowance may be reduced.

The second exception relates to married couple's allowance, if either or both of you were entitled to claim this. Regardless which regime applies to your claims or what elections are in place, no reallocation can be made, but any part of the allowance due to the deceased that cannot be used for the period to the date of death will be transferred to you. Again, a full year's allowance will be available, however early in the year the death occurs.

You will not be entitled to any married couple's allowance in future years unless you enter into a fresh marriage or civil partnership.

6.8 Divorce or separation

If you are divorced or permanently separated you are regarded as a single person for tax purposes. This means that the personal reliefs for single persons will apply to your income. If, however, you were separated but maintained your wife by voluntary maintenance payments for which you got no tax relief, prior to 6 April 1990, you obtained the married man's personal allowance. Subsequent to that date, married couple's allowance (£1,970 for 1999–2000) applied in the tax year of separation only, subject to transitional relief and from 6 April 2000 relief has continued only if you or your separated spouse were born before 6 April 1935 (6.8.3).

You are treated as being permanently separated if you are separated under a court order or deed of separation; also if you are separated in such circumstances that the separation is likely to be permanent.

6.8.1 Divorce or separation during the tax year

The independent taxation rules mean that after 5 April 1990, each of you is a taxpayer in your own right in any event.

Where a couple are divorced or permanently separated after 5 April 1990, each of you obtains the full personal relief for the year and any share of the full year's married couple's allowance that is appropriate. From 5 December 2005 members of a civil partnership that is dissolved or who separate permanently during the year are treated similarly.

6.8.2 **Claiming additional personal relief** (TA 1988 S260)

This relief for certain individuals having care of or contributing to the maintenance or education of children ceased after 5 April 2000. Information on the relevance of the relief to divorced or separated spouses can be found in previous editions.

6.8.3 **Alimony and maintenance payments** (ITA 2007 S343)

In general, tax relief for alimony and maintenance payments was severely curtailed in 1988 and largely withdrawn for 2000–01 and subsequent years.

From 6 April 2000 generally (5 December 2005 for civil partners) all maintenance payments to separated or former spouses or civil partners or to or for the maintenance of children are treated as the income of the payer and not the recipient and should be paid in full without any deduction for tax.

If either of the separated or former spouses or civil partners was born before 6 April 1935, relief may be available up to an annual limit as shown in the table below. Relief is calculated at 10 per cent of the lower of the maintenance payment and the maximum married couples allowance (10 per cent of £2,960 for 2012–13).

Subject to detailed rules, maintenance payments qualify for relief if they arise under a court order, Child Support Agency assessment or binding legal agreement.

The recipient of a maintenance payment can neither be assessed to tax nor claim any tax repayment in respect of it.

The maximum relief is 10 per cent of the relevant annual limit, which is as follows:

	£		£
2002–03	2,110	2007–08	2,440
2003–04	2,150	2008–09	2,540
2004–05	2,210	2009–10–11	2,670
2005–06	2,280	2011–12	2,800
2006–07	2,350	2012–13	2,960

If you maintained your separated spouse by voluntary payments and you separated before 6 April 1990, you will normally continue to obtain married couple's allowance (6.1). This does not apply if you are divorced.

6.8.4 Foreign divorces

If the divorce is effected by a foreign court then different rules relate to the receipt or payment of alimony by residents of this country. Normally no tax will be deductible from the payments by a United Kingdom resident but a recipient resident in this country may be assessed to tax on the amount arising.

Tax relief (6.8.3) has been progressively extended to payments under court orders of countries which are members of the EC, EU and EEA; also written agreements enforceable under the law of those countries. Payments must be to a divorced or separated spouse or (from 5 December 2005) civil partner for their maintenance, or for the maintenance of a child of either of them or whom they have voluntarily treated as a member of their family.

6.9 Civil partners (FA 2005 S103)

Civil partners in accordance with the Civil Partnership Act 2004 (CPA) are treated as married couples for tax purposes. The new rules took effect from 5 December 2005, when CPA commenced.

CPA allows single-sex partners the opportunity of obtaining the new legal status of civil partners. This entitles them to similar tax treatment to married couples.This is particularly useful regarding freedom from capital gains tax and inheritance tax on asset transfers between two CPA partners.

Parties to certain same-sex legal relationships validly registered under the law of another country or territory will, subject to the detailed rules, be treated as having formed a civil partnership without the need for any further registration in the UK.

Chapter 7

INCOME FROM LAND AND PROPERTY

The amount of income that you derive during the tax year from letting property such as a house, flat, factory or shop, less the deductions you may claim represent your net income from letting property and must be shown separately on your tax return. You must return your gross property income including certain lease premiums and also give full particulars of your expenses. If up to 5 April 1995 the income was derived from furnished lettings then the assessment was under Schedule D Case VI (15.1); otherwise it was generally under Schedule A. From that date to 31 March 2009, Case VI on furnished lettings only continued for corporation tax purposes.

From 6 April 1995, all property income is pooled and was assessed under Schedule A. This includes income from furnished lettings. Initially, the rules only related to income tax and not corporation tax, but broadly similar rules applying to corporation tax operated from 1 April 1998 to 31 March 2009 (FA 1998 Ss38–41 & Sch 5). From 6 April 2005, the legislation has been consolidated into ITTOIA (2.10.1), mainly in Ss260–364. At the same time the classification as Schedule A income changed to 'property income' (2.10), but overseas property income is dealt with on the '*foreign pages*' of your self-assessment return.

For accounting periods ending on or after 1 April 2009, the classification of income for corporation tax purposes has shifted from the old schedular system to the descriptive titles which have become familiar for income tax purposes. Companies will in future deal with all property income, including overseas property and commercial furnished letting as a single category, subject to the detailed rules (CTA 2009 Ss210–214).

The old rules governing the allowance of expenditure down to 5 April 1995 for income tax and 31 March 1998 for corporation tax can be found in previous editions of this book.

7.1 The current property income tax system (ITTOIA Ss260–364)

New, simplified rules apply to the taxation of the property income of individuals, partnerships, trusts and non-resident companies from 6 April 1995. Similar rules apply to companies subject to corporation tax for accounting periods ending on or after 1 April 2009. Points to note include the following:

(1) All of your property income normally is put into a 'pool' and taxed together, but on trading principles. Thus expenses are deducted on this basis (11.3), although the net is treated as investment rather than trading income. In general, an accruals basis is to be used for income and expenditure.

(2) Your furnished lettings income is no longer taxed as a separate source, but is simply pooled with the other property income.

(3) Any property losses which you brought forward from 1994–95 were offsettable against the combined profits of your property business for 1995–96. Similarly, any unused losses are carried forward to set off against future property business profits.
(4) The capital allowance rules (11.9) broadly continue for property income purposes. However, from 6 April 1997 (1 April for companies), a 'pooling' basis applies. So far as furnished lettings are concerned, you are still able to make the 10 per cent wear and tear claim based on rents (7.5).
(5) Relief for interest payable in respect of a property business is obtained by deducting it like any other expense. Thus any excess of interest over your other net property income produces a loss. Furthermore, the old requirement is removed under which the property must be let or available for letting for at least 26 weeks in a year (4.6).
(6) Remember that under normal trading principles, any proportion of expenses attributable to personal use is not deductible but accrued expenses often would be.
(7) Overseas property income remained (before 2005–06) taxable under Schedule D Case V. However, the rules have been aligned more closely with the system for UK property income. For example, interest payable on a loan to purchase the property is deductible.
(8) The corresponding rules for companies subject to corporation tax effectively preserve the flexibility of reliefs currently available for corporate interest and management expenses (13.9).

7.2 Computing your property income (ITTOIA Ss276–286)

Income tax on property income is charged on:

(1) Profits of a UK property business, whether carried on by a UK resident or non-resident;
(2) Profits of an overseas property business, if carried on by a UK resident;
(3) Profits from rents arising from a wide range of interests in land, including mines, quarries, mineral rights, ironworks, waterworks, canals, waterways, fishing, markets, fairs, tolls, ferries, railways, other ways and any like business;
(4) Profits from rents for wayleaves in respect of UK electric, telephonic or telegraphic wires, cables, poles, pylons or related equipment.

Profits are generally to be computed on the same principles that would apply to a trade (11.3). However, profits arising to a UK resident or ordinary resident from certain mineral leases are taxed as to 50 per cent as property income and as to 50 per cent as chargeable gains. Also, special rules apply where an overseas property business is owned by a UK resident who is either not ordinarily resident or not domiciled in the UK and elects to adopt the remittance basis of assessment (18.0).

Your '*regular property income business*' embraces income from furnished and unfurnished letting, both in the UK and abroad, but not '*furnished holiday letting*'.

7.2.1 Expenses formerly allowed against land and property income (TA 1988 Ss25–33)

The following list of expenditure that was formerly specifically allowable against property income may be helpful as a guide, but this is no longer to be regarded as prescriptive:

(1) Repairs and maintenance including redecorating the premises during the lease.
(2) Insurance premiums against fire and water damage etc. to the building.
(3) Management costs including costs of rent collection, salaries, advertising for new tenants, legal and accountancy charges etc. If your wife takes part in the management, consider paying her a salary (26.2.10).
(4) Services that you are obliged to provide for the tenants but for which you get no specific payment.
(5) Any payments that you make for general, business and water rates, and council tax, but not in general community charge.
(6) Any payments that you make for any rent, rent-charge, ground annual, feu duty or other periodical payment in respect of the land.
(7) The cost of lighting any common parts of office blocks or flats and otherwise maintaining them.
(8) The upkeep of gardens of flats etc. where the lease requires you to be responsible for this expense.
(9) Architects' and surveyors' fees in connection with maintenance but not improvements.
(10) Capital allowances (11.9) on any plant or machinery that you might use in the upkeep of your property (unless a dwelling-house).
(11) The upkeep of any private roads, drains and ditches etc. on your land if part or all of the property is let and the expenditure is for the benefit of your tenants.
(12) In the case of an industrial building which is used by the tenant for industrial purposes (for example manufacturing) you may get capital allowances on the building (11.11). This also applies to some hotels (11.15). These allowances ceased at 5 April and 31 March 2011 (11.14).
(13) When you live in a part of the premises you let to others you may not deduct the full amount of your expenditure from your income. Instead you must subtract from your expenditure some reasonable proportion because the premises were not wholly used to produce the income. You may calculate this proportion as being, for example:

$$\frac{\text{Area (or rooms) used by you}}{\text{Total area (or rooms)}} \times \text{Expenses}$$

(14) From 6 April 2004, capital expenditure on loft and cavity wall insulation in rented residential accommodation up to £1,500. This extends to draught proofing and hot water system insulation from 6 April 2006 and floor insulation from 6 April 2007 (ITTOIA S312). The expiry date has been extended from April 2009 to 5 April 2015.

7.3 Losses

From 6 April 1995 (7.1), for income tax purposes, any property losses carried forward were offsettable against your combined property business profits for the year. Unused losses are available to carry forward to be relieved against future property business profits. If you have property both in UK and abroad, these are taxed as two separate businesses and the losses in respect of the UK and foreign businesses must be separately pooled and considered. (ITA Ss118 & 119).

7.4 Assessment of property income (ITTOIA S260)

Tax under this category is charged by reference to the profits and income of your property businesses for the year, computed on the basis described above (7.2 & 7.3).

Thus your 2011–12 assessment is based on the profits of your property businesses to which you are entitled in the year to 5 April 2012.

For 1996–97 and subsequent years of assessment, the self-assessment rules apply. Payments on account of your total liability are required on 31 January in the year of assessment and the following 31 July, with any balance being due on the next 31 January. However, for 1996–97 itself, only one payment on account was normally required, on 31 January 1997. Each payment on account is generally based on half of the assessment for the previous year.

Income assessable (prior to 2005–06) under the former Schedule A was normally treated as investment income and not treated as 'savings income' and was thus not taxed at the lower savings rate, which applied down to 5 April 2008. From 2010–11, the basic (20 per cent), higher (40 per cent) and additional (50 per cent) rates apply to individuals (50 per cent for trusts).

7.4.1 Example: Assessment of property income

Mr A bought an old house some years ago and divided it into three flats each of which he lets unfurnished. Taking the rents and expenses shown in the example, assuming that Mr A has already used his personal reliefs and starting rate tax band and that he is not liable for the higher rate of tax, his assessments are as follows:

Year ended 5 April:	**2012**		**2013**	
	£	**£**	**£**	**£**
Rents receivable		12,000		13,000
Less expenses:				
Garden upkeep	500		540	
Maintenance, window cleaning, light and heat of hall and stairs	760		850	
Exterior repairs and decorating	1,400		520	
Insurance of structure of building	625		640	
Accountancy	575		590	
Agents' rent collection charges	1,440		1,560	
		5,300		4,700

Net property income assessments		6,700		8,300
Income tax payable		**2011–12**		**2012–13**
	(20%)	1,340.00	(20%)	1,660.00

Note: Income tax will be payable for 2012–13 (together with the self-assessed tax on any other income) as follows:

Provisionally on 2011–12 basis		
31 January 2013 – ½ × £1,340.00	670.00	
31 July 2013 – ½ × £1,340.00	670.00	
		1,340.00
Balance on 31 January 2014		320.00
Total income tax liability for 2012–13		1,660.00

7.5 Furnished lettings (ITTOIA S308)

Since 6 April 1995, (1 April 1998 for companies) furnished lettings income has been automatically assessed under Schedule A (7.1), now redefined as 'property income'.

As well as expenses normally allowable for land and property purposes (7.2), you are also entitled to a deduction to cover depreciation on furniture and furnishings. This may be available as a deduction of the entire replacement cost from year to year, but no relief is available for first-time capital outlays or any improvement element.

However, you may find it preferable to claim a yearly deduction of 10 per cent of your rents less any rates etc. and service costs which you pay. Thus, if your annual rents are £4,000 and you pay £700 in council tax, you can deduct £330 yearly to cover the depreciation and replacement of furniture and furnishings.

If, under the terms of a letting, you provide services such as laundry, meals, domestic help etc. then you can charge the cost of these items against your taxable profit. If you provide such services, then your lettings income might possibly be treated as earned income. However, case law has made this less likely. Otherwise it would be unearned income, subject to special rules for holiday lettings (7.7).

As from 6 April 1992, the existing practice of including within the furnished lettings rules payments under licences was confirmed (F2A 1992 S58).

7.6 'Rent a room' (ITTOIA Ss309 & 784–802)

If you let a room in your house, valuable relief may be available to you for 1992–93 and subsequent years. The relief applies if you are an owner occupier, or a tenant and let furnished accommodation in your only or main home. If you move home during the year or if you let your home whilst abroad, special considerations apply.

The relief covers gross rents of up to £4,250 for 1997–98 and subsequently (previously £3,250). If the gross rent is higher, you have the option of paying tax on the excess over £4,250, without any relief for expenses, or according to the normal furnished lettings rules (7.5). (Where any others share the rents, your exemption is limited to £2,125.)

For example, suppose that you let a room in your house and your gross rent for 2012–13 is £5,250, with allowable expenses of £1,250. If you are a basic rate tax payer, on the conventional basis, your income tax (ignoring any other allowances) would be (£5,250 – £1,250) × 20 per cent = £800. However, if you elect for the 'alternative basis', you only pay (£5,250 – £4,250) × 20 per cent = £200.

You will need to elect for the 'alternative' basis to apply within one year of the end of the tax year to which it applies. After that, it remains in force until you withdraw it. Note that whilst the election is in force, no capital allowances are available, losses from previous years are carried forward to subsequent ones and balancing charges are added to your gross rental income. However, (quite apart from the 'rent a room' provisions) capital allowances are not available on assets such as furniture and equipment that is let for use in residential property.

7.7 Holiday lettings (ITTOIA S325 & CTA S264)

Prior to 6 April 2009, UK furnished holiday letting businesses which satisfied certain requirements qualified for reliefs only normally available where the activity is a trade for tax purposes. For 2009–10 the rules were extended to include qualifying lettings in any EEA country, and the whole holiday lettings regime was due to be abolished with effect from 6 April 2010. However, the outgoing Government was forced to withdraw the abolition and the incoming coalition Government has preserved the extended treatment for UK and EEA properties, subject to more stringent qualifications, which apply from 6 April (1 April for corporation tax purposes) 2011 and 2012.

The accommodation had previously needed to be available for holiday letting for at least 140 days during the year and actually let for at least 70 days (no let to normally exceed 31 days). From April 2012, the letting thresholds increased by half to 210 days and 105 days respectively. Averaging elections are available to iron out variations and adjustments can be made, where premises are unavailable because of damage or repair work.

The income is treated as earned income; also capital gains tax rollover relief (20.25) and (from 6 April 2008) the new entrepreneurs' relief (20.30) apply. In general, although the income is normally assessed under Schedule A the letting activity is treated as a trade for the purposes of many tax provisions. These include payments by instalments, loss relief (11.22), capital allowances (11.9), personal pension contracts etc.

From April 2011, furnished holiday lettings in UK and EU/EEA constitute two separate businesses, whose results must be pooled separately and any overall losses for the year can only be carried forward against future profits of the same business. Even on cessation, there is no terminal loss relief to carry back and no offset against general income.

7.8 The taxation of lease premiums (ITTOIA Ss277–283 & 292–295)

If you obtain a premium in connection with the granting of a lease of not more than 50 years' duration on any property that you own, then you will be assessed to income tax on part of such premium. The amount to be included in your income tax assessment is the premium, reduced by $\frac{1}{50}$ of its amount for each complete period of 12 months (other than the first) comprised in the duration of the lease. The balance of the premium which is not so charged normally attracts capital gains tax (20.1).

If you sell a lease rather than grant one you will normally be assessed to capital gains tax on any profit unless you are a dealer (7.10) or it is an 'artificial transaction' (7.11).

The following are also included with your taxable premiums:

(1) The value of any work that the tenant agreed to carry out to your premises to the extent that the present value of your property is enhanced.
(2) Any premiums paid to you in instalments. You include the aggregate of the instalments in the year that you grant the lease; but you can claim on grounds of hardship to pay the tax by instalments over a period not exceeding eight years, or ending with your last premium instalment if earlier.
(3) If you are granted a lease at a premium (£P) that is less than its market value (£M) and you then assign the lease at a profit, the amount of your profit is charged to income tax to the extent that it does not exceed (£M – £P).

7.8.1 Reverse premiums (ITTOIA Ss101(2) & 311 & CTA 2009 Sch 2(4))

A reverse premium is a payment made by a landlord to induce you to take out a lease. The tax treatment previously had been disputed, but from 9 March 1999, reverse premiums are taxable as income. If you will be carrying on a trade or profession from the premises, your reverse premium will be taxed as part of your business profits. Otherwise, it will be taxed as investment income.

7.9 Woodlands

Prior to 6 April 1988, you were assessed to income tax under Schedule B in respect of woodlands if you occupied them with a view to obtaining a profit and managed them on a commercial basis. Subject to certain transitional provisions, income from woodlands has now been removed from the tax regime. Special treatment for inheritance tax (22.22) continues, but business taper relief for capital gains tax (20.12) was replaced by a new entrepreneurs' relief (20.30), which might be available for disposals after 5 April 2008.

7.10 Dealing in property

Normally when you sell a property which you acquired as an investment you will be liable to capital gains tax on any profit that you make (20.1). The previous maximum tax rate of 40 per cent reduced to a flat rate of 18 per cent from 6 April 2008.

If, however, you carry out a number of purchases and sales of land and/or buildings you are likely to be treated as dealing in property and you will be taxed accordingly. This means that your profits must be computed as if you were conducting a trade (11.1) and you will be taxed on your adjusted profits as trading income. This income will be treated as being earned and you will be charged to income tax at the basic, higher and additional rates where applicable.

7.11 Transactions in land (ITA Ss752–772)

Previously entitled 'Artificial transactions in land', this legislation may operate wherever you make a capital profit from selling land (or buildings) that you had purchased with a view to selling later at a profit. The provisions also apply to sales of land indirectly held as trading stock and the sale of land (and buildings) that had been developed with the intention of selling them at a profit. However, it does not apply to trading profits from land already taxed as income.

Any capital profit arising in the above circumstances can be treated by HMRC as being income on which you will be liable to pay income tax instead of capital gains tax. How significant this is varies from time to time, according to the relationship between the top rates of income tax and capital gains tax.

These provisions do not apply to any purchase or sale by you of the house or flat in which you reside provided that it is your principal private residence (20.23).

If you believe that Ss752–772 might apply to any property sale that you have made or are planning, then you can apply for a clearance under S770 ITA 2007 to the Commissioners for HMRC. It appears that this is currently still submitted via the Tax Office, to the Inspector of Taxes to whom you submit your annual tax return, but this should be checked. You should give the Commissioners full written particulars of how the gain has arisen or how it will arise. They must then let you know within 30 days whether or not they are satisfied that your gain is outside the ambit of Ss752–772. If the Commissioners do give you a clearance then provided your transaction proceeds exactly as you have described it to them, you will not be taxed under these sections in respect of your gain.

7.12 Agricultural land etc. (ITTOIA Ss9 & 335–343)

Basically farmers are chargeable to income tax in the same way as persons who carry on a trade or business (11.1). Certain special rules apply, however

(15.6), but agricultural buildings allowance (11.13) is to be phased out over a four-year period commencing 6 April 2008 (11.14).

If you own any sand or gravel quarries, any rents and royalties to which you are entitled should now be received gross. (Prior to 2 May 2005 such payments were subject to the deduction at the source of basic rate income tax at 20 per cent.) See also aggregates levy (7.15).

7.13 Land sold and leased back (ITTOIA Ss284–286, TIOPA Sch 4 & CTA 2010 Ss850–854)

Special provisions may apply when you sell a lease with less than 50 years to run and take a fresh lease on the same premises. If you had been obtaining tax relief for your rent payments under the old lease and your new lease is for a term of less than 15 years, you will be charged to income tax on a proportion of the capital sum that you receive for your old lease.

The proportion is given by the formula $\frac{16-n}{15}$ where n is the term in years of your new lease. Thus if you have, say, a 40-year lease, which you sell for £15,000 and take back a ten-year lease you will be charged to income tax on

$$£15,000 \times \frac{16-10}{15} = £6,000.$$

The balance of £15,000 – £6,000 = £9,000 will be treated as capital on which you may be liable to pay capital gains tax.

The portion chargeable to income tax forms part of the profits of your UK or overseas property business (as appropriate) unless the premises are used in your trading business, in which case your taxable trading profits are correspondingly increased.

The above rules are applicable to trusts and partnerships. They also apply to companies in which case the corporation tax charge (13.2, 13.2.1) may be adjusted.

There are certain rules for treating leases for longer periods than 15 years as being periods shorter than that time. This applies if you sell a lease and take a new one under which the rent for the earlier years of the lease is greater than that for the later years. For example, suppose you sell a 45-year lease for £30,000 and take back one for 20 years at £3,000 annual rent for the first ten years and £1,000 per annum for the remainder. Your new lease will then be treated as being for ten years and you will be charged to income tax on

$$£30,000 \times \frac{16-10}{15} = £12,000$$

7.14 Landfill tax (FA 1996 Ss39–71 & Sch 4)

A tax on waste disposals in and on landfill sites in the UK was introduced on 1 October 1996. Details are included in the 1996 Finance Act and these are supplemented by legislation in the summer of 1996 and subsequently. (New rules tax controllers of sites even if they are not the operators.) Exemption for product from the clean-up of contaminated land is to be phased out over the period 1 December 2008 to 1 April 2012.

There are two rates of tax. Inactive waste (which does not decay, pollute groundwater or contaminate land) is taxed at £2.50 per tonne from 1 April 2008 (previously £2) and the Government announced in the 23 March 2011 Budget their intention to freeze this rate from 1 April 2012. Generally, a higher rate applies. From 1 April 2011, this rate is £56 per tonne, increasing to £64 per tonne from 1 April 2012.

Standard rates of landfill tax applicable in previous years, currently in force and announced are set out in the following table.

From	Rate per tonne £	From	Rate per tonne £
1 April 2006	21	1 April 2010	48
1 April 2007	24	1 April 2011	56
1 April 2008	32	1 April 2012	64
1 April 2009	40	1 April 2013	72

The Government announced in the 23 March 2011 Budget their intention to freeze the low rate at £2.50 from 1 April 2012 and to increase the standard rate by £8 per tonne annually up to and including 1 April 2014, when £80 per tonne will become a floor, below which this rate will not fall before 1 April 2020.

From 1 April 2011, the maximum credit against landfill tax liabilities for contributions to bodies concerned with the environment was increased to 6.2 per cent (previously 5.5 per cent from 1 April 2010). Recent rates are set out in the following table.

From	Maximum credit %	From	Maximum credit %
1 April 2007	6.6	1 April 2010	5.5
1 April 2008	6.0	1 April 2011	6.2

From 1 September 2009 certain gaps in the existing law (exposed in litigation) were repaired by secondary legislation. The outgoing Government announced in the March 2010 Budget an intention to revise the definitions of inactive waste that qualifies for the lower rate of levy with effect from autumn 2010. The new coalition Government included enabling legislation in F2A 2010 and the new subsidiary regulations operate from 1 April 2011, prior to which the previous rules applied.

7.15 Aggregates levy (FA2001 Ss16–49 & Schs 4–10)

Operative since 1 April 2002, aggregates levy applies to sand, gravel or crushed rock extracted in the UK (including its territorial waters) or imported. The aggregate becomes liable when it is commercially exploited. Exclusions include metal, coal, gemstones and industrial minerals.

An increase in rate to £2.10 per tonne originally due to take effect on 1 April 2011 has been deferred for a further 12 months and is now due to start on 1 April 2013. This leaves the rate at £2.00 per tonne (introduced on 1 April 2009, previously £1.95 from 1 April 2008 and £1.60 before that).

7.16 Real estate investment trusts (REITs) (CTA 2010 Ss518–609)

(1) From 1 January 2007 a special regime has been available to UK REITs. The rules were modified from 22 April 2009, to inhibit unintended exploitation of the scheme and regulatory powers should enable further abuses to be stopped quickly.

(2) Subject to the rules, companies and groups can become REITs paying an entry charge on 2 per cent of the value of their investment properties (spread over 4 years if desired, subject to a finance charge). This is taxed at the main rate of corporation tax or, if the company is not UK-resident, the basic rate of income tax.

(3) Provided a REIT distributes at least 90 per cent of its property income and capital gains, these are subjected to no tax in its hands. With effect from 16 December 2010 these distributions can be made by way of stock dividends. Also the 90 per cent distribution requirement can be modified, where meeting it would require an illegal distribution.

(4) Distributions to investors made out of tax exempt property income and gains are taxed in their hands as UK property income, none of which attracts capital gains tax.

(5) Dividends paid out of other profits are taxed under the normal rules.

(6) To become a REIT, a company must be listed on a recognised stock exchange, no investor may have a 10 per cent stake, and 75 per cent or more of its assets and income must be in or from property.

(7) Owner occupied properties were excluded from 22 April 2009 as was abuse of the relief by groups of companies adopting 'artificial' restructuring schemes.

(8) The Government announced in the March 2011 Budget an intention to modify the rules for REITs, so as to accommodate certain genuine commercial requirements of well-managed property companies. A short consultative document published in May and due to close on 27 June 2012 addresses the possibilities of facilitating REIT involvement in long-term finance of new social housing and modifying the present rules to permit investment by an REIT in other REITs. The requisite legislation is planned for Finance Bill 2012.

Chapter 8

INCOME FROM DIVIDENDS AND INTEREST

8.0 Introduction

This chapter broadly covers savings income and dividends, including certain tax efficient investments. From 6 April 2005 the legislation contained in ICTA and subsequent Finance Acts was broadly consolidated into ITTOIA Ss365–573 and Parts 5–7 of Sch 2 and references to schedules for income no longer apply although the basic rules remain.

8.1 How dividends are taxed (ITA Ss8, 9, 13–15 & 19 & ITTOIA Ss382–385)

Any dividend paid to you by a United Kingdom company does not have tax deducted. The amount paid carries with it a tax credit of currently 1⁄9th (13.6). Special rules may apply to any shareholders who live abroad (19.1.5).

The following are examples of payments by companies to their shareholders (distributions) that are treated in this way:

(1) Dividends on ordinary shares.
(2) Dividends on shares with special rights such as preference and deferred shares.
(3) Capital distributions made in cash, such as dividends, paid out of the capital profits of a company.
(4) Scrip dividend options (8.9).

The gross amounts of your dividends including tax credits (and taxed interest) receivable in the tax year are included with your investment income for total income purposes (5.2).

8.1.1 Rules applying after 5 April 1999

Where your dividends, taken to be the top slice of your income, fall within your basic rate (20 per cent) band, although the tax credit is only 10 per cent, you pay no more tax. To achieve this effect, the income tax rate on your dividends is taken to be 10 per cent. Any dividends in the higher rate band (40 per cent) effectively bear the same tax burden (25 per cent of the cash dividend) which is achieved by charging 32.5 per cent on the grossed dividend and offsetting the 10 per cent tax credit (8.1.7). However, from 6 April 2010 dividends falling in the new 50 per cent rate band (5.6.2) attracts a charge of 42.5 per cent on the grossed amount, subject to the 10 per cent offset.

From 6 April 2004, a special tax rate of 32.5 per cent (previously 25 per cent) applied to the dividend income of those trusts which were liable to the 40 per cent rate (21.2.1). From 6 April 2010 those trusts face a dividend trust rate of

42.5 per cent and a trust rate of 50 per cent. This particularly applies to discretionary and accumulation and maintenance trusts.

8.1.2 **Example: Income tax on dividends**

Mr A has a taxable income for 2012–13 of £42,370 after allowances. This comprises dividends of £9,000 together with tax credits of £1,000 and £32,370 salary.

Mr A will be liable to tax as follows for 2012–13:

	£		£
Salary	32,370*	at 20%	6,474.00
Dividends	2,000*	at 10%	200.00
	8,000	at 32.5%	2,600.00
			9,274.00
Credits			1,000.00
Net tax payable			8,274.00

* Basic rate band £34,370.

8.1.3 **Tax credits on dividends after 5 April 1999** (TA S231 & F2A 1997 S30)

Successive reforms have taken place regarding the repayment of tax credits on dividends. This was stopped from 2 July 1997 as regards dividends on shares held by pension funds, including occupational (14.3) and personal pension (14.6) schemes, and from 6 April 1999 for individuals. From that date, if you have no tax liability, you are no longer able to reclaim tax credits on dividends.

If you pay income tax, the intention is that the change results in your paying no more tax. From 6 April 1999, the tax credit was halved to 10 per cent. For 2010–11, if you are a lower or basic rate payer, your tax on the dividend plus tax credit is 10 per cent, leaving nothing to pay after setting off the 10 per cent tax credit. However, as a higher rate payer, you are taxed at 32.5 per cent on your gross dividends, leaving 22.5 per cent to pay net of the tax credit and as an additional rate payer, you are taxed at 42.5 per cent on your gross dividends, leaving 32.5 per cent to pay net of the tax credit. Your dividends are treated as the top slice of your income in determining which rate(s) to apply (5.6).

Charities are no longer able to reclaim dividend tax credits, but transitional relief applied up to 5 April 2004 (15.2.1). Dividend tax credits also ceased to be reclaimable by pension funds and the position of trusts was also affected (21.5).

8.1.4 **Dividends etc. and your return**

You must enter the totals of your dividends and tax credits in your income tax return (16.2).

As well as dividends etc. from companies, you must include in your return the totals of the gross amounts of any payments due to you for taxed interest on government securities, trust income, and the income proportion of annuities etc. Most of these will have been taxed by deduction at the source before you receive them. Also include in this section any loan interest that has been taxed before you receive it and all unit trust dividends including those converted into new units instead of being paid to you in cash. You should watch for any interest payments which reach you without deduction of tax and show them separately (8.4).

8.1.5 **Income tax deduction vouchers**

Dividend vouchers show the actual dividend payment made to you together with the tax credit.

Different certificates (form R185) are provided for interest payments under deduction of income tax. These show the gross interest and the tax which is certified to have been deducted on the payment of the net interest to you. In the case of income distributions from trusts, tax deduction certificates are provided by the trustees – form R185 (Settlor or Trust Income or Estate Income). All of these tax deduction certificates are accepted by HMRC in connection with income tax repayment claims (16.7).

8.1.6 **Dividends from overseas companies** (ITTOIA Ss402–404)

The gross amounts of your overseas dividends are included in your total income (5.2) but you may get some double tax relief in respect of the overseas taxes against your tax liability.

From 6 April 2008, the non-reclaimable dividend tax credit (8.1.3) extends to dividends from non-UK companies paid to individual investors holding less than 10 per cent of the shares. This applies if you are UK resident and/or a Commonwealth or EEA national. As previously announced, individuals with larger shareholdings are included from 6 April 2009, subject to certain conditions – namely that the company is located in an approved jurisdiction with which the UK has a tax treaty with a non-discrimination clause and that the company is NOT an offshore fund. The effect is that if your top tax rate is no more than 20 per cent, your net UK rate on these overseas dividends is zero and otherwise it is 25 per cent of the amount received, if you are a higher rate payer, but 36 per cent if you pay additional rate.

Before 6 April 2008, any dividends that you received from overseas companies were normally net of both overseas tax deducted at source and United Kingdom income tax at 10 per cent.

You should enter on your 2010–11 tax return the total of the gross amounts of your overseas dividends and also show the amounts of foreign and UK tax deducted at source on the Foreign pages. However, if your total overseas dividends are £300 or less and you do not wish (or need) to claim relief for foreign tax, you can enter the net amount in the appropriate box (Box 5 on Page TR3) on the main tax return (SA 100).

Reclaiming any foreign tax suffered requires a study of any relevant tax treaty and the local administrative rules. You may receive guidance from the company in which you hold the shares, but, unless the amount at stake is large, it will often prove not be cost-effective to pursue it.

The treatment of distributions from offshore funds is similar to other foreign dividends, where the fund invests mainly in equities, because the non-payable tax credit previously withdrawn for 2008–09 was restored from 22 April 2009. However, if an offshore fund invests as to 60 per cent or more in interest bearing (or equivalent) assets, its distributions will carry no tax credit and will be taxed as interest.

In cases where the offshore fund is treated as fiscally transparent, the distributions will continue to be ignored and the underlying income attributed to the investor and taxed according to its nature.

8.1.7 **Authorised unit trusts** (ITTOIA Ss376 & 389)

Dividends which you receive from an authorised unit trust carry a tax credit of currently 1/9th (1/4 before 6 April 1999). As with other dividends, if you are a basic rate tax payer you pay no further tax. (Previously the trust paid a special corporation tax rate of 25 per cent, but from 1 April 1996, this has been 20 per cent.)

For distribution periods beginning after 31 March 1994, special interest distributions may be made. These were originally net of income tax at the basic rate (25 per cent) for which you obtained a tax credit. The tax deduction and credit from 6 April 1996 is 20 per cent. The trust obtains relief for the interest payments against its corporation tax on its interest income.

The tax treatment of foreign investors in authorised unit trusts has improved. Payments to them from certain underlying income, such as from Eurobonds, is now free of UK tax. Otherwise relief is often available under the interest article of the relevant UK tax treaty.

8.1.8 **Financial services compensation scheme** (ITTOIA S380A & ITA S979A)

Payments made to depositors by the FSCS (or HM Treasury) since 6 October 2008 in respect of the failures of banks or other financial institutions include an interest element. New rules ensure that individuals, trustees and other income tax payers will be taxable on the interest element and able to receive credit or repayment of the income tax deducted, for which forms R185 should be issued.

Corporation tax payers will be dealt with under the loan relationship scheme.

8.2 Interest paid on government securities etc. (ITA Ss877 & 890–897)

From 6 April 1998, interest on 'gilts' is normally paid gross, subject to the right to elect for payment less tax. Normally, income tax is payable under self-assessment by UK residents, unless the interest is covered by their personal reliefs.

8.3 Bond washing – accrued income (ITA Ss615–681)

(1) Rules exist to prevent tax saving by selling *securities* with accrued interest and thereby receiving extra capital instead of income. Previously, this would have at most only have borne capital gains tax.
(2) The accrued income scheme covers transfers after 27 February 1986. In addition, anti-avoidance rules cover the previous year. A special new regime regarding companies was included in the 1996 Finance Act, mainly affecting corporation tax for accounting periods ending after 31 March 1996 (13.27).
(3) *Securities* excludes shares in a company but covers loan stocks etc. whether issued by the UK or other governments or companies. Thus 'gilts' are included and 'corporate bonds' (20.19). National savings certificates and war savings certificates are excluded, as are certain securities redeemable at a premium. Certificates of deposit are also excluded but profits on disposal are assessable as miscellaneous income (15.1).
(4) If you transfer *securities* with accrued interest, so that the purchaser receives the next interest payment, you are taxed on the same basis on a portion of that interest. The proportion is A/B, where 'B' is the total days in the period for which the interest is paid and 'A' is the part of the period during which you held the *securities*. When the purchaser receives his first interest payment, his taxable amount is reduced by the proportion A/B.
(5) If you transfer *securities* but receive the next interest payment, your taxable amount is reduced by the proportion (B – A)/B. The purchaser is taxed on the same proportion, which actually corresponds to his ownership.
(6) The above rules do not apply if you trade in securities, nor if you are neither UK resident nor ordinarily resident (17.3.1). You are also excluded if the nominal value of your securities does not exceed £5,000 at any time in the year of assessment or previous year. A similar rule applies to the estates of deceased persons and trusts for the disabled.
(7) If you sell foreign securities but are not permitted to have the proceeds remitted to you, your tax charge is delayed until they can be sent.
(8) Transactions taxed under these rules are normally excluded from other anti-avoidance provisions.
(9) Special rules apply to the issue of securities in tranches. Accrued interest included in the issue price qualifies for relief and tax relief for the interest deemed to be paid by the issuer is restricted to the amount taxable in the hands of the subscriber.

(10) The accrued income scheme no longer normally applies to transfers under sale and repurchase agreements (ITA Ss654–655).
(11) For deaths after 5 April 1996, the accrued income scheme no longer applies to the transfer of a person's securities to his or her personal representatives, or normally to legatees.

8.4 Interest not taxed at source (ITTOIA S369)

Subject to the deduction of tax at source (8.6 and 8.7), income tax is charged on the following. (For years prior to 2005–06, Schedule D Case III applied).

(1) Any interest whether receivable yearly or otherwise.
(2) Any annuity or other annual payment received without the deduction of tax.
(3) Discounts.
(4) Income from securities payable out of the public revenue unless already charged.
(5) Various kinds of investment income as specifically directed.
(6) The discount portion of the proceeds of 'deep discount securities' (8.8).

8.4.1 Examples of interest etc. not taxed at source

- Bank deposit interest generally up to 5 April 1985. (Composite rate rules then applied up to 5 April 1991 followed by tax deduction at source – 8.7).
- Discount on treasury bills.
- National or Trustee Savings Bank interest (TA S349) apart from the £70 tax-free portion from National Savings Bank Ordinary Deposits (2.6.1).
- Income from government securities in general (8.2).
- Gross payment of share and loan interest by a registered industrial and provident society.

8.5 Basis of charge for interest etc. not taxed at source (ITTOIA Ss369–381)

Since 6 April 1997, interest has generally been taxable by reference to the amount arising in the year. No deductions are allowed in computing the assessable income.

Note that after 2004–05, the Schedule D Case III classification was dropped but the rules still apply.

A company is assessed to corporation tax on its actual interest not taxed at source for each of its accounting periods (13.6.2).

As an individual, your income is normally included when it is due to be paid to you whether or not it is actually paid. For example, if interest is payable for each year ended 31 December in June and December, your assessment for 2010–11 would normally be based on the income for the year to 31 December 2010.

Your liability in respect of interest normally forms part of your general self-assessment (5.7), which is usually payable by two provisional instalments, based on the previous year and a balancing adjustment approximately 10 months after the close of the tax year.

8.6 Building society interest (ITA Ss7, 12, 18 & 875)

Building society interest is normally paid to you less the deduction of 20 per cent income tax at source. The system is similar to that which applies for bank interest (8.7). If your income is sufficiently low (8.7) you can request that the interest is paid to you gross. As mentioned, income tax is deducted from the interest at 20 per cent and unless you are a higher rate (40 per cent) or additional rate (50 per cent) tax payer, you pay no further tax.

As an exception, from 6 April 1983, interest has been paid gross by building societies in respect of 'qualifying certificates of deposit' and 'qualifying time deposits'. Broadly, these must be for at least £50,000 and (under current rules) be repayable after less than five years. However, from 6 April 2012, new deposits will no longer enjoy this treatment. Building societies are permitted to pay interest gross to non-resident individuals and quoted Eurobond holders; also to charities and registered Friendly Societies.

In 1991, rules were introduced to deal with permanent interest bearing shares (PIBS). You are taxed as if they are 'debt' rather than 'equity'. Thus income tax is deducted from your interest. No capital gains tax arises but the bond washing and accrued income scheme (8.3) apply.

8.7 Bank interest (ITA Ss7, 12, 18 & 878)

From 6 April 1991, bank deposit interest is normally paid subject to the deduction of income tax at source. From 6 April 1996, tax is deducted at 20 per cent and you pay no more tax on the interest unless your top rate reaches 40 or 50 per cent. Where appropriate, you are able to reclaim the tax. If your income is sufficiently large, higher and additional rate tax will apply, any assessments being on an actual basis.

There are arrangements under which if you are not liable to tax you may receive the interest gross. You need to complete a certificate enabling each financial institution to pay you gross. You must certify that, to the best of your knowledge, you do not expect to be liable to tax and the information which you have given in the form is correct. If you knowingly make a false declaration, you may be subject to penalties. This also applies where you later deliberately fail to inform your bank or building society that you have become liable to tax.

If you are not ordinarily resident in the UK (17.3.1), you can be excluded from the tax deduction arrangements, so that deposit interest is paid to you gross. However, you need to supply the bank etc. with a declaration regarding your residence status and you must tell them if this changes. Note also that under ITA Ss 811–826, if you are not resident in the UK and receive bank interest etc. without the deduction of income tax, in certain circumstances, the Inland Revenue will take no steps to pursue your liability to income tax.

Normally excluded from the tax deduction rules are debentures, loans by a deposit taker in the course of business, certain quoted loan stocks and also 'qualifying certificates of deposit' and 'qualifying time deposits', both of which (broadly) must be for at least £50,000 when issued and (under current rules) be repayable after less than five years. The income on such deposits is normally payable gross, even if now in 'paperless' form. Lloyd's premium trust funds and solicitors' and estate agents' undesignated client accounts were also excluded. Here too (see 8.6), from 6 April 2012, new deposits will no longer enjoy this treatment.

8.8 Deeply discounted securities (ITTOIA Ss427–459)

Special rules now applicable to 'deeply discounted securities' originally targeted deep discount securities issued after 13 March 1984. These are securities issued at a discount of more than half of one per cent for each year of their life or more than 15 per cent overall. Effectively the discount is treated as income accruing over the life of the security and when you dispose of your investment, you are normally charged income tax on the accruals (under Schedule D Case III before 2005–06).

Exceptionally, you are taxed on the 'income element' arising on certain securities issued after 19 March 1985 from 'coupon stripping operations'. These are where a company acquires securities and issues its own related stocks – normally deep discounted with varying maturity dates.

The company issuing the security gets *annual* relief for the accruing discount. The rules do not apply to certain securities exchanged for others issued before that date, not of the deep discount type, provided the new redemption date and price do not exceed the original ones.

For disposals after 13 March 1989, the rules apply to certain variable deep discount securities, but not index-linked bonds satisfying various conditions. These conditions include a limit on capital profits on redemption equal to the rise in the retail price index. Also, the interest rate must be reasonable and commercial; payments being at least annual. The securities must be issued for a period of at least five years.

A security issued after 31 July 1990 is not a 'deep discount security' if under the terms of issue there is more than one date when the holder can require it to be redeemed. Where securities are issued in tranches after 18 March 1991, any accrued interest included in the issue price is excluded from the price used to compute the 'deep discount' or 'deep gain'.

'Deep gain securities' issued after 13 March 1989 are treated in a similar way to deep discount securities. A 'deep gain' means that the redemption price exceeds the issue price by more than 15 per cent or half of one per cent for each completed year.

A security is not to be classed as a 'deep gain security' solely because it may be redeemed early if the issuer fails to comply with the issue terms, is taken over or is unable to pay its debts. Also, 'qualifying convertible securities' are excluded. These are, in general, bonds issued from 9 June 1989 which are convertible into ordinary shares of the issuing company and give the investor an option to 'put' the bond back to the issuer. Bonds issued from 12 November 1991 are not caught simply through the potential operation of default or event risk clauses.

From 1996–97, one set of rules broadly covers the above ground, relating to securities which have effectively been issued at a discount and are held by private investors. (Unstripped gilts are not covered.) In general, you are assessed under income tax (not capital gains tax) on any profits on the disposal or redemption of such securities.

8.9 Scrip dividend options (TA 1988 Ss249–251)

Your taxable dividend income (8.1) includes any shares in UK resident companies (17.3.3) which you obtain by exercising an option to take a dividend in such a form. In this case, you are treated for tax purposes as if you had received the dividend in cash. If, however, the cash equivalent is substantially less than the market value of the shares on the day when market dealings commence, HMRC may substitute that market value for the cash value.

8.10 Personal equity plan (PEP) (TA 1988 Ss151 & 333 & FA 1998 S6)

A scheme to encourage the purchase of shares in UK incorporated companies commenced on 1 January 1987. It was called the personal equity plan (PEP). After 5 April 1999, you can make no further investment in PEPs. However, you are allowed to keep those which you have and continue to enjoy their tax advantages, as indicated below, without prejudicing your ISA investment potential (8.12). For previous details please see previous editions of this book.

Re-invested dividends (and accompanying tax credits) are free of income tax. (Also, tax can be recovered on dividends distributed.) Similarly re-invested capital profits are not subjected to capital gains tax.

As from 6 April 2001, the rules regarding remaining PEPs have been aligned with the ISA rules. Single company and general PEPs can now be merged. PEPs may now invest in the less restricted range available for ISAs, for example listed shares worldwide. Written withdrawal requests are no longer required. Notification by telephone, fax or Internet will suffice. Part of a PEP can now be transfered to a new fund manager, rather than just the whole PEP.

8.11 Tax exempt special savings accounts (TESSAs) (TA Ss326A–326C)

Investment into a TESSA was allowed with a bank or building society, subject to the following rules:

(1) You were able to invest in one TESSA only.
(2) The account needed to run for a five year period and maximum total deposits of £9,000 were allowed.
(3) No capital could be withdrawn before the five year period expired, otherwise the tax advantages were lost.
(4) Income could be withdrawn subject to a notional basic rate deduction (22 per cent).
(5) When your TESSA matured, you could open a new one in accordance with the above rules. Alternatively, if you had held your TESSA for the full five year term, you could open up a new one within 6 months, with a maximum first-year deposit of the capital from your first TESSA.
(6) No new TESSAs could be taken out after 5 April 1999, but those taken out by that date were allowed to run their full course. When your TESSA matured, you were able to transfer the capital (not interest) into an ISA without affecting the amount you could otherwise subscribe.

8.12 Individual savings account (ISA) (FA 1998 Ss75–77)

The ISA scheme operates from 6 April 1999. Significant changes were made from 6 April 2001 and again from 6 October 2009.

If you are resident, ordinarily resident (prior to abolition) and now 16 or over, you are able to invest through an ISA each tax year. The scheme also applies to Crown servants and their spouses. In recent years only half the permitted limit of subscription could be invested in cash (including National Savings) but the rest had normally to be invested in shares or certain single premium life assurance policies and only one ISA could be used in any tax year.

Special relief applied if you withdrew cash from a Northern Rock ISA between 13 and 19 September 2007, when there was a run on that bank. This allowed you to reinvest the cash in another ISA before 6 April 2008, even if you had otherwise reached the limit.

From 6 October 2009 the rules are relaxed to enable you to use two separate ISAs each year and to move cash from existing ISAs into shares. Also from 6 October 2009, if you were already 50 or more or due to be so by 5 April 2010, your subscription limit for 2009–10 was £10,200 (£5,100 as cash). If you were younger than that, the 2008–09 limits of £7,200 and £3,600 continued until 6 April 2010.

Subsequent limits (for all adults*) have been:

	Stocks and shares £	Cash £
2010–11	10,200	5,100
2011–12	10,680	5,340
2012–13	11,280	5,640

* Savers under the age of 18 are only eligible to invest in Cash ISAs.

From 2011–12, the limits will be indexed annually for inflation, adopting always a multiple of 120, so as to facilitate monthly savers. Initially, indexation was by reference to RPI, but from 6 April 2012 CPI will be applied.

Everything in your ISA is income tax-free. There is no capital gains tax and the 10 per cent tax credit on dividends accrued to ISAs until 5 April 2004, when this ceased to be refundable. Another advantage is that you are able to make withdrawals as you please.

ISAs are administered by managers in accordance with detailed government regulations. These include for example, rules for making annual returns and HMRC determining the recovery of tax relief wrongly given. Furthermore a penalty might be levied instead of recovering the relief. Sometimes interest might be charged on the ISA investments rather than taxing an individual investor directly.

8.12.1 Junior ISAs

It was intended that Junior ISAs (6.6.3), which became available in autumn 2011, would serve as a replacement for Child Trust Funds (CTFs) (6.6.2) in autumn 2011.

The new accounts are intended to offer parents a simple tax-free way to save for their children's future. Their key features are to be tax-free status and offer a choice of cash or stocks and shares, but they will be restricted to those under 18 and will receive no Government contributions. Funds will be locked in until the child reaches adulthood and annual contributions will be capped.

8.13 Venture capital trusts (VCTs) (ITA Ss258–332)

This form of highly tax efficient investment was introduced in 1995–96. After their issue to you, the actual shares in VCTs must be quoted, but because they invest mainly in smaller non-quoted companies, there is a tangible degree of risk. However, the tax benefits are substantial. From 6 April 2006, the maximum annual investment, on which you may claim income tax relief is £200,000, if you have sufficient income, but relief is capped at the lower of 30 per cent or your actual tax rate. For 2004–05 and 2005–006 an optimum rate of 40 per cent applied, prior to which relief was limited to £100,000 at 20 per cent.

Dividends are exempt from tax in your hands and, if held for 5 years or more (3 years for shares issued before 6 April 2006), disposals are exempt from capital gains tax.

From 6 April 2011, in order to ensure their approval for state aid under EU regulations, it is permitted that the listing of the VCT's ordinary shares be on any EU or EEA regulated market (replacing the previous UK listing requirement).

Changes introduced by F3A 2010 and FA 2011 are now reflected in the numbered paragraphs below, as too are certain further technical changes to the rules for eligibility of VCT, ESI and EMI companies that are included in FA 2012 and take effect from 6 April 2012.

(1) VCTs need Inland Revenue approval, which can be provisional for up to three years.
(2) The established conditions for approval include the VCT's income being mainly from shares or securities and at least 70 per cent of its investment being in 'qualifying holdings' of which at least 30 per cent consists of ordinary shares. The holding in any one company may not exceed 15 per cent of the VCT's investments, nor must it retain more than 15 per cent of its income from shares and securities. At least 10 per cent of a VCT's total investment in any company must be held in ordinary non-preferential shares. In general, VCTs may not provide majority funding for companies, ignoring all fixed rate preference shares and loans. From 6 April 2011, the minimum portion of the VCT's 'qualifying holdings' that must comprise 'eligible shares' was raised from 30 per cent to 70 per cent, but the definition of 'eligible shares' was simultaneously modified to include shares with certain preferential rights to dividends.
(3) 'Qualifying holdings' are in unquoted companies which exist wholly for the purpose of carrying on one or more qualifying trades. This is broadly defined as for EIS purposes (11.26) and needed to be wholly or mainly carried on in the UK. From 27 November 1996, investment in the parent of a group may qualify where non-qualifying activities do not form a major part of the group's activities as a whole. From 6 April 2011, the trading requirement was redefined as a 'permanent establishment' in the UK or, in the case of a parent company, at least one company in its group that is carrying on a 'qualifying trade' and has a 'permanent establishment' in the UK.
(4) Investments of no more than £1 million in any one company count towards the 70 per cent requirement mentioned above, but not if its gross assets (or those of its group) broadly exceeded £10 million before 6 April 1998. For investments made in qualifying companies after 5 April 1998 the gross asset limit per company was increased to £15 million before the investment and £16 million afterwards. However, after 5 April 2006, these limits were reduced to £7 million and £8 million. If any of the companies become quoted after holdings are acquired by a VCT, their shares are treated as qualifying for a further five years. For shares issued from 6 April 2012, the gross assets limit was restored to £15m before and £16m after the VCT's funding injection.
(5) Various property backed activities are excluded (also for EIS purposes). These include farming, market gardening, forestry, property development and running hotels, guest houses and nursing/residential care homes. Also excluded are investments by VCTs of funds raised after 5 April 2008 in shipbuilding and coal and steel production.
(6) The following tax benefits are available to you provided you are at least 18 years of age, invest no more than £200,000 from 2004–05 (previously £100,000) in VCTs each tax year (to 5 April) and hold your VCT

shares for at least five years. Regarding VCT shares issued after 5 April 2000, you only need hold them for three years. However, for shares issued after 5 April 2006, the holding period is once again five years.

(7) You obtain 30 per cent relief on your investments in new VCT shares, which you deduct from your income tax liability. Previously 40 per cent applied for 2004–05 and 2005–06 (originally the rate was 20 per cent).

(8) Any dividends which you receive from a VCT will be free of income tax.

(9) Your disposals of VCT shares will be free of capital gains tax.

(10) If you subscribed for new VCT shares up to 5 April 2004, you were able to defer paying tax on a corresponding amount of capital gains on any asset disposals after 5 April 1995. The gains must arise during the year before and the year after the VCT shares were issued. This reinvestment relief (maximum 40 per cent) was available in addition to the 20 per cent relief (see (7) above). However, the relief will in general be recalled if you dispose of your VCT shares without replacing them by others.

(11) If a VCT makes an issue of shares, it will have had 12 months in which to invest 80 per cent of the money in companies which qualify for the scheme, with the remainder being invested in the following year. From 22 April 2009, two years is allowed for making the whole of the investment.

(12) From 16 June 1999 VCTs are allowed to retain shares received in exchange for an existing holding in preparation for a stock market flotation and also shares from exercising conversion rights in qualifying shares or securities held as investments.

(13) From 17 April 2002 relief is not lost on account of VCTs being wound up or merging.

(14) FA 2007 made various technical amendments, including from 6 April 2007 a rule that the company raising money under the scheme must have less than 50 full-time employees when its shares are issued and, from 19 July 2007, a new limit of £2m on the money raised during the 12 months up to any investment from all EIS, VCT and Corporate Venturing schemes. For shares issued from 6 April 2012, the above limits increased to 'fewer than 250 employees' and '£5m annual funding'.

(15) As from 6 April 2011, shares in a company are ineligible for VCT (or EIS) investment, if it is reasonable to assume that the company would rank as an 'enterprise in difficulty' for the purposes of the EU Rescue and Restructuring Guidelines.

8.14 Proposed Saving Gateway

The coalition Government are not proceeding with their predecessors' proposal to introduce the Saving Gateway, due to have commenced in July 2010. This was to have been a Government-sponsored savings plan aimed at people with low income and would have enabled them to save up to £25 per month for 2 years and would have attracted a Government contribution of 50p for every £1 saved.

Chapter 9
LIFE ASSURANCE

9.1 Introduction

Earlier in this book, certain tax aspects of life assurance are touched on. This chapter deals with them in more detail, together with related subjects such as permanent health insurance and purchased life annuities.

Life assurance used to enjoy a highly favoured status for tax purposes. Since 1984, this has been reduced but some benefits still remain and these are examined below.

Remember, you should not enter into life assurance arrangements merely to save tax, but for the primary benefits they confer. However, the tax benefits certainly make them more attractive.

9.2 Types of life assurance

There are three main kinds of assurance policy which you can take out on your life:

(1) Term assurance: the sum assured is only payable if the event insured occurs during the term of the policy.
(2) Whole of life: the sum assured is payable if the event insured occurs at any time in your life.
(3) Endowment: the amount insured is payable on your death within the term of the policy or otherwise at its end.

However, the tax treatment of your life assurance premiums and policy proceeds mainly depends upon whether the policies are 'qualifying' or 'non-qualifying'. (*Single premium bonds* are probably the most important type of non-qualifying policy.) But for both categories, whilst the policy is in force, the income and gains are the responsibility of the insurance company.

Most insurance policies pay the benefits when the life assured dies, but *critical illness policies* pay the benefits when the life assured suffers from and survives a serious illness from a range which typically includes heart attack, cancer and stroke.

9.3 Qualifying policies (TA 1988 Sch 15)

Qualifying policies have various tax advantages. For example, if you took out the policy before 14 March 1984, subject to the rules (3.2.4) tax relief will be available on the premiums at the rate of 12.5 per cent.

It is intended that there will be a limit of £3,600 per annum on premiums to qualifying policies issued on or after 6 April 2013. The limit will apply to the total premiums paid to all policies issued from that date, not to each policy. There is to be no limit for policies issued before 21 March 2012.

If you realise any gains under your policy, you are not liable to basic rate tax. Furthermore, the proceeds are generally completely tax-free provided you have been paying the premiums for at least ten years (9.5). In the case of an endowment policy, this period is three-quarters of the policy term, if less than ten years.

For policies issued on or after 21 March 2012, the relief (i.e. freedom from tax on any proceeds) will only apply to gains attributable to premiums paid from 21 March 2012 to 5 April 2013, and up to £3,600 per annum of the premiums payable from 6 April 2013.

9.4 Life assurance relief (TA 1988 Ss266–274)

Tax relief is only available in respect of premiums which you pay on qualifying policies which were effected before 14 March 1984. The detailed rules are described earlier (3.2.4). It is the current intention that tax relief on life assurance premiums will no longer be available from 6 April 2015.

Subject to these rules and until 5 April 2015, you may deduct the relief from your premium payments at the rate of 12.5 per cent of the eligible premiums.

Where a qualifying policy was made paid-up or surrendered during its first four years, the life assurance premium relief could be clawed-back in whole or part. These rules are now outdated, but partial surrenders from policies effected after 26 March 1974 and before 14 March 1984 may give rise to a 'claw-back'.

The rules only apply if there is a surrender of part of the policy rights later than its fourth year and this has happened at least once previously. The claw-back is limited to relief on the premiums for the year of the surrender etc. and the insurance company will pay it over to HMRC.

9.5 The taxation of life assurance policy proceeds (TA 1988 Ss539–552 & TCGA 1992 S210)

Whether your policy is qualifying (9.3) or not, there is an assumption that tax at 20 per cent has been paid. In addition, you would pay no basic rate income tax (20 per cent) on the proceeds. However, you may be liable to the excess of higher rate tax over the 20 per cent assumed rate. This applies particularly for non-qualifying policies (9.2). Thus, for the tax year 2011–12, if your top rate of tax is 40 per cent you could have a liability of 40 per cent minus 20 per cent = 20 per cent on any gain made on a UK non-qualifying policy. If you pay tax at 50 per cent (because your taxable income exceeds £150,000), the tax charge could be 50 per cent minus 20 per cent = 30 per cent.

The position with qualifying policies is that you will normally incur no income tax on the proceeds in any event, provided you pay premiums for a required period. This is at least ten years (or until death, if earlier). For an endowment policy, the required period is limited to three-quarters of the term of the policy.

In the normal course of events, you will have no capital gains tax liability on the proceeds of a life assurance policy (22.8.1). However, if you are not the original beneficial owner and purchased the policy for money or money's worth, the exemption does not apply.

Income tax on your policy proceeds may arise, if a *chargeable event* occurs. As mentioned earlier, no basic rate income tax is payable. However, if your income, together with the appropriate proportion of your policy gain is large enough, higher rate tax will arise (9.6) and the excess over the basic rate is payable.

Chargeable events in the case of a non-qualifying policy include its maturity or total surrender, where you assign it for money or money's worth and the death of the person whose life was assured. Also included are 'excesses' on partial surrenders. However, if you assign a policy to your husband or wife, this is not a chargeable event.

The above chargeable event rules are modified for qualifying policies. Maturity or death is only included where the policy had been made paid up within its first ten years (limited to three-quarters of its term for an endowment policy).

Similar modified rules apply for an assignment for money or money's worth, a surrender, making the policy paid up within the policy period, or an 'excess' on a partial surrender. These will only be chargeable events if they take place within that period (ten years etc.).

If you borrow money against a non-qualifying policy at an uncommercial rate of interest, this could be treated as a chargeable event if the policy dates from after 26 March 1974.

9.5.1 Assignment of joint policies

There are special rules that apply when a policy is currently held by two or more people and the ownership is transferred to one of them, or the policy is owned by one person and is to be subsequently owned by two or more people. Typically, this can often happen on divorce.

The assignment of a part of the policy from one joint owner to the other can result in a chargeable gain arising and tax being charged on the person assigning their interest. Similarly, assignments from a sole owner into joint names of the assignor and another will be affected.

These rules will only apply to assignments that are treated as assignments for money or money's worth. Assignments that are gifts are not affected by these rules.

9.6 How the gains on chargeable events are computed and taxed (TA 1988 S541)

(1) The gain on a chargeable event must be ascertained and in general the details will be supplied by the life assurance company. It is their duty to send a certificate to HMRC giving detailed information about your policy and the gain made (TA 1988 S552).

(2) In general, the gain is the investment profit on the policy, taking account of earlier capital benefits (other than any related to disability).
(3) Any benefit from death included in the proceeds is not treated as part of the taxable gain.
(4) No basic rate income tax, nor normally capital gains tax will be payable (9.5).
(5) 'Top slicing relief' is often available on your gain. This is described below (9.7) and effectively adjusts the tax taking account of the number of complete years for which you have held the policy. However, since no basic rate income tax is payable, you only pay the excess over the 20 per cent tax assumed already paid.
(6) A gain is regarded as the top part of your income for tax purposes and higher rate income tax is calculated, taking account of any top slicing relief. A credit of 20 per cent of the gain is allowed, resulting in your paying tax at 30 per cent at the most.
(7) Normally it is the policyholder who will be liable for any tax on a gain. However, if a policy is held on trust, it is normally the settlor who is taxed but he can recover the tax from the trustees (TA 1988 Ss587 & 551).
(8) Life insurance companies will tell the policyholder the amount of any gain he or she has made in the previous tax year. This will help taxpayers complete their self-assessment tax return.

9.7 Top slicing relief (TA 1988 S550)

This relief is available to individuals but not companies. The rules include the following:

(1) The tax on your gain is payable for the fiscal year when it arises, but you obtain spreading relief on the basis of the number of complete years (Y) for which you have held the policy.
(2) What you do is to divide your investment gain (G) by (Y). This gives the 'slice'.
(3) Next, calculate the tax (T) payable for the year on your other income plus the 'slice' (G÷Y).
(4) You then calculate the tax payable on your other income by itself and deduct it from (T). This gives the total tax on the 'slice' (G÷Y).
(5) The total tax on the 'slice' is then divided by the 'slice' to give the tax rate on it and the special rate (20 per cent) is deducted, since this is not payable on your gain. The remaining percentage is applied to your gain (G) to give the tax payable.
(6) Certain categories of income and relief are ignored for the purposes of the above. Examples are lease premiums charged as rent (7.8) and compensation for loss of office (10.12). EIS relief is not ignored.

9.8 Example: Top slicing

Mr A purchased a single premium bond for £15,000 in February 2007 and realises it in March 2013 for £27,000, his gain being £12,000. His other taxable income for 2012–13 is £33,370. The tax on the gain is as follows:

	£	£
'Slice' = gain £12,000 ÷ 6 (complete years held)		2,000
Other taxable income + 'slice'		36,000
	£	£
Tax rate on 'slice'		
£33,370–£34,370 at 20%	200	
£34,370–£35,370 at 40%	400	
Total tax on 'slice'	600	
Average tax rate on 'slice'		
$\frac{600}{2000} \times 100\%$	30%	
Less: assumed rate of 20%	20%	
Rate applicable to gain	10%	
The tax payable on the gain is thus 10% × £12,000 =		1,200

9.9 Partial surrenders and excesses (TA 1988 S546)

If you make a partial surrender of a life policy (often by cashing in part of a single premium bond) it may give rise to tax, subject to the following rules:

(1) You have an allowance of 5 per cent for each 'policy year' (which starts with the day you took it out and each subsequent anniversary). This is calculated on the premium(s) (normally a single premium on a bond) and is set against your partial surrenders.

(2) Your total allowances are limited to 100 per cent of your premium(s).

(3) Unused allowances and partial surrenders are carried forward from previous years. When a partial surrender is made, you only pay tax on any excess.

(4) When your policy ends, you may have an overall gain on it which is less than the excesses which have previously been added to your income. If so, you can normally obtain higher rate relief (the excess over the 20 per cent rate) on the difference. This is called 'deficiency relief'. (However, deficiency relief will only be allowed where the previous gains formed a part of your income and not someone else's. If they did not, for example where the policy was owned by someone else previously when the earlier gains arose, then those earlier gains will not be taken into account, restricting the deficiency relief available to you). In addition,

the relief may be restricted if the main purpose of the arrangement is to secure a tax reduction greater that the amount of tax due on previous chargeable gains.

(5) When there is an excess in a policy year, you obtain top slicing relief (9.7). As usual, you pay tax for the fiscal year in which the policy year ends based on your highest rate, less the special rate (20 per cent).

(6) For the first partial surrender or on final termination, the period which you use for the purposes of top slicing is the number of policy years since your policy started. Otherwise, you take the number of complete policy years since the last 'excess'.

(7) If any of your policies were issued before 14 March 1975, special rules apply. Broadly, withdrawals used to be fully taxed with no 5 per cent allowance each year. Such policies only obtain the benefit of this allowance for partial surrenders in policy years beginning after 13 March 1975.

9.10 Example: Partial surrenders – excesses

Mr A takes out a £20,000 single premium bond and withdraws £2,000 after each of policy years 3, 4, 5 and 7. He then surrenders the remainder for £20,000 after the end of policy year 8. His gains will be as follows:

Years	Allowances available £	Cumulative withdrawals £	Gain £
1	1,000 (5% × £20,000)	0	0
2	2,000	0	0
3	3,000	2,000	0
4	4,000	4,000	0
5	5,000	6,000	1,000
6	1,000	0	0
7	2,000	2,000	0
8		*surrender*	*see below*

When the bond is surrendered after eight policy years, Mr A will have a further gain of £7,000. This is the excess of the bond proceeds (£28,000) over the original cost (£20,000), less the earlier gain (£1,000).

The earlier gain of £1,000 will be top-sliced (9.7) over five years and the £7,000 gain over eight years. The excess of higher rate tax over the 20 per cent rate will then be charged as appropriate.

The earlier gain of £1,000 will only be allowed as a deduction in the example above, if it previously formed a part of the income of an individual. This new rule generally only applies to contracts made on or after 21 March 2012. It can apply to ealier policies in certain circumstances, for example where it is assigned to someone else.

9.11 Inheritance tax

There are two aspects of inheritance tax in relation to life assurance. There is the incidence of the tax on life assurance policies, particularly the proceeds on death. There is also the important use that can be made of life policies in inheritance tax planning. These subjects are dealt with in Chapter 22 (22.27).

9.12 'Key man' policies

These are policies taken out by a company on the lives of its directors or executives. The following points should be noted:

(1) The normal purpose is to protect the company against the death of the 'key man', although in certain cases where the employee and company are unconnected the proceeds can be paid out free of inheritance tax to the next of kin.
(2) Provided the 'key man' is not 'connected' with the company and a term policy is used for not more than about five years, the premiums are allowable for tax but the company will be taxed on any proceeds.
(3) Where the 'key man' has a substantial holding of the company's shares so that he is 'connected' with it, the premiums will not be deductible. Any proceeds will normally only be taxable if there is a chargeable event (9.5).
(4) This treatment (in (3) above) is also likely where the policy has one or more of the following attributes: a term of more than about five years; is for a capital purpose; has a surrender value.
(5) The treatment of the proceeds of pre-14 March 1989 policies held by companies is broadly similar to those owned by individuals.
(6) For new 'investment' policies, that is, policies that can acquire a surrender value, taken out by a company on or after the first day of the first accounting period that starts on or after 1 April 2008, the company will be taxed on realised and unrealised gains on a year by year basis.

    Example: An investment policy is effected with a UK insurer in May 2008, after the start of the investing company's accounting period. The company pays tax at the main rate of corporation tax, 28 per cent.

    The investment is £100,000. At the end of the company's accounting period, the value of the policy is £110,000. Thus there is an unrealised gain of £10,000. To calculate the tax, this gain is grossed up at 20 per cent, that is, giving a gross gain of £12,500. The gain of £12,500 is taxed at 28 per cent, the rate for this particular company, which is £3,500. Relief of £2,500 is allowed to reflect the tax assumed to have been paid by the insurance company on its funds. Thus the tax charge will be a net £1,000. If the company has not surrendered the policy, it will have to find this sum from its general funds.

    Conversely, had the value of the policy fallen, the loss would have created a non-trading loss which could be offset against the trading profits of the company, or carried forward to offset against future non-trading profits. Special rules apply to policies already in force before the commencement of the investing company's first accounting period that starts on or after 1 April 2008.

9.13 Permanent health insurance

This is intended to provide you with an income should illness or disability prevent you from working. Contracts frequently take the form of non-qualifying life assurance policies. For taxation purposes, disability benefit payments are not regarded as rights surrendered (9.5).

If your employers pay the premiums on your policy, they would normally obtain a tax allowance on the basis that it is part of your own taxable remuneration package. Where you pay the premiums, you will not usually obtain any tax relief.

Any permanent health benefits paid to you from personally owned policies are tax-free.

9.14 Purchased life annuities (TA 1988 Ss656–658)

When you buy an annuity from a life assurance company, the effect is the reverse of a life assurance policy. Instead of paying periodic premiums and getting back a lump sum, you pay a lump sum to receive an annuity periodically. This is based on your age when you purchase it. However, you may have a joint annuity together with your spouse and then the younger of your respective ages would be used.

Annuities are of great importance to pension arrangements (Chapter 14). When you retire, one or more annuities are often purchased for you by the pension fund(s) and special tax rules apply.

The normal tax rule for a purchased life annuity is that it is treated as comprising a non-taxable capital element and the rest is taxable income. The capital part is regarded as a return of the premium and is fixed from the start of the annuity. The life company will normally inform you of the split and deduct basic rate income tax from the income part of each payment.

For example, suppose you pay £10,000 for an annuity of £1,000 for the rest of your life. The company tell you that the capital part of each instalment is £400 and the income part is £600 from which they will deduct basic rate tax of £120. You will thus be paid £880. If you are a higher rate payer, you will pay further income tax of £600 × (40% – 20%) = £120.

Because of the tax-free element, annuities are useful tax-planning tools. This is particularly true as you become older, since the rates improve. But remember that you will be parting permanently with the capital. Some annuities compensate for this by guaranteeing a minimum span, even if you should die meanwhile. One point to watch is that you will not be able to save tax through the independent taxation rules by assigning an annuity to your spouse (TA1988 S685 (4A)).

9.15 Guaranteed income bonds

Guaranteed income bonds normally provide you with a fixed income for a stated period. After that, your original investment is returned to you, or you might be able to take an annuity for life. These bonds resemble annuities but have various structures.

For example, there could be a combination of a temporary immediate annuity and a deferred lifetime one. Another common arrangement is to have a series of term or endowment life policies.

Considering an annuity combination, you would receive a temporary annuity for, say, ten years. The income element would be subject to income tax, but not the capital portion of each instalment. You would then either take an annuity for life under the deferred contract or receive your original outlay.

If you choose the money-back option, you will be charged basic rate income tax (and higher rate if your income is sufficiently high) on the excess of the proceeds over the original cost of your deferred contract. This applies for contracts effected from 26 March 1974. Profits on earlier contracts are not subject to the basic rate.

9.16 European insurance policies

If you take out a policy with a European insurance company, rules will ensure that you only pay the difference between the higher rate and the basic rate of tax (currently 20 per cent) provided tax of at least 20 per cent has been paid within the company's funds. This puts European policies on a broadly similar tax basis to UK policies.

9.17 Miscellaneous aspects

(1) Policies owned by trusts

There are differences to the way any gains made from non-qualifying policies are taxed, when owned by trustees.

Normally any gains will be added to the income of the person who created the trust, and he or she will have an excess tax liability at either 20 per cent if their highest rate of tax on other income is 40 per cent, or at 30 per cent if they pay tax at 50 per cent.

However, when the person who created the trust died before 17 March 1998 and the policy started before that date, the gain will usually be free of all taxes, provided the policy is not increased. This is known as the 'Dead Settlor Rule'.

For trusts where the person who created the trust dies on 17 March 1998 or later, the gain will usually be treated as income of the trust and taxed at 20 per cent of the first £1,000 of the income and 50 per cent on the excess. The trustees are liable in this situation.

If the trustees are non-resident, the gain will be treated as income of the trust and taxed on any UK beneficiaries entitled to benefit under the trust, to the extent that they receive benefit from the trust.

Normally any gain made on a policy held by trustees is taxed on the person creating the trust. In some cases, for example where the person creating the trust is dead, the gain will be taxed on the trustees.

Loans taken by trustees will be treated as part surrenders and taxed in the same way.

(2) Personal Portfolio Bonds

Personal Portfolio Bonds are usually single premium insurance bonds, often arranged with offshore life assurance companies, which allow the owner to choose the underlying investments, rather than investing in a fund available to other investors as well. Thus the fund is unique to the policyholder.

There is an annual tax charge on a 'deemed gain' of 15 per cent of the premium paid. Thus if the original investment is £100,000, the deemed gain at the end of the first year will be £15,000. If the owner is a UK taxpayer and pays tax at 40 per cent, the tax charge will be £6,000 (£15,000 × 40 per cent) assuming the investment is with a non-UK insurance company. At the end of each subsequent year the gain – and thus the tax – is increased by 15 per cent.

The object of the tax charge is to discourage UK residents from investing in these very specialised investments. These rules do not apply to other investments with insurance companies, where the investor chooses one or more funds which are available to other investors.

These rules apply to Personal Portfolio Bonds taken out before 17 March 1999.

(3) Commission arrangements

A loophole was closed with effect from 21 March 2007, involving the rebating of the commission earned by an adviser on a large policy to the client/policyholder. In effect, this generated a tax-free income from the policy. This will no longer work if the premium to the policy exceeds £100,000 and the policy is not owned for at least three years.

9.18 Policies held by charities

Occasionally, life assurance policies are held by charities. With effect from 9 April 2003, a charity will usually have no tax liability on any gain made on a UK policy.

9.19 Policies effected by non-residents with UK companies

Policies effected by non-residents with UK life assurance companies benefit from the fact that there is no tax payable within the funds. On return to the UK, they are only taxed at the higher rate, with a credit equal to the basic rate of tax.

For policies taken out or enhanced from 17 March 1998, there will be a tax charge at all rates, including basic rate.

Chapter 10

INCOME FROM EMPLOYMENTS AND PAYE

10.1 Background

The taxation of your income from employments or from any office that you hold derives mainly from earlier legislation. Until 5 April 2003, such income was normally taxed under Schedule E and generally a receipts basis applied (10.13). Schedule E was divided into three 'Cases' which focused on your resident, ordinarily resident and domiciliary status (TA S19).

That legislation, together with rules previously existing as concessions and practice, was consolidated into ITEPA, which aims at increased clarity and took effect from 2003–04. Thus, from 6 April 2003, although there was no classification of income into cases, the new rules (ITEPA Ss14–26) had broadly similar effects (see previous editions).

From 6 April 2008 the rules were refocused in order to tie in with the extensive provisions introduced from that date to discourage the use of the remittance basis of assessment (18.0) by certain UK residents. *The following paragraphs (10.2–10.5) address the regime applicable from 6 April 2008.*

10.2 Taxation of employment income

A summary of ITEPA follows, so as to provide a broad overview of its contents. You will see that this statute embraces the taxation of 'pension income' and 'social security income' which are both taxed under the PAYE system, but are otherwise outside the scope of the present chapter.

10.2.1 Income Tax (Earnings and Pensions) Act 2003 (ITEPA)

Part			Sections	Schedules
1	Overview – abbreviations etc.		1–2	1
2	Charge to tax on employment income		3–61	
3	Earnings and benefits treated as earnings		62–226	
4	Employment income –	exemptions	227–326	
5		deductions from earnings	327–385	
6		not earnings or share related	386–416	
7		share-related income and exemptions	417–554	2–5
8	Former employees – deductions for liabilities		555–564	
9	Tax on pension income		565–654	
10	Social security income		655–681	

11	PAYE	682–712	
12	Payroll giving	713–715	
13	Supplementary, definitions etc.	716–725	6–8

10.2.2 The distinction between self-employment and employment

This distinction is sometimes very fine – for instance in the case where you have a number of part-time employments and do some of the work at home. If you can show that you are in fact working on your own account and are self-employed (not an employee) then you will be assessed under the rules for trading income which normally results in your being able to deduct more of your expenses from your taxable income than if you are treated as employed. Divers and diving instructors are normally assessable as trading (ITTOIA S15). HMRC remain keen to ensure that entertainers, journalists and many others should be assessed as employed. When this happens, agents' fees will still be allowable as expenses (ITEPA S352), subject to a cumulative limit of 17.5 per cent of the taxable earnings. It was hoped that uncertainties and difficulties in this area would be addressed by the 'wholesale review' of small business tax and administrative burdens, but progress seems to be impeded by the extent of apparent abuse that has emerged (10.16.1).

10.3 UK resident employees (ITEPA Ss15–19)

You are normally taxable on your 'general earnings' for any tax year in which you are a UK resident. Your liability is based on the amounts received in the tax year, whether or not the employment is held in that year.

However, if those general earnings consist of money, the detailed rules may permit their reallocation to more appropriate years and, where they are received before the particular employment starts or after it finishes, they will generally be reallocated to the first or the final year respectively. These reallocations do not apply to other forms of remuneration, such as benefits in kind, cash vouchers, non-cash vouchers and credit tokens, to each of which a specific time of provision is ascribed (ITEPA Ss73–226 & 693–702), nor to deemed employment income or disguised remuneration (10.17).

10.3.1 Working outside the UK in course of UK employment

If your UK employment involves you in work abroad this is normally treated as being derived from your employment in this country and is included in your taxable income. However, in respect of any work that you do abroad, special rules apply which may result in you paying less tax (18.5). From 1 April 2006, operational allowance paid to members of the UK Armed Forces is tax-free.

10.4 UK resident employees who are not ordinarily resident or not domiciled in the UK (ITEPA Ss15, 22(6) & 26(7))

If you are resident in the UK, but are either not ordinarily resident or not domiciled here, any foreign earnings to which the remittance basis rules (18.0 *et seq.*) apply are taxed in accordance with those rules and removed from the general rules (10.3).

10.5 Categories of employment earnings

For clarity and ease of assimilation, the layout used in previous editions of this book has been retained in describing the effects of the tax provisions (10.6 *et seq.*).

10.6 Amounts included in your income

Any amount that you derive from your office or employment is normally included in your taxable income. This applies to the value of any payments in kind as well as cash.

10.6.1 Typical items

- Normal salary or wage.
- Overtime pay.
- Salary in lieu of notice (often tax-free – see 10.12).
- Holiday pay.
- Sick pay from your employer, including statutory sick pay.
- Sickness insurance benefits paid to you (all sickness benefits are taxable immediately except to the extent that you have paid for these yourself).
- The value of luncheon vouchers until 5 April 2013 (limited to the excess over 15 pence per day).
- Cost-of-living allowance.
- Christmas or other gifts in cash excluding personal gifts such as wedding presents.
- Annual or occasional bonus.
- Commission.
- Director's fees.
- Director's other remuneration.
- Remuneration for any part-time employment.
- Salary paid in advance.
- Payment for entering into a contract of employment.
- Tips from employer or from customers or clients of employer.
- Settlement by employer of debts incurred by employee.
- Payment by employer of employee's National Insurance contributions.
- Value of goods supplied free of cost to employee by employer.
- Value of shares or other assets received from employer for no charge, or amount by which their market value exceeds any payment made for them.
- Fringe benefits (see below).

- Unregistered pension scheme contributions.
- Travelling allowances in excess of expenditure incurred for business use (10.6.4).
- Share options (10.9.2).
- Job release allowances capable of beginning earlier than a year before pensionable age.
- Maternity pay.
- Statutory paternity and adoption pay, from April 2003 (FA 2002 S35).
- Payments under *restrictive covenants* including (after 9 June 1988) where separate from the contract of employment.
- Various non-cash benefits such as tradable assets and readily convertible assets (ITEPA S19).

10.6.2 **Fringe benefits – the 'Benefits Code'** (ITEPA Ss62–289 & Schs 2–5)

Fringe benefits is a wide non-technical term used colloquially to describe any benefit which you obtain from your employment that is not actually included in your salary cheque. Fringe benefits are taxable according to the rules now subtitled the 'Benefits Code' and outlined below.

If you are an employee earning less than £8,500 each year, including the value of any benefits, then the taxation of your fringe benefits is on a comparatively favourable basis. If, however, you earn over £8,500 or are a director, then you are normally taxed more strictly on the actual value of the benefits obtained. If you fall into this latter class then your employers must submit to HMRC a form P11D for you every year. This form covers your expenses and benefits (10.7).

You are not caught by the rules as being a *director*, if you own no more than 5 per cent of the company's shares and work full time for it. Any shares owned by relatives and associates count towards your 5 per cent. (In the case of charities etc. you do not need to work full time.) If you work for several companies which are connected, your earnings including benefits must be taken together for the purposes of the rules.

The taxation of certain fringe benefits is summarised in the following table according to whether or not you are a P11D employee (that is, a director or earning over £8,500).

10.6.3 **Fringe benefits – taxation 2012–13**

	Details	Non-P11D employee	P11D employee or director
(1)	Free private use of motor car supplied by your employers. Car mileage allowance	Tax-free (provided some business use is made)	Taxable (10.6.5 & 10.6.6)

	Details	Non-P11D employee	P11D employee or director
(2)	Provision of motor van	Tax-free (provided some business use)	Taxable (10.6.7)
(3)	Company house occupied rent free	Taxed on annual value of benefit (that is, open market rental and expenses paid) unless you need to occupy house to do your job properly	Taxed on annual value unless you must live there to perform your duties (10.6.13)
(4)	Board and lodging	If you receive cash you are taxed on it. Otherwise tax-free	Taxed on cost to employer of board and lodging subject to a limit (10.6.13)
(5)	Working clothing, for example overalls	Tax-free	Tax-free
(6)	Suits and coats etc.	Taxed on estimated second-hand value	Taxed on full cost to employer
(7)	Private sickness insurance cover	Tax-free	Taxed on premiums paid by your employer (10.6.11)
(8)	Interest-free loan	Tax-free	Taxable subject to certain exemptions (10.6.9) – to participator etc. of close company (13.17.3) – employee shareholdings (10.9.4)
(9)	Share options	Taxable with certain exceptions (10.9)	Taxable with certain exceptions (10.9)
(10)	Employee's outings	Tax-free	Normally tax-free
(11)	Luncheon vouchers (10.1.6.1)	Tax-free up to 15p per day – excess taxable	Tax-free up to 15p per day – excess taxable
(12)	Subsidised staff canteen	Tax-free	Tax-free provided facilities available to all staff
(13)	Pension and death in service cover	Normally tax-free (10.11)	Normally tax-free (10.11)
(14)	Cash vouchers	Taxable (10.6.12)	Taxable with some exceptions (10.6.12)
(15)	Season tickets and credit cards	Generally taxable (10.6.12)	Generally taxable (10.6.12)
(16)	Assets at employee's disposal	Normally tax-free	Taxable with some exceptions (10.6.8)

	Details	Non-P11D employee	P11D employee or director
(17)	Scholarships from employer for children of employee	Normally tax-free	Taxable with some exceptions (10.6.14)
(18)	Long service awards of articles or employer company shares; after 20 years' service and each further 10 years; maximum £50 for each year	Tax-free	Tax-free
(19)	Security assets and services provided after 5 April 1989 (10.6.8)	Tax-free	Tax-free
(20)	Childcare	Tax-free	Tax-free subject to conditions (10.6.15)
(21)	Mobile telephones	Tax-free	Tax-free subject to conditions (10.6.16)
(22)	In-house sports and recreational facilities	Tax-free	Tax-free (10.6.17)
(23)	Removal expenses and benefits	Tax-free up to limit (10.6.18)	Tax-free up to limit (10.6.18)
(24)	Employee liabilities and indemnity insurance	Tax-free (10.6.19)	Tax-free (10.6.19)
(25)	Work-related employer-funded training	Tax-free	Tax-free
(26)	Corporate loan	Tax-free	Tax-free up to limit (10.6.9)
(27)	Works buses	Tax-free	Tax-free (10.6.21)
(28)	Bicycles	Tax-free	Tax-free subject to rules (10.6.21)
(29)	Education and training	Tax-free	Tax-free subject to conditions (10.6.23)
(30)	Payments by employers towards incidental homeworking costs	Tax-free	Tax-free subject to rules (10.6.24)
(31)	Payments of council tax relief to members of Armed Forces from 1 April 2008 and continuity of education allowance from 6 April 2012	Tax-free and NIC free	Tax-free and NIC free

10.6.4 **Travelling and entertainment allowances** (ITEPA Ss337–342, 356–358 & 369–376)

An allowance or advance that you derive from your employer to meet the costs of travelling, entertaining or other services you perform on his behalf is not taxable provided that you actually incur expenditure for these purposes. (Your employer is able to deduct the payments from his taxable profits. Entertaining expenses, however, are not normally deductible.) Should you incur expenditure of less than the full allowance or advance and are not required to pay back the unexpended portion to your employer, this excess must be included in your taxable income.

If you are a P11D employee (10.6.2) any allowance made to you by your employers for travelling etc. is normally included in your taxable income in full. If you incur travelling expenses etc. in the course of your employment you must make a claim to that effect and you will be allowed to deduct from your taxable income the amount of your expenses. If you are not a P11D employee (or director) any expense allowances or payments on your behalf are not normally included in your taxable income.

Your employer can pay you free of tax up to 20p for each mile for which you use your own cycle for business travel. If you use your own bicycle for business travel you can claim capital allowances on a proportion of the cost (11.9).

Payments made to you by your employer to cover your personal incidental expenses when you stay away from home overnight on business are now tax-free up to certain limits. The expenses covered include newspapers, personal telephone calls and laundry. The exemption runs from 6 April 1995 and the limits are £5 each night in the UK and £10 overseas.

You are not in general allowed any deduction for your travelling expenses between your home and your employer's place of business. Thus if your employer makes you any allowance for this expense it is wholly taxable in your hands. However, certain benefits are tax-free (10.6.21). No tax is payable on travel facilities provided for *servicemen* and *servicewomen* going on and returning from *leave* (ITEPA S296).

From 6 April 1998, site-based employees get relief for the cost of travelling to and from a site and for subsistence when staying there, provided no more than 24 months is spent at that location. Also, from that date, the position is improved regarding travel and subsistence between home and a temporary place of work. You now obtain relief for your full costs without having to offset any saving through not doing your normal commuting. (ITEPA S338).

If you *travel abroad* in connection with your employer's business, the cost is allowable. If you also have a holiday abroad during the same trip you will be taxed on an appropriate proportion of the cost of your trip as a personal benefit. If your employers pay for your wife to accompany you (and she is not an employee herself) her own trip would normally be taxed as a personal benefit although some allowance could be obtained if, for example, she acted as your secretary during the trip or it was necessary for her to go for reasons of your health.

No benefit is assessed on you if your employer pays for the actual journeys of your family in visiting you, provided you *work abroad* for at least 60 continuous days. This applies to your wife (or husband) and any of your children who are under 18 on the outward journey. Also covered are journeys by your family in accompanying you at the beginning of your overseas period or by you back to the UK at the end. Two return trips for each person are covered by the rule, in any tax year (ITEPA Ss369–375).

Any travel expenses paid by your employer covering journeys to and from the UK will be tax-free where you are UK resident and working abroad.

Members of Parliament are allowed no deduction for expenditure incurred to cover staying away from home in London or the constituency. However, the Additional Costs Allowance paid to meet these expenses is not taxable (ITEPA S292). Exemption now extends to payments for travelling and related expenses when MPs visit an EU institution or agency or the National Parliament of another EU state, on Parliamentary duties. Candidate or applicant countries are also included. From April 1999 members of the Scottish Parliament, Welsh and Northern Ireland Assemblies are treated in the same way for tax purposes as MPs.

Certain payments by employers to their employees for travel between work and home are tax-free. This exemption (formerly by concession A66 – now *ITEPA S248*) covers working until at least 9 pm on no more than 60 occasions in a tax year. Furthermore, there must be no regular pattern. Subject to these points, the cost of a taxi or hired car will not give rise to tax on the employee. This now extends to where your car sharing arrangements for commuting fail through unforeseen circumstances (breakdown or late working etc.) and your employer pays for your journey home.

Another concession concerns non-cash gifts from third parties (that is, not the employer). These are tax-free in an employee's hands providing the cost is no more than £250 in the tax year from any one source (previously £150). There is a similar exemption regarding entertainment provided by third parties. Credit tokens and non-cash vouchers are included. There is no limit but the person providing the benefit must not be the employer or anyone connected with him, nor must it be provided in recognition of particular services regarding the employment.

Employees are not taxed on annual staff parties such as for Christmas if the total expenditure per head is no more than £150 (previously £75).

10.6.5 **Motor cars** (ITEPA Ss114–153, 167 & 169–172)

With effect from 2003–04, a new method of calculating car benefits applies to you if yours is a director's or *higher paid* employment (10.6.2):

(1) The new method originally targeted 15–35 per cent of the car's 'list' price, depending on its level of carbon dioxide emissions. There is a 3 per cent supplement for diesel cars, but the 35 per cent maximum still applies. From 2008–09 a new 10 per cent rate applied for very low emission cars (QUALECs) and separate reductions applied to other cars which are hybrid-powered (3 per cent) or use gas or E85 biofuel (2 per cent), but these stopped on 5 April 2011. FA 2010 introduced incentives for even lower emission levels for five years from 2010–11, halving the charge to 5 per cent for QUALECs with emissions up to 75g/km and extending the electric vehicles exemption to any vehicle that cannot produce any CO_2. The table below shows the main rates from 2008–09 to 2013–14 and 2014–15 rates appear in footnote:

	2008–09 to 2009–10 g/km	**2010–11 g/km**	**2011–12 g/km**	**2012–13 g/km**	**2013–14 g/km**	**Percentage of list price for tax****
Zero CO_2 cars from 6 April 2010		–	–	–	–	nil
Cars registered from 1.1.98						
CO_2 emissions g/km						
not more than:	–	–	75	75	75	5
CO_2 emissions	76–120	76–120	76–120	76–99	76–99	10
by 5 g/km steps				100–119	100–114*	11–14
not exceeding:	140	135	130	120	115*	15
each additional	5	5	5	5	5	1 extra
maximum from:	235	230	225	220	215*	35
Cars registered before 1.1.98						
with no CO_2 emission figures:						
Electric only***						9***
Engine size up to 1400cc						15
1401–2000cc						22
over 2000cc						32

* Levels of 99–109, 110 and 210 g/km have been announced for 2014–15.
** 'List' price cap at £80,000 expired on 5 April 2011.
*** From 6 April 2010 the general zero rate apples for five years.

(2) From 2003–04 a new car fuel basis applies, directly linked to CO_2 emissions. The percentage derived from the above scales (1) is applied to a fixed price, which will be £20,200 for 2012–13 and will then be indexed by RPI plus 2 per cent annually (previously £18,800 for 2011–12, £18,000 for 2010–11, £16,900 for 2008–09 to 2009–10 and £14,400 for 2003–04 to 2007–08).

(3) Special rules apply if you own your car but are paid a mileage allowance (10.6.6).

(4) Changes in motor vehicles provided for staff must be notified to the Tax Office quarterly, but your code is not altered automatically and intervention may be needed to avoid incorrect tax deductions.

(5) If you would otherwise be within the car benefit scheme and you are offered an alternative to the car of say cash, the offer of an alternative

will not, of itself, alter your tax. You will be taxed on what you actually get, car benefit or cash.

(6) Provided you do not have the use of a particular car but simply take one from a car pool and do not garage it at home overnight, you will not normally be assessed to any benefit; subject, however, to the further condition that any private use of the car is merely incidental to your business use thereof.

10.6.6 **Car mileage allowances** (ITEPA Ss229–236)

(1) You are entitled to relief for travelling expenses concerning your employment. Mileage allowances paid to you where you use your own car for work are taxable to the extent that they exceed your allowable expenses, including capital allowances.

(2) To reduce the administrative work involved there is the *approved mileage allowance payments scheme* (AMAP) (previously *fixed profit car scheme* (FPCS)). Under this, your taxable mileage 'profit' may be calculated using the excess of the mileage rate paid to you over the appropriate AMAP 'tax-free' rate.

(3) The main approved mileage rate increased to 45p (previously 40p) per mile from 2011–12, but the other rates continue at their 2002–03 levels:

Cars and vans:	On the first 10,000 miles in the tax year (2002–03 – 2010–11 40p)	45p
	On each additional mile over 10,000 miles	25p
Motor cycles:		24p
Bicycles:		20p
Each business passenger:	(that is, fellow employee or from 2011–12 a volunteer) per mile	5p

(4) Capital allowances were available to you if you used your car for work, but this does not apply for 2002–03 and subsequently. The allowances were based on the proportion relating to business use.

(5) If you borrowed money to buy a car to use for work, interest relief was available on a more general basis from 6 April 1990. This does not apply after 2001–02.

10.6.7 **Vans etc.** (ITEPA Ss154–166, 168 & 248A)

From 6 April 1993, you have been taxed on any benefit that you obtain from having the use of a company van. The charge is apportioned if several employees share a van. Furthermore, vans over 3.5 tonnes are usually outside the benefit charge, as in general are other commercial vehicles above that weight.

Initially, the standard benefit was £500 p.a., but only £350 p.a. for vans which were at least four years old at the end of the tax year, and you could elect to be taxed instead on £5 for each day that you had the use of a van.

Moreover, no extra charge was made for any fuel provided by your employers.

From 6 April 2004, you are no longer taxed on any benefit where you are required to take an emergency vehicle home, when you are on call. This might apply if you work for the fire, police or ambulance services. A similar exemption applies from 6 April 2005, provided you are not allowed other private use.

From April 2007, changes in detailed rules were made, the standard benefit was increased to £3,000 and an additional charge of £500 was imposed for use of private fuel. From 2010–11, the fuel charge increased to £550 and is due to be increased by RPI for 2013–14.

From 2010–11 to 2014–15, the provision of a van which produces no CO_2 is exempt from van benefit charge.

10.6.8 **Use of assets** (ITEPA Ss201–210)

If your employer places an asset at your disposal for your personal use (for example a television set) your annual taxable benefit is 20 per cent of its market value when you first began to use it. (For assets placed at your disposal prior to 6 April 1980, the benefit is 10 per cent.) This rule does not apply to cars (see above) nor to land for which 'annual value' is used (S531) and only relates to those in director's or *higher paid* employment (10.6.2).

For assets provided after 5 April 1980 by your employer, a special rule applies if you subsequently become the owner. You will then have a taxable benefit of the excess over what you pay for the asset, of the original market value less the previous annual benefit assessments. This is increased to the excess of market value over price paid when you obtain the asset from your employers.

From 6 April 1989, employees (and self-employed people) who face a special threat to their *personal physical security* obtain special relief. However, the threat must arise directly out of their particular job or business. The relief extends to services and assets provided by the employer, such as alarm systems, security guards, bullet-resistant windows etc. In appropriate circumstances, no benefit charge will be made.

If your employer loans you computer equipment, it is likely that no tax charge resulted for 1999–2000 or subsequently. The first £500 of annual benefit was exempt. If the loaned computer was sold to you at market value after 5 April 2005, there will be no taxable benefit in kind. However, no tax exemption applies for computers loaned for private use after 5 April 2006.

10.6.9 **Beneficial loan arrangements** (ITEPA Ss173–191)

(1) If you or a 'relative' have a loan by reason of your director's or *higher paid* employment at no interest or at a lower rate than the 'official' one then you will be taxed on the benefit of your interest saving compared with the official rate, subject to the following rules.
(2) The 'official rate' varies periodically. Recent rates are:

From	%	From	%
6 November 1996	6.75	6 April 2007	6.25
6 August 1997	7.25	1 March 2009	4.75
6 March 1999	6.25	6 April 2010	4
6 January 2002	5		

(3) 'Relative' means parent, grandparent, child, grandchild etc., brother, sister or spouse of yourself or any of the relatives aforementioned.
(4) For 1994–95 and subsequent years, the benefits from loans totalling up to £5,000 are exempted.
(5) From 6 April 1994, you are taxed as if you had been given the equivalent in cash of a cheap or interest-free loan. Where appropriate you are then given tax relief as if you had paid interest on the loan at the 'official rate'.
(6) Up to 1994–95, any loan which replaced a beneficial loan was treated as the original one and was thus potentially taxable. From 1995–96, this no longer applies for arm's-length replacement loans.
(7) From 2000–01, if your beneficial loan qualifies for full tax relief, it no longer needs to be reported. Also, the exemption for loans made on normal commercial terms is extended where their terms are varied.

10.6.10 **Director's PAYE** (ITEPA S223)

Where a company accounts for PAYE (10.14) to HMRC in respect of certain directors and this exceeds the amounts which they suffer, the excess is treated as their income. This does not apply to directors owning less than 5 per cent of the company's shares who work full time for it, nor to directors of charities etc.

10.6.11 **Medical insurance** (FA 1989 Ss54–57, FA 1994 S83 & Sch 10 & F2A 1997 S17)

Non-directors earning less than £8,500 annually are not taxed on medical insurance premiums borne by their employer. Otherwise, employees and directors are taxed on such premiums (an exception being regarding overseas service).

From 1990–91 relief for private medical insurance was available for those aged 60 and over. From 6 April 1994, relief was limited to the basic rate. Where a contract covered a married couple and one died, the other could claim relief for its remainder.

Relief was withdrawn for private medical insurance premiums paid on policies taken out or renewed after 1 July 1997. An exception was made for contracts arranged before 2 July 1997 but not executed until later.

10.6.12 **Vouchers and credit tokens** (ITEPA Ss73–96)

All employees (and directors) are normally taxed on the value of cash vouchers received as a result of their employment. That value is the money for which the vouchers are capable of being exchanged. The rules include cheque vouchers and credit tokens such as credit and charge cards. However, lower paid employees of transport undertakings are not taxed on transport vouchers provided under arrangements existing at 25 March 1982.

Rules in the 1994 Finance Act aim to ensure that vouchers and credit tokens are properly valued for tax purposes. This must be according to the expense to those paying for the vouchers etc. From 6 April 2002, vouchers evidencing entitlement to minor benefits which are exempted under these regulations are free of tax.

From 6 April 2006, vouchers for eye tests and spectacles for VDU work are exempted from tax.

10.6.13 **Living accommodation provided for employees** (ITEPA Ss97–113)

In general, living accommodation provided to you because of your employment results in a taxable benefit. You are taxed on the open market rental value of the property, or the actual rent paid by your employer, if this is more. Amounts which you pay towards the cost are deducted. From 22 April 2009 lease premiums paid by your employer for a new or extended lease of 10 years or less will be spread over the term of the lease and added to the amount of rent (if any) paid, when calculating the amount of your benefit. However, the new charge will not apply where you occupy part of a property which is used mainly for your employer's business.

You are exempted from the charge, however, if any of the following circumstances apply:

(1) You have to live in the accommodation in order to perform your duties properly.
(2) It is customary in your type of employment to have accommodation provided and it helps you to do your job better.
(3) Your employment involves you in a security risk and special accommodation is provided with a view to your safety.
(4) From 6 April 2000, minor amounts of private use of assets and services which you mainly use for work purposes are exempted.

The above exemption also covers rates paid for you, but does not apply in circumstances (1) and (2) if you are a director, unless you have broadly no more than a 5 per cent shareholding and work full time or work for a charity etc.

If your employment is 'director's or *higher paid*' (10.6.2), you will still be assessed on payments by your employer for your heating, lighting, cleaning, repairs, maintenance and decoration etc. as well as on the value (20 per cent – 10.6.8) of domestic furniture and equipment provided. A limit applies, however, which is 10 per cent of your net emoluments from your job which is after deducting capital allowances, pension contributions and expenses claims, and excludes the expenditure for your benefit.

An additional charge applies to houses costing the employer more than £75,000 or, if purchased more than six years previously, worth more than that figure when first occupied by the employee after 30 March 1983. The additional benefit is broadly based on the excess of the cost etc. over £75,000. This is subjected to the rate of interest in force in relation to beneficial loans (now 4 per cent) at the start of the year of assessment (10.6.9). (From 6 April 1996, the above special rules take precedence and only the balance is charged as basic Schedule E income, if that is in point.)

10.6.14 **Scholarships** (ITEPA Ss211–215)

You will be assessed on the value of any scholarships awarded by your employer to your children, provided you are a director or *higher paid* employee (10.6.2), subject to certain exceptions. However, the scholarships will remain tax-free in the hands of your children.

An exception is where a scholarship comes from a fund or scheme from which at least 75 per cent by value goes to scholars otherwise than by reason of their parents' employment. (Overseas employees who are the parents of scholars are not included in the 75 per cent.)

10.6.15 **Childcare** (ITEPA Ss270A & 318)

From 6 April 1990, subject to certain rules, childcare facilities provided by your employer will not give rise to any benefit charge on you. You must either be a parent or foster parent of the child and the care may not be provided on domestic premises. Other conditions include your employer running the nursery at your workplace or elsewhere; or jointly with other employers. Childcare benefits also remain free from any charge to National Insurance contributions. From 6 April 2011, a higher or additional rate paying parent or foster parent joining such a scheme for the first time will receive a capped tax allowance, which effectively limits relief to the basic rate on the normal maximum.

From 6 April 2005, your employer is able to contract direct with a nursery, child-minder or after-school club thereby providing you with tax-free benefits or childcare vouchers up to £55 (previously £50) weekly plus associated administrative costs. From 6 April 2011, a higher or additional rate paying parent or foster parent joining such a scheme for the first time will be limited to £28 or £22 (according to their top tax rate) benefits or vouchers weekly.

10.6.16 **Mobile telephones** (ITEPA S319)

From 6 April 1991 to 5 April 1999 you were taxed on a standard amount of £200 yearly, on each mobile phone provided by your employers. (This included car phones – 10.6.5.) However, if you had no private use, or were required to make good the full cost of such use and did so, there was no tax charge. As from 6 April 1999, the charge was removed. From 6 April 2006, relief is restricted to one mobile phone.

From 6 April 2012, smart-phones will be regarded as mobile telephones and some retrospective relief may be available back to 2007–08, if they have been treated as benefits. However, devices such as tablets that use Voice over Internet Protocol to make telephone calls will continue to be viewed by HMRC as computers and potentially within the benefits regime.

10.6.17 **Sporting and recreational facilities** (ITEPA Ss261–263)

From 6 April 1993, benefits in kind are not taxable in connection with workplace sports and recreational facilities provided by your employer for use by staff generally. The exemption covers in-house facilities and those provided by outside firms for the staff in general. However, the exemption does not extend to yachts, cars and aircraft, or overnight stays.

10.6.18 **Removal expenses and benefits** (ITEPA Ss271–289)

If you start a new job or move with your present employer after 5 April 1993, statutory relief is available for relocation expenses and benefits. (Previously there was certain extra-statutory relief.) The relief covers such items as disposal and acquisition expenses, transporting belongings, travelling and subsistence and bridging loans. However, there is an overall limit of £8,000 per relocation, which also applies to freedom from benefit charge where your employer bears the costs. The £8,000 limit does not cover existing reliefs for expenses concerning work overseas (18.5.3).

If your employer provides you with a bridging loan, any unused part of your £8,000 expense allowance will result in reducing the beneficial loan charge (10.6.9). There is a formula that converts unused allowance into a number of days which reduces the period for which the charge is made.

10.6.19 **Employee liabilities and indemnity insurance** (ITEPA Ss346–350)

From 1995–96, if you incur expenditure on indemnity insurance or legal costs etc. relating to your employment, you obtain tax relief. Similarly you are not taxed if your employer meets these costs. Relief extends six years after you leave the employment for any years when you incur such expenses relating to your former employment.

10.6.20 **PAYE settlement agreements** (ITEPA Ss703–707)

Under 'annual voluntary settlements', employers may meet their employees' tax liabilities on a range of minor benefits in kind and expense payments. From 1996–97, these are known as 'PAYE settlement agreements' to which specific regulations apply.

10.6.21 **Commuting benefits** (ITEPA Ss237 & 242–249)

From 6 April 1999 you are not liable to tax on the following benefits provided by your employer:

(1) Works buses with at least 12 seats used to bring you and other employees to and from work. From 2002–03 minibuses taking 9 to 11 passengers are included.
(2) General subsidies to public bus services used by you and other employees provided you pay no less than the general public, unless it is a local stopping service.
(3) Bicycles and cycling safety equipment provided for your commuting.
(4) Parking facilities for cycles and motorcycles at work. Meals and refreshments can now be provided tax-free on official cycle-to-work days.
(5) From 6 April 2005, where you sell at market value a cycle loaned to you by your employer.

10.6.22 **Income from employment and your return**

HMRC significantly changed the appearance of many tax returns as from 2007–08 and the degree of detail required. You should be careful to ensure that you provide what is requested rather than what you used to provide previously.

The supplementary employment pages have been reduced to a single side, thus accommodating up to two employments on each sheet. As previously, a separate page is required for each employment or directorship.

The information requested falls into three blocks:-

(1) Total pay pre-tax, which will usually be net of any pension contributions; total tax deducted; tips and other payments not included on P60; employer's PAYE tax reference; employer's name; and three boxes to tick if you are a company director, if the company is a close company (13.18) or if you are a part-time teacher in the Repayment of Loan Scheme.
(2) Summary of benefits received grouped into eight boxes, which may require you to combine figures from your P11D. You must give details of your benefits-in-kind including goods and vouchers received as well as living accommodation. If the Inspector has granted a dispensation to your employer, however, you may leave the relevant expenses payments out of your return. (A dispensation will be granted if the Inspector is satisfied that all of the expenses payments are covered by allowable expenses.)
(3) Summary of the employment expenses (10.8) you wish to deduct from your taxable earnings including fees or subscriptions to professional bodies and superannuation contributions (if not already netted from your taxable pay) – all these are grouped into four boxes, which again may leave you combining figures from your P11D and elsewhere. If you are a P11D employee (10.6.2), it is essential that you claim relief for the deductible expenses appearing on your P11D in addition to those which you pay from your own resources.

HMRC have relegated to a new 'Additional information' set of supplementary pages 'SA 101' a wide range of less common but vital details for 'complex taxpayers', which could span many different aspects of their affairs.

The employment income items that you would need to enter there, if applicable are:

Taxable amounts from share scheme (10.9) and the tax deducted; other taxable lump sums; lump sums from pension schemes; redundancy, other lump sums and compensation; tax deducted from the above; exemptions claimed against pensions; compensation and lump sum exemptions; disability and foreign service deduction; seafarers' earnings deduction and the list of names of vessels; details of foreign earnings not taxable in UK, foreign tax for which double tax relief has NOT been claimed and exempt employers' contributions to any overseas pension scheme. If your duties are performed wholly abroad, this must be indicated.

Also show any part-time or casual earnings. If your spouse or civil partner has any income of this kind, it must be shown separately in his or her own return.

10.6.23 **Education and training** (ITEPA Ss250–260)

From 6 April 2000, new training relief operates where your employer contributes to your education or training and you are an individual learning account holder. The contributions are exempt from tax and National Insurance contributions provided the training or education qualifies for a grant or discount from the Department for Education and Employment etc. Your employer must also make similar contributions available to all employees on similar terms.

10.6.24 **Incidental homeworking costs** (ITEPA S316A)

From 6 April 2003, if you work all or part of your time at home and your employer contributes to any additional household costs, subject to the rules, this is tax and NIC free, up to a prescribed amount – £3 per week from 2007–08 (previously £2). No supporting evidence is needed and, beyond this, evidence must be provided to the effect that the payments are wholly in respect of your additional household expenses incurred in carrying out your duties at home. Although this arrangement does not apply to the self-employed, HMRC have previously agreed that the old rate of £2 may be claimed as an estimate, where a self-employed person does some work from home. It would be logical for them to accept such claims at the new rate in future.

10.6.25 **Benchmarked meal allowances**

From 6 April 2009 HMRC has set advisory scale rates for particular day subsistence expenses that it will accept for any employer who first notifies his intention to adopt them on Form P11DX (10.7). Subject to detailed rules, an employee who incurs subsistence expenses for meals bought on an allowable business journey, may be paid tax and NICs free subsistence payments of up to the following advisory rates:-

Breakfast rate –	£5.00 if you leave home earlier than usual and before 6.00 a.m.
One meal (five hour) rate –	£5.00 if away from home or normal workplace for at least five hours.
Two meal (ten hour) rate –	£10.00 if away from home or normal workplace for at least ten hours.
Late evening meal rate –	£15.00 if you work later than usual and after 8.00 p.m. having worked your normal day.

At a more significant level, HMRC now publish annually an extensive schedule of benchmarked subsistence rates for numerous countries worldwide. The content runs wider than just for meals and can enable employers and employees to overcome difficulties in obtaining comprehensive evidence of every item and for vouchers going astray in transit.

10.6.26 Subsistence allowances to certain visiting EU experts

From 1 January 2011, subsistence allowances will be exempt from income tax, if paid by a body of the EU located in UK to experts seconded by their employers to work here for that body. Initially there were three such bodies – The European Medicines Agency (EMA), Police College (CEPOL) and Banking Authority (EBA).

10.7 Expense payments for directors and others (form P11D)

If you have a director's or higher paid employment (10.6.2), your employers must complete a form P11D for each tax year in respect of all benefits in kind and expense payments made to you or on your behalf.

For 2010–11, particulars to be entered by your employer on your form P11D regarding any expenses payments made and benefits etc. provided by him would include the following, unless covered by a dispensation. (Form P11DX initiates and explains the procedure under which your employer can request a dispensation from the Tax Office regarding various business expenses such as scale rate payments for travelling and subsistence.) The amounts entered must include VAT even though this is recovered by the employer.

(1) Cars owned or hired by employer:
   - (i) Make, model and date of registration.
   - (ii) Price of car and optional extras provided originally and those added later.
   - (iii) Period for which car available to you in year.
   - (iv) Payment by you towards running costs.
   - (v) Fuel type, engine size and date from which free fuel made available or withdrawn.
   - (vi) Approved CO_2 emissions if registered after 31 December 1997.
   - (vii) Capital contributions towards cost (maximum £5,000).
   - (viii) Cash equivalent of each car and of fuel.

(2) Cars owned by you:
 (i) Excess mileage and passenger allowances over the maximum permitted rates and any other allowances from employer towards your running expenses.
 (ii) Contribution from employer towards purchase price, depreciation or hire.
(3) Entertainment – all payments made exclusively for entertaining including the amount of any round sum allowance, specific allowances, sums reimbursed and sums paid to third persons (entertaining disallowable to your employer must still be included).
(4) General round sum expense allowances not exclusively for entertaining.
(5) Travelling and subsistence – fares, hotels, meals etc. and payments from your employer for travel between your home and work from which no PAYE has been deducted – expenses regarding overseas employments.
(6) Subscriptions.
(7) Private medical and dental attention, treatment and insurance.
(8) Educational assistance for self or family including scholarships awarded to you or your family.
(9) Goods and services supplied free or below market value – equivalent cash benefit.
(10) Work done to your own home or other assets by your employer.
(11) Wages and upkeep of personal or domestic staff provided by your employer.
(12) Cost of vouchers and credit cards given to you by your employer.
(13) House, flat etc. provided by employer – cash equivalent.
(14) The market value of any cars or other assets given to you by your employer (other than personal gifts outside the business).
(15) Home telephone – cost of provision or contributions towards.
(16) Child care and nursery places provided for your children (10.6.15).
(17) Other expenses and benefits including your own National Insurance contributions (if paid by your employer), holidays.
(18) Beneficial loans – particulars of loans (if total exceeds £5,000) giving rise to benefit assessment including the maximum amount during the year (10.6.9).
(19) Should you have any share-related benefits, a box is provided to be ticked.
(20) Vans available and van fuel provided for private use (10.6.7) – enter the standard charge (£3,000 and £550) for van and fuel and reduce this for shared vehicles etc.
(21) Tax paid on your behalf.
(22) Non-qualifying relocation expenses.
(23) Tax on notional payments not borne by you within 90 days.

The order in which these details appear in the P11D vary from time to time. Optional working sheets are available to employers regarding cars and fuel, vans, relocation expenses, mileage and passenger payments, living accommodation and beneficial loans. Whether preparing a P11D or checking one issued to you, be alert for instances where the form asks only for the excess payments made over approved maximum allowances, but the whole of unapproved payments.

The above items are entered on your P11D and then your employer deducts the following:

(1) The amounts of any of the above expenses that you have repaid to your employer (unless already deducted from the items shown).
(2) Amounts included above from which tax has been deducted under PAYE.

Forms P11D were due to be sent to HMRC by your employer so as to arrive by 6 July 2011. Employees should receive copies by the same date. Although it is possible to lodge P11Ds by Internet, HMRC do not appear to be pressing for this just yet.

It is also necessary for employers to complete a simple confirmation that all necessary forms P11D have been completed and returned to the Tax Office.

10.8 Deductions you may claim (ITEPA Ss327–385)

You may claim any expenses which you have to incur wholly, exclusively and necessarily in performing the duties of your employment. These do not include:

(1) The cost of travel between home and work (but see 10.6.4 and 10.6.21).
(2) The cost of business entertainment except where the expense is disallowed in computing your employer's tax assessment or is reasonable entertainment of an overseas trading customer.

If you are a director or a P11D employee (10.6.2) you should make a claim to the Tax Office in respect of any allowable expenses that have been included by your employer in your form P11D. The claim should certify that the expenses covered were incurred 'wholly, exclusively and necessarily' in performing the duties of your employment. You will not then be taxed on payments for such expenses made by your employer whether made to you or third parties.

Any expenses that you personally incur in connection with your employment should be included on your return and these include:

- Overalls, clothing and tools.
- Travelling.
- Business use of your own car, van or cycle, but not capital allowances (10.6.6).
- Home telephone and other expenses.
- Professional fees and subscriptions relating to your work.
- Your own contributions to any approved superannuation (pension) scheme operated by your employers (10.12).
- In certain employments (for example entertainment industry) such expenses as hairdressing, make-up, clothes cleaning etc.
- Certain relocation expenses (10.6.18).

10.9 Share option and share incentive schemes (ITEPA Ss417–554 & Schs 2–5)

Over the years, there have been a variety of relieving provisions relating to tax on share option and share incentive schemes. The following pages describe some of these and reflect important changes brought about by the Finance Act 2000, including a new all-employee share plan (10.9.7) and an enterprise management incentives scheme (10.9.8). From 2003–04, ITEPA has regrouped the legislation and used certain new abbreviations such as SIPs (share incentive plans), CSOPs (company share option plans) and EMIs (enterprise management incentives). Note that where income tax remains payable, there may also be National Insurance contributions, although the employer's position is being improved.

10.9.1 Unapproved share option schemes

As a director or an employee of a company, you may be granted an option to take up shares in the company. When you exercise your option, the notional 'gain' will be included in your Schedule E assessment for the tax year in which you exercise the option. (This does not apply if you exercise your option under an approved scheme – see below.) You thus pay income tax on the 'gain' (as earned income) calculated thus:

	£	£
Market value of shares on day you exercise option (that is, when you take up the shares)		A
Less: Price paid by you for the shares	B	
Price paid by you for the option (if any)	C	D
Assessable 'gain'		E

If you subsequently sell the shares themselves at a profit, subject to the share incentive scheme rules (10.9.3), this will be liable to capital gains tax (20.1) calculated as follows:

	£	£
Net proceeds obtained on the sale of the shares		F
Less: Price paid by you for the shares	B	
Price paid by you for the option (if any)	C	
Gain already assessed under Schedule E	E	A
Capital gain		G

10.9.2 Approved company share option plans (CSOPs) (ITEPA Ss521–526 & Sch 4)

Special rules apply to options granted under an approved scheme, which can extend to groups. In particular, the gain will only be taxable when the shares are sold and capital gains tax (not income tax) will apply. On the grant of an option to an employee, the company's capital gain is the amount (if any) paid.

Important changes apply for options granted after 16 July 1995, otherwise they continue to be within the old rules. The conditions for HMRC approval include the following:

(1) Each participant may hold options over shares with a maximum value at the time of grant of £30,000. (Under the old rules, the limit applying to options granted before 17 July 1995 was £100,000 or four times the current or previous year's emoluments if greater.)
(2) The options may not now be granted at an exercise price which is 'manifestly' less than the market value of the shares at the date of the grant.
(3) You cannot exercise your option earlier than three years or later than ten years after its grant.
(4) You must be a full-time director or employee when the option is granted to you but may leave before its exercise. Part-timers may be included in schemes approved from May 1995.
(5) Before 9 April 2003, you could only exercise approved options once every three years (FA 2003 Sch 21).
(6) No participant can have a 'material interest' (broadly 10 per cent of the shares) in the company or group if close (13.17).
(7) The options must be non-transferable and the shares fully paid ordinary shares. These shares must form part of the capital of the company (G) granting the option, or its parent, or a consortium company owning at least 5 per cent of the ordinary shares of G.
(8) Shares subject to special restrictions may not be used, although employees may be required to sell their shares when their employment ends.
(9) Where a company has two classes of issued ordinary shares, most of the class of shares used in the scheme needed to be held by outsiders. However, a class of shares can now be used of which the majority is held by directors or employees and gives them control of the company.
(10) Redeemable shares cannot be used, except in the case of registered worker co-operatives.
(11) If a company with an approved share scheme is taken over by another company, it is possible for the options to be exchanged for options over shares in that other company. Certain conditions must be satisfied, including having the replacement options governed by the rules of the original scheme.
(12) Where loans are obtained by employees to exercise their options, conditions regarding security and repayment are not regarded as 'restrictions'. Thus the shares are not debarred on this account.
(13) From 24 March 2010, shares in a company that is controlled by a listed company are no longer 'eligible shares'. Schemes were allowed 6 months to come into line with HMRC approval.

10.9.3 **Approved savings related share option schemes** (ITEPA Ss516–520 & Sch 3)

Any notional or real gains from an approved savings related share option scheme will be free of income tax. However, some capital gains tax may be payable. Under such a scheme you are given an option to buy shares in the company which employs you or its controlling company. (You would not be eligible if you controlled more than 25 per cent of the shares and it is a close company – 13.17.)

You must save the money to buy the shares through a special SAYE contract set to produce the required cost of the shares on its maturity. (The proceeds from SAYE linked schemes set up under earlier legislation may also be used.) SAYE contracts may now be arranged by banks and building societies.

Early exercise of the option is normally only allowed in special circumstances, such as death, disability, retirement or redundancy. Early exercise is also allowed if the company or part of its business in which you work leaves the group operating the scheme. You may exercise an option at the due time, even though you then work for a company which is only associated with the company granting the option, providing it is under its control.

The maximum permitted monthly contribution is £250 and no minimum monthly contribution below £5 can be stipulated. Also, the future purchase price of the shares must not be manifestly less than 80 per cent of the market value of the shares when the option is granted. You must normally exercise the option within six months of reaching an age between 60 and 75 specified for the scheme.

10.9.4 **Share incentive schemes (pre-2001)** (ITEPA Ss723–724 & Schs 7–8)

These are schemes under which you are allowed to purchase shares in the company where you work because of your employment or directorship and not simply because of a general offer to the public. If you obtain shares under certain incentive schemes, you are broadly assessed to income tax on the increase in the market value of your shares between their acquisition date and the earliest of the following:

(1) seven years from when you bought the shares;
(2) the time when you cease to be a director or an employee of the company;
(3) the time when you sell the shares; and
(4) the time when your shares cease to be subject to any special restrictions.

The above rules apply to shares from incentive schemes acquired before 26 October 1987. Certain *profit sharing schemes* (10.9.6) were excluded provided various conditions were satisfied. For acquisitions of shares or interests in shares after 25 October 1987, the previous rules apply in essence with some changes. However, those not charged under previously Schedule E Case I in respect of the employment are excluded. Also excluded are acquisitions arising from public offers.

Income tax may be chargeable in certain circumstances, such as the removal or variation of restrictions over the shares; or the creation or variation of rights in the shares owned or other shares in the company.

However, this does not apply if the company is employee-controlled because of holdings of shares of the same class, nor if it is a subsidiary (but not a 'dependent subsidiary' – see below); nor if a majority of the shares of the same class are held other than by directors and employees, associated companies etc. The tax is levied on the value increase resulting from the removal of restrictions etc.

Special benefits, such as a capital distribution or the sale of rights in a rights issue, may be taxable. However, unless the company is a 'dependent subsidiary' wider exemption applies. Broadly, employee shareholders are not taxed on their special benefits where they are available to at least 90 per cent of shareholders and a majority of the shares are held by non-employees.

A 'dependent subsidiary' is one whose business is mainly carried on with group members. Furthermore, any increase in the value of the company during its accounts period must be limited to 5 per cent. The directors must give HMRC a certificate within two years of the end of the accounts period. You are liable on shares in a 'dependent subsidiary' in the same way as other shares (see above).

10.9.5 **Employee shareholdings** (ITEPA Ss417–446 & 542–548)

Special rules apply if you are a director or *higher paid* employee (10.6.2) and you acquire shares at an undervalue by reason of your employment. The shares need not be in the company which employs you.

You are treated as obtaining shares at an undervalue if you pay less than the market value of fully paid shares of the same class at that time. This applies whether or not you are under any obligation to pay more at a future time. Subject to certain relaxations (see below) you are taxed on the shortfall of what you pay for the shares compared with market value when you bought them. This shortfall is treated as an interest free loan (10.6.9) and you are treated as if your taxable earnings were increased by the benefit of such a loan. This continues until the shortfall is ended or the shares are sold, even if you cease your employment.

In general, relief is not completely withdrawn if the price is too low; it simply does not apply to the benefit represented by the difference in price. Also, if there are several offers to the public of shares of the same class, a 10 per cent overall limit applies but up to 40 per cent of the shares comprised in one offer may go to employees. Furthermore, different directors or employees can obtain a different mix of shares offered to the public at the same time, provided the aggregate benefit is similar. This exemption extends to a public offer comprising a package of shares in more than one company and also 'special benefits' such as bonus shares.

If you obtain shares through a priority allocation to the employees of your company, when it offers shares to the public, special rules apply. You will not be assessed on any benefit provided no more than 10 per cent of the offer goes to employees, all entitlements are on similar terms and the arrangement is not exclusively for directors or highly paid employees. In the case of a fixed price issue the employees must subscribe at that price, whilst for a tender issue the lowest price successfully tendered applies.

From 17 March 1998, certain shares subject to forfeiture are taxable on issue to employees (the rules are modified for acquisitions after July 1999 to prevent a double charge). Similarly, convertible shares issued to employees from that date are taxed on conversion. This differs from the previous practice.

10.9.6 **Profit sharing schemes (pre-2001)** (TA 1988 Ss186–187 & Sch 9)

Tax relief is available for employees participating in a company share scheme which has been approved by HMRC. Under such a scheme, trustees are allowed to acquire shares in the company to the value of up to £3,000 or 10 per cent of salary, subject to a ceiling of £8,000. For this purpose you take your salary for the current or previous year, whichever is the higher. If the trustees receive qualifying corporate bonds as the result of a takeover or reconstruction, they can keep these. Alternatively they can distribute them in due course to the participants.

A participant must agree to his shares remaining with the trustees for at least two years unless he dies, becomes redundant or reaches normal retirement age. However, for schemes approved after 25 July 1991 an age must be specified between 60 and 75 for all members.

The scheme must be open fairly to all employees within the company or group with five years' service or more. The employers may allow those with shorter service to join, however. Any dividends on the shares are paid over to the participants.

When the trustees sell any of a participant's shares after two years, a percentage will be charged to income tax. The percentage is calculated on the original value (less any capital receipts already charged to income tax as below), or the proceeds of the shares if less, as follows:

Period held – years	% taxable post 7.85	% taxable post 4.96
2–3	100	100
4–5	75	Nil
5 or more	Nil	Nil

The appropriate percentage (see above) of capital receipts less an allowance is charged to income tax. The allowance is £20 for each year until disposal plus £20 in addition, with a maximum of £60 (£100 before 1997–98). There is a special 50 per cent abatement of the charge for employees leaving due to injury, disability, redundancy or reaching pensionable age.

No new schemes will be approved after 5 April 2001, unless a full application was submitted by that date. Furthermore, approval of a scheme may be withdrawn where appropriations from both a scheme and an all-employee share plan are made in the same year. Appropriations to you of shares after 31 December 2002 no longer command income tax relief and by that date corporation tax relief on payments to the scheme was phased out. From 21 March 2000, anti-avoidance rules bite regarding the approval of certain schemes involving controlled service companies and loans to employees.

10.9.7 **All-employee approved share incentive plans (SIPs)** (ITEPA Ss488–515 & Sch 2)

Previously entitled 'employee share ownership plans' (ESOPs), the scheme operates from 28 July 2000, but free shares can be awarded for performance periods beginning earlier. The rules are lengthy, and the following are some of the main details:

(1) Your employer can put into a plan for you up to £3,000 of shares each year, free of income tax and National Insurance. (The shares could be awarded for reaching performance targets.)
(2) The plan must be open to all staff on a fair basis, according to the rules.
(3) Instead of providing free shares, a plan can be set up to supply partnership shares. You will then be able to buy partnership shares out of your pre-tax salary. The maximum amount is £1,500 each year and this is free of tax and National Insurance.
(4) Your employee can give you up to two free shares for each of your partnership shares.
(5) The company obtains corporation tax relief on the cost it bears in providing you with shares.
(6) Dividends held by a plan on your behalf may be reinvested up to a limit of £1,500 in any tax year.
(7) If you keep your shares within the plan for five years, you pay no income tax or National Insurance on them. Keeping them for at least three years means that you only pay tax and National Insurance on the initial value and not on any increase.
(8) Where you keep the shares in the plan until you sell, you pay no capital gains tax. Otherwise, this arises on any increase in value outside the plan.
(9) If you leave your job, your shares must come out of the plan. Where you leave within three years, your employers can decide whether you lose your free shares.
(10) You obtain capital gains tax rollover relief (20.25.2) where you sell company shares to a plan.
(11) Approved profit sharing schemes are being phased out (10.9.6), subject to transitional measures such as where a new plan provides partnership shares.

(12) From 6 April 2000, business assets taper relief extends to shares owned by employees in certain non-trading companies where they work.
(13) From 2003–04, with the introduction of ITEPA, the schemes have become known as approved share incentive plans (SIPs).
(14) From 24 September 2010, rules were modified to reduce the risk of changes being made for tax avoidance purposes to the rights of shares subject to the plan.

10.9.8 **Enterprise management incentives (EMIs)** (ITEPA Ss527–541 & Sch 5)

(1) These are share option incentive schemes operating from 28 July 2000.
(2) Subject to the rules, options on up to £100,000 worth of shares each can be granted to originally no more than 15 key employees. FA 2001 removed the limit on the number of employees and allows up to £3m of shares in total. If your own limit is reached, no more options can be granted to you under the scheme for three years.
(3) Normally no income tax or National Insurance is payable when you exercise an option under the scheme.
(4) When you sell the shares you obtain capital gains tax taper relief generally going back to the date of grant of the option.
(5) A simple notification process applies instead of a formal approvals system. This entails notice of the option being given to the Tax Office within now 92 days of its grant.
(6) To be eligible for the scheme, you need to work at least 25 hours weekly (or if less, 75 per cent of your working time) for the company (or its subsidiary). Also, together with your 'associates' including family, you must not have a 'material interest' in the company or any group company (broadly 30 per cent).
(7) The scheme is available only for small higher risk companies. Initially they had to be independent trading companies with gross assets of no more than £30 million, but groups of companies are now eligible. There are detailed rules for qualification, similar to those for VCT and EIS companies (8.13 & 11.26).
(8) From 16 December 2010, F3A 2010 made various technical changes to the rules for VCT and ESI companies, to ensure their approval as state aid under EU regulations. Similarly, from the same date, a company wishing to grant EMI options must have a 'permanent establishment' in the UK or, in the case of a parent company, have at least one company in its group that is carrying on a 'qualifying trade' and has a 'permanent establishment' in the UK. This replaces the current requirement to be carrying on a 'qualifying trade' 'wholly or mainly in the UK'.
(9) From 21 July 2008, in order to grant EMI options, a company or group must now have fewer than the equivalent of 250 full-time employees at the date of the grant of the options.
(10) From the same date, the list of excluded activities for a company granting EMI options is extended to preclude shipbuilding and coal or steel production.

10.9.9 **Shares in research institution spin-out companies** (ITEPA Ss451–460 & TCGA S119A)

New measures concern research institution employees who acquire employment-related shares in spin-out companies into which the employer transfers intellectual property. Starting from 2 December 2004, the value of the intellectual property is ignored on transfer to the spin-out company, PAYE and National Insurance only being charged on benefit later flowing to the employee. (Transitional relief is available on election before 16 October 2005).

10.9.10 **Setting-up costs of employee share schemes** (TA 1988 S84A & 85A)

The costs of setting up various types of employee share schemes are allowable for tax purposes. These include all-employee profit sharing schemes (10.9.6), all-employee share ownership plans (10.9.7), all-employee savings-related share option schemes (10.9.3) and discretionary share option schemes (10.9.2). If HMRC approval is obtained more than nine months after the end of the period of account when the expenditure was incurred, allowance is given for the period when approval is given.

10.10 Employee share ownership trusts (ESOTs) (ITEPA Ss549–554, TA 1988 S85A, FA 1989 Ss67–74 & Sch 5, TCGA 1992 Ss227–235 & FA 2000 S54)

Tax relief for ESOTs (employee benefit trusts) applies to contributions made to qualifying trusts from 27 July 1989. The main features are:

(1) ESOTs may borrow to acquire their shares rather than relying on funds provided by the employer company.
(2) ESOTs may provide a market in unquoted shares and may distribute larger amounts of shares than under Profit Sharing Schemes (10.9.6).
(3) All employees of the company and its subsidiaries, who work 20 or more hours weekly and have been employed for at least five years must be beneficiaries of the ESOT.
(4) Beneficiaries may also include ex-employees and ex-directors within 18 months of leaving; and employees and directors who work at least 20 hours weekly. (Part-timers may be included in trusts established from-May 1995.) However, those with a 'material interest' in the company (broadly 5 per cent) must be excluded.
(5) Funds from the company must be used within nine months after the end of the company's accounting period in which they were received. The funds must be used in buying ordinary shares in the company, servicing and repaying borrowings, paying benefits and paying expenses.
(6) The shares must be distributed within seven years of their acquisition to all accepting beneficiaries on similar terms. This period is 20 years for ESOTs set up after April 1994.

(7) Payments to an ESOT by the company or a subsidiary are allowed for corporation tax. However, the trust itself is taxable on its income and capital gains. Also, employees receiving shares at less than market value will be liable to income tax.
(8) Capital gains tax rollover relief (20.25) was available, subject to certain conditions, for disposals of your company shares to an ESOT before 6 April 2001. Replacement assets must be purchased within six months of the sale. (Broadly, your dwelling house and BES shares are not allowed as replacement assets qualifying for relief.) If the replacement assets are disposed of without other assets being acquired, the deferred gain will be brought into charge.
(9) An ESOT may transfer shares to a new employee share ownership plan, provided the ESOT owned the shares on 21 March 2000 or bought them with funds held on that date. There is no claw-back of earlier corporation tax relief.
(10) The costs of setting up an ESOT are an allowable deduction for tax purposes.
(11) Prior to 1 January 1992, a tax charge could arise from a share-for-share exchange. Subsequently, there is no tax charge provided the new holding stands in place of the old for capital gains tax purposes (20.18.6).
(12) Broadly from May 1996, it is possible to operate savings related share option schemes in conjunction with qualifying ESOTs.

10.11 Retirement pension schemes (ITEPA Ss386–400 & 565–654, TA 1988 Ss590–617 & 630–655; FA 1989 Ss75–77 & Schs 6 & 7 & FA 1993 S112)

Any National Insurance contributions that you pay as an employee are not deductible from your taxable income. Your employer, however, deducts his share of such contributions from his taxable profits. On your retirement your state pension is taxable as employment income, on the basis of the actual amount for the tax year, and any pension payable to your wife or widow is also taxable in this way. There is an Earnings Related component in the State Scheme, out of which you may be contracted (14.2.1). 'Contracting-out' using an occupational scheme relieves you and your employer of the obligation to pay higher rate National Insurance contributions (25.2) but its availability has been much curtailed from 6 April 2012.

Any pension paid to you out of your employer's own staff superannuation scheme is taxable as earned income. The same applies to any retirement pension paid by your employer that has not been provided for under any scheme. Reference should be made to Chapter 14 for a fuller treatment of pensions.

Retirement schemes are either 'contributory' or 'non-contributory'. In the latter case the employer bears the entire cost and in the former case the employee makes his own regular contributions to the scheme. If you work for a big company it may run its own registered pension scheme which will put aside funds to provide pensions for its employees. A separate pension trust is set up and investments are made on which generally no UK tax is payable either on income or capital gains. The employees' contributions (if any) are deductible from their taxable earnings, subject to certain limits, and amounts paid by the company are deductible from its taxable profits. Furthermore no 'benefit in kind' assessments are made on the employees. To qualify for this taxation treatment HMRC approval must be obtained (14.3.2).

Instead of managing their own registered pension scheme many employers arrange for it to be operated by an insurance company. In return for annual premiums paid to it based on the salaries of the employees covered, the insurance company provides retirement pensions and also sometimes lump sum payments in the event of the death in service of any employee. Subject to continuing registration with HMRC (see below) the company deducts the contributions that it pays from its taxable profits and the employees deduct their contributions (if any) from their taxable earnings. However, special rules have been introduced with effect from 22 April 2009, which are aimed at limiting tax relief for pension contributions if your income exceeds £150,000 per annum (14.13).

From 1 July 1988, *personal pension schemes* (14.5) have been available for those not in staff superannuation schemes (or for the purposes of 'contracting-out'). Contributions may be paid by the employer or employee. From October 1987, 'freestanding' AVC contracts operate (14.4).

If a new scheme is to maintain its registration with HMRC it must satisfy various conditions (14.3.2). Separate rules apply to personal pension schemes. For further details please refer to Chapter 14 (14.5 and 14.6).

Important changes to the rules for the approval of pension schemes and regarding tax relief on contributions operate from 6 April 2001 with the aim of creating an integrated tax regime for personal pensions and stakeholder pensions. Radical reforms of the pension system took effect from April 2006, including a shift from prior approval by HMRC to registration with them.

10.12 Compensation for loss of office (ITEPA Ss401–416)

If a 'golden handshake' payment is made to you on your retirement, resignation, redundancy or removal from that office etc. at least the first £30,000 will normally be tax-free. However, this exemption depends on the payments being not otherwise taxable.

From 1 November 1991, Inland Revenue practice changed regarding *ex gratia* payments made on retirement or death. These may now be taxed under the rules relating to pension schemes (Chapter 14). However, HMRC (PSS) approval will be available if the normal retirement benefits scheme requirements are satisfied and the lump sum *ex gratia* payment is the only lump sum relevant benefit potentially payable from your employment. The tax treatment of *ex gratia* termination payments other than on retirement or death is generally unchanged and the excess (if any) over £30,000 will be taxed as your earned income.

Benefits are now taxable only to the extent that they actually arise. Furthermore both payments and benefits now are taxable for the year in which they are enjoyed or received, rather than for the year of termination.

The employer is usually able to deduct 'golden handshake' payments from his taxable profits unless for example they are abnormally high payments to controlling directors or are made in connection with a sale of the actual business or made just before its cessation.

If you have a service contract that provides for a lump sum payment to be made to you when you leave your employer this payment will not be tax-free because it is treated as arising out of your employment. This point should be borne in mind when service contracts are drawn up.

However, severance schemes for Members of Parliament, members of the devolved parliamentary bodies or (from 6 April 2008) the Greater London Authority Assembly and the Mayor of London all carry exemption for the first £30,000.

From 6 May 2010, the rules covering MPs' tax, National Insurance contributions and expenses have been revised and consolidated, to reflect the technical and administrative changes that flowed from the implementation of the Parliamentary Standards Act 2009 (F2A 2010 Sch 3). From 1 April 2012, IPSA resettlement payments to MPs who are defeated at an election are specifically granted exemption for the first £30,000.

From 6 April 2013, a special relief will be created for travel costs of spouses or partners of members of devolved parliaments, where they share caring responsibilities for a dependant. FB 2013 will also deal with the travel and accommodation expenses of the members themselves.

Any payments received by a former employee in the following circumstances are normally tax-free:

(1) *Ex gratia* payments on the death or permanent disability of the employee.
(2) Terminal grants and redundancy payments to members of UK Armed Forces.
(3) *Ex gratia* payments on the termination of a job where the employee worked abroad either:
    (a) for three-quarters of his entire term of service; or
    (b) for the whole of the last ten years; or
    (c) where the total service is more than 20 years, for half the total service period including any ten of the last 20 years.

From 16 March 1993, *counselling services* provided by your employer on your redundancy are tax-free. (Previously, they would normally have counted towards the £30,000 exemption.) The services include advice on adjusting to job loss, writing CVs, interview skills, job searches and providing office equipment (ITEPA Ss310 & 311). The arrangements have now been extended to part-time employees and courses of two years' duration.

10.13 The assessment basis (ITEPA Ss3–37)

Up to 5 April 1989, many directors and certain others were assessed to income tax on their emoluments on what was known as the 'accounts basis'. This involved paying tax for a tax year based on your director's remuneration etc., for the accounts year ending therein. Thus, if your remuneration for the year to 31 December 1987 was £25,000, this was assessed for 1987–1988.

From 6 April 1989, the earnings of *all* directors and employees are assessed for the year in which they are received and not (as previously) for the year for which they were earned. However, certain pensions, including state retirement pension and widows' pension, continue to be assessable (previously under Schedule E) on the amount accrued in the year, whether or not paid. Transitional provisions dealt with situations where income was either taxed twice or not at all. In general, the earnings were taken out of assessment for the year when earned and taxed only in the year received, provided relief was claimed.

Where emoluments for an accounting period ending after 5 April 1989 are paid more than nine months after the end of that period, they must be added back in the employer's tax computations and only allowed as a deduction when paid. This applies where the remuneration relates to any period after 5 April 1989.

10.14 The PAYE system (ITEPA Ss682–712)

Real time information (RTI) – implementation 2013–14

HMRC's strategy to accelerate the use of electronic PAYE filing by even the smallest of employers, *Real Time Information (RTI)*, is now under way. Most employers will be legally required to report payroll information in real time from 6 April 2013 with all employers doing so before October 2013, in accordance with individually notified starting dates.

This dramatically changes the way employers and HMRC interact. Employers will be required to report payments electronically as they are made, generally weekly or monthly. From November 2012, all new PAYE schemes must use RTI from the outset. If you already use commercial payroll software, it will need updating and you may then join the RTI pilot scheme immediately (from November 2012). If you have nine or fewer staff, HMRC will be issuing a new version of their free Basic PAYE Tools, which will enable you to calculate tax and National Insurance and to transmit the RTI data. Employees should be able to inspect their tax account on HMRC's computer and employers should be relieved from having to issue year-end returns (P35) or movement forms (P45 or P46). Due dates for tax payment should not change for most employers, but electronic payment will generally be required, and quarterly or annual accounting in small cases will disappear. If timely reporting of changes in circumstances, including entitlement to benefits, could be achieved, in theory tax codes would be adjusted within the tax year and fewer employees would need to lodge personal tax returns.

The following paragraphs address the current system.

10.14.0 The current system

Most of the income tax payable on earnings from employments in this country is collected under the 'pay as you earn' system (PAYE), which covers starting, basic and higher rate income tax. Your employer is responsible for administering the PAYE on your own wages and that of your fellow employees. From each wages payment that you receive, whether it be weekly or monthly, your employer must deduct the relevant income tax and National Insurance contributions, paying to you the net amount. (If income tax has been previously over-deducted by your employer or if you suddenly become entitled to higher relief you may be due to receive a repayment which your employer will make to you.)

10.14.1 Payment

Your employer has to pay over to the HMRC Accounts Office the total PAYE income tax deductions (less refunds) and National Insurance contributions in respect of the previous month. The 2012–13 time limit is arrival by the nineteenth day of the following month or the twenty-second day if sent electronically. If payment is not made, it is now open to the Collector to send an estimated demand which must be paid within seven days unless:

(1) The correct PAYE is paid.
(2) The Collector is satisfied that nothing further is due.
(3) The Collector is invited to inspect the PAYE records.

Since 1992–93, interest has been due on any amounts outstanding after the following 19 April (that is, 19 April 1993 etc.). Interest is also calculated in retrospect for all late payments, once the annual return P35 has been lodged. FA 2009 introduced an incremental penalty regime with effect from 2009–10, addressing in-year payment delays. FA 2011 will empower HMRC to require security from employers, if they have grounds to consider payment of PAYE to be at risk. From the date of Royal Assent (summer 2011) Regulations can be expected to be laid, whereby failure to provide such security within a specified time limit will be a criminal offence, carrying a fine of up to £5,000.

After 5 April 1992, employers whose monthly payments of PAYE and National Insurance contributions are less than a fixed amount are allowed to pay quarterly. From 6 April 2000 the figure is £1,500 (previously £1,000).

Payments are then made to HMRC for the quarters ending 5 July, 5 October, 5 January and 5 April, and each is due within 14 days.

10.14.2 Records

Your employer is required to keep separate tax details for each of his employees (including directors but not partners). However, he is allowed to use his own records which may be computerised, in which case the structure of the PAYE calculations described below will not be visible to him. If the payroll is not fully computerised, your employer may use the official Deductions Working Sheet (form P11). This can be used for weekly or monthly paid employees. For a weekly paid person the following particulars are entered and calculated:

(1) National Insurance contributions.
(2) Statutory sick pay and statutory maternity pay.
(3) Student loan deductions.
(4) Gross pay for the week.
(5) Cumulative pay for the tax year to date.
(6) Total 'free pay' to date (see below).
(7) Total taxable pay to date (5) minus (6).
(8) Total tax due to date (see below).
(9) Tax to be paid or repaid for the week (see below).
(10) Tax credits.

(Similar details for each month are entered for monthly paid employees.) The total 'free pay' to date is obtained from 'Table A' in the tax tables provided by HMRC. This table shows for each week the 'free pay' applicable to each code number (see below). If your total pay is less than your 'free pay' to date then you pay no more tax for that week and would normally get a refund.

From 6 April 1993, 'Tables A' are known as 'Pay Adjustment Tables' and also give the amounts to add to your pay where you have a K code (10.14.3). From 6 April 2001, student loan deductions and tax credits (3.4) are included.

The tax to be paid or repaid for the week (see (9) above) is calculated by subtracting the total tax due to date for the previous week from that for the current week (see (8) above). The total tax due to date is found each week from the tax deduction tables. These show the tax attributable to the relevant total taxable pay to date.

The tax deduction tables in use are designated Tables B, C and D. (Table SR applied before 6 April 2008, showing the tax due at the starting rate of 10 per cent.) Table B shows tax due at the basic rate. Tables C show for each week or month (see below) the amounts to be taxed at the higher and additional rates, whilst Tables D show the tax due at these rates.

If you have only one employment your tax is calculated from Table B if your earnings are below the higher rates level. (Before 6 April 2008, starting rate applied.) Should your earnings make you liable for higher or additional rate income tax, however, your PAYE tax payable is calculated from Tables C and D, which are in fact supplementary to Table B.

Where your earnings are substantial and you have more than one employment, HMRC will normally direct that Tables B, C and D are used for your main employment. For your other employments, however, they might issue you with code D0 or D1, which procure respectively that tax at 40 or 50 per cent is applied to those employments. The 'D' codings merely provide HMRC with a very approximate method of taxing at source your salaries from employments other than your main one.

HMRC no longer issue hard copy monthly tax deduction tables for use where salary payments are made on a monthly basis but they are available for electronic download. The Deductions Working Sheet has a column in which to enter the amount deductible for earnings-related National Insurance contributions, which are collected through the PAYE system.

10.14.3 Your code number

Your code number is calculated from your income tax allowances and reliefs. It is allocated to you by the Tax Office and takes into account all the reliefs to which you are entitled against which some of your other income may be set off. Account may also be taken of any Schedule E income tax underpaid or overpaid for the previous year.

Coding notices are only sent to cover changes. Otherwise the code for the previous year must be used. The notice itemises the various allowances and reliefs to which you are entitled (3.0). Any other necessary adjustments are also shown on your coding notice which shows at the bottom the adjusted balance of your allowances and also the code number which corresponds to that figure. HMRC will probably obtain the details for your coding notice from your last income tax return.

In order to convert your total allowances and adjustments into your code number, you simply divide by ten and round down to the nearest whole number. Thus if your allowances etc. for 2012–13 total £8,015, your code number is 801. For administrative purposes, your code number in respect of your main employment will normally end in L, P, T or Y depending on your main personal reliefs (single, married couple's, age etc.). When these reliefs increase, instructions are issued by HMRC to employers to augment the relevant codes accordingly. In these cases revised coding notices are not needed. There are also codes with a prefix D or K or comprising only letters 'BR' or 'NT' (see below).

If you have additional employments and HMRC consider that your taxable earnings after deductions for the year 2012–13 will not exceed £34,370, you will be coded 'BR' in respect of each of your other employments. This means that Table B (10.14.2) is applied to your total earnings from each employment except your main one. No deductions are normally made for your allowances etc. because these are included in your coding for your main employment. If, however, your earnings are likely to exceed £34,370 then the Tax Office is likely to allocate you with 'D' codings (10.14.2) in respect of your supplementary employments.

For 2010–11, the annual recording process for many employees and pensioners with multiple sources of employment income was distorted by data errors in HMRC's new computer system. You should therefore be alert for inconsistencies and seek amendments, if you wish to avoid incorrect tax deductions during the year. This may also have affected late coding amendments for 2009–10, giving rise to year-end over- or under-payments. Vigilence remains advisable, as there have been further reports of heightened frequency of year-end adjustments for subsequent years, with many instances, where coding adjustments duplicate the collection of tax already paid on account under the self-assessment regime.

From 6 April 1993, a system of K codes operates. These cover car and other benefits etc., which increase your taxable pay. Another application is where your state retirement pension exceeds your personal allowances. It is hoped that this arrangement will facilitate the collection of tax on benefits. If you have a K code instead of a normal one, your employer simply adds the appropriate amount to your taxable pay rather than deducting it. This amount can be checked by adding 9 to the code – e.g. over 12 months, code K123 adds £1,239 to your taxable pay.

As from 6 April 2004, unless you object, HMRC are empowered to take account of your untaxed income from any source in determining your code number. This may result in a higher percentage of your earnings provisionally being paid in tax, but this is subject to an overriding limit of 50 per cent.

10.14.4 **Employers' PAYE returns**

Electronic filing

From 2007–08, employers who had 50 or more employees on 30 October 2006 were required to submit their PAYE annual returns online. Submission of these or of any supporting documents in magnetic form or on paper attracts a penalty.

New employers and those with less than 50 employees on 30 October 2006 are being encouraged to submit online by the offer of a tax-free payment of £75 in 2008–09 (previously £100). 2009–10 is the last year for which small employers will be able to continue to submit returns on paper and larger new employers should be prepared for earlier notification to join the online system.

On 12 April 2008 HMRC announced plans to introduce a new and improved online system in October 2008 for in-year and year-end operations. For data protection reasons, certain information will NOT be retained – primarily that lodged before 6 April 2005 and current unsubmitted work in progress at the changeover date. To avoid data loss, it was important that, before October 2008, existing users of the previous system downloaded and archived any such data, which they did not hold in their own archives. Implementation was deferred until summer 2009, when major changes took place.

From 2009–10 almost every employer is required to file the year-end P35 and P14s electronically. Small employers, who ceased to operate PAYE during 2009–10 and submitted these forms manually before 6 April 2010 were excused.

For 2010–11 onwards the only exceptions will be individuals who:

- cannot operate computers for genuine religious reasons;
- only employ people who provide them with personal care and support; or
- operate the simplified PAYE system for domestic staff and have not previously accepted the cash incentive to file online. (See references to RTI at 10.14). However, HMRC have announced the closure of the simplified system on 5 April 2013.

Manual filing

If you are eligible to file on paper, the documentary process is as follows.

At the end of each tax year your employer must complete a form P35 and send this to the Tax Office. End of year returns P14 must be completed for each employee and sent with the P35. The P14s are completed from the Deductions Working Sheets (P11) or other records and include National Insurance number, date of birth, final tax code, total pay, tax and National Insurance contributions, as well as any Statutory Sick Pay and Statutory Maternity Pay. Also any forms P11D required for the year (10.7) should be sent to the Tax Office.

The form P35 is a summary of the total tax due to be deducted for the tax year in respect of all of the employees. The earnings-related National Insurance contributions are also entered for each employee. The total Statutory Sick Pay and Statutory Maternity Pay details are also included. The details are obtained from the tax deduction cards. The total income tax due to be paid over for the year by the employer is then found by adding up all of the tax entries on the form P35 and from this is deducted the total of the actual payments made. A similar procedure is followed regarding the earnings-related National Insurance contributions except that the amount to be paid over also includes the employer's contributions.

The recent development of the duplex Question 6 of the P35 (which aims to identify certain service sector companies and to distinguish those that are 'IR35' and 'MSC' service companies (10.16 & 10.16.1) from the rest) coupled with a related question on page TR4 of the personal self-assessment tax return (16.2.1), has caused considerable concern because of a lack of consistency and clarity in the original official guidance. Representations by the tax professional bodies has resulted in greater consistency in the current guidance, together with clarification from HMRC as to their intended responders. Although the answers on the self-assessment return are said to be intended for statistical purposes, those on the P35 can affect tax and NIC liabilities. It is important to answer the P35 questions, if you are an employer, and to provide the TR4 data, where applicable. If you have any doubt as to whether these questions apply to you or what answers are appropriate to your circumstances, you should take professional advice.

The balances shown by the form P35 represent underpayments or overpayments of PAYE income tax and earnings-related contributions: if the employer has underpaid he should send a cheque with the form and if he has overpaid a repayment will subsequently be received.

There are time limits for submitting the forms which must be carefully watched. Penalties (16.9.3) may arise on forms P14 and P35 not submitted by 19 May following the tax year. Thus the 2011–12 forms should have been submitted by 19 May 2012. (From 2009–10 HMRC no longer waive penalties for paper forms received by the last business day within seven extra days.) For 2009–10, non-filing penalties for employers with 5 or less employees were set at zero per cent.

At the end of each tax year the employer should issue to each of his employees a form P60 which is a certificate of gross earnings for the year and of income tax deducted under PAYE and now forms part of the P14 pack (P14/P60). This must be done by 31 May.

10.14.5 **Change of employer**

Traditionally, if you leave your employment your old employer should complete a form P45 for you showing your name, district reference, code number, week or month number of the last entries on your tax deduction card, total gross pay to date and total tax due to date. Your old employer sends part 1 of the form P45 to his Tax Office and hands to you parts 2 and 3 which you must give to your new employer and part 4 for you to keep. Your new employer enters your address and date of starting on part 3 and sends it to his Tax Office. Much of this will normally be done electronically.

Your new employer should prepare a tax deduction card for you in accordance with your form P45 and deduct PAYE tax from your wages in the normal way.

If you are not able to give a form P45 to your new employer, he will normally deduct tax under the 'emergency' system which assumes you are single and gives you no other allowances. If this happens you should make an income tax return to the Inspector of Taxes or supply the necessary details to him, so that he can issue you with your correct code number which your employer will then use, making any necessary tax repayment to you.

Form P46 is available for you to complete if you do not have a P45 when you start a new job. It covers whether you are a school leaver or whether it is your main job or an additional one which you are starting. The P46 enables you to indicate your circumstances so that your employer will know whether to deduct basic rate tax from your salary or use an emergency code. (There is also a coding claim form P15 for use in establishing your coding.) From 6 April 2009, two specialised forms P46 apply to all new pensioners – P46 (Pen) and to certain seconded employees from abroad – P46 (Expat).

Also from 6 April 2009, employers with 50 or more employees have been required to submit all forms P45 and P46 online. Small employers were required to do so from 6 April 2011, but encouraged to start sooner. However, hard copy P45s are required to be issued to the departing employee.

10.14.6 **Extension of scope of PAYE** (ITEPA Ss696–702)

Rules were introduced operative from May 1994 to prevent employers avoiding PAYE by paying staff in assets. Payments through third parties such as offshore trusts are also targeted. Similar rules operate in relation to National Insurance contributions from 1 December 1993.

If you are paid income by an intermediary, this is treated as paid by your employer for PAYE purposes. Also, if you are given part of your income as 'tradable assets', this is now caught by the PAYE net. Examples of 'tradable assets' are gold and commodities. The rules extend to vouchers and credit tokens used to provide these assets. From 3 July 1997, the assignment by employers of trade debts to employees is also caught.

From 9 December 2010 and 6 April 2011, additional anti-avoidance legislation has been introduced in respect of payments through third parties (*Disguised remuneration*) (10.17).

10.15 Profit related pay

From 1 January 2000 any performance or profit related pay is taxable like any other bonus and PAYE applies on payment.

10.16 Service companies etc. providing personal services (ITEPA Ss48–61)

Rules (widely referred to as the IR35 legislation) operate from 6 April 2000 to counter the avoidance of tax and National Insurance contributions by supplying personal services through service companies, partnerships and other intermediaries. Broadly, the intermediary is responsible for deducting any extra tax and National Insurance as well as that on salary already paid to you as follows:

(1) The rules apply where your services are contracted to a client by an intermediary, without whom you would have been treated as being an employee of the client.
(2) Existing case law is used to define 'employee'.

(3) Engagements are excluded where your client is an individual who is not in business or your only income from the intermediary is fully taxed under Schedule E and you are entitled to no further income or capital (with minor exceptions).
(4) Intermediaries are responsible for operating the legislation. If you work through a service company, it will deduct PAYE and National Insurance from your salary in the normal way. At the end of each tax year, you will be charged income tax and National Insurance on any balance of the income for your services received by the intermediary and not paid to you as salary and benefits in kind. You are allowed to deduct certain expenses (5 below).
(5) As well as all expenses otherwise deductible under the normal rules, the intermediary can deduct certain approved scheme employer pension contributions; also an extra 5 per cent on the relevant gross income and employer's National Insurance including that on the deemed payment to you. Also treated as expenses from 2002–03 are reimbursements and mileage allowances.
(6) Where the intermediary is a partnership, it might be caught by the rules if you have a close connection, like being entitled to at least 60 per cent of its profits or where partners share profits according to their relevant engagements. Where the rules apply, income received gross from all of your relevant engagements (net of expenses) are deemed paid to you at the end of the tax year and charged to tax and National Insurance contributions. Your taxable partnership share (if any) will then exclude the deemed amount already taxed.
(7) From 10 April 2003, certain domestic workers such as nannies and butlers were brought within the rules for income tax. This applies normally where personal service companies are being used.

10.16.1 **IR35 Regime**

The 'IR35' regime continues to attract much criticism and, despite its inclusion in the coalition Government's 'wholesale review' of the tax and administrative burdens applicable to small businesses, the new *Office of Tax Simplification* (OTS) excluded this from its first list of superfluous legislation issued in March 2011. However, steps towards improving its application and administration are expected. These include publication of situations regarded as outside its scope, pre-transaction clearance facilities, establishment of an *IR35 Forum* and limiting taxpayer reviews to high risk cases, which will be handled by specialist HMRC teams. On 9 May 2012, HMRC published fresh clarified guidance, which was felt by professional commentators not to have gone far enough. It was reported in June 2012 as this edition went to press that HMRC had written to a number of service company contractors (thought to be viewed by them as high risk), drawing attention to their recent publications and inviting them to consider their status and to furnish explanations as to why they consider themselves outside the scope of IR35.

On 23 May 2012 a consultative document was published concerning the engagement through personal service companies of individuals who fulfill controlling roles in public or commercial sectors without creating employment income. Further movement can be expected in the Autumn and, subject to consultation, the Government proposes to require individuals who control entities with more than 10 staff and turnover in excess of £1.7m to be subject to PAYE by the engaging entity. This would not tamper with the commercial aspects of their contractual arrangements, but would place the application of PAYE in the hands of the engager rather than the personal service company, taking precedence over IR35.

In addition, one of OTS's priority areas for action, in order to clarify true tax rates and ease administration, is the integration of income tax and national insurance, on which the consultation announced in 2011 is now scheduled to commence in autumn 2012. Such an integration could remove the scope for one of the major perceived tax abuses that IR35 is supposed to combat.

10.16.2 **Managed Service Companies (MSCs)** (ITEPA Ss64A–64J & 688A & Sch 1)

From 6 April 2007, different rules apply if you supply personal services through a Managed Service Company (MSC), and these may affect you, the providers of the MSC and persons who actively encourage, facilitate or are otherwise actively involved in the provision of your services. If this code applies:

(1) All payments you receive will be deemed to be employment income and the MSC will be expected to account for income tax from 6 April 2007 and NIC from 6 August 2007 under PAYE.
(2) You will NOT be allowed to claim tax relief for the costs of travelling to the MSC's client.
(3) HMRC will be able to collect unpaid PAYE incurred after 6 August 2007 from you or the MSC provider, after 6 January 2008 from any other persons actively involved (see above), except for accountants, lawyers or employment agencies etc., who do not influence and control the company or the way you are paid.

Despite HMRC guidance issued in July 2007 and 'clarification' issued in December 2008, their interpretation of this legislation is far from clear. At the outset, these rules were not expected to apply to 'umbrella' companies offering services of a portfolio of individuals but were seen to be aimed at mass-marketed companies. HMRC appear to be hoping to review the nature of providers' standard business patterns rather than analyse contractual terms amongst you, the MSC and client on a case-by-case basis.

It remains important to take professional advice on any contractual arrangements proposed and consider using bespoke rather than standard documentation.

10.17 Disguised or third party remuneration (ITEPA Part 7A & FA 2011)

Although the title *Disguised Remuneration* was originally used in promulgating this topic, the sixty pages of legislation that came into effect on 6 April 2011 carry the rubric *Remuneration through Third Parties.* Forestalling provisions in respect of steps taken on or after 9 December 2010, when the draft legislation was published, and 5 April 2011 will have given rise to tax liabilities on 6 April 2012, unless those steps were undone, where permissible – generally within 90 days (but see (3) below regarding loans).

(1) This complex anti-avoidance legislation aims to tax benefits provided through third parties in connection with past, present or future UK employment. Those third parties include employment benefit trusts (EBTs), employer-financed retirement benefit schemes (EFRBS), employment intermediaries and fund managers, but could embrace any third party (including another group company) which holds or handles funds or other assets. Registered or approved pension, share option or share incentive schemes are excluded and there are exemptions for commercial transactions where tax avoidance is not a motive.

(2) The legislation creates employment income, which is subject to income tax and national insurance by reference to the date at which funds or other assets are earmarked or applied for the benefit of past, present or future employees or their families or nominees and does so regardless of the resident status of the parties concerned at the time of assessment.

(3) Loans in place at 9 December 2010 will continue to be taxed on the established benefit in kind basis, but those made between 9 December 2010 and 5 April 2011 will be treated as employment income arising on 6 April 2012, if not repaid before that date. Loans made from 6 April 2011 will be treated as employment income when made.

(4) These provisions may also provide tax relief to the employer in respect of the cost of providing the benefits concerned as a trading expense.

(5) Other technicalities are beyond the scope of this book, but certain of the structures in which HMRC are interested are mentioned in *Anti-Avoidance Spotlights 5 & 6* (15.10.23).

Chapter 11

INCOME FROM BUSINESSES AND PROFESSIONS

11.1 Trades, professions and vocations

The profits from trades, professions and vocations were normally assessed for 2004–05 and previous years under Schedule D Case I (trades) and Schedule D Case II (professions and vocations). However, from 2005–06 onwards, with the introduction of ITTOIA (2.10), the income is no longer classified for income tax purposes into schedules, although the basic rules remain. (ITTOIA does not apply for corporation tax purposes.) There are certain special rules which apply to partnerships (Chapter 12) and companies (Chapter 13).

Trade includes manufacturing, retailing, wholesaling and all kinds of trading ventures.

A profession is defined as an occupation requiring special intellectual skills, sometimes coupled with manual skills (for example doctor of medicine, architect, accountant, barrister).

A vocation has been defined as the way that a person passes his life (for example composer, author, actor, singer).

11.2 What is trading?

Your regular business will normally be treated as a trade. There are, however, certain other activities which might constitute trading depending on the circumstances. The following are some general guidelines:

(1) Regular buying and selling normally constitutes trading although this does not usually apply to purchases and sales of shares by an individual.
(2) An isolated transaction might be held to be trading if it is by its very nature commercial. For example, a single purchase and sale of a quantity of unmatured whisky is normally treated as a trading transaction. This is because the ownership of unmatured whisky is mainly for commercial purposes.
(3) Isolated transactions involving the purchase and sale of works of art are not normally trading. Here the works of art are owned to be admired and not exclusively (if at all) for commercial purposes. Capital gains tax, however, might be payable on sales of works of art for over £6,000 each (20.24).
(4) Isolated transactions in income producing assets are not usually treated as trading. Capital gains tax would normally apply (20.1).
(5) If you do something to your purchase before selling it the sale might be considered to be trading. For instance, if you buy a ship, convert it and then sell it you will be treated as trading.
(6) Repetition of the same transaction is evidence of trading.
(7) If you deal in property this is likely to be treated as trading (7.10).

(8) The possession of expert business knowledge in connection with a transaction that you carry out will increase your chances of being treated as trading.

11.3 What business expenses are allowed?

In computing the amount of your profits to be charged to tax, you are allowed to deduct any sums wholly and exclusively incurred for the purposes of the trade, profession or vocation, subject to various special rules (see below). Only expenses of a revenue nature are deductible, however, and these must be distinguished from capital expenditure (2.6).

11.3.1 Allowable business expenses

To the extent that they are incurred wholly and exclusively for business purposes the following are deductible (the list is not exhaustive):

(1) The cost of goods bought for resale and materials used in manufacturing.
(2) Wages and salaries paid to employees, together with National Insurance payments. This includes employees seconded on a temporary basis to charities (ITTOIA S70) and to certain educational bodies including local authorities (ITTOIA S71).
(3) Pensions paid to past employees and their dependants.
(4) Redundancy payments to employees including certain voluntary payments on business cessation, up to three times the statutory amount (ITTOIA Ss76–79).
(5) The running costs of any premises used for the business including rent and rates, light and heat, repairs (not capital improvements), insurance, cleaning etc.
(6) Discounts allowed on sales.
(7) Carriage, packing and delivery costs.
(8) Printing, postage, stationery and telephone.
(9) Repairs to your plant and machinery.
(10) Staff welfare expenses.
(11) Insurance regarding loss of profits, public liability, goods in transit, burglary etc.
(12) Advertising.
(13) Trade subscriptions.
(14) Professional charges of a revenue nature – for example audit fees.
(15) Legal charges of a revenue nature, for example debt collection, preparing trading contracts and settling trading disputes.
(16) If you pay a premium for the lease of your business premises and the recipient is taxed under previously Schedule A you can claim the cost of the premium as a deduction from your business profits spread over the term of the lease.
(17) VAT on your purchases and expenses if you are not registered for VAT. (If you are registered you set this VAT against that on your sales and only charge your purchases etc. excluding VAT.)
(18) Travelling expenses including hotel bills and fares on business trips but excluding the cost of travelling between your home and business (unless you also do business from home).
(19) The entertaining of your own staff but not entertaining UK or overseas customers.
(20) Gifts which incorporate an advertisement for your business provided that the value for each recipient each year does not exceed £50 (ITTOIA S47).

(21) Bad debts which arose in the course of trading. Also provisions made for specific debtors whom you anticipate may not pay. Also, any debt which you release after 29 November 1993 as part of a formal voluntary arrangement. Special rules limit the relief available for doubtful sovereign debt due from overseas governments etc. normally to banks. Broadly, the allowable amount for 1990–91 is limited to the 1989–90 level and scaled up by 5 per cent annually thereafter.

(22) A trader's expenses of obtaining patents are normally allowable. The outright purchase of a patent is a capital expense, however, which normally qualifies for capital allowances.

(23) Running expenses of motor vehicles excluding such proportion as is attributable to private use.

(24) Interest payments including hire purchase interest. Relief for bank and other interest is normally given on the basis of payments rather than accruals.

(25) The incidental costs of obtaining loan finance which carries deductible interest (ITTOIA S58). Costs concerning repayment, providing security and abortive exercises are covered; but not stamp duty, foreign exchange losses, issue discounts or repayment premiums. This relief extends to certain convertible loan stocks.

(26) Pre-trading expenditure, of a revenue nature, incurred within seven years before starting to trade (ITTOIA S57). For companies it is treated as falling on the first day of trading; for individuals it was regarded as a separate loss (11.22). However, for businesses set up after 5 April 1995, individuals are treated like companies in this respect.

(27) Work training provided by an employer for employees about to leave their current jobs, or who have just left. Training courses must provide improved skills or knowledge for use in new jobs or business and the employee is not taxed on the benefit. Courses must not exceed one year and must take place within the UK (TA 1988 S588).

(28) Security expenditure (ITTOIA S81). This is allowed for the self-employed (including partners) regarding assets or services to meet personal security threats arising from their businesses.

(29) Certain revenue expenditure incurred concerning waste disposal sites (ITTOIA Ss165–168). Expenditure on preparing a site is allowed according to the proportion of its capacity filled with waste in the accounts year. Expenditure on making good a site is given in the year of payment or on commencement of trade if later. However, no allowance is given for expenditure on which capital allowances (11.8) are given.

(30) Certain payments for football ground improvements made by pool promoters (FA 1990 S126).

(31) Gifts of equipment, manufactured, sold or used in the trade, to schools and other educational establishments. The relief has now been extended so as to cover all charitable causes (ITTOIA Ss107–110).

(32) The setting-up costs of certain employee share schemes (10.9.6).

(33) Class 1A and Class 1B National Insurance contributions on car benefits for employees (ITTOIA S53).

(34) Contributions to the Individual Learning Accounts of employees, subject to the rules, after 5 April 2000 (10.6.23).

(35) Contributions to the running costs of Urban Regeneration Companies from 1 April 2003 (ITTOIA S82).

11.3.2 Expenses not deductible from business profits (ITTOIA S34)

(1) Any payments or expenses not wholly and exclusively laid out for the purposes of the business.
(2) Expenses incurred for the private or domestic purposes of yourself or family.
(3) Where expenses contain some business and some private element the proportion attributable to the latter is not deductible. In the case of a private dwelling house used for business purposes the deductible proportion is not normally allowed to exceed two-thirds of the rent and other costs.
(4) Any capital used for improvements to your business premises.
(5) Any loss not connected with the business.
(6) Any reserves and provisions made for anticipated expenses such as repairs, retirement benefits etc. including general bad debts reserves but not reserves for specific bad debts (nor contributions under approved pension plans).
(7) Any annuity or other annual payment (other than interest) payable out of the profits (4.2).
(8) Payments of income tax, capital gains tax and corporation tax etc.
(9) Your own drawings as the owner or part owner of the business.
(10) Depreciation and amortisation of plant and machinery, motor vehicles, buildings etc. Capital allowances are normally available however (11.9).
(11) Any royalty payment from which you deduct income tax.
(12) Entertaining expenses unless in connection with your own staff.
(13) Professional charges of a capital nature. For example legal fees in connection with a new lease, architects' fees for designing a new building, accountants' fees connected with the purchase of a new business. These expenses can often be added to the cost of the assets for capital gains tax purposes (20.10).
(14) Fines for illegal acts and connected legal expenses.
(15) Charitable donations, unless wholly for business purposes (TA 1988 S577). (Note special rules for non-close companies (15.2.1) and gift-aid.)
(16) Political donations.
(17) The cost of acquiring capital assets such as plant and machinery, motor vehicles, buildings etc. Capital allowances are frequently available however (11.9).
(18) Expenditure involved in payments which are criminal offences and payments resulting from extortion by terrorist groups or other criminals and payments overseas, such as bribes, which would be criminal if made in the UK (ITTOIA S55).

11.4 The computation of your assessable profits (ITTOIA Ss34–94)

If you conduct a business or profession you will normally have annual accounts prepared on a commercial basis including a profit and loss account or an income and expenditure account. Your annual accounts should normally be drawn up to the same date in each year but need not coincide with the tax year (which ends on 5 April).

Simpler accounts were permitted for 'small businesses' with a turnover originally less than £15,000 for accounts submitted after 6 April 1992. A simple three line account was needed showing total turnover, purchases and expenses and net profit. Tax returns from April 1991 allowed the three line account to be incorporated therein. However, accurate business records must still be kept. 2011–12 tax returns now permit you to enter only turnover and total expenses if turnover is below £73,000 (previously £70,000).

The profit shown by your annual accounts will form the basis of your assessment, but it will normally require adjustment in some or all of the following ways:

(1) Add to your profit any non-deductible expenses that have been charged in your accounts (11.3.2).
(2) Deduct from your profit any items included in your accounts which are not taxed as trading income either because they are non-taxable or because they are otherwise liable to tax. Examples are:
    - Capital profits liable to capital gains tax (20.1).
    - Interest receivable (8.4).
    - Rents receivable (7.1).
    - Interest received net, income tax having been deducted at source (8.2); also dividends (8.1).
    - Amounts originally set aside as reserves and now recredited in your accounts provided the original amounts were not allowed against your taxable profits.
(3) Deduct from your profit any allowable expenses not already charged in your accounts.
(4) Exclude from your profits government grants towards the cost of specified capital expenditure or compensation for loss of capital assets. Other grants under the Industries Act 1972 etc. are now generally taxable. However, regional development grants under the Industrial Development Act 1982 and certain grants to assist industry in Northern Ireland are normally exempt.
(5) If you have recently left the unemployment register to set up a business you may be receiving Enterprise Allowances. These are paid for one year at a weekly amount and are taxable as miscellaneous income (15.1). They should therefore be eliminated from your assessable trading profits. (However, Enterprise Allowances are liable to Class 4 National Insurance.)
(6) Add to your profit any trading profits not already included.
(7) From your profits adjusted as above, deduct your capital allowances for the year (11.8).
(8) Under the current year basis (11.7.1 and 11.8.2) capital allowances are based on the accounting period and treated as deductible expenses.

11.4.1 Example: Trading income computation

Mr A carries on a manufacturing business. His accounts for the year to 31 December 2012, which show a net profit of £39,000, include the following:

	£		£
Expenses		**Income**	
Depreciation of motor vehicles	4,300	Bank deposit interest	70
Depreciation of plant and machinery	6,700	Profit on sale of motor car	1,050
Bad debts provision (5% × sales debtors)	1,650	Bad debts provision no longer required (general)	200
Legal expenses re debt collection	200		
Legal expenses re new lease (not a renewal)	270		
Charitable donations (non-business nor under gift-aid)	90		
Entertaining expenses	2,250		

Assuming capital allowances of £10,500 for the year ended 31 December 2012, compute Mr A's adjusted trade profit.

Mr A – Trading income computation based on accounts for year ended 31 December 2012

	£	£
Net profit per accounts		39,000
Add: Disallowable expenses:		
Depreciation (£4,300 + £6,700)	11,000	
General bad debts provision	1,650	
Legal expenses re new lease	270	
Charitable donations	90	
Entertaining expenses	2,250	15,260
		54,260
Less:		
Bank deposit interest	70	
Profit on sale of motor car (capital)	1,050	
Bad debts provision no longer required	200	
Capital allowances	10,500	11,820
Adjusted profit		42,440

11.5 Basis change – adjustment (ITTOIA Ss226–240)

Special rules apply where a business has a change of accounting basis or in the way in which tax adjustments are made to accounting profits, whether through change in the law or practice. These rules apply to changes of basis in accounting periods ending after 31 July 2001.

The rules are to ensure that on a change of basis, profits are only taxed once and trading expenses only relieved once. Also, spreading relief is given regarding tax payable on prior year adjustments.

11.6 Stock valuation

An important factor in the preparation of business accounts is the valuation of stock and work in progress. This is the amount of unsold raw materials, finished goods and work in progress that was owned at the end of the accounts period. The stock etc. must be valued at each accounting date and the profits are augmented by the excess of the closing stock over the opening stock or decreased by the deficit. It is clear that if the closing stock is valued on a more generous basis than the opening stock then the profits shown will be higher than the true profits and vice versa.

HMRC pay careful attention to the manner in which businesses value their stock and they normally insist that for tax purposes the opening and closing stocks are valued on the same basis. The usual basis adopted is that each item in stock is valued at the lower of its cost or net realisable value. The exact cost to be included may or may not contain an addition for expenses depending on the exact basis adopted. The general rule in ascertaining cost is that identical items should be identified on the basis that the earliest purchases were sold or used first (FIFO). In all cases the method chosen must be used consistently. 'Net realisable value' is what it is estimated will be obtained from disposing of the stock in the ordinary course of business at the balance sheet date, after allowing for all expenses in connection with the disposal.

Rules operate to prevent the manipulation of stock values for discontinued businesses. These are to stop tax advantages being obtained from selling the stock to a connected party at an untrue valuation (TA S100 (1A–1G)).

From 12 March 2008, statutory effect is given to a long established rule that where goods are appropriated to or from a trading stock other than by way of trade, their market value is to be used in calculating the taxable profits.

11.7 Basis of assessment (ITTOIA Ss196–220)

The present system has operated since 1996–97. The assessment for that year was based on the average profits for the two years ending in 1996–97. After that, the assessment for any year is based on the accounts for the year ending within the year of assessment. Thus, if your accounting date is 31 December, your 2012–13 assessment will be on your profits for the year to 31 December 2012.

11.7.1 **The current year basis** (ITTOIA Ss196–220)

(1) If your business commenced *after 5 April 1994*, the new basis applied at once. Otherwise, it applied for 1997–98 and future years with special rules for 1996–97.
(2) The basic rule is that you are assessed on the adjusted profits for your accounts year which ends in the year of assessment. Thus if you make up your annual accounts to 30 September, your 2012–13 assessment is based on your profits for the year to 30 September 2012.
(3) Under the present rules, the first year of assessment for a business is based on the profits to the next 5 April (apportioned in days). Say you *commenced trading* on 1 July 2011, your 2011–12 assessment is based on your profits from that date to 5 April 2012.
(4) The assessment for your second tax year of trading is normally based on the profits for the year ended on your accounting date falling within that tax year. Thus, if 30 June is your accounting date, your 2012–13 assessment is usually based on your profits for the year to 30 June 2012. However, say your commencement date was 1 September 2011, the 2012–13 assessment will be based on the profits for the first complete year, to 31 August 2012.
(5) When your business ceases, the assessment for the final period will be on an actual basis from the end of your previous base period. Thus suppose you stop trading on 30 April 2012 and your accounting date is 30 June, your 2012–13 assessment will be on the profits from 1 July 2011 to 30 April 2012.
(6) Where a business changes its accounting date the aim will be to tax 12 months' profits for all years except the first and last. This may mean that some profits are taxed twice. However, the intention is that over the lifetime of a business, its profits are fully taxed, but only once. Hence 'overlap relief' will be given where the business ends or a basis period exceeds 12 months, in respect of profits taxed more than once.
(7) 'Overlap relief' often results where a business starts after 5 April 1994. For instance, if you started to trade on 1 July 1994 with a 30 June accounting date, the period 1 July 1994 to 5 April 1995 would be taxed twice. Supposing your proportionate profits for that period are £20,000, you will get relief of this amount when your business eventually ceases.
(8) Special rules cover such areas as losses (11.22.1), capital allowances (11.8) and partnerships (12.2).

11.8 Capital allowances (CAA etc.)

You are not normally allowed to deduct from your taxable profits the cost or depreciation of capital assets. You can, however, deduct capital allowances in respect of the cost of certain assets used in your business or profession including the following:

(1) Plant and machinery (11.9) – this category also includes furniture, fittings, office equipment and motor vehicles, together with the thermal

insulation of industrial buildings and of making certain buildings comply with the fire regulations. Other categories of included expenditure relate to safety at sports grounds and stadia (11.9.10) security (11.9.11) and computer software and IT equipment (11.9.16).

(2) Industrial buildings (11.11) – this includes factories and some warehouses etc. (phased out by 2010–11).
(3) Agricultural and forestry buildings etc. (11.13) (mainly phased out by 2010–11).
(4) Hotel buildings etc. (11.15).
(5) Scientific research expenditure (11.17).
(6) Patents and 'know-how' (11.18).
(7) Mines, oil wells etc. (11.20) and dredging (11.19).

If you have expenditure which qualifies for allowances under more than one of the above heads, you will be able to make an irrevocable choice. This applies for accounting periods ending after 27 July 1989 (FA 1989 Sch 13).

From 6 April 2008 (1 April for companies) sweeping changes took effect as detailed with further changes operating for subsequent years.

11.8.1 **Base period** (CAA S6)

For a business, profession or vocation (including partnerships) the capital allowances are computed according to the assets purchased and those used in the annual accounts period (that is, the base period). For these purposes, you must take the date when the expenditure was incurred. This is now generally when the obligation to pay becomes unconditional, unless, for example, part of the capital expenditure is payable more than four months later. Under the old system, a deduction was made from the Schedule D Case I or Case II assessment in respect of the total capital allowances for that tax year. (See 11.8.2 below for the rules introduced with the current year basis.)

Under the old system, special rules applied where there were base periods of less than one year. Where one base period applied to two tax years, the additions during the base period were allocated to the earlier tax year for the purposes of calculating the allowances. If there was a gap between base periods, it was added to the second base period unless this marked a cessation of trading – in this case you added the gap to the first period.

11.8.2 **Current year assessment rules** (FA 1994 Ss211–212 & Sch 20)

The capital allowances rules were changed in line with the current year basis. These took full effect for 1997–98 and future years, regarding businesses existing at 5 April 1994. Capital allowances are treated as trading expenses. Similarly, balancing charges are regarded as trading receipts. Capital allowances have to be claimed in the tax return.

Capital allowances are now related to the period for which accounts are drawn up, rather than the year of assessment. However, any unrelieved amounts from 1996–97 and earlier years are included with the allowances for the first accounts ending after 5 April 1997.

11.8.3 **VAT Capital Goods Scheme adjustments** (CAA Ss234–246 etc.)

Extra VAT paid under the VAT Capital Goods Scheme qualifies for capital allowances in the year of payment. Similarly, VAT repaid from that date reduces the appropriate expenditure pool for capital allowances purposes in the year of receipt. This particularly affects businesses which are partly exempt (23.3) from VAT such as those in banking, finance, insurance and property.

The items covered are limited to computers and computer equipment worth at least £50,000 and land and buildings worth at least £250,000. From 1 January 2011, the list also includes aircraft, ships and boats. The VAT adjustments generally arise on changes of use.

11.9 Capital allowances on plant and machinery

In general, expenditure qualifies for 18 per cent writing down allowance each year from 2012–13 (previously 20 per cent). However, special rules apply to long-life assets (11.9.8), motor vehicles (11.9.12), plant which you lease out (11.9.15) and computer equipment etc. (11.9.16). Expenditure before 6 April 2008 on plant and machinery may also attract first year allowance (11.9.1).

Balancing charges and allowances can arise when plant is sold (11.9.4). The main allowances available on plant purchased new or second-hand between 26 October 1970 and 1 April 1986 were normally a first year allowance for the year of purchase and a writing down allowance for each subsequent year.

11.9.1 **First year allowances** (CAA Ss39–51)

Expenditure on plant and machinery after 1 July 1997 and before 6 April 2010 obtained first year allowance subject to certain conditions. The rates were 50 per cent to 1 July 1998 and then 40 per cent on expenditure thereafter. A special 100 per cent rate applied for spending on machinery or plant for use in Northern Ireland in the four years starting 12 May 1998. The relief was limited to small and medium-sized businesses, including companies and groups, broadly satisfying two of the following three conditions:

(1) turnover not more than £11.2m
(2) assets not more than £5.6m
(3) not more than 250 employees.

For 'small businesses' (11.9.15) the rate increased to 50 per cent for the year to 31 March 2005 for companies and to 5 April 2005 for other businesses. After that, it reverted to 40 per cent for one year and then back to 50 per cent for two years. From 6 April 2010 (1 April for companies) it is abolished (see table below).

Exclusions included machinery and plant for leasing, cars, long-life assets (11.9.8), seagoing ships and railway assets. If you wish you can disclaim all or part of your first year allowance. If first year allowance is taken, writing down allowance is not available until the second year.

From 1 April 2001, expenditure on certain designated energy-saving products (including hand dryers) and water technologies attracts 100 per cent first year allowance. Such expenditure after 16 April 2002 also qualifies for 100 per cent first year allowance where the asset is for leasing, letting or hire. The categories which qualify are revised periodically.

Expenditure after 16 April 2002 and before 1 April 2015 on new low emission cars (except for leased cars) which are either electrically propelled or emit no more than 110 g/km of carbon dioxide (11.9.13) (120 g/km before 1 April 2008) obtains 100 per cent first year allowance. Also included are purchases before 1 April 2015 of plant and machinery to refuel cars with natural gas or hydrogen fuel. Furthermore, for expenditure after 16 April 2002, the capital allowance restrictions for cars costing over £12,000 and leased cars (11.9.1) are removed for low emission cars, qualifying for the 100 per cent allowance.

After 31 March 2003, 100 per cent first year allowance is available on expenditure on designated environmentally beneficial technologies and products (CAA S45H).

From April 2012, 100 per cent first year allowance is available for trading companies buying plant or machinery for use in designated assisted areas within enterprise zones.

First year allowance rates are summarised below and further details are given in the 1989–90 and earlier editions of this book.

Expenditure date	**Rate of allowance %**
After 31.3.86 and before 1.11.92	nil
After 31.10.92 and before 1.11.93	40
*After 1.7.97 and before 2.7.98	50
*After 1.7.98	40
# From April 2004	50
# From April 2005	40
# From April 2006 for two years	50
# From April 2008 for one year	–
§ From April 2009 for one year	40

* restricted to small and medium-sized businesses – 100% applies where used in Northern Ireland and expenditure is after 11 May 1998 (also certain IT expenditure).

\# For 'small businesses' only.

§ on the excess over the first £50,000 which qualifies for AIA (11.9.9).

11.9.2 **Writing down allowance** (CAA Ss11–20 & 55–70)

Each asset is put into a 'pool' at its cost price (previously less any first year allowance obtained) and a writing down allowance of 20 per cent was given on the balance up to April 2012. You can take less than 20 per cent in any year and this also applies to companies (13.10). Prior to 6 April 2008 (1 April for companies) the rate was 25 per cent. Writing down allowance was not normally given for the first year, if first year allowance was obtained. Only 6 per cent may be available on long-life assets bought after 25 November 1996 (11.9.8) and 10 per cent after 5 April 2008 (1 April for companies). For chargeable periods ending after 5 April 2012 (1 April 2012 for companies), the rates are 18 per cent and 8 per cent respectively. This may result in a hybrid rate for periods spanning April 2012.

See also *small plant and machinery pools* (11.9.9(9)).

The 'pooling' rules normally apply to what were Schedule D businesses. However, from 6 April 1997 (1 April for companies) capital allowances are also to be computed on a 'pooling' basis regarding machinery and plant used for a property letting business. This will normally relate to all your previously Schedule A income (7.1).

Where you obtain no first year allowance, writing down allowance runs from the first year. Unlike first year allowances, writing down allowances previously only applied when the assets concerned were brought into use. However, from 1 April 1985, they are available from when the expenditure is incurred.

If the base period is less than a year, the rate of writing down allowance is proportionately reduced. Thus, if the base period for a business is only six months for a given year of assessment, then any writing down allowances for that period would be at the rate of 18 per cent × $^{6}/_{12}$ = 9 per cent.

From 2008–09, a new annual investment allowance was introduced for the first £50,000 of expenditure on plant and machinery in the general pool (11.9.9). This was increased to £100,000 from April 2010, but then reduced to £25,000 from 5 April 2012 (1 April 2012 for companies).

11.9.3 **Ships** (CAA Ss127–158)

Free depreciation by postponing first year allowances was available with regard to new ships. This extended to expenditure on second-hand ships incurred after 31 March 1985. The same principle still applies regarding writing down allowances on expenditure on new ships after 13 March 1984 and second-hand ships after 31 March 1985. The allowances can be 'rolled-up' and used at will. These rules do not apply, however, to certain leasing situations where capital allowances are restricted (11.9.15).

You can claim to defer a balancing charge on a ship disposal. It is now necessary that you reinvest the proceeds in other shipping within six years and relief is available across groups of companies.

11.9.4 Sales of plant and machinery – balancing allowances and charges (CAA Ss55–70)

If you sell an item of plant from your 'pool' of purchases, you simply deduct the sale proceeds from the 'pool' balance. If the proceeds exceed the original cost of the plant, however, you only deduct the cost from the pool and the excess is a capital gain. Should the sale proceeds exceed your 'pool' balance, the excess is treated as a balancing charge and it is added to your assessment for the relevant year. By means of the balancing charge, HMRC recoup the excess of capital allowances that would otherwise have been given to you. Note that your time of sale is taken as the earlier of completion or when possession is given. This rule is of general application for most capital allowance purposes.

Regarding plant etc. (apart from some motor cars) purchased after 26 October 1970, balancing allowances normally only occur in the event of a cessation. If you cease permanently to trade during a period then you receive for that period a 'balancing allowance' equal to the remainder of your 'pool' (of expenditure on assets after 26 October 1970 less allowances already obtained) less its disposal value.

If assets are sold from one person (company etc.) to another, both being under common control, both may elect within two years that the tax written down value is passed from one to the other. The effect is that there is no balancing allowance or charge. (These provisions must now be assumed always to have had effect regarding qualifying hotels, scientific research assets and commercial buildings in enterprise zones, providing both parties are entitled to capital allowances.) A similar election may be made within two years after the succession of a trade between connected persons (for example where a trade passes from one company to another under common control).

Balancing charges and other balancing adjustments are not applicable regarding certain transfers of UK trades from a company situated in one EC member state to a company situated in another. The consideration must consist of shares or securities and the transfer must be for commercial reasons and not with a main purpose of saving tax.

An anti-avoidance measure prevents a balancing charge being obtained where the proceeds have been reduced by means of a tax avoidance scheme (CAA S570A).

11.9.5 Example: Capital allowances on plant and machinery

Mr A has been carrying on a small manufacturing business for many years and makes up his accounts to 31 December each year. At 31 December 2006 the capital allowances written down value of his plant etc. was £8,100. Mr A purchased the following new plant:

Date	Description	Cost £
on 2 February 2007	Typewriters	1,000
on 1 May 2007	Machinery	5,000
on 30 November 2007	Machinery	2,000

Compute Mr A's capital allowances from 2006–07 to 2010–11.

		'Pool' £	Total allowances £
Balance forward		8,100	
2006–07 writing down allowance		2,025	2,025
Balance forward		6,075	
2007–08 (base period year to 31 December 2007)			
Additions:			
2 February 2007		1,000	
1 May 2007		5,000	
30 November 2007		2,000	
		14,075	
First year allowance £8,000 at 50%	4,000		
Writing down allowance £6,075 at 25%	1,518	5,518	5,518
Balance forward		8,557	
2008–09 writing down allowance			
£2,227 at 25%	557		
£6,330 at 20%	1,266	1,823	1,823
Balance forward		6,734	
2009–10 writing down allowance 20%		1,347	1,347
Balance forward		5,387	
2010–11 writing down allowance 20%*		1,077	1,077
Balance forward		4,310	

* From 2012–13 the rate is 18 per cent.

11.9.6 Annual investment allowance (AIA)

FA 2008 introduced a new annual investment allowance (AIA) for expenditure after 5 April 2008 (1 April for companies). Qualifying activities for individuals include trades, professions, vocations, ordinary property business and employments. AIA is also available to companies and partnerships consisting only of individuals.

The first £50,000 of expenditure on plant and machinery each year (normally excluding motor cars) qualified for 100 per cent AIA relief and any excess was dealt with under the normal capital allowances regime, attracting writing down allowance. There are special rules for limiting relief to a single AIA for groups of companies and businesses under common control.

If the chargeable period was more or less than 12 months, the £50,000 figure was increased or reduced proportionately. However, where it bridged 6 April 2008 (31 March for companies) only the fraction falling after that date qualified. Thus a company with a chargeable period from 1 January 2008 to 31 December 2008 had maximum AIA for that year of £50,000 × 9⁄12 = £37,500.

From 1 April 2010 for companies and 6 April 2010 for unincorporated businesses, AIA was available on the first £100,000 of expenditure on plant and machinery. Any excess attracts writing down allowance. Where a business had a chargeable period spanning the increase, a proportion was taken. Thus if a company prepares accounts to 30 September, its AIA limit for the year to 30 September 2010 was ½ × £50,000 + ½ × £100,000 = £75,000. From April 2012, the limit has gone down to £25,000.

11.9.7 **Short-life assets** (CAA Ss83–89)

A special rule applies to short-life plant and machinery which you buy for your trade. You can elect to have the writing down allowances on that plant calculated separately from your 'pool' (de-pooling). The election must be made within two years of the year of acquisition. De-pooling does not normally apply to assets leased to non-traders, or to cars or ships.

When you sell the assets, there will be a balancing allowance or charge, not normally otherwise arising. However, if the machinery or plant has not been sold within five years, it must be transferred to your 'pool' at its tax written down value. From April 2011, the election extends to an 8-year cut-off period.

11.9.8 **Example: Short-life assets – de-pooling**

Mr B makes up his business accounts to 5 April and bought plant for £100 on 30 June 2007, for which he made a de-pooling election. The plant is sold for £10 on 15 May 2011. The capital allowances computations are as follows:

Year ended 5 April		£
2008	cost	100
	25% writing down allowance	25
		75
2009	20% writing down allowance	15
		60
2010	20% writing down allowance	12
		48
2011	20% writing down allowance	10
		38
2012	Sale proceeds	10
	Balancing allowance	28

Note: If the plant had not been disposed of by 5 April 2012, the written down value would be transferred to the general plant pool.

11.9.9 **Long-life assets and the new special rate pool** (CAA Ss90–104)

On assets bought after 25 November 1996, your writing down allowance was only 6 per cent, subject to the following:

(1) The 6 per cent rate applied to plant and machinery with an expected life when new of at least 25 years.
(2) From 6 April 2008 (1 April for companies) a new *special rate pool* has been introduced to contain expenditure on long-life assets, thermal insulation and integral features (11.10). Writing down allowance is given at 8 per cent (10 per cent prior to April 2012), any balance on the existing 6 per cent pool being transferred in, subject to transitional rules where a business's accounting period spans 5 April (31 March) 2008.
(3) Your business is outside the rules if it spends no more than £100,000 each year on such assets (reduced pro rata for associated companies).
(4) Other exclusions are motor cars and machinery and plant in a building used as a dwelling house, shop, showroom, hotel or office.
(5) Ships attract 18 per cent (previously 20 per cent) as do railway assets bought before 2011.
(6) Expenditure before 2001 under contracts effected before 26 November 1996 continues to attract 20 per cent relief (25 per cent before 6 April 2008 – 1 April for companies).
(7) If applicable, a separate pool was needed for your long-life assets.
(8) Where you sell a long-life asset for less than its tax written down value, in order to gain a tax advantage, it is treated as sold for that value.
(9) From 6 April 2008 (1 April for companies) *small plant and machinery pools* operate. A writing down allowance of up to £1,000 each is available where the unrelieved expenditure in either or both of the main (11.9.2) or special rate pools does not exceed that limit. However, this does not apply to single asset pools.

11.9.10 **Safety at sports grounds** (CAA Ss27, 30–32 & 63)

If relief is not otherwise available, you can claim capital allowances at 20 per cent (25 per cent before 6 April 2012 – 1 April for companies) on the reducing balance on certain safety expenditure at sports grounds. You must be trading and the grounds designated under the Safety of Sports Grounds Act 1975. From 1 January 1989 this was extended to include 'regulated stands' (broadly providing covered accommodation for 500 or more spectators). This relief was repealed in FA 2012.

11.9.11 **Security assets** (CAA Ss27, 33 & 63)

Expenditure after 5 April 1989 on 'security assets' may qualify for capital allowances (now 18 per cent on reducing balance). Before 6 April 2012 (1 April for companies) the rate was 20 per cent. You must acquire the assets to meet a special threat to your personal security which arises by virtue of your trade or profession. Partnerships and sole traders are covered by the rules.

11.9.12 **Motor vehicles – pre April 2009 rules** (CAA Ss74–82)

If you bought a car for use in your business you obtained the 20 per cent writing down allowance – 25 per cent before 6 April 2008 (1 April for companies) for every year including the first. Special rules applied, however, to cars costing over £12,000 in which case your allowance for any year is restricted to 25 per cent × £12,000, that is, £3,000. Each car that cost over £12,000 must be treated as a separate 'pool' which, when sold, gives rise to its own balancing allowance or balancing charge.

Cars purchased for no more than £12,000 were all put into a separate pool (CAA S41). This rule abolished from the start of the chargeable period including 1 April 2000 for corporation tax and 6 April 2000 for income tax. The balance on the separate pool was then included in the main pool. However, you had the option of delaying this for one year.

First year allowances are not given on motor vehicles unless they are designed to carry goods; or are of a type unsuitable for use as private vehicles; or are vehicles for hire to the public such as taxis or certain hire cars; or are provided for the use of the recipients of certain mobility allowances and supplements; otherwise, they are available for small and medium enterprises (11.9.1). From 17 April 2002 100 per cent first year allowance applies to low emission cars (11.9.1).

If your car was leased through your business (or company) and its equivalent retail cost price exceeded a given limit, the rental deduction from the taxable business profits was correspondingly restricted. The limit was £12,000 retail cost equivalent if the car was first rented after 10 March 1992 and £8,000 if earlier. New rules apply for lease periods starting from April 2009 (below).This restriction is not to apply to hire purchase arrangements where there was an option to purchase for 1 per cent or less of the original retail cost.

The actual deductible rental is found by multiplying the true rental by $(12{,}000 + \frac{RP - 12{,}000}{2})$ and dividing it by the RP (retail price of the car when new).

11.9.13 **Scheme for motor vehicles from April 2009**

If you buy a car for use in your business after 5 April 2009 (1 April for companies), new capital allowances rules apply. You ignore whether or not the cost exceeds £12,000 and simply consider whether or not its emissions are above or below 160 grams per kilometre. Up to 160g/km the cost went into the ordinary 'pool' on which writing down allowance at 20 per cent was available. Higher emissions went into a special pool attracting only 10 per cent allowance. Cars costing over £12,000 bought before 6 April/1 April 2009 continue under the old system for about five years, any remaining written down value then being transferred into the main pool.

From the same dates, motorcycles are treated as general plant, rather than cars. Also, for leased cars, the special treatment is applied for carbon emissions over 160 g/km rather than £12,000 value and only 85 per cent of the expenditure is deductible. This applies for lease periods starting from April 2009. From April 2012, the rates are reduced to 18 per cent and 8 per cent respectively.

From April 2013, the carbon dioxide emission threshold will be drastically reduced to 130 g/km, so that more cars are likely to go into the 8 per cent pool.

The carbon dioxide emission threshold for receiving 100 per cent first year allowances on motor vehicles is 110 g/km before 1 April 2013 and will be 95 g/km for the next two years.

11.9.14 **Hire purchase** (CAA Ss67–69)

If you buy plant or machinery on hire purchase you are entitled to full capital allowances as soon as you bring it into use in your business. You receive allowances on the capital proportion of the total instalments – the interest proportion is allowed against your business profits in the year that the respective instalments are paid. Thus if you buy under hire purchase a machine whose cash cost would be £1,000 and you are paying a total of £1,600 over three years, you get capital allowances on £1,000 as soon as you start to use the machine. You would also deduct the interest of £600 from your profits for the three years during which you are paying off the instalments (that is about £200 each year).

11.9.15 **Machinery for leasing** (CAA Ss70 & 105–126)

You are normally able to obtain 18 per cent writing down allowance (11.9.2) on expenditure to buy assets which you lease out. However, subject to the rules, first year allowance may have been available (11.9.1). A separate pool was used for all such assets purchased before 1 April 1986 and certain cars (11.9.12).

Where an asset ceased to be used for qualifying purposes during the *requisite period* (above), the capital allowances were recomputed as if no first year allowance had been given. This normally gave rise to a balancing charge when use for *qualifying purposes* ceased.

Broadly for chargeable periods ending after 1 July 1998 expenditure on assets used in 'finance leasing' only qualifies for writing down allowance in the year of purchase according to the time held in that year. However, no such restriction applies subsequently.

Where new plant or machinery is sold and leased back, the lessor can claim capital allowances, provided the lessee does not do so, the parties are not connected and the sale is within four months of the equipment being brought in to use. This rule operates from 28 July 2000.

Over the years, various anti-avoidance measures have been introduced regarding leasing and capital allowances (15.10.6).

11.9.16 **IT equipment and computer software** (CAA Ss71–73 & FA 2003 Ss165–166)

Eighteen per cent writing down allowance (11.9.2) is available (previous rates were 20 per cent and 25 per cent) for capital expenditure on the outright acquisition of computer software. This extends to capital expenditure on software licences and access to electronic transmission. The expenditure is treated as if on plant and may rank for first year allowances in the case of a small or medium-sized business (11.9.1).

'Small businesses' could claim 100 per cent first year allowances on their investment in the three years to 31 March 2004 in information and communication technology (IT). This broadly comprises computers, equipment and peripherals such as printers and keyboards, high-tech communications technologies (third generation mobile phones etc.) and related software (unless acquired after 25 March 2003 with a view to sub-licensing).

The relief is limited to 'small businesses', including companies and groups, broadly satisfying two of the following conditions:

(1) turnover not more than £2.8m
(2) assets not more than £1.4m
(3) not more than 50 employees.

11.9.17 **Definition of plant and machinery** (CAA Ss21–25)

Special rules were introduced which provide that buildings and structures do not qualify as plant for capital allowances purposes, nor does land. These rules cover expenditure incurred from 30 November 1993, unless under a contract made before that date and incurred before 5 April 1996. Earlier expenditure is not affected and established exceptions under case law are preserved.

The expression 'building' includes such items as walls, gates, main services, waste disposal and fire safety systems, sewerage, drainage and lift shafts. Items not affected include electrical and water systems provided for the trade, manufacturing equipment, furniture and fittings, cookers, dishwashers etc., other machinery, movable partition walls, decorative assets for hotels etc. and advertising displays.

'Structures' include tunnels, bridges, pavements, roads, inland navigations, dams, sea walls and weirs. Items not affected include altering land to install machinery, dry docks, jetties etc. to carry plant, pipelines, indoor and outdoor swimming pools, fish tanks and railway lines. The rules only mention what is not plant; otherwise, existing law must be followed.

11.10 Fixtures – entitlement to capital allowances – integral features (CAA Ss33A & 172–204)

Detailed rules apply to clarify who is entitled to capital allowances where machinery or plant is installed in a building or on land and becomes a fixture.

The rules may treat the plant as belonging to you for capital allowances purposes even though you are not the owner. This includes boilers and radiators installed in a building as part of a central heating system. These rules prevail where they conflict with the hire purchase ones.

The rate of writing down allowances on certain fixtures integral to a building is 8 per cent from 2012–13; 10 per cent from 2008–09 (1 April 2008 for companies). The list of *integral features* comprises electrical (including lighting) and hot water systems; space or water heating systems; powered ventilation air cooling or purification systems and related flooring or ceilings; lifts, escalators and moving walkways; external solar shading and active facades. *Expenditure on integral features* is to be included in the *special pool* (11.9.8).

Note that the 8 per cent rate applies to both the initial and replacement expenditure (where over 50 per cent of an integral feature is replaced in a 12 month period).

If you lease a piece of equipment and it becomes a fixture at a building, you will obtain capital allowances if you jointly elect with the lessee. Where you pay to be granted a lease including a fixture on which the lessor would obtain capital allowances, you can jointly elect that you receive the allowances.

Lessors can claim capital allowances on heating equipment installed under the Government's affordable wealth programme where the expenditure is after 27 July 2000 and before 2008.

Modifications to the rules took effect from 24 July 1996 with a view to:

(1) Provide for a joint election of purchaser and vendor as to the amount of the sale price to be apportioned to fixtures.
(2) Prevent the acceleration of allowances on fixtures.
(3) Stop allowances exceeding the original cost of a fixture.
(4) Bar allowances on fixtures leased to non-taxpayers if the lessor has no relevant interest in the land.

The rules are reinforced by FA 2012.

Expenditure on designated energy-saving equipment which a business is contracted to provide and operate under an energy services agreement came within the above rules from April 2001. Normally the equipment would be attached to land in which the business holds no interest.

11.11 Industrial buildings (CAA Ss271–360)

The cost of new industrial buildings used in your business (that is, factories, warehouses etc. and some repair shops) qualified for industrial buildings allowances. However, by 2010–11, industrial buildings allowances had been phased out and generally removed (11.11.3). (Qualifying expenditure also included additions and improvements to industrial buildings. Industrial buildings allowance extended to the construction of toll roads.)

Also included were import warehouses which store goods or materials imported into the UK. The relief also covered privately financed public roads under the Design Build Finance and Operate initiative.

Each year (including the first) a writing down allowance of 4 per cent of the original cost was obtained. Up to 25 per cent of the capital cost of an industrial building could relate to a non-qualifying use without restricting the allowances.

Prior to 1 April 1986, expenditure qualified for initial allowance at various rates. Building costs after 31 March 1986 normally did not attract initial allowances apart from in enterprise zones (11.12). However, 20 per cent initial allowance was available for qualifying buildings constructed under a contract entered into between 1 November 1992 and 31 October 1993. Also, the buildings must have been brought into use for the purposes of the trade by 31 December 1994. In cases where the expenditure was in the same year as the building was brought into use, both initial and writing down allowance were available.

If a building on which industrial buildings allowances had been obtained is sold then the sale proceeds must be compared with the balance of original cost less initial allowances and writing down allowances obtained. Any excess proceeds will be assessed as a balancing charge and any deficit will be allowed as a balancing allowance. This now applies even if you had ceased to use the building for industrial purposes. Any excess of the proceeds compared with the original cost must be disregarded for this purpose but may give rise to a capital gain (20.2).

11.11.1 **Space above shops etc.** (CAA Ss393A–W)

Subject to the rules, 100 per cent initial allowance is given on expenditure after 11 May 2001 on renovating or converting space above shops and other commercial buildings to flats for letting.

(1) The property must be pre-1980.
(2) There must be no more than five floors and those above ground level originally constructed for mainly residential purposes.
(3) At the time of the conversion the ground floor must be rated for broadly shops, offices, restaurants and medical use.
(4) The upper floors need to be empty or used as storage for at least a year before the conversion.
(5) Each new flat must be self-contained with its own access and have no more than four rooms apart from kitchen and bathroom.
(6) High-value flats are excluded. For example the rent limit for a four-room flat in Greater London is £480 per week.
(7) The rules resemble those for industrial buildings, but are simplified.

11.11.2 **Business premises renovation allowances** (CAA Ss360A–Z4)

An initial allowance of 100 per cent is available on renovating and converting business property in a 1997 designated disadvantaged area of the UK. A condition is that the property has been unused for at least a year. The relief applies to expenditure from 11 April 2007 to 10 April 2012 and now extended to April 2017.

11.11.3 **Phasing out industrial buildings allowance**

From 2008–09, writing down allowances on industrial buildings and agricultural buildings (11.14) were withdrawn, with final removal by 2010–11. To prepare for this, balancing adjustments and the recalculation of writing down allowances in respect of balancing events from 21 March 2007 were withdrawn. Exceptions are regarding an existing contract and certain qualifying enterprise zone expenditure (11.12).

11.12 Enterprise zones (CAA Ss281 & 298–304)

The Government have designated a number of enterprise zones. One of their attractions is that expenditure on industrial and commercial buildings including hotels qualifies for 100 per cent initial allowance. Unusually shops and offices are included. Less than the full initial allowance may be claimed in which case 25 per cent writing down allowance (straight line) is available on the original expenditure until used up.

Enterprise zone allowances are now restricted to exclude expenditure incurred more than ten years after the expiry of the zone. Expenditure payable after 15 December 1991 on an unused building is no longer denied enterprise zone allowances because it is bought after the expiry of the zone's ten-year life. Also, allowances are to be available on used buildings sold, within two years of being brought into use after that date.

Where you own the freehold and sell a long lease in your property for a capital sum, this has not given rise to a balancing charge. However, buildings purchased by you in enterprise zones on or after 13 January 1994 may produce balancing charges if disposed of in this way. The new rules provide for balancing charges on sales of the long leases within seven years (25 years in cases with guaranteed exit arrangements).

One hundred per cent initial allowance will not be available on expenditure after 5 April 2011 (31 March 2011 for companies). However, if a business's accounting period spans these dates and writing down allowance is being claimed, it will be restricted on a time basis. From those respective dates, balancing charges are removed, except within seven years of first use, where initial allowance or writing down allowance had been claimed. However, from April 2012, 100 per cent first year allowance is available for trading companies buying plant or machinery for use in designated assisted areas within enterprise zones. Plans for 21 new enterprise zones were mentioned in the 2011 Budget.

11.13 Agricultural buildings allowance (CAA Ss361–393)

If you were the owner or tenant of any farm or forestry land, you obtained allowance for your expenditure on certain constructions on that land. These included farmhouses, farm or (generally only up to 19 June 1989) forestry buildings, cottages, fences etc.

The allowance was given in the form of an annual writing down allowance of 4 per cent on your original expenditure. (Previously, an initial allowance of up to 20 per cent could also be claimed. The balance was eligible for writing down allowance of 10 per cent of the original cost for each year including the first.) With the exception of the year to 31 October 1993, for expenditure incurred from 1 April 1986, there was no initial allowance and the writing down allowance was reduced to 4 per cent.

Expenditure after 31 March 1986, attracting 4 per cent writing down allowance was generally written off within 25 years. However, if you sold or demolished the building within that time, you could elect for a balancing adjustment (that is, balancing allowance or charge – 11.9.4). This also applied if the building is destroyed. The election must be made within two years after the end of the relevant year of assessment (accounting period for a company).

If your expenditure was on a farmhouse, then your allowance was normally based on only one-third (maximum) of the total cost to take account of the personal benefit. The allowance was phased out from 2008–09 to 2010–11 (11.14).

11.14 Phasing out of industrial buildings and agricultural buildings allowances

Up to 5 April 2011 (31 March 2011 for companies), the basis of calculating allowances was unchanged, but where an accounts period bridged those respective dates, there was a corresponding reduction. Furthermore, only a percentage of the full allowances was due as follows:

Financial year from 1 April	Tax year	%
2008	2008–09	75
2009	2009–10	50
2010	2010–11	25
2011	2011–12	0

FA 2008 contains an anti-avoidance rule to limit writing down allowance where property qualifying for industrial buildings allowance was transferred between connected parties to obtain a tax advantage.

11.15 Hotel buildings (CAA Ss277, 279 & 317)

Expenditure incurred on the construction or improvement of certain hotel buildings qualified for an annual writing down allowance of 4 per cent of the original cost, subject to phasing out (11.14). If the hotel is in an enterprise zone (11.12), expenditure qualifies for relief at special rates (100 per cent initial allowance etc.). To qualify for the allowance, the hotel must have at least ten bedrooms for letting to the public and provide breakfast and an evening meal. Also, it must be open for at least four months in the season from April to October inclusive.

11.16 Assured tenancies (CAA Ss490–531)

A 75 per cent initial allowance followed by 4 per cent writing down allowance (phased out from April 2008 – 11.14) was available on qualifying expenditure incurred between 9 March 1982 and 14 March 1984. From 14 March 1984, the initial allowance was phased out, but the writing down allowance remains for expenditure incurred before 1 April 1992. The allowances were given on dwellings let on assured tenancies by bodies approved by the Secretary of State for the Environment under the Assured Tenancies Scheme. Assured tenancies allowances are treated as capital allowances, which enables them to be included in group relief claims (13.13).

The expenditure on each house or flat qualifying for allowance is limited to £40,000 (£60,000 in Greater London). Regarding expenditure after 4 May 1983 (unless under existing contracts) only landlords which are companies qualify for the allowance.

11.17 Research and development (R&D) relief (CAA Ss437–451 & FA 2003 S168 & Sch 31)

From 6 April 2000 (1 April 2000 for companies) a new definition is brought in for R&D as being activities that fall to be so treated in accordance with normal accounting practice in relation to UK companies. However, the Treasury are empowered to make altering and supplementary regulations.

From 1 April 2000, 'small and medium companies' (SMEs) (11.9.1) are entitled to R&D relief, subject to the rules:

(1) The qualifying R&D expenditure must be at least £10,000 (previously £25,000) in a 12-month accounting period (scaled down for shorter accounting periods). The £10,000 expenditure threshold also applies to 11.17.1 and 11.17.2 below but is planned to be abolished from April 2012.

(2) The expenditure must relate to a present or projected trade of the company and not be capital, nor subsidised and can include staffing costs (including certain externally provided workers), consumable stores and certain intellectual property.

(3) Relief against taxable profits was given at 150 per cent of the R&D expenditure.
(4) Companies which are not yet in profit may elect to take a non-taxable R&D tax credit of up to 16 per cent of the relief, that is, 24 per cent etc. of the R&D cost. This may be encashed.
(5) The R&D credit is limited to PAYE and NIC liability for the period.
(6) From 1 April 2004, a wider definition of R&D applies and qualifying expenditure now also includes software, power, fuel and water.
(7) From April 2006, for big companies and later for small and medium enterprises, relief extends to payments to clinical trial volunteers.
(8) FA 2007 broadens the requirements for companies to be entitled to relief by including those with fewer than 500 employees, annual turnover no more than €100m and/or a balance sheet value not exceeding €86m.
(9) From 2008, the enhanced rate for 'small and medium companies' goes up to 175 per cent, whilst the value of the payable credit remains at about 24 per cent of the qualifying expenditure.
(10) From 1 April 2011, the total rate increases to 200% and 225% applies from 1 April 2012.

11.17.1 **Larger companies' R&D relief** (FA 2002 S53 & Sch 12)

For expenditure from 1 April 2002, larger companies obtain R&D tax credit at 25 per cent, in addition to relief for their actual expenditure. Thus they obtain relief for 125 per cent of their expenditure. From 2008–09, the enhanced deduction for larger companies becomes 130 per cent. Subject to consultation, FA 2013 will include 'above the line' R&D tax credits. This will be introduced in FA 2013 for larger companies. The credit will be paid in cash from April 2013 and will be at least 9.1 per cent of the pre-tax qualifying expenditure.

11.17.2 **Vaccines research relief (VRR)** (FA 2002 S54 & Schs 13 & 14)

The 2002 Finance Act brought in 150 per cent relief for corporation tax on expenditure for certain vaccines and medicines in the fields of TB, malaria, HIV infection and AIDs. FA 2012 has abolished VRR for SMEs.

11.17.3 **EC restrictions on R&D relief and VRR**

The schemes need to comply with the EC guidelines before approval is granted for the above rate increases. Also companies whose latest accounts have not been prepared on a going concern basis cannot claim relief and there is a cap for relief on each project of €7.5m. Furthermore, the VRR relief rate for companies has come down to 40 per cent.

11.18 Patent rights and 'know-how' (CAA Ss452–483)

The 1985 Finance Act changed the allowance basis for both patent rights and 'know-how', so that from 1 April 1986, only a 25 per cent writing down allowance applies and this is reduced to 20 per cent from April 2008 (18 per cent from April 2012). (Note that costs in connection with creating and registering your own patents are treated as deductible revenue expenses (TA 1988 S83).)

If you purchase patent rights from a connected person, your allowances may be limited, by reference to the vendor's disposal value for capital allowance purposes. Otherwise, it is necessary to use your capital expenditure, or if smaller, the market value of the rights on your acquiring them, or normally the original acquisition costs of the vendor.

Regarding companies, the revised intellectual property rules (13.29) apply to assets created or acquired by them after 31 March 2002 in place of the above. From April 2013, a new 'Patent Box' scheme applies to companies (13.29).

11.19 Dredging (CAA Ss484–489)

For dredging expenditure after March 1986, an annual writing down allowance of 4 per cent on the original amount is due. Previously an initial allowance of 15 per cent applied, together with writing down allowance at 4 per cent each year on a straight line basis.

11.20 Mineral extraction (CAA Ss394–436)

Expenditure before 1 April 1986 attracted initial and writing down allowances related to output etc. These have been replaced by writing down allowances at 18 per cent (previously 20 per cent and 25 per cent before April 2008) or 8 per cent (10 per cent before April 2012), depending on the nature of the expenditure. Pre-1 April 1986 balances qualify for the new reliefs. Balancing allowances or charges arise under the present system where mineral deposits cease to be worked or the mine etc. is sold.

11.21 Films etc. (F2A 1992 Ss40–42, F2A 1997 S48, CAA Sch 2 & FA 2002 Ss99–101)

Films, tapes and discs with at least a two-year life normally qualified for capital allowances. However, this was withdrawn from 10 March 1982 for overseas films but continued for British made films (including those for television). Unless the film etc. is trading stock, the rules provide for the production expenditure not qualifying for capital allowances to be written off over the film's income-producing life. Film investment is sometimes made by means of limited partnerships. However, relief for limited partners' losses after 19 March 1985 was severely restricted (12.3).

The production of qualifying films (those with sufficient EC content) obtains special relief from 11 March 1992. Pre-production costs incurred from that date attract relief at once, up to a limit of 20 per cent of total budgeted cost; production expenditure on films completed after 10 March 1992 is to be written off as to one-third each year starting with the completion of the film, as is the cost of acquiring qualifying films.

Special relief applies for British qualifying films costing no more than £15m. For production expenditure and certain acquisition costs incurred after 2 July 1997 and before 1 January 2007, 100 per cent write-off is allowed when each film is completed. New rules of a clarifying nature operate generally from 6 April 2000 (FA 2000 S113). Generally from 17 April 2002, 'British qualifying films' must be intended for release in the commercial cinema and the production expenditure relievable must be paid no later than four months after the films' completion.

From 10 December 2003, rules took effect aimed at preventing tax avoidance through contrived exits from businesses where tax relief has resulted from trading losses generated from film tax reliefs.

Further anti-avoidance provisions operate from 2 December 2004 (FA 2005 Ss59–71 & Sch 3). These are designed to prevent relief being given for more than the entire cost of a film; also using film relief alongside tax deferral for more than 15 years.

FA 2006 brought in new rules operating broadly from April 2006 regarding British films produced by a film production company. Such a company is responsible for the principal photography, postproduction and delivering the completed film. Each film is taxed as a separate trade. However, FA 2007 introduced powers to elect to be taxed according to general tax rules.

Relief is on a maximum of 80 per cent of the total UK qualifying expenditure, which must be at least 25 per cent of the total production expenditure on the film. However, the relief is increased to 100 per cent for films with total qualifying production expenditure of £20m or less. Where a loss is created, it can be taken as a tax credit of 20 or 25 per cent.

11.22 Relief for losses (ITA Ss60–101)

11.22.1 Losses under the current year basis

The previous system under which relief was allowed for business losses is outlined in the next section (11.22.2). Broadly, this system still applies but with some alterations.

Among the changes relating to the move to the current year basis (11.7.1) are the following:

(1) Losses are computed on the basis of the periods for which the accounts of the business are prepared, instead of the fiscal year basis.
(2) Relief for trading and professional losses under S380 (11.22.2) is allocated differently. It now goes against your income either of the year of loss or the preceding year and you can choose which has priority.

(3) Similarly, the rules regarding losses on certain unquoted shares (20.14) changed, as did those for terminal losses (11.24) and losses in new businesses (11.23).
(4) In general, the new rules took effect from 1997–98 for businesses existing at 5 April 1994 and otherwise from commencement.
(5) An election to HMRC must be made within 12 months from 31 January following the year of assessment.

Various rules remain from the old system including:

(1) If you make a trading loss in the year and have insufficient other income for the year to offset it, you can claim relief against capital gains for that tax year. If there are still unused trading losses after absorbing other income for the following year, relief is available against the capital gains for that year (20.13).
(2) Note that you are not allowed to carry a loss forward from one trade to another. You should remember this if you change businesses. A move to a nearby shop in the same trade may be in order, however.
(3) Your loss in the first year of assessment of a new business includes *pre-trading expenditure* of a revenue nature (11.3.1). This applies to individuals and partnerships regarding such expenditure within seven years before trading commences.
(4) Income tax relief is claimable for certain losses on disposals of *unquoted shares in trading companies* by original subscribers (20.14). These losses take precedence over claims under ITA S64.
(5) Loss relief is given before personal reliefs and allowances (3.0 etc.) which cannot be carried forward. Thus these may be lost through your income being absorbed by losses. If possible, carry the losses forward in these circumstances so that your allowances are not wasted.

11.22.2 **The previous system**

If the adjusted results for your business, profession or vocation showed a deficit of income compared with expenditure for a particular year then your assessment was nil for the related tax year. The loss for the year was augmented by your capital allowances and the resultant total loss was available for relief. This was first given against (a) your other income for the tax year in which you suffered the loss and (b) that for the following tax year. ((a) includes your business assessment on the profits for the year prior to the loss.)

If your loss was not entirely relieved as above then you could and can still claim that the balance should be carried forward and set off against future profits from the *same* trade, profession or vocation.

11.22.3 Example: Relief for losses

D makes a loss of £20,000 in his profession for the year to 31 December 2012 having made a profit of £6,000 for 2011. For 2013 his profit is £22,000. His only other income is taxed dividends, which including tax credits amount to £5,000 for 2011–12 and £6,000 for 2012–13. What loss relief can D obtain?

D's loss of £20,000 for the year to 31 December 2012 will be allocated as follows.

	£
2011–12 loss relief (S64)	
Against 2011–12 assessment on trading income	6,000
Against 2011–12 dividends	5,000
2012–13 loss relief (S64)	
Against 2012–13 dividends	6,000
2013–14 loss relief (S89)	
Against 2013–14 assessment on trading income	3,000
	20,000

(The assessment for 2013–14 becomes £22,000 – £3,000 = £19,000)

11.22.4 Temporary extension of loss carry-back period

An extended carry-back applied to the losses of unincorporated businesses, professions and vocations in 2008–09 and 2009–10; companies for accounting periods ending between 24 November 2008 and 23 November 2010. For these periods, losses could be carried back three years instead of one. However, where the original one year period was exceeded, a £50,000 cap applied to the remainder and the set-off could only be against profits from the same trade.

11.23 Loss in new business (ITA Ss72–74)

If you carry on a business or profession personally or in partnership, a special relief is available. This applies to any loss which you make in your first year of assessment, or in any of the next three years. A written claim is required within two years of the end of the year of assessment.

The losses include capital allowances, and certain pre-trading expenditure (see 11.3.1(26) above). They are offset against your income for the three years of assessment prior to the year in which the losses are made, taking the earliest first.

11.24 Terminal losses (ITA Ss89–94)

If you cease to carry on a trade, profession or vocation and make an adjusted loss in your last complete year of trading, you get relief for this so-called 'terminal loss'. The relief is augmented by your capital allowances apportionable to your last 12 months of trading. The terminal losses are allowed against your business assessments for the three years of assessment prior to that in which you cease to trade. Under the current rules (11.22.1) this is extended to include the tax year of cessation.

11.25 Business expansion scheme (BES)

Under the BES, subject to the rules, you obtained income tax relief in a year of assessment in respect of amounts subscribed for shares in a qualifying company during that year up to £40,000 in total. A qualifying company existed to carry on one or more *qualifying trades*. The BES operated regarding shares issued from 6 April 1983 up to 31 December 1993. From 1 January 1994, the enterprise investment scheme (EIS) operates (11.26). This has many common features such as mainly similar rules for qualifying trades (11.26(5)).

Further details of the BES are given in previous editions of this book.

11.26 Enterprise investment scheme (ITA Ss156–257)

Regarding new investment from 1 January 1994, the enterprise investment scheme (EIS) replaced the business expansion scheme. The EIS is available for purchases of ordinary shares in 'qualifying' unquoted trading companies. Important features are:

(1) The relief is 30 per cent on shares issued after 5 April 2011 before which it was 20 per cent.
(2) From 2004–05 the investment limit was £200,000. From 2006–07 it was £400,000, from 2008–09 it is £500,000 and from 2012–13 it is £1m.
(3) Subject to a maximum of £50,000 (£25,000 before 2006–07), half of the amount that you invest between 6 April and 5 October in any year could be carried back to the previous tax year. From 2009–10, up to the entire amount subscribed can be carried back to the previous year.
(4) From 6 April 1998, participation was limited to companies with gross assets of under £15m before an investment and £16m after it. Generally from 6 April 2006, these limits were reduced to £7m and £8m. However, from 6 April 2012, the respective limits are £15m and £16m.
(5) 'Qualifying companies' are unquoted trading companies which carry on a qualifying activity for at least three years. The range of qualifying activities was broadly similar to that for BES (11.25), but does not include private rented housing. The following rules regarding qualifying trades and companies apply broadly both for VCTs (8.13) and EIS:
    (a) A trade whose income is mainly from royalties and licence fees does not qualify but exceptions are film production and distribution and for shares issued after 5 April 2000, intangible assets created under the corporate venturing scheme (13.28) by a small company.
    (b) Companies whose business consists of certain research and development in general qualify.

(c) Prior to 6 April 2008 only, ship chartering was a qualifying trade. Charters must not have exceeded one year and the ships must have been UK registered and owned, managed and navigated by the company. (Pleasure craft were excluded.)
(d) Wholesaling or retailing goods normally collected or held as investments is not a qualifying trade, unless the company actively tries to sell them. Examples are fine wines and antiques.
(e) Certain parent companies are qualifying companies if all their subsidiaries are wholly owned. This extends to tiers of companies provided they are each at least 90 per cent owned. Subsidiaries can even be resident abroad if the group's trade is mainly within the UK.
(f) Various property backed activities are excluded (also for VCT purposes). These include farming, market gardening, forestry, property development and running hotels, guest houses and nursing/residential care homes.
(g) From 6 April 2008, coal and steel production are excluded.

(6) You must hold your EIS shares for at least three years or else your relief will be withdrawn.
(7) For EIS shares on which relief has not been withdrawn, there is capital gains tax exemption when they are first sold. Any loss you make in these circumstances is available against capital gains or on election against income.
(8) Investment in the parent of a group of companies may qualify where non-qualifying activities only form a minor part of the group activities as a whole.
(9) To obtain relief, you need to be a 'qualifying investor'. That means that during the period you are not 'connected' with the company (holding over 30 per cent of the shares or an employee). This applies from incorporation (or if later, two years before issue) to three years after the issue of the shares.
(10) You can become a paid director and still qualify for EIS relief, provided you were not connected with the company or its trade before the shares were issued.
(11) The scheme extends to companies trading in the UK, whether or not incorporated and resident here. Furthermore, you will be entitled to relief on EIS shares, provided you pay UK income tax, even if you are not UK resident.
(12) If you subscribe for EIS shares you will be entitled to unlimited reinvestment relief where you realise capital gains on other assets, when you are UK resident and ordinarily resident. The EIS shares must be purchased within one year before and three years after the disposals and a claim to HMRC is needed. Subject to the rules, your gains are deferred until you dispose of the EIS shares.
(13) If you defer a capital gain on one EIS investment by investing in another and so on, you obtained taper relief (20.12) for the cumulative period.
(14) EIS reliefs are not lost where its qualifying trade is affected by the company being liquidated or going into receivership.

(15) Companies have 24 months to employ all of the money raised, provided that 80 per cent of this has been applied during the first 12 months. This can extend to two years from the start of the qualifying activity.
(16) Companies which float on a recognised stock exchange after an EIS share issue from 7 March 2001 no longer normally cease to qualify.
(17) EIS companies must have fewer than 250 full-time employees (previously 50). There is also an investment limit of £5m (previously £2m) in any 12 month period. Furthermore, the investment period in which a manager has to invest 90 per cent of the funds raised goes up from 6 to 12 months.

11.26.1 SEED Enterprise Investment Scheme (SEIS)

SEIS relief applies to investments made fom 6 April 2012 in companies with no more than 25 employees and no more than £200,000 assets, which are starting new businesses.

Provided your stake is less than 30 per cent, you will obtain 50 per cent relief, even if you are a director. Your maximum annual investment is £100,000, and unused amounts can be carried back to the previous year.

A SEIS company has a cumulative tax favoured investment limit of £150,000. As an investor, you have an exemption from capital gains tax on SEIS shares and relief for gains realised in 2012–13 which are invested in SEIS shares (20.36).

11.27 Earnings basis and cash basis (FA 1998 Ss42–46 & Sch 6 & ITTOIA S160)

If you are carrying on a trade, you will normally be taxed on an 'earnings basis'. This means that your sales for each accounts period are included as they arise and not when you receive the money. Sales normally arise when they are invoiced. In a retail shop the sales usually arise as the customers pay over the counter. Your expenses are also deductible on an arising basis and the actual date of payment is not relevant. Your profit or loss will also reflect any increase or reduction in your stock and work in progress.

If you are carrying on a profession or vocation, however, HMRC may have taxed you on a 'cash basis', which means by reference to the actual cash received, taking no account of uncollected fees at the end of each accounts period. (Sometimes a mixed earnings and cash basis was allowed.)

The cash basis was usually used for barristers. Other professions prepared their opening accounts on an earnings basis but had the option of later switching to a cash basis. Often the expenses were calculated on an arising basis but in some small cases the actual expense payments were used ignoring accruals.

The cash basis has generally been withdrawn. The withdrawal normally first applied to your accounts for the accounts year beginning after 6 April 1999.

However, special rules apply for accounts for more or less than twelve months. In the case of new barristers (and advocates in Scotland), the cash basis can be used for their first seven years of practice.

Suppose that your accounts are prepared to 30 June each year. Your accounts to 30 June 2000 would have been prepared on an 'earnings basis' and the excess of the taxable profits on that basis (reflecting any increase or decrease in work in progress) calculated as compared with on the 'cash basis'.

You were normally taxed on the excess spread over 10 years starting with 2000–2001. This was restricted to 10 per cent of the profits for each particular year, if less, with the balance payable for the tenth year.

11.27.1 Cash basis for smaller businesses

The Government will consult on introducing a voluntary cash basis for incorporated businesses with a turnover below the VAT threshold (currently £77,000). Other simplifications are also planned.

11.28 Post-cessation receipts (ITA Ss349–356)

If, after you permanently cease your trade, profession or vocation, you receive amounts relating to those activities, they are known as 'post-cessation receipts'. An example is a late fee payment that had not been included in your accounts because they are prepared on a cash basis or the fee was not included in your outstandings.

Post-cessation receipts are usually taxed under the miscellaneous profits rules (15.1). They are normally treated as earned income and you can set off unrelieved losses and capital allowances from before the cessation. You can, however, elect that any post-cessation receipts for the first six years after cessation should be added to your income from the business etc. on its last day of trading.

Relief is available for those born before 6 April 1917 and in business on 18 March 1968 who are taxed on a fraction of their post-cessation receipts varying between $^{19}/_{20}$ and $^{5}/_{20}$. The latter fraction applies if you were born before 6 April 1903; if you were born before 6 April 1904 the fraction is $^{6}/_{20}$ and so on.

11.29 Class 4 National Insurance contributions (TA 1988 S617 & FA 1996 S147)

You will be liable to pay the contributions if you are self-employed in accordance with the rules in Chapter 25 (25.5). For 1985–86 and subsequent years up to 1995–96, you could claim relief for half of your Class 4 contributions. Your total income (5.2) was reduced accordingly. However, this relief was withdrawn for 1996–97 and subsequent years, the Class 4 rate being reduced from 7.3 per cent to 6 per cent to compensate, although it has now gone up to 9 per cent.

11.30 Remediation of contaminated land (FA 2001 S70 & Schs 22 & 23)

Companies which acquire contaminated land for the purposes of their trade or land business are now able to claim 150 per cent of their clean-up costs as follows:

(1) Expenditure after 11 May 2001 is covered and the land can be held as a capital asset or trading stock.
(2) Land is in a contaminated state if, because of substances in, on or under the land, harm is or might be caused or controlled waters polluted and nuclear sites are excluded.
(3) Only expenditure on remediation which is in addition to normal site preparation costs comes within the scheme.
(4) If any loss results, the normal loss and group relief provisions apply.
(5) Should a loss result, a cash payment can be opted for.
(6) Bringing long-term derelict land and land contaminated by previous industrial use back into productive use (FA 2009).

11.31 Foster carers (ITTOIA Ss803–828)

If you provide foster care services, directly or through an agency, to local authorities, from 2003–04 you will be treated as having no profit and no loss for the tax year if your turnover is less than a given limit. This comprises a fixed amount of £10,000 per residence for a full tax year plus £200 per week for each child cared for under 11, increasing to £250 if 11 or over. If your turnover exceeds the limit, you have the option of being taxed on the excess, or according to the normal business profit and loss rules. From 2010–11, similar rules apply for 'shared lives carers' who care for up to three individuals placed at their homes under a local authority scheme.

11.32 Alternative finance arrangements (FA 2005 Ss46–57 & Sch 2)

(1) Special measures take effect regarding the taxation of post 5 April 2005 finance arrangements not involving the receipt or payment of interest.
(2) The rules apply to both individuals and companies investing or borrowing money under arrangements not using interest.
(3) One of the parties to a transaction must be a bank or other financial institution and the usual arrangements involve buying and selling assets.
(4) Alternative finance arrangements will be treated as giving rise to interest for taxation purposes.
(5) After 5 April 2005, banks and building societies offering alternative finance products will have to apply the rules for deduction of tax at source.
(6) The new provisions entail more favourable SDLT (24.4) treatment.
(7) FA 2006 extends the rules to certain agency and partnership arrangements from 1 April 2006.
(8) Rules in FA 2007 bring certain types of investment bonds within the scheme, where they involve paying or receiving no interest.

11.33 Bank payroll tax (BPT)

BPT operated from 12.30pm on 9 December 2009 until 5 April 2010. It covered all discretionary and contractual bonus awards except where there was an existing contractual obligation at the former date. BPT applied to bonuses above £25,000 paid to each employee of a bank, building society, UK branch of a foreign bank, certain financial and related holding companies. The bank, etc. paid BPT at 50 per cent on the excess of each bonus over £25,000.

11.34 Bank levy

A bank levy applies from 1 January 2011 on the total chargeable equity and liabilities of banks, building societies, etc. excluding certain low risk items.

The percentage rates are:

	To 28.2.11	30.4.11	31.12.11	31.12.12	From 1.1.13
Short-term chargeable liabililties	.05	.1	.075	.088	.105
Long-term chargeable equity and liabilities	.025	.05	.0375	.044	.0525

Chapter 12

PARTNERSHIPS

Special rules relate to the taxation of partnerships and these are covered in the following sections. Note that the present system operates generally from 1997–98 and for partnerships *starting after 5 April 1994* (12.2). From 2005–06, rewritten legislation is applied by Ss846–863 in ITTOIA (2.10).

12.1 What is a partnership?

Partnership is the relationship which exists between two or more persons in business together with the object of making profits. There does not necessarily have to be a written partnership agreement but the partnership must exist in fact. If no partnership is in fact operating then, even though there may be a written agreement, it would not make the partnership exist.

Since the assessment of a partnership differs from that of an individual in certain respects, HMRC will seek to establish whether a partnership in fact exists. Points to consider include:

(1) Is there a written partnership agreement?
(2) Can the partners close down the business and are they liable for its debts?
(3) Do the partners' names appear on business stationery?
(4) What arrangements exist for dividing the profits (and property on dissolution)?

12.2 Partnerships under the current year system (TMA Ss12AA–AE, 93A & 95A, TA Ss111–118 & ITTOIA Ss846–863)

In line with the present current year basis, changed rules apply broadly from 1997–98 for partnerships carrying on business on 5 April 1994.

These apply at once for partnerships commencing after that date. Points to note under the new system include the following:

(1) You are assessed on your share of the profits individually, rather than the partnership being assessed on the total.
(2) All partnership expenses and capital allowances are deducted from its profits.
(3) The profits are allocated to the period of account of the partnership, rather than the year of assessment and split according to the profit sharing ratios for the former.
(4) Your assessment is computed as if your profit share were derived from a trade or profession carried on by you alone. This deemed trade or profession runs from when you joined the partnership until you leave it (or it ceases). If you had originally commenced trading by yourself, the deemed trade goes back to when you started.

(5) A change of partners after 5 April 1994 is not regarded as a cessation (12.4), provided there is at least one person who was a partner both in the old partnership and the new one. Consequently, the continuation basis election is no longer needed and has been withdrawn.

(6) With effect from 1996–97, self-assessment rules took effect. These include new partnership returns from 1996–97 and enquiry procedures.

(7) One partner may be made responsible for partnership tax returns etc. If he or she is not available, a 'successor' may so act.

(8) For 1997–98 (and subsequently), you make payments on account on 31 January and 31 July 1998 of normally half your liability for 1996–97, with a balancing payment by 31 January 1999. For example, suppose your 2010–11 liability is £20,000 and your 2011–12 liability is £25,000, you will pay for 2011–12:

	£
on 31 January 2012 (½ × £20,000)	10,000
31 July 2012 (½ × £20,000)	10,000
31 January 2013 (balance)	5,000
	25,000

(9) On the conversion to the 'earnings basis' (11.27) any 'catching-up charge' was allocated to the partners by reference to their profit shares for each of the ten years over which it is spread.

(10) Where a partner is remunerated partly by way of a salary and partly by receiving a share of the profits, the salary is normally not assessed as such but is included in his assessable profit share. Interest paid to partners in respect of their capital is also treated as part of the assessable profit share of each partner. Such interest is not an annual payment (4.1), nor is it taxed as investment income (8.1).

However, there were special rules covering partnership changes (12.4). The 'precedent partner' (normally the senior partner), had to make a joint return of the partnership income each year.

Partnership investment income was and is split between the partners in their profit-sharing ratios and they personally pay any income tax arising.

When the partnership income had been determined for the purposes of Schedule D Case I or Case II, it was split between the partners according to the proportions in which they shared profits during the tax year. These proportions were not necessarily the same as the profit sharing ratios during the year when the profits were actually made.

Under both the old and the new system, where a partner is remunerated partly by way of a salary and partly by receiving a share of the profits, the salary is normally not assessed as such but is included in his assessable profit share. Interest paid to partners in respect of their capital is also treated as part of the assessable profit share of each partner. Such interest is not an annual payment (4.1), nor is it taxed as investment income (8.1).

12.3 Partnership losses (ITTOIA Ss849–851 & ITA Ss62 & 102–116)

Where a partnership has an adjusted loss for any accounting period, that loss is apportioned between the partners in the same ratio as a profit would have been split. Thus the loss is split according to the profit sharing ratios applying to the year of assessment corresponding to the tax year in which the loss is made. For example, if a loss was made in the year to 5 April 2012 this was split between the partners according to their profit sharing ratios for the tax year 2011–12 (assuming that the preceding year basis of assessment applies).

Each partner can use his partnership losses as he chooses according to the various rules for obtaining loss relief (11.22). Thus he can claim for the loss to be relieved against his other income tax assessments for the tax year in which the loss is actually made or the previous year. (Under the old system, relief for the loss was available for the year of the loss and the following one.) Also he can carry forward any unused balance of the loss to be set off against future profit shares from the same partnership; this applies even if the partnership had been treated as discontinued because of a partnership change (see below).

If you are a limited partner, so that your risk is limited to the capital which you have invested, your loss is also restricted in the same way. This applies broadly to losses after 19 March 1985. This was extended to general partners by FA 2004. All partners joining after 25 March 2004 may be affected and for existing partners the rules may restrict trading losses incurred after 9 February 2004.

Provisions in ITA Ss115–116 address the recovery of excess relief and tax avoidance involving films (15.10.21).

The rules normally apply for the first four years of a partner's membership and only bite if he or she works within the partnership for less than a weekly average of ten hours. In that case, loss relief is restricted to the partner's 'contribution' by way of capital introduced, retained profits etc. If a further contribution is made, restricted loss relief may be used in a later period (ITA Ss102–116).

The temporary extension of the loss carry-back period (11.22.4) applied to partnerships.

12.4 Changes of partners (ITTOIA Ss848–850)

If there was any change in the make up of a partnership caused either by a partner leaving or dying or a fresh partner joining, the partnership was treated as ceasing for taxation purposes unless the continuation election described below was made. However, different treatment applies under the rules for changes after 5 April 1994 (12.2). A complete change in the ownership still triggers a deemed cessation. However, a partial change in the identity of the partners is treated as a continuation.

Previously, the effects of cessation caused by a change of partners were similar to any other Schedule D Case I or Case II cessation. Thus the assessment for the final tax year was based on the actual profits for that year and HMRC have the option to increase the assessments for the two previous tax years to the actual profits for those years.

There are some special rules governing partnerships between individuals and a company (TA 1988 Ss114–115 & ITTOIA S863).

12.5 Partnership capital gains (TCGA S59)

When a partnership asset is sold in circumstances that if owned by an individual capital gains tax would have been payable, this tax is assessed on the partners according to their shares in the partnership asset. Thus if a capital gain of £1,000 is made from the sale of a partnership asset on 1 January 2012 and A, B, C and D share equally in the partnership assets, a capital gain of £250 each must be added to the capital gains tax assessments for 2012–13 of A, B, C and D respectively (20.1).

Where a share in a partnership changes hands, a share in all of the partnership assets is treated for capital gains tax purposes as changing ownership and this might give rise to capital gains or capital losses for the partner who is disposing of his share. Thus if A, B and C are equal partners and A sells his share to D, A is treated for capital gains tax purposes as disposing of a one-third share in each of the partnership assets to D.

12.6 Overseas partnerships (ITTOIA Ss857–858)

If you are in partnership carrying on a trade or business and the control and management of the trade or business is outside the UK then the partnership is treated for tax purposes as being non-resident. This follows even if you or some of your other partners are resident here (17.3.4) and some of the business is conducted in this country.

Any profits arising from the partnership trade or business in this country are assessed here under (previously) Schedule D Case I. The firm is assessed in the name of any partner resident in the United Kingdom. Regarding the partnership profits earned abroad, these are assessable in respect of any profit shares of the partners resident here under what was Schedule D Case V according to the special rules outlined in Chapter 18. This now generally applies, even if under a double tax agreement the profits of the overseas partnership arising abroad are exempt from UK tax. From 1997–98 each partner is assessed separately (12.2).

12.7 European economic interest groupings (TMA Ss12A & 98B & TA S510A)

Tax rules regarding European economic interest groupings (EEIGs) operate from 1 July 1989. Such 'groupings' are business entities set up by two or more European community member states with simpler rules than traditional company law bodies – they are more akin to partnerships in some respects. EEIGs may not be formed to make profits for themselves but rather benefit all of their members. Likely activities are packing, processing, marketing and research.

An EEIG is transparent so far as tax on income and capital gains is concerned. Thus these will only be charged to tax in the hands of the members. However, this does not apply to the deduction of tax. Thus an EEIG based in the UK is responsible for operating PAYE.

12.8 Limited liability partnerships (LLPs) (ITTOIA S863 & TCGA Ss59A & 169A)

Measures have been introduced to ensure that LLPs incorporated under the Limited Liability Act 2000 are treated as partnerships for tax purposes. Also, when an LLP goes into liquidation, chargeable gains held over on business gifts will fall into charge. Further provisions prevent tax loss where LLPs are used for investment and property investment.

Chapter 13

COMPANIES

13.1 Introduction

The following is a general outline of the taxation of companies that are resident in the UK or are trading here through a branch or agency. In the latter case it is normally only the profits arising in this country that are taxable here. It must be stressed that the actual provisions are lengthy and many details have been omitted in this summary. Note that ITTOIA (2.10) has no effect for corporation tax purposes. However, consolidating corporation tax legislation (CTA 2009 and 2009–10) has been introduced.

13.2 Corporation tax on profits etc. (TA 1988 S6)

The tax on the profits etc. of companies is called corporation tax which is charged at the present rate of 24 per cent, subject to special relief for companies with profits under £1,500,000 (13.7). Full corporation tax is now charged both on a company's profits and its capital gains (13.15).

Corporation tax applies not only to limited companies, but also to certain associations and unlimited companies. A company's income must be considered for each accounting period (13.4). It is charged to corporation tax on the basis of the actual income assessable for each accounting period according to the rules of the various classes of income (2.3.1) or other Schedules if applicable.

The rate of corporation tax is normally fixed by Parliament in the Finance Act each year for the preceding 'financial year'. A 'financial year' commences on 1 April and, for example, the financial year 2011 is the year to 31 March 2012. The Finance Act 1999 fixed the rate for financial year 2000 at 30 per cent and this rate applies for financial years up to 2007. From 1 April 2008 until 31 March 2011, it is 28 per cent. The following table shows the rates of corporation tax over recent and future years.

13.2.1 Full corporation tax rates

Financial year	Tax rate %
1987–89	35
1990	34
1991–96	33
1997–98	31
1999–2007	30
2008–2010	28
2011	26
2012	24
2013	23
2014	22

13.3 Company dividend payments

If a company pays dividends to its shareholders, no tax is normally deducted. However, there is a tax credit of $^1/_9$ (10 per cent of the gross). The company no longer obtains any set-off against its corporation tax (13.17.3), nor must it pay the tax credit to HMRC.

13.4 Accounting periods for corporation tax (TA 1988 Ss8, 10 & 478 & Sch 30)

Corporation tax is charged in respect of accounting periods. These usually coincide with the periods for which the company prepares its annual accounts but cannot exceed 12 months in duration. Thus, if a company prepares accounts for a period of 18 months, the first 12 months will constitute one accounting period and the remaining six months are treated as another accounting period.

The actual tax is payable nine months after the end of each accounting period, in accordance with the 'pay and file' system (13.4.1).

Interest may arise on overdue corporation tax in accordance with the rules (16.8.2). Interest rates are as follows:

	Accounting periods ending after:	
	30 September 1993 (Pay and file)	30 June 1999 – on income tax on company payments
From	Rate %	Rate %*
29 September 2009	3.0	3.0
24 March 2009	1.75	2.5
27 January 2009	2.75	3.5
6 January 2009	3.5	4.5
6 December 2008	4.25	5.5
6 November 2008	5	6.5
6 January 2008	6	7.5
6 August 2007	6.75	8.5
6 September 2006	6	7.5
6 September 2005	5.25	6.5
6 September 2004	6	7.5

* Tax-deductible.

13.4.1 The pay and file system (TMA Ss59D & 87–87A, TA 1988 Ss8, 10, 4 9 & 826 & FA 1998 S117 & Schs 18 & 19)

Various administrative changes took effect starting with the first accounting period of each company which ended after 30 September 1993. The scheme is called the 'pay and file system'. Particular points are:

(1) Subject to (9) below, companies must pay corporation tax nine months after their accounting dates, whether or not assessments have been raised. For accounting periods ending after 30 June 1999, groups of companies are able to pay on a group-wide basis.
(2) Tax paid late or repaid by HMRC carries interest from the required payment date.
(3) Accounts (and normally, subject to notice being issued, a return) are required to be submitted to HMRC within 12 months from the accounting date.
(4) If accounts are filed late without excuse, penalties are as follows:

	Penalty Basic £	Penalty Persistent failure £	% of unpaid tax
Return overdue by:			
Up to 3 months	100	500	
Over 3 months	200	1,000	
Delay from end of return period:			
Over 18 months			10
Over 24 months			20

(5) FA 2009 contains harsher penalties to be brought in by Treasury order, but no earlier than 2010–11.
(6) Companies should ensure that their accounting systems provide adequate information to comply with the rules.
(7) If a company cannot supply actual figures, estimated ones will be accepted provided all reasonable steps have been taken to provide correct ones. These must then be supplied shortly.
(8) Losses are formally determined by assessment, in the same way as profits. Formal determinations also apply to capital allowances, management expenses and charges available for surrender as group relief.
(9) For accounting periods ending on or after 1 July 1999 corporation tax returns require companies to make self-assessments of their tax. Also there is a new scheme enabling HMRC to make enquiries into returns, subject to giving notice.
(10) A system of quarterly corporation tax payments for large companies took effect for accounting periods ending after 30 June 1999. The payments are based on the estimated liability, with a balancing amount. For example, the payment dates for a large company with a 31 December 2007 year end are 14 July 2007, 14 October 2007, 14 January 2008 and 14 April 2008. A large company (without associated companies) is normally one with

annual profits of at least £1.5m (FA 1998 S30). However, companies whose tax liability is no more than £10,000 are excluded. Interest is payable at rates which change frequently and interest payable is now 1 per cent above the base rate, being 1.50 per cent from 24 March 2009. From the same date interest on overpaid instalments is 0.25 per cent.

(11) In general, from 1 April 2011 corporation tax returns are required to be made online, as are payments including interest and penalties.

13.4.2 Notice of coming within corporation tax

FA 2004 introduced for companies the obligation of informing HMRC when they come within corporation tax for the first time or come within it again, after having been dormant. Notice is required within three months of the start of the first relevant accounting period, together with other information which may be prescribed. Non-compliance could result in penalties of £300 for initial failure and then £50 per day, with up to £3,000 for fraudulently or negligently providing information.

13.5 Repayment supplement and interest on overpaid corporation tax (TA 1988 S825 & 826 & FA 1998 S35 & Sch 4)

This applies for a company if it receives a tax repayment more than a year after the date that corporation tax is due for the relevant accounting period. However, no repayment supplement is due for accounting periods ending after 30 September 1993, although interest is payable (see below). Any repayment supplement is tax-free, and is calculated from the date one year after the due date for paying corporation tax until the end of the tax month (ending fifth day of next month) in which the repayment is made. If the original tax had not been paid by the anniversary of the due date, the interest runs from the anniversary following the payment of the tax. Where loss relief was claimed (13.11), repayment supplement may arise with reference to the accounting period of the loss, rather than any earlier period when the original profits were made. The rates are as on overdue corporation tax payments (13.4).

For accounting periods *ending after 30 September 1993*, tax-free interest is paid on overpaid tax. For corporation tax, interest normally runs from the payment date (or due and payable date, if later) to the date of repayment. The rates are as follows:

	Accounting periods ending after:	
	30 September 1993	**30 June 1999**
From	**Rate %**	**Rate %**
6 December 2003	2	3
6 September 2004	2.75	4
6 September 2005	2	3
6 September 2006	2.75	4

6 August 2007	3.5	5
6 January 2008	2.75	4
6 November 2008	2	3
6 December 2008	1.25	2
6 January 2009	0.5	1
27 January 2009	0	0
24 March 2009	0	0
29 September 2009	0.5	0.5

For accounting periods ending after 30 June 1999, interest on underpaid corporation tax is tax deductible and interest received on overpaid corporation tax is taxable. (Interest rates have been correspondingly adjusted.) Furthermore, interest on income tax repayments is paid from the day after the end of the accounting period.

13.6 Small companies rate (TA 1988 S13, FA 1999 Ss27–29, FA 2000 S36 & FA 2005 S11)

This is the term used to describe the special reduced corporation tax rate which is charged on company profits which do not exceed certain limits for a given accounting period. The rate is 20 per cent from 1 April 2011 and prior rates are shown below. The profits in question comprise those on which corporation tax is paid together with 'franked investment income' (13.17.2) for the period. Small companies rate does not apply to close-investment holding companies for chargeable accounting periods beginning after 31 March 1989 (13.18).

The small companies rate applies to periods after 31 March 1973 and previous rates have been as follows:

	%
8 years to 31 March 1996	25
Year to 31 March 1997	24
2 years to 31 March 1999	21
3 years to 31 March 2002	20
5 years to 31 March 2007	19
Year to 31 March 2008	20
3 years to 31 March 2011	21
From 1 April 2011	20

The small companies rate is to be charged on the profits of a company with no 'associated companies' (see 13.8) provided these do not exceed £300,000. If the profits are between £300,000 and £1,500,000, some marginal relief is given. These figures have been fixed for the year to 31 March 1995 and subsequently.

The tax is then broadly the full corporation tax rate (13.2.1) on the profits less a fixed fraction (currently 3/200) of the amount by which they fall short of £1,500,000 etc. Thus there is now a marginal rate of 27.5 per cent within the £300,000–£1,500,000 profit band. This assumes there are no 'associated companies' (see 13.8). For financial years 2008–2010, the fraction was 7/400.

If a company has 'associated companies', then the above-mentioned figures of £300,000 and £1,500,000 must be divided by one plus the number of 'associated companies' connected with the company under consideration. Thus, if five associated companies comprise a group, they will each pay 20 per cent on their profits for the year to 31 March 2013 if these are no more than £60,000 (£300,000/5) each. If any of the companies has profits between £60,000 and £300,000 (£1,500,000/5), some marginal relief is obtained.

13.7 Starting rate of corporation tax (TA S13AA, FA 1999 Ss28 & 29 & FA 2005 S12)

Beginning with financial year 2000, there was a starting rate of corporation tax which applied where a company's profits did not exceed £10,000 (proportionately less if there are associated companies). The rate for financial years 2000 and 2001 was 10 per cent with 0 per cent applying for 2002, 2003, 2004 and 2005. FA 2006 abolished the starting rate from 1 April 2006.

If the profits were in the £10,000–£50,000 band, marginal relief was available. This was found by calculating tax at the small companies rate and deducting 19/400 of the difference between £50,000 and the profits. (For 2000 and 2001 this fraction was 1/40).

13.7.1 Non-corporate distribution rate (NCDR) (TA 1988 S13AB & Sch A2)

FA 2004 introduced legislation into TA 1988 which in certain cases applied NCDR to at least part of a company's profits where distributions were made after 31 March 2004 to persons other than companies.

NCDR applied at a rate of 19 per cent until it was abolished from 1 April 2006. For NCDR to apply, the underlying rate of corporation tax must have been lower than the NCDR and further details are provided in earlier editions.

13.8 Associated companies (TA 1988 Ss416 & 417)

These are companies which are either under common control or one controls the other. Control broadly comprises voting power or entitlement to the greater part of either the profits, or the assets on liquidation.

In considering whether two companies are under common control, shares held by a husband and wife and their minor children are considered as one. If, however, one company is controlled by an individual and another company is controlled by a more distant relative, such as his brother, the two companies are not normally treated as being 'associated'.

Also 'associated' are the settlor of a trust and its trustees. Furthermore, if you are interested in any shares held by a trust, you are 'associated' with the trustees. Two companies can be associated if both are interested in the same shares.

Prior to 1 April 2008, business partners were considered in assessing conrol for the above purposes. FA 2008 simplified matters, so that this only applies if there are 'relevant tax planning arrangements', which involve the shareholder or director and the partner and secure greater small companies relief.

For the purposes of small companies relief (13.6) HMRC will not normally attribute to you all the rights and powers of your relatives, unless there is 'substantial commercial interdependence' between the companies in question.

13.9 The computation of assessable profits (TA 1988 Ss8–9 & 337–341)

It is strictly speaking necessary to compute the different categories of assessable income and aggregate these to find the total amount chargeable to corporation tax. All corporation tax assessments are made on an 'actual' basis, however, instead of the preceding year basis that sometimes applied for income tax purposes.

The adjustments to the accounts profits that are required for corporation tax purposes follow with some modifications of the normal rules for income tax assessments described earlier in the book. The following are some of the necessary adjustments:

(1) Deduct any franked investment income (13.17.2).
(2) Add back payments made for non-business purposes (11.3.2).
(3) Add back capital losses and payments and deduct capital profits and capital receipts. The capital gain less capital losses of the company must be computed for the accounting period according to the capital gains tax rules (20.1).
(4) Add back legal and other professional charges relating to capital projects.
(5) Add back business entertaining unless in connection with the company's own staff (11.3.2). Gifts of advertising articles such as diaries, pens etc. of less than £50 annual value to each customer are also allowable.
(6) Add back depreciation and amortisation charged in the accounts in respect of fixed assets.
(7) Adjust the interest payable and receivable to the actual gross payments and receipts during the accounting period (if this is different from the amount shown in the accounts).
(8) Deduct capital allowances for the accounting period (see below and 11.8).
(9) Add back any balancing charges and deduct any balancing allowances (11.9.4).
(10) Add income tax at 20 per cent to any building society interest received. This income tax is calculated by multiplying the actual interest received by 20⁄80 (2.7). The tax must then be deducted from the total corporation tax payable.
(11) Add accruals of rent from members of the same group of companies who have already obtained tax relief (15.10.11).

13.9.1 **Withholding tax on interest and royalty payments** (TA Ss349A–D & TMA S98 (4A–C))

Under the old system, tax deduction at source was required where interest or certain royalty payments were made from one company to another. Exceptions included where both companies were in the same group and there was a group income election or interest was paid to a bank.

The following changes took effect from 1 April 2001:

(1) No tax is withheld on international bond interest, nor on most payments of interest or royalties between companies where the recipient is chargeable to corporation tax on that income.
(2) The paying company needs to be satisfied that the recipient is within the charge to corporation tax.
(3) If it later transpires that the recipient is outside the charge to corporation tax, the paying company is liable for the tax and interest.
(4) The administrative burden of deducting tax and accounting for it to HMRC has been relieved.
(5) Payments of interest and royalties from companies to individuals continue to be paid under the deduction of tax.

From 1 October 2002:

(1) Companies do not need to deduct withholding tax from royalties, interest, annuities etc. paid to specified tax-exempt bodies and certain partnerships which include tax-exempt bodies.
(2) UK companies are able to pay royalties without prior Inland Revenue clearance to non-residents whom they reasonably believe will be able to reclaim tax deducted under a double tax treaty. The royalties may be paid gross or less a reduced tax rate in line with the treaty rate.
(3) Yearly interest may be paid gross by a dealer in financial instruments as principal, who is authorised under the Financial Services and Markets Act.

From 1 January 2004, exemption from withholding tax applies for interest and royalties between associated companies in different member states of the European Union. FA 2004 incorporates the relevant EU Directive.

13.9.2 **Management expenses – investment business** (TA 1988 Ss75, 75A & 130)

From 1 April 2004, companies with investment business qualify for relief for their expenses of managing investments, regardless of whether they are investment companies under the legislation, which was a previous condition. Relief is extended to non-resident companies which have a UK permanent establishment. The timing rules are changed so as to bring the relief in line with the accounting treatment.

13.10 Special capital allowances rules for companies

The normal capital allowances rules for businesses etc. (11.8), apply to companies subject to a number of special rules including the following:

(1) An individual in business can claim that his writing down allowances should be at a lower rate than the normal rate of 20 per cent (25 per cent before 1 April 2008). Companies also have this right (CAA S24).
(2) Where there is a 'company reconstruction without change of ownership' as a result of which one company takes over all of the assets and business of another company, the former continues to receive exactly the same capital allowances on the assets transferred as the old company would have got. A reconstruction without change of ownership takes place if at any time during the two years following the reconstruction, no less than 75 per cent of the acquiring company belongs to the same people who owned no less than 75 per cent of the old company. (This is treated for all corporation tax purposes as a continuation of the trade (TA 1988 Ss343–344).)
(3) Special rules now apply where a UK trade is transferred in exchange for shares from one EC company to a company in another EC state. Balancing adjustments are not made, subject to certain conditions (11.9.4).
(4) Under the 'pay and file' system (13.4.1), a formal claim for capital allowances is needed. This is included in the new corporation tax return. You no longer need to disclaim allowances, since you simply claim the required amount.
(5) From 6 April 1995, companies starting further trades may have their capital allowances on plant etc. restricted for the first accounting year (FA 1995 S102).
(6) *First year tax credits* are available on certain expenditure from 1 April 2008 where losses are attributable to 100 per cent first year allowances on designated energy saving or environmentally beneficial plant and machinery. If the loss cannot otherwise be relieved, 19 per cent of it will be paid to the company with a maximum of £250,000 or if greater, its total PAYE and NIC for the loss period.

13.11 Losses (TA 1988 Ss393–396, 768 & 768A–C & Sch 28A)

Company trading losses arising from 2 July 1997 can be carried back against profits for the preceding year. This compares with a previous three year carry back facility. This change also applies to losses on loan arrangements, financial instruments and foreign exchange transactions. However, the carry back period is three years for trading losses in the year before a trade ends (13.14).

As an alternative to the above, a repayment of tax deducted at source from interest received and tax credits on dividends (where applicable) can be obtained. Otherwise the losses will be carried forward and relieved against future profits. (This is subject to possible restriction if the ownership of the company changes, similar to above.) Losses on shares in qualifying trading companies sold by investment companies can be set off against their surplus franked investment income. This follows the general relief against income now available for such losses made by investment companies (20.14).

Anti-avoidance rules may operate to bar relief where there is a change of trade. Furthermore, relief is denied where there is a change of ownership and a major change in the nature or conduct of the trade within a three-year period.

The anti-avoidance provisions relate in modified form to capital losses and formerly ACT (13.17). Investment companies are normally covered where there is a change in the ownership of such a company after 28 November 1994. Excess management charges and charges on income brought forward from before the change will not be allowed against subsequent income and gains if:

(1) During the three years afterwards, the capital (as defined) increases by at least £1m or more than doubles, compared with in the year before, or
(2) There is a major change in the nature or conduct of the business within three years before and three years after the change, or
(3) The business had become small or negligible before the change and subsequently revived.

FA 2007 includes further anti-avoidance provisions regarding losses. Groups of companies are affected where they are buying and selling companies to obtain a tax advantage through accessing their capital losses and gains. Also companies are hindered from profiting from buying tax losses from corporate members of Lloyd's who are ceasing their underwriting activities.

Under the 'pay and file' system, a trading loss in an accounting period ended after 30 September 1993 is normally set off against future profits in the same trade. However, an exception is where claims already have been made to relieve the loss in other ways. The new corporation tax return form includes spaces to keep track of the losses. The company will be able to set aside the carry-forward, so as to use part or all of the losses as group relief.

13.11.1 Temporary extension of loss carry-back period

The extended carry-back (11.22.4) applies to the losses of companies for accounting periods ending between 24 November 2008 and 23 November 2010. For these periods, losses can be carried-back three years instead of one. However, where the original one year period is exceeded, a £50,000 cap applies to the remainder and the set-off can only be against profits from the same trade.

13.12 Reconstructions (TA 1988 Ss343 & 344)

A 'company reconstruction without change of ownership' (13.10(2)) has other advantages apart from capital allowance continuity. In particular where a company takes over the trade and assets of another and they are under at least 75 per cent common ownership, any trading losses are carried over with the trade. However, the unused tax losses may be restricted if the original company is insolvent when its trade is transferred.

13.13 Group loss relief (TA 1988 Ss402–413 & Sch 18 & TCGA Ss170–192A)

In a group of companies (that is, parent and subsidiaries) the trading losses (including capital allowances etc.) of respective group members can be offset by way of group relief against the profits of others provided that:

(1) The necessary claim is made within two years of the end of the accounting period.
(2) The group relationship exists throughout the respective accounting periods of the loss making and profit making companies. Otherwise the relief is only obtained for the period during which the group relationship exists; profits and losses being apportioned on a time basis if necessary.
(3) The parent has at least a 75 per cent interest in each of the subsidiaries. Also the parent company must be entitled to at least both 75 per cent of the distributable profits of each subsidiary and 75 per cent of the assets available on the liquidation of each subsidiary. (FA 2009 excludes certain relevant preference shares). Option arrangements etc. made after 14 November 1991 are to be taken into account in calculating the percentages, as if they had been exercised.
(4) Subject to certain special rules group relief also applies to a consortium where UK companies (and now EEA companies) own between them ordinary shares of a loss making company or of a holding company which owns 90 per cent of a loss making company. It is necessary for 75 per cent or more of the ordinary shares to be owned by the consortium with no less than 5 per cent held by each member (thus the maximum number is 20). Losses for accounting periods made by consortium companies can be surrendered down to a company which is jointly owned.
(5) Where a company joins or leaves a group during its accounting period the time apportionment basis (see above) may be set aside if it operates unfairly. A 'just and reasonable method' is then used. A similar rule applies in consortium situations.
(6) Subject to certain conditions, a loss can be claimed partly as group relief and partly as consortium relief. Also, consortium relief can flow through to other companies in a consortium member's group.
(7) It should be noted that no group relief is available for the losses of dual-resident investment companies (15.10.14).
(8) From 1 April 2000, groups or consortia qualify even where established through overseas companies. Thus the UK subsidiaries can surrender group relief to one another. From the same date, group relief extends to UK branches of non-resident companies.
(9) The scope of the relief was extended to reflect EU law with effect from 1 April 2006. From that date relief extends to UK groups with foreign subsidiaries that have incurred foreign tax losses that cannot be relieved elsewhere, the subsidiaries being EU resident or the losses arising in a permanent establishment there.

13.14 Terminal losses (TA 1988 S394)

These were available to a company in a similar way to an individual who ceases trading (11.24). Thus, a company was entitled to claim to set off a terminal loss incurred in its last 12 months of trading against its profits for the three preceding years.

13.15 Companies' capital gains and capital losses (TCGA Ss8 & 170–192 & Schs 7A & 7AC, TA 1988 Ss345–347, 400 & 435 & Sch 29)

The capital gains of companies are now charged to corporation tax at the normal rates. Thus a gain made by a company with £2m profits bears 26 per cent tax. However, a gain of £20,000 made by a company with £50,000 other taxable profits pays the 20 per cent small companies rate on the gain (13.7).

The previous tapering relief system for individuals etc., was not applied to companies, whose gains continue to be computed by allowing indexation relief up to the time of sale (20.12).

Capital losses in accounting periods may be set off against gains, so that the net gains are taxable. Chargeable gains can be relieved by means of capital losses in the same period or those brought forward from previous periods. Trading losses can be set off against capital profits of the same period or the previous period. Trading losses in accounting periods ending after 31 March 1991 and arising before 3 July 1997 could be set off against gains going back three years (13.11). Capital profits can also be set off by group loss relief claims (13.13). Trading losses brought forward from previous periods, however, can only be set off against future trading profits and not against future chargeable gains.

Capital losses (20.13) incurred by a company can only be set off against any capital gains of the company in the same accounting period or a future accounting period. Unused capital losses can be carried forward to future years even if the company has ceased trading, whereas a cessation prevents trading losses from being carried forward. Companies are prevented from manufacturing capital losses by sales from large holdings (2 per cent upwards) of another company's shares and buying them back within a month if quoted and six months otherwise.

Certain anti-avoidance provisions apply including:

(1) Under TCGA S13 UK resident and domiciled shareholders of an overseas company can have its capital gains apportioned to them if the company would have been close if UK resident. This rule also covers overseas trusts with shares in such companies. The effect is that UK beneficiaries of the trusts can then be taxed, if they receive any benefit (20.32). The apportionment of gains depends on the extent of each UK shareholder's participation in the overseas company.

(2) The exploitation of capital gains tax indexation allowance through inter-group financing is countered. The rules ensure that share exchanges by companies in the same group do not result in capital gains or losses being charged or allowed more than once.
(3) Where a trade owned by one EC company is transferred to another in exchange for shares or securities, various rules apply. Of particular importance is where a UK trade is transferred in this way from a company resident in one EC country to one resident in another. Under these circumstances, the assets are treated as being transferred at values giving no capital gain or loss, provided certain anti-avoidance provisions are not infringed.
(4) Previously, it was possible for a group of companies to buy a company with unused capital losses and then introduce their own assets prior to sale. Any gains on sale would then be offset against the losses. This was stopped for sales after 15 March 1993 regarding losses from a company which joined the group after 31 March 1987. Losses it subsequently realises on assets it held on joining the group after that date are also restricted. Post-11 March 1994 disposals of these assets are included, even if first transferred within the group.
(5) FA 2011 is to contain simplified capital loss rules where a group company changes ownership. Relief will no longer be restricted for capital losses realised before the change.

Subject to certain conditions, including the following, gains on disposals by companies of shares after 31 March 2002 are exempt from tax and losses are not allowable:

(1) During a continuous 12-month period beginning not more than two years before the disposal, broadly at least 10 per cent of the shares must be held.
(2) Subject to the above, disposals of options and convertible securities are also exempt.
(3) The company making the disposal must be a trading company or member of a trading group.
(4) The company whose shares are being sold must be a trading company or the holding company of a trading company or subgroup.

13.16 Groups of companies (TA 1988 Ss402–413, TCGA Ss170–181 & FA 2002 Ss42 & 43)

Various special provisions relate to groups of companies (broadly parent and subsidiaries). A subsidiary company is classified according to the percentage of its ordinary capital owned (directly or indirectly) by its parent. Thus a 51 per cent subsidiary is over 50 per cent owned by its parent; and a 75 per cent subsidiary is not less than 75 per cent so owned. For these purposes, loan financing may play a part in calculating the percentage owned, unless 'normal commercial loans' (TA 1988 Sch 18).

Some of the main rules relating to groups of companies are as follows:

(1) Group loss relief is available in respect of a parent company and its 75 per cent subsidiaries subject to various rules (13.13).

(2) Subject to an election to HMRC, dividend payments from 51 per cent subsidiaries to the parent could be made without having to account for ACT. A similar rule relates to inter-group interest payments. These provisions only apply to companies resident in the UK. Also included are payments from a consortium-owned trading or holding company to the consortium members, where the consortium owns at least 75 per cent of the ordinary shares. Each consortium member must own at least 5 per cent.

    There needs to be a group relationship in an economic sense between the companies. For example, one company needs not only more than 50 per cent of the other but also to be entitled to more than 50 per cent of the distributable profits and of the assets in a winding up.

(3) Transfers of assets within a group consisting of a parent and its 75 per cent subsidiaries do not generally give rise to capital gains tax. Before 1 April 2000, this only applied to UK resident companies, but now the requirement is that the assets remain within the UK tax net. (Certain dual resident companies are excluded.) The parent must be effectively entitled to over 50 per cent of the profits of the subsidiary and of its assets on winding up.) When the asset leaves the group, however, capital gains tax is paid on the entire chargeable gain on the asset whilst it was owned by any group company (TCGA S171). Also, rules restrict schemes to reduce tax on selling subsidiaries (15.10.16).

    Assets are charged when a company leaves the group (TCGA Ss179 & 179A). Also, capital gains tax on an asset can be charged where two companies are degrouped together. For a company leaving a group after 31 March 2002 all or part of its gains or losses arising on that account may be reallocated to other members of that group. Furthermore the degrouping charge can be postponed by applying a modified form of business rollover relief.

(4) Capital gains tax 'rollover relief' (20.25) applies to a UK group consisting of a parent company and its 75 per cent subsidiaries. The gain on an asset sold by one trading company may be 'rolled over' against the purchase of an asset by another trading company (excluding certain dual resident companies) in the group (TCGA S175). (Property holding and non-trading companies which hold assets used for trade by trading companies in the group are also included.) Also, relief applies for disposals under compulsory purchase orders where another group company acquires replacement land.

(5) If a parent company holds more than 50 per cent of the ordinary shares of a subsidiary and is entitled to more than 50 per cent of its distributable

profits and more than 50 per cent of its assets on liquidation, the parent could transfer to its subsidiary relief for ACT. If the subsidiary ceases to be owned by the parent, any unused ACT is lost unless the companies remain in the same overall group.

(6) A special rule applies to interest payments between companies under common control, including a parent and 51 per cent (or more) subsidiaries. To prevent relief for the payer occurring in one year and tax being paid the next, the interest is to be treated as received on the day when paid. This rule applies where the paying company obtains relief for the interest as a charge on income and the recipient is taxed under Case III (8.4).

(7) The 1998 Finance Act introduced various anti-avoidance measures which took effect from 17 March 1998. Where a company with capital gains joins a group from that date, the group losses which it can offset are restricted.

(8) For disposal from April 2000, group companies can elect to bring together gains and losses into a single company without transferring the asset within the group. Any payment of the gain or loss between the group companies concerned is tax neutral (FA 2000 S101).

(9) From 21 March 2012, the group status of a company is not affected where it issues loan notes which carry rights to be converted into shares or securities of unconnected quoted companies.

13.16.1 **Group rules introduced with 'pay and file'** (FA 1989 S102, FA 1998 Sch 18)

With the introduction of 'pay and file' (13.4.1) for accounting periods ended after 30 September 1993, revised rules operate for groups, including the following:

(1) In a group of companies, a refund of tax in one company can be set off against liabilities in other companies by election. The object is to avoid companies being penalised by the differential between interest payable and receivable under the new system.
(2) Improved and more flexible procedures operate concerning group relief claims (which must be included in the claimant company's tax return).
(3) Claims may be made and be capable of being withdrawn within two years of the end of the accounting period. If later, this is to be extended to the date that the profits and losses for the period are determined, but no more than six years from the end of the period.
(4) Trading losses which have been relieved against the profits of a later period will be allowed to be reallocated and surrendered as group relief.
(5) There are rules concerning reductions in group relief surrenders for accounting periods ending after 30 June 1999. If unpaid, the resultant extra tax can be recovered from group companies to the extent that they benefited from the surrender.

13.17 ACT on dividends, distributions etc. (TA 1988 Ss14, 209, 238 & 239, FA 1998 Ss31–32, Sch 3 & FA 1999 S91)

Companies had to pay 'advance corporation tax' (ACT) at $^{20}/_{80}$ on their payments of dividends (13.3). This tax was also payable on other 'qualifying distributions'. ACT was abolished for dividends and other qualifying distributions made after 5 April 1999. For further details, please see previous editions of this book.

13.17.1 Distributions

There are two different classes of distribution known as qualifying and non-qualifying distributions. Qualifying distributions are dividends and similar payments. Other examples are interest on certain securities and equity notes. Non-qualifying distributions are those which are really distributions of special sorts of shares etc. which carry a potential future claim on the company's profits: for example bonus debentures or bonus redeemable shares. Whereas qualifying distributions were subjected to ACT, in the case of non-qualifying distributions no ACT was payable by the company.

13.17.2 Franked investment income (TA 1988 S238)

This consists of income from a UK resident company (17.3.3) being distributions in respect of which tax credits are obtained. A company's franked investment income is the amount including the relevant tax credits. Thus if a company receives a dividend of £900, this is treated as being franked investment income of £1,000 (that is, £900 + £900 × $^{1}/_{9}$).

13.17.3 Setting off ACT against 'mainstream' corporation tax (TA 1988 Ss238–246)

As its name suggests, advance corporation tax was a pre-payment of the main or mainstream corporation tax bill of a company. The latter was only ascertained when accounts were submitted to the Revenue after the end of the accounting period and the ACT was offset.

13.17.4 Carry-back and carry-forward of ACT (TA 1988 Ss239 & 245 & FA 1998 S32)

Any ACT which was not relieved against corporation tax payable for the accounting period in which the relevant distribution was made, because of the restriction mentioned above, was known as 'surplus ACT'. This surplus ACT could be carried back and offset against corporation tax payable for any accounting periods beginning in the six years preceding that in which the relevant distribution was made.

Any surplus ACT which was not carried back as above may normally be carried forward without time limit to be set off against future corporation tax payable. Relief was restricted if within three years there was both a change in the ownership of the company and a major change in the nature or conduct of its trade (or this becomes negligible). ACT relating to an accounting period before the change in ownership cannot be carried forward to a period after that change. Furthermore, ACT arising after such a change cannot be carried back before the change, where this occurs after 15 March 1993.

Following the abolition of ACT for qualifying distributions made after 5 April 1999 (13.17), the benefits of surplus ACT carried forward are preserved by '*shadow ACT*'. As a result, subject to a limit of 20 per cent of its corporation tax profits, a company can obtain relief for surplus ACT from previous years, allowing for notional ACT on dividend payments.

13.18 Close companies (TA 1988 Ss414–430 & Sch 19 & FA 1989 Ss103–107 & Sch 12)

Special provisions relate to 'close' companies, more particularly for periods beginning before 1 April 1989, and are described in greater depth in previous editions of this book. Close companies are broadly those under the control of five or fewer persons and their 'associates'. The latter term includes close family such as husband, wife, child, father, mother, brother, sister etc. A quoted company is not 'close', however, if not less than 35 per cent of its voting shares are owned by the general public.

There is also an alternative test by reference to whether five or fewer persons and their 'associates' would receive broadly the greater part of the company's assets on liquidation which would be available for distribution.

A UK subsidiary of an overseas parent company is 'close' if the latter would have itself been 'close' if resident here. It is thus seen that most small or medium companies are likely to be 'close' companies unless they are subsidiaries of non-close companies. The majority of 'family' companies are 'close'.

13.18.1 Apportionment of income under the imputation system (TA 1988 Ss423–430 & Sch 19 & FA 1989 S103 & Sch 12)

For periods beginning *before 1 April 1989*, the Revenue could apportion among the shareholders the excess of the 'relevant income' of a close company over its distributions.

13.18.2 Loans and distributions for close companies (CTA 2010 Ss455–465)

A special provision regarding close companies which remains operative is that if they make loans to their 'participators' (see below) or associates of the latter, the companies are charged tax at 25 per cent on the amounts. (If the loan is repaid to the company, the tax will be repaid.) Thus if a loan of £8,000 is made to a participator the company will be assessed to tax of 25 per cent × £8,000 = £2,000. Loans by companies controlled by or subsequently acquired by close companies are also covered by this rule.

Under rules which apply for loans made in accounting periods ending on or after 31 March 1996, the tax is due nine months after the end of the accounting period.

If the loan is repaid before the tax is due, it is not necessary to pay the tax. Previously, the due date was only 14 days after the end of the accounting period in which the loan was made and the Revenue could assess loans even if repaid.

Should a close company lend money to a participator or his associate and then release the debt, higher rate tax is assessed on the recipient if applicable in respect of the grossed up equivalent of the loan. Thus in the above example, if the company releases the participator from his debt he could pay higher rate tax on £10,000 (£8,000 + £2,000). A deduction of £2,000 will be made, however, from the total tax payable.

The meaning of the term 'distribution' (dividend etc.) is extended in the case of close companies to include living expenses and accommodation etc. provided for a 'participator' (or his associate). A 'participator' means broadly a person having a share or interest in the capital or income of a company, including, for example, a shareholder or loan creditor. The effect of treating a payment as a distribution is that it is not deductible from the taxable profit of the company.

13.19 Close investment holding companies (CICs) (TA S13A)

(1) Provisions having effect for accounting periods beginning after 31 March 1989 imposed harsher taxation on certain close investment holding companies (CICs).

(2) A CIC is a close company which is neither a 'trading company' nor a member of a trading group, nor a property investment company (which lets to non-connected persons).

(3) Broadly, a trading company is one which exists wholly or mainly for the purpose of trading on a commercial basis.

(4) Dealing in property or shares does not cause a company to be a CIC. Similarly, mixed property dealing and investment companies are not CICs.

(5) CICs are now subject to 24 per cent corporation tax regardless of their level of profits. They do not obtain the benefit of the 20 per cent small companies rate or the start up rate.

(6) If a shareholder waives, or does not receive a dividend, the extent to which someone else is entitled to be repaid a tax credit may be restricted. HMRC may request information and make 'just and reasonable' restrictions. This does not apply where, for example, there is only one class of shares.

(7) Where a CIC takes out a life assurance policy after 13 March 1989, profits subsequently realised will be taxed, subject to the rules.

13.20 Non-resident companies trading in the UK (CTA 2009 Ss5–15 etc.)

Where a non-resident company (17.3.3) carries on a trade in this country through a branch or agency here, corporation tax is charged in respect of the profits of the branch or agency. If those profits are also subject to tax in the country of residence of the company, double tax relief may be available (18.6). (Special rules apply where companies become non-resident (17.3.3).)

Regarding accounting periods of non-resident companies which begin after 31 December 2002, the rules for applying UK corporation tax on income and chargeable gains substitute 'permanent establishment' for 'branch or agency' (in this country). Subject to certain provisions and any relevant double tax treaty, a company has a permanent establishment in a territory if it has a fixed place of business there through which the business of the company is wholly or partly carried on; or an agent acting there on behalf of the company has and habitually exercises authority to do business on behalf of the company.

For accounting periods starting after 31 December 2002, UK branches of overseas companies are subjected to rules which restrict the debt and effectively the interest deduction claimable for tax purposes.

13.21 UK companies with overseas income

Any overseas income of a company that is resident in this country is subject to corporation tax on the gross amount of such income. Double tax relief is frequently available in respect of overseas income that is taxed both in the UK and abroad.

If a UK company receives a dividend from an overseas company from which withholding tax has been deducted, the gross dividend is included in the taxable profits subject to corporation tax. Normally, double tax relief for the withholding tax suffered is given against the corporation tax payable. (Withholding tax is tax that is 'withheld' from the dividend when the latter is paid. It is thus a form of tax deducted at source.) In addition, if at least 10 per cent of the voting capital of the overseas company is owned by the UK company, relief is given for the 'underlying tax' (that is, the proportion of the total tax paid by the foreign company attributable to its dividends). Also in these circumstances, in certain cases no basic rate tax is to be charged on the paying and collecting agents (F2A 1992 S30). In no case, however, can the double tax relief rate exceed 45 per cent (18.6).

FA 2005 introduced further restrictions, limiting foreign tax credit to the UK tax on so much of the trade profit as is derived from the income suffering foreign tax. There are also new anti-avoidance rules.

FA 2009 provides that:

(1) From 1 July 2009 the rules governing the tax treatment of foreign and UK dividends and other distributions are changed. In general, a UK company will be exempt from corporation tax on them.
(2) From 1 January 2010 there is a restriction of the charge for interest and other finance expense which may affect a group other than one consist-

ing only of small and/or medium-sized companies. There will be a cap of the consolidated gross finance expense of the group.

(3) The Treasury consent rules are repealed (ICTA Ss 765–767) and replaced by a post-transaction information reporting requirement for companies undertaking certain transactions involving foreign investments.

13.21.1 Foreign branches

For accounting periods beginning from the date of Royal Assent to FA 2011, subject to the rules, UK resident companies can irrevocably elect for all their foreign branches to be exempt from UK corporation tax. However, no relief will normally be available for foreign branch losses.

13.22 Controlled foreign companies (CFCs) (TA 1988 Ss747–756 & Schs 24–26 & FA 2002 Ss89 & 90)

HMRC are able to impose extra tax on UK companies with interests in CFCs, subject to certain rules, including the following:

(1) The overseas company must be under overall UK control. This is now satisfied if two companies etc. control it and only one is UK resident, each having at least 40 per cent.

(2) The overseas company must be subject to tax in its country of residence which is less than 75 per cent of that payable if it were UK resident.

(3) A UK company (together with associates etc.) has at least a 10 per cent interest in the overseas company.

(4) Acceptable dividend payments which are made by a company not resident at the time of payment, will exclude the charge. The requirement for trading companies is 90 per cent of the profits, calculated as for UK tax purposes. For investment companies this figure has always been 90 per cent but capital profits and foreign tax are deducted from the profits. Also, investment companies are now able to make distributions for such periods out of profits of earlier periods not yet taxed under the CFC rules.

(5) The charge is excluded if the CFC satisfies an 'exempt activities' test. For this, the company must have a business establishment where it is resident and be managed there. Also it must broadly be a trading or qualifying holding company rather than an investment company.

(6) Exclusion is also available through a motive test. The foreign company's transactions must be carried out for commercial reasons and not for the main purpose of saving UK tax or diverting profits from the UK.

(7) Certain foreign companies quoted on foreign stock exchanges are also excluded.

(8) There is no charge if the foreign company's profits for the year are less than £50,000 (but see (20)).

(9) A list has been published of excluded countries which will not be regarded as low tax countries for the purposes of the above rules. In general, the list excludes tax havens and normally applies where at least 90 per cent is 'local source' income.

(10) Where applicable, the profits of the overseas company are apportioned to any UK companies with at least a 10 per cent interest and corporation tax is charged at the appropriate rate for each. A deduction is then made for any 'creditable tax' (overseas tax etc.) which is similarly apportioned. Appropriate relief is then given where dividends are paid by the overseas company.
(11) Various anti-avoidance provisions have been introduced (15.10). For example, CFCs can include dual resident companies.
(12) Where profits need to be calculated for the CFC rules, they are expressed in the currency used in the company's accounts.
(13) CFC charges are brought into the corporation tax self-assessment system.
(14) Dividends paid by a CFC to the UK do not count towards the acceptable level (90 per cent etc.) if they are paid out of UK dividends (or other distributions) not counting towards its chargeable profits.
(15) Further anti-avoidance provisions cover holding companies, intra-group service companies, control (see (1) above) 'designer' tax rates and artificial schemes to exploit the acceptable dividend policy rules.
(16) The Treasury have reserve powers to specify countries for which the CFC exemptions will not apply. Also, UK resident companies from 1 April 2002 can be caught by the CFC rules, even if treated as non-resident under a double tax agreement. From 22 March 2006 this extends to certain companies becoming non-resident in this way before 1 April 2002.
(17) FA 2003 introduced further modifications. Eligible companies in Hong Kong and Macao continue to claim CFC exemption through the 'exempt activities test'. Also, a loophole was closed which had been exploited by companies carrying on warranty or credit protection business.
(18) FA 2005 (Ss89 & 90) restricts relief involving certain related companies and regarding CFCs for which exemption is available under the acceptable distribution policy test.
(19) FA 2008 blocks various artificial avoidance schemes which use partnerships or trusts to avoid a CFC charge by misusing a CFC exemption or arranging for the profits to be earned allegedly outside the rules.
(20) FA 2011 includes some interim improvements before full reform in 2012. A particular item is an alternative to the current lower limit ((8) above) of £200,000.
(21) For accounting periods beginning after 31 December 2012, a new CFC scheme operates. It will better reflect the way that businesses operate in a global economy and general commercial business will be excused as well as incidental finance income.

13.23 Demergers (TA 1988 Ss213–218)

Special rules assist two or more trading businesses in 'demerging' where they are carried on by a single company or a group. In demergers, subject to the detailed provisions:

(1) Where a company distributes shares in a 75 per cent subsidiary (13.17.1) to its shareholders this is not treated as a distribution.

(2) Relief also applies where one company transfers a trade to a second company which in turn distributes its shares to the shareholders of the first.
(3) Capital gains tax relief applies to any distribution which you receive in the above circumstances until you sell the actual shares.
(4) There was also certain relief from development land tax and stamp duty in demergers.
(5) The provisions only apply to the genuine splitting off of trades or trading subsidiaries. There are anti-avoidance provisions to counter, for example the extraction of tax-free cash from companies subject to an advance clearance procedure.

13.24 Unquoted company purchasing its own shares (TA 1988 Ss219–229 & FA 1997 S69 & Sch 7)

The 1985 Companies Act enables companies to purchase their own shares and issue redeemable equity shares. With effect from 8 October 1996, these distributions were treated as foreign income dividends. As a result, recipients were not able to obtain any repayment of tax credit.

With the abolition of both FIDs and ACT from 6 April 1999, the system broadly altered.

Under the rules, in certain circumstances the shareholder's liability is restricted to capital gains tax (unless he is a share dealer, in which case the gain is treated as his income). Stamp duty relief applied up to 27 October 1986, but not subsequently. Broadly, the conditions for relief are as follows:

(1) The company must not be quoted nor be the subsidiary of a quoted company. (Shares dealt with on the Unlisted Securities Market are not treated as quoted.)
(2) The company must be a trading company or the holding company of a trading group.
(3) The purchase or redemption of the shares must be mainly to benefit a trade of the company or its 75 per cent subsidiary.
(4) The shareholder must be UK resident and ordinarily resident, having normally owned the shares for at least five years (three years in specified cases such as inherited shares, where ownership by the deceased is also counted).
(5) If the shareholder keeps part of his shareholding in the company (or its group) his shareholding must be substantially reduced. Broadly, this means reducing his interest by at least 25 per cent and not being 'connected' (that is, holding with 'associates' 30 per cent of the shares etc.).
(6) If the payment is used for inheritance tax within two years after a death, (4) and (5) above do not apply and relief is due, provided that to pay the tax out of other funds would have caused undue hardship.
(7) Advance clearance application may be made to HMRC.
(8) As indicated, the above rules do not apply where a company buys back its shares from a dealer, who is taxed under Schedule D Case I or II (11.4), receiving no tax credit.

Regulations allow listed companies which purchase their own shares to hold them and either sell them back into the market or cancel them. Such 'Treasury Shares' are treated for tax purposes as cancelled when bought and newly issued when sold. When a venture capital trust (8.13) issues shares from 'Treasury', no income tax relief is due to individual investors.

13.25 Foreign exchange gains and losses (FA 1993 Ss92–96, 125–170 & Schs 15–18 & FA 2009 Sch 21)

A special tax system for company foreign exchange transactions applies to companies for their first accounting periods starting after 22 March 1995 and is now substantially revised (10). This replaces the previous system which lacked certainty. Particular features in the new scheme include the following:

(1) Exchange gains and losses on monetary assets (cash bank deposits and debts etc.) and liabilities are taxed or relieved as income as they accrue.
(2) Capital gains tax is no longer to be charged on any monetary assets in foreign currency.
(3) Exchange differences on monetary items are recognised as they accrue.
(4) Where certain conditions are met, the calculation of trading profits before capital allowances, in currencies other than sterling, is permitted and sometimes required (11).
(5) Unrealised exchange gains above certain limits may be deferred, where they arise on long-term capital items.
(6) Where a borrowing matches a monetary asset, exchange differences may be deferred until the asset is disposed of.
(7) For the purposes of the rules, the ECU is to be regarded as a foreign currency.
(8) Transfers of assets by way of security are ignored and the company continues to be regarded as holding them.
(9) Exchange differences on debts must be computed from when the obligation to pay arises rather than when payment is due (if later).
(10) Certain important changes generally apply for accounting periods beginning on or after 1 January 2000 and ending from 21 March 2000.
(11) When calculating their taxable profits, companies are to use the currency of their accounts (or branch financial statements), provided that this accords with normal accounting practice. This is also to apply to exchange gains and losses.
(12) New rules have effect for accounting periods beginning after 30 September 2002, except for certain anti-avoidance provisions. The above foreign exchange legislation is generally repealed and incorporated in the loan relationships provisions (13.27).

13.25.1 Foreign denominated losses

Where a company incurs a tax loss computed in a non-sterling currency, it has been converted into sterling at the exchange rate for the period in which it arose. However, under FA 2009, where such losses are carried forwards or backwards for offsetting against profits of different accounting periods, the losses will be converted at the same rates as the relevant profits. These new rules apply to accounting periods commencing after 28 December 2007 (subject to a deferral election).

13.26 Interest rate and currency contracts and options (FA 1994 Ss147–177 & Sch 18)

The tax treatment of financial instruments to manage interest rates and currency risks for companies was reformed. The rules apply for accounting periods beginning on or after 23 March 1995. Profits and losses on 'qualifying contracts' are normally to be taxed or relieved on an income basis when they accrue. These broadly include currency or interest rate contracts or options acquired under the new rules.

13.27 Loan relationships (FA 1996 Ss80–105 & Schs 8–15)

Detailed rules apply for companies with effect from 1 April 1996, regarding 'loan relationships'. These apply to debts which are loans under general law and whether owed to or by the company. In general, the rules treat all profits and losses on loans made by companies as income, interest payments being taxed or relieved as they accrue rather than as they are paid. Assets covered are taken out of the capital gains tax regime. Certain revised transitional rules apply from 14 November 1996. However, where a trade debt is released between connected companies after 21 April 2009, the debtor company is no longer chargeable on the resultant profit.

The rules apply to corporate bonds, Permanent Interest Bearing Shares and other corporate debt. Gilts held by companies are also covered, apart from profits and losses on 3.5% Funding Stock 1999/2004 and 5.5% Treasury Stock 2008/12.

The Finance Act 2002 introduced new and wider rules for derivative contracts, replacing the old financial instrument rules. As a result, favourable tax treatment is restricted for convertible, exchangeable and asset-linked securities. The loan relationship rules are revised, as are those for connected party bad debts.

For accounting periods beginning after 30 September 2002, the provision preventing exchange gains and losses being taken into account under the loan relationships legislation was removed. At the same time detailed new rules regarding foreign exchange were assimilated into that legislation (FA 2002 Sch 24).

Further changes were introduced by FA 2004, including some relating to certain venture capital limited partnerships, companies with insolvency proceedings and those which emigrate. Certain assets which contain a derivative element are now divided so that such part is subject to capital gains rules and the loan relationship balance taxed according to the loan rules. Exchange gains and losses on certain loans can now be matched, even though not taken to reserve.

Various changes have been brought into effect by FA 2010, so that a close company is not entitled to a deduction for the writing off or release of a loan to its participator. Also, the loan relationship rules applying to impaired debts between connected companies are tightened up, as are those relating to certain manufactured sale and repurchase transactions.

13.28 Corporate venturing scheme (CVS) (FA 2000 S63 & Schs 15 & 16)

A tax incentive scheme operates broadly from 1 April 2000 to encourage companies to invest in small higher risk trading companies and to form wider corporate venturing links.

(1) The focus is on the same types of company as for the EIS (11.26) and VCT (8.13) schemes. For example, the same gross asset limit applies of £7m before investment and £8m afterwards (£15m and £16m before 6 April 2006).
(2) Investment relief, being a 20 per cent reduction in corporation tax, is given on the cost of new CVS ordinary shares held for three years or more.
(3) Gains on sales of CVS shares can be deferred if invested in other CVS shares.
(4) Relief for allowable capital losses net of investment relief can be claimed against gains or income (if gains are insufficient).
(5) A CVS company cannot be controlled by any corporate venturer.
(6) At least 20 per cent of its ordinary shares must be owned by individuals and not more than 30 per cent by a corporate venturer.
(7) CVS relief applies to shares issued from 1 April 2000 to 31 March 2010 provided that at issue, they are unquoted and there are no arrangements to be listed.
(8) Previously, all money raised needed to be used within 12 months but from 7 March 2001, only 80 per cent must be so used with the balance used in the next 12 months. From 22 April 2009 new rules require full use within 24 months, or if later 24 months after the start of the qualifying activity.
(9) From 17 March 2004, the rules were relaxed regarding subsidiaries. Companies qualify under the scheme even if they have 51 per cent subsidiaries or 90 per cent subsidiaries which are property management companies or benefit from the CVS money raised.
(10) FA 2007 introduces a new requirement that a company raising money under a CVS scheme must have less than 50 full-time employees (or their equivalent). Also, the total raised in any 12 months must not exceed £2m.
(11) For shares issued after 5 April 2008, shipbuilding and coal and steel production are excluded activities.

13.29 Intangible fixed assets (FA 2002 S84 & Schs 29 & 30)

A corporation tax regime covers intangible fixed assets, such as intellectual property and goodwill acquired or created from 1 April 2002 (including their preservation and maintenance). The provisions allow tax relief to be obtained normally at the rate at which the assets are depreciated in the same accounts, subject to a minimum annual amount of 4 per cent. Such assets will cease to be within the capital gains rules. However, gains on disposals from 1 April 2002 of assets created or acquired before that date may on election be rolled-over into new qualifying assets acquired before that date and within a year of the disposal.

Goodwill is excluded from the regime if a business commenced before 1 April 2002 unless or until that business is acquired by an unrelated party. Internally generated assets such as goodwill fall within the regime.

Anti-avoidance rules aimed at inter-group transfers operate after 20 June 2003 (FA 2003 S184). FA 2006 includes legislation against avoidance schemes, regarding existing assets which it had not been intended to relieve.

13.29.1 Patent Boxes

FA 2012 allows companies to elect for a 10 per cent corporation tax rate to apply on a proportion of profits attributable to patent and certain other intellectual property. In the first year, from 1 April 2013, the proportion will be 60 per cent, increasing annually to 100 per cent from April 2017.

13.30 International Accounting Standards (IAS)

For periods beginning after 31 December 2004, companies adopting IAS to draw up their accounts can use these for tax purposes, which was not previously the case. However, companies in the same group are barred from obtaining a tax advantage through treating the same transaction as being under IAS rules in one group company and UK practice in another.

Among detailed changes made to the legislation is the introduction of relief for companies which add R&D expenditure (11.17) to the cost of intangible assets in accordance with IAS. FA 2005 contains various technical amendments, generally effective from 1 January 2005. Also, securitisation companies are able to be taxed on the old basis regarding periods of account ending before 1 January 2008 and now extended by FA2007. (Such companies are special purpose vehicles normally involved in issuing securities to the market.)

FA 2006 provides spreading relief over three to six years for certain taxable adjustments arising in the first period of account ending after 21 June 2005.

Chapter 14

PENSIONS

14.1 Introduction

As we live longer, but are left with greater responsibility for our welfare in later life, it becomes more and more important to make the most of the opportunities presented to us by pension tax reliefs.

This chapter is mainly concerned with the tax aspects of pension arrangements as they will affect you. This means that the primary focus of the chapter is the framework of tax reliefs relating to registered pension schemes. However, to provide some context, there is also a summary of the state scheme (14.2) and of private schemes that are not registered for tax purposes (14.3).

The main tax benefits of registered personal pension and occupational pension schemes are:

- Full tax relief at highest marginal rates on member contributions within specified allowances.
- Contributions paid by an employer are not generally taxed as a benefit within specified allowances. Employer contributions are usually allowable as a deductible business expense.
- The pension fund is free of UK tax on investment income, savings income and capital gains (although it is not possible to reclaim tax credits on dividends).
- Retirement benefits may include a substantial lump sum which is currently tax-free.
- A substantial tax-free lump sum is also payable in the event of death before taking the retirement benefits.
- The retirement pension (and any dependant's pension) is taxed as non-savings income, but is not subject to a National Insurance liability.

Contributions are now able to be paid on someone else's behalf, including on behalf of a minor child.

A pension scheme member may also be provided with substantial life assurance cover. Its cost will be met by the employer and will be relievable against tax.

14.2 The state scheme

The state pension scheme provides a basic pension subject to the claimant having an adequate National Insurance contribution record. Employees may also qualify for a graduated pension on contributions from April 1961 to April 1975, the state earnings related pension scheme (SERPS) on contributions between April 1978 and April 2002 and the state second pension (S2P) on contributions from April 2002. The pension credit is designed to ensure that all pensioners and pensioner couples receive a minimum level of income. The basic state pension will increase each year from 2011–12 by the greater of the increase in the index of national average earnings, the increase in the Consumer Prices Index (CPI) and 2.5 per cent, although the 2011 uprating was also underpinned by the rise in the Retail Prices Index (RPI).

The additional earnings-related pension will increase in line with the CPI from 2012. Both elements of the state pension had previously increased in line with the RPI subject to a minimum 2.5 per cent in respect of the basic state pension.

The pension credit increases by the amount of the cash increase awarded to the basic state pension. The pension credit resembles income support in that it is means-tested rather than contributory and comprises a guaranteed credit (in effect the amount needed to ensure a minimum income from all sources and available from age 60) and a savings credit. The savings credit allows a higher level of benefit where income before the credit exceeds the savings credit threshold. However, it will be reduced (by 40 pence in the pound) where income exceeds the 'appropriate minimum guarantee'. The savings credit is available from age 65.

The basic pension is shown later (25.3.1). To obtain the maximum, you need to have paid or to have been credited with National Insurance contributions for 30 years. For those who retired before 6 April 2010, the full pension was only available if you had a contribution record of 90 per cent of a working life (16–60 for a woman; 16–65 for a man).

Your entitlement to the additional (earnings-related) pension is determined by your record of Class 1 National Insurance contributions. Class 1 National Insurance contributions are payable by employees on a band of their earnings.

From 6 April 2002, employees and some disabled people and carers qualify for the S2P. It is earnings related, but will eventually move to a flat rate. Indeed, from 6 April 2012, the contributor becomes entitled to a 'flat rate accrual amount' (FRAA) in respect of earnings to the lower earnings threshold (£14,700 in 2012–13). The FRAA will increase each year with earnings and has been set at £88.40 a week in 2012–13. The next band of earnings qualifies the contributor for a pension of 10 per cent of earnings between the lower earnings threshold and the upper accrual point (UAP). The UAP was introduced with effect from 2009–10 (based on the 2006–07 upper earnings limit) and will not increase. It is set at £770 a week. When the lower earnings threshold increases to the level of UAP in about 2030, S2P will have moved to a flat rate. The Government is looking at ways to accelerate this process or indeed replace all components of the state pension, including the pension credit, with a flat rate (as announced in the 2011 Autumn Statement which gave an implementation date of some time in the next Parliament). It has since confirmed that, having introduced the FRAA in 2012–13, the flat rate 'universal pension' will be implemented in 2015 or 2016. The details of implementation are unclear, but it is assumed that the facility to contract out will be withdrawn.

Your basic state pension is paid gross, but is included in your income in your tax computation and will generally reduce your personal allowances in any PAYE coding you receive. Between April 2010 and April 2018, the state pension age for women will increase to 65: a woman's pension age will depend on when she was born. From April 2018 to April 2020, the equalised state pension age will increase in stages to 66. In the 2011 Autumn Statement, the Chancellor announced that the state pension age would further increase to 67 between April 2026 and April 2028. The state pension age is due to increase to 68 by 2046, but the Government is examining ways of accelerating this and possibly linking state pension age to evidence of improved mortality.

14.2.1 Contracting out of the state second pension (S2P)

Contracting out enables some of your National Insurance contributions to be redirected to an occupational pension scheme so that it can provide an alternative to the S2P.

Whilst some occupational schemes (defined benefit schemes) once had to undertake to provide a pension at least equal to an approximate SERPS pension (the 'guaranteed minimum pension'), the only test now is that the pension displays certain features of a reference scheme. A personal pension scheme or money purchase occupational scheme was required to offer 'protected rights' in respect of the National Insurance rebates, but the option to contract out under a personal pension scheme or money purchase occupational scheme was abolished on 6 April 2012. The protected rights fund could have provided benefits from the same age as other benefits and could provide a lump sum of up to 25 per cent of the fund. The protected rights fund was required to make provision for widows'/widowers' pensions where appropriate and to convert to a pension using unisex annuity rates.

If you are a member of a contracted-out occupational scheme, your National Insurance contribution will be reduced by the rebate. Your employer's National Insurance contribution is also reduced. If you contracted out by way of a personal pension scheme, you and your employer continued to pay the full rate of National Insurance and the 'rebate' (supplemented by a small amount of tax relief) was forwarded directly to your scheme after the tax year to which it related.

Defined benefit occupational schemes must provide benefits that exhibit the features of a 'reference scheme'. Those features include limited inflation proofing of pensions, rules on calculating the minimum accrual rate and, where appropriate, widows'/widowers' pensions.

Contracting out by way of a money purchase or personal pension scheme was abolished from 6 April 2012 and the special rules and features of protected rights were withdrawn. Defined benefit schemes have been given the option of withdrawing contracted-out rights on the basis that members will be no worse off: few have taken the opportunity.

The consequence of withdrawing the facility to contract out on a money purchase basis is that the facility is withdrawn as if it had never existed. This means that:

- There is no distinction in the funds held by a personal pension plan or contracted-out money purchase scheme whether the funds accrued before or after 6 April 2012 and whether or not they were contracted out.

► There are no NI rebates.

There are some minor safeguards for those transferring from defined benefit to money purchase schemes.

If the benefit is in payment by way of an annuity, the annuity will have had to meet certain requirements but annuities cannot be rewritten once established so they will retain the features although not because they are contracted out.

14.3 Registered pension schemes (FA 2004 Part 4 & Schs 28–36, FA 2005 Sch 10 & Welfare Reform and Pensions Act 1999 S3)

14.3.1 Introduction

In order to qualify for the range of tax reliefs described above (14.1), a pension scheme must be registered. A tax-approved scheme that was in existence on 6 April 2006 ('A day') was automatically registered unless the scheme requested that it should not be. All new schemes apply for registration and the same tax regime applies to both occupational and personal pensions schemes.

There remain differences in design between one scheme and another and distinctions are made for other legislative purposes. For example, there is a different framework of governance for personal pension schemes established by a scheme manager from occupational pension schemes established by employer trust. There are further features that are unique to Stakeholder pension schemes which were primarily introduced to provide a low-cost option.

From 8 October 2001, it is compulsory for many employers to provide *access* to a Stakeholder pension scheme for most employees unless they offer a suitable alternative. This can be an occupational scheme or a grouped personal pension scheme. This requirement is being removed with the introduction of the National Employee Savings Trust (NEST) in July 2012.

Your employer may operate an occupational pension scheme. However, you cannot be compelled to join or remain in the scheme. You could, for instance, opt out in favour of a personal pension scheme although you would generally be unwise to do so.

If an occupational pension scheme is non-contributory, employees will not be required to make contributions. Otherwise it will be known as a contributory scheme.

Should an employer offer a group personal pension scheme instead of access to a Stakeholder scheme, the employer must make a minimum contribution of 3 per cent of pay and match member contributions to 5 per cent.

14.3.2 Scheme registration (FA 2004 Part 4 Chap 2)

The special tax reliefs are made available to pension schemes that are registered. There is a statutory basis of registration which supersedes the previous system of approvals. This is significant in itself because it removes most of the discretion previously exercised by HMRC.

Registration is available online and is instantaneous providing that the form is correctly completed. A scheme can subsequently be de-registered if there are substantial breaches of the statutory requirements such as large unauthorised payments, failure to account for significant tax, false declarations or a serious failure to meet the HMRC reporting requirements.

Schemes that were 'approved' on the introduction of the new regime are automatically 'registered' under the new regime unless they have chosen to 'opt out' of registration.

Occupational pension schemes may be established for employees (including directors), employees of other businesses linked by a common interest (such as being in the same industry or the same geographical area) or even self-employed individuals who have perhaps undertaken long-term work for the employer.

Each occupational scheme must be registered in order to enjoy tax privileges. However, each personal pension provider will usually offer one scheme (which they will register). Individuals are invited to become members of the personal pension scheme and are allocated arrangements as evidenced by a policy. So, if you invest in a personal pension plan you can assume that registration has been taken care of.

14.3.3 **The tax framework: an overview** (FA 2004 Parts 4 & 9 & Schs 28–36)

The structure of reliefs and charges has changed to such a degree that an overview becomes necessary. Remember that these rules replace their predecessors for new and existing schemes.

The key features of the current tax regime (introduced in April 2006 and amended regularly since) are:

(1) There is one set of tax rules. A consequence is that contributions to one scheme do not preclude contributions to another.
(2) There is one simple set of input personal allowances. These are not limits and may be exceeded. However tax reliefs are withdrawn in respect of that part of any contribution that exceeds an allowance.
(3) There is one output allowance based on a capital value (lifetime allowance) of pension rights when they are 'crystallised'. If the lifetime allowance is exceeded, there will be an additional tax charge on the 'excess' designed to recover tax reliefs previously allowed. However, again, output rules are based on an allowance not a limit.
(4) Pension funds are exempt from UK tax on investment income, savings income and capital gains (although the dividend tax credit remains irrecoverable). However, income from trading is taxable as are capital gains and income derived from shares in property limited liability partnerships owned by the fund.
(5) There is a set of taxes in respect of 'unauthorised payments'. Instead of a list of banned transactions and investments, a system of tax charges

applies to a range of activities. So, for example, it is theoretically possible to assign a pension, but the tax consequences make it unattractive. Similarly, investment in residential property is not banned, but is heavily penalised by application of tax.

(6) One of the consequences of the authorised payments regime is that there is no 'blanket ban' on transactions with members and their connections. HMRC will simply require that transactions between the scheme and the member are at a commercial value. If there is an undue benefit to the member there will be a tax charge.

(7) The legislation is very specific about what constitutes an authorised payment. This means that there is little discretion and payments that fall outside the legislation will be unauthorised.

(8) There are transitional protections that provide a 'measure of protection' to those individuals who had acquired pension rights before 6 April 2006. These are not necessarily individuals with large funds.

14.4 Input allowances (FA 2004 Ss188–195, 196–202, 227–238 & Sch 33)

The two main ways in which money can be invested in a pension scheme are by way of contributions, or a transfer from another registered scheme or qualifying recognised overseas pension scheme (QROPS).

This section describes the tax rules as they apply to contributions.

14.4.1 Member contributions

Member contributions (which include contributions paid on your behalf) are subject to an annual limit. This is not a limit on contributions, but a limit on tax relief. Tax relief is allowed to a relevant member who makes contributions to a registered scheme. A relevant member is one who is below the age of 75 and is one of the following:

(a) an individual with relevant UK earnings chargeable to income tax for the year of payment;

(b) an individual who is UK resident for tax purposes for part of the tax year;

(c) an individual who has been UK tax resident at some time in the five years immediately preceding the contribution and when he or she became a member of the scheme;

(d) an individual or the individual's spouse or civil partner who has general earnings (defined in S28 ITEPA 2003) from overseas Crown employment subject to UK tax.

Earnings are not regarded as chargeable to income tax if they are not taxable in the UK by virtue of a double taxation agreement. However, contributions by seafarers (excluding floating oil-rig workers) who enjoy 100 per cent foreign exchange deduction against taxable earnings are allowable.

The annual limit is in respect of aggregate personal contributions to all schemes up to 100 per cent of earnings for each tax year.

Contributions may only be relieved against tax in the year of payment and the allowable contribution is calculated in respect of earnings for that year.

If it would produce a higher allowable contribution, you may invest £3,600, but only if your contribution is collected on a 'relief at source' basis. This allows contributions to be paid by or on behalf of non-earners such as non-working spouses and minor children.

This method of regulating tax reliefs on contributions would be inappropriate for defined benefit (for example final salary) schemes that provide 'added years' from voluntary contributions. In order to derive a measurable contribution for these purposes, an adjusted increase in benefit is measured over a period (usually a year) and then multiplied by 16. So, if one added year would increase the pension by £1,000 then in simplistic terms, the contribution would be deemed to be £16,000. (Until 5 April 2011 the factor was 10 and in the example, the derived contribution would have been £10,000.)

An 'adjusted' increase in benefit means, for instance, after adding benefits transferred from the scheme in the previous 12 months, but subtracting benefits transferred to the scheme in the same period. The adjustment also requires the 'opening balance' to be increased with the increase in the CPI.

14.4.2 **Claiming relief**

Personal contributions are usually payable net of basic rate tax. This is the 'relief at source' basis. For example an investment of £3,600 would require you to pay £2,880. The tax is then recovered by the scheme administrator and invested. If you are a higher rate taxpayer you may make a claim for relief against higher marginal rates (usually) through the self-assessment process. The method of giving higher rate relief is to expand the basic rate tax band (and therefore reduce the band subject to the higher rates by the amount of the gross contribution). In effect this could afford relief against tax on investment income.

The relief at source basis allows tax relief at basic rates even if you pay no tax, perhaps because, although you have no earnings, you are UK tax resident, because you are a minor child or non-working partner.

Most occupational schemes operate a system called the 'net pay arrangement'. In this system, the employer deducts contributions from pay and invests them for you. The contributions are deducted after accounting for National Insurance, but before applying tax to the reduced earnings. This is not the same as salary sacrifice (salary exchange) where salary is reduced in order to boost employer contributions and avoid a liability to National Insurance (because the pay is never received as such). Employers may elect whether they wish to operate a relief at source or net pay arrangement for *all* members.

Personal contributions to an occupational scheme may be a requirement of membership (a 'contributory scheme') or the scheme may offer a facility to pay additional voluntary contributions (AVCs). In the private sector, the contributions are paid on a money purchase basis, whilst public sector defined benefit schemes may offer an option to buy added years (i.e. further accrual). The member will usually be offered a limited range of funds under the AVC facility. Until 2006, providers offered freestanding AVC plans that were similar to personal pensions and independent of the 'main scheme'. They were more restrictive than personal pension plans. The easing of eligibility rules from 6 April 2006 has led to these arrangements being withdrawn in favour of the more universal personal pension plan.

The third means of claiming tax relief is known as relief on making a claim. Under this method, the individual pays the full contribution and recovers all tax relief, if available, from HMRC through the self-assessment process. This applies to contributions under the net pay arrangement that exceed pay and UK resident members of qualifying overseas schemes. Relief on making a claim is also the way in which general and dental practitioners claim relief on contributions to the NHS Pension Scheme.

The legislation does not generally allow *in specie* contributions (contributions in the form of assets). The exception is limited to share saving schemes (SAYE) where the transfer to the personal pension is effected within 90 days of your exercising the right to acquire the shares. Similarly shares from an approved profit sharing scheme or share incentive plan may be transferred where the transfer is within 90 days of the exercise of the option or release date if earlier. The transfer is a disposal for capital gains tax purposes, but the transfer is an allowable contribution.

The individual may also transfer property to a pension fund in order to meet an obligation to pay a contribution. The significance of the transfer meeting an obligation (in effect to meet a debt) is that stamp duty may be payable. The transfer will allow tax relief, in effect, as a contribution. Note that the value of the asset should not be less than the obligation and the transfer may have to be supplemented by cash unless properly arranged.

If the annual limit is exceeded, tax relief will be recovered by HMRC. The individual may request a 'refund of excess contributions lump sum' in respect of the unrelieved portion. This is an 'authorised payment' and is tax-free.

14.4.3 **Employer contributions** (FA 2004 Ss196–201)

There are two aspects to the way tax relief works for employer contributions: whether the employer may claim the contribution as a deduction and whether the contribution will be taxed on the employee.

The question of whether a contribution is deductible under Part 2 ITTOIA 2005 will be for the local tax inspector to decide. The inspector's decision will be guided by the HMRC *Business Income Manual* that deals with this topic (and many others).

This represents a summary:

- The expense (the contribution) must be wholly and exclusively incurred for the trade.
- HMRC will consider if the total remuneration package is reasonable.
- The contribution is deductible in the accounting year of payment, not the year recognised in the accounts.
- Contributions for controlling directors, proprietors, close friends and relatives of these people will attract special attention.
- HMRC will examine the taxpayer's objective.
- In doing so it will examine subjective intentions.
- The purpose must be to benefit the trade not the taxpayer (although the taxpayer may benefit as a consequence).
- HMRC will look at the rate for the job by comparing with other similar employees.
- HMRC will look closely at contributions paid immediately before business cessation unless paid to meet an obligation under employment contract.

Where contributions to a scheme exceed contributions paid in the previous accounting period by £500,000, part of the contribution will be relieved in the following year and other equal parts in subsequent years to a maximum of four years in the case of very large 'excesses'. Some excesses can be disregarded for these purposes, such as increases to fund inflation, increases for pensioners and increases to fund benefits for new members.

14.4.4 The annual allowance

The main tax control over input is known as the 'annual allowance'. If aggregate employer and member contributions exceed the annual allowance, the member will pay an annual allowance charge by way of the self-assessment process. Whilst the annual limit measures contributions paid in a tax year, the annual allowance refers to contributions paid in an input period ending in the relevant tax year.

The first input period is deemed to have started on 6 April 2006, or the start of scheme membership if later, or the date of the first contribution and will end on 5 April immediately following unless the member or administrator determines otherwise. If the input period started on 6 April 2006 and ended on 30 April 2006, contributions for that period would have been measured against the annual allowance for the tax year in which the input period ended (2006–07). Subsequent input periods must generally end no earlier than the following 6 April (the next tax year) and no later than 5 April following that. Input periods of more than 12 months (which comply with the rules above) are allowed in order that input periods can be aligned under different schemes. The exception is that if the member dies or becomes incapacitated, the input period ends at that time notwithstanding that the previous input period may have ended in the same tax year.

The annual allowance charge will be at your marginal rate of income tax on the excess. Schemes are required to deduct all or some of the tax from the value of accrued benefits if the tax due exceeds £2,000 and they receive a valid notice from the member. If the charge is less than this amount, the trustees have a discretion within the scheme rules whether to deduct from benefits.

The member must usually notify the scheme that they wish to use the 'scheme pays' facility by 31 July in the year following the tax year in which the charge became due or before benefits are taken if earlier. Exceptionally, for 2011–12, the deadline is extended to 31 December 2013.

The member may not usually notify the scheme before the end of the tax year in which the charge arises.

The member having given notification, liability is joint and several between member and scheme. The tax charge will be reported by the scheme under its accounting for tax (AFT) responsibilities. The scheme should usually account for the charge no later than 31 December following the end of the tax year in which the charge arose. The tax must be paid by the second 14 February following the tax year in which the liability arises. HMRC offers an example.

The liability relates to 2012–13. It must be reported by the scheme by 31 December 2014 and paid by 14 February 2015.

The deadline for 2011–12 has been extended so that the scheme must account for the liability by 31 March 2014 and paid by 15 May 2014.

The member must include the amount of the annual allowance charge on their self-assessment return which will be submitted by 31 January of the year following that in which the tax year ended.

There will have to be a corresponding reduction in benefits, but neither legislation nor HMRC practice dictates when that should be. However, the scheme will be sensitive to the fact that it must provide regular statements of benefits and that under some schemes, the death benefit will be based on the size of the fund.

In 2006–07, the annual allowance was £215,000 and this has increased annually to £255,000 in 2010–11. It can be increased by Treasury Order, but has been reduced to £50,000 for the tax year 2011–12 and succeeding years.

From 6 April 2011, you can increase your annual allowance for a tax year if:

(1) you were a member of a registered pension scheme in at least one of the immediately preceding three years (not necessarily active or contributing); and
(2) your contribution in any of those years fell short of the current £50,000 allowance (not the actual allowance applicable at the time).

The unused allowance can be carried forward from the years in which you were a member to a later year, but must be absorbed at the first opportunity (that is, immediately the £50,000 is exceeded) unless the excess arose before 6 April 2011. No election is needed.

If the contribution is paid in 2012–13, unused allowance from the three years starting 2009–10 may be available and, for these purposes, you must assume that your annual allowance was £50,000 in each of those years.

There were transitional measures for the period from which new rules were announced in October 2010 to 6 April 2011 from which the current rules apply.

If the input period ended before 6 April 2011, the annual allowance was £255,000. If the input period started after 13 October 2010 and ended after 5 April 2011, the annual allowance was £50,000. If the input period started before 14 October 2010 and ended after 5 April 2011, the period was divided into two periods for this purpose. The allowance for the period to 13 October 2010 was subject to an allowance of £255,000. For the remianing period the allowance was £50,000 subject to the aggregate of the two 'periods' not exceeding £255,000.

These rules (of historic interest) should not be confused with the rules implemented after 5 April 2011 which allow unused allowance to be carried forward three years, but for these purposes only, assuming that the annual allowance was £50,000 from 2008–09 onwards. So if £60,000 was paid in an input period ending in 2009–10, it was well short of the allowance when paid, but leaves no scope for carry-forward under the 2011 rules.

The maximum allowable contribution is unlimited in the tax year in which the member dies or on the evidence of a medical practitioner suffers ill health to the extent that he or she will not be able to undertake gainful work in any capacity at any time in the future.

The annual allowance is a personal allowance and has no bearing on deductibility for the employer.

In measuring against the annual allowance, all contributions from all sources (including your employer) to registered pension schemes must be taken into account. Contributions from HMRC as a consequence of contracting out of the S2P through a personal pension scheme could be ignored as could minimum payments via a money purchase occupational pension scheme when that option was available.

Personal contributions that have exceeded the annual limit and therefore which have not been relieved are also ignored in measuring aggregate contributions against the annual allowance.

In order to determine the contribution for a member of a defined benefit scheme (for example a final salary scheme), the contribution is derived from the difference between the adjusted opening (allow for CPI inflation, for example) and closing values (eg add transfers out, deduct transfers in) for an input period. The result is then multiplied by 16. If a member's benefit increases by £1,000 after adjustment, the derived contribution is £16,000.

Recent and current annual allowances are:

Tax year	Annual allowance
2006–07	£215,000
2007–08	£225,000
2008–09	£235,000
2009–10	£245,000
2010–11	£255,000
2011–12 onwards	£50,000

14.4.5 **Pensions and higher rate tax**

In the 2009 Budget, the government proposed restricting higher rate relief on pension contributions. The main rules were to be implemented from 6 April 2011, but in the meantime, pension tax relief would operate in a framework of transitional provisions (the 'anti-forestalling' measures).

The anti-forestalling measures (14.4.6 &14.4.7) ran from 22 April 2009 until 5 April 2011 and were replaced by a cut in the annual allowance (4.4) to £50,000. This was expected to generate the same amount of taxation as the proposed special rules for high earners, which were therefore not introduced from 6 April 2011.

14.4.6 **The anti-forestalling provisions (2009–11)**

The special annual allowance (SAA) charge applies to an individual when:

- Total adjusted income is at least £130,000 in the tax year or the previous two tax years. Until 8 December 2009, the threshold was £150,000 and this threshold continues to apply in respect of contributions paid between 22 April and 8 December 2009 and
- Total pension saving in the tax year from all sources (including you and your employers) exceeds the special annual allowance and the protected input (14.4.7).

These expressions need some explaining.

Total adjusted (relevant) income is derived from taking the following steps:

(1) all taxable income including earnings, interest, rent, taxable redundancy pay, chargeable gains from investment bonds, taxable element of annuities, pensions;
(2) add pension contributions paid under the net pay arrangement (that is, these must be added back);
(3) deduct trading losses and certain business reliefs;

(4) deduct personal pension contributions to a maximum of £20,000 (gross) even if added back under (2);
(5) add back any salary sacrificed to fund an employer contribution where the agreement was made on or after 22 April 2009 (whichever threshold applies);
(6) deduct any amounts paid under the gift aid scheme.

If the income for the current year does not reach the threshold, HMRC may refer to each of the previous two tax years.

For contributions that are paid at least quarterly, the SAA is £20,000.

For contributions that are paid less frequently than quarterly, the SAA is the average contribution for the years 2006–07, 2007–08 and 2008–09, but subject to a cap of £30,000. If infrequent contributions have averaged less than £20,000, the SAA is £20,000. The averaging always requires the total paid in the three years to be divided by three even if nothing was paid in one of those years.

If contributions have been both frequent and infrequent, each SAA applies, but they cannot be aggregated with each other.

Example: Annual contribution paid in each of the last five years is £35,000. The monthly contribution in the same period has been £1,500 a month.

The maximum contribution that will qualify for higher rate relief could be:

- an annual contribution of £30,000 or
- a monthly contribution of £1,666.67 a month plus an annual contribution of £10,000 or a variation on these figures subject to the monthly contribution not exceeding £20,000 a year and the total not exceeding £30,000 a year.

14.4.7 **Protected inputs/savings (2009–11)**

Protected input can only apply to frequent contributions. It enables the rate of contribution (defined contribution – rate refers to cash amount or percentage of earnings) or rate of accrual (defined benefit) to be maintained even though it may exceed the SAA (14.4.6).

In a simple example, if the member was paying £2,500 a month then the maximum fully relievable contribution will be £2,500 a month rather than £20,000 a year.

If contributions fluctuate within a year, the figure for the year (used in the averaging calculation) is the 'median' – the midway figure. So, if there are four payments of £2,000, £3,000, £4,000 and £5,000, the median is £3,500.

The conditions are essentially that the rate (£ or percentage) does not change and that there has been no break in contributions since 22 April 2009. 'No break' usually means no more than two contributions are unpaid.

The input period for the purposes of the SAA is always the tax year.

There is no SAA (the contribution is unlimited) in the tax year in which the member dies or becomes entitled to a serious ill-health lump sum.

In determining input under a defined benefit scheme, the same calculation applies as for the annual allowance. The additional accrual for the year is multiplied by ten.

There are special rules for those who change schemes. The general rule is that changing a scheme loses the protected input unless the member had no choice.

There are special rules for those for whom large contributions were paid before 22 April or 9 December 2009.

14.5 Benefit allowances (FA 2004 Ss214–226)

There is no earnings cap under the new pensions regime. However, if aggregate benefits exceed a lifetime allowance HMRC will recover some of the tax reliefs previously allowed in addition to the usual tax charges. The lifetime allowance is expressed as a capital value of pension rights and measurement against the lifetime allowance is triggered by a 'benefit crystallisation event' (BCE).

The standard lifetime allowance is modified for some individuals who had already accumulated substantial pension rights by 5 April 2006.

14.5.1 Benefit crystallisation events

The BCEs are as follows:

BCE 1 Designation of money purchase funds as unsecured pension fund. This is income drawdown and is described in section 14.7.1. Where an individual has not crystallised money purchase funds by the age of 75 he is deemed to have designated funds under this heading at 11.59 pm on the day before his or her birthday. It would immediately be followed by BCE 5A unless the member determined otherwise.

BCE 2 Member becomes entitled to a scheme pension. A scheme pension is selected and provided by the scheme trustees (rather than the member). Defined benefit schemes may only provide a scheme pension.

BCE 3 Excessive increase to a scheme pension. As a general rule, a scheme pension may not reduce from one year to the next and increases are restricted. An excessive increase is treated as an additional pension.

BCE 4 Member entitled to a lifetime annuity under a money purchase scheme. A money purchase scheme is a scheme that defines a contribution from time to time, but benefits are unknown until crystallised being subject to, for instance, net investment returns.

BCE 5 Member reaches 75, entitled to scheme pension and/or lump sum.

BCE 5A Member reaches 75 having sums or assets held for the purposes of a money purchase arrangement under any of the relevant pension schemes. The fund may comprise crystallised and/or uncrystallised funds. There will be no deadline for taking benefits and no further BCE. The amount is represented by funds designated for drawdown and any unused funds less any amounts crystallised under BCE 1 (to prevent overlap or double counting).

BCE 5B The individual reaching the age of 75 when there is a money purchase arrangement relating to the individual under any of the relevant pension schemes. The amount crystallised is the value of any remaining unused funds.

BCE 6 Member becomes entitled to a relevant lump sum (for example pension commencement lump sum, serious ill-health lump sum).

BCE 7 Lump sum death benefit.

BCE 8 Transfer to qualifying recognised overseas scheme. This is to recognise that funds are leaving the UK system and tax supervision.

BCE 9 Certain commutation events on the grounds of triviality.

No BCE will ever apply to funds that were already providing benefits on 5 April 2006, although those benefits will be taken into account on the first BCE to arise after that date.

Note that a 'scheme pension' is a pension provided by the trustees or managers of a scheme the level of which is determined by the trustees/managers in accordance with the scheme rules. Members do not have a choice of how their scheme pension will be provided (such as with a lifetime annuity chosen under an open market option) because this is decided by the trustees. The most common example of a scheme pension is a pension from a defined benefit scheme which is always a scheme pension.

In the 2010 Emergency Budget, the new Government proposed a review of the pension taxation rules to remove the effective obligation to purchase an annuity by age 75 for those who had not crystallised their money purchase fund or who were in receipt of an unsecured pension. As an interim measure, they increased from 75 to 77 the age by which an unsecured pension was required to convert to an alternatively secured pension, an annuity or a scheme pension. This measure has itself been overtaken by more radical rules which are effective from 6 April 2011 and which remove the requirement to convert what is now called a 'drawdown pension' at age 75 (or age 77) or indeed to take retirement benefits by age 75. Uncrystallised benefits will be subject to a BCE at age 75 and there will be no BCE after that date other than BCE 3. The interim rule only affected individuals who attained age 75 between 22 June 2010 and 5 April 2011.

14.5.2 The lifetime allowance

The lifetime allowance is a capital value of pension rights. If the lifetime allowance is exceeded, the 'excess' is subject to a lifetime allowance charge before any other tax charges are applied. It may also apply to any lump sum in respect of an excess.

The lifetime allowance charge is 55 per cent where the funds are paid as a lump sum to the member and 25 per cent in other circumstances, such as when the excess is paid as income or the member reaches age 75 with uncrystallised money purchase funds.

The standard lifetime allowance was set at £1.8 million for the tax years 2010–11 to 2011–12. From 6 April 2012, it reduced to £1.5 million unless the member has made a prior claim for 'fixed protection'. Fixed protection allows a lifetime allowance 'underpin' of £1.8 million on condition that there is no further benefit accrual or contributions, the member does not join another scheme other than for the purposes of transferring benefits and that transfers are restricted.

Recent and current rates of the standard lifetime allowance are:

Tax year	Standard lifetime allowance
2006–07	£1.5m
2007–08	£1.6m
2008–09	£1.65m
2009–10	£1.75m
2010–11	£1.8m
2011–12	£1.8m
2012–13 to 2016–17	£1.5m

The standard lifetime allowance may, on application to HMRC, be enhanced. This may arise, for instance, because the member had a large fund at 5 April 2006 which he or she elected to protect under transitional provisions. In some circumstances, the standard lifetime allowance is enhanced by a pension credit awarded before 6 April 2006 as part of a divorce settlement.

The new pension regime relies heavily on self-assessment and the member. When a member crystallises benefits he or she will be required to disclose whether the lifetime allowance has been enhanced and how much of the lifetime allowance (standard or enhanced) remains. The scheme will be required to inform the member of how much lifetime allowance has been used in respect of the scheme following a BCE.

The disclosure is based on amounts being expressed as percentages or factors of lifetime allowance.

Example 1: member crystallised £750,000 in 2006–07 when the lifetime allowance was £1.5m. He has not claimed transitional protection.

In this example, the member has used 50 per cent of the standard lifetime allowance. This means that he can use another 50 per cent of a future lifetime allowance (which will have increased) before incurring the lifetime allowance charge.

Example 2: member had funds at 5 April 2006 of £2.25m which she protected. She has a lifetime allowance enhancement factor of 0.5 (1 + 0.5). If she crystallised £750,000 she would retain (1.5 – 0.5) = 1 × the standard lifetime allowance.

If the scheme administrator calculates that the cumulative BCEs will take the latest crystallisation over the lifetime allowance the administrator must account to HMRC for the lifetime allowance charge. If the member has incorrectly disclosed the lifetime allowance used, the member may be directly charged and the administrator will avoid the charge if it took reasonable care to ascertain the situation. If information is not forthcoming from the member, the scheme will either not crystallise or will deduct 55 per cent as a precaution.

There are rules on how to calculate the value of benefits for the purposes of measuring against the lifetime allowance. In the case of money purchase schemes the value is usually the value of funds.

In the case of a defined benefit (for example final salary) scheme, the benefits are not expressed as an individual fund rather a pension and (usually) a lump sum. To derive a capital value, the pension is multiplied by 20 unless the scheme offers pension increases that could exceed 5 per cent in which case a different multiple is agreed between the scheme and HMRC. Higher multiples are likely to be confined to public sector schemes. The capital value of the pension is then added to the lump sum unless the lump sum is simply expressed as a commutation of pension, in which case the value is derived from the full non-commuted pension.

Example: Jane takes a defined benefit pension of £20,000 and a lump sum of £50,000. The value for testing against the lifetime allowance is (£20,000 × 20) + £50,000 = £450,000 (which is 30 per cent of the standard lifetime allowance in 2006–07 leaving 70 per cent for later).

If benefits were in payment at 5 April 2006 they will not themselves be the subject of a BCE, but must be taken into account at the first BCE after that date. This is done by multiplying the pension in payment (at date of crystallisation) by 25.

Example: John was receiving a pension on 5 April 2006 which is now £10,000 a year. He crystallises a further fund of £300,000. The capital value of that pension is (25 × £10,000) = £250,000. This means that 16.67 per cent of the lifetime allowance is deemed to have been used before the further 20 per cent represented by the £300,000. Note that pre-April 2006 lump sums are ignored.

In determining the value of pension rights, state pensions are ignored, but contracted-out rights are included in the funds to be measured.

14.6 Authorised and unauthorised payments (FA 2004 Ss164–185 & FA 2006 S158 & Sch 21)

The legislation is quite specific about what is an authorised payment and what is not. If a payment is unauthorised then it may be subject to a range of taxes that are designed to neutralise tax reliefs and in some cases include a ‘penalty’.

14.6.1 What is an unauthorised payment?

Benefits that meet the requirements of the ‘pension rules’ or the lump sum rule are authorised payments. If they do not meet the requirements then there will be an unauthorised payment.

A payment need not be a physical transfer of cash, but may be a benefit to the member or his family or members of his household for which the member etc. does not pay a commercial rent.

An unauthorised payment may be generated by a transaction with a member or someone connected with the member which is not at a commercial rate (for example sale of an asset at an undervalue or purchase at an overvalue).

Similarly if there is a reduction in value of scheme assets and a corresponding increase in value of assets owned by the member or connected parties, this may constitute an unauthorised payment. This is known as 'value shifting'.

However, direct or indirect investment by an investment-regulated pension scheme in certain assets known as 'taxable property' will be treated as unauthorised payments and taxed on purchase, whilst held and on disposal. An investment-regulated pension scheme is one where the member chooses investments such as a self-invested personal pension (SIPP) or small self-administered scheme (SSAS). Taxable property will include most residential property and 'tangible moveable property'.

Tax-efficient indirect investment in residential property or tangible moveable property may be possible through a 'genuine diverse commercial vehicle'. The requirements of such a vehicle will differ according to whether investment is into Real Estate Investment Trusts or the vehicle is a general investment vehicle or a trading vehicle. The general requirement is that investment must not be for personal use, but there are other rules depending on the type of vehicle. The vehicle may take a number of forms such as a limited company, unit trust or life assurance company fund, but an investment vehicle must not be a close company.

Scheme administration payments may include loans by a small occupational scheme to an employer, but they must comply with a number of requirements to ensure that they are offered on a commercial basis. These include a restriction to 50 per cent of the net value of assets, a commercial rate of interest (1 per cent over an average bank rate), a first charge on company assets to at least the value of the loan, a maximum term of five years and a regular repayment schedule.

The scheme may borrow in order to purchase assets, but the borrowing limit is restricted to 50 per cent of the remaining net assets. Commercial interest and repayment of capital are authorised payments.

FA 2006 S158 & Sch 21 introduced a new unauthorised payment. This can arise where you take a retirement lump sum and reinvest it in another pension scheme in order to claim more tax relief and where the transaction was pre-planned (HMRC has published guidance on what this means). The transaction will be ignored for these purposes if the amount reinvested is less than 1 per cent of the lifetime allowance, or the reinvested contribution is less than 30 per cent of the lump sum, or the contributions have increased by less than 30 per cent as a consequence of what is known as 'recycling'.

14.6.2 **Unauthorised payments: tax charges** (FA 2004 Ss204–213, 239–242)

The range of tax charges that may be applied to an unauthorised payment are:

The *unauthorised payments charge* which is 40 per cent of the payment and is usually payable by the member in a variety of circumstances, including certain investments.

The *unauthorised payments surcharge* which is usually payable by the member where there is an unauthorised payment (or series of such payments in a 12 month period) that exceeds 25 per cent of asset value. It will be at a rate of 15 per cent of the payment. It is unusual for a scheme sanction charge to apply in the absence of an unauthorised payment charge, but it may apply when income or a capital gain accrues to the scheme from an unauthorised transaction such as rent or a capital gain from investment in taxable property (eg residential, tangible moveable property). These are 'chargeable payments'.

The *scheme sanction charge* which is payable by the administrator. It is usually 15 per cent to allow for the payment of the unauthorised payments charge. If there has been no such charge, it will be 40 per cent of the payment.

The *de-registration charge* which is levied on de-registration and is in addition to the above unauthorised payments charges. The rate is 40 per cent of assets immediately before de-registration.

14.7 Retirement benefits (FA 2004 S165 & Sch 28)

As a general rule, retirement benefits are available from age 55 (although there is no upper age limit). There is a measure of transitional protection for earlier ages agreed before 6 April 2006. There is no requirement to retire and no need to take benefits if you do retire.

Retirement benefits will usually take the form of a pension payable for (at least) life and usually a lump sum. The pension is taxed as earned income (but not subject to National Insurance). The lump sum is usually tax-free.

Retirement benefits that do not comply with certain requirements of the legislation will be unauthorised payments.

14.7.1 **The pension rules**

The requirements of a pension are as follows:

Pension rule 1: Minimum pension age. The minimum age from which the pension can be taken is the normal minimum pension age of 55 unless the member meets the ill-health condition. This is that the member by reason of ill health or injury is permanently unable to carry on his or her occupation or one for which they are reasonably suited.

Pension rule 2: 10 year guarantee. This rule allows the pension to be paid for a minimum term of up to ten years whether or not the member survives the term.

Pension rule 3: Defined benefit scheme must offer a 'scheme pension' (see 14.5.1). Defined contribution schemes may offer a scheme pension. The scheme pension must meet certain requirements: it must generally not reduce from one year to the next (the main exception being 'bridging pensions' that reduce when the state scheme becomes payable) and it must not increase by more than inflation (or 5 per cent if greater). In the event of the death of a member after age 75 a scheme pension cannot provide survivor pensions that total more than the member's pension.

Pension rule 4: Pensions available are a lifetime annuity, scheme pension or drawdown pension. If the scheme pension derives from a money purchase scheme, the member must be offered a lifetime annuity (open market option). A drawdown pension allows a variable income to be taken directly from the fund.

From 6 April 2011, there are two types of drawdown: capped drawdown and flexible drawdown. Capped drawdown is subject to a maximum withdrawal from the fund each year. Flexible drawdown allows unlimited withdrawals if you can demonstrate an existing minimum income of at least £20,000 (which must be paid in the tax year that the initial declaration is made) provided by:

(1) a scheme pension payable from a scheme with at least 20 pensioner members;
(2) a pension annuity;
(3) a pension from an overseas scheme that would meet these criteria if paid from the UK;
(4) a state pension; or
(5) a pension payable under the Financial Assistance Scheme.

Pension rule 5: The capped drawdown pension must not exceed 100 per cent of the basis amount determined by the Government Actuary's Department (although there are transitional rules if the drawdown started before 6 April 2011 and subject to a higher maximum). The maximum withdrawal must be reviewed at least every three years (previously five years).

Pensions available from age 75 are a lifetime annuity, a scheme pension or a drawdown pension.

From age 75, the capped drawdown limit is reviewed annually. The maximum capped drawdown is 100 per cent of a basis amount for a person of your age.

The pension in payment will be taxed under the PAYE procedures. An individual who elects for a drawdown pension has the option of subsequently purchasing an annuity with the residual fund.

Annuities are streams of income purchased from life assurance companies and may be guaranteed, partially guaranteed or subject to movements on investment markets. The annuity 'rate' is determined by the performance of underlying investments (usually fixed interest securities such as gilts), expenses and mortality factors (the risk of dying). By historic standards, annuity rates (the rate at which the fund is converted to pension) are low in 2012. This is because annuitants are living longer and because fixed interest yields are low. There are concerns that rates may go lower because the providers are being asked to retain more capital in their reserves to meet guarantees and solvency requirements under EU legislation ('Solvency II').

It is impossible to predict how annuity rates will move in future (especially over the short term). However, pension scheme members will be well advised to use the services of a financial adviser to explain the threats and opportunities presented by the annuity option. If the member decides to purchase an annuity, he or she should consider taking advantage of the 'open market option' which enables the fund to be applied to the provider offering the best rates at time of purchase.

14.7.2 **Lump sums** (FA 2004 Sch 29)

There are a number of allowable lump sums payable to the member grouped under one lump sum rule. They are:

Pension commencement lump sum: tax-free within allowances. It is payable within the six months before and twelve months after your becoming entitled to the related pension (and after age 75 if entitlement arose before that age). It is calculated as the lesser of 25 per cent of the standard lifetime allowance (less lump sums in respect of funds already crystallised) and the lump sum available under the scheme. For money purchase schemes this simply means 25 per cent of the fund being crystallised, whilst the position is more complicated under a defined benefit scheme and influenced by commutation rates. A feature of the new rules is that a lump sum is payable in respect of protected rights (money purchase funds derived from contracting out) and additional voluntary contributions.

Serious ill-health lump sum: this is available at any age in respect of uncrystallised rights if, in the opinion of a registered medical practitioner, the member's expectation of life is no more than 12 months. If the member is below the age of 75 the lump sum is tax-free, but it is only payable to the extent that there is remaining lifetime allowance. At age 75 and beyond, the lump sum is subject to tax at 55 per cent.

Short-service refund lump sum: taxed at 20 per cent on first £20,000 then 50 per cent. This is a lump sum representing a refund of personal contributions where a member of an occupational scheme leaves service before completing two years service and the rules allow the option.

Refund of excess contributions lump sum: tax-free. This is where a member exceeds the annual limit (see 14.4.3).

Trivial commutation lump sum: 25 per cent of fund tax-free. If aggregate funds (not just those being encashed) do not exceed 1 per cent of the lifetime allowance, and the lifetime allowance has not already been exhausted, the funds may be taken as a lump sum within a 12-month period. From 6 April

2012, the limit changed from 1 per cent of the lifetime allowance to £18,000. The trivial commutation rules have been extended by the introduction of more relaxed rules allowing payment of 'small lump sums' (no more than £2,000). The rules were introduced to assist the administration of schemes, especially in relation to 'small pots' that have been 'stranded' such as National Insurance rebates paid after annuitisation.

Winding-up lump sum: as trivial commutation lump sum. This is similar to the previous option, but applies on a scheme wind-up.

Lifetime allowance lump sum: taxed at 55 per cent. This lump sum represents funds that exceed the lifetime allowance.

14.8 Death benefits

Death benefits may be paid as an income to dependants and/or lump sum. The dependant's pension is taxed as income, but is never the subject of a benefit crystallisation event (or taken into account). There will therefore never be a lifetime allowance charge in respect of a dependant's pension. These pensions are unlimited except that total dependants' pensions deriving from a scheme pension must not exceed that paid to a member if the member dies at or after age 75.

14.8.1 **Income benefits** (FA 2004 S167, Sch 28)

There are a number of ways in which a dependant's pension may be paid within the pension death benefit rules. Payment of a dependant's pension in the event of a member's death is not a benefit crystallisation event. Beneficiaries under this heading are confined to dependants who will be defined by the scheme rules, but under the Finance Act 2004 are defined as:

- A person married to the member or a registered civil partner at the date of the member's death.
- A person who was married to the member or a registered civil partner when the member first became entitled to the pension.
- A child of the member (natural or adopted) who has not reached 23 or has reached 23 and in the opinion of the scheme administrator was at the date of the member's death dependent because of mental or physical impairment.
- A person who does not fall into these categories and was financially dependent on the member at the date of the member's death or interdependent or dependent because of mental or physical impairment.

A *dependant's scheme pension* is a pension paid by the scheme or by an insurance company selected by the scheme administrator.

A money purchase scheme may provide a *dependant's annuity*.

No dependant's pension may include a guaranteed payment period.

The dependant may 'inherit' the member's drawdown pension by way of a dependant's drawdown pension.

14.8.2 **Lump sum benefits** (FA 2004 Sch 29)

There are a number of lump sum death benefits payable, some dependent on the scheme design. Payment of a lump sum in respect of uncrystallised funds before age 75 is treated as a BCE and measured against the deceased member's lifetime allowance.

Special lump sum death benefit (defined benefits): taxed at 55 per cent. It pays a lump sum on the death of a member in receipt of a scheme pension before age 75. It is the initial capital value of the member's pension (usually the initial pension multiplied by 20) less instalments paid.

Pension protection lump sum death benefit: taxed at 55 per cent. This pays a lump sum on the death of a member in receipt of a scheme pension before age 75. It is the initial capital value of the member's pension less instalments paid.

Uncrystallised lump sum death benefit: tax-free within the allowances before age 75. On death from age 75, the lump sum is taxed at 55 per cent. This is payable in respect of a money purchase scheme (for example return of fund) on death before retirement benefits are taken.

Special lump sum death benefit (annuity protection): taxed at 55 per cent. This mirrors the pension protection lump sum death benefit where the member purchased an annuity with his money purchase fund.

Special lump sum death benefit (unsecured lump sum): This is payable on death in drawdown and is subject to tax at 55 per cent.

Charity lump sum death benefit: tax-free and payable from a drawdown pension or uncrystallised funds where there is no surviving dependant.

Tax relief on personal pension life assurance

This was withdrawn by section 68 and Schedule 18 FA 2007 for new plans. In summary, if the policy application was received before 14 December 2006 (issued by 31 July 2007) or was part of a pension scheme and the application was received before 29 March 2007 (issued by 1 August 2007) then contributions will continue to receive tax relief. Relief will also be available if the policy was issued before 21 March 2007 within an occupational scheme registered before that date.

Tax relief will continue to be available on contributions to 'group life' schemes established by an employer.

14.9 Transitional protections for pre-A Day pension rights (FA 2004 Sch 36)

It is a common misconception that these rules only apply to individuals with large pension funds. There are many areas where transactions of a long-term nature are protected, such as loans and investments made under the previous regime. The scheme rules will be overridden where compliance with the new regime would require them to be broken, but all schemes must have brought their rules into line with the tax legislation by 5 April 2011.

Under the Finance Act 2004, any scheme that was approved for tax purposes on 5 April 2006 is automatically registered unless the scheme decided to 'opt out', but this is an unlikely scenario.

The problem with the transitional rules is that in order to be fair in respect of past pension rights and to prevent abuse, they are complicated. This section will cover the protection afforded earlier pension rights in three main areas:

- Aggregate pension rights.
- Retirement lump sums from occupational schemes.
- Pension ages.

14.9.1 Aggregate pension rights

Paragraph 14.5.2 described the lifetime allowance and included a table showing the lifetime allowance for every year after 5 April 2006 when it was first implemented. This section explains how the allowance works in more detail.

Under the new regime, a lifetime allowance tax charge will usually apply when the value of pension rights at a benefit crystallisation event exceeds £1.5m in 2012–13. However, there are some individuals who will already have accrued rights of this value at 5 April 2006 and for them, the legislation allows a measure of protection from the lifetime allowance charge.

Any pension in payment at that date will never be subject to the lifetime allowance charge. However, if other 'uncrystallised' benefits are subsequently crystallised, the pension in payment at 5 April will be taken into account in determining how much lifetime allowance is available. Pensions in payment are multiplied by 25 in order to determine their value for these purposes, so a pension of, for example, £10,000 would have a value of £250,000 which is 16.67 per cent of the lifetime allowance in 2012–13. Where income is being taken from drawdown funds, the maximum allowable annual withdrawal is assumed to be the pension in payment.

The individual had until 5 April 2009 to decide whether to claim protection from the lifetime allowance charge by way of primary or enhanced protection.

14.9.2 Transitional protection

The 2006 tax framework allowed individuals until 5 April 2009 to claim primary or enhanced protection from the lifetime allowance charge.

Primary protection is the more limited form of protection, but allows the member future accrual and/or contributions in respect of registered pension schemes. The protection extends to the aggregate value of benefits in respect of approved schemes on 5 April 2006 increased in line with the lifetime allowance. If total funds exceeded HMRC limits under the old rules, then the excess is ignored in determining the protected amount. The valuation of rights under a defined benefit scheme in particular is difficult.

Primary protection was made available by making a claim and HMRC allocating a reference number and a lifetime allowance enhancement factor. It is effective from 6 April 2006 where the value of pension rights at 5 April 2006 exceeded £1.5m.

Example: You have pension rights on 5 April 2006 valued at £2.25m. The enhancement factor is 0.5. When applied in 2006–07, this tells us that the protected rights are (1 + 0.5) × £1.5m. If you were to crystallise £400,000, you would tell the pension scheme the reference number and the lifetime allowance enhancement factor as well as the amount of lifetime allowance used (nil in this case). After the transaction, you would be left with (1.5–0.25) = 1.25 × the standard lifetime allowance for that year (£1.5m in 2012–13). (The £400,000 is 26.67 per cent of the standard lifetime allowance in 2012–13).

Primary protection will only be lost if a pension debit awarded by the court in the event of divorce takes the value of rights below the standard lifetime allowance. If the debit reduces rights to a higher value, then the lifetime allowance enhancement factor is reduced (and therefore the 'personal' lifetime allowance).

Enhanced protection was available whatever the value of pension rights at 5 April 2006 providing that it did not exceed HMRC limits under the old basis. Any excess had first to be surrendered (repaid as surplus subject to tax at 35 per cent). Enhanced protection protects all funds from the lifetime allowance charge whilst it applies providing there is no further significant benefit accrual. Enhanced protection is effective from 6 April 2006, but may be lost in certain circumstances:

- Further contributions are paid to a money purchase scheme.
- There is further benefit accrual to a defined benefit scheme (other than inflation proofing which is measured in a number of ways).
- You take out a new arrangement other than solely to accept a transfer value.
- Your arrangement accepts a transfer from a non-registered scheme.
- You transfer benefits to other arrangements which represent less than the full actuarially defined value of one or more of your plans.
- You transfer benefits from a money purchase scheme to a defined benefit scheme.
- Funds are reallocated to your fund from that of another member, perhaps on their death.

Contributions to a plan that existed at 5 April 2006 and only represented contracting-out contributions to a money purchase scheme did not jeopardise enhanced protection. Similarly contributions to a life cover arrangement or a claim on such an arrangement will not lose your enhanced protection if the arrangement was in place on 5 April 2006 and the benefit formula has not changed.

If enhanced protection is lost, all previous crystallisation events will be ignored, but the crystallised funds will be taken into account in future crystallisations. Protection will be lost completely unless a claim was originally made for the protection to revert to primary protection should enhanced protection be lost and the funds exceeded £1.5m at A Day.

14.9.3 Lump sum protection

Many occupational pension schemes offered an opportunity to take a lump sum that exceeded 25 per cent of the value of pension rights prior to A Day. The new regime offers some protection for these schemes where the accrued lump sum at 5 April 2006 exceeded 25 per cent.

In most cases the protection need not be claimed and there is no need to make a claim for enhanced or primary protection. However, if a claim is made for enhanced or primary protection the protected lump sum may be recorded.

There are two bases of protection.

The most common is when the lump sum exceeds 25 per cent of the value of pension rights under the previous regime. That lump sum, plus increases in line with the lifetime allowance, will be protected if all benefits from the scheme are taken at the same time.

Generally, this lump sum protection will be lost if funds are transferred to another scheme. They will continue to be protected if the transfer is made to a new scheme as part of a 'block transfer' (two or more members transferring from the same scheme to the same scheme as part of the same transaction) or where the transfer is to a deferred annuity ('buy-out' contract) on the winding up of the scheme. The member must not have been a member of the new scheme for more than 12 months in the case of a block transfer.

The second basis of protection only applies when aggregate lump sum rights at 5 April 2006 exceeded £375,000 and the member has claimed enhanced or primary protection. This basis overrides the scheme specific basis above when it applies.

If the basis of protection is primary protection, the lump sum will be the aggregate lump sum entitlement at 5 April 2006 increased in the same proportion as the lifetime allowance. The lump sum can be taken from any scheme although it may have accrued to other schemes.

If the basis of protection is enhanced protection, then the protected lump sum will usually be the same proportion of each arrangement as it was at 5 April 2006.

Note that when calculation of the protected lump provides a lower figure than the standard lump sum calculation (25 per cent etc.), the higher figure can be used, but the standard lump sum can never exceed 25 per cent of the standard lifetime allowance for the year in question in these circumstances.

14.9.4 **Pension age**

The normal minimum pension age was 50 until 5 April 2010 when it increased to 55. These pension ages apply to all types of retirement benefit regardless of whether or not you continue to work and also to contracted-out rights subject to scheme rules. Benefits can be taken earlier than these minima if you have to give up work permanently because of ill health or injury.

However, there are many members of schemes who had a right to take benefits before these minimum pension ages prior to 6 April 2006 and they are generally offered protection.

If you enjoyed a special early pension age because of your occupation then, providing you have left that occupation, you may retain that age whether it applies to a personal or occupational pension scheme.

If you are a member of an occupational scheme that allowed members to retire at 50 on 10 December 2003 (the date the White Paper was published) and you had that right on 5 April 2006, then you continue to enjoy that right.

There are certain conditions such as requiring you to take all the benefits from the scheme simultaneously and not transferring subject to being able to protect the age where part of a block transfer (see lump sums above).

If you take benefits earlier than the 'normal minimum pension age' because you have a protected pension age, then the lifetime allowance is reduced by 2.5 per cent for each year the crystallisation date falls short of the current normal minimum pension age (for example ten years short would reduce the standard lifetime allowance by 10 × 2.5 per cent = 25 per cent). The lifetime allowance reduction is itself reduced as each further year passes so it would be back to 100 per cent at normal minimum pension age. Note that there are some public sector schemes where no reduction is made in the lifetime allowance, but it is in any case unlikely to be relevant.

14.9.5 **Reduction in lifetime allowance**

On 6 April 2012, the lifetime allowance reduced to £1.5 million. You will be able to claim 'fixed protection' from the lifetime allowance tax charge on funds up to £1.8 million or a higher subsequent lifetime allowance. The protection was claimed by writing to HMRC by 5 April 2012 (a standard form), but may be withdrawn if there is further benefit accrual (or further contributions paid) or you join a new arrangement other than to transfer benefits. Some transfers may also not be permitted.

The protection will not affect an existing claim for enhanced or primary protection and primary and lump sum protection will be assumed to be based on a lifetime allowance of £1.8 million. So, for example, if primary protection allows a personal lifetime allowance of 120 per cent of the standard lifetime allowance, it will be calculated as 120 per cent of £1.8 million in 2012–13.

14.10 Divorce

There are certain aspects of pension sharing orders as a consequence of divorce or nullity which are worthy of note. This is not a comprehensive description of the rules on divorce:

(1) If the sharing order was made before A day (6 April 2006) then the member will simply have a smaller fund to measure against the lifetime allowance and if appropriate to protect against the lifetime allowance. The 'ex-spouse member' will be able to include the pension credit in a claim for transitional protection and the personal lifetime allowance will, if appropriate, be increased by a lifetime allowance enhancement factor.
(2) If the sharing order is made under the new regime, the debit will reduce the member's fund for all purposes. If the member has claimed primary protection, the protected allowance will be reduced by the debit and if the funds fall below the standard lifetime allowance primary protection will be lost.
(3) No lump sum is available in respect of a pension credit which is awarded after retirement benefits have started.

14.11 Funded non-registered schemes

These schemes are described as employer-financed retirement benefit schemes in the legislation. The basic rules of tax until April 2011 were:

(1) Employer contributions are not deductible until benefits are taken. If the member has not left service there will be a liability to National Insurance.
(2) Employer contributions will not be taxed on the member.
(3) Benefits will be taxed at marginal rates on the individual.
(4) Income in the fund will be taxed at highest marginal income tax rates.
(5) Capital gains in the fund will be subject to tax at 18 per cent.
(6) Inheritance tax will be applied by treating the scheme as a discretionary trust.
(7) The pre-A Day accrued fund may be 'ring-fenced' and will not be subject to the new inheritance tax regime.
(8) The pre-A Day fund may provide tax-free benefits in most circumstances where contributions were taxed.

The Finance Act 2011 introduced tax charges on what it described as 'disguised remuneration' (10.17) and this includes funded employer financed retirement benefit schemes. The position now resembles that which existed before 1997. Contributions paid by the employer are taxed as a benefit and are subject to national insurance, but lump sum benefits derived from taxed contributions are free from income tax. (Part 7A ITEPA 2003 added by Schedule 2 FA 2011.)

14.12 Automatic Enrolment and NEST

The Pensions Act 2008 is mainly concerned with auto-enrolment and the National Employee Savings Trust (NEST).

1. Auto-enrolment

Employers will be required to offer automatic enrolment in a pension scheme to jobholders who are at least 22 and not already members of a qualifying scheme. Auto-enrolment obligations on the employer will arise every three years although the jobholder will have the option to remain out of the scheme.

The contribution to a money purchase scheme must eventually be at least 8 per cent of qualifying earnings made up of an employer contribution of 3 per cent, a jobholder contribution of 4 per cent and reinvested tax of 1 per cent of qualifying earnings. Qualifying earnings are those falling between (proposed) £5,564 and £39,853 in 2012–13, but these thresholds will be revalued with average earnings.

Defined benefit schemes will be required to pass a quality test that includes a member's pension of at least 1⁄120 of qualifying final pay. This may be increased by the Secretary of State to 1⁄80 of qualifying pay.

Minimum contribution	Employer	Employee (incl. tax relief)
To 30 September 2017	1%	1%
1 October 2017 to 30 September 2018	2%	3%
From 1 October 2018	3%	5%

Employers have been assigned a date for starting automatic enrolment: larger employers will start before smaller employers. The staging dates will start in October 2012 and continue to 'unwind' until early 2018.

2. NEST

The scheme created by the Act is what is being referred to as the National Employee Savings Trust and this will operate under a trust. The Act provides very little other detail, but enables regulations to be made.

Maximum contributions will be £4,400 in 2012–13 (this figure will increase each year and the principle of a 'cap' will be reviewed in 2017).

There will be a ban on transfers from other schemes to NEST; this will be reviewed in 2017.

Retirement benefits will be payable from 55.

NEST is subject to the same tax regime as other registered pension schemes as described above.

Chapter 15

MISCELLANEOUS ASPECTS

15.1 Miscellaneous profits – previously Schedule D Case VI

(ITTOIA Ss 574–689)

The consolidating and rewriting statutes, ITTOIA (2.10), ITA 2007 and CTA 2009 eliminated the classification of income under the previous schedules and cases, Schedule D Case VI being particularly relevant to this chapter. Although the basic rules have largely continued, each type of income taxable under miscellaneous profits is now specified in law, rather than swept up by exception. Such income includes:

(1) Income from underwriting (if not a business), but Lloyd's underwriting profits (15.9) were assessed as a trade (under Schedule D Case I).
(2) Income from guaranteeing loans.
(3) Income from dealing in futures. However, this is now more likely to be subject to capital gains tax (20.31).
(4) Certain capital sums received from the sale of UK patent rights.
(5) Post-cessation receipts (11.28).
(6) Certain 'anti-avoidance' assessments (15.10).
(7) Enterprise allowance payments after 17 March 1986. Previously Case I or II applied. Case VI also applied to payments before 18 March 1986 which continued subsequently (11.4).
(8) Profits on the disposal of certificates of deposit.
(9) Gains on certain life policies held by companies.
(10) The surplus from converting from the cash to the earnings basis from 1999–2000 (11.27).

The basis of assessment for miscellaneous profits is the actual income arising in the tax year. Expenses incurred in earning the income can be deducted in ascertaining the assessable profits.

Losses sustained in any relevant transaction can be set off against other miscellaneous profits of the same or any subsequent year. They cannot, in general, be set off against income of a different category (formerly assessable under any other Case or Schedule (ITA Ss152–153)).

15.2 Tax-free organisations (TA 1988 Ss460–467 & ITA Ss413–446 etc.)

15.2.1 Charities (ITA Ss413–446 & 518–564)

Recognised charities are exempt from tax on any income that is used only for charitable purposes from:

(1) Land and buildings.
(2) Interest, dividends and annual payments.

(3) Trades carried on by the beneficiaries of the charity or trades exercised in the course of executing the actual purposes of the charity. Certain lottery income is included from April 1995 (ITA S530). For these purposes, for periods commencing after 21 March 2006, trades will be split into qualifying and non-qualifying parts.

Since 2000–01 certain trading and sundry income of a charity up to a limit is exempt from tax, provided it is used for its charitable purposes. The limit for a full year is £5,000, which is increased to the lesser of £50,000 and 25 per cent of all of the charity's incoming resources.

Recognised charities are also exempt from capital gains tax.

Gifts to charity out of both capital and income are often afforded favourable tax treatment as described elsewhere in this book. In particular, note capital gains tax (20.31), and inheritance tax (22.5.1 & 22.17.3).

Gifts of qualifying investments to charities from 6 April 2000 for individuals and 1 April 2000 for companies create tax relief on their value. This covers quoted shares and securities, authorised unit trust units, open-ended investment company shares and offshore fund interests. From April 2002 this relief covers gifts of land and buildings providing the charity agrees to accept it.

Historically, deeds of covenant, which were written to last four years or until some later event (for example giving up membership of the charity) were the lifeblood of charitable income. However, from 6 April 2000, deeds of covenant come within the 'gift-aid' rules (see below).

Certain charitable gifts qualify for 'gift aid'. This is income tax or, for companies, corporation tax relief for charitable donations. Basic rate income tax is deducted by the donor and reclaimed by the charity. The donor obtains full tax relief at the higher or additional rate, if applicable. Similarly a company deducts the gross donation from its taxable profits and obtains relief at its corporation tax rate (26 per cent etc.).

Your 'gift-aid' donations can now be of any size, but may fall within a proposed annual cap on 'unlimited reliefs' equal to the greater of £50,000 or 25 per cent of total income from 6 April 2013. Furthermore, the scheme has been extended to foreign donors, crown servants and members of the armed forces serving overseas. Also, your capital gains tax is taken into account in seeing whether you pay enough tax to cover the relief. One simple 'gift aid' form is needed for each charity to which you give, no matter how many donations you make to each.

Thus, suppose you give under 'gift aid' £1,000 gross to a charity during 2012–13, you deduct 20 per cent basic rate and pay £800, the charity reclaiming the £200. You will also obtain £200 or £300 further relief if you are a higher rate or additional rate income tax payer. Your net cost will then be £600 or £500 respectively. Exceptionally, if your 'adjusted net income' would otherwise lie in the bracket £100,00 to £114,950, where the claw-back of personal allowance now takes place, the net cost of additional 'gift aid' payments that do not reduce this below £100,000 may be only £400 (3.2.9–10 & 26.2.22).

Between 6 April 2008 and 5 April 2011, although your deduction was at 20 per cent, HMRC paid the charity an extra 2 per cent transitional relief.

If you make a gift qualifying for 'gift aid' after 5 April 2003, you are able to elect for it to be relieved in the previous tax year. However, there are detailed rules to observe and the election must be made to HMRC no later than the date when your self-assessment return for the earlier year is lodged – and that must not be late. From April 2004 and until 2010–11, you could nominate a charity to receive all or part of your tax repayments. The resulting payment qualified for 'gift aid' by reference to the date when it was received by the charity. This facility ceased in respect of repayments made after 5 April 2012.

From 6 April 2013, it is expected that, subject to formal consultation, for which the closing date was 25 May 2012, recognised charities and CASCs (15.2.2) with a good three-year record within the gift aid scheme will be permitted to claim 'top-up payments' in lieu of tax refunds on an annual total of up to £5,000 of small gifts, none of which exceeds £20, without the need to obtain gift aid declarations.

The original rules for tax relief on covenanted (or gift-aided) membership subscriptions to heritage and conservation charities were relaxed in 1989, so that the right to free or cheap entry to view the property of the charity does not prevent the member from obtaining tax relief. However, there are limits to the benefits which you can receive from a recipient of gift aid donations. From 6 April 2007, these are 5 per cent of your donation, if that is over £1,000 (25 per cent if £100 or less and £25 if £101–£1,000). From 6 April 2011 (periods ending after 31 March for companies), the additional overriding limit on your total gift aid benefits in any one year increased to £2,500 (£500 from April 2007 and £250 previously). This could facilitate incentives to attract donors making gifts of £10,001–£50,000 annually.

A payroll deduction scheme operates from 1987–88. Employees were able to contribute no more than £1,200 each year to charities through an approved agent and obtain tax relief. Employers' expenses in running schemes are allowable business deductions, as are those paid to charitable agencies (FA 1993 S69). From 6 April 2000 the £1,200 limit has been removed and, for four years from that date, the charities received a 10 per cent supplement (FA 2003 S146).

Certain anti-avoidance provisions (TA 1988 Ss506–507 & Sch 20) restrict a charity's tax relief if its *funds* are used for non-charitable purposes, or passed to an overseas body without ensuring that it will use the money for charity. Relief is also restricted if the charity lends or invests the funds for the benefit of the original donor unless for charitable purposes and these rules are expanded after 21 March 2006 for substantial donors (£25,000 annually or £100,000 over a six-year period). From the same time, the income and gains eligible for tax relief are restricted by £1 for each £1 of non-charitable expenditure incurred.

Higher or additional rate relief for gift-aided donations may be restricted where the charity's own relief is limited. These rules do not generally apply if a charity's taxable income and gains are no more than £10,000 in a year. If you pay more than £1,000 of donations under covenant in a year to charities whose relief is limited as above, your own higher rate relief may be restricted.

From 1 April 2011, the substantial donor rules were relaxed in respect of certain transactions with pre-existing substantial donors, to whom the rules will continue to apply, provided the transaction is not 'tainted' for the purposes of a new anti-avoidance code.

Also from 1 April 2011, a new regime has been introduced by FA 2011, which denies tax relief to donors and charities that enter into transactions, of which a main purpose is to obtain an advantage from the charity and which would not have been done, were it not for the prospective tax relief. The donations affected are classified as 'tainted' whilst others will be 'relievable'. Tax relief on tainted donations can be refused, clawed back or cancelled by assessment as appropriate.

15.2.2 **Other tax-free organisations**

Other organisations whose income in certain circumstances may be free of tax include registered and unregistered friendly societies, registered trade unions, mutual associations, pension funds and 'community amateur sports clubs'.

Registered friendly societies are exempt from tax on profits from life assurance business subject to certain limits. The maximum annual premium payable on such a life assurance policy is now £270. The previous limit was based on annual premiums of £200 (FA 1991 Sch 9). Premiums under existing friendly society policies may be increased to the new limit without affecting the tax benefits. In addition, the previous restriction that the cash value on early surrender cannot exceed the premiums paid has also been removed. There remains a limit of £156 annually for each annuity (TA 1988 S464).

Since 31 May 1984, the life business of friendly societies has been treated for tax purposes as being more akin to that of life assurance companies (TA 1988 S466 & FA 1996 S171). The 1992 Friendly Societies Act allows societies to incorporate. The legislation regarding tax exemption now extends to incorporated societies.

Provident benefits paid by *trade unions* to their members are tax-exempt up to certain limits. (Such payments might cover sickness, injury etc.) The limits which apply from 1 April 1991, are £4,000 for lump sums and £825 for annuities (TA 1988 S467 & FA 1991 S74).

Depending on the exact circumstances, tax exemption may apply to government bodies, foreign diplomats and United Nations Organisation officials in this country and the salaries of the members of visiting forces.

Community amateur sports clubs (CASCs) obtain certain tax reliefs from 1 April 2002 and individuals get reliefs from 6 April 2002 (companies from 1 April 2002). A CASC must be open to the whole community, be organised on an amateur basis and provide facilities for and promote participation in eligible sports.

CASCs are exempt from corporation tax on interest, the first £30,000 of trading income, the first £20,000 of property income and on capital gains, provided they are spent on qualifying purposes. Prior to 1 April 2004, these thresholds were £15,000 and £10,000 respectively.

Donors to CASCs will benefit from gift aid as for charities, inheritance tax relief, gifts of assets on a no gain/no loss basis for capital gains tax and business gifts of trading stock, plant and machinery (FA 2002 S58 & Sch 18).

From 17 April 2002 investment by companies or individuals in accredited *community development finance institutions* (CDFIs) normally attracts a tax credit of 5 per cent for each of up to five years. The investment can be by way of debt or shares and the CDFIs must use the funds for small businesses and social enterprises working in disadvantaged communities (FA 2002 S57 & Schs 16 & 17).

The London Olympic Games and Paralympic Games are given tax relief retrospectively from 22 October 2004. For example, the London Organising Committee of the Olympic Games Ltd is exempted from corporation tax. Also, members of the International Olympic Committee and non-UK athletes temporarily here regarding the 2012 Games will be exempted from tax.

15.3 Patent holders (TA 1988 S527, ITTOIA Ss587–602, CAA Pt8 & ITA S461)

If you own a patent (11.18) and you grant the right to use it to somebody else he will normally pay you a periodical royalty in respect of the patent user. This royalty is normally subject to tax by deduction at source at the basic rate (20 per cent). If, however, the payer does not deduct tax then you would generally be assessed to income tax as miscellaneous profits.

The gross equivalent of any patent royalties that you receive must be included in your total income for income tax purposes (5.2), but you get a credit for the basic rate tax already suffered by deduction at source. Where you receive a lump sum payment, in respect of royalties for the past user of your patent, you can spread the payment backwards over the period of use in order to calculate your income tax liability.

If you sell any patent rights for a capital sum, this will normally be taxable as miscellaneous profits provided you are resident in this country. You can, however, spread the payment forward over a period of six years in computing your income tax liability. If, however, you are non-resident, the payer should deduct income tax at 20 per cent in paying you (subject to possible double tax relief and exemptions).

Note that profits from the exploitation of patents acquired or created by companies from 1 April 2002 fall within the new corporation tax rules for intellectual property (13.29.1) rather than the above. Known as the *Patent Box*, this beneficial treatment is only available to companies that either contribute to the creation of the patent or manufacture products covered by it.

15.4 Authors' copyright sales and royalties (ITTOIA Ss221–225)

Unlike patent royalties, copyright royalty payments to authors etc. are made gross without the deduction of any income tax. If you have such receipts and you are an author or composer etc. by profession, then your royalties will be taxed as part of your professional earnings (11.4). Otherwise, any royalties that you receive may be assessed as miscellaneous profits. Different rules have applied for companies since 1 April 2002 (13.29).

Prior to 6 April 2000, where you assigned the copyright in the whole or a part of a work, although any sum that you received was taxable by reference to the tax year or accounting period in which it was received, you could normally obtain relief by electing to spread the payment in accordance with special rules, which can be found in previous editions of this book.

From 6 April 2000, income spreading was replaced by a profits averaging system as follows:

(1) The first years for averaging were 2000–01 and 2001–02.
(2) Individual taxpayers can claim to average the profits of two or more consecutive tax years if the profits are derived from a trade, profession or vocation mainly derived from creative activities.
(3) If the profits of one of the years are 70 per cent or less of the profits of the other, on a claim being made, the average is assessed for each year.
(4) Where the smaller profits (S) are between 70 and 75 per cent of the larger (P), a formula is used to find the adjustment, which is 3D – 0.75P (D = P – S).
(5) An averaging claim may not be made for a year of commencement or cessation.
(6) A claim must be made no later than 12 months after 31 January following the end of the later of the tax years to which it relates.

15.5 Sub-contractors (FA 2004 Ss57–77 & Schs 11–12 & SI 2005 No. 2045)

If you are an independent or self-employed contractor and are not engaged under a contract of employment, you will be taxed as if you are trading, rather than employed. This will normally be advantageous to you because you will be able to deduct various expenses such as travelling from your home or other base of operations to the site etc. where you are working for the time being.

Special rules apply to payments made by a building contractor or similar organisation in the building trade to a sub-contractor in connection with building and construction work. These extend to non-building firms which spend substantial amounts on construction operations (over £1 million on average for the last three years or £3 million in less than three years). These figures can be calculated exclusive of VAT and materials costs. However, from 6 April 1998, all construction workers whose services are supplied by employment agencies etc. are normally taxed as if they are employees. Hence, they are subject to PAYE and NIC deductions.

The current sub-contractors' regime was introduced from 6 April 2007 and readers should refer to previous editions of this book for the rules applicable in earlier years.

Key changes introduced from 6 April 2007 were the substitution of an HMRC verification service for the former registration cards and exemption certificates, the introduction of monthly returns in place of individual vouchers and the requirement for a new employment status declaration.

As part of the verification process, the contractor is instructed whether to pay gross or make deductions at the standard rate of 20 per cent (18 per cent from 6 April 2000 to 5 April 2007) or at a higher rate of 30 per cent (for unregistered sub-contractors).

Subject to transitional rules until 6 April 2009, the verification process did not apply to a sub-contractor who has been included in a scheme return by the contractor concerned for the same year or either of the two previous years.

HMRC's online Employment Status Indicator tool assists contractors to establish the likely HMRC view as to whether new sub-contractors' terms of engagement constitute employment or self-employment. However, it is not intended to be used by company directors or other office holders, or if you work through an agency or your own intermediary (IR 35) vehicle (10.16). A written ruling can be obtained from HMRC in case of doubt. Following the work done by the IR35 Forum since June 2011, HMRC published their *Business Entity Tests* in May 2012 with commentary and risk scoring. It does not improve the law, but provides further insight into HMRC's concerns.

The contractor must deduct tax at the rate notified (if any) for each of them from every payment made to the sub-contractors who work for him except for the element which represents cost of materials or VAT. The tax deducted must be paid over to HMRC. Each sub-contractor then prepares accounts to show his trading profits which include the gross equivalents of the payments made to him. Income tax is computed on the basis of the accounts (11.4) and the tax deducted is credited against his total liability. If the income tax liability is less than the tax deducted a repayment is obtained. Interest is charged where formal assessments are made on contractors for under-deductions from payments to sub-contractors.

The scheme also applies to certain companies, whilst other rules require the deduction of tax from payments made to temporary agency workers. Companies with a sub-contractor gross payment status (see below) will need to notify HMRC of any change in company control.

Companies in the Construction Industry Scheme can set off tax deducted from sub-contract payments received against payments due to HMRC. These include PAYE, national insurance contributions and deductions made as a contractor.

If you are a sub-contractor in the building trade you will normally be able to obtain gross payment status if you complete the necessary application and can satisfy certain conditions including having a regular place of business in this country and having been substantially compliant with your UK tax obligations throughout the twelve months immediately preceding your application. There is also a turnover test (now £30,000 for sole traders and higher amounts for partnerships and companies) for which you can include all of your construction income net of VAT and materials.

15.6 Farming

If you carry on a farming or market gardening business in this country you will be treated as carrying on a trade. You are assessed to income tax under the rules for trading income (11.4).

In addition to the normal computational rules, some special ones apply, including the following:

(1) If you have more than one farm they will all be assessed as one business (ITTOIA Ss9–11).

(2) You may receive *deficiency payments* from the Government in respect of certain crops etc. These are by concession included in your taxable profits for the year when they are received rather than when the crop is sold.

(3) If you have an eligible agricultural or horticultural holding, you may be able to benefit under one of the various Ministry of Agriculture, Fisheries and Food Grant Schemes. Grants received under these schemes are treated as either capital receipts or revenue receipts for tax purposes according to their nature. For example, field husbandry grants are revenue and grants to cover the reclamation of waste land are capital.

(4) Normally all your livestock will be treated for tax purposes as stock-in-trade. If you have any 'production herds', however, you can elect within two years from the end of your first year of assessment that the *herd basis* should apply. 'Production herds' are those kept for the purpose of obtaining products from the living animal (for example wool, milk etc.). Where a herd basis election has been made the initial cost of the herd is not charged against your profits but is capitalised together with the cost of any additional animals. The cost of rearing the animals to maturity is also capitalised. (Capital allowances are not available.) Any sales proceeds are taxable and the costs of replacement animals are deductible from your taxable profits. If you sell your entire herd you are not charged to tax on the proceeds (ITTOIA Ss111–129). The herd basis also applies to shared animals.

(5) Up to 5 April 2011, a special *agricultural buildings allowance* was available, subject to phasing out from 2008–09 to 2010–11 (11.14).

(6) If you carry on any farming or market gardening activities without any reasonable expectation of profit on a non-commercial basis you will normally be treated as conducting merely *hobby farming*. The effect of this will be that you will not be granted tax relief for any losses from your farming against your other income. You will, however, be permitted to carry forward any losses from your hobby farming to be set against

future taxable profits from the same source (ITA Ss67–70). Generally, the restriction applies when you make your sixth consecutive loss.

(7) Relief is available regarding *fluctuating profits* (taken net of capital allowances if under the new scheme – 11.8) of individual farmers or partnerships. You are able to claim to average the profits of any pair of consecutive years of assessment, provided you do so within broadly 22 months of the end of the second year. If the taxable profits for either or both years are later adjusted, the original claim is set aside but a new one can be made by the end of the year of assessment following that in which the adjustment is made. Another condition is that the profits in the lower year must be no more than 70 per cent of the profits of the better year. If the lower profits are 70 per cent to 75 per cent of the higher, however, limited spreading is allowed. Where a loss is made in any year, for the purposes of the spreading rules, the profits are treated as nil and the loss is relieved in the usual ways (11.22) (ITTOIA Ss221–225).

(8) Capital gains tax rollover relief (20.25) was extended to include first milk and potato quotas and then ewe and suckler cow premium quotas (TCGA S151 & FA 1993 S86). Rights under the EU *single payments scheme* have been added retrospectively as from 1 January 2009 (FA 2012).

15.7 Building society arrangements (TA 1988 S476–483 & ITA S874)

From 6 April 1991 building societies (as well as banks etc.) deduct income tax from interest payments and account for it to the Inland Revenue. The rate was 25 per cent up to 5 April 1996 and then 20 per cent. Non-taxpayers are able to reclaim tax deducted. However, building societies may pay interest and dividends gross to individuals ordinarily resident outside the United Kingdom (8.6). This also applies to payments to charities, friendly societies, pension funds etc.

15.8 Insolvents

When a person becomes bankrupt, a bankruptcy or interim order is made on a certain date and all income tax and capital gains assessments that have been made by that date for previous years are treated as debts in the bankruptcy. Also any assessments made for the tax year ending on the following 5 April will rank as debts in the bankruptcy provided the assessments were made before the date of the receiving order. PAYE and sub-contractors' deductions made within the previous year will rank as preferential debts. This means that they will be paid in full before any payment is made on the non-preferential debts. The remaining assessments will rank as non-preferential debts.

In the case of VAT (23.11.9) tax payable for the six months prior to the date of the order etc. ranks as a preferential debt.

Any future income of the bankrupt individual will be charged to tax in the normal way. Thus any salary would be subjected to PAYE (10.14) – also income tax would be payable on other income.

15.9 Lloyd's underwriters (FA 1993 Ss171–184 & Schs 19–20, FA 1994 Ss219–230 & Sch 21, FA 1995 S143, FA 1999 Ss82–84 & FA 2000 S107)

The special rules which apply to the taxation of Lloyd's underwriters were substantially altered by FA 1993, FA 1994 for companies and subsequent legislation, the main changes being:

(1) A new tax deductible reserve replaced the limited special reserve. This enables you to put aside profits free of tax to meet future losses. Up to 50 per cent of your profits can be transferred in this way each year, provided the value of the reserve fund is no more than half your overall premium limit. Income and gains within the reserves will be tax-free.
(2) Gains on assets representing your invested premiums are no longer specially treated and are incorporated in trading profits.
(3) In general, your taxable receipts and allowable expenses are now within the rules for taxation of trades (11.1), together with gains and losses on assets in premium trust funds.
(4) Although syndicate accounts for each trading year are drawn up annually, they are closed off after the third year to allow members to join and leave. At that stage the members for that year pay those for the new year appropriate insurance premiums and the new year's syndicate members take over the outstanding liabilities. This is known as 'reinsurance to close'.
(5) Starting with the 1985 account, 'reinsurance to close' is tax deductible only to the extent that it is shown not to exceed a fair and reasonable assessment of the liabilities. This means aiming at having neither a profit nor loss accrue to the recipient of the premium. These rules were introduced in 1987 and were modified in 1988 and 1993.
(6) For accounting periods beginning after 31 December 1993, profits from corporate membership of Lloyd's are charged to corporation tax under FA 1994. In general, these are treated as trading income except for non-syndicate profits otherwise taxable as income. 'Reinsurance to close' relief is available as for individuals (above).
(7) From 6 April 1999 individual members participating in syndicates through 'members agent pooling arrangements' may treat their shares of the various syndicate capacities so held as being single direct holdings for capital gains tax purposes. Also, capital gains tax rollover relief will apply for all syndicate capacity.
(8) The benefits of tax deferral may be clawed back where provisions for unpaid claims are not properly discounted and those for future claims are overestimated. This applies to individual members of Lloyd's from 2000–2001 and companies' accounting periods beginning after 31 December 2000. (Individuals participating in only a very small proportion of a syndicate's business will be exempted.)
(9) A type of reinsurance is known as a quota share contract. Where a premium is payable under such a contract from 17 April 2002, by a Lloyd's member, tax relief is restricted to take account of that already given for declared but unpaid losses. At the same time, members paying

cash calls before entering into share quota contracts will be helped by extending the relief available to losses covered by the cash call.

(10) Lloyd's Names, who after 5 April 2004 transfer their underwriting to a company (or Scottish Limited Partnership in which they are the only underwriting partner), will be able to obtain relief for trading losses from previous underwriting years against income from the company or limited partnership. Capital gains tax deferment may also be available regarding assets transferred in exchange for shares.

15.10 Anti-avoidance provisions (ITA Ss682–809 etc.)

There is an important distinction between *tax evasion* and *tax avoidance*. Tax evasion refers to all those activities illegally undertaken by a taxpayer to free himself from tax which the law charges upon his income, for example the falsification of his returns, books and accounts. This is illegal and subject to very heavy penalties (16.9.2). Tax avoidance, on the other hand, denotes that the taxpayer has arranged his affairs in such a way as to reduce his tax liability legally – for example, by investing in tax-free securities such as national savings certificates.

Tax avoidance is also attempted in more complicated and devious ways with particular use being made of overseas trusts and companies. In order to prevent abuse of the UK tax rules in this way various anti-avoidance provisions have been introduced. Also, certain Court decisions such as *Ramsay* and *Furniss* v. *Dawson* have barred tax relief from artificial circuitous schemes. Much of the legislation was included in TA 1988 Ss703–786, which has (in the main) been rewritten in ITA Ss682–809.

Unfortunately, some of the rules introduced to counter sophisticated avoidance schemes penalise quite innocent commercial activities, not carried out with a view to tax saving. It is thus important to consider the anti-avoidance provisions, particularly when involved in overseas operations and company reorganisations or takeovers. The following are some of the more important provisions to consider.

15.10.1 Transactions in securities (ITA Ss682–713 & FA 2010 S39 & Sch 12)

These provisions charge you to income tax as miscellaneous income any 'tax advantage' that you obtain as a result of one or more 'transactions in securities'. For these purposes a 'tax advantage' is a saving of income tax or corporation tax (including, from 11 October 1996, the payment of a tax credit), but it does not apply to capital gains tax. 'Transactions in securities' include the formation and liquidation of companies as well as purchases and sales of shares etc. A frequent application of this legislation is to prevent tax savings being effected by obtaining the use of the undistributed profits of companies by means of schemes involving 'transactions in securities'.

Under the original rules, you could avoid being assessed under these provisions if you could show that the transactions concerned were carried out for commercial purposes and one of your main objects was not tax saving. However, the legislation has been rewritten with effect from 1 April 2009, 24 March 2010 and 1 April 2010, to express the provisions in terms of four positive conditions. Two of these are that one of the main purposes is to secure a tax advantage and the fact that such a tax saving has been made. The previous commercial purpose and absence of tax saving as a main purpose is replaced by an exception where there is a 75 per cent change in ownership involved. These changes make it all the more important that, if you are planning to carry out transactions which you fear may be covered by these provisions, you should exercise your right to apply for clearance to HMRC giving all relevant facts and they must let you know within one month whether such clearance is granted.

15.10.2 **Transfer of assets abroad** (ITA Ss714–751)

The object of these provisions is to prevent you from avoiding tax by transferring some of your assets abroad. The provisions normally, but not exclusively, apply to transfers of assets made by persons ordinarily resident in this country (17.3.1). If as a result of such transfer of assets, income is payable to persons resident or domiciled abroad (to avoid UK income tax) then if anyone ordinarily resident in the UK has the 'power to enjoy' any of the income, he can be assessed to income tax as miscellaneous profits on all or part of the income. 'Power to enjoy' the income is widely defined.

For income arising from 26 November 1996, confirming normal practice, the legislation applies whatever your ordinary residence status is when you make the transfer, and where a purpose is to avoid any form of direct tax.

There are no provisions under which clearance can be obtained and this particular legislation must be most carefully considered regarding all overseas schemes. You can even be assessed on a benefit if you did not make the original transfer. However, no income can be assessed more than once.

From 5 December 2005 the rules are clarified and tightened, particularly regarding the motive test (either no tax avoidance purpose or the transactions all being commercial with any tax avoidance being only incidental to the general design).

It is expected that from 6 April 2013 the status of *ordinarily resident* will be abolished and these rules will then apply, if you are simply *tax resident* in UK (17.6).

A consultation on proposals to modernise this legislation and also the treatment of gains on UK assets held by foreign companies was due to be published in June 2012. Unfortunately, insufficient was known about content of these proposals when this edition went to press for us to include any early warning to readers.

15.10.3 **Sales at undervalue or overvalue** (TA 1988 S77A & Sch 28AA)

Important rules apply where any sale takes place between people who are connected with each other (this can include partnerships and companies) and the price is less than the open market value of the goods (or services). Then in calculating the tax liability on the trading income of the seller, the sales proceeds must be adjusted to the true value of the goods if HMRC so direct. This does not apply if the purchase is made by a taxable business in this country as a part of its trading stock. If the purchaser is an overseas trader, however, the sale is not exempted from these provisions.

A similar adjustment must be made for the buyer if the price is more than the open market value of the goods. Other provisions cover capital gains on sales between connected persons. For chargeable periods ending after 1 July 1999, the above transactions are brought within the self-assessment framework. The legislation has been revised in line with international practice and a particular feature is the facility for taxpayers to agree transfer prices with the tax author ities in advance. Advance pricing agreements may be made between taxpayers and the Inland Revenue from August 1999 regarding chargeable accounting periods ending from that time. These enable problems to be cleared in advance so as to remove the risk of extra tax being imposed.

From 1 April 2004, the general transfer pricing rules encompass thin capitalisation (excessive loan finance between connected companies). Neither normally continue to apply for small and medium-sized enterprises. However, the scope of the transfer pricing requirements for other businesses now extends to UK and cross-border transactions, but dormant companies are excluded.

15.10.4 **Sale of income derived from personal activities** (ITA Ss773–789)

The object of these provisions is to prevent you from saving tax by contriving to sell your present or future earnings for a capital sum, thereby paying no tax or only capital gains tax instead of income tax at basic and higher rates. Subject to the precise rules, any such capital sum is to be treated as earned income arising when it is receivable and is chargeable as miscellaneous profits.

These provisions might apply if you receive a capital sum from the sale of a business which derives part of its value from your personal services. From 6 April 1988, the provisions are not so penal because broadly the same tax rates apply to income and capital gains.

15.10.5 **Artificial transactions in land and 'sale and leaseback'** (ITA Ss752–772)

These provisions are considered in detail in the chapter which deals with income from land and property (see 7.11). Note that tax advantages from sales of land with the right to repurchase are also countered.

15.10.6 **Leasing and capital allowances** (TA 1988 Ss384 & 395 etc. & CAA 2001 Ss213–233)

Complicated anti-avoidance provisions operate concerning the claiming of relief for capital allowances in certain contrived situations. These provisions were designed to counter certain tax saving schemes involving leasing arrangements in group situations and consortia; also leasing partnerships between individuals and companies.

Wider provisions prevent your setting off losses created through claims for capital allowances on leasing assets, against non-leasing income. An exception is made for a leasing trade to which you devote substantially all your time, provided this trade continues for at least six months.

Leasing assets normally qualifies for a 20 per cent writing down allowance (11.9.15). However, the rate is restricted to 10 per cent where the assets are leased to non-residents. Similarly, a writing down allowance of only 10 per cent is available on expenditure after 9 March 1982 where ships or aircraft were let on charter to non-residents in order to obtain first year allowances.

Two new measures counter tax-saving through finance leasing schemes. Under a finance lease, a bank etc. buys an asset and leases it to you so that you have substantially all the benefits of outright ownership.

Also hit are new leases made after 26 November 1996, where the rentals are concentrated towards the ends of their terms. In both cases from that date, for tax purposes the rentals are as appears in the lessor's commercial accounts, rather than the rentals receivable. Furthermore, the assets concerned do not attract capital allowances (FA 1997 S82 & Sch 12).

FA 2004 blocks capital allowance loopholes with effect from 17 March 2004 concerning sale and leaseback or lease and leaseback of plant and machinery. The new rules are to prevent any double tax advantage to a business from obtaining capital allowances and deductions for lease rentals. They restrict the rental deduction in computing profits. The tax consequences of termination leases are also dealt with.

Measures are introduced by FA 2006 with effect, with some exceptions, from 5 December 2005 which counter the avoidance of tax where a company carrying on the business of leasing plant or machinery is sold etc. to another such company. However, the purchaser normally obtains extra relief.

New rules in FA 2008 counter artificial tax advantages obtained by leasing in and leasing out the same plant and machinery; also where a lease is granted in exchange for an otherwise tax-free premium.

FA 2008 legislates against a corporation tax avoidance scheme crystallising a balancing allowance on plant and machinery to make it available to a profitable group not intending to trade in the long term.

15.10.7 **Group relief restrictions** (TA 1988 Ss409–413 & FA 1989 Ss97–102)

These provisions can act to restrict or prevent group loss relief being available for one group company (13.13) in respect of trading losses of another. A particular point to watch is that if a group of companies has arranged to sell a loss-making company, relief for the losses of that company may not be available to the other group members for periods prior to the accounting period in which the sale actually takes place.

Special rules apply where companies join or leave a group. Instead of the normal time apportionment to fit the losses or profits to the respective old and new groups, a just and reasonable basis will be substituted in obviously distorted cases. This could involve separate accounts before and after the date of changing groups. Modifications of the rules regarding groups took effect during 1989 and are mentioned elsewhere (13.16).

15.10.8 **Interest schemes** (ITA Ss578–580)

Complicated tax avoidance schemes were developed concerning 'manufactured' interest relief. Anti-avoidance rules operate regarding the interest payments.

15.10.9 **Capital gains tax** (TCGA Ss27, 29, 71, 137, 138 & 169 & Sch 7A)

Various rules counter the avoidance of capital gains tax in certain situations. The latter include 'value-shifting' schemes, where an allowable loss has been created artificially by moving value out of one asset and possibly into another.

There are also anti-avoidance rules concerning capital gains tax resulting from company reconstructions, takeovers and amalgamations (20.18.6). A clearance procedure applies, however, which is similar to that applying for transactions in securities (15.10.1). Also, the rules do not apply if you can show that the arrangements were carried out for commercial, rather than tax-saving purposes.

Provisions prevent the artificial creation of capital losses by inflating the purchase price of assets for capital gains tax purposes above their true value, so that by selling for the true worth a capital loss results. This artificial effect sometimes resulted from the rule that transactions between connected persons are treated as being for a consideration equal to market value and sometimes through reorganisations of share capital (20.18.6). The capital gains tax cost of the purchaser is only increased to the extent that the capital gains tax position of the vendor is affected.

Gifts relief (20.28) does not apply to non-resident donees. Dual-resident trusts are regarded as non-resident for this purpose.

Capital gains tax rollover relief is not available where a non-resident replaces a business asset within the UK charge with one which is outside it.

With effect from 16 March 1993, tax benefits from buying capital loss companies (13.15) were legislated against. From the same date, capital gains no longer fall out of charge where shares are exchanged for debentures which are outside the tax net.

FA 2004 introduced measures effecting certain disposals after 9 December 2003. Gifts relief (20.28) was withdrawn regarding transfers to a settlement in which the settlor has an interest. Furthermore, private residence relief (20.23) may be lost where gifts relief was obtained on the earlier disposal of the property.

New rules operate from 5 December 2005 regarding corporate capital losses. These flow from FA 2006 and redefine allowable capital losses to exclude losses generated by a company as part of a tax avoidance scheme. Other targeted areas include the buying and selling of capital gains and losses and the conversion of income streams into capital gains.

15.10.10 **Commodity and financial futures** (TA 1988 S399 & TCGA S143)

Losses created by means of certain artificial dealing partnerships may not be relieved against general income. (Note that a commodity deal not forming part of a trade is liable to capital gains tax rather than income tax as miscellaneous profits as before.)

15.10.11 **Bank lending etc.** (TA 1988 S798)

There are rules to prevent certain tax advantages being obtained by exploiting the double tax relief system. Also, the creation of 'equity loans' where the interest paid is partly dependent on a company's results no longer produces a 'distribution'. This affects banks and the loss-making companies they were able to lend money to at lower rates. The double taxation rules relate mainly to banks.

15.10.12 **Controlled foreign companies (CFCs)** (TA 1988 Ss747–756 & Schs 24–26 etc. & TIOPA 2010 Ss 371AA-VJ)

HMRC have powers to assess additional tax on certain UK resident companies with interests in CFCs. Fuller details are given earlier (13.22) but the circumstances where a charge might arise are where a foreign subsidiary in a low tax area is paying insufficient of its profits as dividends etc. to its UK parent company. FA 2008 blocked certain avoidance schemes using a partnership or trust to escape a CFC charge, either by misusing a CFC exemption or arranging for profits to purportedly fall outside the CFC rules.

Pending the completion of a comprehensive review of the CFC regime, FA 2011 made a number of relaxations to assist genuine commercial needs of large companies and groups. These apply from 1 January 2011 and include raising the *de minimis* exemption from £50,000 to £200,000 and basing this on the accounts profit. FA 2012 includes a comprehensive rewrite of the CFC regime operative from the commencement of the first accounting period of each CFC on or after 1 January 2013.

15.10.13 **Offshore funds and other savings income** (TA 1988 Ss757–764 & Schs 27–28, TCGA Ss102, 212, FA 2003 Ss198–199 & FA 2009 S44 & Sch 22)

Broadly, if you dispose of an investment in an offshore fund which does not distribute enough of its income, you will be taxed on your entire gain as if it were income as miscellaneous profits (15.10.2). Gains on switches of holdings in offshore 'umbrella' funds by UK investors, attract capital gains tax. Since 29 November 1994 only 'collective investment schemes' are covered by legislation and the distribution test is waived if the income is no more than 1 per cent of the average value of the assets. From 1 December 2009 a new approach will reclassify offshore funds on a purposive basis.

FA 2003 enables certain EU proposals regarding the exchange of cross-border information to be implemented in order to help ensure that savings income is properly reported. However, they do not take effect until after 1 January 2005. Reports will be required regarding non-residents from banks, building societies, other deposit takers, registrars, authorised unit trusts, stockbrokers etc.

15.10.14 **Dual resident companies** (TCGA Ss159, 160 & 188)

Special provisions apply to prohibit a dual resident investment company from surrendering losses to other members of a UK group (13.13). The companies concerned are UK resident and also taxed in another country because of place of incorporation, management or residence. Furthermore, the definition of such dual resident investment companies extends to those which either do not trade or are mainly used to borrow or to purchase or hold shares in another group member.

Where an asset of a dual resident company ceases to be within the UK capital gains tax charge due to a double tax agreement, the company is deemed to have disposed of the asset. Regarding replacements of business assets (either the disposal or replacement) rollover relief is not available if a UK asset within the capital gains tax charge is replaced by an asset which is not.

Certain dual resident companies are treated as resident outside the UK for some tax purposes. This is to counter avoidance of tax through controlled foreign companies (13.22) and transfers of assets abroad.

Also, rules operate which are designed to prevent a company transferring assets tax-free to a dual resident company in whose hands any gain would be outside the UK tax charge. Similarly, rollover relief (20.25) is denied on the replacement of business assets where one member of a group disposes of an asset and a dual resident group member replaces it with an asset outside the UK tax charge.

15.10.15 **International capital movements – migration of companies** (TA 1988 S765 & FA 2009 Sch 17)

From 1 July 2009, the long-standing regime for advance notification of 'migration of companies' was replaced by a potentially wider requirement for 'reporting companies' to notify certain transactions within (generally) six months after the event. However, this only applies to transactions in excess of £100 million. There are numerous specific exemptions (broadly repeating and extending the former general consents).

Previously, TA 1988 S765 contained penal provisions to prevent a UK company from becoming non-resident without Treasury consent being obtained. Such consent was also required to transfer part or all of its business to a non-resident and for certain share transactions. From 15 March 1988, such consent was no longer needed (except for certain share transactions) and it was replaced by a tax charge on unrealised gains. Companies intending to emigrate had to notify the Inland Revenue in advance, providing an estimate of their UK tax commitments including tax on unrealised gains, and details of arrangements to settle such tax. If the tax was not paid, penalties could be charged. Furthermore, former directors and group companies could be held responsible for tax and interest.

After 30 June 1990, Treasury consent was no longer needed regarding certain transactions relating to companies within the European Community. This applied to issues and transfers of shares and debentures of overseas subsidiaries within the EC. Where special Treasury consent was previously needed, reporting to the Revenue was required with non-compliance penalties of up to £3,000.

15.10.16 **Capital gains tax – sales of subsidiaries** (TCGA Ss31–34 etc.)

Certain schemes to save tax on capital gains where a group disposes of one or more subsidiaries are blocked. For example, the value of a subsidiary may be reduced before sale by distributing assets to fellow group members at less than market value; such undervalue will be added to the sale proceeds in calculating the capital gain on the sale of the subsidiary. However, the legislation is not intended to catch distributions which could be made out of normal profits and reserves.

The above rules have been widened to catch situations where a subsidiary is sold to another group company which is non-UK resident, which in turn sells it to the eventual non-group purchaser. The new rules apply where the transfer to the overseas group company takes place after 8 March 1999.

Another situation which has been countered, is where the commercial control of a subsidiary is sold, whilst keeping it within the group for capital gains relief on inter-group transfers etc. through using special shares. The benefits of group membership only apply if the parent company of the group has, directly or indirectly, an interest of over 50 per cent in the income and assets of the company.

The sale of a subsidiary can also give rise to capital gains on assets previously transferred to it from other group companies. Conversely, gain buying by groups with losses has been countered. These and similar anti-avoidance rules are considered earlier (13.16).

15.10.17 **Capital gains tax – non-resident trusts** (TCGA Ss80–98 & Sch 5)

From 19 March 1991, sweeping changes have effect regarding the capital gains tax rules relating to offshore settlements. The rules (21.9.1) involve the settlor and beneficiaries. Among other changes, the use of such settlements to delay the onset of capital gains tax has been much curtailed. Further detailed changes, sometimes retrospective to 1991 have been introduced by the 1998 Finance Act.

From 21 March 2000, rules take effect to stop capital gains tax being avoided where an offshore trust is made UK resident and then non-resident again. Also acted against is the situation where gains are sheltered through the double tier of a trust and an offshore company and the existing anti-avoidance laws are set aside by a double tax agreement (FA 2000 Ss94–96).

15.10.18 **Interest within multinational groups** (FA 1993 Ss61–66)

Special rules apply to interest payable within multinational groups to UK companies by non-resident associated companies on certain loans etc. The interest is taxable as it accrues, rather than when it arises as hitherto. This applies to interest accruing from 1 April 1993.

The rules apply where under the financial arrangements, the interest payable in any 12 month period is less than the amount accruing pro rata to the lender in that period. However, if you can satisfy the Inspector of Taxes that saving tax was not the main motive for using the arising basis and similar terms would have been agreed at arm's length, exemption is available from the rules.

15.10.19 **Capital gains tax – UK trusts**

From 16 June 1999, the avoidance of capital gains tax by purchasing trust losses has been countered. The new rules apply to transfers of trust property to beneficiaries from that day.

The set off of losses against trust gains arising after 20 March 2000 is restricted where gains on the original transfer to the trust were deferred by gifts relief (FA 2000 S93).

Where a beneficiary of a trust sells his interest in it to someone else after 20 March 2000, in certain circumstances there may be a capital gains tax charge. (This particularly applies to UK trusts where the settlor has an interest.) The underlying assets to which the interest relates are treated as disposed of by the trust at market value and immediately reacquired (FA 2000 S91 & Sch 24).

From 21 March 2000, where trustees are in debt and transfer funds to another person and the borrowings have not all been used for trust purposes, the trust assets are in whole or part treated as being disposed of and reacquired at market value, so as to crystallise a capital gain. This is to prevent avoidance schemes involving loans and new trusts (FA 2000 S92 & Schs 25 & 26).

15.10.20 **Manufactured dividends and interest** (TA Sch 23A)

From 17 April 2002, the tax deductibility of manufactured payments made by individuals (and others not charged to corporation tax) has been restricted. Such payments might arise where the current holder of say loan stock receives a payment of interest or dividend but has agreed to pay an equivalent amount to the original owner. Relief will be restricted to cases where the underlying real payment would be deductible or the recipient is taxed on an equivalent amount from the same UK securities. FA 2004 has strengthened these provisions to ensure that the dividends are taxed at the same rate as relief is given for the manufactured payments and has extended the rules to trusts.

FA 2008 legislates against various schemes involving investment products for tax avoidance, such as disguised interest. These include where interest is received in the form of non-taxable distributions and relief is obtained for non-existent overseas tax credits. FA 2009 is to legislate for a generic approach to ensure that all such arrangements will be taxed in the same way as interest.

15.10.21 **Avoidance involving partnerships etc.**

Various anti-avoidance measures are included in FA 2004 regarding partnership and related arrangements. Certain of the provisions concern film relief (11.21), licence exploitation, companies in partnership and restricting the loss relief of non-active partners (12.3).

FA 2005 introduces various anti-avoidance provisions regarding partnerships. Ss72–78 limit the amount of relief which partners can claim against their other income and capital gains and give the rules for calculating the excess relief, which is taxable. S79 defines 'capital contribution to the trade' for partners' film relief purposes and enables the countering of avoidance schemes in which partners obtain more tax relief than the capital which they introduced.

15.10.22 **Disclosure of tax avoidance schemes (DOTAS)**

FA 2004 imposed new disclosure obligations on scheme promoters and taxpayers. The arrangements covered are those where the main advantage is a tax benefit and further conditions, which are being specified, are met. The disclosure rules came into effect on 1 August 2004, but apply to schemes promoted or sold from 18 March 2004, or 23 April 2004 where no promoter or an offshore one is involved.

The promoters are required to provide full details of their tax schemes, which HMRC will register and allot reference numbers. As a purchaser of such a scheme, you will merely need to enter the reference number in your tax return, unless the promoter is based offshore or no promoter was involved. In those cases, you must provide the scheme details to HMRC. If you render professional advice in respect of a scheme, you should consider thoroughly the extent of and time limit for any reporting obligation you have.

Initially the taxes covered were restricted to income tax, corporation tax and capital gains tax and the schemes to be disclosed were limited to those based on employment or financial products, which met further conditions.

New regulations apply from 1 July 2006, containing hallmarks which make schemes notifiable. (However, SMEs and individuals are excluded regarding in-house schemes.) Subject to the rules, targets include new and innovative schemes, mass-marketed products and areas of particular risk; also certain schemes to create losses and leasing schemes. Other changes include reducing the time limit to 30 days from the implementation of a scheme and wider powers to exchange information internationally, now to include both direct and indirect taxes.

From 1 January 2011, further changes have been made to expedite early disclosure, including enhanced non-compliance penalties for promoters (up to £5,000 daily 10 days after imposition by a Tribunal and a further possible maximum of £1 million in large cases), power to require intermediaries to identify promoters, submission of periodic lists of scheme clients and revised hallmarks. Notification is generally needed within 5 working days (30 days continuing where there is no promoter). From 6 April 2011, certain transfers into relevant property settlements, where an inheritance tax advantage is anticipated, have been brought within the regime, if the scheme is new or innovative.

A consultation paper was due to be released in June 2012, setting out proposals to further extend the existing hallmarks of schemes, requiring notification to HMRC. No further details are available for inclusion as this edition goes to press.

15.10.23 'Spotlights' on schemes under challenge

On 22 April 2009 HMRC announced a change in their policy of not commenting publicly on tax avoidance activities. They now intend to publicise a small selection of the schemes under scrutiny, in order to put the public on notice that they view them as unlikely to be effective and, subject to the particular facts, intend to challenge them and seek full settlement of tax liabilities through enquiry and litigation. These announcements (entitled 'Spotlights') may be coupled with fresh legislation to clarify or change the existing law either retrospectively or from the date of any Ministerial announcement. Brief details of the eleven Spotlights so far published are:

(1) Goodwill – companies acquiring businesses carried on prior to April 2002 by a related party (FA 2009 S69 from 22 April 2009).
(2) VAT – artificial leasing of pleasure craft within EU (April 2009).
(3) Pensions schemes – artificial surpluses arising from certain surrenders of rights (April 2009).
(4) Contrived employment liabilities and losses (FA 2009 S67 as from 12 January 2009).
(5) Using trusts and similar entities to reward employees without payment of NI contributions or income tax (10.17).
(6) Employer financed retirement benefits schemes (EFRBS) (10.17).
(7) Avoidance using gift aid for certain share transfers (6 January 2010).
(8) Investments to obtain trade loss relief ('sideways relief') (8 February 2010 – FA 2010 S24).
(9) Gift Aid with no real gift (29 March 2010).
(10) Stamp duty land tax avoidance (7 June 2010).
(11) Avoiding income tax on pay (3 March 2011) (10.17).
(12) Rewards for work carried out for UK based employer (23 August 2011).

HMRC will continue to monitor and challenge other activities that have NOT been the subject of a Spotlight.

15.10.24 General attack on tax avoidance

FA 2009 continued the Government's targeting of tax avoidance over a wide front. In addition to the items given specific mention, there are further provisions aimed at specialised schemes designed for large groups of companies and for financial institutions, which are beyond the scope of this book.

FA 2010 contains numerous items under the general caption 'anti-avoidance and revenue protection'. These include provisions to introduce by statutory instrument a special table of penalties for non-disclosure of offshore income, with maximum penalties of 200 per cent of the underpaid tax in the severest cases.

FA 2011 included anti-avoidance provisions to prevent groups of companies exploiting timing differences in accounting treatments for inter-company loans and hedging agreements to manipulate their tax liabilities. Also, new rules for plant leasing businesses pre-empt tax anomalies that would otherwise arise from prospective changes to UK and International accounting standards. With effect from 6 April 2011, further measures in FA 2011 prevent UK residents from taking advantage of tax treaty exemptions in UK for foreign pensions, where pension funds have been exported from UK for that purpose.

In June 2010 the Government first indicated its intention to reconsider the possibility of introducing a *general anti-avoidance rule* (GAAR), which had been soundly rejected some years earlier. It later commissioned Graham Aaronson QC to head a study group, which reported similar conclusions in November 2011, but steered Government towards the introduction of a carefully focused *general anti-abuse rule* (also GAAR). A public consultation on this was published on 12 June 2012 and remains open until 14 September 2012. Detailed legislation is expected in the Autumn 2012 draft FB 2013 and commencement would be from 1 April 2013, with exclusion of any transaction wholly completed before that date.

An essential element of the proposals is to ensure that the GAAR does not create uncertainty of tax outcome for taxpayers' normal transactions. There is to be no advance clearance procedure, but there is to be an independent Advisory Panel, which, at the initiative of HMRC, would issue non-binding opinions to HMRC and taxpayer before any application of the GAAR. Any transaction that falls within a self-assessment will presumably be notified by the taxpayer, if he wishes to protect himself against non-disclosure penalties – and it is possible that DOTAS (15.10.22) may apply in some cases. The usual tribunal and court appeal mechanism will apply. The declared intention is to target transactions that meet both a *tax arrangements test* and an *abusiveness test*. If it can be proved that there was no tax purpose, the GAAR will not apply. Often the transactions will be novel and complex and unlikely to have been contemplated by tax legislators. Therefore the tax advantage of offending arrangements will be counteracted on a *just and reasonable* basis. If successful, this approach may eventually reduce the need for reactive targeted anti-avoidance rules.

The GAAR will apply to a wide range of taxes – income, corporation and inheritance taxes, CGT, SDLT, NIC and the new annual charge on enveloped properties (15.10.25), but not to VAT, which has its own concept of tax abuse.

15.10.25 High value residential property

A consultation document issued on 31 May 2012 set out detailed proposals for a dual strategy to counteract perceived tax losses in respect of UK-located, high value residential properties held in offshore structures (envelopes) owned by persons other than individuals. The consultation runs to 23 August 2012 and fuller draft legislation can be expected in the Autumn 2012 draft of FB 2013.

These proposals complement the special rate of SDLT imposed on purchases of such properties from 22 March 2012 (24.4.2) and apply only to properties (or parts thereof):

- whose market value exceeds £2 million; and
- which constitute a *dwelling* as defined for SDLT, even if let on a commercial basis or used by the owner or tenant as accommodation for others, including employees.

Their two components are:-

(1) Annual charge – proposal at 31 May 2012

- applies to specified 'non-natural' persons (broadly companies, partnerships including companies and collective investment vehicles);
- does not apply to trust companies holding solely as trustees of a settlement, nor to established property developers with a two-year trading history;
- liability to be for years 1 April to 31 March commencing 1 April 2013;
- initial value to be self-assessed as at 1 April 2012 or subsequent acquisition cost and revalued at intervals of 5 years;
- initial flat amount of tax payable to be based on a scale of values as follows:

Market value	£m 2–5	5–10	10–20	20 upwards
Tax 2013–14	£15,000	35,000	70,000	140,000

- tax to be pro-rated for part-years and indexed by reference to CPI annually for subsequent years;
- tax due annually on 15 April, except for 2013, which may have to await Royal Assent to FA 2013.

(2) Capital Gains Tax – proposal at 31 May 2012

- to extend to disposals or part-disposals by non-resident, non-natural persons of high value residential property or interests in such property or in the envelopes in which they are held;
- the definition of these persons has yet to be decided and may not precisely follow that for the annual charge;

- charities exempt from CGT on their assets will be exempt from this extension;
- a deliberate departure (for economic reasons and on the grounds that most jurisdictions claim primary taxing rights over immovable property in their territory) from our established principle of exempting non-residents from CGT;
- appropriate anti-avoidance provisions for non-residents have yet to be considered;
- the rate of CGT payable has not been decided and is not a matter intended for consultation;
- will generally be within the self-assessment regime for non-resident companies;
- will apply to disposals on or after 6 April 2013 with tax due by 31 January 2015.

15.11 Tax defaulters

15.11.1 Serious tax defaulters – 'Name and Shame' (FA 2009 S53)

FA 2009 permits HMRC to publish the names of certain tax defaulters from a date to be announced. The rules apply across a wide range of taxes (excluding tax credits) to any individual, business or corporate taxpayer who is penalised for deliberately understating tax due or overstating claims or losses, where the resultant tax loss exceeds £25,000. First publication cannot be deferred more than twelve months from the date when the penalty becomes final and, once published (by quarterly list) names will be displayed for precisely twelve months. Those who make an unprompted disclosure or a full prompted disclosure within the required time will not be affected and the provisions will not apply to defaults prior to the commencing date.

15.11.2 Deliberate tax defaulters – 5-year reports

The 2009 Budget included an announcement of proposals to enable HMRC to require additional information in support of income tax returns for up to five years from taxpayers who have been subjected to a penalty for tax understatements in excess of £5,000, in order to ensure that they have adequate records and systems, to enable future returns to be prepared to an adequate standard.

Chapter 16

RETURNS, ASSESSMENTS AND REPAYMENT CLAIMS

This chapter covers administrative matters, largely to be found in the Taxes Management Act 1970 (TMA). With effect from 1996–97, radical changes took effect, with the introduction of the new self-assessment system. This is dealt with below.

16.1 Self-assessment – an overview (TMA Ss7–9D, 12, 12D, 19A–21, 25–41, 42–43, 59A–D & Schs 1–4 etc.)

FA 1994 contained the framework for the self-assessment system which applies for 1996–97 and future years. FA 1995 and FA 1996 contained further relevant provisions, mainly amending those in the TMA. Points to note include the following:

(1) New filing dates were introduced for 2007–08 and subsequent tax returns. If they are filed online, this must be done by 31 January in the following year. However, for paper returns, an earlier date applies which is 31 October, whether or not you are computing the tax.
(2) Previously, individuals and trustees needed to submit their returns to HMRC by 31 January after the end of the tax year of the return or if later, three months after its issue, including a self-assessment of your tax liabilities.
(3) You did not need to work out your tax bill if you submitted your return by 30 September after the tax year or if later, two months after its issue.
(4) Special tax returns are sent to partnerships to show the income and its division between the partners.
(5) Late returns may give rise to penalties including £100 at once and again after six months; also if the Tax Tribunal (formerly the Commissioners) agree, £60 per day. From April 2011, if your return is 3 months late, there is an automatic penalty of £10 each day (maximum £900). For each of 6 months and 12 months late, your penalty is £300 or 5 per cent of the unpaid tax if greater.
(6) HMRC are able to correct minor errors within nine months of your sending in a return although you can object. You are able to make amendments within one year and HMRC have the same time for notifying you that they are making enquiries. They may then delay making any repayment reflected in your return. For returns from 2007–08 the 'enquiry window' is changed to one year after the return is submitted.
(7) An enquiry may be limited in scope or so wide as to resemble a back duty investigation (16.9), although confined to the year of the tax return. HMRC will issue you with a formal notice after completing an enquiry. You are then able to appeal. However, prior to the formal notice, disputes about points of law can be resolved by litigation.

(8) If you have not submitted your return in time, HMRC are able to make an estimated assessment and you cannot appeal against the tax charge. However, this is displaced when you send in your return and self-assessment.

(9) Your income tax and capital gains tax are normally due for payment on 31 January after the year of assessment. However, except where most of your income is taxed at source, you normally make income tax payments on account on 31 January in the tax year and the following 31 July. These will generally be of equal amount and based on the final liability for the previous year, but may be reduced to reflect circumstances.

(10) Interest runs from the due date. Also you may incur a 5 per cent surcharge on your unpaid tax for a year of assessment if it is not paid by the next 28 February. A further 5 per cent surcharge may arise on any tax outstanding at the following 31 July. However, HMRC pay interest on tax overpayments from the original tax payment dates (or due dates if later). Twelve months late, a further 5 per cent is now chargeable on unpaid tax.

(11) Where a settlement has more than one trustee, each is able to make a return and be accountable for errors and omissions. Any liable trustee can be required to meet liabilities to income tax and capital gains tax.

(12) Your return and self-assessment need to reflect the taxable position after allowing for claims to reliefs and tax credits. Where the necessary conditions exist for a relief, you are able to claim it in your self-assessment without prior HMRC approval.

(13) You must claim any allowable loss for capital gains tax purposes in relation to the year when it accrues. This means you can include it in your tax return and must claim it within 5 years 10 months of the end of the year of assessment when the loss arises.

(14) Your employers must provide you and HMRC with details of your expenses payments and benefits in kind, including cash equivalent calculations, unless a dispensation has been given by HMRC. The deadline is 31 May following the end of the tax year.

(15) In general, in cases where previously the time limit for income tax and capital gains tax claims has been two years, this becomes 31 January after the year following the year of assessment. Thus a claim for 1997–98 was needed by 31 January 2000 instead of 5 April 2000. During this period you are also allowed to revoke or amend any claims and elections made ahead of this time limit.

(16) Various reliefs, such as loss relief, farmers' averaging (15.6), spreading of literary and artistic receipts (15.4) and post-cessation receipts may relate to more than one year. Where this is the case, relief is given in the assessment for the later (latest) year when the claim is made but taking account of the tax figures of the earlier year(s). This will avoid reopening the earlier years.

(17) There is a wide range of revised time limits applying for income tax and capital gains tax but not corporation tax. In general, the changes involve

reductions of just over two months. Thus two years from the end of the year of assessment will become 31 January in the next year but one. Similarly six years thereafter becomes 31 January in the sixth year.

(18) You are required to keep and preserve adequate records on which to base your tax return and failure to do so may result in penalties.

16.2 Your tax return (TMA Ss7–12B)

If your income includes property and/or self-employed earnings you will usually have to submit a tax return each year. If, however, all your income is taxed under PAYE (10.14) you may only be required to complete a return about every three years or not at all. Husbands and wives must submit separate returns.

Apart from individuals, trusts, partnerships and companies etc. also have to submit tax returns. In the case of companies, previously, provided HMRC received the annual accounts and tax computations they did not normally insist on the submission of corporation tax returns. However, with the introduction of 'pay and file', for the first accounting periods ending after 30 September 1993 (13.4.1), corporation tax returns are mandatory if notices are issued.

If no return is submitted, sources of income and capital gains must broadly be notified to HMRC. The time limit is one year from the end of the year of assessment or accounting period and there is a penalty of up to the amount of the unpaid tax (FA 1988 Ss120–122).

If you have not been sent a tax return for the previous tax year and you have received income for that year apart from your wages or salary, you should request that HMRC send you a return form for completion. This request should be made to the Inspector of Taxes who deals with your affairs – if you are employed it will be the tax district that handles your employer's PAYE affairs.

As well as including details of your income for the previous tax year your tax return also constitutes a claim for income tax allowances and reliefs. Thus your tax return for the year to 5 April 2012 must show your income for the year to 5 April 2012 and the income tax allowances that you are claiming for the year to 5 April 2012. A further reason for you to request a tax return from your Inspector of Taxes is thus to ensure that you are granted all of the income tax reliefs to which you are entitled.

The 1996 and earlier tax returns were comprehensive and consisted of up to 12 pages. Fuller details are included in earlier editions of this book. Your tax returns are now to be completed under the self-assessment rules. You probably receive your return in April each year and it is described below for the year to 5 April 2012.

16.2.1 Your tax return for the year to 5 April 2012

Your tax returns for 2007–08 and subsequently are completely different from previous ones, for which details appear in earlier editions. The basic tax return now consists of 6 pages, together with 4 pages for **additional information** and 8 classes of **supplementary pages**, if needed.

Page 1 is informative, telling you about the filing dates (16.1) and £100 etc. penalty for late returns. It also has space for your personal details, being date of birth, confirmation that your name is correctly stated, contact phone number and National Insurance number.

Page 2 lists the available supplementary pages and has boxes for you to select which apply to you. These will already be provided in your tax return by HMRC, or you will need to request them. The supplementary pages listed are as follows:

Employment	–	A separate form is needed for each, including salary, tax, benefits and expenses.
Self-employment	–	You must show your business turnover, expenses and capital allowances. If your turnover is less than £73,000 (previously £70,000) only the total of your expenses need be entered.
Partnership	–	You must complete a form for each partnership of which you are a member showing your profit share and shares of other classes of income and tax.
UK property	–	Income and expenses.
Foreign	–	All forms of income, capital gains and overseas tax credits. If you are non-domiciled (17.2) there is a box to tick to claim the remittance basis and you should not enter unremitted income.
Trusts etc.	–	Discretionary and non-discretionary income receipts. Income chargeable on you as a settlor. Income from UK and foreign estates and tax.
Capital gains summary	–	Computations of gains and losses must also be sent.
Non-resident	–	You must complete this form if any of the following apply; you are non-resident, not ordinarily resident, entitled to split-year treatment; non-domiciled.

Page 2 ends with a space for student loan repayments, including the amount deducted by your employer.

Page 3 is for *other income* as follows:

UK interest etc. and dividends
Dividends from authorised unit trusts and open ended investment trusts
UK pensions, annuities and other State benefits
Other UK income not included on supplementary pages
Benefit from pre-owned assets.

Page 4 mainly deals with tax reliefs and in particular:

Relief for UK and overseas pension contributions
Charitable giving including gift aid and shares, land and buildings given to charities
Blind person's allowance
You must also give the total income included anywhere in the return derived from the provision of your services through a *service company* (10.14.4, 10.16 & 10.16.1).

Page 5 concerns your tax position. You must state any refund you have had for 2011–12 and whether you want any amount (up to £3,000) which you owe for that year to be collected through your 2013–14 PAYE tax code (if you have one). Also, there are spaces to give details of your bank or building society account into which any repayment to you should be paid.

Page 6 has spaces for details of your tax adviser (if any), any other information and your signature, with a warning that false information may lead to penalties and prosecution.

Additional information

You need only complete this 4-page form if you have any income or reliefs which it covers, such as:

Interest from gilt edged securities
Stock dividends and loans written off
Business receipts taxed as income of an earlier year
Share schemes and employment lump sums, compensation and deductions
Other tax relief, for example VCT and EIS
Age related married couples' allowance
Income tax losses
Pension savings tax charges and taxable lump sums from overseas pension schemes
Tax-avoidance schemes – reference numbers etc.
Additional information

16.2.2 New simplified tax returns

A new simplified four-page tax return form was sent out in April 2004 to about 400,000 taxpayers. This is used on a much wider scale subsequently and is known as the *short tax return*. There is no requirement to calculate the tax on the form. It is aimed at those with simple affairs, modest investment and non-furnished holiday letting property income (under £73,000) including:

- Employees other than directors.
- Self-employed people with turnover under £73,000 for 2011–12 (previously £70,000).
- Pensioners with income from a state, occupational or retirement pension.

Also a trial return was sent in some larger cases from 2005–06.

16.2.3 Filing online

If you are computer literate, there are various advantages from filing your tax return online. These include a 31 January filing deadline compared with 31 October, having the tax payable computed automatically and having a clear record. You can either use software provided by HMRC or commercially.

16.3 HM Revenue and Customs (TMA Ss1 & 55)

The overall control and management of income tax, corporation tax and capital gains tax is carried out by HM Revenue and Customs. This resulted from the merger of the Board of Inland Revenue with HM Customs and

Excise on 18 April 2005 by CRCA 2005. They are responsible for administering the relevant law as contained in TA 1988 and the various Finance and Taxes Acts.

The Finance Acts are normally enacted annually about July, the main items having been announced by the Chancellor of the Exchequer in his Budget speech in March or April. However, in 2010, the regular Budget was on 24 March and an 'emergency Budget' followed on 22 June, some weeks after the general election.

HM Revenue and Customs (HMRC) is made up of the Commissioners and officers of Revenue and Customs. The day-to-day administration, however, is carried out by various officers of Revenue and Customs who are civil servants, appointed by the Commissioners. They may be appointed for general purposes or specific purposes, at the discretion of the Commissioners.

HMRC is organised into various tax districts, to one of which you will have to send your income tax return. An area director heads each district under whom are a number of officers, who obtain and verify as they think fit the information that is necessary to accept self-assessments and raise assessments to income tax, capital gains tax and corporation tax. (Prior to 18 April 2005, the Inland Revenue mainly included inspectors and collectors of taxes.)

16.3.1 **The assessment mechanism** (TMA S29)

When you had submitted your income tax return for 1995–96 and earlier years, the Inspector of Taxes issued a 'notice of assessment' to income tax in respect of your various types of income. A capital gains tax assessment was also raised by your Inspector of Taxes (20.15) if appropriate.

If the Revenue had not received sufficient information to raise accurate tax assessments prior to the date on which the tax was due for payment, they would normally make estimated assessments in respect of the taxpayer's sources of income.

Since the introduction of self-assessment, the rules encompass being assessed to tax or being charged under the new regime. For 1996–97 and subsequent years, the self-assessment system applies (16.2). If you submitted your return by 30 September 2007, HMRC could be asked to calculate your 2006–07 tax; otherwise you needed to do so. However, if you are required to complete a simplified tax return (16.2.2) you do not need to calculate the tax nor do you if you file online. In general, HMRC will now calculate your tax unless you request otherwise.

16.3.2 **Due dates for payment of tax** (TA 1988 S5)

For 1996–97 and subsequently, the due dates for paying income tax and capital gains tax are generally 31 January following the year of assessment. For 1997–98 and subsequently, you make payments on account on 31 January and 31 July, each based on half the self-assessed amount for the year before (excluding tax paid at source). (Generally you will not make payments on account if your tax for the previous year is less than £500.)

16.3.3 **Discovery** (TMA S29 (3))

Any estimated assessments will be made by HMRC to as great a degree of accuracy as possible according to any information in their possession such as particulars for previous years. If, however, HMRC make a *discovery* that:

(1) profits which ought to have been assessed to tax have not been assessed, or
(2) an assessment to tax is or has become insufficient, or
(3) excessive relief has been given

HMRC may make an assessment of the amount or further amount which ought in their opinion to be charged.

16.3.4 **Time limits for assessments etc.** (TMA Ss30, 34 & 36)

Normally an assessment to corporation tax may be made at any time not later than six years after the end of the chargeable period to which the assessment relates. For income tax and capital gains tax the time limit is five years from 31 January following the year of assessment.

Broadly, the same time limits apply to claims for overpaid tax. FA 2004 legislation aims at preventing any extension of this period for bringing an action based on a mistake in law.

In cases, however, of any fraudulent or negligent conduct by the taxpayer (16.9.1) HMRC have more time to make assessments.

A special rule applies to the recovery by HMRC of excessive repayment claims etc. The time limit is then extended to the end of the tax year when the original repayment etc. was made or the closing date of any enquiry into the self-assessment return which gave rise to the repayment.

16.3.5 **Tax remission – official error**

If you send in full returns of your taxable income and you receive no assessments, so that you are led to believe that your tax affairs are in order, it is the practice of HMRC to excuse you all or part of the tax.

For tax arrears notified prior to 11 May 1996, certain income limits applied. However, from that date there are no such limits.

16.4 Appeals against assessments (TMA Ss31D & 44–57)

If you are not in agreement with an assessment to income tax, capital gains tax or corporation tax you may appeal to HMRC within 30 days of the date of the assessment. Your appeal must be in writing and state the grounds on which you object to the assessment; most frequently these are that 'the assessment is estimated and excessive'. Should you not be able to appeal within 30 days for some good reason such as absence from home or ill-health, HMRC will normally allow you to make a late appeal.

The majority of appeals are settled by agreement. This normally follows when the accounts and/or returns have been submitted to HMRC and any queries that they raise are answered. If, however, you are not able to agree with HMRC or if you or your accountants have not submitted all of the required information, the appeal will be listed for personal hearing before a Tax Tribunal (formerly the Commissioners) (16.5).

All the tax charged by an assessment is treated as due and payable (16.3.2) unless, within 30 days, you estimate how much you are being overcharged and apply to HMRC for the balance to be postponed.

The 30-day time limit is extended where your circumstances change so that your tax liability reduces. It will then be determined by agreement with HMRC how much of the tax should be held over with only the balance being collected. This collectable balance is payable within 30 days after HMRC have dealt with the application for postponement. Any unpaid tax normally becomes due 30 days after the date on which, following the agreement of the assessment, HMRC issue a notice of the tax payable. An interest charge could run from an earlier date, however (16.8.2), especially in the case of a long-drawn-out appeal.

16.5 Tax appeal tribunals

A dramatic change has taken place in the jurisdictions for tax appeals. This is part of a move necessitated by human rights law, to bring consistency to the arrangements for all appeals by citizens or other claimants against official decisions of any arm of Government. Eventually, all such matters will fall under the auspices of The Tribunals Service. Moreover, before you even start the appeal process, you now have the right to ask HMRC for an independent internal review of any disputed decision. Time limits for reviews and appeals are generally 30 days.

16.5.1 **The First-Tier and Upper Tribunals (Tax)** (TCEA Schs 1–5 & SI 2009 Nos. 56 & 1590)

A common feature is the division of most appellate work between First-Tier and Upper Tribunals. These Tribunals comprise various specialist streams or Chambers, including a 'Tax Chamber' at the First-Tier and a 'Finance and Tax Chamber' (to be renamed 'Tax and Chancery Chamber' from 1 September 2009) at the Upper Tribunal. The tribunals consist of judges and other members with relevant professional knowledge and experience, who may sit singly or as a panel of two or three. All hold judicial appointments under the Lord Chancellor and must meet statutory criteria for appointment.

From 1 April 2009 most appeals on direct taxation (income, capital gains, corporation or inheritance tax) matters come within the jurisdiction of the

Tax Chamber of the First-Tier Tribunal. The former General and Special Commissioners (16.5.2) were abolished on 31 March 2009 and transitional arrangements provide for transfer of existing appeals and, where necessary, for continuity of attention to part-heard cases and the like. As with the former Special Commissioners, tribunal venues are in London, Edinburgh, Belfast and Manchester. Although appeals on some specialised matters may fall to be made direct to the Tribunals Service, in most instances direct taxation appeals are to be made to HMRC.

It may be possible to ask the First-Tier Tribunal to review its own decision, including a question of fact. Subject to its own review, the decision of the First-Tier Tribunal is final regarding questions of fact. If either the taxpayer or HMRC is dissatisfied with a First-Tier decision, they may request a review or lodge an appeal on a point of law within the time permitted – generally 56 days, but a full written decision may need to be requested in 28 days.

The first venue for any appeal (on points of law only) would normally be the Finance and Tax Chamber of the Upper Tribunal, from which any further appeal would lie to the Court of Appeal (or Court of Session in Scotland) and House of Lords. However, before you appeal from the Upper Tribunal, you should weigh very carefully the strength of your case and the potential tax saving if you succeed in the higher Courts against the high legal costs involved.

16.5.2 **Former General and Special Commissioners** (TMA Ss2–6 & 44–57)

Until 31 March 2009, most direct tax appeals were heard by either the General or Special Commissioners. The General Commissioners were similar to lay magistrates and needed no special legal or accountancy qualifications, but were assisted by a Clerk, who was usually a solicitor. The Special Commissioners were full-time civil servants, who for 25 years had all been lawyers of at least ten years' standing. For more detail please see our previous editions.

16.5.3 **Appeal hearings** (TCEA Sch 5 & SI 2009 No. 273)

The tribunals manage their caseload according to weight and complexity. At the lower end, they will seek to deal with some cases on paper without any hearing, in which case you would need to request a hearing, if it were important to have your case presented orally. At the top end, other cases may go direct to the Upper Tribunal.

The Tribunal Clerk will advise you of the time and place for your appeal hearing. If you are unable to attend for some good reason or if you or your accountants or other advisors require more time to prepare, it should normally be possible to have the matter adjourned at least once until a later date. If you need an adjournment, you or your agent may be able to agree this with HMRC, if your reasons are acceptable to them, but otherwise you should deal directly with the Clerk, who will consider your request impartially.

At the appeal hearing you may represent yourself or be represented by an accountant, solicitor or barrister or by any friend you wish to take. If your appeal is on a point of law which you anticipate may go to the Courts (see below) it is wise to be represented at the outset by a barrister who can act for you in the Courts.

HMRC are normally represented by an Inspector of Taxes, but on difficult legal points a member of their Solicitors' Office may appear. Proceedings before the Tribunals resemble those in the Courts in many ways – for example, witnesses may be summoned and examined and cross-examined under oath. When the hearing has been completed, the Members will withdraw to consider their decision. Even if they deliver this orally, they will usually issue it in full or in summary in writing at a later date. Tribunals may confirm, reduce or increase the disputed assessment.

16.6 Investigatory powers of HMRC (TMA Ss20, 20C & Sch 1AA etc., FA 1988 S127 & FA 2000 Ss148–150)

The powers of HMRC to obtain papers and search premises were strengthened by the 1976 and 1989 Finance Acts. Subject to the consent of a Tax Tribunal (formerly the Commissioners), HMRC may require you by notice in writing to supply documents in your possession or power, which they consider have a bearing on your tax liability. However, the Tribunal is not to consent unless you have failed or may have failed to comply with any provisions of the Taxes Acts; and as a result your tax position has been seriously affected.

HMRC may also require documents from certain other people. These other people include your spouse and any of your children. In general these rules do not apply to pending appeals, but they do include access to computer records.

If any of your income comes from a business which you either carried on yourself or you managed, then any person who is or was carrying on a business may be directed to provide documents concerning their dealings with your business. The same applies if your wife carries on a business or manages one.

These rules also apply to a past business and any companies of which you or your spouse are, or were, directors, such companies not needing to be carrying on business. Furthermore, the Director of Savings is within the net.

In order for HMRC to obtain information about your affairs from other people, they must obtain the consent of a Tax Tribunal (formerly a General or Special Commissioner) (16.5) and the latter must ensure that HMRC are justified in their request. FA 1994 S255 provides that the same judge or panel (formerly Commissioner) cannot later hear an appeal involving the same information. HMRC must tell you why they require documents unless they can convince a Tax Tribunal that disclosure might prejudice collecting the tax.

A barrister, advocate or solicitor cannot be compelled to yield up documents without your consent provided these are covered by professional privilege. This even applies to such a lawyer acting as your tax accountant (see below).

From 27 July 1989 various changes took effect including:

(1) The protection of personal records and journalistic material from disclosure.
(2) A requirement for HMRC to allow not less than 30 days for requested information to be produced.
(3) The putting of written questions to the taxpayer.
(4) It being a criminal offence to falsify, conceal or destroy documents called for under HMRC powers.

FA 2000 introduced revised measures to combat serious tax fraud. Where there are reasonable grounds for suspecting this, HMRC may apply for an order from a judge directing that documents needed as evidence are supplied, normally within ten working days. However, documents subject to legal professional privilege are exempt, whoever holds them. Where this new legislation applies, a search warrant will not be issued. Also covered is a right of HMRC to use National Minimum Wage information.

FA 2008 introduced legislation which aligns and modernises record keeping requirements and time limits for assessments and claims. Also, HMRC are provided with new inspection and information powers. Information powers and penalties for failing to comply with these obligations are to operate from 1 April 2009 whilst the new time limits will be fully operational from 1 April 2010 (16.9.6).

16.6.1 Tax accountants' papers

Your tax accountant is not obliged to reveal his working papers to HMRC subject to the following.

Where a tax accountant is convicted of an offence in relation to tax by a UK court or has a penalty awarded against him for assisting in making incorrect returns etc. subject to certain rules, HMRC may require him to surrender documents relating to the tax affairs of any of his clients. Notice is required in writing and the permission of a circuit judge, Scottish sheriff or Irish county court judge must be obtained. The power of HMRC to give this notice generally ceases 12 months after the conviction or penalty award, and does not have effect whilst an appeal is pending.

Not less than 30 days must be allowed for a convicted tax accountant to deliver documents required by HMRC. Also from that time, personal records and journalistic material are protected as are, in general, audit papers and records of tax advice. At the same time, taxpayers must be notified of requests for information from third parties, unless fraud is involved.

From 1 April 2013, if your tax accountant or other tax agent is dishonest, new rules will apply which provide for a civil penalty. Also, subject to Tribunal approval, HMRC will have access to the agent's working papers and may reveal those penalised.

16.6.2 Entry warrant to obtain documents

If HMRC obtain an entry warrant in a case of suspected fraud they may enter specified premises, seizing and removing any documents or other things required as evidence for relevant proceedings. However, note the new judicial order rules introduced by FA 2000 (16.6).

A warrant is valid for 14 days and can only be granted by a circuit judge etc. who is satisfied on information given on oath by an officer of HMRC, that evidence concerning a tax fraud is to be found on the premises in question.

HMRC search powers are broadly restricted to the investigation of 'serious fraud' and are subject to a detailed code of conduct. Also, taxpayers have rights of access to property removed under the search powers.

16.6.3 Returns of information (TMA Ss13–19)

HMRC are empowered to request returns of certain information from traders and others. For example, you may be required to give particulars of any lodgers you may have.

Your bank may be required to return details of interest paid to you during a tax year. Furthermore, HMRC are empowered to obtain from any business details of its payments of fees, commissions, royalties etc.

There is a three-year time limit regarding many of HMRC's powers to request information returns. However, they can extend their enquiries to certain government departments and public authorities.

16.7 Repayment claims (TMA Ss42–43B & TA 1988 S281)

Repayment claims arise in connection with many different facets of taxation. You will normally, however, find that any income tax repayment to which you become entitled arises in one of the following ways:

(1) Most of your income has been taxed at the source and your personal reliefs and allowances exceed your other income. (Also, you may not have received the full benefit of the starting and lower rate income tax bands.) If your income tax return reveals this position and you send in the required simple repayment claim form together with dividend vouchers etc. in respect of the income tax credits, you will receive an income tax repayment. The repayment will reduce your income tax bill for the tax year to its correct level.

(2) Some of your income has been taxed both in the UK and in another country. You are frequently able to make a double taxation relief repayment claim of either UK tax or overseas tax depending on the circumstances (18.6).

(3) You may have already paid an assessment for a tax year and, as described elsewhere in this book, you make an election to HMRC which results in your assessment for that year being reduced.

(4) You make a business loss which you claim to be offset against your other income for the year (11.22). Some of this income has suffered income tax by deduction at the source and on making the required claim and submitting the tax vouchers or receipts you will be repaid an appropriate amount of such tax, as well as tax credits on dividends.

(5) You discover that an 'error or mistake' has been made in a return or statement or schedule that you have previously submitted as a result of which you have been over-assessed to tax. Within six years after the end of the tax year in which the original assessment was made, you may make a claim to your Inspector of Taxes for the repayment of the tax previously overpaid.

(6) Repayment claims often arise in respect of minors (under 18) all of whom are taxpayers in their own right and so are entitled to at least the personal allowance for a single person. Thus if a minor's only income for 2012–13 consists of non-dividend investment income of say £400 and none of the investments were gifted to him by his parents, then he can reclaim all of the relevant tax credits (that is, $^{20}/_{80} \times$ £400 = £100). Similarly, if the trustees of a settlement apply income for the education and maintenance of a minor, that income is treated as belonging to the child. The income is treated as having suffered basic rate income tax at the source (and additional rate tax if applicable). This enables an income tax repayment claim to be made for the minor unless he has already obtained the full benefit of his tax reliefs and allowances or the settlement had been actually created by one of his parents.

(7) HMRC may raise an additional assessment and if this is not related to fraud or negligent conduct, you may be able to claim additional reliefs as a result. Such claims, elections etc., even though out of time according to the normal rules, are valid if made within one year of the end of the tax period in which the assessment is made.

(8) For claims made from 1 April 2010, your means of reclaiming tax have been widened, and non-statutory routes withdrawn. Also, the 'error or mistake' rules are changing to provide you with more safeguards.

The procedure for making repayment claims is normally very simple. A repayment claim form to list your income and allowances (R40) is available. If HMRC have already received a full return of your income, or in the case of a business or company its accounts and tax computations, it will generally only be necessary to sign a short form in which you claim the tax repayment to which you are entitled.

The self-assessment tax returns have a box to tick if you would like tax overpaid to be repaid to you. There is now also a space to nominate a charity to receive all or part of the repayment. You may be required to send dividend vouchers or tax deduction certificates or receipts to cover the amount of your repayment.

Special forms are usually required for double tax relief claims on which you must enter particulars of the dividends. Special forms are also provided by HMRC for use in connection with various other repayment claims, for example concerning minors.

Income tax repayment claims should normally be made to your HMRC branch. If you are, for example, a British citizen resident abroad or a foreign entertainer, your repayment claims should be made to HMRC Residency in Bootle, who also run the international telephone help-desk, but non-resident Crown employees and pensioners are dealt with by South Wales Area office in Cardiff. HMRC Residency in Nottingham attend to written enquiries on tax treaties and dual residence and recovery of UK tax suffered on overseas dividends etc.

Note that for 1999–2000 and subsequent years, the 10 per cent tax credit on dividends is not reclaimable. However, it is offsettable against other tax so as to reduce your liability.

16.7.1 **Example: Income tax repayment claim**

Miss A is 24 years of age and during the year to 5 April 2013 she only had occasional employment from which her gross earnings were £5,030, no PAYE being deducted. During 2012–13 she pays allowable loan interest of £55. Miss A's only other income for 2012–13 consists of £2,250 dividends (tax credit £250) and an income distribution of £500 (net) from a discretionary trust. Calculate the amount of the income tax repayment claim of Miss A for 2012–13.

Miss A – Income tax repayment claim 2012–13:

Details	£	Gross income £	Tax credits £
Earned income		5,660	
Taxed dividends including tax credit		2,500	250
Trust income – net	500		
Grossed up equivalent at 40%		1,000	500
		9,160	
Less: Personal allowance	8,105		
Loan interest (paid gross)	55		
		8,160	
Taxable amount		1,000	
Total tax credits			750
Less: Income tax liability £1,000 at 20%			(200)
Tax credit restriction (£250 – £100)			(150)
Income tax repayable for 2012–13			400

Note: The repayment excludes any dividend tax credit.

16.7.2 **Repayment supplement** (TA 1988 Ss824–826)

This used to apply if you received a tax repayment more than a year after the end of the year of assessment to which it relates. Interest at the appropriate rate(s) free of tax normally runs from the later of the end of the assessment year in which the tax was paid or 5 April following the year for which repayment is made, until the end of the tax month of repayment.

From 6 February 1997, separate repayment supplement and overdue tax rates apply. An important change is that the repayment supplement runs from when you paid the tax. (It remains a requirement that you are UK resident.)

FA 2001 S88 confirmed that interest is to be added to repayments which arise when relief from one year is set against income of an earlier one. An example is where pension contributions are carried back; also regarding the averaging of profits for farmers and creative artists.

Recent rates are:

From	Rate %
29 September 2009	0.5
27 January 2009	0
6 January 2009	0.75
6 December 2008	1.5
6 November 2008	2.25
6 January 2008	3
6 August 2007	4
6 September 2006	3

16.8 The collection of tax (TMA Ss60–68)

Under the self-assessment system (16.1), generally applying for 1996–97 and subsequent assessments, once the tax has been ascertained by HMRC, they will send you a statement of account incorporating a payslip. You should then pay your liability before the respective due dates (normally 31 January and 31 July). However, if you have not received a statement of account, you should pay by the relevant due date so as to avoid interest and particularly surcharge (16.8.3), estimating your liability if necessary.

HMRC have certain powers to take action in Magistrates' Courts for the recovery of tax. Otherwise, action must be in the County Courts (up to the 'County Court limit') or the High Court.

16.8.1 Payments on account

If you receive a large tax demand which you find difficult to meet out of your available funds, HMRC can in cases of hardship allow you to settle the outstanding tax by instalments payable at say monthly or quarterly intervals. You should contact them and explain the position. Interest will probably be payable, however (see below). A standard payments on account system has come in with self-assessment (16.1).

Voluntary managed payment plans (MPPs) will allow payments of income tax or corporation tax to be spread equally over a period straddling the normal due dates. Although the legislation is in FA 2009, the MPP system was not introduced until April 2011.

16.8.2 **Interest on overdue tax** (TMA Ss86–92)

The following rules apply to assessments issued after 31 July 1975. Assessments issued earlier are covered by different rules (even if still unpaid), and details are given in previous editions. For 1996–97 and subsequent tax years, the self-assessment rules apply (16.1). The rules were clarified and modified by the 1989 Finance Act. For example, the mechanics for altering the interest rate have been made more automatic, rather than needing a statutory instrument, as previously.

Interest is payable at the appropriate rate(s) from the 'reckonable date' until the tax is settled. Some recent rates are:

From	Rate %	From	Rate %	From	Rate %
29 September 2009	3.0	6 September 2005	6.5	6 August 1997	9.5
24 March 2009	2.5	6 September 2004	7.5	6 February 1997	8.5
27 January 2009	3.5	6 December 2003	6.5	6 February 1996	6.25
6 January 2009	4.5	6 August 2003	5.5	6 March 1995	7.0
6 December 2008	5.5	6 November 2001	6.5	6 October 1994	6.25
6 November 2008	6.5	6 May 2001	7.5	6 January 1994	5.5
6 January 2008	7.5	6 February 2000	8.5	6 March 1993	6.25
6 August 2007	8.5	6 March 1999	7.5		
6 September 2006	7.5	6 January 1999	8.5		

The 'reckonable date' for 1995–96 and earlier assessments, is the date when the tax becomes due and payable (16.3.2) unless you appeal and obtain a deferment of tax. In that case the 'reckonable date' is when the tax becomes due and payable or the date given by the following table whichever is earlier:

Description of tax	Date applicable
(1) Previously Schedules A or D	1 July following the end of the year of assessment
(2) Additional rates of income tax	1 June following the end of the next year of assessment
(3) Capital gains tax	1 June following the end of the next year of assessment
(4) Corporation tax	Usually the normal payment date (13.4)

The above table applies to all amounts, even if not covered by the original assessment.

No interest paid on overdue tax is allowed as a deduction from your taxable income or business profits nor is it allowed as a deduction for corporation tax or capital gains tax purposes.

Interest arises on overdue formal assessments, which have to be raised for PAYE and sub-contractor deductions (15.5). The interest charge runs from 14 days after the end of the tax year to which the assessment relates. With effect from 19 April 1993, interest is chargeable on late payments to HMRC of PAYE deductions made by employers.

For 1996–97 and subsequently the self-assessment rules apply (16.1). These normally direct that interest runs from the due date for the tax. In general, this means that interest at currently 3.0 per cent (see above) applies to overdue income tax and capital gains tax from each due date (31 January, 31 July etc.).

16.8.3 **Surcharge on unpaid tax** (TMA S9c)

An additional charge has been introduced under the self-assessment system. Any *balancing* payments unpaid after 28 days from the due date (31 January 1998 etc.) will normally carry a surcharge of 5 per cent. An additional 5 per cent will be levied on tax still unpaid after six months and again after twelve months.

16.9 Back duty investigations and enquiries

If you have not disclosed to HMRC your true income or if you have claimed tax reliefs and allowances to which you were not entitled the discovery of such facts by the authorities might give rise to an enquiry. Some years ago this was more commonly known as a 'back duty' case.

It is open to HMRC to take criminal proceedings against you resulting in a fine and/or imprisonment but this is rare. The normal course will be for HMRC to obtain full particulars of the income omitted by you and raise assessments on you in respect of the further tax that is due. You will also normally be charged interest on the tax from when it should have been paid if your income had been properly declared. HMRC may also charge you to penalties (see 16.9.2) depending upon whether your omissions were due to pure carelessness or ignorance or on the other hand were due to some fraudulent intention.

In order to ascertain the amount of your undisclosed income HMRC will frequently require that capital statements be drawn up at the beginning and end of the period under review. The increase in your net worth between those two dates is then added to your living expenses for the period to give your total income (subject to adjustments for known capital profits, purchases and sales, betting winnings etc.). Your total income less income already taxed will give your total income requiring still to be taxed. This should be split between the various intervening tax years by considering your assets and living expenses etc. for each tax year.

You may have been able to avoid an investigation by taking advantage of disclosure opportunities (18.7).

16.9.1 **Fraud, wilful default or neglect; fraudulent or negligent conduct** (TMA S36)

Tax lost through the 'fraudulent or negligent conduct' of a taxpayer may be assessed up to 20 years after the end of the period to which it relates. This rule also applies to partners and where agents are culpable. These provisions apply to assessments for 1983–84 onwards and, regarding companies, for accounting periods ending after 31 March 1983.

'Neglect' is defined as 'negligence or a failure to give any notice, make any return or to produce or furnish any document or other information required by or under the Taxes Acts'.

For years of assessment prior to 1983–84 and accounting periods ending before 1 April 1983, the normal six-year time limit for making assessments (16.3.4) is extended indefinitely in any case where there is fraud or wilful default. This does not apply, however, in the case of the personal representatives of a deceased person (21.2).

A statutory offence of evading income tax took effect from 1 January 2001 (FA 2000 S144). This is tried summarily in the Magistrates' Court or on indictment in the Crown Court, with serious penalties (10.9.3).

16.9.2 **Interest and penalties** (TMA Ss55, 56, 70, 86–107 & 283)

Where an assessment has been made for the purpose of making good a loss of tax through fraud, wilful default or neglect, interest at 3.0 per cent (2.5 per cent before 29 September 2009 and 3.5 per cent prior to 24 March 2009 etc. 16.8.2) is charged on the underpaid tax from the date that the tax should have been paid. This also covers tax lost through 'fraudulent or negligent conduct' and was extended from 27 July 1989 to tax assessed late as the result of an incorrect return. Prior to 6 February 1997, various other interest rates applied as for overdue tax (16.8.2).

The maximum penalties are laid down in the legislation but frequently the Board of HMRC are prepared to accept less according to the particular facts of each case.

Regarding tax years after 1987–88 (or accounting periods ending after 31 March 1989 for companies), relief is given where more than one penalty arises on the same tax. In no case is the total amount of penalty to exceed the maximum possible amount for any one of the penalties involved.

The 1989 Finance Act introduced a simpler procedure for charging default interest and penalties. HMRC may make formal determinations of the amounts due rather like assessments. You have full rights of appeal to the Appeal Commissioners and Courts. These rules do not apply to the initial penalties under the compliance rules which continue to be awarded by the Appeal Commissioners.

16.9.3 **Penalties – details** (TMA Ss93–107)

Subject to further changes below (16.9.6) generally operating from 1 April 2010, the following are examples of some of the maximum penalties:

Offence	Penalties
Failure to submit personal tax returns (pre-self-assessment)	£300 plus £60 per day after a court declaration
Failure to submit self-assessment tax returns (limited to tax due)	£100 after the filing date (31 January) and £100 after 31 July (and £60 per day etc.)
Failure to submit return continuing beyond tax year following that in which issued	Additional penalty of up to the amount of tax on income and gain, for year. However, if there is no assessable income or gains, the maximum total penalty is £100
Incorrect returns	Up to 100% of tax lost
Assisting in the preparation of incorrect returns or accounts	£3,000
Supplying incorrect information to HMRC	£3,000
Failure to keep records under self-assessment	£3,000
Failure to give notice of liability to tax	From 6 April 1989 the penalty is the amount of tax if notice is more than one year overdue
Failure to make (when required) a return of information for HMRC	£300 plus £60 for each additional day in default
Statutory offence of evading income tax from 1 January 2001 (16.9.1)	Summarily in Magistrates' Court, £5,000 and/or six months. Indictment in Crown Court, unlimited fine and/or seven years
Late submission of employers' year-end PAYE returns (10.14.4)	Initial penalty of up to £1,200 per 50 employees and £100 per 50 employees per month for further delays up to one year; beyond which up to 100% of tax underpaid or paid late
Fraudulent or negligent certificate of non-liability to tax re building society or bank deposit	Up to £3,000
False statement made by sub-contractor to obtain exemption from tax deduction (15.5)	£5,000

16.9.4 **Penalties – previous rules** (TMA Ss93–107)

Many of the selected penalties shown in the previous table, (16.9.3), operate from 1989 and others came in with the self-assessment system (16.1). Details of penalties for earlier years are given in previous editions of this book. In general, the fixed penalties were lower. Also, failing to give notice of liability to tax before 6 April 1989 attracted only a £100 penalty, but now if notice is more than one year overdue, the penalty can go up to the amount of the tax.

16.9.5 **Penalties – disclosure**

Provided you have notified undisclosed tax liabilities under the offshore account arrangements (18.7), there is no serious criminality and the time limits (18.7) are kept, your penalty should be limited to 10 per cent. A parallel system applies to 'onshore disclosure' (where no offshore account is involved).

16.9.6 **Further changes – from 1 April 2010**

FA 2008 includes new rules generally taking effect from 1 April 2010 relating to penalties and time limits for reopening assessments regarding a wide spectrum of taxes including VAT (23.2.2).

The new maximim penalty scale based on the understated tax in a return is 30 per cent for failure to take reasonable care, 70 per cent for deliberate understatement and 100 per cent for deliberate understatement with concealment. Similar maximum percentages apply for failure to notify new taxable activities after 1 April 2009. Substantial reductions will follow from disclosure, particularly if voluntary.

The new rules align the time limits for assessments as follows:

Tax	Mistake	Discovery	Failure to take reasonable care	Deliberate understatement or failure to notify liability
VAT	4 years	n/a	4 years	20 years
IT & CGT	n/a	4 years	6 years	20 years
Corp. tax	n/a	4 years	6 years	20 years
PAYE	4 years	n/a	6 years	20 years

FA 2009 extends the compliance framework to various other taxes including inheritance tax, stamp duty reserve tax, stamp duty land tax, petroleum revenue tax and certain environmental taxes. In general, the above time limits for making assessments are operative from 1 April 2010.

Penalties for late filing and paying tax late have been intensified by FA 2009. The new rules are being implemented over a number of years, starting with in-year PAYE from April 2010. It is planned to include in FA 2013 powers to increase fixed penalties in line with inflation.

Chapter 17

DOMICILE AND RESIDENCE

17.0 Prospective changes from 6 April 2013

Certain fundamental aspects of the UK taxation of non-residents and non-domiciliaries were under discussion between HMRC and professional bodies before the May 2010 General Election. Proposals for more extensive changes intended to operate from 6 April 2012 were announced in outline. by the new Government in the March 2011 Budget, but only on 17 June 2011 were detailed principles revealed by way of consultative documents, which were expected to lead to draft legislation for formal enactment in FA 2012.

In the circumstances, we included last year the key features of the proposals as seen at 17 June 2011 in order to give readers who might be affected advance notice of the significant change that could impact on their tax status before this edition would reach them part way through 2012–13.

In the event, the consultation was extended and , although some important changes were made to the remittance basis (18.0.3(5)), no change in law concerning the statuses of resident or of ordinarily resident took place on 5 April 2012. The summary of responses to the 2011 consultation were published on 21 June 2012 together with the Government's replies and draft legislation for public consultation until 13 September 2012. A further draft will be included in the Autumn consultative draft of FB 2013, which will be followed by a final draft following the Spring Budget. The *statutory residence test* and key concepts are said to be 'near final', though subject to the outcome of the further consultations.

In the circumstances, we have updated the key features as seen at 21 June 2012, in order to update readers of how the change could impact on their their tax status before publication of our next edition. Because of the ongoing consultations and aspects still under consideration, further changes and detailed provisions will need to be taken into account when dealing with tax liabilities for 2013–14. *If your tax affairs are sensitive to the topics covered in Chapters 17, 18 or 19, and you wish to review your future personal plans for periods beyond 5 April 2013, it will be vital to take account of the ongoing legislative developments and consider taking appropriate professional advice.*

17.0.1 Specific topics expected to change from 6 April 2013

The Government's consultation proposals of 21 June 2012 include:

- a completely novel statutory test of *Residence* for individuals, which may increase complexity as well as certainty (17.3.8 & 17.5)
- abolition of the status of *Ordinary Residence* of individuals and consequent changes to the various tax rules that currently depend upon whether or not you are *ordinarily resident* (17.3.8)
- further changes affecting the taxation of some *Non-domiciled or Not ordinarily resident* individuals who adopt the remittance basis (17.6)

- withdrawal of the remittance basis from domiciliaries who are *not ordinarily resident*, except for certain new or returning residents (after a five-year absence) and then only for three tax years (17.3.8)
- generally to replace *ordinary residence* by *residence* as a tax criterion.

but they do not include any proposal to alter the basic law of *Domicile* (17.2.4).

17.1 The importance of domicile and residence

Your domicile and residence can have a considerable effect on your liability to UK income tax, capital gains tax and inheritance tax. The position is summarised in the following table and dealt with in more detail in Chapters 18 and 19. (Domicile is defined in 17.2 and residence in 17.3.) Note that after 2004–05, ITTOIA (2.10) generally removes the classification into schedules for income tax purposes, but the basic rules remain.

17.1.1 The tax effects of domicile and residence to 5 April 2012

Tax applicable and class of income	Situation of assets or where income arises	Tax treatment depending on taxpayer's residence and domicile		
		Taxed on arising basis (18.1.1)	**May be taxed on remittance basis** *(see Note 1)*	**Tax-free**
Income Tax *Self-employment*	UK Abroad	All classes Not normally applicable		
Interest	UK Abroad	Normally all classes Not normally applicable		
Foreign property and other income	UK Abroad	Not applicable UK domiciled resident and ordinarily resident	Not applicable Non-domiciled, UK domiciled resident but not ordinarily resident	Special rules (18.0 etc.)
Foreign self-employment and pensions	UK Abroad	Not applicable UK domiciled resident and ordinarily resident (90% pensions)	Not applicable Non-domiciled, UK domiciled resident but not ordinarily resident	Special rules (18.0 etc.)
Miscellaneous income	UK Abroad	All classes Not normally applicable apart from anti-avoidance rules (15.10)		
Employment		See 10.1–10.4		
Capital Gains Tax	UK or Abroad	UK domiciled and resident or ordinarily resident	Non-domiciled but resident or ordinarily resident (UK assets on arising basis)	Neither resident nor ordinarily resident *(see Note 2)*
Inheritance Tax (residence is normally immaterial)	UK Abroad	UK domiciled or non-domiciled UK domiciled or deemed domiciled (22.4)		Non-domiciled

Notes: (1) From 6 April 2008, long-term UK residents may elect to be assessed on the arising basis, in order to avoid fiscal disadvantages which now attach to use of the remittance basis (18.0 & 18.0.4).
(2) If you leave the UK for tax residence abroad after 16 March 1998 an absence of five complete tax years is normally required for this treatment (20.3 & 20.34).

17.2 What is domicile?

Although your domicile may affect your tax treatment, it is not a tax concept, but a basic legal concept that reaches out into matrimonial and testamentary law and can determine which country's courts have jurisdiction in determining disputes and which law should be applied. Your domicile is the country which you regard as your natural home. It is your place of abode to which you intend to return in the event of your going abroad. For most people it is their country of birth. Everyone has one domicile only. Unlike dual nationality, it is not possible to have two domiciles for the general purposes of English law. There are three main categories of domicile:

(1) Domicile of origin.
(2) Domicile of choice.
(3) Domicile of dependency.

Exceptionally, however, for some anti-avoidance or tax treaty purposes, you could have a fiscal domicile that differs from your legal domicile.

17.2.1 Domicile of origin

You receive a domicile of origin at birth; it is normally that of your father at the date of your birth. In the case, however, of an illegitimate child or one born after the death of his father, his domicile of origin is that of his mother.

Your domicile of origin can be supplanted by a domicile of choice (see below), but your domicile of origin will revive if you abandon a domicile of choice without acquiring another or resume permanent residence again in your country of origin.

17.2.2 Domicile of choice

If you abandon your domicile of origin and go and live in another country with the intention of permanently living there, the new country will become your domicile of choice. You will normally have to abandon most of your links with your original country of domicile (above). However, from 6 April 1996, registration for and voting in UK or EU parliamentary elections as an overseas elector are generally disregarded for all tax purposes (ITA 2007 S835B & IHTA S267) unless you prefer them to be taken into account for the purposes of any particular liability.

If you lose or abandon your domicile of choice, your domicile of origin automatically revives, unless you establish a new one.

17.2.3 Domicile of dependence

Certain dependent individuals are deemed incapable of choosing a new domicile and the latter is always fixed by the operation of the law. Dependants for this purpose include infants, married women before 1 January 1974 and mental patients.

A child under 16 years of age automatically has the domicile of his father if he is legitimate, and otherwise that of his mother. If, however, a girl of under 16 marries then she takes on her husband's domicile. (Prior to 1 January 1974 the relevant age was 18.) In Scotland a boy has an independent domicile from age 14 and a girl from age 12.

Prior to 1 January 1974 a wife assumed the domicile of her husband while they were married. After the end of the marriage (by death or divorce) the woman kept her former husband's domicile unless she took on a fresh domicile of choice. Since 1 January 1974, however, a wife's domicile is independent of that of her husband. If married before that date, the husband's domicile remains as the wife's deemed domicile of choice until displaced by positive action. An exception to this rule arises under the UK/USA tax treaty, which deems pre-1974 marriages of US wives to have taken place on 1 January 1974. This enables them to nominate their domicile of origin or subsequent domicile of choice to apply for UK income tax purposes.

17.2.4 **Previous prospective changes**

The law of domicile has been under a cloud since before 1993 and a review for individuals covering domicile and residence was announced in Budget 2002.

It did appear that the then Government felt it had achieved its tax ambitions by revising fiscal law and intended to keep the law of domicile intact, as it had said that there would not be any further changes in this area. However, in May 2010, the incoming Government's five-year policy programme included a review of the taxation of non-domiciled individuals, which was amplified at the time of the 22 May 2010 budget as an intention to 'assess whether changes can be made to the current rules to ensure that non-domiciled individuals make a fair contribution to reducing the deficit, in return for greater certainty and stability for those bringing skills and investment to the UK'. The consultation document *'The reform of taxation of non-domiciled individuals'* published on 17 June 2011 indicates that the tax proposals therein are designed to achieve the Government's objectives and that there is no intention to change the law of domicile.

17.3 What is residence?

Your residence for tax purposes is something which is fixed by your circumstances from year to year and you may sometimes be treated as being resident in more than one country (under their respective rules) at the same time.

In the UK, residence depends on the facts of each case and is currently determined by your presence in this country, your objects in being here and your future intentions regarding length of stay. Until 5 April 2013, the main criterion is the length of time spent in the country during each tax year and another important point can still be whether a 'place of abode' is kept in the country (17.3.6).

17.3.0 New regime to decide residence of individuals from 6 April 2013

As explained above (17.0), radical changes to the rules determining the *Residence* of individuals previously expected to take effect from 6 April 2012 will now apply from 6 April 2013, but are still subject to consultation and further draft legislation is expected in FB 2013. Key features of the new regime as seen at 21 June 2012 appear below (17.5).

Abolition of the status of *Ordinary Residence* and consequent revision of the rules linked to it are also proposed (17.0.1, 17.3.8 & 17.6).

17.3.1 What is ordinary residence?

If you have always lived in this country you are currently treated as being ordinarily resident here. This means that your residence is not casual and uncertain but is an essential feature of the ordinary course of your life. It implies residence with some degree of continuity, according to the way your life is usually ordered.

If you come to this country with the intention of taking up permanent residence here, it is Revenue practice to regard you as being both resident and ordinarily resident in the UK from your date of arrival. If, however, you originally did not intend to take up permanent residence here, you would not be considered ordinarily resident unless you stay here for two complete tax years and keep a place to live in this country.

17.3.2 The residence of an individual to 5 April 2013 (ITA Ss829–832)

If you visit this country for some temporary purpose only and not with the intention of establishing your residence here, you are not normally treated as being a UK resident unless you spend at least six months here during the tax year.

As an overseas visitor, however, you might be treated as acquiring UK residence if you pay habitual substantial visits to this country. The normal requirement would be to come here for at least four consecutive years and stay for an average of at least three months each year. If you wish to remain non-resident you must avoid such habitual visits.

If you come to this country during a tax year with the intention of staying for two years or more, a Revenue concession will apply. You will only be treated as UK resident from your date of arrival, rather than from the beginning of the tax year when you come. A similar concession applies for your year of departure if you leave the UK for permanent overseas residence.

If you pay only short casual visits abroad you will not lose your UK residence, but if an entire tax year is included in any continuous period spent abroad you will normally be treated as being non-resident for at least the intervening tax year (17.3.7).

17.3.3 The residence of a company (TA 1988 S749 & CTA 2010 Ss13–18 & Sch 2(13–15))

Subject to transitional provisions (see below), a company which is incorporated in the UK is treated for tax purposes as being resident here. Prior to 15

March 1988, a company was deemed to be resident where its central control and management were carried out. This was not necessarily where the company was registered although normally the central control and management would be exercised in the country in which the company was registered.

Where a company simply had its registered office here but carried on all its business from offices abroad and held its board meetings abroad, it was non-resident. Such companies did not come within the new rules for determining residence until 15 March 1993, provided they were already non-resident on 14 March 1988 or became non-resident later with Treasury consent. (In general, such companies needed to continue to carry on business.)

Under the controlled foreign company rules (13.22), where a company is resident abroad, it is necessary to establish in which country. Broadly, it is regarded as resident in the country where it is liable to tax because of its domicile, residence or place of management.

If a company registered abroad transacts some of its business in this country, it will not normally be treated as being UK resident provided its management and control are exercised abroad, which includes all board meetings being held abroad.

From 1 July 2009, Taxes Act 1988 S765, which imposed criminal sanctions if UK compnies become non-resident without Treasury consent, was repealed. Notifications are still required by regulation (15.10.15).

Where a company is resident in two countries, a double tax agreement often determines which residence applies for its purposes. If such a dual resident company is non-UK resident under the double tax agreement, it is so regarded for all UK tax purposes from 30 November 1993.

17.3.4 **The residence of a partnership** (ITTOIA Ss857–858)

Where any trade or business is carried on by a partnership and the control and management of the trade is situated abroad, the partnership is deemed to be resident abroad. This applies even if some of the partners are resident in this country and some of the trade is carried on here (12.6).

17.3.5 **The residence of a trust** (ITA Ss474–476 & Sch 2)

Until 2006–07, a trust was generally treated for capital gains tax purposes as being resident and ordinarily resident in the UK unless its general administration was ordinarily carried on outside this country and a majority of the trustees were neither resident nor ordinarily resident here. Stricter rules generally applied for income tax. For these purposes, special rules applied where at least one trustee was UK resident and one was not, depending on the settlor's status when he created the settlement or introduced further funds. If the settlor was then resident, ordinarily resident or domiciled in the UK, for determining the residence of the trust, all of the trustees were treated as being UK resident. Otherwise, they were all treated as being resident outside the UK. (A similar rule concerns the residence of executors etc.) (FA 1989 Ss110 & 111).

From 6 April 2007, there is a common set of trust residence rules for the purposes of income tax and capital gains tax, more in line with tests previously applying for income tax.

Similar rules have applied throughout to determine the residence of executors etc. (now ITA Ss718, 834 & 989).

17.3.6 **Place of abode in the UK** (ITA Ss830–832)

Prior to 6 April 1993, if you maintained a house or flat in this country available for your occupation this was usually a factor towards deciding that you were resident here. Your residence position, however, was decided without regard to any place of abode maintained for your use in the UK in either of the following circumstances:

(1) You worked full-time in a trade, profession or vocation no part of which was carried on in this country.
(2) You worked full-time in an office or employment, all the duties of which (ignoring merely incidental duties) were performed outside the UK.

For 1993–94 and subsequent years of assessment, your residence position may not be affected by your having a place of abode here. Such accommodation will be ignored in considering whether or not you have come to the UK for a temporary purpose (17.3.2). However, if you leave the UK and retain a home here, your reasons for this may be a factor in deciding your residence.

17.3.7 **The effect of visits abroad to 5 April 2013** (ITA S829)

If you are a citizen of the Commonwealth or the Republic of Ireland and your ordinary residence has been in the UK you are still charged to income tax if you have left this country only for the purpose of occasional residence abroad. In order to obtain non-residence for UK tax purposes your overseas residence must be more than merely occasional, it must have a strong element of permanency. The normal HMRC requirements are as follows:

(1) A definite intention to establish a permanent residence abroad.
(2) The actual fulfilment of such intention.
(3) Normally a full tax year should be spent outside this country before you are considered non-resident. Short periods in the UK may be disregarded by HMRC, however. Thus if you left the country permanently on 30 September 2006 you would only be confirmed as non-resident after 5 April 2008. If you go abroad for the purposes of employment or to carry on a trade, once you are accepted by HMRC as being no longer resident here, your non-residence is made retrospective to the day after your date of departure. In other cases of permanent departure, non-residence will normally run from the day after departure, but in some instances may run only from the following 6 April. In general, HMRC have less stringent rules regarding those working abroad under contracts of employment.

17.3.8 **Recent and prospective changes**

The law of residence has been subject to much uncertainty since it appeared that HMRC were not interpreting long-standing published guidance as had previously been generally understood (17.4.1).

From 6 April 2008, significant changes were made to:

(1) the manner of counting days presence here when testing UK resident status (17.4.1) and

(2) the remittance basis of assessment for foreign income and gains of long-term UK residents who are not ordinarily resident or are not domiciled here (18.0 & 18.0.4).

Also, fresh guidance was published (17.4.1) and judicial commentary in appeal cases has brought some clarity to the situation.

As indicated earlier (17.0 & 17.3.0) the future taxation of non-residents and non-domiciliaries was under discussion between HMRC and professional bodies before the 2010 general election, and radical changes to the rules determining the *Residence* of individuals previously expected to take effect from 6 April 2012 were held back until 6 April 2013. These will take the form of a statutory code, to be included in FB 2013. Details are well advanced, but remain subject to consultation and further draft legislation is expected in Autumn 2012. Key features of the new regime as seen at 21 June 2012 appear below (17.5).

From 6 April 2013, the proposed treatment of UK residents who have been not ordinarily resident is complex (17.6). Except for certain new residents, who have not been resident here in the past five years, the remittance basis will be withdrawn from UK domiciliaries who are *not ordinarily resident*. The exception applies to new or returning residents (after a five-year absence), whose eligibility will be limited to three tax years.

17.4 How to change your domicile and residence to 5 April 2013

As has been already indicated, domicile and residence normally run together but domicile is much more difficult to change.

The way in which to change your residence is summarised on the previous page. You simply establish a permanent residence abroad and remain out of this country for a complete tax year. (In certain circumstances short visits to the UK are allowed.) After that you must avoid returning to this country for as much as six months in any one tax year, averaging less than three months here every year. Even if you do not work abroad, it is now less necessary to avoid having a place of abode available for you in the UK (17.3.6), but HMRC comments following the *Gaines-Cooper* decision in 2006 suggest that it could be a problem for recent UK residents who make frequent return visits to the UK.

The general rule is that you will be charged to UK tax for the entire year of assessment as being either resident here or non-resident. However, in certain circumstances, by Inland Revenue Concession, the year of assessment is split for this purpose, namely where, being not ordinarily resident:

(1) You come to the UK to take up permanent residence or stay at least two years (previously three years).
(2) You cease to reside in the UK because you have left for permanent residence abroad.

The concession (A11) also applies if you go abroad under a contract of employment which includes a complete tax year. However, you may not spend 183 days or more in the UK in any tax year, nor an average of 91 days over a maximum period of four years. Counting days spent in the UK is no longer simple (17.4.1).

In order to establish a fresh domicile, you should take as many steps as possible to show that you regard your new country as your permanent home.

The following points are relevant to establishing a particular country as your new domicile:

(1) Develop a long period of residence in the new country.
(2) Purchase or lease a home.
(3) Marry a native of that country.
(4) Develop business interests there.
(5) Make arrangements to be buried there.
(6) Draw up your will according to the law of the country.
(7) Exercise political rights in your new country of domicile (17.2.2).
(8) Arrange to be naturalised (not vital).
(9) Have your children educated in the new country.
(10) Resign from all clubs and associations in your former country of domicile and join clubs etc. in your new country.
(11) Any religious affiliations that you have with your old domicile should be terminated and new ones established in your new domicile.
(12) Arrange for your family to be with you in your new country.

The above are some of the factors to be considered. The more of these circumstances that can be shown to prevail, the sooner you will be accepted as having changed your domicile or, it seems, even your residence (17.4.1).

17.4.1 Counting days spent in the UK to 5 April 2013

For very many years, it was customary to *exclude days of arrival AND departure*, when testing under Concession A11 (17.4) whether or not on average you had spent more than 91 days each year in the UK. However, following the *Gaines-Cooper* case in 2006, it became clear that HMRC wished to stop a perceived abuse of this practice by regular 'visitors' to the UK, who were counting two-day or three-day trips as zero or as a single day respectively. It is important to be prepared to prove a settled purpose to change your former residence pattern and explain the reasons for retaining your UK home.

From 6 April 2008, in determining your UK resident status, any day when you are present in the UK at midnight will be a day of residence. Thus the rule is now to *count days of arrival, but NOT days of departure*. This is the method that always applied for the purposes of the foreign earnings deduction now available only to seafarers (18.5.2).

Also from 6 April 2008, there is now a statutory exception for passengers in transit between two places outside the UK. Your single overnight stays in the UK will be disregarded, provided you leave the UK the next day and do not engage in activities that are substantially unrelated to your transit. In short, if your presence here is solely to change between flights, ships or a continental train, it should be disregarded as should any unplanned delay days. However, if you build business meetings or even family visits into your UK time, you may forfeit the exception. The 2010 disruptions of airline flights by volcanic ash and by cabin crew strikes have been recognised in principle by HMRC as potentially acceptable causes of delay, subject to documentary evidence to support individual claims.

Regular 'return visitors' to the UK should remain wary of comments made by HMRC after the *Gaines-Cooper* case and in booklet HMRC 6. These warn that, if you have not actually shed your resident status, it may not even be relevant to count days, to determine whether you are taxable as a resident (17.3.7). It appears that HMRC intend to apply some of the domicile criteria (17.4) to would-be non-residents. Subsequent cases make it clear that the counting of days spent in UK is generally only one of the facts to be considered in deciding whether there has been a change in your pattern of life. However, the day count remains of overriding significance, if you spend 183 days in UK in any tax year, because that makes you statutorily resident for that year.

Revised official guidance operative from 6 April 2009 can be found in booklet HMRC 6 entitled *Residence, Domicile and the Remittance Basis*. For greater detail, there is also a new HMRC manual under a similar title. In May 2008 HMRC published a partially updated version of IR 20 on their website only. That did NOT address the FA 2008 changes, in respect of which HMRC 6 was promised later in 2008–09. The last printed version of IR 20 of December 1999 reflected the law and practice as at October 1999.

The 2011–12 Residence, remittance basis etc. pages to the Self-assessment Return specifically ask (among many other questions):

a) in respect of that year

- Number of days spent in UK excluding ***only days of departure***.
- How many days' presence you attribute to exceptional circumstances.
- How many were workdays on which you performed any work duties.
- How many separate visits you made to the UK excluding eligible ***transit visits***.

b) retrospectively to 5 April 2012

- Total number of days spent in UK since 5 April 2008 or your date of departure from UK, if later. In previous years, this was on a mixed basis, excluding days of arrival as well as of departure up to 5 April 2008 but not thereafter and also excluding ***exceptional circumstance*** and eligible ***transit days***.

However, reference should be made to the explanatory notes before completing these supplementary pages.

A practice statement informally circulated by HMRC in April 2011 indicates the relevance of the information about 'working days' on the tax return and that they will not generally enquire into non-residents who spend no more than 10 working days in UK. In other cases, they may look closely at the nature of your UK duties so as to establish whether they were a substantial part of or merely incidental to your duties overseas. This primarily affects the extent to which your pay is taxable in UK. It was feared that there was an implication that non-residence might be challenged by reference to 10 working days in UK, rather than by reference to the 91-days or 183-days rules. Although that was refuted by HMRC, it could be that in some cases a greater UK work pattern might lead to a challenge that you did not make a clean break with the UK, on leaving to take up your foreign employment. However, HMRC have indicated that such a challenge would be based on an overall view of all relevant factors and not by reference solely to the number of working days spent here.

The current consultations relating to periods commencing 6 April 2013 seem likely to change and clarify the underlying rules on working days and the records that you ought to keep.

17.5 New statutory residence test for individuals from 6 April 2013

As explained above (17.0 & 17.3.0), radical changes to the rules determining the *Residence* of individuals previously expected to take effect from 6 April 2012 were held back to 6 April 2013, but are still subject to consultation and further draft legislation is expected in Autumn 2012. In the circumstances, only the key features of the new regime as seen at 21 June 2012 are set out below and further changes and detailed provisions will need to be taken into account when dealing with tax liabilities for 2013–14.

These key features may be of assistance, if your tax affairs are sensitive to residence issues and you wish to review your future personal plans for periods beyond 5 April 2013. However, it will be vital to take account of ongoing developments and consider taking appropriate professional advice.

17.5.1 Key aspects of conclusive residence tests from 6 April 2013

Part A – Automatically not resident in UK for a tax year, if you meet any of:

(1) were resident in the UK in one or more of the previous three tax years and are present in the UK for fewer than 16 days in the relevant tax year; or
(2) were not resident in the UK in all of the previous three tax years and are present in the UK for fewer than 46 days in the relevant tax year; or
(3) work full-time overseas for the relevant tax year, provided you are present in the UK for fewer than 91 days in the relevant tax year and there are fewer than 21 days on which you work for more than 3 hours in

the UK in that tax year except that (1) shall not apply to the tax year in which you die and (3) shall not apply to you, if at any time in the relevant tax year you have been an *international transportation worker*.

Part B – Automatically resident in UK for a tax year if you do not meet any of the tests under Part A and you do meet any of:

(1) are present in the UK for at least 183 days in that tax year; or
(2) have only one home and that home is in the UK (or have two or more homes and all of them are in the UK) for at least 91 days during the year; or
(3) carry out full-time work in the UK for a period of 276 days, all or part of which falls within that tax year, more than 75 per cent of the days on which you work for more than three hours are days when you work in the UK and that there are no *significant breaks* from work during the period – a *significant break* being a period of 31 days or more when there is no day on which you work for more than three hours in the UK and your absence from work is not due to annual leave or sick leave;
(4) you die during the relevant tax year, having been resident in the UK under an automatic test for each of the three previous tax years, the preceding tax year would not have been a split year, even if you were not resident in the relevant tax year, and at the time of your death your normal home was in UK (even if your were temporarily overseas at that time), except that (3) shall not apply to you, if at any time in the relevant tax year you have been an *international transportation worker*.

Only if you do not fall within Parts A or B would you need to consider Part C of the test, which is expected to apply only if you have 'complex tax affairs'.

17.5.2 **Key aspects of alternative residence tests from 6 April 2013**

Part C: applies differently to UK 'Arrivers' and 'Leavers' and combines specified '*UK Ties*' with a graduated count of days spent in the UK.

Part C(i): Arrivers

– applies if you were not resident in all three previous tax years
– the *UK Ties* may count if at any time in the relevant tax year you:
  (a) have a UK resident family;
  (b) have accessible accommodation in the UK;
  (c) have substantive UK employment or self-employment;
  (d) spent more than 90 days in the UK in either of the previous two tax years.

Days spent in UK	Impact of *UK Ties* on residence status
Fewer than 46 days	Always non-resident
46–90 days	Resident only if 4 ties apply
91–120 days	Resident only if 3 ties or more apply
121–182 days	Resident only if 2 ties or more apply
183 days or more	Always resident

Part C(ii): Leavers

- applies if you were resident in one or more of the three previous tax years
- the *UK Ties* may count if at any time in the relevant tax year you:
  - (a) have a UK resident family;
  - (b) have accessible accommodation in the UK;
  - (c) have substantive UK employment or self-employment;
  - (d) spent more than 90 days in the UK in either of the previous two tax years;
  - (e) spend more days in the UK in the tax year than in any other one country.

Days spent in UK	Impact of *UK Ties* on residence status
Fewer than 16 days	Always non-resident
16–45 days	Resident only if 4 ties or more apply
46–90 days	Resident only if 3 ties or more apply
91–120 days	Resident only if 2 ties or more apply
121–182 days	Resident only if 1 tie or more applies
183 days or more	Always resident

17.5.3 Replacement of concessions by statutory rules from 6 April 2013

From 6 April 2013, it is intended to replace various long-standing extra-statutory concessions by statutory rules. In some cases, the detailed qualifications will need to be changed, so as to avoid subjective or imprecise tests and ensure certainty.

Split-year treatment (17.3.2 & 17.4) for arrivers and leavers will be preserved, where you:

(1) become resident in the UK by virtue of your only home being here;
(2) become resident in the UK by starting full-time employment here;
(3) establish your only home in a country outside the UK, become tax resident in that country and do not come back to the UK in that tax year;
(4) lose UK residence by virtue of working full-time abroad;
(5) return to the UK following a period of working full-time abroad; or
(6) go (or return from) abroad with or following your spouse or civil partner, who is (or has been) working full time abroad, provided your sole or main home is then (or has been) outside the UK.

17.6 Proposed abolition of Ordinary Residence of individuals from 6 April 2013

An integral part of the proposed new regime for *residence* of individuals is the abolition of the status of *ordinary residence*. The table below indicates the main provisions currently affected by that status and the manner in which Government intends to approach each area in future. In some cases transitional reliefs are expected to be offered. Most of the legislation will be available in the Autumn 2012 draft of FB 2013.

Provision	Current application	Future application
General remittance basis	Available if tax resident and non-domiciled *or* not ordinarily resident	Available only if tax resident and non-domiciled (18.0 *et seq.*)
Overseas workday relief	Available if tax resident and ordinarily resident	Replaced with a statutory relief which will only be available if non-domiciled (19.8 (8))
Transfer of Assets Abroad	Applies to individuals who are ordinarily resident	Will apply to individuals who are tax resident (15.10.2)
Seafarers Earnings Deduction	Available if ordinarily resident in the UK or tax resident in an European Economic Area state (other than the UK)	Available if tax resident in the UK (or resident in an EU or EEA state) or tax resident in an European Economic Area state (other than the UK) (18.5.2)
Foreign service relief for termination payments	Applies in respect of earnings related to UK duties for individuals who are not ordinarily resident	Will apply only in respect of earnings for overseas duties.
Capital gains tax	Applies to UK gains if individual is tax resident *or* ordinarily resident	Will apply to UK gains only if individual is tax resident (20.3)
Capital gains tax and temporary non-residence rule	Applies to individuals who are tax resident or ordinarily resident	Will apply to individuals who are tax resident (20.3.1)
Taxable lump sums from pension schemes (ESC A10)	Applies in respect of earnings related to UK duties for individuals who are not ordinarily resident	Will apply only in respect of earnings for overseas duties (19.8)
Individual Savings Accounts (ISAs)	Available to individuals who are tax resident and ordinarily resident	Will apply to individuals who are tax resident (8.12)
FOTRA securities	Applies where the holder is not ordinarily resident	Will apply where the holder is not tax resident (19.2)

Chapter 18

TAX ON FOREIGN INCOME

18.0 Remittance basis from 6 April 2008

18.0.1 Background

Many UK residents who are not domiciled in any part of the UK or are not ordinarily resident here have hitherto enjoyed the facility to pay tax in respect of certain foreign income and gains by reference to amounts actually or deemed to be remitted to the UK in each tax year, rather than by reference to the amounts arising for the year.

However, mainly from 6 April 2008, significant changes were made, which are described here. So as to preserve your ability to refer to the previous regime, when reviewing your tax affairs for 2007–08 or earlier, our commentary on the old rules remains unchanged (18.1.1–18.1.3).

From 6 April 2013 new statutory tests of tax residence are proposed to take effect and the status of *ordinarily resident* abolished for tax purpose, so the grounds of entitlement to the remittance basis and to selected tax advantages hitherto linked to *not ordinarily resident* status will be redefined. However, there are purposes for which UK domiciliaries who are currently resident and not ordinarily resident here will become exposed to additional liabilities, subject to transitional reliefs.

18.0.2 New single regime (ITA Ss809A–809Z)

Over the years, as can be seen from the remainder of this chapter, different rules have built up governing the application of the remittance basis to various classes of income and gains. However, from 2008–09 a single regime was substituted, which includes detailed rules concerning remittances. These aim to reduce the scope for avoiding tax by remitting income or gains in years after the source had ceased or in a form other than cash or by an indirect route that was not hitherto taxable, including the use of third parties, companies or trusts. Many established pathways were closed either from 12 March or (mainly) 6 April 2008.

Another major change is the introduction of detailed rules specifying the order in which remittances are to be notionally attributed to previously unremitted foreign income and gains. That allocation will supplant the true origin of the remittances. The rules also provide for the treatment of mixed funds, containing different categories of income, capital, capital gains or amounts from different years. However, there are a number of transitional reliefs to protect selected aspects of your affairs as at 5 April 2008. There is a mechanism for reducing unremitted gains by losses realised on foreign assets, provided that you elect for this to apply from the first year after 5 April 2008 in which you use the remittance basis.

18.0.3 **Long-term UK residents – disadvantages and reliefs for claimants**

From 2008–09, if you had been resident in the UK for at least 7 out of the 9 years preceding the year to be assessed, use of the remittance basis might (subject to extensive detailed rules) carry a range of new tax disadvantages as follows:

(1) These disadvantages do *not* apply if you qualify for *automatic* access to the remittance basis (18.0.4).
(2) Otherwise, you forfeit any right you would have had to claim personal, age-related, blind persons or married couples' allowance or life assurance relief for income tax.
(3) Additionally, you lose the annual exemption for capital gains tax.
(4) Also, until 5 April 2012, unless you were aged under 18 throughout the year, you were liable to pay the new *remittance basis charge* of £30,000 per annum, which is a payment of income tax or capital gains tax or both, according to an allocation which you make. Although in subsequent years remittances out of the income or gains that you have nominated can in principle be remitted without any fresh tax charge, your remittances will first be attributed to your *untaxed* unremitted income and gains until they are exhausted.
(5) Several changes from 6 April 2012 (outlined in the March 2011 Budget and subjected to formal consultation process) are in FA 2012. The most significant reliefs remove the tax charge on remittances made for the purposes of commercial investment in qualifying UK businesses and on any capital gains therefrom, provided the proceeds are promptly removed from UK once realised or reinvested in other qualifying businesses here. Detailed rules apply and include time limits for reinvestment or re-export of the proceeds, but they do permit these investments to be made via offshore companies. Smaller changes, including the disregard of remittances of up to £10 of previously *nominated income*, should significantly reduce the administrative burdens of the present remittance basis rules. However, longer-term residents who use the remittance basis will face an increased remittance basis charge of £50,000 if they have been resident in UK for at least 12 years out of the 14 years preceding the year to be assessed.

18.0.4 **Whether a claim is necessary and other issues**

From 2008–09, the remittance basis applies automatically (without the need for you to make a claim) and without your suffering the disadvantages (18.0.3 (2)–(4)) in two situations:

(1) If you are UK resident in the year, but non-domiciled or not ordinarily resident, have no UK income or gains for the year, have made no relevant remittances in the year and are either under 18 or have been resident in the UK for no more than 6 of the 9 immediately preceding years.
(2) If you are UK resident in the year, but non-domiciled or not ordinarily resident, and your unremitted foreign income and gains for the year are less than £2,000.

A claim to adopt the remittance basis is required, if you are UK resident in the year, but non-domiciled or not ordinarily resident, are aged 18 or over in the year and have been resident in the UK in at least 7 of the 9 immediately preceding years. If you are in this category:

(1) You can choose between the remittance basis and the arising basis each year.
(2) Although the remittance basis can be claimed at any point up to 5 years and 10 months after the end of the tax year, the remittance basis charge (18.0.3 (4) & (5)) is payable as part of your self-assessment tax due on the normal dates and, if you were subsequently to decide to withdraw your claim to use the remittance basis, this would have to be done not later than 12 months after the normal submission date for your return.
(3) You can use the remittance basis charge to frank gift aid payments and to claim any benefits available under double taxation treaties.
(4) If the remittance basis charge is paid *direct to HMRC* by cheque or electronic transfer from an overseas source, that payment will not be taxed as a remittance, but any subsequent refund would be treated as a remittance at that time.

These rules are extensive and complex and merit careful study if you have been enjoying the remittance basis and are or may soon become a long-term or longer-term UK resident (18.0.3); more especially so, if you are affected by double taxation treaties and particularly that with the USA. A number of minor adjustments were made retrospectively by FA 2009, to ensure that the rules operate as intended and to dispense with the need for remittance basis users to file UK returns, if their foreign employment income and foreign bank interest are under £10,000 and £100 respectively and have been fully taxed abroad.

Once you make use of the remittance basis, the new rules impose what may be a significant record-keeping burden upon you, if you are to comply with your responsibility to have available for production to HMRC, if required, all the evidence needed to support your tax returns.

The cumulative nature and complexity of calculation of unremitted income and gains, the fact that your tax affairs could come under investigation by random selection as well as by risk assessment and the increased severity of penalties for compliance lapses all underline the wisdom of starting these records as soon as you form an expectation that you are eligible to and actually may make use of the remittance basis.

Early suggestions that HMRC would generally be content to collect your remittance basis charge without requiring details of your unremitted income and gains should be regarded as unrealistic in the long term. *Potential claimants may prefer to await the outcome of the consultation process which commenced in June 2011 (17.0 & 18.0.3(5)) on the taxation of non-domiciled individuals before incurring significant costs on building retrospective records. However, if you are already using the remittance basis, you should take advice if you are at all uncertain as to the adequacy of your current remittance records.*

In addition to the main leaflet HMRC 6 (*Residence, Domicile and the Remittance Basis* – updated February 2010 and again in December 2010), HMRC guidance on detailed aspects of compiling records of mixed funds and allocating and prioritising remittances is publicly available as Part 3 of the *Residence, Domicile and Remittances Manual* and HMRC Statement of Practice SP1/09 (*Employees resident but not ordinarily resident in the UK*). From 6 April 2013, much of the above guidance is likely to be revised to reflect the administrative changes to the remittance basis (18.0.3 (5)) and the proposed statutory residence test (17.5) and abolition of *ordinary residence* (17.6).

18.0.5 Rate of higher rate tax on foreign dividends

From 6 April 2008 an error created by faulty drafting of ITTOIA was rectified, so that the rate of tax payable under the remittance basis on foreign dividends became 40 per cent and *not* 32.5 per cent. From 2010–11, the 50 per cent additional rate will apply as appropriate.

18.1 Overseas income from investments and businesses

(ITTOIA Ss5, 7, 261, 268–270, 357, 370, 402–403, 422, 424, 428, 572, 579–580, 582, 610, 612, 614–617, 683–684, 687–689, 830 & 838–845)

Up to 2003–04, if you obtained any income from investments and businesses situated overseas, you were normally charged to income tax under the former Case IV or Case V of Schedule D, but income from overseas employments fell under Schedule E (18.5).

After 2004–05, the classification into schedules for income tax purposes no longer applies in view of ITTOIA (2.10). However, the basic rules have remained in place.

Frequently your overseas income will have already suffered tax in its country of origin. If you also have to pay UK income tax on this income you will normally be entitled to some relief to limit the extent that you are taxed doubly on the same income (18.6).

If you are UK resident and suffer 'special withholding tax' on savings income from abroad, you will be able to credit it against your UK tax liability and have any excess repaid. Also you can ask the Inland Revenue for a certificate for the paying agent to pay you gross. 'Special withholding tax' is broadly levied under an EU directive of 3 June 2003 or corresponding legislation of a non-EU state.

From 1997–98, the normal basis of assessment under the former Cases IV and V of Schedule D has been the amount of income arising in the year of assessment.

In certain special circumstances (18.1.2) the 'arising basis' was not used and the historically more favourable 'remittance basis' applied (18.1.1). However, from 2008–09, significant changes to the remittance basis have taken place (18.0).

If you are UK domiciled and ordinarily resident, however, your assessments on overseas pensions are based on only 90 per cent of the income arising.

From 1 December 2009, the taxation of income and gains from qualifying offshore funds has changed. Those funds that choose to become '*reporting funds*' must allocate their income to participants regardless of whether or not it has been distributed and, if you are a UK resident, you will be subject to income tax on the amount allocated. However, on disposal, your capital gain will be reduced by any undistributed income on which you have paid income tax. If you participate in a fund that becomes a '*non-reporting fund*' you will pay income tax on the distributions you receive and also on any capital gain on disposal. There are further rules for remittance basis and for non-resident participants.

18.1.1 **The remittance basis before 2008–09**

Up to 2007–08, under the remittance basis you were only taxed on the amount of income actually brought into this country in the year of assessment (whilst you still possessed the source of overseas income). If you were assessed on the remittance basis and brought income into the UK in a tax year after the source had come to an end, you were not liable to UK tax on it at all (18.1.2). Remittances can be made in cash or kind (18.1.3).

Prior to 6 April 2008, if you made no remittances you will have had no liability to UK tax on your overseas income that was taxable on the remittance basis, no matter how high your income was in any year, although you might well have suffered foreign tax. From 6 April 2008, that will no longer necessarily be the case, because of the significant changes made to the remittance basis (18.0).

18.1.2 **When did the remittance basis apply?** (ITTOIA S831)

Your assessments on foreign businesses and investments were based not on the 'arising' basis but on the remittance basis:

(1) If you were resident in this country but not domiciled here (17.3.2); or

(2) If you were a British subject or a citizen of the Republic of Ireland and were resident in this country but not ordinarily resident here.

Prior to 6 April 2008, you may have had some overseas income that was taxed on a remittance basis and some that was taxed on an arising basis. In this case you should have clearly segregated the two sources of income by using separate bank accounts since income from the latter could be brought into this country without paying any additional tax here because it had already been charged to UK tax. However, from 2008–09, the new rules for attributing remittances to unremitted income could override the facts (18.0.4).

If you were not resident in the UK (17.3.2), you would not normally be charged to tax in respect of your income from foreign businesses and investments, even if it was remitted here.

18.1.3 **What were classed as remittances?** (ITTOIA Ss831–837)

Even prior to 6 April 2008, whilst you had any continuing sources of overseas income in respect of which income arising abroad had not been fully transmitted to this country, any sums brought into the UK would normally be first considered to be remittances of overseas income.

Although prior to 6 April 2008, that would not have applied if you kept separate bank accounts for income and capital, bringing in funds from the latter only (possibly giving rise to capital gains tax) from that date, the new rules permit the allocation of these remittances to unremitted foreign income and gains, although provable pure capital may be tax-free (18.0.4).

As well as cash and cheques, any property imported or value arising here from property not imported will have been classed as remittances. Thus if you bought a car abroad out of your overseas profits and brought it into this country this was a remittance (although strictly speaking, if intended for your own use, the second-hand value of the car at the time of importation should have been used instead of the cost of the car). Similarly, if you hired an asset abroad out of unremitted overseas income, any use that you had from the asset in this country would be valued and treated as a remittance.

If you borrowed money against sums owing to you for overseas income and brought the former into this country, this was a remittance. Similarly, if you borrowed money here and repaid it abroad out of overseas profits, this was known as a 'constructive remittance' and was taxable. Other forms of 'constructive remittances' included the payment out of overseas income of interest owing in this country, and the repayment out of such income, of money borrowed overseas which was made available to you in this country.

If you used non-remitted overseas income to buy shares in UK companies this was normally treated as a remittance unless a third party abroad actually acted as the principal in the transaction.

You were able to use non-remitted overseas income to cover the costs of overseas visits (including holidays) and provided you bring none of the money back to this country there was no taxable remittance. For this purpose the Revenue allowed you to receive traveller's cheques in this country provided they are not cashed here.

If overseas profits were remitted to the Channel Islands or the Isle of Man this was not treated as a taxable remittance since those countries are not regarded as part of the UK for taxation purposes. They were, however, treated as being part of the UK for the purposes of exchange control and, until the abolition of UK exchange control rules from 24 October 1979, these islands played an important compliance role in providing a useful home for income earned abroad which had to be remitted to the UK. However, you are now free to keep money in other countries, subject to their own regulations.

From 2008–09, detailed rules (18.0.2 *et seq.*) address the above principles and a variety of other means of introducing to the UK value from unremitted income and gains, including the provision of benefits to closely connected individuals or to beneficiaries of trusts and the sale in the UK of imported assets.

18.2 The basis of assessment for investments and businesses (ITA 2007 S95)

As previously mentioned, from 1997–98, the normal measure of assessment has been the amount of income arising in the year of assessment. In certain cases, however, the assessment was based on the remittances in the tax year (18.1.2). Details of the preceding year basis of assessment for earlier years can be found in previous editions of this book, together with the special rules for new or ceasing sources of income.

If you have an overseas business and the remittance basis does not apply, the assessment rules will generally follow those for UK businesses (11.7.1). Thus you are assessed on the adjusted profits for your accounts year ending in the year of assessment.

Under the current system, income from property outside the UK has been aligned with that within the UK by importing some of the rules (7.1). Thus interest payable for the purposes of your property business is allowed as a deduction. Income from overseas property remains assessable as such and separately from your UK property income pool. However, from 6 April 1997, your overseas property income is itself pooled.

Deductions allowed in computing the income arising include the following:

(1) Any annuity paid out of the income to a non-resident of this country.
(2) Any other annual payment (not being interest) out of the income to a non-resident.
(3) Normal trading expenses against the income from any trade etc. which you have abroad.
(4) Normal maintenance costs against rental income arising abroad.
(5) Ten per cent of any pensions.
(6) If you pay any overseas taxes for which you get no form of double tax relief then you can deduct such payments in computing your overseas income arising.
(7) If your overseas pension (or part of it) arises under the German or Austrian law relating to victims of Nazi persecution, such income is totally exempt. This includes cases where refugees from Germany were later credited with unpaid social security contributions thereby getting higher pensions.

18.3 Professions conducted partly abroad

If you are engaged in any profession or vocation that is conducted partly within this country and partly overseas, you will normally be assessed on your entire 'global' profits as UK self-employment income. It is only if you conduct a separate profession or vocation entirely abroad that rules for a foreign business will apply.

This rule is particularly applicable to actors and entertainers etc. who travel widely in the conduct of their professions. The rule does not apply, however, to income from an office or employment the duties of which are conducted entirely abroad.

18.4 Relief for overseas trading by individuals

Prior to 1985–86 a special relief applied against assessments on the profits of trades, professions or vocations including partnerships, if you resided in the UK and were absent from it for at least 30 'qualifying days' in the tax year. Details can be found in earlier editions of this book.

18.5 Earnings from employment overseas (ITEPA Ss22–28, 38–40, 328–334, 342, 355, 376 & 382–384)

Overseas earnings generally arise from employment with a foreign employer where your duties are performed wholly outside this country, but can include specially designated Crown employment. Duties performed in the UK which are purely incidental to the performance of your overseas employment are normally disregarded.

If you are *not domiciled* (17.2) within the UK, you are taxable only on remittances from *overseas earnings* even if you are resident and ordinarily resident (18.5.3). Other special rules may apply (19.1.7).

If you are UK resident, but *not ordinarily resident*, earnings from any employment, the duties of which are carried out outside the UK, qualify for the remittance basis, as do those from specially designated Crown employment (18.5.3). If you are *not resident* here, such earnings will not be taxable, whether or not remitted.

If you are a UK resident and the duties of your UK employment are performed partly here and partly abroad, you will normally be taxed on the income arising as part of your general earnings (10.3.1).

From 6 April 1974 to 5 April 1985, your assessable earnings from any overseas employment were generally discounted by 25 per cent (1984–85 – 12.5 per cent). Thereafter, a 100 per cent deduction applied for extended periods of absence (18.5.1) until 16 March 1998, when this relief was withdrawn for all except seafarers (18.5.2)

18.5.1 The 100 per cent deduction up to 16 March 1998

Prior to 17 March 1998 you were not normally liable to UK tax on any income from *overseas employments* which you earned during a 'qualifying period' of absence from this country of at least a year. The detailed rules varied from time to time and are described in previous editions of this book.

18.5.2 The 100 per cent deduction after 16 March 1998 (ITEPA Ss378–385)

With effect from 17 March 1998, the general 100 per cent foreign earnings deduction (18.5.1) was removed, except for foreign-going seafarers, but excluding those employed on offshore installations for oil/gas exploration or extraction.

The rules for seafarers are broadly that, if you are resident and (until 5 April 2013) ordinarily resident in the UK (or from 6 April 2011 the EU or EEA), you may be entitled to exemption from UK tax on certain income from an employment carried out wholly or partly abroad, which you earn during an 'eligible period' of absence from this country *of at least a year*. This does not need to be a tax year and may be built up from any number of absences. You are allowed to spend up to one-half of the period in the UK, but no more than 183 days in any one visit. The one-half test must be applied cumulatively from the start of your 'eligible period' as at the end of each overseas trip – and meticulously monitored.

For this purpose, days in the UK have always been counted on the basis adopted from 6 April 2008 for testing UK residence (17.4.1) – *count days of arrival, but not days of departure*.

Supposing that, as you approach the end of your first year, you have a potential 'eligible period' of 340 days including actual visits to the UK totalling 170 days, but spend 20 days in the UK, followed by 16 days overseas, bringing your total period to 376 days, including 190 days in the UK. Your 'chain' would be broken, because you would have spent 2 days more in the UK than the permitted maximum of 188 (one-half of the 376) days – frustrating and potentially costly, because the test is applied absolutely strictly and there are no concessions, leaving you to start building a fresh 'eligible period' from the date when next you go overseas again.

Once you have established an 'eligible period' of 365 days or more, your earnings from qualifying activities, which essentially are duties of your employment carried out on board ship at sea or in port in the course of an international voyage will be eligible for the 100 per cent deduction. The deduction applies to your net earnings after deducting expenses claims and pension contributions. Where appropriate, duties incidental to your overseas work will be eligible, even if performed in the UK. However, earnings from substantive UK duties will be taxable.

To claim this deduction you currently require the *Additional Information* pages (SA 101) to the 2011–12 self-assessment return. Complete Box 11 on page Ai 2 under '*Share schemes and employment lump sums, compensation and deductions*' and then list the names of all vessels on which your qualifying activities were carried out (this is required annually from 2006–07) in Box 20 on page Ai 4.

18.5.3 **Remittances**

The rules concerning the remittance of income from employment are exactly the same as for income from foreign businesses and investments (18.0 etc.; formerly 18.1.2). The remittance basis now broadly only applies for overseas employments if you are UK resident and not domiciled here and/or not ordinarily resident (18.5). Note that you are assessed on remittances made after 5 April 1990 whether or not the employment has ceased.

Remittances of income from overseas employments carried out abroad are not taxable here in either of the following situations:

(1) If made during a tax year in which you are not resident here (whether or not you are ordinarily resident in this country).
(2) If made when you are UK domiciled and ordinarily resident (normally taxed on an arising basis).

18.5.4 **Expenses concerning work overseas** (ITEPA Ss328–330, 341–342 & 369–375)

Provided your employer ultimately bears the cost, normally you are not taxed as a benefit on any of the following expenses concerning overseas employments:

(1) Travelling to take up your overseas employment or returning on its termination. (Expense relief is available if you bear the cost yourself.)
(2) Board and lodging overseas.
(3) Certain visits by your family (10.6.4).
(4) Unlimited outward and return journeys between your overseas employment and the UK.

Similar rules apply to the travel and subsistence of UK residents with businesses carried on wholly abroad. The rules cover travel between overseas trades as well as between the UK and abroad.

18.6 Double taxation relief (TIOPA Ss2–145)

The UK government has entered into agreements with the governments of other countries for the purpose of preventing double taxation under the UK tax law and under the tax law of such other countries in respect of the same income (This can now apply even if the UK does not recognise the other government). A further object of certain of those agreements is to render reciprocal assistance in the prevention of tax evasion.

Under particular double taxation conventions certain classes of income are made taxable only in one of the countries who are party to the agreement, for example, that in which the taxpayer resides. Certain other income is taxable in both of the countries concerned, but in the case of UK residents the overseas tax is allowed as a credit against the UK tax. If after 16 March 1998 your overseas tax on such income is reduced, you must tell HMRC.

Double tax relief is restricted for UK banks lending to non-residents to 15 per cent of the gross interest. However, it is now necessary to look at each loan separately. Foreign tax credit relief is only to be offset against the corporation tax on a particular loan.

If there is no double tax convention between this country and another one then 'unilateral relief' may be available. This means that if you are a UK resident and obtain income from the other country, you are normally allowed to set off any overseas tax suffered against your UK tax liability on the same income. If you are not allowed to do so then you can deduct the overseas tax in computing the overseas income taxable in this country.

Various changes have effect after 31 March 2000 regarding mainly multinational companies. For example, the rate of underlying tax attributable to an intra-group dividend is capped at 30 per cent (45 per cent against other dividends not themselves capped). The on-shore pooling rules were extended from 1 April 2001 to allow relief for foreign tax rates paid up to 45 per cent even if this is at more than one level in a chain of companies. FA 2005 Ss85–89 made rule changes. These include denying underlying tax relief if a tax deduction is given in another jurisdiction calculated by reference to the relevant dividend.

Double tax agreements may include provisions for the exchange of information about taxpayers, between the UK and the overseas country concerned. This is particularly aimed at countering tax evasion and numerous treaties devoted entirely to this have recently been negotiated with '*Tax Havens*'.

18.6.1 Double taxation relief – list of countries which have general agreements with the UK

Antigua & Barbuda
Argentina
Armenia
Australia
Austria
Azerbaijan
Bangladesh
Barbados
Belarus*
Belgium
Belize
Bolivia
Botswana
Brunei
Bulgaria
Burma (Myanmar)
Canada
Cayman Islands
Chile
China*
Cyprus
Czechoslovakia (Czech & Slovak Republics)
Denmark
Egypt
Estonia
Falkland Islands
Faroes
Fiji
Finland
France
Gambia
Georgia
Germany
Ghana
Gilbert Islands (Kiribati and Tuvalu)
Greece
Grenada
Guernsey
Guyana
Hong Kong
Hungary
Iceland
India
Indonesia
Irish Republic
Isle of Man
Israel
Italy
Ivory Coast
Jamaica
Japan
Jersey
Jordan
Kazakhstan
Kenya
Korea
Kuwait
Latvia
Lesotho
Libya
Lithuania
Luxembourg
Macedonia
Malawi
Malaysia
Malta
Mauritius
Mexico
Moldova
Mongolia
Montserrat
Morocco
Namibia
Netherlands
New Zealand
Nigeria
Norway
Oman
Pakistan
Papua New Guinea
Philippines
Poland
Portugal
Qatar
Romania
Russian Federation*
Saudi Arabia
Sierra Leone
Singapore
Slovak Republic under Czechoslovakia
Slovenia
Solomon Islands
South Africa
Spain
Sri Lanka
St Kitts & Nevis
Sudan
Swaziland
Sweden
Switzerland
Taiwan
Thailand
Trinidad & Tobago
Tunisia
Turkey
Uganda
Ukraine
USA
USSR*
Uzbekistan
Venezuela
Vietnam
Yugoslavia (Bosnia Herzegovina, Croatia, Serbia & Montenegro, Slovenia & Tajikistan)
Zambia
Zimbabwe

* The convention with the USSR has become known as being with the Russian Federation, but also applies to most other states which used to make up the USSR until superseded by new agreements. However, from April 2002, Armenia, Georgia, Kyrgyzstan and Moldova are excluded.

Note: In addition to the above general agreements, arrangements of a more restricted kind have been entered into with Brazil, Lebanon and Zaire covering the double taxation of profits from shipping and air transport. Agreements with Algeria, Cameroon, Ethiopia and Iran cover only air transport and China has a separate air transport agreement.

18.7 Disclosure facilities for unreported offshore accounts etc.

18.7.1 Offshore disclosure facility (ODF)

On 17 April 2007 HMRC announced arrangements enabling investors with offshore accounts to disclose related income and gains previously omitted from their tax returns. Disclosure had also to cover any unreported UK income or gains. If no serious criminality has occurred, disclosure under this facility should carry a penalty of only 10 per cent of the unpaid tax. To match the published terms, if you needed to make a declaration under this facility, you should have given Notification of Intent to disclose by 22 June 2007, following which an identification number should have been issued, and you should then have made Disclosure and Payment (of the tax, interest upon it and 10 per cent of the tax by way of mitigated penalty) by 26 November 2007. Only income and gains for 2005–06 and earlier should have been reported in this way.

HMRC reserved the right to investigate further if the disclosure appears incomplete or if serious criminality is involved, but planned to accept satisfactory disclosures as soon as possible and before 30 April 2008, which was the date by which they announced that they would open formal investigations, where they consider that necessary. HMRC had to fight hard for judicial confirmation of their right to obtain information from offshore banks and indicated that taxpayers who failed to make use of their Disclosure Facility could expect to face penalties of 30–100 per cent of the unpaid tax.

18.7.2 New disclosure opportunity (NDO)

The 2007 ODF (18.7.1) was introduced following discovery of details from the offshore branches of the major UK banks and the *New Disclosure Opportunity* (NDO) announced in the Budget on 22 April 2009 followed discovery of details from other offshore institutions. The NDO ran from 1 September 2009 to 12 March 2010. Essentially, the terms were similar to those in the ODF, but participants were required to address and correct their tax affairs for the 20 years ended 5 April 2008. The key deadlines were 30 November 2009 for registration and 31 January and 12 March 2010 respectively for making disclosure on paper or online.

18.7.3 Liechtenstein disclosure facility (LDF)

On 11 August 2009 a major initiative was announced following agreement between the Governments of the UK and Liechtenstein. This combines the imposition of a full compliance and reporting regime by the finance and trust sector in Liechtenstein with a modified version of the NDO entitled the *Liechtenstein disclosure facility* (LDF) in the UK.

Over the period 1 September 2009 to 31 March 2015 a full reporting system will be introduced in Liechtenstein in respect of all entities with known connections to UK residents. Liechtenstein financial intermediaries will provide UK taxpayers with all the information necessary to enable them to remedy any tax arrears on income or transactions since 1 April 1999.

Although those liabilities are restricted to 10 years' retrospection, in general you would be expected to disclose any omissions in the past 20 tax years in respect of other liabilities. Exceptionally that degree of retrospection may be reduced to four or six tax years, where the omissions are accepted not to have been deliberate.

If affected, you can register for the LDF at any time from 1 September 2009, but time limits for registration and for disclosure are geared to the timing of notifications that you receive from the Liechtenstein intermediary.

Full disclosure of worldwide assets held at 1 September 2009 is normally required, but, if you are not domiciled in the UK, this is limited to UK assets. As for the NDO, full interest on underpaid tax has to be paid, together with a fixed penalty of 10 per cent of the underpayment, but the penalty is waived in proven cases of innocent error. Unlike the NDO, there is an option to apply a composite rate of tax of 40 per cent to all tax calculations made and there is an assurance that criminal prosecutions will not be pursued in respect of tax offences, but this does not extend to other financial offences.

Chapter 19

NON-RESIDENTS, VISITORS AND IMMIGRANTS

This chapter has been kept as short as possible, in order to provide a simplified introduction to the UK's approach to taxing your income, if you are a non-resident, visitor or immigrant. We have many more taxes, for which you should refer to the relevant chapters.

For many years no preamble was needed, but, in recent years, the professions have been concerned that taxpayers can no longer rely on what had for many years been understood to be the settled official approach to the key issue of 'residence'. As we go to press, we are on the brink of a major change, because a statutory definition of 'residence' is due to take effect from 6 April 2013. So, please read this preamble in full and bear it in mind as you refer to those paragraphs which seem relevant to your affairs.

The concept of 'residence' is of fundamental importance to your liability to UK income tax, but 'residence' has not hitherto been clearly defined in UK law. With one exception, you cannot ascertain your resident status simply by counting the number of days that you spend in the UK. The exception is that, if you are physically present in the UK on 183 days or more in any particular tax year (running from 6 April to the next 5 April), you will be resident here for that year and taxable on that basis. For this purpose you are regarded as present in the UK on any day, if you are here at midnight.

Various appeal cases aroused concern that HMRC had moved away from what was understood to be their long-established practice in deciding questions of residence. Consultations commenced in June 2011 as to the future tax treatment of individuals who are non-domiciled or are not ordinarily resident and on the introduction of a codified statutory definition of residence. The date of commencement originally proposed (6 April 2012) has been delayed to 6 April 2013. Although the detailed rules have yet to be finalised, they are now at an advanced stage of public consultation and the broad outline of the proposals and the key features of the statutory residence tests are set out at 17.5. *The present situation makes it even more important than usual to take professional advice at an early stage, if you are contemplating living, working or making a major investment here.*

19.1 On what income are non-residents liable to UK tax?

If, for a given tax year, you are not a UK resident (17.3.2) you will normally be liable to UK income tax only on income arising in this country. If your income arising here is also taxed in your country of residence you will in many cases be entitled to double taxation relief (18.6). Should there be a double taxation agreement between your country of residence and the UK (18.6.1) this agreement may provide that certain categories of income arising in this country should only be taxed in your own country and not here. The following paragraphs cover the position if such relief is not obtained. Remember that for tax years after 2004–05, classification into schedules for income tax purposes normally no longer applies, in view of ITTOIA (2.10). However, the basic rules remain.

19.1.1 **Business profits in the UK** (ITTOIA Ss6 & 269)

If you are non-resident but carry on a business in this country you will be charged to tax here on your profits. You will be assessed to income tax on trade profits (11.2) at the basic rate (20 per cent), higher rate (40 per cent) and additional rate (currently 50 per cent, but reducing to 45 per cent for 2013–14) if your total income liable to UK tax is sufficiently high (2.2).

If your UK business is operated by a manager etc., he is charged to the tax on your behalf, but if your only business in this country consists of selling through a broker or agent who acts for various principals, you will not be chargeable. From 6 April 1996, your branch or agent in the UK was made jointly responsible with you for all that needs to be done concerning the self-assessment of the profits.

19.1.2 **Income from property and land in the UK** (ITTOIA S269)

Income tax on property income is charged on the profits of your property business (7.1). If you are non-resident you will nevertheless have to pay UK income tax on these profits and income tax at the basic rate normally should be deducted at source by the tenant or agent in paying you the gross rent, unless you register with HMRC under the non-resident landlords' scheme. Furthermore the UK's right to tax such property income is usually protected by our double taxation agreements.

19.1.3 **Interest received from sources in the UK** (ITTOIA S368–369 & ITA S858)

You are liable to income tax on interest as savings income (8.5). If you are not ordinarily resident, you can sign a declaration and obtain your interest gross from banks, building societies and other deposit takers, but you will then have to pay UK tax for any year when you are resident here within the rules (17.3 & 17.5).

19.1.4 **Interest on UK securities** (ITA Ss890–897)

Income tax at 20 per cent will be withheld from interest payments made to you unless some lower rate (or nil rate) is specified in any relevant double taxation agreement (18.6). (See also exempt gilts, 19.2.)

19.1.5 **Dividend payments to non-residents** (ITTOIA S397)

If you are non-resident, your dividends from UK companies normally carry no tax credits unless you qualify for UK personal reliefs and allowances (19.7) or come within certain double taxation arrangements (see below). Thus if you receive a dividend of £90, you will normally pay overseas tax on this amount with no deduction for the £10 tax credit which you would have got, if you were a UK resident. You may also be liable here to the excess of the higher or additional rate income tax over the tax credit (5.0.1) on the actual dividend payments, if your total UK income is high enough. Such tax could qualify for relief against your overseas tax subject to the relevant double tax arrangements (18.6).

Provided the relevant double tax agreements have been revised to permit it, special arrangements can be made between UK companies and HMRC. These enable a UK company, when paying a dividend to an overseas resident, also to pay him an amount representing the excess over his UK tax liability on the dividend of the UK tax credit to which he is entitled under the relevant double tax agreement (18.6.1). Comparable rules apply to companies. However, the right of certain non-resident companies to payments of tax credits has since been withdrawn. This broadly covers various situations involving 'unitary taxation'.

19.1.6 **Investment managers acting for non-residents** (FA 1995 Ss126 & 127 & Sch 23 & ITA Ss814–828 & TIOPA Sch 6)

Casual agents and brokers, investment managers, such as banks and other financial concerns, are exempted from any tax liability as agents for non-residents. The exemption applies provided, for example, the agent is in the business of providing investment management services to a number of clients, on a normal commercial basis. It extends to stocks and shares, interest on deposits and futures, commodities, financial futures and options contracts (not involving land).

Generally from 6 April 1996 (and in some cases 1995) a Revenue concession became law, which may be of benefit to you if you are non-resident. Your UK income tax is then limited to that deducted at source regarding investing and trading through a broker, investment manager etc. A condition is that the investment manager acts as your independent agent.

19.1.7 **Income from employments in the UK** (ITEPA Ss14–41 etc.)

If you are not resident in this country (or not ordinarily resident) you are assessed to UK tax as employment income in respect of any emoluments during the relevant tax year regarding duties performed here. Non-domiciled employees obtain relief for travel expenses between their UK jobs and their home countries similar to that afforded to UK personnel working abroad (10.6.4). However, the relief is only available for five years from the arrival of the employee in the UK (ITEPA S373). The remittance basis (18.0) may be relevant to foreign earnings, if you are non-domiciled, but resident and ordinarily resident in the UK (18.5.3).

19.1.8 **Higher and additional rate income tax**

If you are not resident in this country but are liable to UK income tax on part or all of your income, this may be taxed at the basic, higher and additional rates. This will depend on the amount of your income liable to UK income tax. Thus if for 2012–13 this is trading or property profits and comes to £155,000 after allowable deductions, you will pay income tax at 20 per cent on £34,370 and 40 per cent on £115,630 and 50 per cent on £5,000. Thus your total UK income tax will be £6,874 + £46,252 + £2,500 = £55,626 (subject to possible double tax relief).

19.2 Interest paid to non-residents in respect of certain UK government securities (ITTOIA Ss 713–716)

From 6 April 1998, 'free of tax to residents abroad' (FOTRA) status extends to all gilts (8.2). Previously, the interest on certain specified UK government securities (19.1.4) could be paid to you gross without the deduction of any UK income tax provided certain conditions were satisfied.

19.3 Rules for taxation of visitors' income (ITA Ss831–832)

If you come to this country as a visitor only and you do not intend to establish your residence here, you will not normally be charged to UK income tax on income arising elsewhere. This applies provided you have not actually been in this country for 183 days or more (in total) during the relevant tax year. This test is likely to change from 6 April 2013 (17.5 *et seq.* & 19.4).

Until 5 April 2013, as a general rule you are not subject to UK income tax unless you are chargeable as a person resident here (17.3.2).

Even if you are not resident in this country during a given tax year you will normally be chargeable to UK income tax on your income arising from sources within the UK. However, interest on certain government bonds is exempted if you make the required application to HMRC (8.2). You may also be entitled to double taxation relief in respect of your income arising in this country (18.6).

19.4 When does a habitual visitor become a UK resident?

From 6 April 2013, new rules are very likely to apply. Although they are not yet finalised, the published proposals are at an advanced stage. Please see the preamble to this chapter (also 17.5 *et seq.*). The question of whether or not you will be treated as *resident* in the UK will be resolved by working through the new statutory residence tests, which combine a series of day-counts with different numbers of specific *UK Ties*. You need to remember that, as an habitual visitor to the UK, your *non-resident* status will no longer be determined simply by a day-count. *If you wish to maintain your current status or to monitor your position, you should take stock of your position and consider taking professional advice in advance of 6 April 2013.*

As from 6 April 2008 the law changed, so that for all residence tests (17.4.1 & 17.5.1–2) HMRC no longer exclude days of arrival. The new rule is *COUNT days of arrival, but NOT days of departure*. If you have previously made frequent trips to the UK of three days or less, you should by now have reviewed your arrangements.

Under the rules applicable until 5 April 2013, if you are a visitor to the UK you are treated as resident here for tax purposes in any year of assessment in which you spend 183 days (in total) in this country.

Even if you do not stay for 183 days in any tax year, you will be regarded as becoming resident if you come here year after year (so that your visits become in effect part of your habit of life) and those visits are for a substantial period or periods of time. HMRC normally regard an average of 91 days as being substantial and the visits as having become habitual after four years, but they may take account of other factors. In particular, if your arrangements indicated from the start that regular visits for substantial periods were to be made HMRC would regard you as being resident here in and from the first tax year.

Historically, if a place of abode was available to you in this country, subject to certain specified exceptions, you were regarded by HMRC as being resident here for any year in which you paid a visit to the UK, however short. This was relaxed from 1993–94, but not necessarily for recent former UK residents (17.3.6). In the light of recent appeal cases (see preamble to this chapter), it seems that ignoring a place of abode does not preclude taking account of the use made of it.

19.5 The position of visiting diplomats (ITA S841)

Special tax exemptions are given to visiting diplomats including agents-general, high commissioners, consuls and official agents. Consular officers and employees of foreign states who visit this country are afforded certain tax exemptions here, even if they stay in the UK for sufficiently long normally to be treated as resident here.

Regarding consular officers and employees of foreign states, the conditions for the exemptions to apply are that:

(1) the individual is not a citizen of the UK or colonies;
(2) he is not engaged in any trade, profession or employment in this country (apart from his diplomatic duties); and
(3) he is either a permanent employee of the foreign state or was not ordinarily resident in the UK immediately before he became a consular officer or employee here.

The tax concessions which apply when appropriate arrangements have been made with the foreign state concerned, include the following:

(1) Any income of the individual from foreign businesses or investments (previously taxable under Cases IV and V of Schedule D (18.2)) is not subject to income tax here.
(2) Certain overseas dividends and interest on securities are not taxed in this country.
(3) Emoluments of the individual from his consular office or employment are not taxed here.
(4) No capital gains tax (20.3) is payable on disposals of assets situated outside the UK.

19.6 Visiting entertainers and sportsmen (ITTOIA Ss13–14 & SI 1987 No 130)

Rules apply from 1 May 1987 under which UK appearances by non-resident sportsmen and entertainers are taxed at source. Payments of £1,000, or more, are subjected to basic rate (20 per cent) income tax, but it is possible to agree a lower or nil rate with the Tax Office where it can be established that the eventual UK tax liability will be less than 20 per cent.

Special rules apply regarding the 2012 Olympic Games and to the 2013 UEFA Champions League (15.2.2).

19.7 The entitlement of certain non-residents to UK tax reliefs

(ITA Ss35–56 & 457–460)

Unless you are resident here or fall within the categories listed below,you will not obtain any UK personal reliefs and allowances (3.0.1) against your income tax liability in this country.

If you fall within the undermentioned categories, however, you will qualify for personal relief against your income taxable in this country.

(1) Subjects of Great Britain or the Republic of Ireland.
(2) Employees of the Crown or Crown protectorates or missionary societies.
(3) Residents of the Isle of Man or the Channel Islands.
(4) Previous residents of the UK who have gone abroad for reasons of their own health or that of a member of their families.
(5) Widows of Crown servants.
(6) A national of any European Economic Area state.

Alternatively, your country of residence may have a tax treaty with the UK which permits you to claim UK personal allowances and reliefs despite being non-resident here. To get this relief, you must submit a claim to HMRC giving details of your UK and world income. From 6 April 1990 full personal allowances are available for those in the above specified categories. However, as from 6 April 2009, in order to transfer allowances between spouses or civil partners, you will both need to be in the *same category* (above). The list is modified with effect from 6 April 2010, so as to exclude Commonwealth citizens (FA 2009 S5 & Sch 1). This will mainly affect citizens of the Bahamas, Cameroon, Tanzania and various islands in the South Pacific or amongst the Windwards.

19.8 Immigrants

If you come from abroad to this country prior to 6 April 2013 with the intention of taking up permanent residence, here the following tax consequences will result:

(1) You will normally enjoy a full year's UK personal reliefs and allowances for income tax for the tax year during which you arrive.
(2) If you have any British government securities on which you had been receiving interest gross as a non-resident (8.2), you will be liable to tax on interest becoming payable from the date of your arrival.
(3) You will not be taxed here on certain lump sum payments that you receive from a former employer or overseas provident fund in respect of termination of an overseas employment (17.6). If you do not adopt the remittance basis, the tax liability on your foreign pensions will be based on 90 per cent of the amount arising in the tax year.
(4) If you have any income from foreign businesses or investments assessable (under what was previously Case IV or V of Schedule D) on a remittance basis (18.1.1) and the source ceased before you arrived here prior to 6 April 2008, you would have had no liability on any sums remitted. If the

source ceased in the tax year of your arrival but after you took up permanent residence here, your liability would have been on the lower of your total remittances in the tax year and the income arising from your date of arrival until the date that the source closed. A major change in the remittance basis took place as from 6 April 2008 and the handling of your pre-residence income and capital needs to be considered in the light of the new regime and its transitional rules before making remittances and before deciding whether or not to adopt the remittance basis (18.0–18.0.5).

(5) If you had a source of income outside this country before coming here, this source is not treated as being a fresh one on your arrival.

(6) Subject to the above comments, you will generally be taxed here only in respect of income arising from your date of arrival.

(7) Unless you have a foreign *domicile of origin* and are careful to preserve this, you will generally come within the ambit of UK capital gains tax and inheritance tax (Chapters 20 and 22) from the date of arrival.

(8) If you retain a foreign *domicile* or (until 5 April 2013) remain *not ordinarily resident* here, your UK earnings attributable to days wholly devoted to work whilst abroad will be exempt from UK income tax. This is known as *overseas workday relief* and is due to be given statutory force as part of the proposed new rules for tax residence.

If you become resident here under the new tests applicable from 6 April 2013, your exposure to UK taxation will be broadly similar.

Chapter 20

CAPITAL GAINS TAX

20.1 Introduction

FA 2008 includes major changes to the capital gains tax rules which apply to individuals, trustees and personal representatives, but not companies. For disposals after 5 April 2008, there is a rate of 18 per cent, indexation was withdrawn, as was taper relief. Furthermore, all assets held on 31 March 1982 are deemed to be acquired on that date at market value. However, from 23 June 2010, there is also an additional rate of 28 per cent.

Subject to the specific rules that are summarised in the following pages, you will be charged to capital gains tax in respect of any chargeable gains that accrue to you on the disposal of assets during a given tax year. You deduct from your capital gains any allowable capital losses (20.13) and then for disposals before 6 April 2008, indexation allowance (20.11) and/or taper relief (20.12). (The taper relief system applied for realisations from 6 April 1998.) For individuals, capital gains tax previously was charged at the same rates as on investment income (10 per cent, 20 per cent and 40 per cent for 2007–08).

For 2011–12, an annual exemption of £10,600 applies for individuals and broadly £5,300 for trusts (21.6). Companies pay corporation tax at corporation tax rates on their capital gains (13.15), subject to special rules for authorised investment trusts and unit trusts (20.18.7).

Most references throughout this chapter are to the Taxation of Chargeable Gains Act 1992 which consolidates the relevant legislation.

20.2 What is a chargeable gain? (TCGA S15)

A chargeable gain is a gain which accrues after 6 April 1965 to a taxpayer (including a company, trust, partnership, individual etc.) such gain being computed in accordance with the provisions of the relevant legislation. There must, however, be a disposal of an asset in order that there should be a chargeable gain.

20.3 Who is liable? (TCGA Ss2, 10 & 12)

Any taxpayer (including a company, trust, partnership, individual etc.) is chargeable to capital gains tax on any chargeable gains accruing to him in a year of assessment during any part of which he is: (a) resident in this country (17.3), or (b) ordinarily resident here (17.3.1).

Also, even if neither resident nor ordinarily resident here, a taxpayer who carries on a trade in the UK through a branch or agency is generally liable to capital gains tax accruing on the disposal of: (a) assets in this country used in his trade, or (b) assets held here and used for the branch or agency. This rule extends to professions and vocations, as well as trades (20.35).

If you are resident or ordinarily resident here during a tax year you will be liable to capital gains tax on realisations of assets throughout the world. An exception is made, however, if you are not domiciled in this country (17.2); in that case you are only charged to capital gains tax on your overseas realisations of assets to the extent that such gains are remitted here (18.1). For these purposes, if you are non-domiciled and have a non-sterling bank account, this is treated as located outside the UK unless both the account is held at a UK branch and you are UK-resident (TCGA S275).

20.3.1 **Temporary non-residents** (TCGA Ss9 & 10A)

If you leave the UK for tax residence abroad (17.3) after 16 March 1998, stiffer capital gains tax rules apply regarding sales of assets you had owned when you departed. You will be liable to capital gains tax on such disposals if you become neither resident nor ordinarily resident for less than five tax years. However this does not apply unless you were a UK tax resident for any part of at least four of the seven tax years before departure.

Your gains as above in the year that you leave are charged for that year and otherwise for the tax year when you resume UK residence. Gains made on assets acquired after you become tax resident abroad and before your return, will normally be exempt.

For disposals after 15 March 2005, the above even applies if you are 'Treaty non-resident' (resident outside the UK for the purposes of a double tax agreement).

20.4 Capital gains tax rates (TCGA Ss4–6)

Originally, capital gains tax was charged by means of a single rate of 30 per cent. This was changed from 6 April 1988 and further modified from 6 April 1992, with the introduction of the lower rate band:

20.4.1 **Rates from 23 June 2010**

Where your total taxable income and gains for the tax year less all allowable deductions, including losses, personal allowance and capital gains tax annual exemption are more than the higher rate threshold (£34,370 for 2012–13), whatever part of your net gains less annual exemption falls within your £34,370 basic rate band is taxed at 18 per cent and the excess at 28 per cent. The rate for trusts and the estates of deceased persons is 28 per cent. In working out the tax, you are allowed to deduct losses and the annual exemption in the most favourable way. One exception is any gain attracting entrepreneurs relief (20.30), which will be taxed at 10 per cent.

Example: Suppose that in 2012–13 your taxable income after personal allowance etc. is £24,370. This leaves £10,000 of your basic rate band. You sell an asset in

May 2012 realising a chargeable gain of £5,000, which is taxed at the lower 18 per cent rate. In November you realise a gain of £25,600 and to minimise the tax, you reduce that by the annual exemption of £10,600, leaving £15,000 taxable. You pay tax on this at 18 per cent on £5,000 and 28 per cent on £10,000.

20.4.2 Rates before 23 June 2010

(1) For disposals after 5 April 2008 and before 23 June 2010 by individuals and trustees, a single rate of 18 per cent applied.
(2) Prior to 6 April 2008, the rates were 10 per cent, 20 per cent and 40 per cent, the same as the income tax rates on investment income. (For 1999–2000, the rates were 20 per cent and 40 per cent).
(3) From 6 April 1992 to 5 April 1999, the capital gains tax rates for individuals were 20 per cent, 23 per cent and 40 per cent.
(4) The rates for accumulation and maintenance trusts and discretionary settlements from 2004–05 were 40 per cent (previously 34 per cent) (21.6).
(5) Other trusts in general paid 23 per cent up to 5 April 1998, then 34 per cent and now 40 per cent from 2004–05. However if the settlor or his or her spouse has any interest in or rights relating to a settlement, any capital gains will be subjected to his or her rates (21.6).
(6) The capital gains of companies continue to bear corporation tax at the appropriate rate (13.15).
(7) To find the rate or rates payable by an individual for 2007–08 and earlier years, you took the total gains less losses (20.13) for the tax year, deducted capital losses brought forward and the annual exemption, and considered this together with taxable income after reliefs and allowances. (From 1991–92, certain trading losses may also be deducted – 20.13.) For 2007–08, the first £2,230 was taxed at 10 per cent, the next £32,370 was taxed at 20 per cent and the remainder attracted 40 per cent. (Your income was taxed at your lower rates first and your capital gains attracted your highest rates.)

20.5 Annual exemptions (TCGA S3 & Sch 1)

The previous system for relieving small gains was changed from 6 April 1980, when an annual exemption was introduced. The following rules apply and the rates shown are for 2011–12 and 2012–13.

(1) The first £10,600 of your net gains is exempted from capital gains tax. This applies no matter how high are your total gains for the year.
(2) Any set-off for losses from previous years (20.13) is restricted to leave £10,600 of gains to be exempted. In this way your exemption is protected and you have more losses to carry forward. All losses for the year must be deducted, however, in arriving at the net gains.
(3) These rules apply to personal representatives for the tax year of death and the next two years.
(4) The rules also apply to trusts for the mentally disabled and for those receiving attendance allowance.

(5) For other trusts set up before 7 June 1978 the first £5,300 of net capital gains each year is exempt (21.6).
(6) Trusts set up after 6 June 1978 by the same settlor each have an exemption of £5,300 divided by the number of such trusts. Thus if you have set up two trusts since that date, they each have an exemption of £2,650. In any event each trust obtains an exemption of at least £1,060.
(7) Any set-off for trust losses from previous years is restricted so that the appropriate exemption (£5,300 etc.) is not wasted.
(8) The above figures apply to future years subject to indexation in line with the increase in the Consumer Prices Index (previously the Retail Prices Index). This applies unless Parliament otherwise directs.
(9) From 1990–91 onwards, husband and wife each have their own annual exemptions and the above rules apply to their own gains and losses alone. Previously, unless they were separated, only one annual exemption applied to their combined net gains.
(10) The corresponding annual exemption figures for previous years have been:

	Individuals etc. £	Trusts £
1999–2000	7,100	3,550
2000–01	7,200	3,600
2001–02	7,500	3,750
2002–03	7,700	3,850
2003–04	7,900	3,950
2004–05	8,200	4,100
2005–06	8,500	4,250
2006–07	8,800	4,400
2007–08	9,200	4,600
2008–09	9,600	4,800
2009–10 and 2010–11	10,100	5,050

20.6 What assets are liable? (TCGA Ss21–27)

Subject to various exemptions (see 20.7.1) all forms of property are treated as 'assets' for capital gains tax purposes including:

(1) Investments, land and buildings, jewellery, antiques etc.
(2) Options and debts etc.
(3) Any currency other than sterling (special rules for companies – 13.25).
(4) Any form of property created by the person disposing of it or otherwise coming to be owned without being acquired. (This would cover any article which you made or work of art created by you.)

20.7 What assets are exempted? (TCGA – see below)

The following classes of assets are exempted from charge to capital gains tax subject to the relevant rules:

20.7.1 Assets exempted from capital gains tax

(1) Private motor vehicles (S263).
(2) Certain gifts covered by an election (20.27).
(3) Your own home – this is known as your 'main private residence' (20.23).
(4) National Savings Certificates, Defence Bonds, Development Bonds, Save-as-you-earn etc. (S121).
(5) Any foreign currency which you obtained for personal expenditure abroad (S269).
(6) Any decoration for gallantry (unless purchased) (S268).
(7) Betting winnings including pools, lotteries and premium bonds (S51).
(8) Compensation or damages for any wrong or injury suffered to your person or in connection with your profession or vocation (S51).
(9) British government securities (S115). Disposals prior to 2 July 1986 were only exempt if the 'gilts' had been held for at least one year, or had passed to you on death or from a trust.
(10) Life assurance policies and deferred annuities provided that you are the original owner or they were given to you. If you bought the rights to a policy from its original owner you may be liable to capital gains tax on the surrender, maturity or sale of the policy, or death of the life assured (S210). Certain policies assigned after 25 June 1982 may give rise to income tax instead of capital gains tax, however (TA 1988 Ss540 & 544).
(11) Chattels sold for £6,000 or less (20.24).
(12) Assets gifted to charity (20.31).
(13) The gift to the nation of any assets (for example paintings) deemed to be of national, scientific or historic interest; also land etc. given to the National Trust (S258).
(14) The gift of historic houses and certain other property of interest to the public, provided they are given access – also funds settled between 2 May 1976 and 6 April 1984 for the upkeep (S258). (Now covered by the gifts exemption – 20.28.)
(15) Tangible movable property which is a wasting asset (that is, with a predictable life of 50 years or less). This includes boats, animals etc., but not land and buildings (S45) nor assets qualifying for capital allowances.
(16) Disposals by a close company (13.17) of assets on trust for the benefit of its employees (S239).
(17) If you sell a debt this is not liable to capital gains tax provided you are the original creditor and the debt is not a 'debt on a security' (a debenture etc.). Otherwise capital gains tax applies. The 'debt on security' requirements do not apply, however, to certain business loans (excluding those from associated companies). Loss relief may be available on such debts and also on certain business guarantees made after that date (S251).
(18) Land transferred from one local constituency association to another, which is taking over from it, as a result of the Parliamentary constituency boundaries being redrawn (S264).
(19) Certain corporate bonds issued which you held for more than 12 months (20.19). Disposals after 1 July 1986 are exempt without time limit (Ss115–117).
(20) Transactions in futures and options in gilts and qualifying corporate bonds (S115).
(21) Business expansion scheme shares issued to you after 18 March 1986, provided you are the first holder of those particular shares (11.25).
(22) Certain 'deep discount' (8.8) and from 14 March 1989, 'deep gain' securities (S117).
(23) Profits from the sale of timber and uncut trees (TCGA S250).
(24) Sales of PEP units, subject to the rules (8.10).
(25) Venture Capital Trust shares held for at least three years (five years if issued before 6 April 2000), subject to the rules (8.13).
(26) EIS shares held for at least three years (previously five), in accordance with the rules (11.26.).
(27) Withdrawals from foreign currency bank accounts after 5 April 2012.

20.8 What constitutes a disposal? (TCGA Ss21–26)

The following are examples of circumstances in which you will be treated as making a disposal or a part disposal of an asset:

(1) The outright sale of the whole asset or part of it.
(2) The gift of the asset or a part of it – the asset must be valued at the date of gift and this valuation is treated as the proceeds. An election for holding-over the gain is sometimes possible (20.28).
(3) If an asset is destroyed, for example, by fire, it is a disposal.
(4) If you sell any right in an asset, for example, by granting a lease, this is a part disposal although if you obtain a fair rent there is normally no capital gains tax liability.
(5) If any capital sum is received in return for the surrender or forfeiture of any rights, this is normally a disposal. For example, you may receive a sum of money for not renewing a lease in accordance with a renewal option which you possessed.
(6) If you die, you are deemed to dispose of all of your assets at your date of death but no capital gains tax is payable. Whoever inherits your assets does so at their market value at your death.
(7) A part withdrawal from a life policy of the original owner and for which you gave money or money's worth (TCGA S210).

The following are not treated as disposals of assets for capital gains tax purposes:

(1) If you give or sell an asset to your spouse this is not treated as a capital gains tax disposal, provided he or she is living with you during the relevant tax year. In that case your spouse is charged to capital gains tax on any subsequent disposal that he or she makes of the asset as if bought when you originally acquired it at the actual cost to yourself (plus any indexation allowance – 20.11). From 5 December 2005, this also applies to transfers between civil partners in accordance with the Civil Partnership Act 2004 (6.9).
(2) If you transfer an asset merely as security for a debt but retain the ownership this is not a capital gains tax disposal. This would apply, for example, if you mortgage your house.
(3) If you transfer an asset to somebody else to hold it as your nominee, this is not a disposal provided that you remain the beneficial owner.
(4) Gifts of assets to charities are effectively not treated as disposals (20.31).

20.9 How your chargeable gains are computed (TCGA Ss15–20 & 37–40)

The following general rules should be followed:

(1) If the asset sold was originally acquired before 7 April 1965, special rules applied (20.17).

(2) Special rules apply in the case of leases and other wasting assets (20.32).

(3) Ascertain the consideration for each of your disposals during the tax year – this will normally be the sale proceeds but in the following cases it will be the *open market value* of the assets (20.16):
   (a) Gifts of assets during the tax year.
   (b) Transfers of assets (by gift or sale) to persons connected with you including your business partner and close relations other than your wife. This also applies to other disposals of assets not at arm's length. (Anti-avoidance rules operate to prevent losses being manufactured artificially in this way (15.10).)
   (c) Transactions in which the sale proceeds cannot be valued, or where an asset is given as compensation for loss of office etc. to an employee. If, for example, you give your friend a picture from your collection on condition that he paints your house each year for the next ten years, then since this service cannot be accurately valued you are treated as disposing of your picture for its market value.

(4) Deduct from the disposal consideration in respect of each asset its original cost (or value at acquisition) together with any incidental expenses in connection with your original acquisition and your disposal of each asset. For disposals after 5 April 1988, if it gives a better result, you normally deduct the value at 31 March 1982 instead of the cost (20.10). Also deduct any 'enhancement' expenditure, that is, the cost of any capital improvements to the assets not including any expenses of a 'revenue nature' (2.6).

(5) For realisations before 6 April 2008, deduct (if applicable) indexation allowance (see below).

(6) For realisations before 6 April 2008, apply taper relief as appropriate for periods after 5 April 1998 (20.12).

(7) Your incidental costs of acquisition and disposal (see (4) above) include surveyors', valuers' and solicitors' fees, stamp duty, and commission in connection with the purchase and sale. Also the cost of advertising to find a buyer and accountancy charges in connection with the acquisition or disposal. No expenses are deductible, however, if they have already been allowed in computing your taxable revenue profits (2.6).

20.10 Re-basing to 31 March 1982 values (TCGA Ss35–36 & Schs 3–4)

20.10.1 Re-basing rules for disposals from 6 April 2008

All assets held at 31 March 1982 must be valued at that date for the calculation of capital gains and losses. This major simplification does not apply to disposals by companies, but results in the removal for individuals and trustees of various special reliefs and rules mentioned in the following paragraphs.

20.10.2 Re-basing rules for disposals before 6 April 2008

If you disposed of an asset after 5 April 1988, which you owned on 31 March 1982, its base value was automatically taken as its value at that date, provided this exceeded the cost. Thus, if you bought some shares for £1,000 in 1970 and they were worth £4,000 on 31 March 1982, you used £4,000 as their base value for capital gains tax purposes. Assuming you sold the shares for £10,000 in August 2007, your capital gain was £10,000 – £4,000 = £6,000 (ignoring indexation and taper relief).

Before 6 April 2008, re-basing to 31 March 1982 did not increase a gain or loss compared with what it would have been under the old rules. Furthermore, where there was a gain under the old system and a loss through re-basing, or vice versa, the transaction was treated as giving rise to neither gain nor loss. For example, if you sold an asset for £1,000 which had cost £500 and was worth £1,500 at 31 March 1982, ignoring indexation you had a gain of £500 under the old rules and a loss of £500 through re-basing; you were therefore treated as having no gain and no loss.

The existing rules for assets held at 6 April 1965 could themselves give rise to disposals being treated as producing no gain and no loss (20.17). This was not affected by re-basing.

Even if you did not hold an asset at 31 March 1982, it may still have qualified for re-basing if you received it from someone else in circumstances that there was neither a gain nor loss under the old rules and their acquisition was before that date. A particular example was where one spouse acquires an asset from another.

If you held assets at 31 March 1982, but subsequently realised them in circumstances such that your gain was deferred, re-basing did not apply. However, special relief was available regarding disposals after 5 April 1988 (excluding no gain/no loss disposals). Provided you made a claim to the Inland Revenue within two years of the end of the year of assessment in which the disposal was made, your original held-over, rolled-over or deferred gain was halved (TCGA S36 & Sch 4).

You had the right to elect that all of your assets were re-based as at 31 March 1982. There was a two year time limit for this irrevocable election (that is, before 6 April 1990). However, this was extended to two years after the end of the tax year in which you made your first sale after 5 April 1988.

20.11 Indexation allowance (TCGA Ss53–57 & Sch 7A & FA 1998 S122)

Indexation relief does not apply to realisations by individuals and trustees after 5 April 2008. However, it still applies to companies at the rates shown later (20.11.1).

If your disposal was after 5 April 1982 (31 March 1982 for companies) the original cost and enhancement expenditure could be increased by *indexation*. For disposals between 5 April 1985 (31 March for companies) and 6 April 1988, you had the option of basing indexation on the value of the asset sold, at 31 March 1982. After 5 April 1988, disposals were automatically re-based to their 31 March 1982 values if this was beneficial and so indexation was taken on the base value (20.10).

Indexation does not apply for the period of ownership after April 1998 (20.12) except for companies. Thus if you sold an asset after 6 April 1998 which you acquired before that date, you obtained indexation up to April 1998 only.

The expenditure was scaled up in proportion to the increase in the Retail Price Index from the month of acquisition (or March 1982, if later) until the month of disposal. Values for the *Retail Prices Index* are shown in 20.11.1.

For disposals from 6 April 1986 to 29 November 1993, you obtained the full benefit of indexation relief, even to the extent that it created or enlarged a loss (20.13). Special rules apply regarding assets held on 6 April 1965 (20.17) and shares (20.14). Any disposals that you made after 29 November 1993 obtained full indexation relief if the end result was a gain. However, subject to transitional relief for individuals and trustees, indexation no longer created or increased a capital loss.

Transactions between husband and wife do not normally give rise to capital gains tax (20.9). Thus if you acquired an asset from your spouse, your deemed acquisition cost was taken to be his or hers, augmented by any indexation allowance attaching to it at the transfer date. When you sold the asset, you obtained full indexation allowance on your deemed acquisition cost, from the date you took over the asset from your spouse. Similar treatment applies to company intra-group transfers (13.15) and certain reconstructions. Legatees obtained indexation allowance as if they had acquired the assets at the date of death. (Apart from assets held by companies, indexation only runs to April 1998.)

20.11.1 **Retail prices index (adjusted)**

	Jan	Feb	Mar	Apr	May	June	July	Aug	Sept	Oct	Nov	Dec
1982			79.4	81.0	81.6	81.9	81.9	81.9	81.9	82.3	82.7	82.5
1983	82.6	83.0	83.1	84.3	84.6	84.8	85.3	85.7	86.1	86.4	86.7	86.9
1984	86.8	87.2	87.5	88.6	89.0	89.2	89.1	89.9	90.1	90.7	91.0	90.9
1985	91.2	91.9	92.8	94.8	95.2	95.4	95.2	95.5	95.4	95.6	95.9	96.0
1986	96.2	96.6	96.7	97.7	97.8	97.8	97.5	97.8	98.3	98.5	99.3	99.6
1987	100.0*	100.4	100.6	101.8	101.9	101.9	101.8	102.1	102.4	102.9	103.4	103.3
1988	103.3	103.7	104.1	105.8	106.2	106.6	106.7	107.9	108.4	109.5	110.0	110.3
1989	111.0	111.8	112.3	114.3	115.0	115.4	115.5	115.8	116.6	117.5	118.5	118.8
1990	119.5	120.2	121.4	125.1	126.2	126.7	126.8	128.1	129.3	130.3	130.0	129.9
1991	130.2	130.9	131.4	133.1	133.5	134.1	133.8	134.1	134.6	135.1	135.6	135.7
1992	135.6	136.3	136.7	138.8	139.3	139.3	138.8	138.9	139.4	139.9	139.7	139.2
1993	137.9	138.8	139.3	140.6	141.1	141.0	140.7	141.3	141.9	141.8	141.6	141.9
1994	141.3	142.1	142.5	144.2	144.7	144.7	144.0	144.7	145.0	145.2	145.3	146.0
1995	146.0	146.9	147.5	149.0	149.6	149.8	149.1	149.9	150.6	149.8	149.8	150.7

	Jan	Feb	Mar	Apr	May	June	July	Aug	Sept	Oct	Nov	Dec
1996	150.2	150.9	151.5	152.6	152.9	153.0	152.4	153.1	153.8	153.8	153.9	154.4
1997	154.4	155.0	155.4	156.3	156.9	157.5	157.5	158.5	159.3	159.5	159.6	160.0
1998	159.5	160.3	160.8	162.6§	163.5	163.4	163.0	163.7	164.4	164.5	164.4	164.4
1999	163.4	163.7	164.1	165.2	165.6	165.6	165.1	165.5	166.2	166.5	166.7	167.3
2000	166.6	167.5	168.4	170.1	170.7	171.1	170.5	170.5	171.7	171.6	172.1	172.2
2001	171.1	172.0	172.2	173.1	174.2	174.4	173.3	174.0	174.6	174.3	173.6	173.4
2002	173.3	173.3	174.5	175.7	176.2	176.2	175.9	176.4	177.6	177.9	178.2	178.5
2003	178.4	179.3	179.9	181.2	181.5	181.3	181.3	181.6	182.5	182.6	182.7	183.5
2004	183.1	183.8	184.6	185.7	186.5	186.8	186.8	187.4	188.1	188.6	189.0	189.9
2005	188.9	189.6	190.5	191.6	192.0	192.2	192.2	192.6	193.1	193.3	193.6	194.1
2006	193.4	194.2	195.0	196.5	197.7	198.5	198.5	199.2	200.1	200.4	201.1	202.7
2007	201.6	203.1	204.4	205.4	206.2	207.3	206.1	207.3	208.0	208.9	209.7	210.9
2008	209.8	211.4	212.1	214.0	215.1	216.8	216.5	217.2	218.4	217.7	216.0	212.9
2009	210.1	211.4	211.3	211.5	212.8	213.4	213.4	214.4	215.3	216.0	216.6	218.0
2010	217.9	219.2	220.7	222.8	223.6	224.1	223.6	224.5	226.8	228.4	225.3	225.8
2011	229.0	231.3	232.5	234.4	235.2	235.2	234.7	236.1	237.9	238.0	238.5	239.4
2012	238.0	239.9	240.8									

* At January 1987 the index base was changed to 100.0 and the above table shows figures before that date adjusted to the same base.

§ From April 1998, indexation only applies to companies.

20.11.2 **Example: Computation of chargeable gain**

Mr A sells a block of flats on 15 July 2012 for £260,000. The flats were bought in May 1981 for £100,000 and subsequent capital expenditure amounted to £17,000 (all pre-April 1982). Also £10,000 had been spent on decorations and maintenance. The legal costs on purchase were £1,500 and stamp duty was £1,000. Surveyors' fees prior to purchase amounted to £500. At 31 March 1982, the market value was £130,000. £100 was spent in advertising the sale and agents' commission amounted to £6,000. Legal costs on sale were £900. Assuming that Mr A's profit is taxed as a capital gain, what tax will he pay on it? Assume also that for 2012–13 Mr A has no other capital gains or losses and his top income tax rate was 40 per cent:

	£	£
Cost of block of flats		100,000
Add:		
Enhancement expenditure		17,000
(decorations and maintenance not relevant)		
Legal costs on purchase		1,500
Stamp duty on purchase		1,000
Surveyors' fees on purchase		500
Total cost		120,000
Re-based 31 March 1982 value		130,000

Proceeds		260,000
Less:		
Re-based value	130,000	
Advertising	100	
Agents' commission	6,000	
Legal fees on sale	900	
		137,000
Chargeable gain		123,000
Less: annual exemption		10,600
		112,400
Capital gains tax at 28%		31,472

20.12 Taper relief (TCGA Sch A1)

A time-related relief system regarding the capital gains of individuals, trustees and personal representatives, applied for disposals from 6 April 1998 to 5 April 2008. However, the old system continues for companies. The following basic rules are subject to certain anti-avoidance provisions. For fuller details please refer to earlier editions.

(1) Under these rules, indexation (20.11) does not apply for periods after 5 April 1998. Thus if you sell an asset after that date which you acquired beforehand, you obtain indexation up to April 1998 only.

(2) Taper relief applied to gains realised from 6 April 1998 to 5 April 2008, subject to the rules. According to the number of complete years that the asset had been owned after that date, a percentage only of the gain was chargeable. Different percentages applied for business and other assets as follows:

Gains on disposals of business assets				**Gains on disposals of non-business assets**	
Number of whole years in qualifying holding period	Percentage of gain chargeable. Disposal date			Number of whole years in qualifying holding period	Percentage of gain chargeable
	pre-6.4.00	from 6.4.00 to 5.4.02	from 6.4.02		
1	92.5	87.5	50	–	–
2	85	75	25	–	–
3	77.5	50	25	3	95
4	70	25	25	4	90
5	62.5	25	25	5	85
6	55	25	25	6	80
7	47.5	25	25	7	75
8	40	25	25	8	70
9	32.5	25	25	9	65
10 or more	25	25	25	10 or more	60

(3) Any assets which you acquired before 17 March 1998 and disposed of after 5 April 1998 had an extra year added for taper relief purposes.

(4) Business assets which attracted increased taper relief were broadly defined as those used in your own or your partnership's trade (including profession) or your 'qualifying company'. Also included were assets held for the purposes of a qualifying full-time employment and shares which you held in a 'qualifying company'.

(5) Taper relief applied to your net gains for a tax year after deducting any losses for that year and then previous losses (20.13). Your losses were allocated on the basis that produced the lowest tax charge. Your annual exemption was set off after taper relief.

(6) If you transfered an asset to your spouse, taper relief on a later disposal was based on the combined period for which you both held it. However, in the case of other no gain/no loss disposals and gifts hold-over relief, you only took the holding period of the new owner.

(7) In the case of reinvesting in a Venture Capital Trust before 6 April 2004 and other instances where your gain on an asset was deferred, taper relief was based on the holding period of your original asset.

20.13 Capital losses (TCGA Ss2, 16, 111 & 253–255 Schs A1 & 7A)

If your capital gains tax computation in respect of any disposal during the tax year produces a loss, such loss is normally deductible from any chargeable gains arising during the year. Any remaining surplus of losses is then available to be carried forward and set off against any future capital gains. For 1989–90 and previous tax years, any unrelieved losses were offset against gains of your spouse in the same year. Any surplus losses were then carried forward to offset against your respective gains.

'Qualifying loans' made to traders which later prove irrecoverable rank as capital losses, subject to the rules. However, after 19 March 1990, any amounts subsequently recovered are taxed.

Your net capital gains are reduced by losses brought forward down to the tax-free amount of currently £10,600 (20.5) and any balance of the losses is carried forward (TCGA S3(5)).

In computing your capital losses note the special rules for assets owned at 6 April 1965 (20.17). Also note that losses may be reduced by 1982 re-basing (20.11). For disposals before 30 November 1993 but (apart from transitional relief) not subsequently, indexation allowance could both create and augment a loss (20.11).

The 1995 Finance Act (S100) introduced the necessity to claim capital gains tax loss relief, which can be done through your tax return. (A special section is included in the supplementary page dealing with capital gains.) You must claim your losses within five years and 10 months of the end of the year of assessment when they arose. (For companies, this period is 6 years from the end of the relevant accounting period.)

Where you make a loss after 9 April 2003 on disposing of an unascertainable 'earn out' right to deferred consideration (20.18.6). Subject to certain conditions, you will be able to elect to take the loss back to the tax year of the original gain on the asset sale (FA 2003 S162).

Before computing taper relief (20.12) you had to reduce your chargeable gains by losses for the same tax year and then losses carried forward. However, the set-off was in the order that produced the best result for you and only so as to reduce the untapered gain to the amount of your annual exemption. Thus losses would first be set against gains not eligible for taper and then against those with the least entitlement such as perhaps non-business assets.

20.13.1 **Relief for trading losses against capital gains** (FA 1991 S72 & FA 2002 S48)

For many years, companies have been able to set off trading losses against capital gains (13.15), but not vice versa. A similar relief operates from 1991–92 for individuals with losses from unincorporated businesses.

If you make a loss in your trade, profession or vocation and do not have enough income to cover it, you can elect for the unused losses for say 2012–13 to be set against your capital gains for that year. Any trading losses still unused would then be carried forward to 2013–14 and any not covered by your income for that year are available against 2013–14 capital gains. The relief does not cover 'hobby farming' and other businesses not carried out on a serious commercial basis.

Previously, the gains available to be relieved by trading losses were after taper relief. However, for 2004–05 and subsequent trading losses, the available gains were taken before taper relief and for 2002–03 and 2003–04, you had the right to elect for the new treatment to apply.

20.13.2 **Restriction of relief for artificial losses** (TCGA S16A)

FA 2007 introduced a general rule covering income tax, corporation tax and capital gains tax which replaced and broadened legislation regarding companies. Capital losses on disposals from 6 December 2006 are caught, if they result from contrived schemes aimed at obtaining tax advantages.

20.13.3 **Reallocation of chargeable gains in groups**

FA 2009 facilitates groups of companies matching gains and losses on asset disposals without needing to move the asset from one group company to another. This applies to disposals after 21 July 2009 where an election is made.

20.14 Losses on unquoted shares in trading companies (TA 1988 Ss573–576)

Beneficial rules apply to disposals of shares in 'qualifying trading companies'. Provided you were the original subscriber, you can elect to obtain income tax relief (11.22) for any loss on a fully priced arm's length sale, liquidation etc.

For disposals in 1994–95 and subsequently, losses on unquoted shares in trading companies are available against your income of the current or preceding year. You must claim within 12 months from 31 January following the tax year of disposal.

A 'qualifying trading company' is broadly one which has always been UK resident but never quoted and has traded for at least six years, or from within a year of incorporation if less. The company is permitted to have stopped trading within the previous three years provided it has not become an investment company in the meantime. 'Trading' excludes dealing mainly in shares, land or commodity futures with retrospective effect, qualified trading companies now exclude building societies and registered industrial and provident societies. The relief applies to individuals and certain investment companies.

20.15 Assessment and payment of capital gains tax (TMA S29, TCGA Ss7, 48, 59B–59C & 279–281)

Assessments to capital gains tax were raised on the taxpayer concerned in respect of each tax year as soon thereafter as the Revenue obtained the necessary information. In the case of a company, however, its gains are included in its corporation tax assessment which is due for payment according to the special company rules (13.2).

Your capital gains for 1996–97 and subsequent years come within the current self-assessment rules (16.1). Your capital gains tax is then payable by 31 January following the tax year of the gains.

Your capital gains tax assessment for 1994–95 was due for payment on 1 December 1995 or 30 days after the assessment was issued, if later. A similar interval applied for 1995–96 gains and those for earlier years.

The date on which a capital gain arises is the actual date of sale or gift etc. In the case of a transaction in which a sales contract is used, such as the sale of shares or property, it is the date of the contract which applies. It is not the completion date if this is different. Similar considerations apply to fixing the date of acquisition for capital gains tax purposes.

Certain gifts after 13 March 1989, for which gifts relief is not available (20.28) qualify for the payment of any capital gains tax by instalments. The assets concerned are land, unquoted shares and controlling holdings of quoted shares. Subject to making an election, the tax becomes payable by ten equal yearly instalments. If the instalments are paid on time, the tax on gifts of agricultural property will carry no interest, otherwise, interest runs from the normal date when the total liability would have been due.

Normally, even if the sales consideration is paid by instalments over a number of years the gain is assessed for the tax year in which the sale arises. If, however, you can satisfy HMRC that you would otherwise suffer undue hardship, payment of the tax can be spread over the period of the instalments (maximum eight years).

20.16 Valuations (TCGA Ss272–274 & Sch 11)

It is necessary to value assets in various circumstances for capital gains tax purposes including gifts, transactions between connected persons, acquisitions on death and valuations at 6 April 1965. However, the most important date for valuations is 31 March 1982, for re-basing purposes (20.10).

The general rule for valuing assets for capital gains tax purposes is that you must take the 'market value' of the assets at the relevant time. 'Market value' means the price which the assets might reasonably be expected to fetch on a sale in the open market.

It is necessary to value only the assets actually being disposed of even though they form part of a larger whole. This is particularly important regarding the shares in a non-quoted company. Suppose you hold 90 per cent of the shares in such a company which are together worth £90,000. If you gift 10 per cent of the company's shares to your son you might assume that their value is £10,000. This would, however, probably not be true since your 90 per cent holding carried with it full control of the company whereas 10 per cent of the company's shares is a minority holding which would be normally worth considerably less than £10,000 in the circumstances mentioned. The true market valuation of the gifted 10 per cent holding might only be £1,000 depending on the profits of the company and dividends paid. Note that different valuation rules apply for inheritance tax purposes (22.12).

An HMRC concession applies where you acquire shares on a no gain/no loss transfer from your spouse, who had held them at 31 March 1982. It also applies to transfers in similar circumstances between group companies. Two years' written notice is needed from the end of the year of assessment or accounting period of the disposal. The 31 March 1982 value will then be taken as a proportionate part of the value of the transferor's *entire* holding at that time. This applies to disposals after 15 March 1993 and assessments open at that time. If notice is not given, the shares may be valued at 31 March 1982 as if held by the *transferee*.

Unquoted share valuations must take account of all information which a prudent arm's-length purchaser would obtain.

Particular rules relate to the valuation of quoted securities such as shares and debenture stocks. (These apply in most cases, including 31 March 1982 valuations.) In this case you must normally take:

(1) the lower of the two prices shown in the Stock Exchange Official Daily List plus one-quarter of the difference between them, or
(2) halfway between the highest and lowest prices at which bargains (other than at special prices) were recorded in the shares or securities for the relevant day.

In valuing quoted shares at 6 April 1965, however, you needed to take the *higher* of:

(1) midway between the two prices shown in the Stock Exchange Official Daily List (that is, the middle market price), and
(2) halfway between the highest and lowest prices at which bargains (other than at special prices) were recorded in the shares or securities for 6 April 1965.

Apart from quoted shares other valuations will normally require to be agreed with HMRC valuation officers such as the district valuers who are concerned with valuing land and buildings.

20.17 Relief on sales of assets owned on 6 April 1965 (TCGA Sch 2)

Rules were introduced with the purpose of relieving such part of your capital gains as could be related to the period before 7 April 1965. For realisations *after 5 April 2008, re-basing to 31 March 1982 values automatically applies* so no assets will be valued as at 6 April 1965.

The general rule was that you assumed that your asset increased in value at a uniform rate and you were relieved from capital gains tax on such proportion of the gain as arose on a time basis prior to 7 April 1965. This was known as the 'time apportionment' method. Your time apportionment benefit was limited to 20 years prior to 6 April 1965. Instead of using 'time apportionment' you had the option of substituting for the cost of the asset its market value at 6 April 1965 (Sch 2(17)).

The 'time apportionment' basis *did not* apply to quoted shares and securities (20.18). Nor did it apply to land with development value when sold (or which had been materially developed after 17 December 1973). Such land was normally automatically dealt with on the 6 April 1965 valuation basis. For further details please refer to previous editions of this book.

20.18 Quoted shares and securities (TCGA Ss104–117)

For disposals of quoted shares and securities prior to 6 April 2008, complicated identification rules applied. However, compulsory re-basing at

31 March 1982 and the abolition of indexation and taper relief have led to a much simpler system for individuals and trustees (but not companies) which is described below, together with notes on the previous rules. For more detailed coverage of the earlier systems, reference should be made to previous editions of this book.

The following rules do not apply to *UK government securities* which are exempt from capital gains tax if sold (or otherwise disposed of), nor do they create allowable losses. However, any compensation stock received on a nationalisation after 6 April 1976 may give rise to a gain or loss on sale reflecting that on your original shares up to the date of issue of the compensation stock.

20.18.1 **Identification – sales from 6 April 2008**

Quoted shares and securities which you sell after 5 April 2008 are:

(1) first matched with purchases on the date of disposal; then
(2) with acquisitions in the next 30 days and then
(3) those in a 'pool' (defined by TCGA as amended by FA 2008 to include all quoted shares or securities of that particular type).

20.18.2 **'Pooling' – pre-6 April 1998 acquisitions**

All shares of the same company and class that you held prior to 6 April 1982 (1 April for companies) were put into a 'pool'. With the introduction of indexation allowance, however, pooling no longer applied to new purchases. However, pooling was reintroduced regarding share *disposals* after 5 April 1985 (20.18.4) for individuals and trusts etc. (after 31 March 1985 for companies). You were then treated as having one pool of shares purchased after 5 April 1982 and another before that time.

Shares which you acquired after 5 April 1998 were no longer to be pooled (20.18.5). However, this does not apply to companies.

20.18.3 **Indexation and identification – sales from 6 April 1985 to 5 April 1998** (TCGA Ss104–114)

Revised rules applied to share disposals by individuals after 5 April 1985 and by companies after 31 March 1985. However, securities covered by the accrued income provisions to combat bond-washing (8.3) only came within the indexation and identification rules after 27 February 1986.

As previously mentioned indexation ran immediately (20.11). An exception was where you bought and then sold the same shares within 10 days; your transactions were matched and you obtained no indexation relief.

Under the revised rules, you kept separate pools of shares acquired after 5 April 1982 (and before 6 April 1998) and those obtained from 6 April 1965 to 5 April 1982. Furthermore, acquisitions prior to 6 April 1965 were kept separately (20.18.1), unless there was a pooling election (20.18.9), in which case they were included in the 31 March 1982 pool.

If you sold shares after 5 April 1985 and before 6 April 1998, they were to be identified with your acquisitions of the same shares on a 'last in first out' basis. If it produced a better result for you, disposals out of your pre-April 1982 and pre-April 1965 pools were re-based (20.10), the market value at 31 March 1982 being taken.

From 19 March 1991, disposals of 'business start up scheme' (11.25) shares could not be pooled with shares of the same type.

Every additional purchase carried indexation relief until sale. This was done on a pooled basis by adding indexation relief to the pool prior to each purchase or sale. The total indexation relief in the pool was then found by deducting the total cost and the relief on the sale was simply the proportion appropriate to the number of shares sold. (Holdings acquired before 1 April 1982 could be valued at 31 March 1982 for indexation purposes if you made the required election (20.11).)

20.18.4 **Share identification – sales from 6 April 1998 to 5 April 2008** (TCGA Ss104–110)

Pooling (20.18.2) ceased for share acquisitions after 5 April 1998 by individuals and trustees (but not by companies). New rules also applied for disposals after that date and before 6 April 2008, which were to be identified with acquisitions in the following order:

(1) acquisitions on the same day
(2) acquisitions within the next 30 days (countering 'bed and breakfasting')
(3) previous post-5 April 1998 acquisitions on a 'last in first out' basis
(4) shares in the pool at 5 April 1998 (if any)
(5) any shares held at 5 April 1982
(6) shares acquired before 6 April 1965
(7) subsequent acquisitions (that is more than 30 days later).

Regarding a part disposal after 5 April 2002 of shares acquired on the same day after that date, some of which came from an employee share scheme, you can elect on the earliest disposal that shares with the smaller gain are disposed of first.

Note that item (2) above does not apply to acquisitions after 21 March 2006 by individuals or trustees who are neither resident nor ordinarily resident in the UK at that time, nor Treaty non-resident. This is to block certain avoidance schemes.

20.18.5 **Bonus issues, take-overs and company reorganisations** (TCGA Ss116, 117 & 126–140 & 251)

If you receive a free scrip (or bonus) issue of shares of the same class as those that you already hold, you must treat the additional shares as having been bought when your original shares were bought. Thus if you bought 100 shares in A Limited for £2 each in 1960 and you now receive a bonus issue of 100 shares you will have 200 shares at a cost of £1 each which are all treated as having been bought in 1960. Note, however, the special rules for scrip dividend options (8.9).

Your company may have a capital reorganisation, in the course of which you receive shares of a different class either instead of or in addition to your original shares. You are not normally charged to capital gains tax on any old shares in your company which you exchange for new ones. Any capital gains tax is only payable when you sell your new holding. The rules for reorganisations including bonus issues hold good under the 'indexation' system unless new consideration is given.

If you take up 'rights' to subscribe for additional shares in a company of which you are a shareholder, your rights shares are treated as having been acquired when your original shares were purchased and the cost of the rights shares is added to the original cost of your holding. If you sell your 'rights' on the market without taking up the shares this is considered to be a 'part disposal' of your holding and accordingly is charged to capital gains tax (20.21). If the proceeds are small (normally no more than 5 per cent) in relation to your holding, however, you can elect not to pay tax then but set off the proceeds against the original cost of your holding. Under the indexation rules (20.18.4), however, any new consideration (for rights shares etc.) is treated effectively as a new acquisition so that indexation runs accordingly.

Anti-avoidance rules act to prevent you from obtaining capital gains tax loss relief artificially from reorganisations. Any increase in the capital gains tax acquisition value of shares which you obtain through the reorganisation is limited to the actual increase in value.

In the case of a take-over you may receive cash for your shares in which case this is taxed as an ordinary disposal. If, however, you receive shares or loan stock etc. in the acquiring company, you will not normally be liable to pay capital gains tax until you actually sell your new shares or loan stock, subject to certain conditions and anti-avoidance laws (15.10). One of the conditions is that the acquiring company already held, or obtains as a result of the takeover, over 25 per cent of the ordinary share capital of the other company.

If you receive qualifying corporate bonds (20.19) on the takeover of your shares, the above relief is modified. You are treated as disposing of your shares at that time, but your gain is deferred until you sell the bonds. From 16 March 1993, these rules extend to certain debentures which are not debts on security (and so previously may have escaped tax). Securities later becoming QCBs may also be covered (20.19(11)).

Sometimes, the consideration for the sale of a company might include an element which is deferred and unascertainable, perhaps related to future profits ('earn out rights'). Broadly, from 26 November 1996, a previous concessional treatment was legislated for. This concerns an 'earn out right' being treated as a security for capital gains tax purposes including deferment.

From 10 April 2003, treating 'earn out rights' as a security applies automatically, subject to certain conditions and an election to disapply them (FA 2003 S161).

All of the above rules concerning bonus issues, takeovers and company reorganisations apply equally to unquoted shares (20.20).

20.18.6 **Investment trusts and unit trusts** (TCGA Ss99–103)

Special rules apply regarding all disposals both of shares owned *by* the trusts and of shares and units *in* the trusts by their shareholders and unit holders. Authorised unit and investment trusts are exempt from tax on their capital gains. However, any disposals which you make of units and investment trust shares carry full capital gains tax with no credit (subject to your £10,600 annual exemption).

From 20 March 1990, capital gains tax indexation did not apply to units in certain unit trusts and offshore funds. This mainly applied to gilt funds and sterling money funds, with at least 90 per cent invested in such funds or building society shares.

20.18.7 **Holdings at 6 April 1965** (TCGA Sch 2)

'Time apportionment' (20.17) has never applied to quoted shares. Instead you considered the mid-market price at 6 April 1965 (20.16). Subject to the election described below, your gain on any sales after 6 April 1965 of shares held at that date was the difference between the proceeds and the higher cost of the shares and their value at 6 April 1965. Similarly any allowable capital loss on such share sales was the difference between the proceeds and the lower of the cost of the shares and their value at 6 April 1965. However, *for disposals after 5 April 1988, 1982 re-basing* (20.10) *was likely to occur. As a result, the value at 31 March 1982 would be used and this is automatic for sales after 5 April 2008.*

If the price at which you sold the shares held at 6 April 1965 was between their value at that date and their cost, then you were normally treated as having no gain and no loss for capital gains tax purposes.

20.19 Exemption for corporate bonds (QCBs) (TCGA Ss115–117 & 132)

The exemption for capital gains tax for gilt edged securities (20.7.1) was extended to certain QCBs satisfying the following conditions:

(1) The bonds were acquired or issued after 13 March 1984.
(2) They are debentures, loan stocks or similar securities, not necessarily secured but 'debts on security'.
(3) They are normal commercial loans, expressed in and redeemable in sterling. Denomination in foreign currency is being allowed with the introduction of the FOREX scheme (13.25).

(4) At least some of the shares or debentures of the issuing company are quoted.
(5) The bonds are capable of being marketed but are not issued by a company to another company in the same group.
(6) Disposals after 1 July 1986 are exempt regardless of the time for which the bonds have been held. Similarly losses have ceased to be available. Prior to that date, normally exemption only applied if you held the securities for at least one year before disposal.
(7) If you sustain a loss on a QCB held on or issued after 14 March 1989, you will obtain relief where part or all of the loan is irrecoverable. However, this relief has been withdrawn regarding loans issued after 16 March 1998.
(8) Regarding disposals after 18 March 1991, bonds convertible into other QCBs are exempt. However, those convertible into shares or securities of the issuing company's quoted parent are not.
(9) From 29 November 1994, the QCB capital gains tax exemption no longer applies to certain indexed securities which are linked to an index of quoted share prices.
(10) Where shares are exchanged for a mixture of cash and QCBs, the cash is liable to capital gains tax but re-investment relief (20.25.2) is available on appropriate share purchases. This relief is also available where a held-over gain comes into charge on a QCB disposal.
(11) After 26 November 1996, the change of status of a security from a non-QCB to a QCB (and vice versa) is treated as a conversion of securities (20.18.7). This could give rise to a capital gains tax charge where the terms of a security change. FA 1999 (Ss59 & 60) expanded this to cover artificial options.

20.20 Unquoted shares (TCGA S273 & Sch 2)

Many of the above points regarding quoted shares and securities apply also to unquoted shares but the following special rules should be noted:

(1) Regarding holdings of shares at 6 April 1965 the 'time apportionment' rule normally applied to sales after that date and before 6 April 2008, subject to the right of election for valuation at 6 April 1965 (20.17). This was not a 'blanket' election for all your non-quoted shares as was the case for quoted shares. (For disposals after 5 April 1988, 1982 re-basing was likely to prevail – 20.10.)
(2) If after 6 April 1965 there was a capital reorganisation or takeover regarding a non-quoted company in which you had shares 'time apportionment' normally stopped at that time and on any future sales you had a time apportioned gain or loss to the date of reorganisation or takeover and the full gain or loss after that time. This did not apply, however, in the case of a bonus issue of the same class of shares (20.18.7).
(3) Prior to 6 April 1982 (1 April for companies) the 'pooling' rules (20.18.2) applied to shares acquired after 6 April 1965 but not to acquisitions

before that time which needed to be separately considered on a 'first in first out' basis.

(4) The indexing and identification rules (20.18.4–8) applied to non-quoted shares as for quoted ones.

(5) Any relief which you obtain against your income, for business expansion scheme investment (11.25) is not also available to create a capital loss. Thus if you eventually sell the shares at a profit, you will obtain full relief for the cost in calculating your capital gain, but not if you sell at a loss.

(6) Subject to the rules (20.25.2) rollover relief applied on reinvestment where qualifying shares in one company were sold after 15 March 1993 and qualifying shares in another were purchased before 6 April 1998.

20.21 Part disposals (TCGA Ss42 & 242–244 & Sch 3)

Where part of an asset is disposed of (including part of a 'pool' holding of shares in a particular company) it is necessary to compute the cost applicable to the part sold. This is normally done by multiplying the original cost by the fraction A/(A+B) where A is the consideration for the part disposed of and B is the market value of the remaining property at the date of the part disposal. If indexation applies (20.11), the cost apportionment formula is applied before computing the indexation allowance (if any) and the same applies for taper relief (20.12). No indexation is calculated on the costs attributable to the undisposed of part (until that is sold).

For part disposals after 5 April 1988, the fraction A/(A + B) is applied to the value at 31 March 1982 if more than the cost. If a part disposal has already taken place between 31 March 1982 and 6 April 1988, the gain on a further disposal after 5 April 1988 must be computed on the basis that 1982 re-basing applied to the earlier part disposal.

A special rule applies to small part disposals of land (only a small part of the whole being sold etc.). Provided that such proceeds during the tax year exceed neither £20,000 nor 20 per cent of the total market value of the land, you may deduct the proceeds from your base cost rather than pay tax now.

20.22 A series of disposals (TCGA Ss19 & 20)

Before 20 March 1985, if you acquired a series of assets (shares etc.) from one or more people connected (20.9) with you, all of the assets were valued together to find the relevant proceeds and your acquisition figure. After 19 March 1985, however, the rule operates only from the viewpoint of a person splitting up an asset or collection of assets by two or more transactions to connected persons. The transactions must be within a total period of six years.

20.23 Private residences (TCGA Ss222–226)

The house or flat where you live is normally exempt from capital gains tax when you sell it, subject to the following rules:

(1) The house must have been your only or main residence during the time that you owned it subject to various allowable periods of absence (see below). You ignore all periods before 6 April 1965 for these purposes.

(2) You are allowed to be absent from the house which is your main residence for the following maximum periods without losing your exemption:
   (a) The last 36 months of ownership. For disposals before 19 March 1991, this period was 24 months.
   (b) Periods of absence totalling three years.
   (c) Any period throughout which you worked abroad.
   (d) Any periods up to four years in aggregate when you are prevented from living in your house due to your employment being elsewhere.
   (e) Any period during which you live in job-related accommodation, but intend to return to your main residence.

   Provided you have no other residence which you claim to be exempt during the above periods they are taken cumulatively and so you could have a long period of absence and still not lose your exemption. You must, however, return to your main residence at the end of periods (b), (c) and (d) above or else you will lose part of your relief.

(3) Any periods of absence subsequent to 31 March 1982 in excess of the periods allowed (see above) result in the relevant proportion of your sale profit being charged to capital gains tax. (For disposals before 6 April 1988, all periods of absence after 6 April 1965 must be considered.) For example, if you bought your house in June 2004 and sold it in June 2012 at a profit of £7,000, having lived elsewhere for reasons unconnected with your employment for the middle six years, your chargeable gain is £7,000 × $1/7$ = £1,000. (You are only allowed three years of absence and the last three in any event, leaving one year taxable.)

(4) If a specific part of your house is set aside for business purposes then that proportion of your profits on sale of the house will be taxable. Thus if you have eight rooms of which two are wholly used for business purposes you would normally claim 25 per cent of your house expenses against your business profits and when you sell your house you will pay capital gains tax on 25 per cent of your total gain (arising after 6 April 1965). If, however, you use no rooms exclusively for business purposes you will not normally be liable for any capital gains tax if you sell your house even though you claim part of your house expenses against your business profits. You also ignore any rooms set aside exclusively for use under a local authority adult placement scheme for disposals after 8 December 2009.

(5) If you dispose of your main residence and part has been let for residential purposes, you obtain some exemption for the let portion. This is not

to exceed the exemption on the part occupied by you, or £40,000 if smaller. Note that you will be exempt for the periods mentioned in 2(a)–(e) in any event.

(6) If you have two residences you can give written notice to HMRC within two years as to which of the two should be treated as your main private residence and thereby be exempted from capital gains tax. The election should be given within two years of acquiring your second residence. If you do not elect then HMRC will decide in the light of the time that you spend at each of your residences which of these is your main private residence.

(7) For the purposes of the exemption, your main residence is taken to include land of up to half of a hectare (including the site of the house). If the house is large and its character requires a larger garden, this is likely to be allowed. Note that the exemption covers the disposal of part of your main residence; for example a strip of your garden. However, take care not to sell the house before the garden, since this would not then be part of your main residence.

(8) For disposals after 9 December 2003 by an individual or settlement, private residence relief is not generally available where, in computing the gain, account must be taken of gifts relief in respect of an earlier disposal.

Previously, you also obtained capital gains tax exemption on no more than one residence owned by you and occupied by a dependent relative, rent-free and without any other consideration. Relief was withdrawn for disposals after 5 April 1988 unless the dependent relative had remained in occupation from an earlier date (TCGA S226).

20.24 Chattels sold for £6,000 or less (TCGA S262)

A chattel is an asset which is tangible movable property such as a chair, a picture, or a pair of candlesticks. For these purposes a set is treated as one chattel. If you dispose of a chattel for no more than £6,000 you pay no capital gains tax and if your proceeds exceed £6,000 your capital gain is restricted to ⅝ of the excess. Thus if you sell a set of antique chairs for £6,300 (original cost £500) your capital gain is restricted to ⅝ × (£6,300– £6,000) = £500.

If you bought a chattel for more than £6,000, and sold it for less than £6,000, your allowable loss is restricted to the excess of the cost over £6,000.

20.25 Replacement of business assets – rollover relief (TCGA Ss152–160 etc.)

You are liable for capital gains tax in respect of any sales of assets used in your business. Similarly a company is liable on any sales of its business assets. If further business assets are purchased within one year preceding and three years after the sale, 'rollover' relief is obtained as a result of which the gain on the disposal is deducted from the cost of the new business assets.

Thus, the gain is 'rolled over' and no tax is paid until the new business assets are sold, unless the latter are in turn replaced. (Note the special 50 per cent reduction for certain rolled-over pre-31 March 1982 gains – 20.10.)

To obtain rollover relief, both your old and new assets must be 'qualifying'. This implies being within the following classes:

(1) (a) Land and buildings (but not trading stock).
    (b) Fixed plant and machinery not forming part of a building.
(2) Ships, aircraft and hovercraft.
(3) Goodwill.
(4) Satellites, space stations and spacecraft etc.
(5) Milk and potato quotas.
(6) Ewe and suckler cow premium quotas.

Note, however, that regarding plant and machinery, rollover relief is only available if it is fixed and so, for example, motor vans and fork lift trucks do not qualify.

In spite of changes to the EU rules, Single Payment Scheme entitlements continue to qualify for rollover relief.

To get the relief you must use the old and new assets in the same business. However, if you carry on several trades, they are treated as one for this purpose. (Relief is still available if you cease one trade and start another.) Also, rollover relief applies regarding purchases and sales by you of personally owned assets used in your 'family company'.

If you are non-resident and replace a business asset chargeable to UK tax with one which is not, rollover relief is generally no longer available. This covers the situation where you sell an asset used in your business in the UK and buy one overseas.

Note that to obtain total relief, the entire proceeds must be invested, otherwise you pay tax on your capital gain up to the extent of the shortfall.

If the new business asset is a wasting asset it must be replaced by a non-wasting asset within ten years. Otherwise the rolled-over gain becomes chargeable. This also applies to assets which will become 'wasting' within ten years, such as a lease with 59 years to run. However, this clawback does not apply to a held-over gain arising before 31 March 1982 and becoming chargeable after 5 April 1988 (TCGA Sch 4).

'Rollover' relief is applicable to companies (13.16). Also a special extension of the rules covers 'gilts' obtained by companies in exchange for group companies in the aircraft and shipping industries on compulsory acquisition through nationalisation. An election is required within four years of the exchange and then the normal new compensation stock rules do not apply.

Dual-resident companies obtain no rollover relief where they replace a UK business asset with one overseas. Also rollover relief is denied where the replacement asset is outside the UK tax charge and is acquired by a dual resident group member (15.10.15).

To fit in with the new self-assessment rules, provisional rollover relief claims are allowed, including on compulsory purchase (20.25.1). You need to declare in your tax return that you intend to re-invest the proceeds in qualifying assets and will lose your relief unless you reinvest within three years of the disposal.

20.25.1 **Rollover relief on compulsory purchase** (TCGA Ss247 & 248)

A form of rollover relief, similar to that available on business assets (20.25) applies to certain land which is sold to local authorities. The property must either be compulsorily bought from you or the purchasing local authority must have compulsory acquisition powers. The relief is available if your replacement property is business or non-business land but not if it qualifies for main residence relief (20.23).

20.25.2 **Rollover relief on reinvestment** (TCGA Ss164A–164N)

An important extension to rollover relief (20.25) applied regarding the disposal of certain shares in unquoted trading companies after 15 March 1993. You needed to have owned at least 5 per cent of the voting shares (making it your 'personal company') and broadly qualify for retirement relief (apart from the age requirement) (20.29).

The relief extended to any assets of which you disposed. Also, your new investment could be in any number of ordinary shares in the 'qualifying company' before 6 April 1998.

The shares purchased needed to be in 'qualifying' companies. These had to carry on 'qualifying trades' and not be controlled by another company etc., whilst any subsidiaries had to be directly owned and trading. The definition of 'qualifying trades' was similar to that for EIS companies (11.26), with some changes.

Your replacement expenditure was first allocated to your gain. Thus your relief was the lower of your gain and the cost of the new asset. However, you could claim a lower amount of relief.

Rollover relief was withdrawn for re-investment in shares after 5 April 1998, but improved EIS relief is available (11.26). For futher details please see previous editions.

20.25.3 **Re-investment into EIS and VCT units**

Subject to the rules, a type of reinvestment relief is available where you subscribe for EIS (11.26) and VCT (8.13) units. You could defer capital gains on other assets by investing up to £150,000 in EIS shares and up to £100,000 in VCT shares each tax year. However, for 2004–05 the EIS limit became £200,000 and the VCT deferal facility was withdrawn. The EIS limit from 2008–09 was £500,000 and is £1m from 2012–13.

For EIS relief, the capital gains must arise no earlier than 29 November 1994 and the EIS shares purchased within one year before and three years after the disposals. With VCT reinvestment, gains must be after 5 April 1995 and the VCT units purchased within one year before and one year afterwards, but no later than 5 April 2004.

20.25.4 **Rollover on transfer of business to a company** (TCGA S162 & 162A)

If you carry out a business and incorporate it, you may be entitled to automatic rollover relief, related to the proportion of the consideration which you take in shares. However, for business transfers after 5 April 2002, you are able to elect that the rollover does not apply, which might have increased taper relief. This opt-out election rule also applies where trustees incorporate a business which they carried on.

20.26 Gifts of business assets

A form of 'hold-over' relief applied to certain transfers of assets, other than bargains at arm's length, made after 11 April 1978. The assets covered were any used in your trade or 'family company'; also shares in such a company.

A more general relief applied for individuals after 5 April 1980 and for settlements after 5 April 1981 (below). The old relief still applied for gifts to companies. From 14 March 1989, the old rules for gifts of business assets were expanded (20.28), following the cancellation of the general relief for gifts (20.27).

20.27 General relief for gifts

In general, transfers of assets which you made after 5 April 1980 and before 14 March 1989, other than bargains at arm's length, were covered by comprehensive 'hold-over' rules. Only UK resident or ordinarily resident individuals (17.3.1) were covered up to 5 April 1981 but after that date, gifts *to* UK trusts were included. From 6 April 1982 gifts *from* trusts were also included. There was a special 50 per cent reduction for certain held-over pre-31 March 1982 gains (20.10). Please refer to previous editions for further details.

20.28 Gifts relief from 14 March 1989 (TCGA Ss165–169 & 260 & Sch 7 & FA 2000 S90)

With the removal of general gifts relief from 14 March 1989, the business gifts relief (20.26) was expanded so that it now includes other items. The scope is now:

(1) Business assets used in a trade, profession or vocation carried on by the giver or his family company etc.
(2) Certain agricultural property (normally where the giver has vacant possession).

(3) Shares and securities in family trading companies or non-quoted trading companies. (These categories include the holding companies of trading groups.)
(4) Gifts of heritage property and to maintenance funds.
(5) Gifts to political parties which qualify for inheritance tax exemption.
(6) Gifts which give rise to an immediate charge to inheritance tax, for example, into (or out of) a discretionary settlement (22.30.2). However, the revised treatment of settlements for inheritance tax purposes (22.30.3) radically increases the range of trusts which qualify for gifts relief in view of the new regime, each situation needing careful study. Potentially exempt transfers (22.3) do not qualify for this relief. However, if a gift is covered by the nil rate band and exemptions for inheritance tax but would otherwise be taxed, the gifts election is available.
(7) Distributions of capital from accumulation and maintenance settlements may also qualify for the election. However, the beneficiary must not obtain the capital later than the income entitlement.
(8) Subject to an election by donor and recipient, gifts to a housing association (TCGA S259).
(9) Certain assets not mentioned above, which are not eligible for gifts relief may qualify for the tax on disposal to be paid by instalments (20.15).
(10) The relief is only available if the donee is UK resident and/or ordinarily resident.
(11) Should you receive some consideration the claim covers only the gift element, if this is less than your total gain. If you are entitled to retirement relief (below) this reduces the held-over gain.
(12) If you received a gift and made the election, then the held-over gain may be assessed on you, should you become neither resident nor ordinarily resident in the UK before having disposed of the asset. However, this only applies if emigration is within six years of the end of the year of assessment of the gift.
(13) From 9 November 1999, the relief is not available on transfers of shares or securities to companies.
(14) Gifts relief is generally denied regarding disposals to settlor-interested trusts after 9 December 2003. (Such a trust is one for which you both provided settled property and have an interest).

20.29 Business retirement relief (TCGA Ss163–165 & Sch 6)

If you were over 50 and disposed by gift or sale of the whole or part of a business which you had owned for the past ten years, subject to the rules, you were exempted from capital gains tax on the first £250,000 of any gain arising before 6 April 1999 in respect of the 'chargeable business assets' of the business. However, the relief was phased out after 5 April 1999 (20.29.1) – for fuller details see previous editions. For disposals after 5 April 1988, not only was the first tranche of gains exempted from capital gains tax; the second tranche was given 50 per cent relief.

From 1999–2000 onwards, capital gains tax retirement relief was withdrawn in stages until it was nil in 2003–04.

20.30 Entrepreneurs' relief

(1) FA 2008 introduced a new form of relief operating for certain qualifying disposals after 5 April 2008 by individuals, partnerships and trustees.
(2) The relief applies to disposals of all or part of a trading business which the individual carries on alone or in partnership; assets of such a business following its cessation; shares in the individual's 'personal' trading company (or holding company of a trading group) and assets used by such a company but owned by the individual.
(3) Relief was given by reducing the first £1m of gains by 4/9, which equates to a tax rate of 10 per cent. The £1m figure was a lifetime limit and post-5 April 2008 gains must be cumulated for this purpose. For disposals after 5 April 2010, the lifetime limit became £2m, whilst after 22 June it is £5m and the rate 10 per cent. From 6 April 2011, the rate is 10 per cent and the lifetime limit is £10m.
(4) You have shares in a 'personal company' if during a one-year qualifying period, you are one of its officers or employees and own at least 5 per cent of its ordinary shares. Unless trading ceases, the one-year qualifying period ends when the shares are sold.
(5) Entrepreneurs' relief is also available when certain deferred gains are crystallised after 5 April 2008. Examples are where gains had been held over or deferred by EIS or VCT investment and the new shares are sold.

20.31 Charities (TCGA Ss256 & 257)

Charities are exempted from capital gains tax in respect of any gains on the disposal of assets provided that such gains are applied to charitable purposes.

If you make a gift of an asset to a charity you pay no capital gains tax on this disposal. If the gifts are of qualifying investments, you also obtain income tax relief (15.2.1).

20.32 Leases and other wasting assets (TCGA Ss45, 240 & Sch 8)

A 'wasting asset' is defined as an asset with a predictable life not exceeding 50 years, not including freehold land and buildings etc. Leases with no more than 50 years still to run are a special kind of wasting asset and are separately treated for capital gains tax (see below).

'Wasting assets' which are also movable property (chattels) are normally exempted from capital gains tax. In the case of other wasting assets apart from leases, you must reduce their original costs on a straight line time basis over the respective lives of the assets. Thus if you buy a wasting asset for £10,000 with an unexpired life of 40 years and sell it after 20 years for £20,000, assuming the residual value after 40 years would have been nil, your allowable cost is £10,000 × $^{20}/_{40}$ = £5,000; thus your chargeable gain is £20,000 – £5,000 = £15,000.

In the case of a lease with no more than 50 years of its original term unexpired (including leases for shorter terms) the original cost must be written off according to a special formula under which the rate of wastage accelerates as the end of the term of the lease is reached. If you sell such an interest in property and lease back the premises at a lower rent for less than 15 years, you may be taxed on all or part of the proceeds either as a trading receipt or other income (prior to 2005–06 under (previously) Schedule D Case VI) (19.1.2).

From 6 April 1996, capital sums paid to a landlord for varying, waiving or surrendering a lease, or commuting the rent are taken into account in the year when payable. Previously they were related to the year when the lease was first granted.

20.33 Traded options (TCGA Ss115, 143, 144A, 148 & 271)

Options to buy or sell quoted shares are dealt with on the Stock Exchange. They are not treated as wasting assets, which means that the entire cost is deductible on sale. The abandonment of a traded option is treated as a disposal so that its cost is an allowable loss. This treatment extends to all traded options quoted on the London International Financial Futures Exchange and recognised stock exchanges.

Transactions in futures and options in gilts and qualifying bonds are exempt from capital gains tax. A further rule provides that if you write a traded option and later extinguish this obligation by buying another option, the cost is allowable against the original sale. Where options are settled in cash, such expenditure is fully allowable.

20.34 Commodity and financial futures (TCGA Ss72, 143 & 271)

Profits from futures which are not part of a trade less losses which you realise are normally covered by capital gains tax and not income tax. This rule applies to commodity futures or financial futures dealt in on a recognised futures exchange.

There is broadly similar capital gains tax treatment for commodity and financial futures and qualifying options (20.33), which are dealt in 'over-the-counter'. Income and gains from futures and options are exempt from tax in authorised unit trusts and pension schemes. Where financial and commodity futures are settled in cash, full relief is given for this expenditure.

20.35 Overseas aspects (TCGA Ss9–14, 25, 80–98, 140, 159–160, 185–188, 275–279 & Sch 5)

As already mentioned (20.3) provided you are resident and/or ordinarily resident in this country (or your non-residence is only temporary (20.3.1)), you are liable to tax on capital gains anywhere in the world. An exception is where assets are realised in a country which will not allow the proceeds to be remitted to the UK. You can then claim that your gain is deferred until the year when it becomes possible to remit the proceeds. If you are non-domiciled in the UK, you are only liable to capital gains tax on overseas gains to the extent that they are remitted here (18.1).

Non-residents carrying on a trade in the UK through a branch or agency are liable to capital gains tax on assets used in the business. This also covers professions and vocations; however, assets are re-based to their values at that date. Furthermore from that date deemed disposals may take place for capital gains tax purposes. This happens if the assets are moved out of the UK or the trade etc. ceases.

If you are UK domiciled, HMRC have powers to apportion to you the capital gains of certain overseas trusts from which you benefit (21.9) and companies. This extends to overseas companies owned by foreign trusts. Regarding overseas companies, relaxations applying from 7 March 2001 include exemption if your interest is no more than 10 per cent.

The *market value* rule (20.9) applies in general to gifts and other dispositions of overseas assets for less than full consideration involving neither resident nor ordinarily resident persons.

Where a company is being 'exported' (17.3.3), there is a deemed disposal of all of its assets at market value for capital gains tax purposes. This broadly applies to companies migrating after 14 March 1988, from which time only those incorporated outside the UK are able to become non-resident. Furthermore, rollover relief (20.25) does not apply where assets are sold before and replaced after migration. If a company which migrates continues to trade in the UK through a branch or agency, any connected assets will be exempted from the deemed disposal.

If a foreign registered 75 per cent subsidiary of a UK company migrates, tax on the capital gains attributable to its foreign assets can be deferred. Parent and subsidiary must make a joint election and the tax becomes payable if any of the foreign assets are sold or if the parent–subsidiary relationship ceases.

If a dual-resident company owns an asset which ceases to be within the UK capital gains tax charge through a double tax agreement, it is deemed to have disposed of the asset. Thus a capital gain may result. Also, for disposals after that date by a non-resident company, tax on the capital gains can be collected from other companies in the same group or from controlling directors. This applies if the original company does not pay within six months of the due date.

If you are a UK resident investor in an offshore 'umbrella fund' you will be subjected to a capital gains tax charge when you switch holdings.

Non-resident companies may transfer their UK branch or agency business to UK resident companies without any immediate capital gains tax charge. This hold-over relief applies if the companies are in the same worldwide group.

Sweeping changes operate from 19 March 1991 regarding the capital gains tax rules for overseas trusts and the rules extended to earlier settlements. These are considered later (21.9.1) as are subsequent changes (21.9.2).

Various relieving provisions came into effect regarding cross-border reorganisations of businesses within the EC. As a result, capital gains tax may be deferred where there is a share exchange and on transfers of UK and non-UK trades, subject to the rules. For a share exchange, voting control must be acquired for shares with not more than 10 per cent of the nominal value in cash. Regarding a UK trade, this must be transferred from a company situated in one EC country to one situated in another, in exchange for securities.

The FOREX legislation (13.25) (now absorbed into the loan relationships legislation – 13.27) came into force for the accounting periods of companies beginning after 22 March 1995. One result is that capital gains tax is no longer charged on monetary assets in foreign currency. Legislation was introduced for asset disposals from 1 January 1995, to block saving tax from the rules coupled with no gain/no loss transfers.

20.35.1 **Offshore funds**

From 1 December 2009, an interest in a transparent offshore fund is treated as an asset for capital gains tax purposes and you are no longer required to consider the disposal of the underlying assets. Elections into the new treatment can be made from 22 April 2009 and retrospectively back to 2003–04.

20.36 SEED Enterprise Investment Scheme (SEIS)

SEIS relief applies to certain investments made from 6 April 2012 in companies, with no more than 25 employees and no more than £200,000 assets, which are starting new businesses. The income tax relief is described at 11.26.1.

As an investor, if you claim SEIS relief from income tax, you will have an exemption from capital gains tax on disposal of your SEIS shares, once you have held them for three years. Additionally, capital gains on other assets that you realise in 2012–13 may be relieved from capital gains tax up to the amount you invest in SEIS shares.

Chapter 21

THE TAXATION OF TRUSTS AND ESTATES

21.1 Trusts

A trust is brought into existence when a person (the settlor) transfers assets to trustees for the benefit of third parties (the beneficiaries). Another word for a trust is a settlement. A trust may also be created under a will when a person (the testator) sets aside the whole or a portion of his estate to be administered (by trustees) for the benefit of his heirs or other beneficiaries. (Where an individual declares himself to be a trustee of certain of his assets a trust will also come into existence.)

Important changes resulted from FA 2006, effective from 6 April 2006. These generally apply for income tax and capital gains tax and include the scope of settled property, settlement, settlor and when a settlement is 'settlor-interested' (21.3.2 etc.); as well as residence rules changes from 6 April 2007. Also, an election procedure has been introduced regarding treating sub-funds as separate settlements (21.2.3).

The definitions of settlor and settled property were aligned for income tax and capital gains tax from 6 April 2006, a settlor including one who enters into a settlement directly or indirectly or reciprocally etc. Where a settlement arises on death etc., the deceased is treated as the settlor, except in certain cases where there is a deed of variation (21.10.4). See Chapter 22 (22.30) for guidelines to the inheritance tax rules concerning trusts.

In certain circumstances, the settlor can be assessed to tax in respect of trust income or capital gains (which he does not actually receive) and he is entitled to reclaim this from the trustees. As from 6 April 2010 rules were introduced (F3A S7) that require the settlor to account to the trustees, where he recovers tax because his rate is lower than theirs. The draft legislation was published on 12 July 2010 for technical consultation, closing on 3 September.

21.2 Trusts – current tax system (ITA 2007 Ss6, 8 & 462–517)

For 2004–05 to 2009–10, the tax rates applying to various trusts, including discretionary and accumulation ones, were a 40 per cent 'trust rate' (previously entitled 'rate applicable to trusts') and a 'dividend trust rate' of 32.5 per cent. From 2010–11, the 'trust rate' and the 'dividend trust rate' have increased to 50 per cent and 42.5 per cent respectively (FA 2009) and further changes from 2013–14 are included in FA 2012. Recent and future proposed rates are as follows:

	Trust rate %	Dividend trust rate %
2004–05 to 2009–10	40	32.5
2010–11 to 2012–13	50	42.5
2013–14	45	37.5

From 2006–07, the first £1,000 (previously £500) of the income of such trusts is charged only at the income tax rate generally applicable to the sources making up to that slice of income and if tax was deducted at source, no more might be payable.

However, the nature of the trust income and the order in which it is allocated to the first slice of the 'trust rate band' may limit its benefit. For example, suppose that for 2010–11 and 2012–13, a trust chargeable at the special trust rates received (in the order laid down by statute) (1) £600 income from property, (2) £350 building society interest (less £70 tax deduction) and (3) £270 dividend income, on which the non-repayable tax credit is £30. The tax payable would be:

	2010–11			2012–13		
Income £	**Tax rate**	**Tax £**	**Credit £**	**Tax rate**	**Tax £**	**Credit £**
(1) 600	at 20%	120.00	–	at 20%	120.00	–
(2) 350	at 20%	70.00	70.00	at 20%	70.00	70.00
(3) 50	at 10%	5.00	5.00	at 10%	5.00	5.00
250	at 32.5%	81.25	25.00	at 42.5%	106.25	25.00
		£276.25	£100.00		£301.25	£100.00
Deducted at source or covered by tax credit		£100.00			£100.00	
Net amount payable		**£176.25**			**£201.25**	

Where you have created more than one settlement, the £1,000 trust rate band is split equally between those existing during the tax year, but so that they each obtain at least £200.

Capital gains tax is charged on any capital gains of the trust (21.6).

Retrospectively to 6 April 2004, certain trusts with 'vulnerable beneficiaries' (21.2.2) can elect that the trust's tax is no more than it would have been, had the income and gains gone directly to such beneficiaries.

The tax assessments etc. are normally made in the joint names of the trustees who pay the tax out of the trust funds.

Any income distributed to beneficiaries is added to their total income for tax purposes (5.2). The income distributions are normally treated as being net of income tax at the appropriate rate(s). Thus they carry a corresponding tax credit. In the case of discretionary trusts etc. (21.3.4) tax must be paid by the trustees to bring the tax credit up to 50 per cent (previously 40 per cent), but reduces to 45 per cent from 2013–14. (Special rules apply to dividends from 6 April 1999 – 21.2.1.) The trustees should issue with each payment a form R185E which sets out the amount paid and the relevant tax credit. They will then account for the 50 per cent on the distributions (40 per cent for 2005–06 to 2009–10, but only 45 per cent from 2013–14) after setting off any tax suffered, including that on the first £1,000 (£500 for 2005–06).

21.2.1 **Dividend income of trusts** (ITA 2007 Ss6, 8, 9 & 491–2)

The following rules apply for dividend income, whether or not the settlor is living. If you have an 'interest in possession' in the trust, so that for example you receive the income as of right, the trustees receive tax credits of 10 per cent (20 per cent before 6 April 1999) and are charged no further tax on the dividends. When these are distributed to you, the net income carries with it a tax credit of 10 per cent (20 per cent before 6 April 1999). This treatment normally extends to Scottish interest-in-possession trusts with UK resident trustees.

If the trust has other income as well as dividends, this carries a credit of 20 per cent. Distributions to you are regarded as coming first out of the other income carrying 20 per cent tax credit and then out of dividend income, with a 10 per cent credit. Prior to 6 April 1996, a tax credit rate of 25 per cent applied to most savings income (2.2) and prior to 6 April 1999 dividend income carried a credit of 20 per cent.

The trustees of accumulation (21.4) and discretionary settlements (21.5) normally pay the trust rate on their income of 50 per cent from 2010–11 (40 per cent for 2004–05 to 2009–10; previously 34 per cent). There is a special rate of 42.5 per cent on dividend income (32.5 per cent for 2004–05 to 2009–10 and 25 per cent for the five prior years). The 50 per cent and 42.5 per cent rates reduce to 45 per cent and 37.5 per cent respectively from 2013–14 (12.2). This is to take account of the notional tax credits on the dividends.

As a beneficiary you have a 50 per cent tax credit (40 per cent for 2004–05 to 2009–10 and 34 per cent before 6 April 2004) on any income distributions. This is set to change to 45 per cent for 2013–14 (FA 2012).

21.2.2 **Trusts with vulnerable beneficiaries** (FA 2005 Ss23–45 & Sch 1)

(1) From 2004–05 tax relief is available for 'qualifying trusts' with vulnerable beneficiaries.
(2) Particularly covered are trusts for disabled persons (mentally or physically) and children who have lost a parent.
(3) To obtain tax relief, all trustees and the relevant vulnerable beneficiary must so elect by the next 31 January but one after the relevant tax year. Thus for 2009–10, election is needed by 31 January 2012.
(4) Income tax relief operates by bringing the trust's liability into line with that of the beneficiary, calculated as if the latter had received the income direct and taking account of personal relief and lower tax rates.
(5) Capital gains tax is charged directly on UK-resident vulnerable beneficiaries where the trustees are UK-resident or ordinarily resident. However, if the beneficiary is non-resident, the trustees must account for the tax, computed as if the gain arose to the former. (The new regime does not cover gains of the trustees if they are not UK-resident or ordinarily resident.)

21.2.3 **Trusts sub-fund elections** (TCGA Sch 4ZA)

(1) From 6 April 2006, subject to the rules, an irrevocable election to HMRC may be made by all of the trustees, for a fund within the settlement to be taxed in certain respects like a separate trust.
(2) An election can only be made if the main settlement is not itself a sub-fund; the sub-fund does not comprise all of the trust property; after the election the sub-fund settlement includes no interest in any main settlement asset etc. and no person will then be a beneficiary of both. Such beneficiaries generally exclude those resulting from future marriage or civil partnerships and the death of a beneficiary or failure of a protective trust, as well as under certain powers of advancement etc.
(3) An election must specify the date from which it is effective, which must not normally be later than when it is made and the sub-fund settlement is treated as having been created on that date.
(4) The election applies in general for income tax and capital gains tax purposes, but not so as to increase the aggregate capital gains tax annual exception nor income tax basic rate band.

21.3 Trusts where the settlor is still living (ITTOIA Ss629–648)

The taxation of trusts where the settlor is still living follows the general rules outlined above except that in certain circumstances the settlor himself is assessed to tax on the income of the trust. In order to avoid such assessment various rules should be observed including the following.

From 6 April 1995, new and simplified rules apply which broadly have the same effect as the previous ones. However, material changes were proposed regarding the taxation of capital sums paid to the settlor (21.3.6), particularly concerning loans between him or her and the settlement. After widespread objections this part of the draft legislation was withdrawn but is expected to reappear in modified form in the future. Meanwhile the original rules apply.

21.3.1 **Period** (ITTOIA S624 etc.)

The settlement must be set up for a period which is capable of exceeding six years.

21.3.2 **The settlor must not have an interest** (ITTOIA S624 etc.)

In the event that the settlor has retained an interest in the income or assets of the trust, he will be assessed to income tax on the income of the settlement to the extent that it remains undistributed. (The settlor has retained an interest in the trust if he or his spouse can obtain some benefit from it.) Furthermore, if the income is distributed to others, subject to certain exceptions, the settlor and not the recipient will be charged to the excess of higher rate tax over the income tax on the distribution.

For trusts made after 13 March 1989, in which the settlor retains an interest, with some exceptions, he or she is taxed on all of the income at the basic and higher rates. (This applies to the income of pre-existing settlements arising from 6 April 1990.) From 6 April 2006, the definition of 'settlor-interested trusts' is wider and treating the income as that of the settlor and not that of the beneficiaries for tax purposes is generally automatic.

For 1990–91 and subsequent years, simple outright gifts and pension allocations between spouses are not to be treated as settlements for the purposes of these rules. However, this does not apply to gifts of property which do not carry a right to all of the income or where a right to income alone is given.

21.3.3 **The settlement must be irrevocable**

If the settlor or his spouse has power to revoke the settlement or partially revoke it, he is assessed to income tax on its income.

21.3.4 **Discretionary settlements** (ITTOIA S624 etc.)

Discretionary settlements are those under which the application of the income and/or capital of the trust is left to the discretion of the trustees. Under such a trust the settlor or his spouse must not be able to benefit from the income, or else he will be assessed to income tax on that income, whether or not any of it is actually paid to him. This does not apply if only a widow or widower of the settlor may benefit.

21.3.5 **Settlements for benefit of own children** (ITTOIA Ss629–632)

Under a trust created by the settlor, his own unmarried minor children (under 18 years of age) must not receive any income nor must it be used for their upkeep or education. Otherwise the settlor will be assessed to income tax on such income. This does not apply to income which is accumulated, however (see 21.4) nor to income not exceeding £100 per child each tax year.

The above rules are extended to any bare trust which you set up after 8 March 1999, for your unmarried minor children, so that they are entitled to the income and capital. Additions to existing settlements are also caught. You will be taxed on the income whether it is accumulated or paid for the benefit of your children. From 22 March 2006 new inheritance tax rules apply (22.30.3).

21.3.6 **Capital sums paid to the settlor** (ITTOIA Ss619–648)

Where 'capital sums' from a settlement (including loans and loan repayments) are paid to the settlor, he is assessable to income tax. The assessments are limited to the undistributed trust income and the balance is carried forward for matching against future income. The carry forward period is limited to 11 years from the 'capital sum' payment and no income is assessable for any period subsequent to the repayment by the settlor of a loan from the settlement.

The rules extend to companies connected with the settlement (normally where the trustees are participators and the company is close – 13.17). A 'capital payment' from the company to the settlor gives rise to the assessment of trust income on him or her, if there is an associated capital payment or asset transfer within five years from the trust to the company. In all of the above cases there are rules to prevent the double taxation of the trust income so it will not be assessed both on the settlor and the beneficiaries.

21.4 Accumulation settlements for the benefit of the settlor's children

If you wish to create a trust for the benefit of your minor (unmarried) children without being assessed to income tax on its income (see above) this can be done by means of an accumulation settlement. However, the new inheritance tax rules must be noted (22.30.3). The income of the settlement should be accumulated for each child until at least the age of 18 and no payments should be made for their benefit until that age. (The trust deed normally states that the trustees are empowered to accumulate income.) If it is wished to distribute income to adult beneficiaries this can be done, but the income shares of the settlor's minor children must be accumulated, or else the settlor is liable to higher rate income tax on such income.

21.5 Income of discretionary trusts etc. (ITTOIA S568 & Sch2, ITA Ss479–517 & FA 1995 S86 & FA 2005 Ss14, 23–29 & 34–45)

The trustees normally pay on their income the trust rate of 50 per cent from 2010–11 (40 per cent for 2004–05 to 2009-10; previously 34 per cent). There is a special rate of 42.5 per cent on dividend income from 6 April 2010 (32.5 per cent for 2004–05 to 2009–10 and 25 per cent for the five prior years). The 50 per cent and 42.5 per cent rates reduce to 45 per cent and 37.5 per cent respectively from 2013–14 (12.2). This is to take account of the notional tax credits on the dividends.

From 2006–07, the first £1,000 of income (£500 for 2005–06) is chargeable at lower rates (21.2). Trusts with vulnerable beneficiaries have relief from 2004–05 (21.2.2).

The above applies to trusts where the income is accumulated or is payable at the discretion of the trustees but not where the income is treated for tax purposes as being that of the settlor; nor where a person is absolutely entitled to the income.

Where income distributions are made to beneficiaries, the amounts received by the latter are treated as being net of tax at 50 per cent from 2010–11 (40 per cent for 2004–05 to 2009–10 and 34 per cent previously), but is set to reduce to 45 per cent for 2013–14. The recipients can reclaim part or all of this tax if their incomes are low enough. For example, if for 2009–10 a discretionary trust paid £600 to your child (or for his maintenance) and he or she had no other income, there would have been a tax credit of £600 × $^{40}/_{60}$ = £400 which was all reclaimable. If in 2011–12 the same trust were to pay £500 in similar circumstances, the tax credit would be £500 × 50/50 = £500, which would be similarly reclaimable. However, a similar £550 payment in 2013–14 should carry a tax credit of £550 × 45/55 = £450.

From 6 April 1999 the trustees do not receive credit for the 10 per cent (notional) tax credit on dividends when distributing income. However, they must still account for the trust rate amounting to 34 per cent up to 5 April 2004, subsequently 40 per cent and from 6 April 2010 50 per cent, after setting off 25 per cent, 32.5 per cent or 42.5 per cent respectively on any dividends. The 50 per cent and 42.5 per cent rates reduce to 45 per cent and 37.5 per cent respectively from 2013–14 (12.2). This limits the amount of dividend income that can be distributed in many cases, thus reducing the income of the beneficiaries. (This may influence the investment policy of the trustees).

Bank interest on deposits belonging to discretionary and accumulation trusts from 6 April 1996, is paid net of tax at 20 per cent. Overseas trusts with no connection to the UK are able to receive gross interest provided the trustees give the bank a signed declaration.

21.5.1 **Special types of income**

FA 2007 corrected two previous legislative drafting errors. *HMRC Press Release of 9 February 2007* indicated how and when you should deal with your 2007 Trust Return, if affected by either.

(1) A retrospective correction was being made to ensure that, *on a company's purchase of its own shares from trustees*, only the excess over the original share capital was taxed – effective 6 April 2006.
(2) Certain *life policy gains* carry a notional tax credit of 20 per cent, in addition to which the trustees had at that time to pay a further 20 per cent. For 2006–07, both the notional and actual tax were allowed to enter the trustees' pool, but from 6 April 2007 any notional tax credit will be excluded from the pool. Thus, by statute a 40 per cent credit was available for 2006–07 only, but HMRC's 'Tax Calculation' and 'Calculation Guide 2007' wrongly adopted the intended 20 per cent credit limit.

21.6 Trusts' capital gains tax (TCGA Ss4, 5, 68–76, 165–167 & Sch 7)

Regarding realisations by trusts, from 23 June 2010, the rate generally applicable to capital gains increased to 28 per cent, with an actual rate of 10 per cent, where entrepreneurs' relief (21.7) is claimed. Previously, from 6 April 2008, a rate of 18 per cent applied generally, but could in effect be reduced to 10 per cent, where entrepreneurs' relief was claimed.

However, for the years 2004–05 to 2007–08 a 40 per cent capital gains tax rate (previously 34 per cent) applied to all trusts, including discretionary and accumulation trusts and personal representatives. Relief may apply where there are vulnerable beneficiaries (21.2.2). Prior to 6 April 1998, 23 per cent applied except for discretionary and accumulation trusts for which the 34 per cent rate applied. Where the settlor (or spouse) has an interest in or rights relating to a settlement, the rate may be increased to the settlor's top rate. Also, the settlor's annual exemption (currently £10,600) would apply if not used up (TCGA Ss77 & 78).

The full (£10,600 for 2011–12 and 2012–13) annual exemption (20.5) applies to trusts for the mentally disabled and those receiving attendance allowance. (From 6 April 1981 only broadly half the property and income need be applied to the disabled.) Other trusts normally obtain exemption at half the rate (£5,300). However, regarding trusts formed after 6 June 1978, the exemption is split between those with the same settlor. Thus if you had settled two such trusts they each have an annual exemption of £2,650. If there are more than five, however, they each still have an exemption of £1,060. Sub-settlements also count for this purpose if an election has been made (21.2.3).

For recent years the corresponding exemptions were as in the next table:

	Disability trusts £	Other trusts £	Minimum £
2004–05	8,200	4,100	820
2005–06	8,500	4,250	850
2006–07	8,800	4,400	880
2007–08	9,200	4,600	920
2008–09	9,600	4,800	960
2009–10 and 2010–11	10,100	5,050	1,010

From 6 April 2008 indexation allowance (20.11) and taper relief (20.12) were both withdrawn for trustees, but entrepreneurs' relief (21.7) may be available, subject to the rules.

When any chargeable assets are introduced into the trust by the settlor this is a realisation by him on which he pays capital gains tax if applicable (20.9). For example, if A bought 1,000 shares in B Ltd for £1,000 in May 1998 and gave them in June 2012 to a settlement that he created, the shares must be valued at that time. If the shares were then worth £2,000 he has a chargeable gain of £1,000 for 2012–13. If, however, the shares were worth only £600 at that time, he has an allowable loss of £400 (£1,000 – £600), which he can only set off against any capital gains resulting from other transactions between A and his trust. This is because they are treated as being 'connected persons' (20.9), except for certain gifts for public educational, cultural or recreational purposes.

There are trust rules, whereby if you are the settlor, you may be taxed on the trustees'capital gains, particularly where you have or are treated as having an interest in the trust. The rule covers both UK resident settlements (TCGA Ss77 & 78) and non-resident ones (TCGA Ss86 & 86A). Historically, the trust's tapered gains would be attributed to you, with no personal loss relief. However, under FA 2002 S51 & Sch 11 from 2003–04, the gross gains were attributed to you and you then had to offset losses, before applying taper relief. Also, until 31 January 2005, you could elect for similar treatment for any of the three earlier years (2000–01 to 2002–03).

From 6 April 2006, the broader definition of *settlor-interested trusts* for the above purposes, includes one you have created where your existing under-aged children have or may benefit. (Married children or those with civil partners are excluded.) Anomalies in the order of attributing dividend income to beneficiaries, to whom income assessed on the settlor has been distributed, were addressed retroactively in FA 2008.

21.7 Trusts' capital gains tax – business assets, gifts etc.

Where, after 11 April 1978, business assets, including shares in 'family companies' were settled, the trustees and settlor could jointly claim for any gain on the assets to be held over (20.26). The effect was that the settlor had no capital gains tax to pay on the settled business assets etc. and the acquisition value for the trustees was correspondingly reduced. From 6 April 1981 to 13 March 1989, the general gifts relief (20.27) applied to disposals *to* trusts. Regarding gifts *by* trusts, the old business assets rules applied for 1981–82, after which the general gifts relief applied up to 13 March 1989. From 14 March 1989, the old business assets rules apply with some extensions (20.28), for instance concerning discretionary settlements; and certain others from 22 March 2006 etc.

For disposals made after 29 November 1993 and before 6 April 1998 by most trusts, wide rollover relief on reinvestment applied (20.25.2). Thus all chargeable gains of trusts were eligible for relief if reinvested in ordinary shares in qualifying companies. The exception was where the beneficiaries included those who were neither individuals nor charities.

From 6 April 2008, trustees and beneficiaries may jointly claim entrepreneurs' relief (20.30) in respect of gains from the disposal of qualifying assets in which a beneficiary has a qualifying interest. The relief will count towards the beneficiary's personal entitlement of entrepreneurs' relief (£5m from 23 June 2010, previously £2m or £1m). From 23 June 2010 this relief reduces the trustees' rate on the gain to 10 per cent (previously achieved by exempting 4/9ths of the gain and charging 18 per cent on the remainder).

21.8 Trusts' capital gains tax – disposals of interests and distributions

The disposal of an interest in the trust by one of the original beneficiaries is normally exempt from capital gains tax. However, this does not apply to non-resident settlements. Under the new regime for trusts in FA 2006, this treatment will only apply to interest in possession trusts which meet the new conditions.

Where a *life interest* in a settlement ends otherwise than on death, capital gains tax does not arise on the excess of its value over the base cost. However, on a subsequent disposal the original base value must be used. Where a *life interest* in a settlement ends on death, there is similarly no capital gains tax. However, the capital gains tax base value of the assets is adjusted to their market value at that time.

Where a capital asset of a trust is distributed to a beneficiary this is a chargeable event which can give rise to a capital gain in the trust. (This even applies for minors etc. who are not yet legally able to own the property.) Thus if a trust bought 1,000 shares in B Ltd for £2,000 in April 1999 and it distributes them to beneficiary C in July 2012 when their market value is £3,000 the trust will have a capital gain of £1,000 (£3,000 – £2,000), which is assessable for 2012–13 subject to the annual exemption and any entrepreneurs' relief. The beneficiary normally has a base value equivalent to the market value of the asset. (An exception to this rule is where a beneficiary under a will or intestacy receives his entitlement – 21.10.3.)

Various anti-avoidance rules apply (15.10.20). For example, where a beneficiary sells his interest in a trust to someone else after 20 March 2000, in certain circumstances there may be a capital gains tax charge. This particularly applies for *settlor-interested trusts*. The underlying assets to which the interest relates are treated as disposed of by the trust at market value and immediately reacquired, giving rise to trust capital gains accordingly (TCGA S76A & Sch 4A).

21.9 Foreign trusts (TCGA Ss13, 76, 76B, 80–90, 96 & 97 & Sch 5 & 5A)

For taxation purposes a trust was generally treated as being resident abroad if a majority of the trustees are so resident and its administration and management is carried out overseas. Such a trust was generally exempt from capital gains tax on realisations of assets in the UK and elsewhere. However, sweeping changes took effect from 19 March 1991 and that rule no longer applies in certain cases (21.9.1). Further important changes apply from 1998, 1999 (21.9.2) and 2008 (21.9.3).

For income tax purposes, broadly, from 1989–90 to 2006–07 (with some exceptions) if at least one trustee was UK resident and at least one was not, special rules applied (17.3.5), depending on the settlor's status when he introduced funds into the settlement. If the settlor was then resident, ordinarily resident or domiciled in the UK, the non-resident trustees were treated as UK resident for determining the trust's residence for income tax purposes. Otherwise, all the trustees were treated as non-UK resident. From 6 April 2007, the trust residence rules for income tax and capital gains tax are aligned.

If the settlement arises on death, the residence etc. of the deceased at the date of death applies for deeming the residence of the trustees and a similar rule applies concerning the personal representatives.

There are rules under which HMRC can sometimes assess UK resident beneficiaries with their shares of any capital gains (provided that the settlor is UK domiciled and resident or ordinarily resident either when he made the settlement or when the capital gain is made). UK beneficiaries are only taxed to the extent that they receive *capital payments* attributable to such gains. Where the *capital payments* and trust capital gains are in different tax years the beneficiary is taxed in the later one. *Capital payments* made to beneficiaries after 5 April 1992 may attract a supplementary charge (21.9.1).

There are rules to prevent capital gains tax being avoided by transfers between settlements and by a trust changing its residence. For the purposes of the rules, the term 'settlement' includes dispositions, arrangements and agreements; whilst 'settlor' takes in those making reciprocal arrangements or undertakings to provide funds indirectly. From 19 March 1991, there are rules to charge to tax, trust capital gains on settlors who have any interest in the settlement (21.9.1 and 21.9.2).

UK income of foreign trusts is charged to income tax here along roughly the same lines as non-resident individuals are so charged. There is no higher rate liability, however, unless distributions are made to beneficiaries resident in this country or if the anti-avoidance provisions apply regarding transfers of assets abroad (15.10.2). In the latter event, in certain circumstances, HMRC may charge any beneficiaries who are resident in this country with basic, higher and additional rate income tax on the trust income.

Since 6 April 1993, the UK dividends received by foreign discretionary and accumulation trusts carry a notional tax credit which is allowed as a credit against the full 'rate applicable to trusts'. However, this tax credit is not repayable. From 6 April 1999, the notional tax credit became 10 per cent of the gross or 1/9 of the dividend amount (previously 20 per cent and 1/4).

21.9.1 **Foreign trusts – capital gains from 19 March 1991** (TCGA Ss80–87 & 98A & Sch 5 & 5A)

Rules operate from 19 March 1991 aimed at increasing the application of UK capital gains tax to foreign trusts. These rules include a capital gains tax charge when the trustees of a settlement cease to be UK resident after 18 March 1991. This is based on the values of the assets which fall out of the UK capital gains tax net when the trustees change residence (not assets used in a UK trade). The trustees are not able to cover such gains by rollover relief through buying new assets outside the UK tax charge.

As the settlor of a non-resident settlement, you will be charged to capital gains tax if certain conditions are satisfied including the following:

(1) You are UK domiciled and resident or ordinarily resident (17.2 and 17.3).
(2) You have an 'interest' in the settlement. This covers being able to benefit, now or in the future, from the income or property of the settlement. You are also caught if your spouse, children or their spouses can benefit (also in some circumstances grandchildren – 21.9.2).
(3) The rules apply to your settlement, if you set it up after 18 March 1991. Earlier settlements may also be caught, where, for example, property or

income is provided otherwise than by way of arm's length bargains. Other instances include the trustees ceasing to be UK resident after that date and a member of your immediate family ((2) above) becoming a beneficiary for the first time.

(4) Any capital gains and losses made by your settlement before 19 March 1991 are not caught by the new rules. However, subject to the conditions being satisfied, you will be assessed on the subsequent net gains. Also, you will have an obligation to notify the Inland Revenue of events which may involve a charge to tax.

If you are a beneficiary of a non-resident settlement and receive a *capital payment* after 5 April 1992, you may be liable to pay a *supplementary charge* in addition to the normal capital gains tax. The rules include the following:

(1) You must be UK domiciled and resident or ordinarily resident (17.2 and 17.3). Originally the settlor had to have this status when you received the payment or when the trust was established. For gains and capital payments after 16 March 1998, this charge applies regardless of the residence or domicile status of the settlor.
(2) Your capital payments will be matched with trust gains on a 'first in first out' basis.
(3) The supplementary charge runs from 1 December in the tax year following the one when the gain arose, to 30 November following the year of assessment in which your capital payment is made.
(4) You will not be charged if your capital payment falls to be matched with trust gains of the same or immediately preceding tax year.
(5) The supplementary charge will be 10 per cent of the tax for each year up to six. Thus, while the top rate was 40 per cent, the maximum supplementary charge was 24 per cent making a total of 64 per cent. From 6 April 2008 to 22 June 2010 a lower single capital gains tax rate of 18 per cent applied, which carried a maximum supplementary charge of 10.8 per cent, making a total of 28.8 per cent. From 23 June 2010, the rate increased to 28 per cent, taking the maximum supplementary charge to 16.8 per cent, and the maximum total to 44.8 per cent.

HMRC must be provided with information where a non-resident trust is set up after 18 March 1991; property (other than at arm's length) is transferred to an earlier trust; or a trust ceases to be UK resident. This is normally limited to where the settlor is UK resident and/or domiciled and now applies whether or not the settlor has an interest. However, after 16 March 1998, the information rules extend to anyone who transfers property (other than at arm's length) to an offshore trust.

21.9.2 **Foreign trusts – capital gains changes from 1998** (TCGA Ss76, 79A–B, 85–88, 96, 97 & Sch 5)

(1) Regarding disposals after 5 April 1999, the rules for settlements set up after 18 March 1991 (21.9.1) generally extend to earlier trusts. Thus if

you created such a trust and you, your spouse or children can benefit, you will be taxed on the trust gains. This will not apply if you are non-domiciled and not resident and/or not ordinarily resident, nor in certain other cases, such as where children are under age 18 at 5 April 1999.

(2) If you set up a foreign trust after 16 March 1998 from which your grandchildren (or those of your spouse) can benefit, you may be charged on the trust gains. This also applies to earlier trusts where capital is subsequently settled, or after 16 March a trust is exported or varied regarding grandchildren.
(3) Any gain realised after 5 March 1998 from the disposal by a beneficiary of an interest in a trust which is or had been located offshore is no longer exempt.
(4) From 21 March 2000, rules take effect to stop capital gains tax being avoided where an offshore trust is made UK resident and then non-resident again. There will be no uplift in the value of any beneficiary's interest in the trust assets if the trust had a stockpile of gains not attributed to the trust beneficiaries.
(5) Also acted against from 21 March 2000 is the situation where gains are sheltered through the double tier of a trust and an offshore company and the existing anti-avoidance laws are set aside by a double tax agreement.

21.9.3 **Foreign trusts – capital gains changes from 6 April 2008**

The 1991 rules for matching gains to capital payments changed in several respects with effect from 6 April 2008 (TCGA S86 after FA 2008). If you are a beneficiary of a non-resident settlement and receive a capital payment after 5 April 2008, you may be liable to pay a supplementary charge in addition to the normal capital gains tax, but the rules now include the following:

(1) Your capital payments will now be matched as far as possible to amounts of trust capital gains less losses on a 'last in first out' basis. Unmatched payments will be carried forwards and any amounts assessed on the settlor will not also be allocated to any beneficiary.
(2) Because of the general changes to the remittance basis of taxation, this allocation is made regardless of whether or not you are UK domiciled. However, you will only be taxed in the UK on capital payments made in years for which you are resident or ordinarily resident (17.2 and 17.3). If you are UK non-domiciled, you will have the option to be taxed on the remittance basis (18.0–18.5).
(3) The supplementary charge still runs from 1 December in the tax year following the one when the gain arose, to 30 November following the year of assessment in which your capital payment is made.
(4) You will not be charged if your capital payment falls to be matched with trust gains of the same or the immediately preceding tax year.
(5) The supplementary charge will be 10 per cent of the tax for each year up to six. From 6 April 2008 a lower rate of tax on capital gains of 18 per cent applied, so the maximum supplementary charge became 10.8 per cent making a total of 28.8 per cent. However, from 23 June 2010 the rate

increased to 28 per cent, on which the maximum supplementary charge would be 16.8 per cent, bringing the maximum total to 44.8 per cent.

(6) If you are and remain UK non-domiciled, you have the option to elect irrevocably to offset your foreign capital losses against foreign trust gains, provided that you do so in the first year after 5 April 2008 for which you chose to use the remittance basis. In addition, transitional reliefs protect you from being charged to capital gains tax on any capital payment that was either:
   a) received between 12 March and 5 April 2008; or
   b) is matched to trust gains prior to 6 April 2008.

(7) Trustees may elect to limit the gains apportionable to UK non-domiciled beneficiaries to the growth in value subsequent to 6 April 2008.

(8) Trustees may also reduce their apportionable amounts by reference to compulsory rebasing as at 31 March 1982.

Those assessable on trust gains can still benefit from a continuing 10 to 16 per cent rate range for capital gains tax if entitled to the entrepreneurs' relief, but will need to assess the implications of the 28 to 44.8 per cent rate range in the light of all relevant circumstances.

The capital gains tax charge on UK resident or ordinarily resident settlors of settlor interested trusts was unchanged and has applied only to settlors who are UK domiciled (TCGA S86). This may change from 6 April 2013, when ordinary residence is abolished.

21.10 Estates of deceased persons

21.10.1 **The tax liability of the deceased** (TMA Ss40, 74 & 77)

When a person dies, income tax and capital gains tax must be settled on all his income and capital gains up to the date of his death. Any of this tax that is not paid during his lifetime must be settled by his executors or administrators out of his estate. Strictly this can require the submission of a self-assessment return or repayment claim form for one or more tax years, the last of which will usually be a part year ending on the date of death (unless that happens to have been 5 April). However, for smaller or less complex cases, HMRC may prefer to agree liabilities 'informally'.

From 1 April 2010, if the deceased has not been assessed to tax on all his income or capital gains prior to his death, HMRC are allowed to make assessments on such income and capital gains within four years from (previously three years after 31 January following) the end of the tax year in which death occurred. HMRC may make assessments in this way in respect of any tax years ending within six years before the date of death in cases of loss of tax brought about carelessly or deliberately by (formerly by fraud, wilful default or neglect of) the deceased, but no earlier years can be assessed (16.9.1).

21.10.2 **Income tax during the administration period** (ITTOIA Ss649–682)

The administration period of an estate is the period from the date of death of the deceased until the assets are distributed to the beneficiaries according to the will of the deceased or according to the rules of intestacy. Where, however, a trust is set up under a will the administration period only normally lasts until the trust takes over the residue of the estate.

During the administration period, the executors or administrators pay any lower or basic rate income tax assessable on the income arising in that period. The tax paid by self-assessment or deduction at source is subtracted from the amounts of income paid to those entitled to the income of the estate. Non-trading expenses of the executors are also deducted, but normally, any trading expenses will have been deducted from trading income in arriving at its net taxable amount.

Strictly this can require the submission of a self-assessment return or repayment claim form for one or more tax years falling within the administration period, the first of which will usually be a part year commencing on the day following the date of death. However, for smaller or less complex cases, HMRC may prefer to agree liabilities 'informally' and a detailed guideline is published within the relevant official Manual.

The beneficiaries include the income that they receive in their tax returns when the payments are made to them. They must return the gross equivalents allowing for income tax at the 20 per cent lower rate and/or basic rate (20 per cent). Any distributions of estate income out of post-5 April 1993 dividends (21.2.1) and post-5 April 1996 savings income (2.2) must be grossed up at the lower or dividend rate. Initially both carried a 20 per cent tax credit, but distributions from dividends received after 5 April 1999 only carry 10 per cent, so must be grossed up by $\frac{1}{9}$ of the amount received.

Historically, the total income payable to each beneficiary was allocated to the respective tax years for which it arose and they paid (if applicable) higher rate tax on that basis. However, different rules apply to estates in the course of administration at 6 April 1995 and new ones. From that date, income payments made to the beneficiaries are taxable in the year of receipt, any balance normally being taxable on completion of the administration and not subject to spreading.

21.10.3 **Capital gains tax during the administration period** (TCGA Ss3, 4 & 62)

Notification of chargeable gains and claims for capital gains losses are dealt with along with income in formal returns to or by informal agreement with HMRC as described above (21.10.2).

Although before 31 March 1971 all of the chargeable assets of the deceased were considered for capital gains tax purposes to be disposed of at the date of his death, no such liability arises regarding deaths on or after that date. The executors or administrators of the estate are regarded as acquiring the assets at their market value at the date of death and if they later sell any of the assets during the administration period, the estate is assessed to capital gains tax on any surplus. The rate was 30 per cent up to 5 April 1988, 25 per cent to 5 April 1996, 24 per cent for 1996–97 and 23 per cent for 1997–98. From 1998–99 the rate was 34 per cent, increasing to 40 per cent for 2004–05 to 2007–08. From 6 April 2008 to 22 June 2010 a lower rate of 18 per cent applied (10 per cent where entrepreneurs' relief is claimed). However, from 23 June 2010 the main rate applicable increased to 28 per cent although the 10 per cent rate continues, where entrepreneurs' relief is available.

Thus, if part of the estate of A deceased consisted of 1,000 shares in B Ltd valued at his death on, say, 30 June 2010 at £2,000, and if those shares are sold on 1 November 2012 for £3,000 (in order to pay inheritance tax for example), the estate is assessed to capital gains tax on £1,000 (£3,000 – £2,000) for 2012–13 (subject to any losses and annual exemption).

If, however, assets of the estate are given to beneficiaries in settlement of their entitlements under the will of the deceased, no capital gains tax is charged on the estate on such transfers of assets. Instead, each beneficiary is treated for capital gains tax purposes as if he had acquired the assets at the same time as the personal representatives acquired them and at the same value.

Thus in the example mentioned above, if instead of selling the 1,000 shares in B Ltd for £3,000 on 1 November 2012 the executors gave them to C on that day in satisfaction of a legacy provided by the will of A deceased, C is treated as having acquired the shares on 30 June 2010 for £2,000 only. (The value of £2,000 was the probate value of the shares at the date of death.) Thus no capital gains tax is payable by the estate in respect of the transfer. If, however, C then sells shares on 1 December 2012 for £3,500 his chargeable gain (subject to any losses or annual exemption) will be £1,500 (£3,500 – £2,000), although the shares have only gone up in value by £500 since he received them. This is because his entitlement to the legacy is considered for capital gains tax purposes to extend back to the date of death.

For the year of assessment in which death occurs and the next two years, the full personal annual exemption is applied to the net gains (£10,100 etc. – 20.5). In the alternative examples given in the previous paragraphs, annual exemption could be available to the executors or to the beneficiary, C.

21.10.4 **Deeds of variation** (TCGA Ss62 & 68c & ITA Ss472–473)

These effectively rewrite all or part of the provisions of wills or intestacies and, if made within two years after death, can be made operative for the purposes of both capital gains tax and inheritance tax (22.29.6) within two years of death. Previously a separate tax election was needed, but variations made after 31 July 2002 which so direct, automatically apply for capital gains tax and inheritance tax purposes. Settlements created by deeds of variation made after 5 April 2006 may, for capital gains tax and income tax purposes, result in others than the deceased being treated as settlors, such as the original legatees giving up property. It is important to note that a deed of variation does not alter the destination of income arising between the dates of death and variation.

Chapter 22

INHERITANCE TAX

22.1 Introduction

This chapter deals with what was originally known as capital transfer tax, but following sweeping changes in the 1986 Finance Act was renamed inheritance tax. The name applies from 25 July 1986. However, the inheritance tax rules cover transfers on and after 18 March 1986.

The tax is highly complicated and technical. Although many of the basic capital transfer tax rules remain, important innovations such as potentially exempt transfers (PETs) were introduced (22.3). Many of its complexities are beyond the scope of this book. The following is thus only a brief outline.

The rules for inheritance tax are contained in the Inheritance Tax Act 1984 (IHTA) and subsequent Finance Acts. The tax covers transfers on death and certain lifetime transfers, particularly to discretionary settlements. However, lifetime transfers between individuals and to certain trusts are only taxed if death occurs within seven years (22.3). FA 2006 made sweeping changes regarding trusts and the period to 5 April 2008 offered some transitional opportunities.

Before capital transfer tax there was estate duty, which did not apply to deaths occurring after 12 March 1975 (22.14). Where property passed on deaths after 12 November 1974 and before 13 March 1975, estate duty applied at capital transfer tax rates. For details of estate duty, reference should be made to Chapter 19 of the 1974–75 *Hambro Tax Guide* and earlier editions.

22.2 Property chargeable (IHTA Ss1–3 & 103–114)

Subject to various exceptions and reliefs (22.15) inheritance tax will be charged on *chargeable transfers* which you make during your lifetime, as well as on the value of your estate when you die. However, with the introduction of the inheritance tax regime, the scope for tax on lifetime gifts was much reduced by the rules concerning *potentially exempt transfers* (22.3). These escape tax unless death occurs within seven years. As a result, most inheritance tax is payable following death.

Chargeable transfers are evaluated by taking the decrease in your assets less liabilities brought about by the transfer and deducting certain exemptions (22.17). Normally, arm's length transactions are ignored if they are not intended to convey any gratuitous benefit. Any capital gains tax which you pay on the same transaction is ignored in calculating the decrease.

If you are domiciled (17.2) in the UK or deemed domiciled (22.4) here, inheritance tax applies to all of your property, wherever situated. Otherwise it only applies to your property in this country.

22.3 Potentially exempt transfers (ITA S3A & FA 1986 S101 & Sch 19)

If you make gifts to other individuals, or to (previously) accumulation and maintenance settlements (22.30.1) or trusts for disabled persons, they are classed as 'potentially exempt transfers' (PETs). This means that inheritance tax will not be payable on these gifts unless you die within seven years. Should that happen, however, the PETs (less exemptions) become *chargeable transfers*. Your tax must then be recalculated as later indicated (22.5.1) but using the rate scale applying at death and subject to possible tapering relief (22.6).

Previously the scope of PETs included lifetime transfers concerning interest in possession trusts. These are broadly trusts where one or more beneficiaries have the income or use of property as of right. Transfers into such trusts were PETs as were transfers out, except on death. If you make a PET, no inheritance tax return is required.

However, broadly from 22 March 2006 for certain new trusts and 6 April 2008 for existing ones, FA 2006 restricts the application of the PET rules. This mainly covers accumulation and maintenance and interest in possession trusts, fuller details appearing later (22.30).

22.4 Deemed domicile (IHTA S267 & FA 1996 S200)

Solely for the purposes of inheritance tax, you are deemed to be domiciled in the UK if one of the following applies:

(1) You were domiciled here on or after 10 December 1974 and within the three years preceding the date of the chargeable transfer.
(2) You were resident here on or after 10 December 1974 and in not less than 17 of the 20 years of assessment (for income and capital gains tax purposes) ending with that in which you make the chargeable transfer.

22.5 Rate scale (IHTA S7 & Sch 1 & FA 2005 S98)

The inheritance tax scheme applying from 18 March 1986 has a seven year limitation on cumulation. Also, as previously mentioned (22.3) lifetime transfers (excluding transfers to discretionary settlements etc.) were previously not cumulated unless you died within seven years. There are, however, various exemptions from the general rules (22.17).

Capital transfer tax was charged on the cumulative total of all your lifetime transfers after 26 March 1974 together with the property passing on your death. There was a ten year limitation on cumulation (22.7).

Inheritance tax is charged according to the following table (22.5.1) which applies to *chargeable transfers* and property passing on death after 5 April 2009. The threshold is now £325,000, compared with £312,000 for 2008–09 and can be expected to remain at that level until 5 April 2015. Even annual indexation of the threshold has been suspended until 6 April 2014 and an increase to £350,000 from 6 April 2010 (FA 2007 S4) revoked (FA 2010 S8).

There is only one scale but lifetime gifts which are not PETs (22.3) are charged at 50 per cent of the rate. Until 21 March 2006, this applied mainly to transfers into discretionary settlements, charges on such settlements (22.30.2) and chargeable transfers arising from close company transactions. However, from 22 March 2006 most transfers into settlement will be chargeable. Tax is paid on such transfers soon after they are made, cumulating them with others within the previous seven years to calculate the amount. If death occurs within seven years, however, tax is adjusted using the full rates, with possible tapering relief (22.6) where death is later than three years after the transfer. However, the adjustment does not operate to reduce the original tax at lifetime rates.

On death within seven years of a PET (22.3) inheritance tax must be calculated by treating it as a *chargeable transfer* and cumulating with it any chargeable transfers within seven years before the PET. Tax is calculated using the value of the gift when made but using the scale current at the date of death. On gifts more than three years before death, some tapering relief will be available (22.6).

22.5.1 **Inheritance tax rate after 5 April 2009**

Slice of cumulative chargeable transfers	Cumulative total £	% on slice	Cumulative total tax £
The first £325,000	325,000	Nil	Nil
The remainder		40	

Note: The rate of tax is halved for lifetime transfers described above (22.5).

In general, the current rate scale applies to chargeable transfers and on deaths after 5 April 2009. Previously the rate scales have been modified periodically. Each time the burden has been slightly reduced. Historic tables appear in Chapter 27 (27.4).

From 6 April 2012, following formal consultation during summer 2011, a special rate of 36 per cent applies where 10 per cent or more of the net estate (after deducting IHT exemptions, reliefs and the nil rate band) is left or redirected by deed of variation to charity or to a CASC (15.2.2).

22.5.2 **Transfer of unused nil rate band of deceased spouse or civil partner**
(IHTA Ss8A–8C & FA 2008 S8 & Sch 4)

From 9 October 2007, your estate may be able to benefit from such part of the nil rate band as was unused on the prior death of your spouse or civil partner, where that occurred on or after 13 March 1975, when capital transfer tax commenced. The provisions are complex, because they provide for the up-rating of the unused relief to current values and for any interaction with the recent charging provisions for *alternatively secured* or *drawdown* pension schemes or with the past capital gains tax treatment of assets which formed part of the earlier estate. *These interactions mean that that the relief should not be claimed without due consideration of any prospective additional liabilities.*

The general time limit for claiming this relief expires two years after the end of the month in which the second death occurs or, if later, three months after your personal representatives start to act. Should they not claim, then any person liable for payment of the inheritance tax has an opportunity to claim within such further time as HMRC see fit to allow.

22.6 Tapering relief (IHTA S7)

Where an individual dies within seven years of making a potentially exempt transfer (PET) (22.3) only a proportion of the full tax is payable as follows:

Death in years	%
1–3	100
4	80
5	60
6	40
7	20

If a transfer is within the nil rate band, so that it attracts no inheritance tax, no benefit is obtained from tapering relief in that instance. Regarding those lifetime transfers which attract inheritance tax immediately at half the full rates (22.5), the tax is increased to full rates if death occurs within three years. Otherwise, the above tapering scale is applied to the rates current at death unless this produces a lower charge than that originally paid. In that case the original basis of liability holds good.

22.7 The former ten-year cumulation period

FA 1981 introduced a ten-year limitation on cumulations (superseded by a seven year limit from 18 March 1986). If you made a chargeable transfer it was added to all chargeable transfers which you made in the previous ten years and any made before that time dropped out.

22.8 The current seven-year cumulation period (IHTA S3A)

Regarding chargeable transfers and deaths occurring after 17 March 1986, the cumulation period was reduced to seven years. This meant that any transfers which you made in the three years to 17 March 1979 immediately fell out of cumulation regarding transfers after 17 March 1986.

Remember that only a limited category of transfers come into charge immediately (22.5). PETs (22.3) are only cumulated and charged to inheritance tax if you die within seven years. Then the PETs become *chargeable transfers* and are brought into cumulation with previous chargeable transfers within seven years of each PET (including the PETs within seven years of death). The estate left at death (22.14) is then added to the chargeable transfers in the last seven years in order to compute the inheritance tax on those assets.

22.9 Indexation of rate bands (IHTA S8)

For each year to 5 April, the inheritance tax rate or rates (22.5) are to apply subject to indexation. The threshold and the various rate-bands will in general be increased in proportion to the rise in the CPI (until 2011–12 the RPI) from September to September and each new threshold will be rounded up to the nearest £1,000. This applies unless the Treasury or Parliament otherwise directs, as is the case for 2010–11 to 2014–15 inclusive (FA 2010 & FA 2012).

22.10 Valuation (IHTA Ss160–170, 222 & 242)

For inheritance tax purposes your assets are normally valued at their open market value at the transfer date. If the value of an asset which you keep is affected by the transfer, you will need to value your 'estate' both before and after the transfer in order to calculate its resultant fall. Your liabilities must be taken into account in valuing your total 'estate'. Regarding appeals as to the value of land, the former Special Commissioners were always able to refer to the appropriate Lands Tribunal. From 1 June 2009, under the new appeals regime (22.24), in England and Wales such cases should be allocated to the Lands Chamber of the Upper Tribunal.

22.11 Quoted securities passing on death (IHTA Ss178–189)

Relief is available where quoted securities are sold for less than their probate values within 12 months of death. This applies where any quoted shares or securities or holdings in authorised unit trusts are realised within one year of death. The persons liable to pay the inheritance tax can claim that the total of the gross sale prices should be substituted for the original probate values of the investments. Where, however, the proceeds are re-invested by those persons in quoted shares or unit trusts after the death and within two months after the last sale, the above relief may be reduced or lost.

For deaths after 15 March 1992, the relief is extended to investments cancelled within 12 months of the date of death; also where quotation is suspended in the 12 months after death. It is necessary that at the date of cancellation or first anniversary, the shares are still held by the person liable for the tax.

22.12 Valuation of related property (IHTA S161)

Where the value of any of your property is less than the appropriate portion of the value of the aggregate of that and any 'related property' you must value your own property as the appropriate portion of the value of that aggregate.

'Related property' is property belonging to your spouse. It also includes property belonging to a charity, charitable trust, housing association etc. or which had belonged to it during the past five years, and came from an exempt transfer from you or your spouse after 15 April 1976.

This rule is particularly relevant to the valuation of unquoted shares. For example if you and your wife each have 40 per cent of the shares of an unquoted company, then the value of 80 per cent of the shares is normally much higher than twice the value of 40 per cent of the shares. This is because an 80 per cent holding carries with it full control of the company.

Thus the successful estate duty saving device of splitting a shareholding in a non-quoted company between your wife and yourself, so that neither of you has control, is not effective (so far as the first transfer is concerned) in producing a lower aggregate value for inheritance tax purposes.

If you inherit any related property, a special relief applies where you sell the property within three years of the death for less than the value on which tax was originally paid. Subject to various conditions, including the requirement that the sale is at arm's length for a freely negotiated price, you can claim for the related property in question to be revalued at death on the basis that it was not related to any other property.

22.13 Land sold within four years of death (IHTA Ss190–198)

Where the person paying the capital transfer tax or inheritance tax arising on death after 15 March 1990 on land or buildings sells them within four years of the death for less than their probate value, he can claim that the sale proceeds are substituted in the tax calculations. (For sales before 16 March 1993, the period was three years.)

There are a number of conditions, including the requirement that the shortfall is at least the lower of £1,000 and 5 per cent of the probate value of the land. Relief is extended regarding a compulsory purchase notified before the end of three years from death.

22.14 Inheritance tax on death (IHTA S4 & FA 1986 Sch 19)

The general rule is that if you are domiciled (or deemed domiciled – 22.4) in the UK at the time of your death, all of your assets, wherever they may be situated, form part of the *gross value* of your estate for the purposes of determining the inheritance tax payable. (The same applied for capital transfer tax.)

If you are not domiciled in the UK at your death then the tax is only chargeable on those assets which are situated in the UK (22.28).

The *net value* of your estate is determined by making certain deductions (22.14.2) from the *gross value* of all the property passing on your death.

The tax on your death is charged as if immediately before your death you made a chargeable transfer equal to the *net value* of your estate, subject to certain adjustments and exemptions (22.15) if appropriate.

For deaths after 17 March 1986, the inheritance tax rules apply and the tax is calculated from the single scale taking account of your cumulative lifetime gifts within *seven* years of death. These gifts include PETs (22.3) on which no tax was previously paid. As previously explained, death may lead not only to tax on the estate but also on lifetime gifts (22.6).

Your executors will need to apply for probate of your will. Otherwise, if you die intestate, letters of administration must be obtained. In either case, it will be necessary for an inheritance tax account to be completed (normally on Form IHT 200). At least a provisional amount of tax will need to be paid at that time. Further administrative rules appear later in this chapter (22.24).

22.14.1 **Gross value of estate** (IHTA S5)

The gross value of your estate includes all your property situated anywhere in the world, such as land, shares, the goodwill of a business, debts owing to you etc., apart from *excluded property* (22.15).

Certain other amounts must also be included in your gross estate, even though they do not belong to you or only arise after your death, such as the proceeds of a life policy held by you on your own life, or any death benefit under a pension scheme which is payable to your estate (rather than under the more usual discretionary disposal clause contained in most pension schemes).

Other amounts to be included in your gross estate are various interests in trusts (22.30). In these cases the trustees may pay the appropriate tax but the rate is calculated by reference to the value of the estate including the trust funds.

From 6 April 2006, the value of *left-over pension funds* (14.7.2) is generally to be included unless passing to a spouse, civil partner, financial dependant or for charity etc. Such funds as remain after income withdrawal will be charged when the spouse etc., dies, but related back to the original death.

22.14.2 **Net value of estate**

The more common deductions which are made from the gross value of your estate in order to arrive at its net value are as follows:

(1) Certain exempt transfers (22.17.3).
(2) Funeral expenses.
(3) Debts owing by you at the date of death which are payable in the UK. However, certain debts may be disallowed in whole or part if you had made connected gifts to the creditors, or the liability had not been incurred for full consideration for your benefit. (FA 1986 S82).
(4) Debts due to persons outside the UK are normally only deductible from the value of assets situated outside this country.
(5) Whilst legal and other professional fees owing at the death may be deducted as debts, no deduction is given for probate and executors' expenses.
(6) Liabilities for income tax and capital gains tax up to the time of death, whether or not assessments were made before that time. No deduction can be made for inheritance tax payable on your death, however, nor can tax liabilities be deducted regarding income and capital gains arising for periods subsequent to your death.

22.15 Excluded property (IHTA S6)

The following 'excluded property' must be left out of the value of your estate for capital transfer tax and inheritance tax purposes, regarding both lifetime transfers and property passing on death:

(1) Property outside the UK if you are neither domiciled nor deemed domiciled in this country.
(2) A reversionary interest unless either you bought it or it relates to the falling in of a lease which was treated as a settlement (22.30). Certain anti-avoidance rules apply to prevent misuse.
(3) Cash options under registered retirement pension schemes (14.3.2), provided an annuity becomes payable to your dependants instead of the cash option itself.
(4) Originally, certain UK government securities on which interest may be paid gross to non-residents (8.2), provided you are neither domiciled, deemed domiciled, nor ordinarily resident here. From 6 April 1998 all of your gilt-edged securities are excluded property and thus free of inheritance tax if you are neither UK domiciled nor deemed domiciled.
(5) Certain overseas pensions from former colonies etc. including death payments and returns of contributions.
(6) Savings such as national savings certificates and premium bonds, if you are domiciled in the Channel Islands or the Isle of Man.
(7) Certain property in this country belonging to visiting forces and NATO headquarters staff.

22.16 Double taxation relief (IHTA Ss158 & 159)

Various other countries also operate systems of capital transfer tax/inheritance tax and the government of the UK is empowered to enter into agreements with them for the avoidance of the double payment of such tax both here and in the other country.

Concerning capital transfer tax or inheritance tax payable on death, relief is continued for estate duty payable on the same property in other countries if there was a 'double estate duty' agreement with the countries in question as at 12 March 1975. The following countries have agreements with the UK covering estate duty and/or capital transfer tax or inheritance tax:

France	Pakistan
India	South Africa
Ireland	Sweden
Italy	Switzerland
Netherlands	United States of America

Unilateral double taxation relief is available for overseas tax paid on death or a lifetime transfer. The tax must be of a similar nature to inheritance tax and if the property is situated in the overseas country, a credit is given against the

UK tax of the amount of the overseas tax. If the property is either situated *both* in the UK and the overseas country, or in *neither* of those places, the credit against the UK tax is C × A/(A + B). A is the amount of inheritance tax, B is the overseas tax and C is the smaller of A and B.

22.17 Exempt transfers (IHTA Ss18–27)

Broadly, exempt transfers can be divided between those which apply both on death and during your life and those which are only exempt if the transfers are during your life. The first category includes transfers between your spouse and yourself.

22.17.1 Transfers between husband and wife

Transfers between your spouse and yourself both during your lives and on death were exempt from capital transfer tax and are exempt from inheritance tax. (Thus lifetime gifts are not even treated as PETs – 22.3.) From 5 December 2005, this also applies to transfers between civil partners in accordance with the Civil Partnership Act 2004 (6.9).

Currently, full exemption does not apply if the recipient of the property is not domiciled (or deemed domiciled) in this country (17.2) (unless the donor is also neither domiciled nor deemed domiciled here). In this case, only the first £55,000 transferred to the non-domiciled spouse is exempt. This resembles the previous estate duty relief.

The Government has announced, but given no details of two proposed changes in this respect in FA 2013, so as to:

(1) increase the exemption available for such gifts and
(2) provide an option for a non-domiciled individual to elect to be treated as domiciled here solely for UK inheritance tax purposes.

Under the estate duty rules, if you left property in trust for your wife for life, when you died duty was paid; but none was payable on her subsequent death. (If her death is after 12 November 1974, no capital transfer tax or inheritance tax applies.) If, however, the first death occurs after 12 November 1974, relief applies so that no tax is payable on property passing to the surviving spouse and this is preserved under the FA 2006 rules (22.30). For this reason, when the latter dies, full inheritance tax is payable on the trust property at that time.

22.17.2 Exempt transfers – lifetime gifts

The following transfers are only exempt if made by an individual during his life. They do not normally apply to transfers made by trustees nor to assets passing on death. In any one fiscal year to 5 April, you can make all of these exempt transfers cumulatively and so can your spouse. The rules apply not only to chargeable transfers but also to PETs (22.3). Thus if a transfer which would otherwise be a PET is an exempt transfer, it will not attract inheritance tax, even if you die within seven years.

(1) *Transfers each year up to a value of £3,000.* If you do not use up the full £3,000 allowance in one year, you can carry the unused part forward for one year only. If your transfers taken against this exemption reach £3,000 in any year, you have nothing available to carry forward, even though you may have had £3,000 brought forward from the previous year.

For example if you made no chargeable transfers in the year to 5 April 2012, you have £6,000 available for exempt transfers under this category in the year to 5 April 2013. If, however, you transferred £500 in the year to 5 April 2012 you have £2,500 carried forward and so can transfer £5,500 in the year to 5 April 2013.

In any year to 5 April, your annual exemption first reduces those lifetime transfers which are not PETs; and then your PETs (FA 1986 Sch 19). (Deaths within seven years may cause the reallocation of your annual exemptions, particularly regarding amounts originally set against your 'non-PETS' for the following year.)

(2) *Small gifts.* Outright gifts to any one person not exceeding £250 for each year to 5 April are exempt. The £250 exemption cannot be used against gifts larger than that amount. Thus you can make an unlimited number of exempt gifts of £250 to different people but any gifts of £251 or more must be set against the £3,000 and other exemptions with the excess being potentially taxable (if the nil rate band has been exhausted).

(3) *Normal expenditure out of income.* To qualify under this exemption, a transfer must be part of your normal expenditure. This means that there must be an element of regularity. Life assurance premiums (9.2) are particularly suited for this. Further conditions are that the transfer is out of your after-tax income and you are left with enough income (taking one year with another) to maintain your usual standard of living.

Life policy premium payments will not qualify for this exemption, however, if they are made out of an annuity purchased on your life, unless you can show that the policy and the annuity were effected completely independently of each other. This rule even applies if you make gifts out of your annuity receipts and the donee pays the premiums on the policy on your life.

If you buy an annuity, and make transfers from it, only the income proportion of the annuity (9.14) is treated as your income for the purposes of the normal expenditure rule; the capital element is not.

(4) *Gifts in consideration of marriage* made to one of the partners of the marriage or settled on the partners and their children etc. The limits are £5,000 if the donor is a parent of one of the marriage partners, £2,500 if a grandparent or great-grandparent or one of the parties themselves, or otherwise £1,000. (Eligibility for relief extends to marriage gifts from settlements where an interest in possession ends (22.30).)

22.17.3 Other exempt transfers

Subject to the particular rules, the following transfers are exempt both if made during your life and on death. They also apply to trusts (22.30).

(1) *Transfers in the course of trade etc.* are exempt if allowed as deductions in computing the profits for income tax purposes (11.3). This applies equally to professions and vocations, as well as allowable deductions against other forms of profits or gains for the purposes of income tax and corporation tax.
(2) *Gifts to charities* are exempt without limit. Gifts to settlements for charitable purposes are covered by the exemption, as are gifts to charities from other trusts.
(3) *Gifts to political parties* are wholly exempt. For these purposes, a 'political party' is one with at least two members sitting in Parliament or one member and not less than 150,000 votes for its candidates at the last General Election.
(4) *Gifts for national purposes etc.* made to the National Trust, National Heritage Memorial Fund, National Gallery, British Museum and similar organisations, including universities and their libraries as well as museums and art galleries maintained by local authorities or universities.
(5) *Gifts for public benefit* of property deemed by the Treasury to be of outstanding scenic, historic, scientific or artistic merit including land, buildings, pictures, books, manuscripts, works of art etc.
(6) *PETs (22.3) of property held for national purposes etc.* This exemption applies where, prior to the death of the recipient, the property is sold by private treaty (or gifted) to an organisation as mentioned in (4) previously.
(7) *Gifts of shares* to an employee trust, provided it will then hold at least half of the ordinary shares of the company (IHTA S28). Exemption now extends to share ownership plans (FA 2000 S134).
(8) *Gifts to housing associations* or sales of land to them at undervalue (IHTA S24A).

22.18 Relief for business property (IHTA Ss103–114)

In general, 'relevant business property' qualifies for business property relief. 'Relevant business property' includes a business or part of a business; shares and securities owned by the controller of a company; unquoted minority shareholdings and land, buildings, plant and machinery used in your partnership or a company which you control. Control of a company for these purposes includes shareholdings which are 'related property' (22.12) in relation to your own shares.

Normally, investment company and land or share-dealing company shareholdings do not qualify for the relief. However, UK stockjobbing and 'market making' qualify for the relief. You must normally own the business property, or property which has directly replaced it for at least two years prior to the transfer, until which time it is not 'relevant business property' and no relief is due.

The rates of relief are 100 per cent and 50 per cent. Prior to 10 March 1992 the relief was 50 per cent and 30 per cent. The scope of the 100 per cent relief became wider on 6 April 1996.

Relief is available as follows (pre-6 April 1996 figures in brackets where different):

(1) The whole or part of a business:	100 per cent
(2) Quoted shares or securities in a trading company which you control:	50 per cent
(3) Property transferred by you which is used in a trade by a company controlled by you or partnership in which you are a partner:	50 per cent
(4) Unquoted shares in a trading company	
Over 25 per cent voting power:	100 per cent
25 per cent or less without control (including related property):	100 per cent (50 per cent)
(5) Holding in a USM company	
Over 25 per cent voting power:	100 per cent
25 per cent or less without control (including related property):	100 per cent (50 per cent)

The 50 per cent relief category is extended to cover the transfer of land or buildings owned by a trust. Immediately before the transfer, the assets must have been used in his own trade by a person beneficially entitled to an interest in possession in the trust.

Business property relief is available against PETs which fall into charge following the donor's death within seven years. However, the relief is lost if the recipient disposes of the property before the donor's death. But relief is not lost if the gifted business property is disposed of, but replaced by other qualifying assets within three years. Also, the property must remain 'relevant business property' during the seven-year period. If these conditions are satisfied for only part of the property, the relief is proportionately reduced. These rules also apply to other lifetime transfers within seven years of death.

Where part of an estate is left to the surviving spouse and thus attracts no tax, and part to others, the allocation of business property relief and relief for agricultural property (22.21) was open to abuse. However, from 18 March 1986 specific gifts of such property must be reduced by the relief. Otherwise, the relief is spread proportionately over the estate.

22.19 Waivers of dividends and remuneration (IHTA Ss14 & 15)

If you waive any remuneration to which you are entitled this normally does not produce any capital transfer tax or inheritance tax liability, provided the amount waived would otherwise have been assessable to income tax under

Schedule E (10.1) and your employer obtains no income tax or corporation tax relief for the waived remuneration.

No inheritance tax accrues on the waiver of any dividend to which you have a right, provided you waive the dividend within the 12 months before it is due. These waiver rules apply from the inception of capital transfer tax.

22.20 Conditional exemption for certain objects and buildings etc. (IHTA Ss27, 30–32A, 57A, 78–79A & Sch 4)

Property similar to that mentioned in (4) and (5) above (22.17.3), is exempted from inheritance tax on death, provided the recipient undertakes to keep it in the country, preserve it and allow reasonable access to the public. If it is later sold, the tax becomes payable unless the sale is to an institution such as the British Museum, National Gallery or National Trust.

For relief claims made after 16 March 1998, there is normally a 2-year time limit. Furthermore, chattels associated with heritage buildings will need to be of pre-eminent quality and future undertakings must give access to the public without prior appointment.

A similar relief applies to lifetime transfers subject to various conditions. The recipient must give the required undertaking. The relief extends to historical and artistic buildings and objects comprised in settlements. It also applies to settlements set up to maintain historic buildings and now objects historically associated with them, together with land of outstanding interest. Such settlements must tie up the capital for at least six years for maintenance purposes only, but after that funds may be withdrawn subject to inheritance tax in certain circumstances.

From an Appointed Day (on or after 1 April 2012) FA 2012 provides that no charges to or claw-backs of relief from inheritance tax shall arise as a result qualifying gifts of pre-eminent assets to appropriate institutions, so as to qualify for income tax or corporation tax relief as *Gifts to the Nation.*

Special rules apply regarding maintenance settlements for approved objects and buildings etc. Provided the HMRC (previously the Treasury) are satisfied that the trusts and trustees comply with certain requirements, transfers to such a settlement are exempt (22.17.3) for inheritance purposes. In general the trust funds must be used for the maintenance of approved assets for at least six years.

The exemption also applies where someone with a life interest in a trust dies and within two years the property goes into a heritage maintenance fund. Heritage property can be offered in lieu of inheritance tax and, from that date, there is the option of calculating the value of the property at the date of the offer instead of acceptance.

Land is exempted which is essential to a building of historic or architectural interest. Previously exemption depended on the land touching the building, but this is no longer necessary.

22.21 Relief for agricultural property (IHTA Ss115–124A)

Under the rules which apply after 9 March 1981 you must have either occupied the property for the purposes of agriculture for at least two years before transferring it, or owned it for seven years up to that time, with others farming. The rules are relaxed where you inherit the property or where you have replaced one agricultural property by another. Agriculture includes stud farming for the purposes of the relief and also (from 29 November 1994) the cultivation of short rotation coppice (FA 1995 S154). From 26 November 1996, farmland which has been dedicated to wildlife habitats will also be eligible for relief subject to the rules (FA 1997 S94). From 22 April 2009, relief is extended to agricultural property situated in any EEA country (previously the UK, Channel Islands and Isle of Man only). This extension is retroactive and enables values for agricultural property to be recognised and an appropriate part of inheritance tax paid on or after 23 April 2003 to be reclaimed, subject to the rules. The earliest time limit for lodging claims was 21 April 2010, but eventually the new four years time limit will apply (FA 2009).

The relief is 100 per cent if you enjoy the right to vacant possession or can obtain this within the next 12 months. 100 per cent relief also applies to transfers of tenanted farmland where the tenancy starts after 1 September 1995. Where a tenancy is acquired by succession following the previous tenant's death, it is treated as a tenancy starting from the date of death.

Otherwise, the relief is normally 50 per cent, which applies to existing tenanted situations etc. Prior to 10 March 1992, the rates were 50 per cent and 30 per cent. If you qualified for the higher relief under the old but not the new rules, you still obtain this regarding property held at 9 March 1981 and transferred after that date, up to the old limit of £250,000 or 1,000 acres if more valuable. The excess is then relieved at the lower rate which is now 50 per cent.

By concession, 100 per cent relief (not 50 per cent) applies on your transfer of tenanted agricultural land, where you have the right to vacant possession within 24 months; also where the value transferred is broadly the vacant possession value of the property. This concession applies for transfers after 12 February 1995 and earlier cases which were still open. Another concession, operative from the same time, allows 50 per cent relief on certain farm cottages even though the occupier has retired.

The grant of a tenancy of agricultural property is not to be treated as a transfer of value if it is made for full consideration (IHTA S16).

Similar rules to those for business property relief apply regarding lifetime gifts within seven years of death and the allocation of relief to partially exempt estates (22.18). Thus the relief is lost if the recipient disposes of the agricultural property before the donor's death, unless it is replaced within three (previously one) years by other agricultural property.

22.22 Woodlands (IHTA Ss125–130)

Inheritance tax relief against the charge at death on growing timber is available, provided you either owned the woodlands for at least five years, or you acquired them by gift or inheritance. From 22 April 2009, relief is extended to woodlands situated in any EEA country (previously the UK only). This extension is retroactive and enables inheritance tax paid on or after 23 April 2003 to be reclaimed, subject to the rules, where the timber remains unsold. The earliest time limit for lodging claims was 21 April 2010, but eventually the new four years time limit will apply (FA 2009).

Under the relieving provisions, provided the inheritor elects within two years of it, tax is not charged on your death. If, however, before the recipient dies, the timber is sold or given away, tax is charged on the proceeds or value of the gift. The tax rate is found by adding such proceeds to the estate at your death. Remember that the relief applies only to the timber and not the land on which it grows.

Business property relief is normally available on woodlands managed on a commercial basis.

Where the disposal follows a change in tax rates the respective new rates (26.4) are applied, even if the death was before they took effect.

22.23 Quick succession relief (IHTA S141)

This relief applies to reduce the tax payable on death where the deceased himself received chargeable transfers on which the tax was paid within five years of his death. The deduction is broadly a proportion of the original tax, being 100 per cent, 80 per cent, 60 per cent, 40 per cent or 20 per cent, depending on whether the period between the transfer and the death is one, two, three, four or five years or less in each case. Where there are more than two transfers of the same property within five years of each other, special rules apply.

22.24 Administration and collection (IHTA Ss215–261 etc.)

Inheritance tax (and capital transfer tax) are under the care and management of the Board of HMRC. Generally speaking the rules for administration, appeals and penalties resemble those for income tax (16.9.2). From 1 April 2009, inheritance tax falls within the new regime for appeals and penalties described elsewhere in this book (16.5–16.5.3 & 16.9.6).

Chargeable transfers must be reported to HMRC in an inheritance tax return within 12 months from the end of the month of transfer or death.

The tax chargeable on death must be paid on at least an estimated figure before probate is granted (22.14). Since FA 2004 permitted the simplification of the accounts rules, except for large estates and a few others, an IHT account will only be necessary if tax is payable. Otherwise, the Probate Service will deal with the formalities for both tax and probate purposes. The first category is the 'low value estate' worth no more than 325,000 (£312,000 before 6 April 2009), provided that overseas assets do not exceed £100,000, settled property passing to others than a surviving spouse does not exceed £150,000 and that a number of further rules, especially regarding gifts made in the last seven years are met. Similar procedures apply to 'exempt estates' (eg due to spouse exemption) which do not exceed £1 million and to estates of 'foreign domiciliaries', who were not born in and have never been domiciled in the UK, provided that their UK estate does not exceed £100,000 and comprises only cash or quoted shares. In other cases, the inheritance tax is payable out of the residuary estate unless there is a contrary direction in the will. However, property situated outside the UK continues to bear its own tax. Recipients of PETs are primarily responsible for the relevant tax.

From 31 March 2003, an optional electronic transfer method has been introduced for paying inheritance tax from bank and building society accounts owned by the deceased.

FA 2004 included certain changes to the IHT penalty regime. For example, where fraudulent or negligent material is submitted, there was no penalty if no additional IHT resulted. Late delivery of an IHT account involved a penalty of £100, unless the tax was less or there was a reasonable excuse.

Interest on unpaid tax runs from when the tax is due. The due date is six months after the end of the month in which death occurs. For lifetime transfers it is six months after the end of the month in which the transfer is made. In the case of transfers between 5 April and 1 October, the due date is 30 April in the following year.

The interest you pay is not deductible for income tax purposes. If you overpay inheritance tax (or capital transfer tax), you will receive non-taxable interest at the appropriate rates, up to the date on which the repayment of the excess tax is made.

From 16 December 1986 to 28 September 2009, a single rate of interest applied to overdue and overpaid inheritance tax. However, from 29 September 2009 rates of 3 per cent and 0.5 per cent respectively have applied. Recent interest rates have varied as follows:

From	Rate %	From	Rate %
6 February 2000	5	6 September 2006	4
6 May 2001	4	6 August 2007	5
6 November 2001	3	6 January 2008	4
6 August 2003	2	6 November 2008	3
6 December 2003	3	6 January 2009	2
6 September 2004	4	27 January 2009	1
6 September 2005	3	24 March 2009	0

From	Overdue rate %	Overpaid rate %
29 September 2009	3	0.5

FA 1999 updated and strengthened certain inheritance tax administration and collection provisions. For example, personal representatives now need to provide extensive information regarding gifts during the seven years before death. Also, HMRC's charge for unpaid tax has been tightened and their information-seeking powers increased.

Higher penalties were introduced. For example, incorrect information provided by those liable to inheritance tax could give rise to penalties of up to £3,000 plus the extra tax in cases of fraud or up to £1,500 plus the extra tax concerning negligence.

22.25 Payment by instalments of tax on death (IHTA Ss227–229 & FA 1986 Sch 19)

Inheritance tax on death on certain assets may be paid by annual instalments over ten years. This applies to land and buildings, controlling holdings of shares in companies and certain other unquoted shares, as well as business assets. Also, shares dealt in on the USM are included. (PETs which become chargeable only qualify for the instalments basis if the recipient had kept the property until the death of the donor.)

Instalments paid on time concerning the shares and business assets mentioned above are free of interest. Land and buildings qualify for this relief only if they are held as business assets, otherwise interest is payable, currently at 3 per cent. Tax in respect of property qualifying for agricultural relief may be paid in interest free instalments as above.

22.26 Payment of tax on lifetime gifts by instalments

The above provisions apply to lifetime transfers if the donee bears the tax and for settled property which is retained in a settlement. If interest is payable it is currently at 3 per cent. The interest free category is extended to include lifetime disposals of timber. In the case of minority holdings of unquoted shares, these must be worth at least £20,000, in order to qualify for the instalments option; also being at least 10 per cent holdings. The instalments basis may also be allowed where paying the tax in one sum would cause undue hardship and the recipient keeps the shares.

22.27 Inheritance tax and life assurance

Life assurance policies can be used to create a fund to pay future inheritance tax and to facilitate gifts to your beneficiaries.

If you effect a policy on your life for your own benefit, the proceeds payable on your death will be taxable as part of your net estate (22.14.1).

22.27.1 **Policies written in trust**

You may effect a policy in a non-discretionary trust for some other person or persons, such as for example your wife and children. In this case the policy proceeds will not be paid into your own estate but will be paid to the trustees for the beneficiaries. Each premium payment, however, will constitute a separate potentially exempt transfer (22.3) by you. Thus they could be taxable if you die within seven years, unless an exemption applies such as the £3,000 or £250 reliefs (22.17.2), or the normal expenditure rule (22.17.2), or the policy is for your wife. If premiums are paid to a discretionary trust, each premium will be chargeable at the time and if no exemption applies, may give rise to recalculation of tax if death occurs within seven years (22.5).

Policies written in trust before 22 March 2006 are protected from the new rules (22.30) even if premiums are paid subsequently. However, such policies effected from that date may give rise to inheritance tax under the new rules, if the *value* exceeds the threshold (£325,000 etc.) but only at a maximum rate of 6 per cent after 10 years. (Bare trusts are still excluded).

22.27.2 **Gifts of policies**

Where you write a policy in trust, this is one way of gifting it. Another way is to assign the policy. Unless it is covered by exemptions (22.27.1) there will usually be a potentially exempt transfer. The transfer value is normally the greater of your gross premium payments and the surrender value of the policy. Your assignment will be potentially exempt if it is to an individual or certain kinds of trust (interest in possession, accumulation and maintenance, or for the disabled). If you make cash gifts to cover subsequent premiums, these gifts will normally be potentially exempt.

However, for policies effected after 17 March 1986, the gifts with reservation rules (22.29.4) may apply. Broadly if you have a retained benefit in the policy the proceeds will form part of your estate at death.

22.27.3 **'Life of another' policies**

If someone else effects a policy on your life and pays the premiums, then the proceeds are not taxable on your death. This is known as a 'life of another' policy. If the person who effects the policy predeceases you, however, then the surrender value of the policy at the date of death of that person is normally included in his taxable estate.

22.28 Property outside Great Britain

Since if you are neither domiciled nor deemed domiciled (22.4) in the UK, you will only normally pay inheritance tax on your assets situated here, it is important to ascertain the situation of particular property. The situation of property for inheritance tax purposes is normally deemed to be as follows:

(1) Cash – its physical location.
(2) Bank accounts – the location of the bank or branch (see also below).
(3) Registered securities – the location of the share register.
(4) Bearer securities – the location of the title documents.
(5) Land and buildings – their actual location.
(6) Business assets – the place where the business is conducted.
(7) Debts – the residence of the debtor.

Foreign currency accounts with UK banks are exempted from inheritance tax if the deceased is not UK domiciled. This also applies if the deceased had an interest in possession (22.30) in a settlement with such an account, unless the settlor was UK domiciled, resident or ordinarily resident, when he made the settlement or the trustees were so situated immediately before the death (IHTA S158).

22.29 Miscellaneous points

22.29.1 **Close companies** (IHTA Ss94–102 & FA 1986 Sch 19)

There are rules under which inheritance tax may be charged where a close company (13.17) makes a transfer of value. Broadly, tax may be charged on the company as if each of the participators (13.17.2) had made a proportionate transfer according to his or her interest in the company. The rules are extended to cover close companies being owned by trusts or being their beneficiaries.

Transfers of values arising as above from alterations in the capital and associated rights in a close company may attract inheritance tax at once. They are not PETs (22.3).

22.29.2 **Free loans** (IHTA S29)

From 6 April 1976 to 5 April 1981, subject to various exceptions, if you allowed someone else the use of money or property at no interest or less than the market rate, you were treated as making a chargeable transfer for each year to 5 April that the arrangement continued. These provisions ceased to have effect after 5 April 1981 although interest-free loans for a fixed stated period can still be treated as a chargeable transfer under general principles.

22.29.3 **Associated operations** (IHTA S268)

Special rules enable HMRC to treat two or more transactions related to a certain property as forming one 'chargeable transfer'. Where transactions at different times are treated as associated operations, the chargeable transfer is treated as taking place at the time of the last of these transactions.

22.29.4 **Gifts with reservation** (FA 1986 S102–102C & Sch 20)

If you make a gift after 17 March 1986 but reserve some benefit, this will normally result in the property remaining yours for inheritance tax purposes on your death. (This could also apply if you later enjoy the benefit of the gifted property.) However, if you subsequently release the reservation, you will be treated as making a PET (22.3) or chargeable transfer at that time. In contrast to PETs, HMRC may require a return to be made for a gift with reservation.

A particular example is where you gift a house but remain living there. The rule does not apply if your benefit is minimal (for example, you do not live in the house but only pay occasional visits). If you give full value for any benefit (for example, pay a full rent for the house), the rule is also set aside. There is also an exception where the reservation represents reasonable provision by a relative for the care and maintenance of an elderly or infirm donor whose circumstances have changed since making the gift.

The rules regarding gifts of homes have been strengthened with effect from 9 March 1999. If you make such a gift, it will be treated as being 'with reservation' if there is an arrangement for you to occupy the property to a material degree without paying full consideration. Exceptions include where you are only allowed to occupy the property once the interest which you gifted has come to an end.

The rules do not normally catch regular premium insurance policies made before 18 March 1986 and not altered since then.

It was held in a decided case (*CIR* v *Eversden*), that gifts made by a married person were not caught if routed through a trust for the spouse. However, such gifts with reservation made after 19 June 2003 are caught.

The FA 2006 trust rules (22.30) include provisions to treat you as making a gift with reservation where you own an interest in settled property which ceases after 21 March 2006, whilst you retain the use of the property.

22.29.5 **Family maintenance** (IHTA S11)

If you make any of the following gifts during your life, they are exempt:

(1) For the maintenance, education etc. of your child, former wife or illegitimate child.
(2) For the maintenance or education of a child not in his parent's care, who has been in your care during substantial periods of his minority.
(3) For the care or maintenance of a dependent relative.

22.29.6 **Deeds of family arrangement** (IHTA S17)

Inheritance tax is not charged on certain variations in the destination of property passing on death. Nor is it charged on the disclaimer of title to property passing on death. The variation or disclaimer must be within two years of the death. An election to HMRC was required within six months of a variation. However, provided a variation made after 31 July 2002 states that it is to take effect for inheritance tax purposes, no election is needed. (The same applies for capital gains tax – 21.10.3.)

This exemption operates similarly, but without time limit, where a surviving spouse's life interest under an intestacy is redeemed. It also applies if an interest in settled property is disclaimed unless there is some consideration in money or money's worth.

Disclaimers are effective for inheritance tax purposes. These involve one or more beneficiaries disclaiming their entitlement. As a result, the assets return to the estate and are dealt with according to the directions of the will or as on intestacy.

22.29.7 **Pre-owned assets**

Legislation in FA 2004 (Sch 15) took effect from 2005–06 and operates by imposing an income tax charge to counter certain estate planning benefits. The rules may catch you if you have disposed of assets since March 1986, but continue to enjoy benefits from them; also where you have funded the purchase of an asset for a third party. The stated objectives are contrived arrangements, but there are various exemptions and the rules are complicated.

An annual cash value will be quantified for your chargeable benefits for 2005–06 and subsequent years, which will be ignored if no more than £5,000, otherwise being added to your taxable income. Market rentals are to be used for land, with imputed percentages of capital value applying for chattels and intangible assets.

If you were caught by the above, transitional rules enabled you to elect by 31 January 2007 that the charge shall not apply for 2005–06 and subsequent years. You will then be regarded for IHT purposes as if the property in question forms part of your estate. This resembles the 'gifts with reservation' rules (22.29.4). Alternatively, you might have taken the option to wind up your original arrangements.

As from 21 March 2007, FA 2007 enables HMRC to accept late elections, including those for 2005–06, which were due on 31 January 2007. Any election must start from the first tax year in which you fall within the scope of these provisions and the normal time limit for electing will be 31 January following the end of that tax year.

22.30 Settled property (IHTA Pt III)

The rules concerning inheritance tax (and previously capital transfer tax) in relation to settled property are most detailed and the following are just a few guidelines, which are subject to important changes introduced by FA 2006. (These mainly cause more trusts to be taxed like discretionary ones):

(1) Broadly any settlement is subject to the inheritance tax rules on its worldwide assets, if at the time it was made the settlor was domiciled in the UK. Otherwise only assets situated in this country (22.28) are caught.
(2) The settlement of any property after 26 March 1974 is itself treated as a chargeable transfer by the settlor. However, after 17 March 1986, settlements on accumulation and maintenance trusts (22.30.1) or for the disabled were classified as PETs (22.3). Thus any property which you settled in this way only attracted inheritance tax if you died within seven years.
(3) If you have a pre-22 March 2006 interest in possession in any settled property for the time being (for example you receive the income as of right), the property itself is treated as yours for inheritance tax purposes. Thus if your interest ends, you will be treated as making a transfer of the value of the property concerned. The tax is calculated on the basis of your cumulative transfers to that time. You can deduct your £3,000 annual exemption (22.17.2) and marriage allowance if applicable (ITA S57).
(4) From 17 March 1987 lifetime transactions involving interest in possession settlements were classed as PETs. This covered gifts setting them up, transfers out and changes in the beneficial interests.
(5) No inheritance tax is payable if you obtain an absolute interest in property in which you previously had a pre-22 March 2006 life interest (or other interest in possession). Similarly, tax normally is not payable on the reversion to you in your lifetime (or your spouse within two years of your death) of property which you previously settled. However, this rule normally no longer applies to discretionary settlements (22.30.2).
(6) Special rules applied to trusts where there was no interest in possession – particularly discretionary trusts etc. and accumulation and maintenance settlements (22.30.1).
(7) Quick succession relief is given if an interest in possession comes to an end within five years of a previous chargeable transfer of the settled property. The relief is now allowed against the tax due on the later transfer etc. but is calculated as a *percentage of the tax payable* on the first transfer. The percentage is 100 per cent, 80 per cent, 60 per cent, 40 per cent or 20 per cent where the interval is not more than one, two, three, four, or five years respectively.
(8) Registered pension schemes and charitable trusts were normally exempted from inheritance tax as are employee and newspaper trusts (IHTA Ss76, 86 and 87); also certain 'protective trusts' and trusts for the mentally disabled (treated as having a life interest in property settled for them after 9 March 1981). Where property was held temporarily on such trusts, the tax charge was proportionately reduced on a time basis (FA 1984 S102).
(9) The above, 22.30.1 and 22.30.2 are subject to changes introduced by FA 2006, which apply for new trusts created from 22 March 2006 and additions to existing ones from that date. Otherwise, existing trusts came

within the new rules from 6 April 2008. The main effect is that the discretionary trust rules (22.30.2) will apply in most cases and so the special treatment for accumulation and maintenance trusts and interest in possession ones generally will cease, except regarding certain will trusts etc. (22.30.3).

22.30.1 Accumulation and maintenance settlements (old rules)

Accumulation and maintenance settlements with no fixed interests in possession for one or more beneficiaries up to an age not exceeding 25 were not subjected to the periodic charge (22.30.2); nor was inheritance tax charged on the capital distributed to those beneficiaries. This relief covered for example a settlement under which your son obtained an interest in possession at the age of 25 and at 35 got the capital, the income being accumulated up to 25 apart from various payments for his maintenance. No inheritance tax was payable during the currency of the trust, nor when your son became entitled to the income at 25 nor the capital at 35.

Relief broadly only applied if either not more than 25 years had passed since the original settlement date (or when it first became accumulating); or if all beneficiaries were grandchildren of a common grandparent (or their widows, widowers, children, step-children etc.).

Any payments into accumulation and maintenance settlements after 17 March 1986 were PETs (22.3). Thus no inheritance tax was payable regarding their creation unless the settlor died within seven years.

22.30.2 Discretionary trusts etc.

The following rules apply where there is no interest in possession in *all or part of the property* and also where the new rules apply (22.30.3), subject to some modifications.

(1) The principal charge to inheritance tax (previously capital transfer tax) is the *periodic* charge. This usually falls on every tenth anniversary of the date of the settlement occurring after 31 March 1983. (Where a transfer requiring court proceedings was made in the year to 31 March 1983, the onset of the periodic charge was delayed until after that date.) The charge is at 30 per cent of the lifetime inheritance tax rate (itself now half of the full 40 per cent rate) which would apply to the assets held on discretionary trusts (taking the $^{N}/_{40}$ fraction for additions during the ten year period – see (3) below).

(2) In calculating the rates of tax which apply, you must accumulate transfers made by the settlor in the seven years immediately prior to the creation of the settlement and other settlements made by him on the same day; but this does not apply to a pre-26 March 1974 trust. For periodic charges before 18 March 1986, you needed to accumulate transfers by the settlor in the *ten* years before the creation of the settlement.

(3) For a settlement made between 26 March 1974 and 9 March 1982, distributions of capital made in the preceding ten years are taken into account in calculating the rate of tax on the first periodic charge. An exemption applies for transfers to charities and benevolent funds for employees (this also applies to pre-27 March 1974 trusts).
(4) Interim charges are made on distributions of capital to beneficiaries between periodic charges, but only $^{N}/_{40}$ of the full tax is charged on each distribution. (N is the number of completed three month periods for which the property has been held on discretionary trusts during the current ten year period – see (1) above.)
(5) Previously, tax was charged on the value of the trust property leaving the trust. However, after 8 March 1982, the charge is based on the reduction in the value of trust property, which could be greater.
(6) If property becomes settled under a will or intestacy it is taken to enter the settlement at death. Where the death is after 12 March 1984 any such property which is distributed within two years of death to a charity, employee trust etc. is treated as if distributed at the time of death (FA 1984 S103).
(7) Property passing directly from one discretionary settlement to another is treated as remaining in the first for the purposes of the discretionary settlement rules. However, after 14 March 1983 this does not apply to certain reversionary interests existing before 10 December 1981 (FA 1984 S104).
(8) Non-resident trustees are liable for the periodic ten-year charge (see above).
(9) Transfers into discretionary settlements are charged to inheritance tax at half the rates applicable at death. If death occurred within three years and the original transfer was before 18 March 1986, the tax was increased by using the full rates at death (22.5.1). Subsequent to that date, if death occurs broadly within five years of a post-17 March 1986 transfer, the tax is likely to be increased, subject to tapering relief (22.6). If death is within three years of the transfer, 100 per cent of tax at full rates is due, 80 per cent in the fourth year and 60 per cent in the fifth year.
(10) HM Treasury announced its intention to publish a formal consultation paper in June 2012 on the possible simplification of the calculation of periodic and exit charges for trusts. Legislation may reasonably be expected to be introduced in FA 2013 – possibly with retrospective effect. No further details were available as this edition went to press.

22.30.3 The new trust rules

New trust rules introduced on 22 March 2006 included a transitional period (see (3) and (5) below) to 5 April 2008, which was retroactively extended to 5 October 2008 by FA 2008.

(1) With the exceptions noted below, accumulation and maintenance (A&M) and interest in possession (IIP) trusts are subject to inheritance tax in the same way as discretionary trusts from 22 March 2006 for new trusts and 6 April 2008 for existing ones. However, additions to trusts from 22 March 2006 came under the new rules at once.

(2) The discretionary trust rules (20.30.2) now apply to capital introduced from 22 March 2006, together with the periodic charge and exit charges. However, ten-year anniversaries will be based on the original date of settlement and the first periodic charge reduced if the period partly falls under the old regime. For example if a trust was set up in November 1998, the first ten-year anniversary will be in November 2008 and the rate of charge will only be one-twentieth of the normal charge.

(3) The main exclusions from the new regime are as follows:
   - Existing A&M trusts which provide for the assets to go to a beneficiary absolutely at 18, or were so modified by 5 October (previously April) 2008.
   - A&M trusts created on death for a child of the settlor vesting at 25. However, a special IHT charge of up to 4.2 per cent may apply.
   - Certain trusts for the disabled which you create during your lifetime or on death.

(4) Existing IIP trusts remain under the old rules until the interest as at 22 March 2006 in the property ends. If someone then takes the property absolutely, the previous beneficiary will be treated as making a PET or it will be a transfer on death. Will trusts for spouses are generally excluded.

(5) You could prolong the time that a pre-existing IIP trust remains under the old rules, if:
   - between 22 March 2006 and 5 October (previously April) 2008, all or part of your IIP was converted into one or more fresh IIPs *(transitional serial interests)* for beneficiaries with a longer life expectancy. The whole of your interest had to be given up, if you wished the transaction to be a PET; or
   - after 5 October (previously April) 2008, your spouse (or civil partner) acquires such an IIP on your death.

(6) FA 2008 clarified retroactively that the beneficiary of a transitional serial interest can be the person who held the IIP on 22 March 2006.

22.31 Avoiding double charges (FA 1986 S104)

Rules were introduced to prevent double charges to inheritance tax on transfers of value and other events occurring after 17 March 1986. The rules in part took the place of the previous rules regarding mutual transfers. The situations covered include where a PET (22.3) becomes chargeable and, immediately before the death, the estate includes property acquired from the person who received the PET for less than full price.

22.32 Example: Calculation of inheritance tax payable

Mr A, having made no gifts relevant for capital transfer tax or inheritance tax, gives £61,000 to his son on 30 June 2012 and £100,000 to his wife on 15 September 2012. He dies on 31 May 2013 leaving an estate valued at £500,000, bequeathed as to £60,000 to his wife, £20,000 to charity and the remainder to his son, including his non-quoted shares in a family trading company valued at £120,000.

Inheritance tax is payable as follows:

	£	£
30 June 2012 – gift to son		61,000
Less: Annual exemption 2011–12		
brought forward	3,000	
Annual exemption 2012–13	3,000	6,000
Potentially exempt (22.3)		55,000
15 September 2012 – gift to wife is exempt provided she is UK domiciled (17.2)		
Estate at death 31 May 2013		500,000
Less: Bequests free of inheritance tax:		
To wife	60,000	
To charity	20,000	80,000
		420,000
Less: Business property relief (22.18)		
100% x £120,000		120,000
		300,000
Potentially exempt transfer 30 June 2012		55,000
		355,000
Inheritance tax on £355,000 : £325,000	Nil	–
£30,000	40%	£ 12,000

Chapter 23

AN OUTLINE OF VAT

23.1 Introduction

VAT was introduced into the UK on 1 April 1973 with an original rate of 10 per cent. On 18 June 1979 a single rate of 15 per cent replaced the then 8 per cent standard and 12½ per cent higher rates. This rate was increased to 17½ per cent from 1 April 1991 (5 per cent now applying in isolated cases – 23.15). As a temporary measure, the standard rate was reduced to 15 per cent from 1 December 2008 reverting to 17½ per cent on 1 January 2010. To combat abuse of the temporary reduction, a supplementary charge of 2½ per cent applied from 25 November 2008 to specified cases of supply to customers who cannot recover all the VAT or from 1 April 2009 where abnormal pre-payments occurred.

From 4 January 2011, the standard rate increased to 20 per cent and detailed anti-forestalling rules applied a 2½ per cent charge to counter a range of abnormal invoicing arrangements between connected parties and any unusual supplies totalling more than £100,000. The rules applied from 22 June 2010, when a detailed guide was published by HMRC.

All other countries now in the European Community have introduced a similar tax and the coverage, but not the rates, has (at least in theory) been harmonised. It is beyond the scope of this book to give more than a brief outline of the provisions of VAT, which has been under the control and management of HM Revenue and Customs (HMRC) since 18 April 2005, when HM Customs and Excise merged with the Inland Revenue (CRCA 2005).

VAT in the UK is imposed:

(1) on imports of goods by any person into the UK (subject to special EC rules – 23.17);
(2) on the supply (such as sale, hire and HP) of goods and services (which together comprise virtually all supplies) by a business in the UK; and
(3) in certain circumstances the import of services by a business.

Hence the tax is payable whenever goods or services pass from one business to another or to a private consumer, although in the former case it is frequently refunded.

After the end of each accounting period for the tax (usually a period of three months) each business has to render a *return* to HMRC of all its 'outputs', that is, the supplies of goods and services it has made during the period to other businesses or to consumers; and has to account to HMRC one month after the end of the period for VAT on the prices (before tax) of those outputs. Each business is, at the same time, normally allowed a credit for the VAT on its 'inputs' in that period, that is, goods imported by it and goods and services supplied to it for the purposes of the business. Unlike income tax or corporation tax, no distinction is made between capital or revenue inputs; the credit generally extends to the tax on its capital purchases as well as on its purchases of stock in trade.

The total tax on the inputs of a business is ascertained from the tax invoices given to it by every other business which has supplied it with goods or services. Amongst other details typical tax invoices would show:

	£
Goods	100.00
VAT at 20%	20.00
Price payable	120.00

	£
Goods	100.00
VAT at 17½%	17.50
Price payable	117.50

	£
Goods	100.00
VAT at 15%	15.00
Price payable	115.00

At the end of each accounting period the business will total all the tax invoices it has received for its inputs in that period, which it must keep for production to HMRC when required, together with its vouchers for tax imports; it will also total all its outputs for the period (keeping copies of all tax invoices it has rendered to other businesses) and a typical return for an accounting period throughout which VAT is all at 20 per cent will show:

	£	£
Total outputs during the period	50,000	
VAT thereon		10,000
Total inputs for the period	20,000	
VAT thereon		4,000
Balance payable to HMRC		6,000

The effect of the credit mechanism is that although VAT is charged on each business in the chain of import, production and distribution, each business in the chain gets a credit for the tax on its inputs, so that the whole tax is passed on to the consumer on the final sale to him. Credit for the VAT on unsold stock will have been given on its purchase and it will therefore be held tax-free until sale.

Because of the credit mechanism outlined above a business does not normally bear much tax; it mainly acts as a collection agency. The ultimate consumer bears all the tax, which is why VAT is described as a sales tax. The difficulty of having a retail sales tax lies in determining when the final retail sale takes place. With VAT it does not matter; if the purchaser is a VAT registered business, he will generally get credit for the tax as input tax, and if he is not he will bear it. Another advantage of the credit mechanism is that the effect is neutral between supplies which go through a number of stages and those where the supplier is vertically integrated. In both cases the tax is on the amount of the final price to the consumer.

A turnover tax charges tax on tax and therefore encourages vertical integration which is not usually in the public interest.

As will be seen later (23.3), businesses which make some 'exempt' supplies do not normally get credit for the VAT on their inputs relating to these supplies.

23.2 VAT in practice

All businesses (23.4), except for the very small, are normally required to be registered with HMRC and they have to make returns every three months. Some businesses which are likely to have repayments of tax, however, because they make zero-rated supplies, are allowed a one-month period. The return has to be completed and the tax paid by the end of the following month. Any amounts due to you will be paid but payments made to you in error may be recovered by assessment.

If HMRC unreasonably delay any repayment to you, a repayment supplement of the greater of 5 per cent of the tax and £50 (previously £30) should be due subject to the detailed rules. Also, you have the statutory right to claim interest on your overpayment of VAT if due to the error of HMRC. Interest rates will generally correspond to those applicable to other taxes (16.8.2).

As from 18 July 1996, the powers of HMRC to assess for undeclared VAT is limited to three years, except in cases of fraud and certain other cases, like 'do it yourself' housebuilders. Furthermore, the right to claim back overpaid VAT is restricted to a maximum of three years. Interest payable by the authorities is similarly limited (FA 1997 Ss44–49).

Businesses with annual turnovers under £1,350,000 (£660,000 before 1 April 2006) which have been registered for at least one year are able to elect for annual VAT accounting. They make nine equal payments on account by direct debit and a tenth balancing amount with their annual return. Businesses already within this scheme can remain until annual turnover reaches £1,600,000 (previously £825,000). Another arrangement open to businesses with outstanding VAT of not more than £5,000 and turnovers under £1,350,000 is to account for VAT on a cash rather than an invoice basis. This new limit (previously £660,000) applies from 1 April 2007.

The voluntary annual accounting scheme was improved for businesses with turnovers below £150,000 from 10 April 2003 (£100,000 from 25 April 2002) who do not need to wait for one year. Such a business has the option of making quarterly interim payments, but normally nine interim monthly payments will be followed with a balancing payment. However, if this total is below £2,000, no interim payments need be made. This scheme can be used in conjunction with the cash accounting scheme (above), the flat rate scheme (23.5.2), and any of the retail (23.10) or margin (23.11.4 & 10) schemes.

Very large taxpayers make monthly VAT payments. This applies to those with VAT of at least £2 million for their four quarters up to 31 March 1991 and they make VAT payments on account of the first two months each quarter. Other businesses join the scheme once it can be seen that their VAT liability will exceed the threshold. As from 1 June 1996, monthly payments are $\frac{1}{24}$ of the annual liability, with an option to pay the true VAT monthly. However, all payments must be made by electronic means and cleared by the month end.

HMRC have inspection powers, widened by FA 2006, regarding goods stored and intended for onwards supply. Also, HMRC can now require additional record-keeping such as regarding mobile phones and computer chips so as to identify potential loss of VAT.

New regulations (SI 2010/599) imposed compulsory online filing of returns and online payment of VAT from 1 April 2010 on all new businesses and on existing businesses with an annual turnover in excess of £100,000. Other traders were encouraged to move from paper returns to electronic filing and up to seven extra days are allowed for online payment in most cases. From 1 April 2012, all businesses are expected to file VAT returns online and penalties will be imposed if paper returns are lodged.

From 1 April 2010 'cleared funds' need to be in the hands of HMRC by the extended date (or last preceding working day). Care should be taken to meet the payment date shown on your online VAT return, in case this practice is tightened as part of the Government's ongoing financial efficiency review.

23.2.1 **Correction of errors**

If you find errors in your VAT return totalling less than £2,000, you can correct them in the next return that you submit. For accounting periods commencing after 30 June 2008, the limit increases to the greater of £10,000 or 1 per cent of turnover, subject to an overall maximum of £50,000. Subject to the rules, it may be necessary to lodge a separate report of the correction in order to protect your compliance standing and penalty exposure. (Notice 700/45; also 700/41–43 re penalties.)

23.2.2 **Penalties**

There are penalties which may be imposed by the courts for overdue VAT returns and payments. Naturally, far heavier penalties apply in cases involving dishonesty. Penalties for inaccuracies in information supplied to HMRC on VAT matters after 31 March 2009 are subject a new behaviour related compliance policy, unless they relate to an accounting period commencing before 1 April 2008. FA 2008 and FA 2009 enable a major realignment of penalties, time limits and interest rates across the whole gamut of UK taxes (16.9.6). This is to be phased in over a number of years, commencing 1 April 2010 and will alter the established regime described below. The new arrangements include a system of suspending penalties for late payment of tax, where you enter into a managed payment plan with HMRC.

The 1985 Finance Act contained stern provisions to counter VAT evasion and speed up tax payment. For example, failure to pay tax on time or submit returns could involve a 'default surcharge'. From 1 April 1993, the maximum penalty is 15 per cent of the VAT involved. However, from 1 October 1993, a new minimum rate of 2 per cent applies for the first default after a surcharge liability notice. (For businesses with an annual turnover of no more than £150,000 there is no longer an automatic penalty on late VAT payments.)

From 1 January 1995, the penalties on late registration for VAT are 5 per cent, 10 per cent and 15 per cent of the tax. These rates apply where registration is late by no more than nine months, 18 months and more than 18 months respectively.

A 'serious misdeclaration penalty' at 15 per cent of the tax operates from 11 March 1992. There is a 'period of grace' extending to the due date for the next return. Also, the penalty will not now normally apply where misdeclarations are compensated for in the next return, nor where the undeclared tax is less than the lower of £1,000,000 and 30 per cent of the 'gross tax'. 'Gross tax' means your VAT on both inputs and outputs.

There is also a 15 per cent penalty on 'persistent misdeclaration resulting in understatements or overclaims'. This penalty will now only be used where a person has underdeclared or overclaimed tax three times within twelve accounting periods and a written warning has been issued. Also, the misdeclaration in each period must be at least 10 per cent of the 'gross tax' or £500,000 if less. (Where a penalty is imposed for 'serious misdeclaration', it will also be included in the reckoning for 'persistent misdeclaration' penalty.)

Giving incorrect certificates of entitlement to zero-rating regarding supplies of fuel and power, new buildings or construction services is liable to a civil penalty. However, this is now subject to mitigation.

23.2.3 Allocation of outputs and inputs to periods

There are rules determining into which period a supply falls. For goods it is normally the date when the goods are removed or made available, and for services it is the date of performance. (There are special rules where VAT rates change.) There are two exceptions. If an invoice (which must contain specified information) is issued within 14 days after that time, the date of the invoice is taken. In practice this will usually apply and the advantage is that the VAT return can be made up from the copy invoices.

The other exception is for payments in advance when it is the date of invoice or payment which counts. This is the only time payment is relevant; normally it is the invoice which matters (see below under 'Special Cases' for the position of bad debts). An arrangement can also be made with HMRC to use the last day of the calendar month or of a VAT accounting period as the time of supply.

The same rules apply for determining into which period the inputs fall. Consequently, relief for input tax will normally be available before the invoice has been paid. The invoices will need to be kept as proof. The VAT return will be a summary of invoices issued and invoices received. If tax is due to HMRC, it will be paid with the return. Inputs of goods and services incurred prior to registration may subsequently be recovered in certain circumstances.

Strictly speaking, tax on *imports* by a business is due at the date of import. However, in practice the VAT is payable by the 15th of the month following importation. (Payment must be by direct debit and covered by bank guarantee.) No tax is due so long as the goods are in a bonded warehouse. Taxable persons pay no VAT on temporary imports for repair, modification etc., provided ownership does not change. Where the reverse happens, VAT on the re-import only applies to the repairs etc. plus freight and insurance. Imports from EC countries are subject to special rules from 1 January 1993 (23.17).

23.3 Zero-rating and exemption

So far we have assumed that all the inputs and outputs of a business are taxable at a positive rate. Certain types of supply are treated specially either because they are 'zero-rated' or because they are 'exempt'. Details of these types are set out in Schedules 8 and 9 to the Value Added Tax Act 1994 and summaries of these Schedules are given later in this chapter.

If a supply is *zero-rated* this means that no tax is charged on the supply but credit is given to the supplier for all tax on his inputs relating to that supply. *Exports* of goods, for instance, are often zero-rated so that these leave the country free of VAT in the UK, although they may be liable to VAT in the country into which they are imported if that country imposes a VAT. However, exports to non-VAT-registered customers in other EU member states may be taxable in the UK.

A business which exports most of its products will probably find that its returns for an accounting period show more tax on its inputs than on its outputs (the majority being zero-rated). In that event, the business can claim back the difference from HMRC. Zero rating also applies to goods shipped for use as stores on a voyage or flight to a destination outside the EU, or for retail sale in transit. However, this does not apply to private voyages and flights.

The EU requires its members to have a VAT with a similar structure although different rates are allowed. One of the reasons is that the similar treatment of imports and exports ensures equality between home-produced and imported goods. Exports to EU countries are subject to special rules from 1 January 1993 (23.17).

In addition to exports, food and many other items sold within the UK (23.14) are also zero-rated. However, *exports of services* (for example professional advice) are often treated as supplied where the recipient resides, thus being outside the UK VAT net. Significant changes to the VAT regime for services and the intra-EU reporting regime for goods (23.17) are to be phased in on 1 January 2010, 2011, 2013 and 2015. From 1 January 2010 most business-to-business services are treated as supplied where the recipient resides. This subjects most imported services to a reverse charge to VAT, the recovery of which depends upon the VAT profile of the recipient. There is also an electronic system of reclaiming VAT paid in the EU on inward services to UK businesses.

Exemption of a supply of goods or services is not so favourable as zero rating, for whilst this means that there is no VAT on the supply (as with zero-rating), there is no credit allowed for the corresponding tax on the inputs of the business. Thus life assurance is one of the exempt items (23.16) so that there is no tax on a premium on a life policy but the life assurance company can get no credit for the tax on those inputs which it uses for its life assurance business. This introduces a hidden tax cost to its business.

A business which supplies both taxable (including zero-rated) and exempt goods and services is a 'partly exempt' business and will have an accounting problem. When claiming credit for the tax on the inputs from HMRC, it is entitled to credit for the tax on those inputs which it uses for its taxable supplies but it is not entitled to credit for the tax on those inputs which it uses for its exempt supplies.

Normally, a proportion of the business's input tax corresponding to its taxable supplies is allowed. After 17 April 2002, this is subject to anti-avoidance rules which may adjust the allowable input tax to reflect the use made of the purchases. However, if exempt input tax is less than £7,500 per year, credit for input tax is not restricted. A requirement from 1 December 1994 is that the exempt input tax is no more than 50 per cent of total input tax. VAT is only recoverable if attributable to:

(1) business taxable supplies;
(2) supplies outside the UK which would have been VATable or zero-rated if made here;
(3) business supplies of certain warehoused goods disregarded for VAT;
(4) overheads supporting the above.

23.4 Business

Central to the working of VAT is the definition of 'business' because the credit mechanism is applied only to a business. It is defined to include any trade, profession or vocation. It also includes clubs and associations, such as sports clubs and members' clubs. The charging of admission fees, for example by the National Trust, is also taxable as a business. VAT is not charged on subscriptions to political parties, trade unions or professional bodies. In general, such subscriptions are now exempt.

23.5 Small traders

23.5.1 Registration

From 1 April 2012 a person whose taxable (including zero-rated) supplies are not more than £77,000 (previously £73,000 from 1 April 2011) per annum is not liable to be registered, although he can apply to be registered voluntarily. A business is required to register if the value of taxable supplies in the past 12 months exceeded £77,000. Alternatively, registration is required if there are reasonable grounds for believing that the value of taxable supplies will exceed £77,000 in the next 30 days.

A small trader who is not registered is in the same position as a business making only exempt supplies. He does not charge tax to his customers and has to bear any input tax.

From 1 April 2012 *deregistration* is in general allowed if HMRC are satisfied that the taxable supplies for the ensuing year will not exceed £75,000 (previously £71,000).

23.5.2 Flat-rate scheme (SI 1995/2518 Regs 55A–V)

From 25 April 2002, an optional scheme operates under which, subject to the rules, you can elect to calculate your VAT due for each period by applying a fixed percentage to your total VAT-inclusive turnover. The actual percentage depends on your trade or profession and various rates were improved in January or April 2004. From 1 December 2008, following the temporary reduction in the standard rate, many of the flat rates changed. Following restoration of the 17½ per cent standard rate, further corrections were made from 1 January 2010, but many of these new rates were clearly not reversions to the 2004 level. From 4 January 2011, the flat rates rose again to reflect the increase in the standard rate to 20 per cent announced on 22 June 2010.

The following examples cover approximately half of the full list (VAT Reg 55K):

Selected rates applicable from	**4.1.11** %	**1.1.10** %	**1.12.08** %	**1.4.04** %
Retail – food, tobacco, newspapers, children's clothing	4	3.5	2	2
Post offices	5	4.5	2	2
Public houses	6.5	6	5.5	5.5
Agriculture services	11	10	7	7.5
Farming or agriculture not listed elsewhere	6.5	6	5.5	6
Forestry, fishing, travel agencies	10.5	9.5	8	9
Retail of goods not listed elsewhere (*check full list first*)	7.5	6.5	5.5	6
Wholesaling agricultural products	8	7	5.5	6
Retailing vehicles and fuel	6.5	6	5.5	7
Building where materials supplied	9.5	8.5	7.5	8.5
Building – labour only	14.5	13	11.5	13.5
Transport including storage, freight, couriers and taxis	10	9	8	9
Hotels or accommodation	10.5	9.5	8.5	9.5
Publishing	11	10.5	8.5	9.5
Estate agency, property management	12	10.5	9.5	11
Real estate not listed elsewhere	14	12.5	11	12
Entertainment or journalism	12.5	11	9.5	11
Laundry or dry cleaning services	12	10.5	9.5	11
Catering including restaurants and takeaways	12.5	11	10.5	12
Hairdressing and beauty treatment services	13	11.5	10.5	12
Computer repairs	10.5	9.5	10	13
Financial services	13.5	12	10.5	11.5
Accountancy, book-keeping, computer and IT consultancy, data processing	14.5	13	11.5	13
Architects, engineers and surveyors	14.5	13	11	12.5
Lawyers and legal services	14.5	13	12	13

Notes: (1) With effect from 1 April 2004, the above rates were reduced by 1 per cent in each case in your first year of VAT registration. This is subject to your notifying your liability to register on time.
(2) Remember to check for any rate changes from time to time and if any change in the standard rate of VAT occurs.

You can elect for the scheme to apply if your expected taxable turnover for the next 12 months is no more than £150,000 (£100,000 before 10 April 2003).

Also, your total business turnover, including exempt supplies (23.3) and other non-taxable income must not be more that £191,500 (£187,500 before 4 January 2011). For example, suppose you are a travel agent and your total VAT-inclusive sales in a quarter are £22,000. If you have elected to join the scheme, you will simply pay 10.5 per cent × £22,000 = £2,310 (9.5 per cent × £22,000 = £2,090 before 4 January 2011) instead of VAT at the full rate on your outputs, less that on your inputs. Once you have joined, you can remain in the flat rate scheme until your total annual business income reaches £230,000 (£225,000 before 4 January 2011).

This scheme can be used in conjunction with the annual accounting scheme (23.2), if you so desire.

23.6 Zero-rated supplies

A person whose supplies are all zero-rated can apply to be exempted from registration. He will not then be able to claim a refund of his input tax but he will not have to make VAT returns.

23.7 Groups and divisions of companies

A group of companies may be registered as a single business and supplies between members of the group will be ignored. The requirement that the companies should be UK resident has now been widened to include overseas companies with a fixed establishment in the UK. One company in the group is responsible for making returns for all the members of the group. Alternatively, a company which is organised in divisions can register each division separately.

The Commissioners of Revenue and Customs can direct that separately registered entities are treated as one for VAT purposes. This applies for companies and other traders. The object is to combat artificially splitting a single business to avoid registration. Similarly, ineligible companies can be removed from groups. Certain avoidance schemes involving the movement of a company or the transfer of assets in or out of a group from 29 November 1995 are also countered. Further anti-avoidance measures take effect from 27 November 1996 and 1 August 2004 regarding groups. The latter makes it more difficult to join a VAT group in limited cases and prevents a company being in two such groups at the same time.

From 1 April 1990, capital items, such as computers, land and buildings and (from 1 January 2011) aircraft, ships and boats, over specified value limits are excluded from the VAT self-supply charge (23.11.3), which otherwise arises when assets are transferred to a partly exempt VAT group as part of the transfer of a going concern.

23.8 Local authorities

Local authorities are in the position of being both in business and also carrying on non-business activities, such as welfare services. Their business activities are treated in the normal way but the input tax on any non-business activities is refunded. In this way there is no hidden tax burden in the rates.

23.9 Charities

Sales in charity shops, fêtes, coffee mornings etc. of donated goods are exempted. This applies to up to fifteen events of each type in a year in one location, not counting small-scale events, with weekly income of no more than £1,000. Apart from this, business supplies of a charity are treated in the normal way; there is no exemption for charities. Non-business supplies such as distribution of free goods are outside the tax unless they are exported, when they are zero-rated. Where a branch of a charity makes business supplies, for example sales at a fête, it may be treated as a separate entity from the charity and be entitled to the £70,000 limit before it is taxable. See zero-rating (23.14) for certain reliefs applicable to charities. The list of zero-rated items related to charities is being increased over the years. Further details may be found in VAT leaflets 701/1 etc.

From 1 April 2001, national museums and galleries can reclaim VAT, even though they allow free admission to the public.

23.10 Retailers

Because retailers often cannot record each sale separately there are special schemes for calculating the amount of the tax which they pay. The schemes also deal with the difficulty of retailers which sell both zero-rated goods (for example food) and standard-rated goods (for example kitchen equipment). Details of the schemes are contained in HMRC Notice No. 727 and supplements describing each scheme.

23.11 Special cases

23.11.1 Motor cars

No deduction of input tax on motor cars is allowed on cars acquired for use in the business. This also applies to the acquisition of hire cars and taxis, except London-type taxis. However, VAT is recoverable for vehicles used in their businesses by private taxi and self-drive firms and driving schools. Businesses may recover input tax on cars used for a demonstrably wholly business purpose, primarily leasing, but must charge VAT on any cars sold.

The VAT on the hire charge is available for credit as input tax. However, this is restricted by 50 per cent where the car is leased from a business which has recovered the VAT and the car is partly used for private motoring. A car dealer is not affected and can claim a credit for input tax in the normal way, but if he takes a car out of stock and uses it in his own business, tax must be paid and it is not available for credit (see 'Self-supply', below). The definition of 'motor car' for this purpose excludes commercial vehicles, vans without rear side windows and vehicles accommodating only one or more than nine persons.

From 12 May 2001, a 5 per cent VAT rate applies to children's car seats. This is extended to the bases for such seats from 1 July 2009.

Petrol supplied at below cost by companies and partnerships etc. for private journeys is not allowable for VAT purposes so far as the input tax is concerned. This creates problems in computing the disallowance and a quarterly scale corresponding to the income tax figures (10.6.5) is used for each person concerned. (There is also a monthly scale.) The company etc. is charged VAT (calculated on a VAT inclusive basis) on the scale figures which effectively cancels the appropriate input tax.

A new scale based on carbon dioxide (CO_2) emissions applies for accounting periods beginning after 30 April 2012 shown below for *3-month periods:*

CO_2 Band	VAT fuel scale £	CO_2 Band	VAT fuel scale £	CO_2 Band	VAT fuel scale £	CO_2 Band	VAT fuel scale £
120 or less	166	150	333	180	433	210	533
125	250	155	350	185	450	215	550
130	266	160	366	190	467	220	567
135	283	165	383	195	483	225	583
140	300	170	400	200	500	or more	
145	316	175	416	205	517		

If a car is wholly used for business purposes, the scale charge does not apply; nor does it apply where a car is used entirely for private purposes, in which case input tax is not deductible.

Special rules affect motor dealers and manufacturers who allow employees to use demonstration cars privately at a nominal fee. VAT will be charged on the open market value.

23.11.2 **Business entertainment**

Input tax on business entertainment is not deductible. Entertainment includes meals, accommodation, theatres and sporting facilities. This does not, however, prevent deduction of input tax on subsistence expenses refunded to employees.

23.11.3 **Self-supply**

It is advantageous for a business which makes exempt supplies to produce its own goods since no input tax will be charged for which it will be unable to obtain a credit. To prevent distortion, an order charging printed stationery to tax even though supplied to oneself has been made. Thus a bank, which is exempt, printing its own stationery would be charged tax on the value of the stationery and it could not obtain relief for the tax. An order also applies to cars to prevent avoidance of the non-deduction of input tax mentioned above.

Regulations may be made to restrict the recovery of input tax on self-supplies by partly exempt businesses. Recovery will only be allowed to the extent governed by the business's partial exemption method. However, from 1 June 2002, partly exempt businesses which produce printed matter for their own use valued above the VAT registration limit no longer have to account for VAT under the self-supply rules.

Developers of certain non-residential *buildings* may be treated as making self-supplies in various circumstances. This applies where, for example, a lease is granted which is an exempt supply; also, when the developer is not a fully taxable person and occupies the building.

In such cases VAT is chargeable based on the land and taxable construction costs, subject to certain exclusions. These include where the value is less than £100,000 and where the construction was completed before 1 August 1989; also, if the freehold had already passed and the non-residential building is new.

23.11.4 Second-hand goods

Second-hand goods are chargeable to tax in the normal way, except that there are special provisions relating to cars, motorcycles, caravans, boats and outboard motors, original works of art, antiques over 100 years old, collectors' pieces, electronic organs and aircraft, which provide that VAT is payable only on the dealer's mark-up. Except in the case of cars these provisions apply only when no tax was charged on the dealer's acquisition or when tax was charged on another dealer's mark-up. Where goods are taken in part-exchange, full VAT is still payable on the new goods supplied.

From 1 January 1995, the dealer's mark-up is chargeable to VAT for all second-hand goods, works of art, antiques and collectors items apart from precious metals and gems. VAT is computed on a global basis and other changes have since been made.

Goods obtained under the special VAT rules for transferring a business as a going concern can now only be sold under the margin scheme if they were so eligible in the hands of the previous owner.

23.11.5 Sales on credit

A separately disclosed credit charge is exempt from VAT.

23.11.6 Gifts

Business gifts of goods are taxable on the cost price but items costing in aggregate under £50 (£15 before 8 March 2001) can be ignored. This applies to samples in general unless more than one identical item is supplied to one person, in which case relief is limited to one item. Gifts of services are not taxable. From 1 October 2002, the £50 rule applies to a series of gifts within a 12-month period not exceeding such aggregate.

23.11.7 Personal use

If a person acquires goods in the course of business and uses them for his own personal use, for example, a shopkeeper who takes goods off the shelf, tax is payable on the cost price of the goods.

Where a business has assets, such as land and buildings which are partly used for non-business purposes, special rules apply which have been adapted by FA 2007 and regulations to comply with European Court of Justice Judgments (VATA Schs 4 & 6). The timing of disallowances, especially on capital outlays, changed from 1 January 2011.

23.11.8 Accommodation for directors

VAT on repairs, refurbishments and other expenses relating to domestic accommodation provided for directors and their families does not rank as deductible input tax. This applies where the accommodation is provided by a business for domestic purposes but not to any rooms used specifically for business where a proportion of the total VAT would be deductible. The timing of disallowances, especially on capital outlays, changed from 1 January 2011.

23.11.9 Bad debts

Relief for bad debts exists where the debtor goes bankrupt or goes into liquidation. The amount excluding VAT is claimed from the liquidator etc. and the VAT from HMRC. Retailers in effect obtain bad debt relief as the special schemes are based on payments. (Relief extends beyond cases of formal insolvency.)

Automatic bad debt relief is now available on debts which are more than six months old (from payable date), and have been written off in the accounts. If you have reclaimed VAT on inputs for which you do not pay, you needed to repay this if your supplier has claimed bad debt relief (FA 1997 S39). However, FA 2002 (S22) removes the connection between the repayment of input tax on unpaid invoices and the supplier claiming bad debt relief. The relief extends to non-monetary (barter) transactions (FA 1998 S23).

23.11.10 Tour operators

Previously, the services of tour operators regarding overseas package holidays were not liable to VAT in the UK. However, FA 1987 S16 introduced a special VAT margin scheme. UK-based tour operators buying in services pay VAT on the margin between their buying and selling prices. This applies if the services are used in the EC, including the UK. Furthermore they are not able to recover any VAT charged by suppliers for those services.

23.11.11 Fuel and power

Fuel and power were originally zero-rated but commercial use was standard rated from 1 April 1989 (23.15). FA 1993 provided that domestic fuel and power were to remain zero-rated until 31 March 1994, then being taxable at 8 per cent for the year to 31 March 1995. After that, the standard rate of VAT (then 17.5 per cent) was to have applied but Finance Act 1995 kept the rate at 8 per cent and from 1 September 1997 it is 5 per cent. This rate now applies to the installation of energy-saving materials and from 1 June 2002, certain grant-funded heating equipment in homes. From 1 June 2004, ground-source heat pumps are also included. This extends to air source heat pumps and micro-combined heat and power units in residential accommodation and certain charity buildings from 7 April 2005.

From 1 January 2005, VAT on wholesale supplies of natural gas and electricity is to be accounted for where the customer receiving the supply is established. Otherwise, the place of supply will be where it is consumed. Other changes include relieving natural gas and electricity from VAT when imported from outside the EC. From 1 January 2011, the regime is extended to include all forms of natural gas and heating and cooling networks, whilst limiting the rules on pipelines to those connecting to EU countries.

23.11.12 **Registration of racehorse owners**

Following the Jockey Club changing the Rules of Racing to allow owners to seek sponsorship and appearance money, racehorse owners are able to register for VAT purposes.

23.12 Documentation

The legislation contained in FA 1972 and nearly all the subsequent Finance Acts was consolidated into the Value Added Tax Act 1983. In turn this, together with further legislation in Finance Acts, has been consolidated into the Value Added Tax Act 1994. Also a large number of statutory instruments have been made under powers contained in the Acts, all of which are available from HMSO.

Detailed information is contained in various Notices issued by HMRC. However, these are constantly updated and the titles often change. They are available free from any HMRC VAT office and include the following:

Number		Number	
48	Extra-statutory concessions	719	Refund of VAT to 'do-it-yourself' builders
700	The VAT guide	723	Refunds of VAT in the European Community and other countries
700/21	Keeping records and accounts	725	The single market
700/50	Default surcharge	727	Special schemes for retailers
700/56	Insolvency	728	Motor vehicles, boats, aircraft: intra EC movements by private persons
700/62	Self-billing	731	Cash accounting
701/1	Charities	732	Annual accounting
702	Imports and warehoused goods	741/A	International services (2010 Rules)
703	Exports	742	Property ownership etc.
704	Retail exports	744	Passenger transport, international freight, ships and aircraft
706	Partial exemption	749	Local authorities and similar bodies
707	Personal exports of new motor vehicles (outside EC)	COP9	Investigations – Statement of Practice
708	Buildings and construction		
714	Young children's clothing and footwear		

It should be emphasised that these Notices are in general guides, and, with certain exceptions such as No. 727, they do not have any legal force. Several of the Notices are supported by numerous leaflets on specific topics.

23.13 Appeals

From 1 April 2009 appeals concerning VAT matters come within the jurisdiction of the Tax Chamber of the First-Tier Tribunal. It may be possible to ask the First-Tier Tribunal to review its own decision, which could include a question of fact. The first venue for any appeal (on points of law only) was the Finance and Tax Chamber (renamed 'Tax and Chancery Chamber' from 1 September 2009) of the Upper Tribunal, from which any further appeal would be to the Court of Appeal (or Court of Session in Scotland) and House of Lords. The Upper Tribunal also has a power to review its own decisions. Before you even start the appeal process, you now have the right to ask HMRC for an independent internal review of the disputed decision.

As with the former VAT and Duties Tribunal, the available venues are in London, Edinburgh, Belfast and Manchester. The tribunal consists of judges and other members with relevant professional knowledge and experience, who may sit singly or as a panel of two or three. All fulfill judicial appointments.

Appeals on the matters listed below are made direct to the Tribunals Service, but appeals against a notice to supply information or against a penalty for failure to do so are to be made to HMRC and will follow the internal procedures applicable to direct taxes (16.5–16.5.3).

The VAT matters over which the tribunals have jurisdiction are as follows:

(1) Registration.
(2) Registration of groups of companies.
(3) Assessment of VAT by HMRC.
(4) The amount of VAT chargeable.
(5) The amount of the deduction of input tax.
(6) Apportionment of input tax by a partly exempt person.
(7) Special schemes for retailers.
(8) The value of certain supplies.
(9) The provision of security.
(10) Repayment of VAT on certain imports.
(11) Refunds to do-it-yourself builders.
(12) Bad debt relief.
(13) Voluntary registration of a person whose turnover is below the limit.
(14) Appeals against certain Commissioners' decisions which in turn depend upon prior unappealable decisions which they made.

23.14 Zero-rating (VATA Sch 8)

The following is a list of the important items. Full details are contained in the General Guide (VAT Notice No. 700) available from HMRC. The group numbers have been changed in some instances by VATA 1994.

- *Group 1: Food* All food except pet foods, alcoholic drinks and certain food products (such as ice cream, chocolate, confectionery including cereal bars, soft drinks and potato crisps). Meals out are, however, taxable and this includes hot take-away food and drink and (from 1 October 2012) consumption in shared adjacent areas.
- *Group 2: Sewerage services and water* Water except for distilled water and bottled water; emptying cesspools. (Standard rated from 1 July 1990 if for industrial use – 23.14.1.)
- *Group 3: Books etc.* Books, newspapers, magazines, music, maps. But diaries and stationery are taxable.
- *Group 4: Talking books and tape recorders for the blind and handicapped and wireless sets for the blind*, including (from 1.4.92) their repair and maintenance.
- *Group 5: Construction of dwellings etc.* Sale of the freehold or grant of a lease for more than 21 years of a building by a builder; construction, and demolition of buildings but not repairs (now basically dwellings for your own, charity and community use – 23.14.1). Sales by a builder's merchant, and architects' and surveyors' fees are, however, taxable. A person building his own house can reclaim tax paid on items purchased. (Conversions, reconstructions, alterations and enlargements for industrial and commercial use are normally standard rated and sales of reconstructed buildings are exempt.) From 1 August 2001, the sale of renovated houses which have been empty for over 10 years is zero rated. From 1 June 2002, new annexes constructed partly for charitable use will be proportionately zero-rated.
- *Group 6: Protected buildings* This includes alterations and reconstructions of listed buildings, ancient monuments and listed churches. Repairs are technically standard-rated, but can qualify for subsidies under a special scheme (23.15 (11)).
- *Group 7: International services* Exports of services, such as an agent arranging the export of goods or certain services outside the EC for a named principal (see also 23.3). Also carrying out work on goods from abroad subsequently exported outside the EC.
- *Group 8: Transport* Passenger transport (inland and international) including travel agents (except in relation to hotels in the UK or package tours), and international freight transport. Taxis and hire cars are, however, taxable, as are pleasure boats and aircraft. Lifeboats and slipways etc. are all included as are spare parts etc. for lifeboats and for zero-rated ships and aircraft. From 1 January 2011, aircraft are expected to be zero-rated, if bought for commercial use on international flights.
- *Group 9: Caravans and houseboats* Caravans which are too large to be used as trailers on the roads (22.9 feet in length or 7.5 feet in breadth). But smaller caravans are taxable.
- *Group 10: Gold* Transactions on the London Gold market.

- *Group 11: Bank notes*
- *Group 12: Drugs, medicines, medical and surgical appliances* Drugs dispensed by a registered pharmacist on a doctor's prescription. Other drugs purchased without a prescription are taxable. Medical and surgical appliances for the disabled. Donated computer equipment is zero-rated, as are lifts and distress systems for the handicapped and necessary work on bathrooms etc. in private homes and in bathrooms for the handicapped in charity residential homes, day centres and other charity premises. More general relief is available for medical equipment, ambulances etc. purchased out of charitable funds or donated. This extends to the sale of donated goods and printed media advertising costs.
- *Group 13: Imports, exports etc.* This group has limited application.
- *Group 14: Tax-free shops* Formerly relating to travellers to other EC countries making purchases on planes, ships, at airports and ports within the limits prescribed and of other goods to be carried in personal luggage (ceased 30 June 1999).
- *Group 15: Charities* (23.9) This includes non-classified advertising (all advertising from 1 April 2000), medical video or refrigeration equipment and motor vehicles with from seven to fifty seats. Also, drugs and chemicals used in medical (and veterinary) research by a charity are zero-rated, also welfare vehicles for the terminally ill and certain rescue equipment. The sale of donated goods is generally included, as is fund-raising and educational advertising on television, radio and cinema. Also covered are toilet facilities in charity-run buildings and boats adapted for the handicapped.
- *Group 16: Clothing and footwear* Clothing for young children, industrial protective clothing (provided meeting UK or EC safety standards and bearing mark) and motor-cyclists' and pedal cyclists' crash helmets. (Protective boots and helmets are standard-rated if supplied to employers for their employees – 23.14.1.)
- *Group 17: Emissions allowances* From 30 July 2009; ceased 30 July 2010 where reverse charge applies.

Note: Zero-rating has priority over exemption if a supply falls into both categories.

23.14.1 Changes to zero-ratings – option to tax

On 21 June 1988, the European Court of Justice ruled that certain zero-ratings did not comply with European Community Law. As a result, the following items are vatable, details being now included in VATA 1994:

(1) construction of buildings for industrial and commercial use;
(2) supplies after 31 March 1989 of fuel and power other than to final consumers for domestic use (domestic use taxable from 1 April 1994 – 23.11.11);
(3) sewerage services and water supplies to industry after 30 June 1990;

(4) supplies after 31 March 1989 of news services insofar as they are not provided to final consumers;
(5) protective boots and helmets supplied to employers from July 2007 for use by their employees.

All contracts entered into before 21 June 1988 continue to be zero-rated. Owners of non-domestic property have the option to elect to charge VAT on rents, and on sales of certain used buildings, from 1 August 1989. Owners can obtain no input tax relief before the election has effect, subject to transitional relief. Certain transactions in non-residential buildings may be treated as self-supplies giving rise to VAT. After 31 July 2009, an option to tax can be revoked (FA 2008) and some procedures have been simplified from 1 May 2009 (FA 2009). The rules in this area are under review and some informal concessions are due to be expire on 30 April 2010 unless given legislative force.

23.15 Reduced rate (VATA Sch 7A)

The following groups of items are now within the 5 per cent reduced rate charge:

- *Group 1:* Domestic fuel or power (23.11.11).
- *Group 2:* Energy-saving materials: installation.
- *Group 3:* Heating equipment, security goods and gas supplies; grant funded installation or connection.
- *Group 4:* Women's sanitary products.
- *Group 5:* Children's car seats (23.11.1).
- *Group 6:* Residential conversions (23.19).
- *Group 7:* Residential renovations and alterations (23.19).
- *Group 8:* Supplies of contraceptives from July 2006, where not zero-rated (Group 12) or exempt (Group 7) as medical care.
- *Group 9:* Welfare advice or information from July 2006.
- *Group 10:* Mobility aids for the elderly: installation from July 2007.
- *Group 11:* Over-the-counter sales of smoking cessation products from July 2007 onwards.

Following post-Budget consultations in 2012 regarding proposals to reduce various VAT rating anomalies, it appears that special arrangements run by the Department for Culture, Media and Sport will continue to repay the difference between the reduced and standard rates on repairs to listed places of worship and on construction, renovation and maintenance of certain memorials to charities.

23.16 Exemptions (VATA Sch 9)

The following is a list of the more important items. Full details are contained in *The VAT Guide* (VAT Notice 700) available from HMRC:

- *Group 1: Land* Sales, leases and hiring out of land and buildings (unless within zero-rating Group 8 or taxable). Examples of taxable items are hotels (excluding conference facilities), holiday accommodation, camping, parking, timber, mooring, exhibition stands, sporting rights and the sale and construction of new non-residential buildings and civil engineering works (23.14.1) – also from 1 October 2012, self-storage warehousing and barbers' chairs.

- *Group 2: Insurance* All types of insurance and insurance brokers and agents. Both premiums and the payment of claims are exempt.
- *Group 3: Postal services* Post and incidental supplies. But telegrams, telephones and telex are taxable. Limited to Royal Mail from 31 January 2011.
- *Group 4: Betting, gaming and lotteries* Bookmakers, charges for playing bingo. But admission or session charges, club subscriptions and takings from gaming machines are taxable.
- *Group 5: Finance* Banking, buying and selling stocks and shares and charges from credit card companies to retailers etc. accepting the cards; also making arrangements and certain intermediary services. Stockbrokers' commissions are taxable but not management fees relating to certain unit trusts nor from 1 October 2008 to certain UK listed investment entities and overseas funds.
- *Group 6: Education* Schools, universities, non-profit-making institutions teaching pupils of any age, or providing job training; private tuition by an independent teacher; government funded training programmes (including from 1 April 1993 where provided for profit). Extension to external providers of university-level courses is subject to consultation during 2012.
- *Group 7: Health* Doctors, dentists, dental workers, nurses, midwives, registered health visitors, registered opticians (including spectacles supplied in the course of treatment), chiropodists, dieticians, medical laboratory technicians, occupational therapists, orthoptists, physiotherapists, radiographers and remedial gymnasts, hearing aid dispensers, registered pharmaceutical chemists, medical and surgical treatment (except health farms etc.).
- *Group 8: Burial and cremation* Undertakers, crematoria.
- *Group 9: Trade unions and professional bodies.*
- *Group 10: Sports competitions.*
- *Group 11: Certain works of art etc.*
- *Group 12: Fund-raising events* Supplies of goods and services by charities and other qualifying bodies (including certain subsidiaries) in connection with fund-raising events.

Note: Zero-rating has priority over exemption if a supply falls into both categories.

23.17 Trading within the EU

F2A 1992 Sch 3 made detailed provisions related to the introduction of the Single Market from 1 January 1993. From that date, import procedures are abolished for movements of goods within the EU. Instead there is a concept of 'acquisition'. Supplies of goods between persons registered for VAT in EU countries continue to be zero-rated. However, the acquirer must account for local VAT in the member state to which the goods are sent.

If you supply goods to persons registered for VAT in other EU countries, you will need to submit quarterly EU Sales Lists (ESLs). (Supplies between the UK and non-EU countries remain largely as before.) From 1 January 2010, this responsibility is extended to supplies of services and the filing time reduced to 14 days (21 days if submitted electronically) from the quarter end. In addition, if the quarterly value of your EU supplies exceeds £70,000 (reducing to £35,000 from 1 January 2012), you will be required to submit ESLs monthly.

Private individuals normally effectively bear VAT at the appropriate rate in the member state of the supplier. However, VAT in the member state of the purchaser (and not the supplier) applies to mail order purchases, new motor vehicles, motor cycles, boats and aircraft; also supplies to non-VAT registered businesses and non-taxable institutions.

If you supply goods from another EU member state to non-VAT registered customers in the UK and are responsible for delivery, this is known as 'distance selling'. Should your annual turnover from distance selling reach £70,000, you must register for UK VAT.

Different rules apply to the supply of services from one EU country to another. In some cases these can require local VAT to be paid in the country of receipt or performance.

Fiscal warehousing operates from 1 June 1996. New provisions allow VAT-free trading within fiscal warehousing regimes for qualifying commodities, such as specified foodstuffs, metals and chemicals. When these are removed from the regime, VAT becomes payable.

A new requirement to register for VAT operates from 21 March 2000 in certain circumstances regarding overseas businesses. The aim is to stop goods being sold free of VAT in the UK where the seller (or a previous owner of the business) has reclaimed the VAT paid on the goods under the rules which allow unregistered overseas businesses to do so (FA 2000 S136 & Sch 36).

From 1 June 2007, a reverse charge mechanism was made available in respect of supplies of goods in respect of which the 'missing trade' fraud was prevalent (so far imposed on mobile phones and computer chips). This has been extended to supplies of goods (FA 2010 S50). It is expected that a reverse charge will be imposed on supplies of emissions allowances from 1 November 2010 and their previous zero-rating has been cancelled from 31 July 2009.

23.18 Optional rate for farmers (VATA S54)

From 1 January 1993, farmers can choose whether to register for VAT or opt to become flat rate farmers. If your taxable supplies are below the registration level (£70,000) you will still have the option of not registering for VAT, nor will you have to become a flat rate farmer.

As a flat rate farmer, you will be outside the VAT system and so obtain no relief for purchases. However, to compensate you, a fixed rate is to be added to your sales and retained by you. The actual rate is 4 per cent. However, you will not be eligible if you would stand to gain £3,000 or more in a year by participating in the scheme.

23.19 Renovations and conversions of residential properties (VATA Sch A1)

From 12 May 2001, a reduced VAT rate of 5 per cent applies to the cost of the following:

(1) Renovating dwellings that have been empty for at least three years.
(2) Converting a residential property into a different number of dwellings (for example flats).
(3) Converting a non-residential property into one or more dwellings.
(4) Converting a dwelling into a care home or house in multiple occupation.

From 1 June 2002, the 5 per cent rate also covers:

(1) Converting a non-residential home into a care home or multiple occupancy building (for example bedsits).
(2) Renovating or altering a care home etc. not lived in for at least three years.
(3) Renovating or altering a multiple-occupancy building not lived in for three years or more.
(4) Constructing, renovating or converting a building which qualifies for the 5 per cent rate into a garage.

23.20 Avoidance schemes – disclosure (VATA S58A & Sch 11A)

Businesses with turnovers upwards of £600,000 are required to inform HMRC if they use certain VAT avoidance schemes, which are recorded on a statutory list. This must be done within 30 days after the first return becomes due which is effected by the scheme after it is listed. A penalty of 15 per cent of the tax avoided will apply if you fail to disclose.

Broadly similar rules will apply to businesses with turnovers over £10 million who use schemes with some of the 'hallmarks of avoidance'. However, in those cases, the non-disclosure penalty is a flat rate of £5,000.

There are also provisions for the promoters of VAT avoidance schemes voluntarily to register those which have the 'hallmarks of avoidance' with HMRC. Provided it has been given the relevant reference number, a business using such a scheme does not need to notify the authorities.

Chapter 24

STAMP DUTY

24.1 Introduction

Stamp duty has long been the most modest of capital taxes but the 'take' has been increasing. Although many of the rates remain very low, stamp duty is likely to arise on some of your major capital transactions and can involve significant sums. Moreover, persistent avoidance has provoked legislative action in respect of high value residential properties, which took effect on 22 March 2012. The brief outline given below concentrates on the *ad valorem* duties, which are charged according to the value of a transaction, rather than the less important *fixed duties*.

The stamp duty rules are contained in the Stamp Act 1891, Stamp Duties Management Act 1891 and subsequent Finance Acts. The 1984 Finance Act (S105) halved the rates of some of the main *ad valorem* duties to 1 per cent from 20 March 1984 (12 March 1984 for most Stock Exchange transactions). The 1985 Finance Act removed certain fixed duties (S79) and abolished contract note duty. Also, *gifts* ceased to be liable to *ad valorem* duty; along with deeds of family arrangement (22.29.6) and divorce transfers. The duty on share transfers was further reduced to 0.5 per cent by the 1986 Finance Act (S58). Also, a new stamp duty reserve tax was introduced (24.5).

Stamp duty is essentially a charge on documents (instruments). (These must be delivered as well as signed.) It is not charged on the transactions and so, if you carry out a transaction without documenting it, no duty should be chargeable. Furthermore if you later make a separate written record of an oral contract, this should not involve stamp duty. However, surrenders of leases are dutiable whether or not they are documented.

The payment of stamp duty is confirmed by a stamp being impressed on the document. The stamp office may need to adjudicate the value of a transaction for duty purposes and you could need to supply balance sheets and other details. If documents are not stamped, you will not always be open to action by HMRC but the instruments will not be admitted in evidence in court. Also, you may be liable for fines if you present the instrument late for filing – in practice after 30 days from when the instruments are first executed (or, if executed abroad, brought into the UK).

Anti-avoidance provisions are being introduced regularly and tightened up year by year. For example, from December 1993, exchanges of land interests are now treated as sales. Also, land interests must be valued if the price payable on transfer cannot then be ascertained. FA 1999 includes stiffer penalties, for example for late stamping, and changes the interest rules. FA 2002 contains a series of anti-avoidance measures regarding commercial property transactions. From 1 December 2003 stamp duty land tax broadly replaced stamp duty on land transactions.

Following consultations over recent years, HMRC have secured the extension of mandatory tax avoidance scheme disclosure to all SDLT schemes and specific legislation against SDLT avoidance by the use of options and sub-sales (FA 2012). FA 2012 also empowers HMRC to incur expenditure in preparing for a new annual tax on high value residential properties owned otherwise than by individuals. This and certain associated capital gains tax proposals were the subject of a further consultation paper published on 24 May 2012 with a view to implementation from April 2013. Further details can be found in our Anti-avoidance chapter (15.10.25).

24.2 Exemptions

The following table lists some of the more important exemptions from stamp duty.

24.2.1 Exemptions from stamp duty

- Transfers of Government Stocks ('Gilts')
- Transfers of units in certain authorised unit trusts invested in UK government securities etc.
- Transfers of short term loans (no more than five years)
- Transfers of certain fixed rate non-convertible loan stocks
- Transfers of bearer loan capital
- Transfers of certain non-sterling loans raised by foreign governments or companies
- Conveyances, transfers or leases to approved charities (FA 1982 S129)*
- Conveyances, transfers or leases to the National Heritage Memorial Fund*
- Transactions effected by the actual operation of law
- Documents regarding transfers of ships (or interests in them)
- Transfers brought about by will (testaments and testamentary instruments)
- Articles of apprenticeship and of clerkship
- Customs bonds etc.
- Certain legal aid documents
- Contracts of employment
- Certain National Savings documents
- Deeds of Covenant and bonds
- Policies of insurance and related documents (excluding life assurance up to 31 December 1989)
- One life assurance policy which is substituted for another according to the rules (FA 1982 S130)
- Transfers (and issue) of certain EC Loan Stocks
- Transfers of Treasury guaranteed stock
- Property put into unit trusts (FA 1988 S140)
- Agreement pursuant to Highway Acts
- Appointment, procuration, revocation
- Letter or power of attorney
- Deeds not liable to other duties no longer liable to 50p duty
- In Scotland, resignation, writ etc.
- Warrants to purchase Government stock etc. (FA 1987 S50)
- Transfers to a Minister of the Crown or the Treasury Solicitor (FA 1987 S55)
- Life assurance policies after 31 December 1989
- Superannuation contracts or grants after 31 December 1989
- Transfers of insurance business under a demutualisation scheme (FA 1997 S96)

- Conversions and mergers of open-ended investment companies and authorised unit trusts up to 30 June 1999
- Certain on-exchange transactions by intermediaries
- Units in a unit trust from 1 February 2000, when liable to stamp duty reserve tax (FA 1999 S122)
- Transactions in intellectual property from 28 March 2000 (FA 2000 S129 & Sch 34)
- Purchases and leases of land and buildings by registered social landlords (FA 2000 S130)
- Transfers of assets to the Northern Ireland Assembly Commission (FA 2000 S132)
- Certain shares in open-ended investment companies and unit trusts held within individual pension accounts (FA 2001 Ss93 & 94)
- Purchase by employees of partnership or dividend shares from an AESOP trust (FA 2001 S95)
- Documents transferring goodwill from 23 April 2002 (FA 2002 S116 & Sch 36)
- Registered social landlords granting short-term tenancy agreements from 1 January 2000 (FA 2003 S129).
- Purchases by certain National Health commissioning bodies (FA 2012)

* Not treated as duly stamped unless they have a stamp denoting not chargeable to duty.

24.3 Relief for takeovers and within groups

Relief applied from *ad valorem* stamp duty (FA 1985 S78) up to 24 March 1986, where a company issued shares etc. in exchange for those of another company, in the course of obtaining control, or if it already had control. *Relief normally remains*, however, where there is a company reconstruction with no real change in ownership unless redeemable shares are involved (FA 2000 S127). Also, relief applies for transfers between associated companies (broadly 90 per cent common control). FA 1995 Ss132–extended the relief to leases granted by one associated company to another and generally reduced the requisite control to 75 per cent, the definitions now following the corporation tax rules (FA 2000 Ss123 & 124). FA 2006 extends the relief to non-UK registered acquiring companies.

From 19 July 2007, stamp duty and stamp-duty land tax reliefs on corporate reconstructions were extended to cases where there is an arithmetical change from the initial ownership proportions, as a result of previous purchases of own shares, which remain uncancelled.

24.4 *Ad valorem* duties

The most important stamp duties with which you may be involved are those which increase according to the consideration involved. These are known as *ad valorem* duties. Normally, *ad valorem* duties are charged at a fixed percentage which is 0.5 per cent for shares, rounded up to the nearest multiple of £5. Also, for some duties, sliding scales apply for small transactions.

The following table gives the basic percentage rates of various *ad valorem* duties:

24.4.1 *Ad valorem* stamp duties

	Rate (%)
Conveyance or transfer on sale other than share transfers	See 24.4.2
Share transfers	½
Certain non-exempt loan transfers	½
Exchanges or partitions of freehold land	1
Inland bearer instruments‡	1½
Overseas bearer instruments‡	1½
Conversion of UK shares into depositary receipts (24.5)	1½
Lease premiums (24.4.2)	1

‡ Bearer loan capital exempt.

24.4.2 *Ad valorem* duty on transfers of property other than shares (FA 1998 S149)

From 1 December 2003, SDLT (24.4.3) generally replaced stamp duty for land transactions. It is important to note that a single rate of tax is determined by the price payable and applies to the whole amount.

From 22 March 2012, SDLT on residential properties over £2m is charged at 7 per cent if purchased by an individual, but at 15 per cent, if purchased by a company, collective investment scheme or a partnership, of which one or more members are either a body corporate or a collective investment scheme. There are exclusions for companies acting in their capacity as trustees for a settlement and property developers who meet certain conditions.

These higher rates do not apply to non-residential or mixed-use properties.

Recent tax rates and thresholds and those currently applicable to transfers of property other than shares are as follows:

From	Designated*	Elsewhere	0%	1%	3%	4%‡
10.3.03	Residential	Commercial	1–150,000	150,001–250,000	250,001–500,000	500,000+
	Commercial		No limit	N/A	N/A	N/A
		Residential	1–60,000	60,001–250,000		
17.3.05	Res/Com	Commercial	1–150,000	150,001–250,000		
		Residential	1–120,000	120,001–250,000		
23.3.06	Res/Com	Commercial	1–150,000	150,001–250,000		
		Residential	1–125,000	125,001–250,000	250,001–500,000	500,000+
22.4.09	Res/Com	Commercial	1–150,000	150,001–250,000		
		Residential	1–175,000	175,001–250,000		
01.1.10	Res/Com	Commercial	1–150,000	150,001–250,000		
		Residential‡	1–125,000	125,001–250,000†		

* Various reliefs have applied to properties in designated 'disadvantaged areas' since November 2001.
† 0% from 25.3.10 to 24.3.12 for first time buyers for own occupation if price £250,000 or less.
‡ From 6.4.11 to 21.3.12 the rate for residential property purchases exceeding £1m is 5% (FA 2010) but from 22.03.12 the 5% rate for residential properties is capped at £2m and new rates of 7% or 15% apply to residential property purchases exceeding £2m (FA 2012).

As regards new leases, the above table is generally applicable to any premium payable, but special rules apply to non-residential property, where the annual rent exceeds £1,000 (£600 until 11 March 2008). Prior to 12 March 2008, those rules also applied to residential property.

In addition, the present value of the rental income attracts a common fixed rate of 1 per cent, again applied to the full amount, if that exceeds the threshold of £125,000 or £150,000 appropriate to the nature and location of the property (see table).

Transfers and leases of property in the most disadvantaged areas of the UK were exempt from stamp duty (FA 2001 S92 & Sch 30 & FA 2002 S110) from 27 November 2001, where the value did not exceed £150,000. Between 10 April 2003 and 16 March 2005 all non-residential property transfers in such areas were exempt, regardless of value. As can be seen from the table, from 17 March 2005 the relief for commercial properties was generally withdrawn and that for residential properties has in effect been eroded to £25,000 by virtue of two increases in the SDLT threshold for residential properties outside those areas.

By a succession of temporary regulations and statutory provisions (FA 2009) any acquisition of residential property of not more than £175,000 made between 22 April 2009 and 31 December 2010 will be exempt from SDLT. From 1 January 2010 the tax threshold reverted to £125,000. However, from 25 March 2010 to 24 March 2012 exemption is restored for first time buyers, where all purchasers will occupy and the consideration is £250,000 or less (FA 2010 S6). At the time of their 22 June 2010 Budget, the new coalition Government indicated their intention to review the benefits of this exemption for first time buyers.

From 6 April 2011, an increased rate of 5 per cent will apply to residential property purchases where the consideration exceeds £1m (FA 2010 S7).

As described in the second paragraph of this section (24.4.2), from 23 March 2012 alternative rates of 7 per cent or 15 per cent (according to the nature of the purchaser) apply to purchases of residential property, where the consideration exceeds of £2m.

24.4.3 **Stamp duty land tax (SDLT)** (FA 2003 Ss58B–C, 73B, 125–126 & Schs 9 & 19–20)

(1) SDLT generally replaced stamp duty in respect of land transactions with effect from 1 December 2003 and minor technical changes have been made subsequently.
(2) For commercial property, the zero rate band upper limit increased from £60,000 to £150,000.
(3) A modernised scheme started and stamp duty was generally abolished on transactions involving land.
(4) New leases bear duty at 1 per cent of the discounted net present value of the rent payments where this exceeds £125,000 (previously £120,000) for residential property generally and £150,000 for non-residential property and residential property in disadvantaged areas (24.4.2).

(5) From 19 July 2007, SDLT is charged on certain transactions relating to land and partnerships which were not previously covered, including land which is transferred into a partnership by an existing partner or in exchange for a partnership share. However, transfers of interests in property among existing partners are SDLT exempt.
(6) From 22 March 2006 'seeding relief' is withdrawn so that SDLT is payable when property is transferred into a newly formed unit trust in consideration for the issue of units.
(7) For five years from 1 October 2007, SDLT relief of up to £15,000 will be granted on the first sale of a new 'zero-carbon' home. This has been retroactively extended to include new flats.
(8) From 19 July 2007 the aggregation of both elements of a property exchange between connected parties was abolished, so that the rate of duty on each element will be based on its separate value.
(9) Special provisions apply to limit the impact of SDLT on purchasers of 'affordable housing', whether under right to buy, a shared ownership lease or (from 19 July 2007) a shared ownership trust. These provisions have been extended and simplified by FA 2009 to encompass several different methods of participating in the affordable housing scheme. They take effect on various dates.
(10) From 13 March 2008, the SDLT group relief claw-back where the purchaser leaves the group within 3 years will also apply if the vendor leaves the group.
(11) From 21 July 2009, transfers of property to and from issuers of land-backed alternative finance bonds are exempted from SDLT.
(12) From 4 July 2011, new style *Land Taxation Returns* introduced in April are mandatory and must then disclose specified unique identification numbers for the lead purchaser, without which they will be rejected.

24.5 Stamp duty reserve tax (FA 1986 Ss86–99, FA 1996 Ss186 & 189 & FA 1999 Ss116–123 & Sch 19)

A charge called stamp duty reserve tax applies at 0.5 per cent on certain transactions in securities otherwise not liable to stamp duty. The charge broadly operates from 27 October 1986 but does not apply to securities exempt from sale duty (for example gifts) or traded options etc. Examples of when the tax applies are renounceable letters of allotment and sometimes where there is no transfer document (for example closing transactions within Stock Exchange accounts). A special rate of 1.5 per cent applies to the conversion of UK shares into depositary receipts after 18 March 1986.

From 1 July 1996, transfers of shares into electronic transfer systems are exempted from stamp duty. However, if the transfers are made for consideration in money or money's worth, the underlying agreement will be liable to stamp duty reserve tax.

A new stamp duty reserve tax framework operates from 1 February 2000 regarding transfers of units in unit trusts. The rate is 0.5 per cent unless the trust is shrinking, when a lesser rate may apply. A similar scheme will apply for open-ended investment companies.

24.6 Abolition of stamp duty on shares etc. (FA 1990 Ss107–111 & FA 1991 Ss110–117)

As described in previous editions of this book, the abolition of stamp duties on shares and marketable securities was originally planned to coincide with the introduction of paperless dealing under a proposed new Stock Exchange share transfer system ('Taurus'), which was ultimately abandoned. At the same time, stamp duty charges on property other than land and buildings were expected to go, including those on patents, goodwill and debt.

In the event stamp duty on goodwill was abolished from 23 April 2002 and on assets other than shares and marketable securities from 1 December 2003.

From 1 July 1996, transfers of securities into an electronic transfer system are exempt from stamp duty, but stamp duty reserve tax (24.5) may apply, according to the rules.

A number of documents remained liable to a fixed amount of stamp duty that amounted to 50p per document, but was, in general, increased to £5 from 1 October 1999. However, from 13 March 2008, fixed £5 charges in respect of documentary share and stock transfers and minimum £5 *ad valorem* charges on sales for less than £1,000 are exempt from stamp duty and from any requirement for submission for 'exempt' stamping.

From 21 July 2008, FA 2008 S97 exempts transfers of certain types of structured loan capital issued on limited recourse terms under 'capital market arrangements'.

24.7 Administrative changes (FA 2008, FA 2009)

Sweeping administrative changes are being phased in, so as to create a consistent approach to all taxes administered by HMRC (16.9.6), including the various Stamp Duties and Taxes. The changes span processes to monitor compliance, penalties for compliance failures, time limits, interest rates and a new behaviour related compliance policy of consistently matching penalties to the degree of non-compliance in each case. This will include a system of suspending penalties for late payment of tax, where you enter into a managed payment plan with HMRC. This regime is to be phased in over a number of years, commencing 1 April 2010.

From 1 April 2009 the appellate jurisdiction in all tax matters has been transferred to the Tribunals Service and the work of the VAT and Duties Tribunal, which has been responsible for all substantive disputes regarding Stamp Duties and Taxes is now handled by the Tax Chamber of the First-Tier Tribunal. The right of appeal is no longer to the High Court, but to the Finance and Tax Chamber (to be renamed 'Tax and Chancery Chamber' from 1 September 2009) of the Upper Tribunal, with further rights of appeal to the Court of Appeal (Court of Session in Scotland) and then the House of Lords. Before exercising those rights of appeal, you may be able to ask either chamber of the two tribunals to review its own decision. Before you even start the appeal process, you now have the right to ask HMRC for an independent internal review of the disputed decision.

However, appeals against notifications to submit information or documents or against penalties imposed by HMRC must be made to HMRC, who will deal with these through a new dedicated unit. This procedure will be applied to all taxes.

Six expired reliefs are to be repealed with effect from 6 April 2013 and a further 36 provisions are destined for like treatment in FA 2013.

Chapter 25

SOCIAL SECURITY

25.1 Introduction

The main social security legislation is now comprised in the Social Security Acts of 1992 and supporting statutory instruments and amendments. The subject is a wide one and only an outline is given below.

Arguably, social security contributions are not a tax but their effect is very similar. Although ultimate benefits such as retirement pensions are secured, when you pay the contributions, you must normally do so out of your after-tax income. Social security contributions payments do not reduce your taxable income any more than do income tax payments.

25.2 National Insurance contributions

Contributions are payable under four categories known as 'Class 1' (employees), 'Class 2' (self-employed), 'Class 3' (voluntary) and 'Class 4' (self-employed earnings related). Classes 2 and 3 are flat rate contributions and Class 4 is dealt with subsequently (25.5). The following points should be noted regarding Class 1:

(1) Contributions are graduated according to earnings up to a certain level and are collected together with income tax under the PAYE system (10.14). They are not allowable for income tax purposes.

(2) Your employer supplements your contributions. Your employers' contributions are deductible for tax purposes.

(3) No contributions are payable by you if the weekly earnings are less than £146 but once this level is reached, your wages carry various percentage contributions which reduce to 2 per cent above £817.

(4) There is no upper earnings limit for employers. They pay contributions on the earnings of employees in excess of £144 weekly.

(5) If your employers operate an approved pension scheme which is contracted out of the state scheme, lower contributions will be due. If you contracted out via a Personal Pension Plan, you still paid full National Insurance contributions. The rebate was paid direct to the pension plan. However, from 2012–13, rebates are available only in respect of salary-related schemes.

(6) You will not have to pay contributions if you have retired and passed normal retirement age (currently 60 for a woman and 65 for a man, but due to increase). If you are still working beyond age 65 you will not be liable for contributions. Your employer remains liable, however.

(7) If you have a company car and earn no less than £8,500 annually, your employer will pay Class 1A National Insurance contributions at currently 13.8 per cent on your taxable benefits. These comprise both your car scale benefit and fuel benefit, where applicable. This is an annual charge, payable for 1991–92 and subsequent tax years normally by the following 19 July.

The following tables give details concerning the rates of contribution.

25.2.1 National Insurance contributions

	Tax year	
	2012–13 **£**	**2011–12** **£**
'Class 1' – employees aged 16 and over	See 25.2.2	See 25.2.2
'Class 2' – self-employed pw	2.65*	2.50**
'Class 3' – voluntary pw	13.25	12.60
'Class 4' – self-employed earnings related	9% on annual earnings in range 7,605–42,475 2% above 42,475	9% on annual earnings in range 7,225–42,425 2% above 42,425

Note: Small earnings exception: *£5,595; **£5,315.

25.2.2 Class 1 National Insurance contributions

2012–13			2011–12		
	Not contracted-out	**Contracted-out**		**Not contracted-out**	**Contracted-out**
Employee weekly earnings	%	%	**Employee weekly earnings**	%	%
Below £146	Nil	Nil	Below £139	Nil	Nil
Above £146			Above £139		
£0–145.99	Nil	Nil	£0–138.99	Nil	Nil
£146–770	12	10.6 (1) (3)	£139–770	12	10.4 (1) (3)
£770–817	12	12	£770–817	12	12
Over £817	2	2	Over £817	2	2
Employer weekly earnings	%	%	**Employer weekly earnings**	%	%
Below £144	Nil	Nil	Below £136	Nil	Nil
£144–770	13.8	10.4 (2) (3)	£136–770	13.8	10.1 (2) (3)
Above £770	13.8	13.8	Above £770	13.8	13.8

Notes:

(1) The employees' rebate of 1.4 per cent (1.6 per cent for 2011–12) deducted in the table refers to salary-related schemes. For money purchase and personal pension schemes, the rebate has now been abolished (1.6 per cent for 2011–12).

(2) The employers' rebate of 3.4 per cent (3.7 per cent for 2011–12) deducted in the table refers to salary-related schemes. For money-purchase schemes, the rebate has now been abolished (1.4 per cent for 2011–12).

(3) The respective rebates apply to earnings within the £146–770 or £144–770 bands (employees or employers) – (£139–770 and £136–770 respectively for 2012–13 and 2011–12).

25.2.3 **National Insurance contributions reforms**

Important reforms to the National Insurance contributions scheme run from April 1999 and later, including the following:

(1) Employers and employees only pay contributions on earnings above the starting point.
(2) The previous 2 per cent rate for employees was removed.
(3) From 2000–01 the starting point for employer contributions was lined up with the income tax personal allowance and there was a single rate of 12.8 per cent from 2003–04 to 2010–11.
(4) The Contributions Agency transferred from the Department of Social Security to the Inland Revenue.
(5) Class 1A National Insurance contributions apply to a far wider range of benefits in kind from 2000–01, similar to those liable to income tax. Contributions will only be payable by employers and details are included in the forms P11D (10.7), due by 6 July each year, the first payments being due by 19 July 2001.
(6) The Classes I, 1A, 1B and 4 contributions for 2003–04 were raised substantially by a general increase of 1 per cent in the main contribution rates, coupled with the abolition of the previous ceilings on contributions for employees and self-employed, but limiting to 1 per cent the rate payable on income or profits above the former ceilings.
(7) From early September 2010 certain new businesses set up after 21 June 2010 are eligible for a partial holiday from Class 1 employers' contributions for up to three years from the later of the start of the business and the start of the scheme. Subject to the detailed rules, exemption can extend to the first 52 weeks' employment of the first 10 employees hired in the first year of business, but cannot exceed £5,000 for any one of them. 'Qualifying businesses' must be outside London, the South-East and East England and will be permitted a wide range of activities, but there are special rules for certain businesses connected with agriculture and fisheries, and some exclusions, such as businesses involved with coal, individuals employing providers of personal services and employers who are within the IR 35 regime or are managed service companies.
(8) For 2012–13, there was no change in the main Classes I, 1A, 1B and 4 contribution rates, leaving employees paying 12 per cent, self-employed at 9 per cent and employers at 13.8 per cent. Similarly, the 'additional rate' of 2 per cent hitherto paid by employees and self-employed on income above the upper earnings limit remained at 2011–12 levels. Numerous threshold adjustments have been made and rebates for employees contracted out the state second pension have been reduced in scope, all of which are reflected in the table above (25.2.2).

25.3 Social security benefits

A wide range of benefits is payable. Some of these are summarised in the following tables and split between those which are taxable and those which are not.

It is beyond the scope of this book to carry comprehensive information on the full range of social security benefits, but there is clearly every possibility that the coalition Government's ongoing spending review will in due course precipitate changes in the present complicated menu.

25.3.1 Taxable social security benefits

	From 6.4.11 to 5.4.12 £	From 6.4.12 £
Retirement pension		
– Single	102.15	107.45
– Wife (or other adult dependant)	61.20	64.40
Old person's pension (non-contributory) (over 80)	61.45	64.65
Carer's allowance		
– Single	55.55	58.45
Severe disablement allowance – age-related additions (only taxable if paid with retirement pension)		
– Higher rate	13.80	11.70
– Middle rate	7.10	5.90
– Lower rate	5.60	5.90
Widow's benefit (bereavement benefits)		
– Pension – basic (variable below 55)	100.70	105.95
– Widowed parent's allowance	100.70	105.95
Jobseekers allowance		
– Single person under 25	53.45	56.25
– Lone parent 18–24	67.50	71.00
– 25 or over	67.50	71.00
Employment and support allowance (contributory)		
– Age 25+	67.50	71.00
– Certain couples	105.95	111.45
Incapacity benefit		
– Short term (higher rate) (under pension age)	84.15	88.55
– Long term	94.25	99.15
Statutory maternity/paternity pay (maximum)	128.73	135.45

25.3.2 Non-taxable social security benefits

	From 6.4.11 to 5.4.12 £	From 6.4.12 £
Severe disablement allowance		
– Single	62.95	69.00

	From 6.4.11 to 5.4.12 £	From 6.4.12 £
Attendance allowance		
– Higher rate	73.60	77.45
– Lower rate	49.30	51.85
Child benefit		
– First child	20.30	20.30
– Each other child	13.40	13.40
Disability living allowance (replaces mobility allowance)		
– mobility component – higher	51.40	54.05
– lower	19.55	20.55
Industrial disablement pension (maximum)	150.30	158.10
– incapacity benefit – long term	94.25	99.15
Maternity allowance		
– standard rate	128.73	135.45
Bereavement payment – lump sum	2,000.00	2,000.00
Housing benefits – various		
War pension – death benefit, disablement, widow's pension, widower's pension – various		

Note: In addition, earnings related unemployment benefit supplement and in-work and return to work benefits are exempt from income tax.

25.4 Statutory sick pay (SSP)

Employers generally pay up to 28 weeks SSP for each employee in any tax year. (The employee does not need to have paid National Insurance contributions.) Only after that is any sickness benefit paid direct by the State. Employers can deduct their SSP payments in any month from the total National Insurance contributions payable to the authorities, subject to the rules.

SSP is paid at the following weekly rates (daily rates are calculated proportionally):

Normal weekly earnings	2011–12 £	Normal weekly earnings	2012–13 £
Less than £102.00	Nil	Less than £107.00	Nil
£102.00 or more	81.60	£107.00 or more	85.85

25.5 Class 4 National Insurance contributions

Self-employed persons and others liable to income tax on the profits of a trade, profession, vocation or other venture may be charged, in addition to their normal flat-rate Class 2 contributions, an earnings related amount under Class 4. The following should be noted.

(1) The contribution rate for 2012–13 is 9 per cent which applies to your self-employment income between £7,605 and £42,475. The maximum on this is thus 9 per cent × £34,870 = £3,138.30. In addition, the excess over £42,475 is charged at 2 per cent.

(2) The rates etc. for recent years were as follows:

Year	% rate	From £	To £	Maximum payable £
2002–03	7.0	4,615	30,420	1,806.35
2003–04	8.0	4,615	30,940	2,106.00*
2004–05	8.0	4,785	31,720	2,158.00*
2005–06	8.0	4,895	32,760	2,229.20*
2006–07	8.0	5,035	33,540	2,280.40*
2007–08	8.0	5,225	34,840	2,369.20*
2008–09	8.0	5,435	40,040	2,768.40*
2009–10–11	8.0	5,715	43,875	3,052.80*
2011–12	9.0	7,225	42,475	3,172.50*

* From 2003–04 to 2010–11 1 per cent was payable on excess earnings. From 2011–12 this increased to 2 per cent.

(3) Prior to 6 April 1975, the charge did not apply.

(4) Class 4 is payable on your self-employment income for the tax year, after capital allowances, but with no deduction of personal allowances, pension contributions etc. Your share of partnership income is thus included.

(5) If your wife has self-employed earnings, these are separately charged to Class 4.

(6) Class 4 does not apply to men over 65 at the end of the previous year of assessment or women then over state retirement age.

(7) Your contributions for each year of assessment are normally collected through your income tax assessment on your self-employed earnings. Thus it is normally payable in two instalments (16.3.2).

(8) It is possible to defer your Class 4 payments in certain cases, such as where you also pay Class 1 contributions.

(9) If you are not resident in the UK (17.3) Class 4 will not apply.

(10) From 6 April 1985 to 5 April 1996, but not subsequently, half of your Class 4 contributions were deductible in computing your taxable profits (11.29).

(11) The rate for 2003–04 was increased by 1 per cent and a 1 per cent 'additional rate' was imposed on any excess of your self-employed profits over the main rate limit.

(12) For 2012–13, the main and additional Class 4 contribution rates remain unchanged at 9 per cent on the first slice of your self-employed profits and 2 per cent on self-employed profits in excess of the main rate limit. The limit of £42,475 remains linked to the higher rate income tax threshold, which was determined when the revised pattern of personal allowances was set. In future, the CPI to the September preceding the tax year will be a relevant factor.

Chapter 26

TAX-SAVING HINTS

26.1 Tax planning

The following pages deal with various ways in which you can arrange your affairs to reduce your tax bill. This should not be done by tax evasion which is completely illegal (15.10) and may result in your tax bill being increased by the addition of interest and penalties (16.9.2). You should always fully disclose your taxable income to HMRC in your income tax return (16.2).

You are fully entitled, however, to arrange your affairs legally in such a way that your tax liability is reduced. This is known as tax avoidance (15.9). There are various anti-avoidance rules (15.9) but providing you are able to steer clear of these provisions you can make substantial tax savings by sensible planning. This chapter covers numerous tax-saving hints with references to fuller explanations earlier in the book.

Tax planning is a very complex subject and many complicated schemes have been evolved. Such schemes are outside the scope of this book and in any event should be treated with great caution, following certain court decisions (*Ramsay, Furniss* v *Dawson* etc.). Furthermore, have regard to the new rules for the disclosure of tax avoidance schemes (15.10.3). If you have substantial income and/or assets you should obtain professional advice on tax planning if you have not already done so.

26.1.1 Tax planning don'ts

(1) DON'T save tax at the expense of commercial benefits. (It is no good losing money in your business just to pay no tax.)

(2) DON'T cause unhappiness to yourself and your family in order to save tax. (Don't emigrate if you know you will not like your new country.)

(3) DON'T enter into tax-saving schemes which run on for a long time. These may be effective when you set them up but could be the target of future anti-avoidance legislation before they are completed.

(4) DON'T jeopardise your future financial security. (Do not give away all of your money just to reduce inheritance tax.)

(5) DON'T make inflexible arrangements. It is always necessary to review your tax planning in the light of changes in your financial position and family. You must also take full account of changes in the tax system, such as the drastic cuts in tax rates.

(6) DON'T forget that the law may change. Particularly remember that with inheritance tax on death it will be the law at your death and not necessarily the law now that will govern the liability.

(7) DON'T rigidly segregate capital and income. Good tax planning sometimes involves saving income and sometimes spending capital. Each has its own taxes and you should aim to maximise both after tax.

26.1.2 **A basic plan**

Before examining in detail ways of saving income tax, capital gains tax and inheritance tax, the following general guidelines are given, which are applicable to the tax and financial planning of many people:

(1) Buy your own house when you marry, or as soon afterwards as you can afford. If you remain single, house purchase is also desirable in appropriate circumstances. Although tax is no longer saved on *mortgage interest payments* (4.7), your home is likely to prove a good long-term tax-free investment.
(2) Divide your assets and income with your spouse so that the best use is made of the independent taxation rules (6.1). Savings of both income tax and capital gains tax can be made in this way.
(3) Whether you are employed or self-employed, you should arrange to have the maximum pension cover possible in your particular circumstances (14.6).
(4) Arrange adequate *life cover* (9.2) to protect your family.
(5) If you have spare funds when your children marry, make outright gifts to them. Provided you survive for seven years no inheritance tax (22.3) will be payable, even if the marriage and other exemptions are exceeded.
(6) When your children have married, if your house is larger than you need, consider selling it and investing part of the proceeds for your retirement.
(7) If you have spare funds over and above your retirement needs you and your wife should each make outright gifts to and certain settlements (26.4.2) on your children and others. In order to cover inheritance tax, which might be payable if you die within seven years (22.3), appropriate term life assurance is advisable.

26.2 Income tax saving

26.2.1 **Personal reliefs and allowances**

Always claim all of the *personal reliefs and allowances* (3.0.1) to which you are entitled. Notify the Revenue as soon as you qualify for an additional allowance. If possible, make sure your spouse and yourself have sufficient income to cover your respective personal reliefs.

26.2.2 **Businesses**

Make sure that you claim all *business expenses* (11.3) to which you are entitled. If you are able to use your car in *your business* (11.9.11) you can claim a reasonable proportion of the running costs (it is sometimes better if your business etc. actually owns the car).

26.2.3 **Capital allowances**

Do not overlook *capital allowances on plant and machinery* (11.9) and *industrial buildings* (11.11). Bear in mind that 100 per cent initial allowance is still available on buildings in certain recent enterprise zones (11.12). Have regard to the projected rate changes in timing asset purchases, so as to maximise relief.

Furthermore, 100 per cent Annual Investment Allowance (11.96) is available on your first £25,000 spent on plant and machinery each year.

26.2.4 **Incorporation**

Once your business profits bring your top income tax rate above 20 per cent, consider incorporation. Operating as a limited company will involve the 20 per cent *small companies corporation tax rate* (13.6), until the limit is passed. (An exception would be if your company is a close investment holding company (13.18) when 24 per cent may be payable.)

You will probably become a director and thus be employed by your company, although you might take some of your income as dividends. The National Insurance burden will change, but on balance, tax savings are likely particularly in view of the further National Insurance increases from 2011–12. Also, you can normally improve your pension cover.

26.2.5 **Employments**

Make sure you claim all *allowable expenses* (11.3). Try to obtain part of your wages or salary in tax-free ways (10.6.3). Tax savings may result if for example you have a company car or are given an interest-free loan or join your firm's pension scheme. However, watch changing tax rules such as the higher car benefit scales (10.6.5). If you are not covered by occupational pension arrangements (10.11) you should consider effecting a *personal pension scheme*.

26.2.6 **Saving tax for your employees**

If you are an employer you can enhance the after-tax income of your employees by various means including the following:

(1) Have a *canteen* for your staff (10.6.3).
(2) Provide *business cars* (10.6.5) for employees (including wives who are employees) where appropriate and tax effective. However, the new rules based on car list prices and CO_2 emissions, together with subsequent increases, may lessen the tax advantages.
(3) Grant *interest free loans* to staff (but see 10.6.9 for restrictions).
(4) Provide *housing accommodation* (10.6.13) if the employees have to live close to their work.
(5) Operate *pension schemes* for staff (10.11). Remember that employers can contribute to personal pension schemes.
(6) Provide workplace *sports and recreation facilities* for your staff – the cost is normally a business expense and the employees will not be taxed on the benefit (10.6.17).

(7) If appropriate, operate a *share option* scheme, particularly since the scope is widening (10.9.2).
(8) If you wish to make leaving payments to any employees make the payments in such forms as to qualify for relief from tax under the *'golden handshake' provisions* (10.12 and 10.12.1).
(9) Provide *childcare facilities* (10.6.15).

Note that (2), (3) and (4) above are subject to the fringe benefit rules for *directors and employees earning over £8,500 annually* (10.6.2). It is still of considerable value to provide such benefits in most cases, however. For example, normally a *car* will involve the appropriate *scale charge* (10.6.5) and employer's National Insurance contributions (25.2) but the employee may obtain a larger benefit from having the use of the car. This includes its capital value, insurance, car tax, repairs and, subject to an additional scale charge (10.6.5), any petrol bought for him.

26.2.7 **Repayment claims**

If you are entitled to make any income tax *repayment claim* (16.7), make sure that you do so at your earliest opportunity. In any event you should not allow the relevant time limit to expire. (This is normally 31 January following the fifth anniversary of the end of the tax year concerned.)

26.2.8 **New businesses and fresh sources of trading income etc.**

Make your accounting date early in the tax year since this will effectively delay the payment of tax.

If you make a *loss in a new business* (11.23), make the best use of it, not forgetting the option of relieving general income going back up to three years before you started to trade. This is particularly useful where income tax rates fall, since your new business losses might be offset against more highly taxed income for previous years.

26.2.9 **Using your home as an office**

If you use your home as an office, make sure that you obtain tax relief as appropriate. If you are an employee, you will need to show that your business use is wholly, exclusively and necessarily required for the purposes of your job. If, on the other hand you have your own business, the 'necessity' test is dropped.

You should be able to claim a proportion of such items as council tax, light and heat, cleaning, insurance and repairs. The proportion is normally calculated on the basis of the main rooms (excluding kitchens and bathrooms) used for your work. A different fraction would be appropriate for claiming your telephone bills. Of course, any expenses reimbursed to you by your employer cannot be claimed.

One word of warning. By claiming that a fixed part of your home is used for business, you might reduce your capital gains tax main residence exemption

(20.23). However, if you use no rooms exclusively for business purposes, this is understood not to apply.

26.2.10 **Spouse's earnings**

If you have a business, pay your husband or wife properly for any work that he or she does for it. In view of independent taxation, it is important that both spouses have adequate income, so as to use their allowances, starting rate (10 per cent), lower rate (20 per cent), basic and now, both higher and additional rate income tax bands. Also, appropriate pension arrangements can be made.

You must be careful that your business does not pay your spouse more than the job is worth, or else HMRC might seek to disallow part of the spouse's wages and so you will be taxed on the amount as a disallowed business expense. Also note that if the spouse's wage is more than £146 per week, National Insurance contributions must be paid.

The separate taxation of husband and wife is automatic and it is most advantageous for each spouse to have income, because each is taxed on his or her own investment as well as earned income.

A satisfactory arrangement is to form a business partnership with your spouse which will give him or her an entitlement to a share in the profits, normally treated as earned income, and to a personal pension plan. However, note that if your spouse's share of the annual profits is over £7,605 the excess is charged at 9 per cent up to £42,475 under the *Class 4 National Insurance Contribution Scheme* (25.5). Above £42,475, a 2 per cent rate applies.

From 5 December 2005, similar comments apply to civil partners under the CPA (6.9).

26.2.11 **Independent taxation – investments**

Ensure that you and your spouse split your investments between you so that you each have investment income and capital gains. In this way, the one with the lower income will be better placed to use his or her allowances and basic rate bands.

A valuable opportunity arises with dividend income, where say you are a higher rate payer and your spouse pays tax at no more than the basic rate. In that situation, you pay an extra 32.5 per cent on each grossed up dividend. If you are an additional rate taxpayer, this becomes 42.5 per cent. However, your spouse pays no more tax, being liable for only 10 per cent on each gross dividend, which is covered by the tax credit (8.1.2). Hence you can make worthwhile tax savings by transferring shares to your spouse. But remember that the 10 per cent tax credit attaching to dividends is not repayable.

The above extends to most other investment income in the hands of a basic rate tax payer who will be taxed at 20 per cent. Thus where you pay 40 per cent and your spouse no more than 20 per cent, transfer investments such as gilts, and building society and bank deposits to him or her. However, from 2010–11, the new additional rate (5.0.2 and 5.6.2) may apply so that even bigger savings will be made where one of you alone pays this.

26.2.12 **Independent taxation-elections**

Make sure that you use the elections under the independent taxation scheme to the best effect (6.1). If you and your spouse jointly own assets, you can elect for the income to be split between you in the ratios that you own them, otherwise the income is split equally for tax purposes.

This election enables taxable income to be diverted to the spouse with unused allowances or a lower income tax rate, thus saving tax. However, the split follows ownership automatically regarding jointly owned shares in close companies (6.1).

26.2.13 **House purchase**

The removal of tax relief for mortgage interest on your main residence, generally from 2000–01 reduced the advantages of buying compared with renting. However, current moderate interest rates and freedom from capital gains tax (20.23) on any gain support buying and you should carefully consider the most favourable way to finance this. But you should act prudently.

As a basic method, you could select the conventional mortgage repayments system. Under this you will normally make monthly payments to the building society etc., partly consisting of the capital advanced to you and partly of interest.

If you have a comfortable income you might consider tying your mortgage to a life assurance endowment policy. Under this system you borrow a fixed sum from a building society or insurance company for a given term (20 years etc.).

You effect a life assurance endowment policy for the sum borrowed, the policy being held by the lender as security. Every year you pay the mortgage interest and policy premiums. At the end of the term your life endowment policy matures and the capital sum is paid to the lender in settlement of the mortgage.

Your policy can be with or without profits. The latter is cheaper but the former might prove a better investment. Make sure that the policy is adequate and carefully monitor it regularly, having regard to the poor performance of some policies in recent years. An advantage of this system is that your life is covered automatically so, if you should die, the mortgage is automatically discharged.

Note, however, that under the endowment system you pay rather more in the earlier years than under a repayment mortgage. Inflation exaggerates this effect because the earlier payments are made in 'dearer' money. Therefore if you are able to invest the difference more profitably, there is a case for choosing a repayment mortgage. A particular instance would be if otherwise you could not afford your total permitted *personal pension* contributions (14.6).

If you make regular *registered pension* payments you may be able to have an interest only mortgage. The capital sum will then be repaid out of the *cash sum on retirement* (14.6.4) which you can receive. This method is attractive for tax purposes since the *pension* contributions (14.6) which you pay qualify for tax relief at your highest earned income rates, subject to the rules.

A more recent development was the use of personal equity plans (PEPs) to repay the capital element in a mortgage. With the annual amount allowed to be invested in PEPs being £6,000 plus £3,000 in single company PEPs (8.10), there was ample scope for ongoing schemes to be set up to repay quite substantial mortgages. ISAs have taken over from PEPs from 6 April 1999 (8.12) the amount allowed to be invested is £11,280 for 2012–13 (8.12).

26.2.14 **Tax-free investments**

Various forms of tax-free income are given in a table in Chapter 2 (2.6.1). Avail yourself of the opportunities open to invest in tax-free situations. However, weigh up the interest you might receive tax-free with the after-tax interest on other investments.

A particular investment on which the income is tax-free is an ISA (8.12).

ISAs took over from PEPs and TESSAs from 6 April 1999 and your annual investment was limited to £7,200 from 6 April 2008 subsequently rising to £11,280 (8.12). So if it is economically sound, hang on to any PEP and TESSA investments which you made prior to that date. However, take account of the removal from 6 April 2004 of the ability of PEPs and ISAs to reclaim the 10 per cent tax credit on dividends.

26.2.15 **Enterprise Investment Scheme (EIS)**

EIS investment normally saves you tax at 30 per cent (11.26). Thus, if you invest say £1,000, the net cost is £700. Provided you are able to select sound investments, the tax advantages are most attractive. These include capital gains tax exemption, tax relief for any losses and the option to carry back part of the relief to the previous tax year (11.26). Even more advantageous, is the facility for rolling over capital gains into the purchase of EIS shares (1.3.6). From 2012–13, your annual EIS investment is limited to £1m.

26.2.16 **Venture capital trusts (VCTs)**

VCTs now save you tax at 30 per cent (8.13). But you are no longer able to hold over gains by investing in VCTs (1.3.6). VCTs have the advantage of being dealt with on the Stock Exchange. Due to impending relaxation of the rules, some VCTs may appear which are dealt with on other EU or EEA markets and the implications should be carefully considered before investing. This means that once you have held them for the required five-year period, disposal should be straightforward. The annual investment limit is £200,000.

26.2.17 **Life assurance (9.2)**

As well as in connection with house purchase, life assurance provides a valuable method of coupling profitable investment with life cover. Subject to the rules (3.2.6) you obtain 12.5 per cent tax relief on qualifying premiums for policies effected before 14 March 1984. However, this relief only runs to 5 April 2015. Normally, the 12.5 per cent would be deducted from your premiums on payment. Since relief is not available for policies effected subsequently, any existing at that date should be continued so that relief is obtained on the premiums. (Of course this does not apply to policies no longer appropriate to your needs.)

There are many schemes in which life assurance is linked to property bonds, unit trusts, shares and combinations of these, under which you obtain life cover. Despite the withdrawal of tax relief on premiums, life assurance policies remain attractive as investments (quite apart from the life cover they provide) because of their ability to provide tax-free proceeds and a wide spread of investments for a small outlay etc.

26.2.18 **Pensions (14.3–7)**

If you have earned income in any year, on which you pay income tax, you obtain full relief from such tax in respect of any pension contributions paid, up to the permitted maximum. The full rules are set out earlier (14.3), subject to which you obtain relief from income tax in respect of your contributions.

You obtain relief at the highest tax rates attributable to your income. Thus suppose on the top £1,000 of your income you pay income tax of £400; if you pay an allowable contribution of £1,000 under a pension scheme, you will obtain £400 tax relief and so your net cost is effectively only £600 (£1,000 – £400). This will secure for you a pension at retirement when your top tax rate may well be lower. Pension contracts provide a very cheap way of obtaining life cover. This is because part of the contributions may provide death benefits.

There are rules which enable you to defer taking your pension. For the deferral period, you can take taxable income from the pension providers. This is a valuable feature which you can use to good advantage where annuity rates are currently low. Subject to the withdrawals, your fund will be available to buy your annuity when rates improve.

Under the new regime (14.6), you can obtain a tax-free lump sum of 25 per cent of the fund when you first take your pension, whether this is an annuity or drawdown pension. The maximum drawdown is reduced, but there is the new opportunity of being able to leave the income stream to your surviving spouse.

Remember that any unused part of your annual allowance, computed on the current basis, is automatically carried forward for 3 years.

The operation of the Stakeholder pension rules from 6 April 2001 has increased the tax-planning opportunities. All personal pension contributions are now paid net of basic rate tax so you generally obtain some relief earlier. Also, since at least £3,600 can be paid each year, lower earners and retired people can generally contribute at that level or more.

26.2.19 **Pension schemes for controlling directors**

If you are a controlling director of a family company, it can implement a *registered pension scheme* (14.3) for you. Contributions paid by the company will enjoy tax relief as a deductible business expense and you can be provided with similar benefits to those of any employee. From 6 April 2006, the new rules apply and, in general, the enhanced contribution levels and more flexible benefits will be to your advantage.

26.2.20 **Gift Aid (15.2.1)**

If you wish to make charitable donations, do so under 'gift aid' (15.2.1). Providing you are a taxpayer, this will result in tax benefits to the charity and to yourself, if you pay higher or additional rate tax, being especially beneficial if your income exceeds £100,000 by £14,950 or less (3.2.9–10 & 26.2.22).

26.2.21 **Gifts and settlements**

If you are a higher rate taxpayer and have more income and capital than you need, you can divest yourself of the surplus altogether and thereby save yourself the income tax on the income concerned. You can probably arrange that the income ends up in the hands of individuals with lower tax rates than yourself. Alternatively the income may be *accumulated in a trust* (21.1) where 50 per cent income tax is payable from 6 April 2010. If trusts are created you should take care that the *settlor* is not *taxed on the income* (21.3). Note that inheritance tax may apply in some circumstances (22.30), particularly under the new rules (22.30.3). Similarly watch the effect of *inheritance tax on gifts* (22.1).

This facility for moving income to basic rate taxpayers, such as grandchildren, remains important even though the trust rate is 50 per cent. For example, accumulation and maintenance settlements can be used to produce worthwhile income tax savings by making payments for the education and maintenance of beneficiaries. Income tax repayment claims are then likely covering the excess of income tax at the 50 per cent trust rate on the distributions, over the lower rates and personal reliefs of those beneficiaries (to the extent not used).

Trust tax planning was made more attractive by two measures in FA 2005. These are the standard rate tax band (21.2) now £1,000 and rules for taxing trusts' income and gains where there are vulnerable beneficiaries (21.2.2).

Gifts to charities under 'gift aid' carry full tax relief. You deduct basic rate tax and the charity reclaims this. At the same time the gross gift carries higher rate tax relief (15.2.1).

If amounts are significant, it is important to consider the CGT and IHT interaction in selecting the type of gift or trust and the assets to be given.

26.2.22 **Lower and starting rate bands**

The removal of the income tax starting rate band from 2008–09 reduces the scope for tax saving through distributing income to your spouse and over-18-years-old or married children. However, there is one compensating factor and that is the special increase in the personal allowance 2009–10 to £6,475, £7,475 for 2011–12 and £8,105 for 2012–13. Thus it remains worthwhile to cover their personal allowances and if you are a higher or additional rate (40 or 50 per cent) payer, to reduce your tax burden by arranging for income to be liable at only 20 per cent in the hands of family members. For 2012–13, if your 'adjusted net income' exceeds £100,000 by £16,210 or less, be aware that the excess bears an effective rate of 60 per cent, due to the progressive claw-back of your personal allowance.

From 5 December 2005, these stratagems also apply to CPA partners (6.9).

26.2.23 **The use of overseas income, taxable on the remittance basis**

Generally speaking the *remittance basis* (18.1.1) only applies in certain limited cases. If, however, you obtain any *income overseas* which is taxable here in respect of foreign business or investment (18.1) or employment (18.5.1), and such income is taxed on the remittance basis, do not bring the income into the country unless you need it to cover your living expenses. Note, however, that any *bank deposit interest* (8.7) or other income derived from any investment made with the funds is normally liable to UK tax on an arising basis, if you are *resident and domiciled* in the UK, subject to the detailed rules.

You can use your overseas deposits for spending on holidays abroad etc. (18.1). Beware of constructive remittances such as meeting UK expenses with an overseas credit card. Furthermore, once your overseas source of income has come to an end you can bring your funds into this country in a subsequent tax year without any charge to income tax.

If you are UK resident and non-domiciled or not ordinarily resident, you must consider the new law taking effect from 6 April 2008. If your unremitted foreign annual income and gains exceed £2,000 and you have been UK resident for more than 7 of the last 10 years, you must either pay tax on an arising basis or bear an annual charge of £30,000. This increases to £50,000 from 2012–13. Thus you will need to decide whether your unremitted income and gains are sufficiently high to warrant paying the special tax charge. Remember that this is a decision that you may revisit annually.

26.2.24 **Planning for 2013–14**

If you have a high income, there are two particular announcements which you might bear in mind regarding tax changes for 2013–14. One of these is that the 50 per cent top income tax rate is going down to 45 per cent. Thus to the extent that you are able, hold over income, such as director's fees, until that year.

The other provision concerns the cap on certain tax reliefs, which is subject to consultation, but if you will be caught by the new legislation, you should consider maximising your reliefs for 2012–13.

26.3 Capital gains tax saving

A number of simple ways are open to you for saving capital gains tax. Some of these are described on the following pages.

26.3.1 £10,600 net gains exemption

Make the best use of this relief. If your sales of chargeable assets produce net gains which are not normally far in excess of £10,600 in any tax year, try to spread your realisations so that your net gains are no more than the annual exemption each year – you will then pay no capital gains tax.

Remember that your spouse and each of your minor children can also realise up to £10,600 of net gains each year and pay no capital gains tax. It is thus a good idea to spread any share dealings etc. throughout your family. This is made easier by *capital gains tax gifts relief* (20.28) which now applies in certain circumstances, subject to the necessary election. However, gift elections are no longer normally of use regarding quoted shares etc. (26.3.3).

Under the system for taxing husband and wife, you each have a capital gains tax exemption now of £10,600. In order to make full use of both reliefs, split your investments between you.

If your net gains are less than £10,600 in any tax year, realise further profits by share sales. The previous 'bed and breakfast' arrangement, under which you could buy back the shares the following day and establish a gain or loss was stopped from 17 March 1998. You now have to wait for at least 30 days, or the sale and purchase are matched. So if you want to keep the shares, your spouse could buy them back or you could buy shares in another company.

26.3.2 Loss relief

Make sure that you keep a proper record of all your capital losses. These are relievable against any capital gains in the same tax year and any balance is carried forward to be used in future years.

If you make a loss in your non-incorporated trade or profession, do not overlook claiming to set this against your capital gains. Trading losses can now be offset against capital gains for the same and next tax years (11.22).

26.3.3 Capital gains tax gifts election

Since the scope for capital gains tax gifts elections is restricted (20.28), it is important to structure your gifts to avoid a capital gains tax charge, if possible. For example, make gifts of cash or quoted securities on which you have little or no capital gains, as well as gilts and loan stocks. Also, chattels worth no more than £6,000 each and gifts within your £10,600 annual exemption.

Furthermore, make gifts still within the scope of the election. These include certain unquoted and family company shares and other business assets (20.28); also gifts which involve immediate inheritance tax. This last category includes discretionary settlements and applies even if no tax arises because the nil rate band has not been exceeded. Under FA 2006 other trusts are also included which fall under the new rules (22.30.3), such as certain accumulation and maintenance and interest in possession ones. However, remember that gifts relief is generally denied for disposals to settlor interested trusts (20.28).

26.3.4 **Husband and wife**

Sales and gifts of assets between yourself and your spouse are not normally liable to capital gains tax (20.9). This enables you to redistribute your assets for inheritance tax purposes without paying any capital gains tax. This also applies to partners within CPA (6.9) from 5 December 2005.

If you each own capital assets, you can minimise capital gains tax by realising gains by the one with the lowest income.

26.3.5 **Entrepreneur's relief usable at retirement**

If you dispose of any business from 6 April 2008 including business assets and shares in personal companies, you can claim entrepreneur's relief. This results in an effective rate of 10 per cent, which applies for the first cumulative £2m of such capital gains. From 23 June 2010, the lifetime amount became £5m with £10m applying from 6 April 2011.

26.3.6 **Rollover relief**

Another important capital gains tax relief related to businesses is rollover relief (20.25). If you sell a business or business assets, consider replacing them within one year before and three years after the disposal. Subject to the rules, you will then pay no capital gains tax until you dispose of the replacements.

26.3.7 **Timing**

Timing your sales of shares or other chargeable assets can have an important bearing on your capital gains tax. If you postpone a sale until after 5 April it means that you delay the payment of your tax for one year. Also if you know that you will be incurring a capital loss during the next tax year you should defer making any potential capital profits until that year because, although capital losses can be carried forward, they cannot be set off against capital profits in earlier tax years.

Similarly if you have already made a lot of capital profits during the current tax year you should consider incurring *capital losses* during the same year which can then be offset. You should not normally sell investments unless it is sound to do so from a commercial point of view.

With the introduction of the higher (28 per cent) capital gains tax rate from 23 June 2010, you may be able to attract the lower rate (18 per cent) or even come within your annual exemption by taking a gain in the following tax year.

26.3.8 **Indexation**

Except for companies, indexation is completely ignored for disposals after 5 April 2008, only being relevant for certain disposals which you make before that date.

26.3.9 **Charities**

Gifts made to charities are completely free of capital gains tax. Thus if you wish to make a generous gift to a charity of a capital amount (rather than recurring annual amounts under gift aid) you will save yourself future capital gains tax if you gift a chargeable asset on which you have a large potential profit. For example if you wish to give £20,000 to a charity and own shares in A Ltd which cost £4,000 in 1993 and are now worth £20,000 you should gift those shares. (If you sold the shares and donated cash they would only produce £17,120 or £15,520 after 18 or 28 per cent capital gains tax.

This valuable relief applies regarding gifts to charity of a range of investments, including quoted shares or securities, authorised unit trusts and open-ended investment companies (15.2.1). The market value of your gift is deducted from your taxable income.

26.3.10 **Main private residence**

Ensure that you gain the maximum benefit from this exemption (20.23). If you have two residences (even if one is rented), claim within two years of the date of acquiring your second abode which should be treated as your main private residence to be free of capital gains tax. You have a free choice in this matter and so should select the house or flat likely to increase in value the most.

26.4 Inheritance tax planning

The essence of inheritance tax planning is the conservation of wealth. Remember that most lifetime gifts are free of inheritance tax provided you survive for seven years (22.3). Thus timely action is advisable. Also, bear in mind that future reforms could radically change the system and make it much harsher.

In broad terms you should aim to spread assets amongst your family to minimise the effects of these two taxes. Do not make gifts which you cannot afford, however, nor give too much money outright to young or irresponsible children, having regard to the divorce and health risks of all concerned. Also, you should have regard for anti-avoidance rules, such as those concerning pre-owned assets (22.29.7).

26.4.1 **Reducing your assets by gifts**

Take advantage of the various *exempt transfers* (22.17). By this means you can gift to your children, and others, considerable amounts over a period of years, free of any inheritance tax charge, even if you die within seven years. Gifts to your wife (or partner under the CPA from 5 December 2005) are normally free of inheritance tax in any event (22.17.1).

If you have funds surplus to your requirements, you can make gifts totalling £3,000 in any year (22.17.2). In addition, you can make outright gifts of up to £250 each year to any number of other individuals and, furthermore, if you have surplus after-tax income you can make *normal expenditure gifts out of income* (22.17.2). Do not overlook the reliefs applied to *marriage gifts* (22.17.2) for your children and grandchildren etc.

By means of all the above transfers you can reduce your estate without risking any inheritance tax liability on your premature death. Furthermore, by making the required election any capital gains tax on the gift (20.28) of certain assets will be held over until the recipient's disposal. The scope of capital gains tax gifts relief now mainly applies to gifts of business assets including shares in family companies etc. and gifts for political or heritage purposes (20.28).

Another important category of gifts qualifying for the above relief is those on which inheritance tax may otherwise be immediately payable, such as regarding certain settlements (22.30).

Remember that the above exemptions apply to both your wife (or CPA partner from 5 December 2005) and yourself. Also, do not forget that unused portions of the £3,000 limit can be carried forward for one year only. Thus your wife should also make gifts, and if her resources are insufficient you should put her in funds. But watch the associated operations rules (22.29.3).

26.4.2 **Larger gifts and settlements**

If you have a large estate, you should consider making more substantial gifts which will entail the payment of inheritance tax, should you die within seven years. The rate would be nil for the first £325,000 of chargeable transfers, however (22.5). Your relief would effectively be more if *business property relief* (22.18) or *agricultural property relief* (22.21) applies. Subject to the inheritance tax charge if you die within seven years, large gifts are now the most tax-efficient method of passing on wealth in many cases. Provided the recipients are sufficiently mature to look after the money etc. large outright gifts are to be strongly recommended. Unless you are in poor health or of advanced years, the contingent inheritance tax liability can be covered by temporary life assurance (26.4.10) at moderate cost.

For elderly people with smaller estates it is not necessarily advisable, however, to gift the £325,000 tax-free band since this is equally tax-free on death and it could be better to retain this sum for contingencies. This is especially so, now that the benefit of any unused tax-free band passes to your spouse or civil partner, if he or she outlives you.

It may be desirable to make larger gifts in the form of settlements, but if these are discretionary or other types, from 22 March 2006, the *periodic charge* (22.30.2) would normally apply at some future time, as well as the tax which you pay when you make the settlement and further tax when benefits are paid to the beneficiaries. Also, you are liable for inheritance tax at half the death rates when you set up the trust.

However, *settlements* (22.30) set up within your £325,000 nil rate band are not likely to give rise to significant inheritance tax liability, subject to the detailed rules. *Small* discretionary settlements of this kind are thus useful for passing funds to your dependants whilst maintaining a degree of flexibility. (Note that you should not be a beneficiary under a new settlement.) A further advantage regarding discretionary settlements (and certain others from 22 March 2006) is that they qualify for capital gains tax gifts relief (26.3.3). This is true whether or not any inheritance is paid on the capital introduced.

Accumulation and maintenance settlements (22.30.1) are useful for the benefit of your minor grandchildren. However, to be taxed under the old rules, they need to be set up for a disabled person and existing trusts must provide for your children to be entitled to the assets at 18. This could be done by varying a settlement before 6 April 2008, but the wisdom of placing too much in the children's hands at that age needed to be considered. Otherwise, the discretionary trust rules apply as above and, in smaller cases, little or no inheritance tax may arise, depending on other gifts and the settlor surviving for seven years.

Fixed trusts are also of use if you wish your grown-up children to have income but no capital until a stipulated time. Thus, if you settle money on your 26-year-old son on 1 July 2006 giving him an entitlement to the annual income until he is 35 and then the capital, you are immediately divested of the capital. This is an interest in possession settlement, treated like a discretionary one. Your son eventually gets the capital at age 35 and an exit charge may arise in larger cases. Your son is fully taxed on the income, however, and if his other income becomes high as he matures, his income tax burden could be heavy.

In establishing settlements, unless they are within the new rules and taxed as discretionary, remember that capital gains tax gifts relief will be limited. Thus either settle cash or assets which will give rise to no capital gains tax, unless you are able to settle assets qualifying for gifts relief (20.28). Also, remember that higher tax rates now apply to trusts, except where income is distributed.

26.4.3 **Gifts to charities etc.**

Gifts to charities and political parties are completely free from inheritance tax. Thus you should consider making such gifts during your lifetime and bequests in your will. Both will reduce the value of your estate for inheritance tax purposes, and capital gains tax relief applies concerning charitable dispositions (20.29.1).

From 6 April 2012, a reduced inheritance tax rate of 36 per cent applies where you have left at least 10 per cent of your net estate (calculated after deducting IHT exemptions, reliefs and the nil rate band) to charity (22.5.1).

26.4.4 Equalisation of assets of husband and wife

Provided the recipient is UK domiciled (or deemed domiciled) no inheritance tax is payable on transfers which you make to your wife or she makes to you, either during your lives or on death (22.17.1). It is now less imperative to avoid keeping all of your assets until you die and leaving them to your wife because the preservation of the unused nil rate band reduces the risk of inheritance tax on her death being more than the combined tax if your estates were equal and you each left your assets to your children. However, there may be good income tax or non-tax reasons for rebalancing your assets.

Administratively, a flexible discretionary trust has a lot of attractions and the latest IHT changes could ensure their popularity. Where shares in a substantial family company are involved, it is most important to take rounded advice on all tax and commercial ramifications, before embarking on any share redistributions – however small.

Now that any unused nil rate band on the death of the first spouse is available on the death of the survivor, it no longer saves inheritance tax by leaving £325,000 to others. Instead, on the first death, the survivor should consider making separate lifetime gifts to members of the family. After 7 years, these will be completely outside the inheritance tax net.

If your wife otherwise has insufficient funds, giving her assets will also enable her to make gifts to your children if she so decides. These will not attract inheritance tax unless she dies within seven years (22.3) and her estate is sufficiently high. This strategy is particularly desirable if your wife is younger and in better health than you are. Note, however, the *associated operations rules* (22.29.3). As mentioned earlier (26.1.2) equalising your assets is likely to produce income tax and capital gains tax savings.

From 5 December 2005, similar planning is appropriate for CPA couples (6.9). Of course, these tax planning considerations must be tempered by practical points, such as making sure your wife has sufficient to maintain her, should you die first. Also, a certain mutual trust is necessary. Your planning should also take account of your respective ages and states of health by arranging for a larger share to be in the hands of the one likely to live longer.

If you are buying a new home, you should ensure that this is put into the joint names of your wife and yourself. Since the matrimonial home often comprises the major part of the assets of a married couple, this is a very useful step towards equalising their respective estates.

If one of you and your spouse is domiciled in any part of the UK and the other is not, you should take into account the outcome of current Government proposals to improve the existing limited IHT exemption for gifts to the non-domiciled partner.

26.4.5 **Wills**

You should think carefully about the preparation of your will and, of course, obtain good legal advice. Substantial inheritance tax savings can result from a well drawn will. However, it no longer is necessary to ensure that both your wife and yourself by your separate wills leave at least £325,000 to other people so that you each get the benefit of the £325,000 nil rate band. Unused nil rate band will be available on the death of the survivor.

Avoid leaving too much directly to your children if they are already wealthy; it may be more beneficial for tax planning purposes to leave money in trust for your grandchildren. Such will trusts, however, will come within the new regime (22.30.3), one particular exception being where your children (but not grandchildren) are absolutely entitled to the assets by age 25 under an A&M trust.

If you have assets abroad, especially land and buildings, it is essential to take first class advice. If you assume that the foreign pattern of administration will follow that in the UK, your family may get some unwelcome surprises.

26.4.6 **Annuities**

If you need to increase your income, annuities provide a means of doing this which at the same time immediately reduces the value of your estate. For example, if you buy an annuity for £10,000 which produces, say, £800 yearly until your death, no part of your original capital outlay is charged to inheritance tax on your death. You have thus saved potential tax on your death. Do not overlook the effects of inflation, however; an unindexed annuity which is sufficient for your present needs soon may be worth too little to maintain you.

26.4.7 **Using business and agricultural relief**

If you have a business, farm or shareholding in an Unlisted Securities Market (USM) company, the further improved relief rates (22.18) offer great potential inheritance tax savings. Subject to the rules, 100 per cent or 50 per cent relief will normally be obtained after two years. You should therefore take advantage of the opportunity to create settlements and make gifts with less, or no, inheritance tax, even if you die within seven years. If any capital gains arise, it will normally be possible to obtain holdover relief. However, in cases where death is imminent, it may be better to keep the assets so as to obtain the tax-free uplift in base value for capital gains tax purposes.

26.4.8 **Protecting family companies**

The *'related property' valuation rules* (22.12) may apply if you transfer valuable holdings in your family company to your children etc. Thus, if you die within seven years, inheritance tax might be payable on the transfers. However, up to 100 per cent *business property relief* (22.18) may be available. The charge (if any) on the shares on your death could be even higher, however, particularly if the rules change and so you should plan to transfer shares to your children before they become too valuable, and your wife should do the same. The best time would be on the formation of a new company or early in its development.

If you are planning a new business venture, then do not put it into your main family company. Form a new company whose shares are owned by your children (or others whom you wish to succeed to your business). The new company should be encouraged to expand as much as possible and you may even let your old company run down. In this way the next generation of your family eventually will be left controlling the major company.

In the case of a partnership, the interest of each partner is valued on the appropriate share of the underlying assets. If, however, the partnership is incorporated into a company, the value of each partner's interest is normally reduced appreciably.

26.4.9 **Deeds of family arrangement**

Variations or disclaimers made within two years of any death not only effectively change the destination of property left by will (22.29.6), they are effective in changing the inheritance tax position. Property might be diverted from the surviving spouse to other beneficiaries, so as to use fully the nil rate band. Alternatively, substantial legacies may go to others than the surviving spouse, resulting in high inheritance tax. Assets can then be diverted to the surviving spouse, who might in turn pass the assets to others at a later stage, with a good chance of saving tax.

However, if you disclaim your legacy, it will revert to the estate and be re-allocated according to the will (or rules on intestacy if there is no will). Thus whether or not inheritance tax can be saved will depend on the facts in each case. Deeds of variation are effective in changing wills after death, provided that those involved take the necessary steps. However, it is better to ensure that your will is effectively drawn up so as to minimise inheritance tax. In this way, you will be more certain that your estate is passed on in accordance with your wishes. Then regular review is essential.

26.4.10 **Providing the funds to pay inheritance tax on death**

You may not be able, or indeed wish, to avoid leaving a large estate when you die. In this case you should ensure that sufficient funds are available for paying the inheritance tax. This avoids forced realisations of assets and, for example, the sale of shares in a family company which it might be desirable to keep.

Life assurance provides one of the best means of providing money to pay inheritance tax arising on your death, as well as being a very suitable vehicle for exempt gifts. Ensure, however, that the policy proceeds themselves are not subject to the tax, which could happen if the policy were taken out (with no trust provisions) by you on your own life. Consider taking out policies in trust for your children where you leave assets to them; this will put cash into their hands to pay the tax. They should be 'whole of life' policies, under which capital sums, with or without profits, or unit-linked to combat inflation, are payable when you die.

However, the new trust rules for inheritance tax (22.30) could bite in larger cases, although the Government has confirmed that those existing before 22 March 2006 are excluded. Also note that the taxable value of the policy is likely to be far less than any death benefit.

If both you and your wife have large estates then you should each insure your respective lives in trust for your children, assuming that you each leave your estates to them. If, however, you each leave your estate to the other by your will, then a joint life last survivor policy could be useful, under which a payment is made only on the second death. If the policy is correctly drawn (in trust for the eventual heirs on the second death) it will not attract inheritance tax. Further, the premium rate for such a policy is usually substantially lower than for two individual policies.

The policy can be written in trust for your heirs, under the Married Women's Property Acts or otherwise. Take care that there is at least one trustee other than you so that the proceeds may be claimed without delay on your death.

Temporary life assurance may be used to cover the five-year period following a gift or settlement on which you have paid tax at the lifetime rate. The amount covered should be the additional tax payable on that transfer should you die within five years (22.6). Temporary life assurance written in trust is also most useful for covering any inheritance tax payable on a gift (potentially exempt transfer (PET)) if you die within seven years.

26.5 Change of residence and domicile

Reference to the table at the beginning of Chapter 17 will illustrate the importance of residence and domicile in ascertaining whether or not an individual is liable to income tax, capital gains tax and inheritance tax. If you are able to become non-resident for tax purposes you will avoid liability to UK income tax on many classes of income and if you are also not ordinarily resident here you may not be liable for any UK capital gains tax on sales of assets here or abroad (see over). However, make sure that there are no vital rule changes arising from the expected Government review.

You should also bear in mind developing policy changes at HMRC, which need to be considered regarding your new lifestyle (17.4.1), if you are successfully to change residence or domicile.

If you become neither domiciled (17.2) nor *deemed domiciled* (22.4) in this country you will only be liable for UK inheritance tax on assets situated here.

A very effective way of avoiding liability from UK taxes is to emigrate and take all of your assets out of this country. Once you have ceased to be resident and are no longer domiciled nor deemed domiciled here you will be outside the UK tax net regarding all income arising and assets situated abroad. (You should note that if you have shares in a UK company with its registered office here, the shares are treated for inheritance tax purposes as located in this country unless they are bearer securities kept abroad.)

If you have a large potential capital gain you should generally defer taking this until the tax year after you have ceased to be resident and ordinarily resident here and you should remain abroad for at least five complete tax years; in this way you will avoid capital gains tax. (If you wish you may then return to this country in a future tax year.)

As a pure tax-saving exercise, you should only consider emigrating if you are a very wealthy person; and even then you should only go to a country where you feel that you will be happy. If, however, you wish to retire to a 'place in the sun', then in choosing to which country you should go, you should take into account the tax which you would have to pay there. Once you have established your foreign residence and domicile, in order to preserve this situation, you must avoid paying regular substantial visits to the UK (19.4).

26.6 Year-end planning

Towards the end of the tax year (5 April), you should consider various tax-saving opportunities.

The following is a list of reliefs to use up and other things to be done on or before 5 April. Further details are given elsewhere in this book.

(1) Capital gains tax annual exemption (20.6).
(2) Realise losses to offset against gains in excess of your annual exemption (26.3.2).
(3) Inheritance tax annual exemption (22.17.2).
(4) Inheritance tax relief of £250 per gift to any one person (22.17.2).
(5) Normal expenditure gifts for inheritance tax (22.17.2).
(6) Nil rate band for inheritance tax (22.5.1).
(7) Take extra dividends and salary for yourself and your spouse from your family company to maximise the benefits of independent taxation (6.1) having regard to the new rules about tax on distributed income from small companies (13.7.1).
(8) Effect single 'gift-aid' donations of any amount (15.2.1), thus getting relief for the current tax year.
(9) Pay pension contributions (14.6).
(10) Pay pension premiums by 5 April 2013 in order to obtain relief for 2012–13.

(11) Make investments qualifying for relief under the Enterprise Investment Scheme (11.26).
(12) Buy plant and machinery to obtain up to £100,000 annual investment allowance (11.9.1).
(13) Buy industrial and commercial buildings in enterprise zones obtaining 100 per cent initial allowance on the building content (11.12).
(14) Increase your contributions to your company pension scheme (10.11). (Your employer's contributions are geared to the company accounting date.)
(15) Ensure you make any necessary tax elections to do with your business and private affairs within the required time limits. A particular instance is trading loss relief (11.22).
(16) Make ISA investments by 5 April each year (8.12).

26.7 The seven ages of tax planning

Although tax planning is important at all stages of one's life, different features may be relevant at particular times. There follows a summary of particular tax planning points to remember at seven selected 'ages':

(1) Childhood.
(2) Student days.
(3) Early working life.
(4) Newly married.
(5) Parenthood.
(6) Middle age.
(7) Retirement.

Much of the advice given earlier in this chapter applies at most times in your life and thus is not highlighted in what follows; for example, tax planning for businesses (26.2.2), employments (26.2.5), companies (13.1) and capital gains tax (26.3). The points now classified under different 'ages' have particular relevance to certain times in your life. References are given to earlier paragraphs in this chapter, which will in turn refer you to further detail in the text.

26.7.1 Childhood

Tax planning for children normally involves other people such as their parents and grandparents. A chief objective is to provide for education and maintenance in the most tax-efficient way. Educational schemes may have become less attractive in view of, for example, the withdrawal of life assurance relief. However, lump sum school fee payments in advance by grandparents may prove of value in saving higher rate income tax and inheritance tax.

Older children may work in the family business at weekends and during the holidays, in which case a reasonable salary should be paid. This will be tax-free to the extent of the unused personal allowance (£8,105). To avoid any National Insurance contributions the salary should be kept below £146 per week. Also, older children might occasionally buy and sell shares and thus make use of their annual capital gains exemption (£10,600).

Other tax planning points to consider include:

(1) Changing wills to include new children (26.4.5).
(2) Settlements by grandparents (26.4.2).
(3) Repayment claims for children (26.2.7).
(4) Gifts to children to save inheritance tax (26.4.1).
(5) Accumulation and maintenance settlements (26.4.2).
(6) Discretionary settlements (26.4.2).
(7) Paying income from settlements for maintenance and education with possible tax repayments (26.2.7).

26.7.2 **Student days**

If you are a student (post-school), you will normally have attained your majority and this facilitates tax planning. In particular, none of your income will be assessed on your parents even though it arises from gifts which they make to you.

Your single personal allowance (£8,105) will normally cover income from jobs, investments etc. before you pay any tax. Also, income distributions from certain settlements are likely to entitle you to reclaim at least part of if not the entire 40 per cent tax already suffered.

Your parents and grandparents might save inheritance tax by making gifts to you or in trust (26.4.2). If you invest the money given to you directly in stocks and shares you will have the annual exemption (£10,600) to cover any capital gains (26.3.1).

26.7.3 **Early working life**

In your early working days you may well be able to benefit from some of the tax planning points regarding employments (26.2.5) and businesses (26.2.2), noting particularly new businesses (26.2.8). If you work overseas in a business or employment, some tax benefits may result (26.2.23).

Make sure that you claim all the expenses to which you may be entitled in your employment (26.2.5) or business (26.2.2) including a proportion of your home expenses if relevant.

Whether you are employed or self-employed, you should consider pensions (26.2.19) or personal pension arrangements (26.2.18) as soon as practicable. These provide a very tax-effective way of providing for your security.

26.7.4 **Newly married**

When you marry, the opportunity arises for the parents and grandparents on both sides to make gifts and settlements (26.4.1 and 26.4.2), using the special inheritance tax marriage exemptions or otherwise. Also they should re-examine their wills.

Particular tax planning matters for you both to consider include:

(1) Wife's salary (26.2.10).
(2) Independent taxation of husband and wife (6.1) – separate rates and allowances for income and capital gains.
(3) House purchase (26.2.13).
(4) Life assurance (26.2.17).
(5) The making of new wills (26.4.5).

26.7.5 **Parenthood**

This is the time when you are likely to have a growing income but also to incur the largest expenses. Gifts (26.4.1) and accumulation and maintenance settlements (26.4.2) made in favour of your children by their grandparents are tax-efficient ways in which the gap can be bridged (but watch the new inheritance tax rules).

As you progress in your employment (26.2.5), business (26.2.2) or profession, the relevant tax planning points become even more important. Particular matters to note include new businesses (26.2.8) and incorporation (26.2.4). Also, you will be well advised to improve your life assurance (26.2.17) and pension (26.2.19) or pension (26.2.18) cover as appropriate. The latter area offers greater opportunities in view of the new regime (14.3) (subject to the withdrawal of higher rate tax relief). You may work overseas (26.2.23) or even completely change your domicile and residence (26.5) if, for example, you become extremely well-to-do.

As you become more wealthy, *capital tax planning* will grow in importance, including capital gains tax (26.3). Inheritance tax planning should include an examination of gifts and settlements (26.4.2), charitable gifts (26.4.3) and equalisation (26.4.4); attention to your will (26.4.5); the protection of family companies (26.4.8) and the provision of funds to pay the tax (26.4.10). Furthermore, assets producing income and capital gains should be split between you, so as to maximise the benefits of independent taxation.

26.7.6 **Middle age**

You will still need to consider the relevant business (26.2.2) or employment (26.2.5) tax planning points as well as life assurance (26.2.17), pensions (26.2.19) and personal pensions (26.2.18). Even if your earlier pension cover was inadequate, there is scope for compensating for this in later life.

As your children come of age, consider passing them income producing assets. When they marry, make use of the appropriate inheritance tax exemptions (26.4.1), thus guarding against tax payable if you die within seven years. Cover larger gifts by life assurance (26.2.17). When they in turn have children, consider modest accumulation and maintenance settlements in favour of your grandchildren (26.2.21), but have regard to the new rules (22.30.3).

Capital tax planning is vital during this period and if you can afford it, you should make gifts and settlements (26.3.3) to pass on your wealth during your lifetime. Also, provide for the payment of any inheritance tax (26.4). If you have a family company try to guard against future heavy inheritance tax on its shares and help succession by passing on shares to the next generation (26.4.8). Should your house be larger than you need, consider selling and re-investing or gifting the proceeds.

26.7.7 **Retirement**

Take advantage of the tax planning opportunities arising when your pension (26.2.18) becomes due, such as taking your full tax-free lump sum entitlement or deferring your benefits.

If you have a family company or business, maximise your capital gains tax entrepreneur's relief (26.3.5) on sale or gift. At the same time, use the limited capital gains tax gifts election (20.28) if appropriate. Also, do not overlook the valuable inheritance tax business relief (22.18) and agricultural relief (22.21). These will eliminate or substantially reduce the inheritance tax payable if you die within seven years of a gift.

Since more of your income is likely to arise from investments, you may be able to claim repayment of the income tax deducted at source (26.2.7) (excluding dividends). If your respective incomes are sufficiently small, you may both be entitled to age relief (3.2.10), together with a higher married couple's allowance.

With the sale of your business and perhaps house (26.2.13), you will have the chance of reviewing your will (26.4.5) and making gifts (26.4.1), including settlements (26.4.2). If you have surplus funds, then gifts to charity should be considered, being free of inheritance tax and capital gains tax; whilst the purchase of an annuity will increase your income but reduce your estate.

26.8 The way ahead

FA 2012 is huge. It is full of changes to the tax rules and you might be forgiven for asking 'will the Government never get it right?'. However, tax legeislation is by it's very nature most fluid. This is so that it can cope with various factors including raising the necessary revenue, controlling the economy, furthering social fairness and blocking tax avoidance.

The Government has included in the 2012 Budget, much detail about 2013–14, including tax rates and allowances for income tax and capital gains tax and also reduced corporation tax. As mentioned earlier (26.2.24) two matters being introduced in 2013–14, which provide planning opportunities are the 45 per cent tax rate and reliefs cap.

We can certainly expect more anti-avoidance provisions and wider use of the avoidance scheme disclosure rules. Thus, as ever, expert professional advice is important in all of these areas. At the same time, basic planning is most important and, with a view to combating coming tax rises, you should make full use of current opportunities, in case these are closed. So use existing lower tax rates and reliefs in case these become less beneficial.

Apart from regarding trusts, one area so far broadly not hit by the Government is *inheritance tax*. Thus, planning in this area is to be recommended, the more so because it is better carried out well before death and thus as early as possible. But watch out for recent anti-avoidance provisions which may affect your tax planning (there are likely to be more). Particular examples are *pre-owned assets* (22.29.7), *trust tax rate* increases (2.1.2) and the interaction of *private residence* and *gifts relief* (20.23). Maximise the benefits of the nil rate band, business property and agricultural reliefs.

However, most gifts are potentially exempt transfers, which are taxed if you die within seven years. The rates applying are those at death. So even if you were within the £325,000 nil rate band when you made the gifts, this band could be reduced by the time you die. Also, a higher rate than the present 40 per cent could apply although this seems less likely with the change of government.

Make good use of your annual and other exemptions. These include the £3,000 annual exemption, small gifts up to £250 per person, relief for normal expenditure out of income and certain marriage gifts. These reliefs normally take effect at once and so should be safe from future changes.

National Insurance contributions have long been regarded as a tax. This is to be acknowledged by continuing consultations later in the course of this year with a view to amalgamating the two.

Chapter 27

TAX TABLES

27.1 Income tax table for 2012–13

Income £	£	Income £	£
5,000	–	20,000	2,379
6,000	–	25,000	3,379
7,000	–	30,000	4,379
8,000	–	35,000	5,379
9,000	179	40,000	6,379
10,000	379	50,000	9,884
12,000	779	70,000	17,884
14,000	1,179	100,000	29,884
16,000	1,579	150,000	53,126 *
18,000	1,979	200,000	78,126 *

Notes:

(1) Personal relief has been taken into account and tax figures marked * reflect total claw-back..

(2) Other reliefs have been ignored.

(3) The above table applies provided you do not qualify for age relief (3.2.10) and normally applies whether you are married or single.

(4) All income is assumed to be earned (until the higher rate threshold has been passed).

(5) The additional rate is 50 per cent on taxable income in excess of £150,000 from 2010–11.

27.2 Tax rates and allowances for 1999–2000 to 2011–12

	99–00	00–01	01–02	02–03	03–04	04–05	05–06	06–07	07–08	08–09	09–10 10–11	11–12
Income tax basic rate	23%	22%	22%	22%	22%	22%	22%	22%	22%	20%	20%	20%
Single personal allowance	4,335ø	4,385ø	4,535ø	4,615ø	4,615ø	4,745ø	4,895ø	5,035ø	5,225ø	6,035ø	6,475*	7,475*
Married couple's allowance												
Age under 66	1,970§	Nil	Nil	Nil	Nil	Nil	Nil	Nil	Nil	Nil	Nil	Nil
Widow's bereavement	1,970	2,000	Nil	Nil	Nil	Nil	Nil	Nil	Nil	Nil	Nil	Nil
Age allowance												
Age 65–74	5,720	5,790	5,990	6,100	6,610	6,830	7,090	7,280	7,550	9,030	9,490	9,940
Age 75	5,980	6,050	6,260	6,370	6,720	6,950	7,220	7,420	7,690	9,180	9,640	10,090
Life assurance relief – normal percentage of premiums (deducted from premiums)	12½%*	12½%*	12½%*	12½%*	12½%*	12½%*	12½%*	12½%*	12½%*	12½%*	12½%*	12½%*

§ Limited to 15 per cent from 1995–96 and 10 per cent for 1999–2000.
ø Available separately for husband and wife from 1990–91.
* Only on pre-14 March 1984 policies.

Note: Allowances for 2011–12 are detailed in Chapter 3 (3.0); income tax rates for 2011–12 are given in Chapter 5 (5.0).

27.3 Income tax rates for 1991–92 and subsequent years

Slice of income £	Rate %	Total income (after allowances) £	Total tax £
for 1991–92			
23,700 (0–23,700)	25	23,700	5,925
Remainder	40		
for 1992–93			
2,000 (0–2,000)	20	2,000	400
21,700 (2,000–23,700)	25	23,700	5,825
Remainder	40		
for 1993–94			
2,500 (0–2,500)	20	2,500	500
21,200 (2,500–23,700)	25	23,700	5,800
Remainder	40		
for 1994–95			
3,000 (0–3,000)	20	3,000	600
20,700 (3,000–23,700)	25	23,700	5,775
Remainder	40		
for 1995–96			
3,200 (0–3,200)	20	3,200	640
21,100 (3,200–24,300)	25	24,300	5,915
Remainder	40		
for 1996–97			
3,900 (0–3,900)	20	3,900	780
21,600 (3,900–25,500)	24	25,500	5,964
Remainder	40		
for 1997–98			
4,100 (0–4,100)	20	4,100	820
22,000 (4,100–26,100)	23	26,100	5,880
Remainder	40		
for 1998–99			
4,300 (0–4,300)	20	4,300	860
22,800 (4,300–27,100)	23	27,100	6,104
Remainder	40		
for 1999–2000			
1,500 (0–1,500)	10	1,500	150
26,500 (1,500–28,000)	23	28,000	6,245
Remainder	40		
for 2000–01			
1,520 (0–1,520)	10	1,520	152
26,880 (1,520–28,400)	22	28,400	6,065.60
Remainder	40		
for 2001–02			
1,880 (0–1,880)	10	1,880	188
27,520 (1,880–29,400)	22	29,400	6,242.40
Remainder	40		

Slice of income £	Rate %	Total income (after allowances) £	Total tax £
for 2002–03			
1,920 (0–1,920)	10	1,920	192
27,980 (1,920–29,900)	22	29,900	6,347.60
Remainder	40		
for 2003–04			
1,960 (0–1,960)	10	1,960	196
28,540 (1,960–30,500)	22	30,500	6,474.80
Remainder	40		
for 2004–05			
2,020 (0–2,020)	10	2,020	202
29,380 (2,020–31,400)	22	31,400	6,665.60
Remainder	40		
for 2005–06			
2,090 (0–2,090)	10	2,090	209
30,310 (2,090–32,400)	22	32,400	6,877.20
Remainder	40		
for 2006–07			
2,150 (0–2,150)	10	2,150	215
31,150 (2,150–33,300)	22	33,300	7,068
Remainder	40		
for 2007–08			
2,230 (0–2,230)	10	2,230	223
32,370 (2,230–34,600)	22	34,600	7,121.40
Remainder	40		
for 2008–09			
34,800 (0–34,800)	20	34,800	6,960
Remainder	40		
for 2009–10			
37,400 (0–37,400)	20	37,400	7,480
Remainder	40		
for 2010–11			
37,400 (0–37,400)	20	37,400	7,480
112,600 (37,400–150,000)	40	150,000	52,520
Remainder	50		
for 2011–12			
35,000 (0–35,000)	20	35,000	7,000
115,000 (35,000–150,000)	40	150,000	53,000
Remainder	50		

Note: The 10 per cent rate only applied to earned income, pensions and savings income.

27.4 Inheritance tax rates from 9 March 1992 onwards

Slice of cumulative chargeable transfers £	Cumulative total £	% on slice
from 9 March 1992 to 5 April 1995		
The first 150,000	150,000	Nil
Remainder		40
after 5 April 1995		
The first 154,000	154,000	Nil
Remainder		40
after 5 April 1996		
The first 200,000	200,000	Nil
Remainder		40
after 5 April 1997		
The first 215,000	215,000	Nil
Remainder		40
after 5 April 1998		
The first 223,000	223,000	Nil
Remainder		40
after 5 April 1999		
The first 231,000	231,000	Nil
Remainder		40
after 5 April 2000		
The first 234,000	234,000	Nil
Remainder		40
after 5 April 2001		
The first 242,000	242,000	Nil
Remainder		40
after 5 April 2002		
The first 250,000	250,000	Nil
Remainder		40
after 5 April 2003		
The first 255,000	255,000	Nil
Remainder		40
after 5 April 2004		
The first 263,000	263,000	Nil
Remainder		40
after 5 April 2005		
The first 275,000	275,000	Nil
Remainder		40
after 5 April 2006		
The first 285,000	285,000	Nil
Remainder		40

Slice of cumulative chargeable transfers £	Cumulative total £	% on slice
after 5 April 2007		
The first 300,000	300,000	Nil
Remainder		40
after 5 April 2008		
The first 312,000	312,000	Nil
Remainder		40
after 5 April 2009 to date		
The first 325,000	325,000	Nil
Remainder		40

Note: The rate of tax is halved for certain lifetime transfers to and many transfers from trusts (22.5).

GLOSSARY

The following is a selection of terms which are explained in more detail in the sections indicated.

Additional rate of income tax Higher rate from 2010–11 at 50 per cent on taxable income above £150,000 (5.0.2)

***Ad valorem* duties** Duties which are charged as a percentage of the subject matter – particularly stamp duty land tax (24.4)

Advance corporation tax Tax formerly payable by companies on dividend payments etc., and offset against their full (mainstream) corporation tax liability, now withdrawn (13.6)

All-employee share ownership plan A scheme to provide tax-free shares for employees (10.9.7)

Back duty Under-assessed tax for previous years, normally due to evasion (16.9)

Basic rate tax Income tax at 20 per cent (2.2)

Business expansion scheme (BES) Government scheme for encouraging investment in smaller companies by giving tax relief on money subscribed, now withdrawn (11.25)

Child tax credit (CTC) Tax credit operating from 2001–02 (3.4)

Claw-back The loss of relief previously obtained, for example, life assurance relief (9.4)

Close companies Companies closely controlled by generally no more than five shareholders and their associates (13.17)

Close investment holding company (CIC) A close company which is neither a trading company nor a property investment company, nor a member of a trading group

Consumer Prices Index (CPI) The index by which various reliefs are to be increased in future

Current use value The value of property on the basis that its use is limited to existing planning consents

Current year basis The uniform basis for assessing income tax liabilities from 1997–98 and sometimes earlier (11.7.4)

Dividend trust rate The tax rate applying to dividend income of discretionary trusts etc. currently 42.5 per cent (21.2.1)

Domicile The country which you regard as your natural home (17.2)

Earned income Income derived from an individual's personal, mental or physical labour and some pensions (3.1)

Enterprise investment scheme (EIS) Government scheme which took over from the business expansion scheme providing revised tax incentives (11.26)

Enterprise management incentives New share option schemes providing options for up to £100,000 worth of shares for each of no more than 15 key employees (10.9.8)

General Commissioners Lay people who used to hear tax appeals (16.5.2)

Higher rate tax Income tax at the higher rate, currently 40 per cent (5.0)

HM Revenue and Customs (HMRC) The integrated Inland Revenue and Customs and Excise department

Indexation allowance Capital gains tax relief for inflation (20.11)

Individual savings account (ISA) A savings scheme which started on 6 April 1999 under which individuals are able to invest free of tax up to at least £10,200 each year (8.12)

Interest in possession Entitlement to receive the income or enjoy the assets of a settlement (22.30)

Lower rate tax Income tax at a lower rate, now abolished (5.1)

Non-corporate distribution rate (NCDR) Former corporation tax charge of 19 per cent on distributed income otherwise taxed at the nil (starting) rate, now abolished (13.7.1)

Partnership The legal relationship existing between two or more persons in business together with the object of making profits (12.1)

Personal allowance Certain deductions from your total income for tax purposes (3.2)

Personal equity plan (PEP) Former share purchase scheme under which up to £9,000 could be invested each year with income tax and capital gains tax advantages (8.10)

Potentially exempt transfers (PETs) Gifts between individuals or to certain trusts which are only considered for inheritance tax if the donor dies within seven years (22.3)

Profit related pay (PRP) Incentive payments to employees which attracted limited income tax relief, subject to the rules, now withdrawn (10.15)

Registered pension schemes Those registered under the new regime for pensions operating from 6 April 2006 (14.3)

Relevant base value Main deduction in computing realised development value on which development land tax was chargeable

Residence Where you are treated as living for tax purposes (17.3)

Seed enterprise investment scheme (SEIS) A tax-favoured scheme for investing in certain small companies (11.2.6)

Self-assessment A system operating from 1996–97 under which taxpayers play a larger part in working out their tax liabilities (16.1)

Special Commissioners Full-time professionally qualified civil servants who used to hear tax appeals (16.5.2)

Starting rate Income tax at the lowest rate, now abolished (5.1)

Taper relief Capital gains tax relief depending on period of ownership, now abolished (20.12)

Tax and Chancery Chamber A judicial Upper Tribunal which takes appeals from the Tax Chamber and also selected tax appeals at first instance (16.5.1)

Tax avoidance Legally arranging your affairs to reduce your tax liability (15.10)

Tax Chamber A judicial First-Tier Tribunal which takes the majority of tax appeals at first instance (16.5.1)

Tax evasion Illegal tax saving (15.10)

Tax exempt special savings account (TESSA) Former savings account with bank or building society which offered tax-free interest (8.11)

Trust Otherwise known as a settlement – assets held by one or more trustees for the benefit of others (21.1)

Trust rate (formerly 'the rate applicable to trusts') The tax rate applying to income and capital gains of discretionary trusts etc. currently 50 per cent (21.2.1)

Unearned income Income from investments as opposed to earned income such as salaries and pensions (3.1)

Venture capital trusts (VCTs) Quoted investment vehicles concentrating on smaller non-quoted companies and offering good tax benefits to shareholders investing for at least five years (8.13)

Vulnerable beneficiaries Certain beneficiaries affording trusts tax reductions (21.2.2)

Working families tax credit (WFTC) Tax credit operating from October 1999 (3.4), now called working tax credit

Year of assessment Year ending 5 April, for which tax is payable (2.8)

INDEX

www.ingramcontent.com/pod-product-compliance
Ingram Content Group UK Ltd.
Pitfield, Milton Keynes, MK11 3LW, UK
UKHW020959050925
462611UK00012B/1073

* 9 7 8 1 3 4 9 3 2 7 2 3 2 *